SO-AHA-678

Toyota Celica Owners Workshop Manual

I M Coomber

Models covered
Toyota Celica ST Coupe
Toyota Celica GT & GT-S Coupe and Liftback
144.4 cu in (2.4 liter)

Covers mechanical features of GT-S Convertible
Does not cover front-wheel-drive models or Supra

ABCDE
FGHIJ
KLMNO
PQR

Haynes Publishing Group
Sparkford Nr Yeovil
Somerset BA22 7JJ England

Haynes Publications, Inc
861 Lawrence Drive
Newbury Park
California 91320 USA

Acknowledgements

Thanks are due to the Champion Sparking Plug Company Limited who supplied the illustrations showing the spark plug conditions. Certain other illustrations are the copyright of Toyota Motor Corporation and are used with their permission. Thanks are also due to Sykes-Pickavant who provided some of the workshop tools, and to all those people at Sparkford who helped in the production of this manual.

A book in the **Haynes Owners Workshop Manual Series**

Printed by J. H. Haynes & Co. Ltd, Sparkford, Nr Yeovil, Somerset BA22 7JJ, England

ISBN 0 85696 935 4

Library of Congress Catalog Card Number 86-81437

Contents

4

Toyota Celica 2.0 ST Liftback

Toyota Celica 2.0 XT Coupe

About this manual

Its aim

The aim of this manual is to help you get the best value from your vehicle. It can do so in several ways. It can help you decide what work must be done (even should you choose to get it done by a garage), provide information on routine maintenance and servicing, and give a logical course of action and diagnosis when random faults occur. However, it is hoped that you will use the manual by tackling the work yourself. On simpler jobs it may even be quicker than booking the car into a garage and going there twice, to leave and collect it. Perhaps most important, a lot of money can be saved by avoiding the costs a garage must charge to cover its labour and overheads.

The manual has drawings and descriptions to show the function of the various components so that their layout can be understood. Then the tasks are described and photographed in a step-by-step sequence so that even a novice can do the work.

Its arrangement

The manual is divided into twelve Chapters, each covering a logical sub-division of the vehicle. The Chapters are each divided into Sections, numbered with single figures, eg 5; and the Sections into paragraphs (or sub-sections), with decimal numbers following on from the Section they are in, eg 5.1, 5.2, 5.3 etc.

It is freely illustrated, especially in those parts where there is a detailed sequence of operations to be carried out. There are two forms of illustration: figures and photographs. The figures are numbered in sequence with decimal numbers, according to their position in the Chapter – eg Fig. 6.4 is the fourth drawing/illustration in Chapter 6. Photographs carry the same number (either individually or in related groups) as the Section or sub-section to which they relate.

There is an alphabetical index at the back of the manual as well as a contents list at the front. Each Chapter is also preceded by its own individual contents list.

References to the 'left' or 'right' of the vehicle are in the sense of a person in the driver's seat facing forwards.

Unless otherwise stated, nuts and bolts are removed by turning anti-clockwise, and tightened by turning clockwise.

Vehicle manufacturers continually make changes to specifications and recommendations, and these, when notified, are incorporated into our manuals at the earliest opportunity.

Whilst every care is taken to ensure that the information in this manual is correct, no liability can be accepted by the authors or publishers for loss, damage or injury caused by any errors in, or omissions from, the information given.

Introduction to the Toyota Celica

Since it was introduced in 1970, the Toyota Celica has been one of the world's best selling Coupés. This manual covers the models produced between 1982 and 1985. These models were produced in two body styles; the two door Coupé and the three door Liftback; and they are distinguishable from their predecessors by their wedge-shape styling and retractable headlights.

The bodywork is of conventional unitised structure. The engine and gearbox are mounted longitudinally, drive being to the rear wheels. The considerable range of standard equipment fitted plus the optional extras offered make the Celica one of the most comprehensively equipped cars on the road.

General dimensions, weights and capacities

Dimensions

	Coupé	Liftback
Overall length:		
UK models	4435 mm (174.6 in)	4450 mm (175.2 in)
USA models	4475 mm (176.2 in)	4485 mm (176.6 in)
Overall width:		
UK models	1665 mm (65.6 in)	1665 mm (65.6 in)
USA models – with FLS	1665 mm (65.6 in)	1665 mm (65.6 in)
USA models – with IRS	1720 mm (67.7 in)	1720 mm (67.7 in)
Overall height:		
UK – ST models	1310 mm (51.6 in)	1310 mm (51.6 in)
All other models	1320 mm (52.0 in)	
Wheelbase:		
All models	2500 mm (98.4 in)	
Front track:		
UK – ST model	1390 mm (54.7 in)	
UK – other models	1395 mm (54.9 in)	
USA – with FLS up to 1984	1395 mm (54.9 in)	
USA – with IRS up to 1984	1435 mm (56.5 in)	
USA – 1982 models with over-fender	1435 mm (56.5 in)	
USA – 1985 with FLS	1400 mm (55.1 in)	
USA – 1985 with IRS	1440 mm (56.7 in)	
Rear track:		
UK – ST models	1365 mm (53.7 in)	
UK – other models	1385 mm (54.5 in)	
USA – with FLS	1365 mm (53.7 in)	
USA – with IRS up to 1984*	1405 mm (55.3 in)	
USA – 1985 models with IRS	1440 mm (56.7 in)	

* Also 1982 models with over-fender

Kerb weight

UK models:

ST Coupé with manual transmission	1135 kg (2502 lb)
ST Coupé with automatic transmission	1150 kg (2535 lb)
ST Liftback with manual transmission	1150 kg (2535 lb)
ST Liftback with automatic transmission	1165 kg (2568 lb)
1984 XT Coupé with manual transmission	1150 kg (2535 lb)
1984 XT Liftback with manual transmission	1165 kg (2568 lb)
1984 XT Liftback with automatic transmission	1170 kg (2579 lb)
1985 ST Sport Coupé	1134 kg (2500 lb)
1985 GT Liftback	1166 kg (2570 lb)

USA models .... 1162 to 1260 kg (2562 to 2778 lb) – according to model and year – check with dealer

Capacities

Engine oil – UK models:
    Drain/refill with filter change .... 4.3 litre (7.6 Imp pints)
    Drain/refill without filter change .... 3.6 litre (6.4 Imp pints)
    Dry refill with filter change .... 4.8 litre (8.4 Imp pints)
Engine oil – USA models:
    Drain/refill with filter change .... 4.6 litre (4.9 US qt)
    Drain/refill without filter change .... 3.8 litre (410 US qt)
    Dry refill with filter change .... 4.8 litre (5.1 US qt)
Cooling system:
    Total capacity:
        UK models .... 7.5 litre (13.2 Imp pints)
        USA models .... 8.4 litre (8.9 US qt)
Manual transmission:
    UK models .... 2.4 litre (4.2 Imp pints)
    USA models .... 2.4 litre (2.5 US qt)
Automatic transmission:
    UK and USA models (drain and refill) .... Up to 2.4 litre (4.2 Imp pints; 2.5 US qt)
    UK and USA models (dry fill) .... 6.3 litre (11.0 Imp pints; 6.7 US qt)
Rear axle:
    UK models:
        Four link suspension (FLS) axle .... 1.3 litre (2.2 Imp pints)
        Independent rear suspension (IRS) axle (6.7 in) .... 1.0 litre (1.8 Imp pints)
        Independent rear suspension (IRS) axle (7.5 in) .... 1.3 litre (2.2 Imp pints)
    USA models:
        1982 model with unitized axle .... 1.2 litre (1.3 US qt)
        1982 model with conventional axle .... 1.3 litre (1.4 US qt)
        1983 and 1984 models with independent rear
        suspension (IRS) .... 1.0 litre (1.1 US qt)
        1983 and 1984 models with four link rear
        suspension (FLS) .... 1.3 litre (1.4 US qt)
        1985 model with independent rear suspension and
        manual gearbox .... 1.2 litre (1.3 US qt)
        1985 model with independent rear suspension and
        automatic transmission .... 1.0 litre (1.1 US qt)
        1985 model with four link rear suspension .... 1.3 litre (1.4 US qt)

Jacking and towing

Jacking points

For emergency roadwheel changing, use the jack supplied with the vehicle tool kit. Always engage the jack with the jacking points located under the side body sills. The Celica tool kit also includes a pair of wheel chocks (blocks) and these should be positioned fore and aft of the wheel diagonally opposite the one to be changed before raising the vehicle (photo).

To remove a roadwheel, apply the handbrake fully and loosen the roadwheel nuts **before** raising the vehicle. Once the vehicle is jacked up, remove the nuts completely and remove the wheel.

When carrying out repairs or adjustments jack up and support the vehicle under the support points shown in the illustrations. Always make sure the vehicle is securely supported before working underneath it.

Towing

In an emergency your vehicle may be towed or you may tow another vehicle by attaching the tow line to the transportation lash down hooks (photos).

If a vehicle is equipped with automatic transmission, it should not be towed further than 50 miles (80 km) or in excess of 30 mph (45 kph) otherwise disconnect and remove the propeller shaft.

Before towing the vehicle ensure that the ignition key is not set in the locked position! Turn the key to the position marked ACC and have it in this position for the duration of the journey. Check that the handbrake is released.

When being towed with the engine off, the brake servo unit will not be operating so allow for a greater braking effort.

On models with power-assisted steering, the steering pump unit will not be operating when the engine is off so allow for extra steering effort.

Do not tow or attempt to drive the vehicle if any part of the steering, suspension or brakes are damaged or faulty.

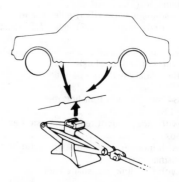

Jacking point locations under body sills

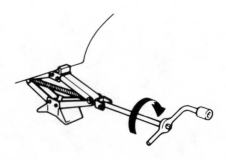

Turn handle in direction shown to raise the vehicle

Chock the wheels before jacking up

Vehicle lash down hook – front

Vehicle lash down hook – rear

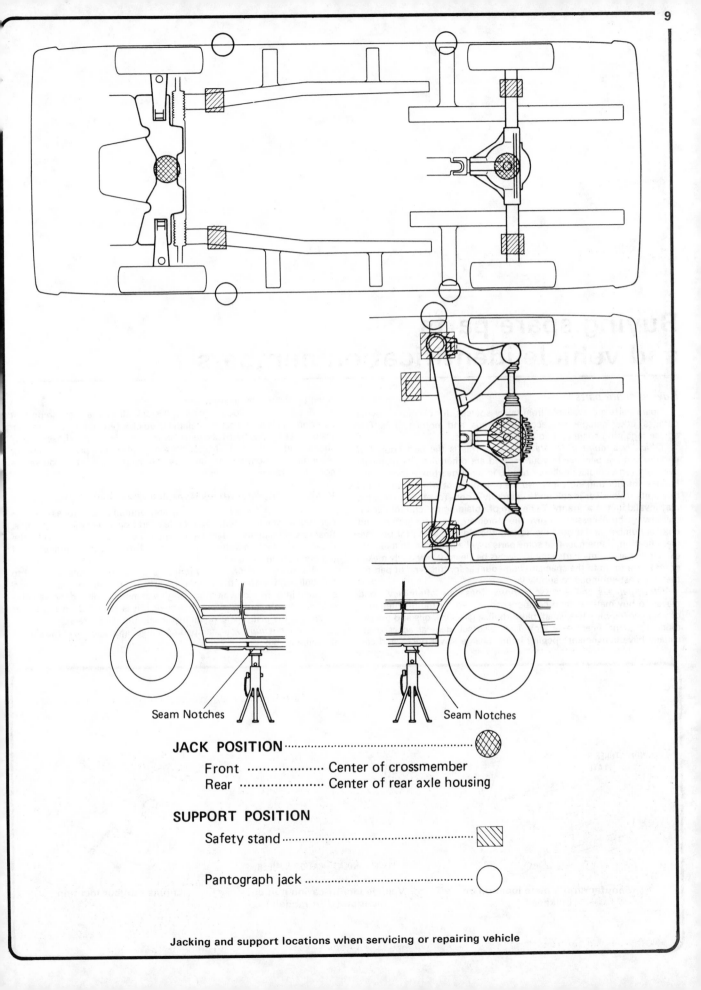

Seam Notches

Seam Notches

JACK POSITION ·· ⬤

    Front ················· Center of crossmember
    Rear ·················· Center of rear axle housing

SUPPORT POSITION

    Safety stand ··· ▨

    Pantograph jack ··· ◯

Jacking and support locations when servicing or repairing vehicle

Buying spare parts and vehicle identification numbers

Buying spare parts

Spare parts are available from many sources, for example: Toyota garages, other garages and accessory shops, and motor factors. Our advice regarding spare part sources is as follows:

Officially appointed Toyota garages – This is the best source of parts which are peculiar to your car and are otherwise not generally available (eg complete cylinder heads, internal gearbox components, badges, interior trim etc). It is also the only place at which you should buy parts if your car is still under warranty - non-Toyota components may invalidate the warranty. To be sure of obtaining the correct parts it will always be necessary to give the storeman your car's engine and chassis number, and if possible, to take the old part along for positive identification. Remember that some parts may be available on a factory exchange basis – any parts should always be clean! It obviously makes good sense to go to the specialists on your car for this type of part for they are best equipped to supply you.

Other garages and accessory shops: These are often very good places to buy materials and components needed for the maintenance of your car (eg oil filters, spark plugs, bulbs, fan belts, oils and grease, touch-up paint, filler paste etc). They also sell general accessories, usually have convenient opening hours, charge lower prices and can often be found not far from home.

Motor factors: Good factors will stock all of the more important components which wear out relatively quickly (eg clutch components, pistons, valves, exhaust systems, brake cylinders/pipes/hoses/seals/shoes and pads etc). Motor factors will often provide new or reconditioned components on a part exchange basis – this can save a considerable amount of money.

Vehicle identification numbers

Modifications are a continuing and unpublicised process carried out by the vehicle manufacturer quite apart from major model changes. Spare parts manuals and lists are compiled upon a numerical basis, the individual vehicle number being essential to correct identification of the component required.

The *vehicle identification number* is shown on a plate attached to the bulkhead within the engine compartment. This number is also stamped into the sidewall of the engine compartment and, on vehicles destined for operation in North America, it is repeated on the upper surface of the instrument panel just inside the windscreen.

The *engine number* is stamped on a machined surface at the side of the cylinder block.

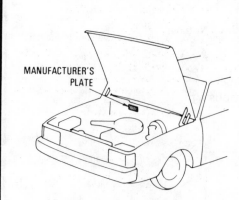

Manufacturer's plate location on bulkhead

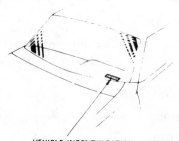

Vehicle identification number location (USA models)

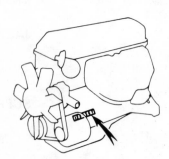

Engine number location

Use of English

As this book has been written in England, it uses the appropriate English component names, phrases, and spelling. Some of these differ from those used in America. Normally, these cause no difficulty, but to make sure, a glossary is printed below. In ordering spare parts remember the parts list may use some of these words:

English	American	English	American
Accelerator	Gas pedal	Leading shoe (of brake)	Primary shoe
Aerial	Antenna	Locks	Latches
Anti-roll bar	Stabiliser or sway bar	Methylated spirit	Denatured alcohol
Big-end bearing	Rod bearing	Motorway	Freeway, turnpike etc
Bonnet (engine cover)	Hood	Number plate	License plate
Boot (luggage compartment)	Trunk	Paraffin	Kerosene
Bulkhead	Firewall	Petrol	Gasoline (gas)
Bush	Bushing	Petrol tank	Gas tank
Cam follower or tappet	Valve lifter or tappet	'Pinking'	'Pinging'
Carburettor	Carburetor	Prise (force apart)	Pry
Catch	Latch	Propeller shaft	Driveshaft
Choke/venturi	Barrel	Quarterlight	Quarter window
Circlip	Snap-ring	Retread	Recap
Clearance	Lash	Reverse	Back-up
Crownwheel	Ring gear (of differential)	Rocker cover	Valve cover
Damper	Shock absorber, shock	Saloon	Sedan
Disc (brake)	Rotor/disk	Seized	Frozen
Distance piece	Spacer	Sidelight	Parking light
Drop arm	Pitman arm	Silencer	Muffler
Drop head coupe	Convertible	Sill panel (beneath doors)	Rocker panel
Dynamo	Generator (DC)	Small end, little end	Piston pin or wrist pin
Earth (electrical)	Ground	Spanner	Wrench
Engineer's blue	Prussian blue	Split cotter (for valve spring cap)	Lock (for valve spring retainer)
Estate car	Station wagon	Split pin	Cotter pin
Exhaust manifold	Header	Steering arm	Spindle arm
Fault finding/diagnosis	Troubleshooting	Sump	Oil pan
Float chamber	Float bowl	Swarf	Metal chips or debris
Free-play	Lash	Tab washer	Tang or lock
Freewheel	Coast	Tappet	Valve lifter
Gearbox	Transmission	Thrust bearing	Throw-out bearing
Gearchange	Shift	Top gear	High
Grub screw	Setscrew, Allen screw	Trackrod (of steering)	Tie-rod (or connecting rod)
Gudgeon pin	Piston pin or wrist pin	Trailing shoe (of brake)	Secondary shoe
Halfshaft	Axleshaft	Transmission	Whole drive line
Handbrake	Parking brake	Tyre	Tire
Hood	Soft top	Van	Panel wagon/van
Hot spot	Heat riser	Vice	Vise
Indicator	Turn signal	Wheel nut	Lug nut
Interior light	Dome lamp	Windscreen	Windshield
Layshaft (of gearbox)	Countershaft	Wing/mudguard	Fender

General repair procedures

Whenever servicing, repair or overhaul work is carried out on the car or its components, it is necessary to observe the following procedures and instructions. This will assist in carrying out the operation efficiently and to a professional standard of workmanship.

Joint mating faces and gaskets

Where a gasket is used between the mating faces of two components, ensure that it is renewed on reassembly, and fit it dry unless otherwise stated in the repair procedure. Make sure that the mating faces are clean and dry with all traces of old gasket removed. When cleaning a joint face, use a tool which is not likely to score or damage the face, and remove any burrs or nicks with an oilstone or fine file.

Make sure that tapped holes are cleaned with a pipe cleaner, and keep them free of jointing compound if this is being used unless specifically instructed otherwise.

Ensure that all orifices, channels or pipes are clear and blow through them, preferably using compressed air.

Oil seals

Whenever an oil seal is removed from its working location, either individually or as part of an assembly, it should be renewed.

The very fine sealing lip of the seal is easily damaged and will not seal if the surface it contacts is not completely clean and free from scratches, nicks or grooves. If the original sealing surface of the component cannot be restored, the component should be renewed.

Protect the lips of the seal from any surface which may damage them in the course of fitting. Use tape or a conical sleeve where possible. Lubricate the seal lips with oil before fitting and, on dual lipped seals, fill the space between the lips with grease.

Unless otherwise stated, oil seals must be fitted with their sealing lips toward the lubricant to be sealed.

Use a tubular drift or block of wood of the appropriate size to install the seal and, if the seal housing is shouldered, drive the seal down to the shoulder. If the seal housing is unshouldered, the seal should be fitted with its face flush with the housing top face.

Screw threads and fastenings

Always ensure that a blind tapped hole is completely free from oil, grease, water or other fluid before installing the bolt or stud. Failure to do this could cause the housing to crack due to the hydraulic action of the bolt or stud as it is screwed in.

When tightening a castellated nut to accept a split pin, tighten the nut to the specified torque, where applicable, and then tighten further to the next split pin hole. Never slacken the nut to align a split pin hole unless stated in the repair procedure.

When checking or retightening a nut or bolt to a specified torque setting, slacken the nut or bolt by a quarter of a turn, and then retighten to the specified setting.

Locknuts, locktabs and washers

Any fastening which will rotate against a component or housing in the course of tightening should always have a washer between it and the relevant component or housing.

Spring or split washers should always be renewed when they are used to lock a critical component such as a big-end bearing retaining nut or bolt.

Locktabs which are folded over to retain a nut or bolt should always be renewed.

Self-locking nuts can be reused in non-critical areas, providing resistance can be felt when the locking portion passes over the bolt or stud thread.

Split pins must always be replaced with new ones of the correct size for the hole.

Special tools

Some repair procedures in this manual entail the use of special tools such as a press, two or three-legged pullers, spring compressors etc. Wherever possible, suitable readily available alternatives to the manufacturer's special tools are described, and are shown in use. In some instances, where no alternative is possible, it has been necessary to resort to the use of a manufacturer's tool and this has been done for reasons of safety as well as the efficient completion of the repair operation. Unless you are highly skilled and have a thorough understanding of the procedure described, never attempt to bypass the use of any special tool when the procedure described specifies its use. Not only is there a very great risk of personal injury, but expensive damage could be caused to the components involved.

Tools and working facilities

Introduction

A selection of good tools is a fundamental requirement for anyone contemplating the maintenance and repair of a motor vehicle. For the owner who does not possess any, their purchase will prove a considerable expense, offsetting some of the savings made by doing-it-yourself. However, provided that the tools purchased are of good quality, they will last for many years and prove an extremely worthwhile investment.

To help the average owner to decide which tools are needed to carry out the various tasks detailed in this manual, we have compiled three lists of tools under the following headings: *Maintenance and minor repair*, *Repair and overhaul*, and *Special*. The newcomer to practical mechanics should start off with the *Maintenance and minor repair* tool kit and confine himself to the simpler jobs around the vehicle. Then, as his confidence and experience grow, he can undertake more difficult tasks, buying extra tools as, and when, they are needed. In this way, a *Maintenance and minor repair* tool kit can be built-up into a *Repair and overhaul* tool kit over a considerable period of time without any major cash outlays. The experienced do-it-yourselfer will have a tool kit good enough for most repair and overhaul procedures and will add tools from the *Special* category when he feels the expense is justified by the amount of use to which these tools will be put.

It is obviously not possible to cover the subject of tools fully here. For those who wish to learn more about tools and their use there is a book entitled *How to Choose and Use Car Tools* available from the publishers of this manual.

Maintenance and minor repair tool kit

The tools given in this list should be considered as a minimum requirement if routine maintenance, servicing and minor repair operations are to be undertaken. We recommend the purchase of combination spanners (ring one end, open-ended the other); although more expensive than open-ended ones, they do give the advantages of both types of spanner.

Combination spanners - 10, 11, 12, 13, 14 & 17 mm
Adjustable spanner - 9 inch
Spark plug spanner (with rubber insert)
Spark plug gap adjustment tool
Set of feeler gauges
Brake bleed nipple spanner
Screwdriver - 4 in long x 1/4 in dia (flat blade)
Screwdriver - 4 in long x 1/4 in dia (cross blade)
Combination pliers - 6 inch
Hacksaw (junior)
Tyre pump
Tyre pressure gauge
Oil can
Fine emery cloth (1 sheet)
Wire brush (small)
Funnel (medium size)

Repair and overhaul tool kit

These tools are virtually essential for anyone undertaking any major repairs to a motor vehicle, and are additional to those given in the *Maintenance and minor repair* list. Included in this list is a comprehensive set of sockets. Although these are expensive they will be found invaluable as they are so versatile - particularly if various drives are included in the set. We recommend the ½ in square-drive type, as this can be used with most proprietary torque wrenches. If you cannot afford a socket set, even bought piecemeal, then inexpensive tubular box spanners are a useful alternative.

The tools in this list will occasionally need to be supplemented by tools from the *Special* list.

Sockets (or box spanners) to cover range in previous list
Reversible ratchet drive (for use with sockets)
Extension piece, 10 inch (for use with sockets)
Universal joint (for use with sockets)
Torque wrench (for use with sockets)
'Mole' wrench - 8 inch
Ball pein hammer
Soft-faced hammer, plastic or rubber
Screwdriver - 6 in long x 5/16 in dia (flat blade)
Screwdriver - 2 in long x 5/16 in square (flat blade)
Screwdriver - 1 1/2 in long x 1/4 in dia (cross blade)
Screwdriver - 3 in long x 1/8 in dia (electricians)
Pliers - electricians side cutters
Pliers - needle nosed
Pliers - circlip (internal and external)
Cold chisel - 1/2 inch
Scriber
Scraper
Centre punch
Pin punch
Hacksaw
Valve grinding tool
Steel rule/straight-edge
Allen keys and keys for Torx screws
Selection of files
Wire brush (large)
Axle-stands
Jack (strong trolley or hydraulic type)

Special tools

The tools in this list are those which are not used regularly, are expensive to buy, or which need to be used in accordance with their manufacturers' instructions. Unless relatively difficult mechanical jobs are undertaken frequently, it will not be economic to buy many of these tools. Where this is the case, you could consider clubbing together with friends (or joining a motorists' club) to make a joint purchase, or borrowing the tools against a deposit from a local garage or tool hire specialist.

The following list contains only those tools and instruments freely available to the public, and not those special tools produced by the vehicle manufacturer specifically for its dealer network. You will find occasional references to these manufacturers' special tools in the text of this manual. Generally, an alternative method of doing the job without the vehicle manufacturers' special tool is given. However, sometimes, there is no alternative to using them. Where this is the case and the relevant tool cannot be bought or borrowed, you will have to entrust the work to a franchised garage.

Valve spring compressor (where applicable)
Piston ring compressor
Balljoint separator
Grease gun
Universal hub/bearing puller
Impact screwdriver
Micrometer and/or vernier gauge
Dial gauge
Stroboscopic timing light
Dwell angle meter/tachometer
Universal electrical multi-meter
Cylinder compression gauge
Lifting tackle
Trolley jack
Light with extension lead

Buying tools

For practically all tools, a tool factor is the best source since he will have a very comprehensive range compared with the average garage or accessory shop. Having said that, accessory shops often offer excellent quality tools at discount prices, so it pays to shop around.

Remember, you don't have to buy the most expensive items on the shelf, but it is always advisable to steer clear of the very cheap tools. There are plenty of good tools around at reasonable prices, so ask the proprietor or manager of the shop for advice before making a purchase.

Care and maintenance of tools

Having purchased a reasonable tool kit, it is necessary to keep the tools in a clean serviceable condition. After use, always wipe off any dirt, grease and metal particles using a clean, dry cloth, before putting the tools away. Never leave them lying around after they have been used. A simple tool rack on the garage or workshop wall, for items such as screwdrivers and pliers is a good idea. Store all normal wrenches and sockets in a metal box. Any measuring instruments, gauges, meters, etc, must be carefully stored where they cannot be damaged or become rusty.

Take a little care when tools are used. Hammer heads inevitably become marked and screwdrivers lose the keen edge on their blades from time to time. A little timely attention with emery cloth or a file will soon restore items like this to a good serviceable finish.

Working facilities

Not to be forgotten when discussing tools, is the workshop itself. If anything more than routine maintenance is to be carried out, some form of suitable working area becomes essential.

It is appreciated that many an owner mechanic is forced by circumstances to remove an engine or similar item, without the benefit of a garage or workshop. Having done this, any repairs should always be done under the cover of a roof.

Wherever possible, any dismantling should be done on a clean, flat workbench or table at a suitable working height.

Any workbench needs a vice: one with a jaw opening of 4 in (100 mm) is suitable for most jobs. As mentioned previously, some clean dry storage space is also required for tools, as well as for lubricants, cleaning fluids, touch-up paints and so on, which become necessary.

Another item which may be required, and which has a much more general usage, is an electric drill with a chuck capacity of at least 5/16 in (8 mm). This, together with a good range of twist drills, is virtually essential for fitting accessories such as mirrors and reversing lights.

Last, but not least, always keep a supply of old newspapers and clean, lint-free rags available, and try to keep any working area as clean as possible.

Spanner jaw gap comparison table

Jaw gap (in)	Spanner size
0.250	$\frac{1}{4}$ in AF
0.276	7 mm
0.313	$\frac{5}{16}$ in AF
0.315	8 mm
0.344	$\frac{11}{32}$ in AF; $\frac{1}{8}$ in Whitworth
0.354	9 mm
0.375	$\frac{3}{8}$ in AF
0.394	10 mm
0.433	11 mm
0.438	$\frac{7}{16}$ in AF
0.445	$\frac{3}{16}$ in Whitworth; $\frac{1}{4}$ in BSF
0.472	12 mm
0.500	$\frac{1}{2}$ in AF
0.512	13 mm
0.525	$\frac{1}{4}$ in Whitworth; $\frac{5}{16}$ in BSF
0.551	14 mm
0.563	$\frac{9}{16}$ in AF
0.591	15 mm
0.600	$\frac{5}{16}$ in Whitworth; $\frac{3}{8}$ in BSF
0.625	$\frac{5}{8}$ in AF
0.630	16 mm
0.669	17 mm
0.686	$\frac{11}{16}$ in AF
0.709	18 mm
0.710	$\frac{3}{8}$ in Whitworth; $\frac{7}{16}$ in BSF
0.748	19 mm
0.750	$\frac{3}{4}$ in AF
0.813	$\frac{13}{16}$ in AF
0.820	$\frac{7}{16}$ in Whitworth; $\frac{1}{2}$ in BSF
0.866	22 mm
0.875	$\frac{7}{8}$ in AF
0.920	$\frac{1}{2}$ in Whitworth; $\frac{9}{16}$ in BSF
0.938	$\frac{15}{16}$ in AF
0.945	24 mm
1.000	1 in AF
1.010	$\frac{9}{16}$ in Whitworth; $\frac{5}{8}$ in BSF
1.024	26 mm
1.063	$1\frac{1}{16}$ in AF; 27 mm
1.100	$\frac{5}{8}$ in Whitworth; $\frac{11}{16}$ in BSF
1.125	$1\frac{1}{8}$ in AF
1.181	30 mm
1.200	$\frac{11}{16}$ in Whitworth; $\frac{3}{4}$ in BSF
1.250	$1\frac{1}{4}$ in AF
1.260	32 mm
1.300	$\frac{3}{4}$ in Whitworth; $\frac{7}{8}$ in BSF
1.313	$1\frac{5}{16}$ in AF
1.390	$\frac{13}{16}$ in Whitworth; $\frac{15}{16}$ in BSF
1.417	36 mm
1.438	$1\frac{7}{16}$ in AF
1.480	$\frac{7}{8}$ in Whitworth; 1 in BSF
1.500	$1\frac{1}{2}$ in AF
1.575	40 mm; $\frac{15}{16}$ in Whitworth
1.614	41 mm
1.625	$1\frac{5}{8}$ in AF
1.670	1 in Whitworth; $1\frac{1}{8}$ in BSF
1.688	$1\frac{11}{16}$ in AF
1.811	46 mm
1.813	$1\frac{13}{16}$ in AF
1.860	$1\frac{1}{8}$ in Whitworth; $1\frac{1}{4}$ in BSF
1.875	$1\frac{7}{8}$ in AF
1.969	50 mm
2.000	2 in AF
2.050	$1\frac{1}{4}$ in Whitworth; $1\frac{3}{8}$ in BSF
2.165	55 mm
2.362	60 mm

Conversion factors

Length (distance)
Inches (in)	X	25.4	= Millimetres (mm)	X 0.0394	= Inches (in)
Feet (ft)	X	0.305	= Metres (m)	X 3.281	= Feet (ft)
Miles	X	1.609	= Kilometres (km)	X 0.621	= Miles

Volume (capacity)
Cubic inches (cu in; in^3)	X	16.387	= Cubic centimetres (cc; cm^3)	X 0.061	= Cubic inches (cu in; in^3)
Imperial pints (Imp pt)	X	0.568	= Litres (l)	X 1.76	= Imperial pints (Imp pt)
Imperial quarts (Imp qt)	X	1.137	= Litres (l)	X 0.88	= Imperial quarts (Imp qt)
Imperial quarts (Imp qt)	X	1.201	= US quarts (US qt)	X 0.833	= Imperial quarts (Imp qt)
US quarts (US qt)	X	0.946	= Litres (l)	X 1.057	= US quarts (US qt)
Imperial gallons (Imp gal)	X	4.546	= Litres (l)	X 0.22	= Imperial gallons (Imp gal)
Imperial gallons (Imp gal)	X	1.201	= US gallons (US gal)	X 0.833	= Imperial gallons (Imp gal)
US gallons (US gal)	X	3.785	= Litres (l)	X 0.264	= US gallons (US gal)

Mass (weight)
Ounces (oz)	X	28.35	= Grams (g)	X 0.035	= Ounces (oz)
Pounds (lb)	X	0.454	= Kilograms (kg)	X 2.205	= Pounds (lb)

Force
Ounces-force (ozf; oz)	X	0.278	= Newtons (N)	X 3.6	= Ounces-force (ozf; oz)
Pounds-force (lbf; lb)	X	4.448	= Newtons (N)	X 0.225	= Pounds-force (lbf; lb)
Newtons (N)	X	0.1	= Kilograms-force (kgf; kg)	X 9.81	= Newtons (N)

Pressure
Pounds-force per square inch (psi; lbf/in^2; lb/in^2)	X	0.070	= Kilograms-force per square centimetre (kgf/cm^2; kg/cm^2)	X 14.223	= Pounds-force per square inch (psi; lbf/in^2; lb/in^2)
Pounds-force per square inch (psi; lbf/in^2; lb/in^2)	X	0.068	= Atmospheres (atm)	X 14.696	= Pounds-force per square inch (psi; lbf/in^2; lb/in^2)
Pounds-force per square inch (psi; lbf/in^2; lb/in^2)	X	0.069	=.Bars	X 14.5	= Pounds-force per square inch (psi; lbf/in^2; lb/in^2)
Pounds-force per square inch (psi; lbf/in^2; lb/in^2)	X	6.895	= Kilopascals (kPa)	X 0.145	= Pounds-force per square inch (psi; lbf/in^2; lb/in^2)
Kilopascals (kPa)	X	0.01	= Kilograms-force per square centimetre (kgf/cm^2; kg/cm^2)	X 98.1	= Kilopascals (kPa)

Torque (moment of force)
Pounds-force inches (lbf in; lb in)	X	1.152	= Kilograms-force centimetre (kgf cm; kg cm)	X 0.868	= Pounds-force inches (lbf in; lb in)
Pounds-force inches (lbf in; lb in)	X	0.113	= Newton metres (Nm)	X 8.85	= Pounds-force inches (lbf in; lb in)
Pounds-force inches (lbf in; lb in)	X	0.083	= Pounds-force feet (lbf ft; lb ft)	X 12	= Pounds-force inches (lbf in; lb in)
Pounds-force feet (lbf ft; lb ft)	X	0.138	= Kilograms-force metres (kgf m; kg m)	X 7.233	= Pounds-force feet (lbf ft; lb ft)
Pounds-force feet (lbf ft; lb ft)	X	1.356	= Newton metres (Nm)	X 0.738	= Pounds-force feet (lbf ft; lb ft)
Newton metres (Nm)	X	0.102	= Kilograms-force metres (kgf m; kg m)	X 9.804	= Newton metres (Nm)

Power
Horsepower (hp)	X	745.7	= Watts (W)	X 0.0013	= Horsepower (hp)

Velocity (speed)
Miles per hour (miles/hr; mph)	X	1.609	= Kilometres per hour (km/hr; kph)	X 0.621	= Miles per hour (miles/hr; mph)

Fuel consumption*
Miles per gallon, Imperial (mpg)	X	0.354	= Kilometres per litre (km/l)	X 2.825	= Miles per gallon, Imperial (mpg)
Miles per gallon, US (mpg)	X	0.425	= Kilometres per litre (km/l)	X 2.352	= Miles per gallon, US (mpg)

Temperature
Degrees Fahrenheit = (°C x 1.8) + 32   Degrees Celsius (Degrees Centigrade; °C) = (°F - 32) x 0.56

*It is common practice to convert from miles per gallon (mpg) to litres/100 kilometres (l/100km), where mpg (Imperial) x l/100 km = 282 and mpg (US) x l/100 km = 235

Safety first!

Professional motor mechanics are trained in safe working procedures. However enthusiastic you may be about getting on with the job in hand, do take the time to ensure that your safety is not put at risk. A moment's lack of attention can result in an accident, as can failure to observe certain elementary precautions.

There will always be new ways of having accidents, and the following points do not pretend to be a comprehensive list of all dangers; they are intended rather to make you aware of the risks and to encourage a safety-conscious approach to all work you carry out on your vehicle.

Essential DOs and DON'Ts

DON'T rely on a single jack when working underneath the vehicle. Always use reliable additional means of support, such as axle stands, securely placed under a part of the vehicle that you know will not give way.

DON'T attempt to loosen or tighten high-torque nuts (e.g. wheel hub nuts) while the vehicle is on a jack; it may be pulled off.

DON'T start the engine without first ascertaining that the transmission is in neutral (or 'Park' where applicable) and the parking brake applied.

DON'T suddenly remove the filler cap from a hot cooling system – cover it with a cloth and release the pressure gradually first, or you may get scalded by escaping coolant.

DON'T attempt to drain oil until you are sure it has cooled sufficiently to avoid scalding you.

DON'T grasp any part of the engine, exhaust or catalytic converter without first ascertaining that it is sufficiently cool to avoid burning you.

DON'T allow brake fluid or antifreeze to contact vehicle paintwork.

DON'T syphon toxic liquids such as fuel, brake fluid or antifreeze by mouth, or allow them to remain on your skin.

DON'T inhale dust – it may be injurious to health (see *Asbestos* below).

DON'T allow any spilt oil or grease to remain on the floor – wipe it up straight away, before someone slips on it.

DON'T use ill-fitting spanners or other tools which may slip and cause injury.

DON'T attempt to lift a heavy component which may be beyond your capability – get assistance.

DON'T rush to finish a job, or take unverified short cuts.

DON'T allow children or animals in or around an unattended vehicle.

DO wear eye protection when using power tools such as drill, sander, bench grinder etc, and when working under the vehicle.

DO use a barrier cream on your hands prior to undertaking dirty jobs – it will protect your skin from infection as well as making the dirt easier to remove afterwards; but make sure your hands aren't left slippery.

DO keep loose clothing (cuffs, tie etc) and long hair well out of the way of moving mechanical parts.

DO remove rings, wristwatch etc, before working on the vehicle – especially the electrical system.

DO ensure that any lifting tackle used has a safe working load rating adequate for the job.

DO keep your work area tidy – it is only too easy to fall over articles left lying around.

DO get someone to check periodically that all is well, when working alone on the vehicle.

DO carry out work in a logical sequence and check that everything is correctly assembled and tightened afterwards.

DO remember that your vehicle's safety affects that of yourself and others. If in doubt on any point, get specialist advice.

IF, in spite of following these precautions, you are unfortunate enough to injure yourself, seek medical attention as soon as possible.

Asbestos

Certain friction, insulating, sealing, and other products – such as brake linings, brake bands, clutch linings, torque converters, gaskets, etc – contain asbestos. *Extreme care must be taken to avoid inhalation of dust from such products since it is hazardous to health.* If in doubt, assume that they *do* contain asbestos.

Fire

Remember at all times that petrol (gasoline) is highly flammable. Never smoke, or have any kind of naked flame around, when working on the vehicle. But the risk does not end there – a spark caused by an electrical short-circuit, by two metal surfaces contacting each other, by careless use of tools, or even by static electricity built up in your body under certain conditions, can ignite petrol vapour, which in a confined space is highly explosive.

Always disconnect the battery earth (ground) terminal before working on any part of the fuel or electrical system, and never risk spilling fuel on to a hot engine or exhaust.

It is recommended that a fire extinguisher of a type suitable for fuel and electrical fires is kept handy in the garage or workplace at all times. Never try to extinguish a fuel or electrical fire with water.

Fumes

Certain fumes are highly toxic and can quickly cause unconsciousness and even death if inhaled to any extent. Petrol (gasoline) vapour comes into this category, as do the vapours from certain solvents such as trichloroethylene. Any draining or pouring of such volatile fluids should be done in a well ventilated area.

When using cleaning fluids and solvents, read the instructions carefully. Never use materials from unmarked containers – they may give off poisonous vapours.

Never run the engine of a motor vehicle in an enclosed space such as a garage. Exhaust fumes contain carbon monoxide which is extremely poisonous; if you need to run the engine, always do so in the open air or at least have the rear of the vehicle outside the workplace.

If you are fortunate enough to have the use of an inspection pit, never drain or pour petrol, and never run the engine, while the vehicle is standing over it; the fumes, being heavier than air, will concentrate in the pit with possibly lethal results.

The battery

Never cause a spark, or allow a naked light, near the vehicle's battery. It will normally be giving off a certain amount of hydrogen gas, which is highly explosive.

Always disconnect the battery earth (ground) terminal before working on the fuel or electrical systems.

If possible, loosen the filler plugs or cover when charging the battery from an external source. Do not charge at an excessive rate or the battery may burst.

Take care when topping up and when carrying the battery. The acid electrolyte, even when diluted, is very corrosive and should not be allowed to contact the eyes or skin.

If you ever need to prepare electrolyte yourself, always add the acid slowly to the water, and never the other way round. Protect against splashes by wearing rubber gloves and goggles.

When jump starting a car using a booster battery, for negative earth (ground) vehicles, connect the jump leads in the following sequence: First connect one jump lead between the positive (+) terminals of the two batteries. Then connect the other jump lead first to the negative (–) terminal of the booster battery, and then to a good earthing (ground) point on the vehicle to be started, at least 18 in (45 cm) from the battery if possible. Ensure that hands and jump leads are clear of any moving parts, and that the two vehicles do not touch. Disconnect the leads in the reverse order.

Mains electricity

When using an electric power tool, inspection light etc, which works from the mains, always ensure that the appliance is correctly connected to its plug and that, where necessary, it is properly earthed (grounded). Do not use such appliances in damp conditions and, again, beware of creating a spark or applying excessive heat in the vicinity of fuel or fuel vapour.

Ignition HT voltage

A severe electric shock can result from touching certain parts of the ignition system, such as the HT leads, when the engine is running or being cranked, particularly if components are damp or the insulation is defective. Where an electronic ignition system is fitted, the HT voltage is much higher and could prove fatal.

Routine maintenance

Maintenance is essential for ensuring safety and desirable for the purpose of getting the best in terms of performance and economy from the car. Over the years the need for periodic lubrication – oiling, greasing and so on – has been drastically reduced if not totally eliminated. This has unfortunately tended to lead some owners to think that because no such action is required the items either no longer exist or will last for ever. This is a serious delusion. It follows therefore that the largest initial element of maintenance is visual examination. This may lead to repairs or renewals.

The following maintenance schedules are for European market models and are sub-divided into service intervals. The service intervals and requirements for USA market models differ and are therefore listed separately.

The specified time intervals should be used as a guide where low mileages are covered. For further details on individual maintenance procedures, refer to the Routine Maintenance section of the applicable Chapter(s).

Underbonnet view – UK model with 21R engine

1 Engine oil filler cap	6 Suspension strut top
2 Petrol pump	mounting
3 Battery	7 Brake master cylinder
4 Fuel filter	8 Clutch master cylinder
5 Carburettor	9 Heater control valve

10 Windscreen wiper motor	14 Washer reservoir
11 Power steering fluid	15 Coolant reservoir
reservoir	16 Drivebelt
12 Ignition distributor	17 Radiator cap
13 Ignition coil	

Underside front view – UK model with undertray removed for clarity

1 Sump drain plug
2 Strut bar
3 Bottom hose-to-radiator connection
4 Stabilizer bar
5 Alternator
6 Lower steering balljoint
7 Suspension arm
8 Tie-rod
9 Steering gear
10 Exhaust downpipe
11 Propeller shaft universal joint
12 Gearbox mounting
13 Speedometer cable
14 Gearbox drain plug
15 Clutch housing

Underside rear view – UK model with IRS suspension

1 Rear axle drain plug
2 Rear silencer
3 Fuel tank
4 Shock absorber bottom mounting
5 Driveshaft
6 Suspension arm
7 Propeller shaft and rear end universal joint
8 Handbrake cable
9 Stabilizer bar

SERVICE SCHEDULES – EUROPEAN MODELS

Weekly or before a long journey

Engine

Check oil level and top up if necessary (Chapter 1)
Check coolant level and top up if necessary (Chapter 2)
Check battery electrolyte level and top up if necessary (Chapter 12)

Brakes and clutch

Check both master cylinder reservoir fluid levels (Chapters 5 and 9)

Steering and suspension

Check tyre pressures. Pressure requirements according to model are given in Chapter 10
Check tyres visually for wear or damage

Lights, wipers and horns

Check operation of all lights front and rear
Check operation of windscreen wipers and horns
Check and top up windscreen washer reservoir fluid

After first 1000 miles (1600 km) – new vehicle

Engine

Check and if necessary adjust the valve clearances (Chapter 1)
Check and if necessary adjust the drivebelt(s) (Chapter 2)
Check and if necessary adjust the idle speed, fast idle speed and idle mixture (Chapter 3)

Brakes and clutch

Check and if necessary adjust the clutch pedal, brake pedal and handbrake (Chapters 5 and 9)
Check both master cylinder reservoir fluid levels (Chapters 5 and 9)
Check the brake lines and hoses for security and any signs of leakage (Chapter 9)

Chassis/body unit

Check tightness of all nuts and bolts

Every 6000 miles (10 000 km) or six months – whichever comes first

---

Engine

Check and if necessary adjust the drivebelts (Chapter 2)
Drain the engine oil (when warm) and refill with the correct quantity and grade of oil. Renew the oil filter (Chapter 1)

Ignition system

Remove, clean, and inspect the spark plugs. Clean and adjust the electrode gap (Chapter 4)
Clean and inspect the ignition HT leads and LT wires. Check for security (Chapter 4)
Remove, clean, and inspect the distributor cap and rotor. Clean and if necessary adjust the distributor contact breaker points (where applicable) (Chapter 4)
Check and if necessary adjust the ignition timing and dwell angle (where applicable) (Chapter 4)

Brake and clutch

Check and if necessary adjust the clutch pedal, brake pedal and handbrake (Chapters 5 and 9)

Inspect the brake pads and discs for signs of excessive wear (Chapter 9)
Check both master cylinder fluid levels.
Check the brake lines and hoses for security and any signs of leakage (Chapter 9)

Transmission and rear axle

Check the oil level in the gearbox (or automatic transmission) and the rear axle. Top up if necessary (Chapters 6 and 8)

Suspension and steering

Inspect the tyres for excessive or uneven wear or damage. Check the pressures (Chapter 10)
Check the power steering fluid level (where applicable) and top up if necessary.
Check the power steering system hoses for condition, security and any signs of leaks (Chapter 10)
Examine the steering and suspension joints and dust covers for signs of excessive wear or damage (Chapter 10)

Every 12 000 miles (20 000 km) or 12 months – whichever comes first

---

Engine

Check the cooling system hoses for condition and security. If a coolant without corrosion inhibitor has been used, drain the system and renew the coolant (Chapter 2)
Inspect the exhaust system for condition and security (Chapter 3)
Clean and inspect the positive crankcase ventilation system (Chapter 3)
Remove and renew the spark plugs (Chapter 4)

Ignition system

Renew contact breaker points (where applicable) (Chapter 4)

Brakes

Clean and inspect the brake linings on the rear drum brakes, renew if necessary (Chapter 9)

Suspension and steering

Examine the steering linkages for excessive wear, and check that the steering wheel free play is within the specified limit (Chapter 10)
Check all front and rear suspension components for condition and security. The securing nuts and bolts should be tightened to their correct torque settings (Chapter 10)
Check the rack and pinion steering gear gaiters for condition and leakage (Chapter 10)

Every 24 000 miles (40 000 km) or two years – whichever comes first

---

Engine

Check all vacuum hoses and connections for condition and security (Chapter 1). The emission control hoses are shown in Chapter 3.
Drain and renew the engine coolant (Chapter 2)
Renew the fuel filter (Chapter 3)
Renew the air filter element (Chapter 3)

Transmission

Drain and renew the gearbox oil (manual transmission) (Chapter 6)
Drain and renew the automatic transmission fluid (where applicable) (Chapter 6)

Brakes

Drain the fluid from the hydraulic system and renew it (Chapter 9)

Suspension and steering

Lubricate the wheel bearings and the steering balljoints with grease (Chapter 10)

SERVICE SCHEDULES – USA MODELS

The Routine Maintenance procedures with distance/time intervals listed below are for vehicles operating under normal conditions. On 1985 models, the maintenance intervals differ in some instances, and owners of these models are advised to check against the intervals specified in the manufacturer's Owners Manual supplied with the vehicle for clarification.

Where a vehicle is used under severe driving conditions, the service intervals will need to be more regular for some items. The items concerned are listed in the Section headed 'Additional maintenance – vehicles used in severe conditions'.

Weekly or before a long journey

Carry out those items listed in the weekly service checks for European models

Every 10 000 miles (16 000 km) or eight months – whichever comes first

Engine

Drain and renew the engine oil (Chapter 1)
Renew the engine oil filter (Chapter 1)

Every 15 000 miles (24 000 km) or twelve months – whichever comes first

Engine

Check and if necessary adjust the valve clearances (Chapter 1)

Fuel system

Check the exhaust system pipes and connections for condition and security, Repair or renew as necessary (Chapter 3)
Check the engine idle speed and, on carburettor models, the fast idle speed and choke system. Adjust if necessary (Chapter 3)

Ignition system

Remove and renew the spark plugs
Check the condition and security of the HT and LT leads

Transmission

Check the oil level in the manual gearbox. Top up level if necessary (Chapter 6)
Check the fluid level in the automatic transmission. Top up level if necessary (Chapter 6)

Rear axle

Check the oil level in the differential housing. Top up the level if necessary (Chapter 8)

Brakes

Check the front brake discs and pads for excessive wear. Renew if necessary (Chapter 9)
Check the rear brake linings and drums or discs and pads (as applicable), and renew if necessary (Chapter 9)
Check for satisfactory operation of the handbrake (Chapter 9)
Examine the brake system pipes and hoses for security and condition. Renew where necessary (Chapter 9)

Suspension and steering

Check the suspension components for excessive wear, condition and security (Chapter 10)
Inspect the steering gear gaiters for signs of damage or leakage
Check the steering linkages and balljoints for excessive wear or damage (Chapter 10)
Check the steering wheel for excessive play (Chapter 10)
On power steering models, check the fluid level in the reservoir and check the system hoses and connections for security and condition

(Chapter 10)

Chassis/body unit

Check the bodywork, particularly the underside, for signs of damage and corrosion. Repair as necessary. If serious corrosion or damage has occurred around the steering or suspension mountings consult your Toyota dealer.

General checks

Check the windscreen and rear window wiper blades for wear and deterioration and renew if necessary
Detach the battery leads, clean terminals and connectors and apply petroleum jelly when reconnecting
Check the lights, horn and wipers for satisfactory operation

Every 30 000 miles (48 000 km) or two years – whichever comes first

Drivebelts

Inspect the condition of the drivebelts and check their tension. Renew/adjust if necessary as described in Chapter 2

Fuel system

Renew the air filter element (Chapter 3)
Inspect the fuel lines and hoses for condition and security (Chapter 3)
Inspect the fuel filler cap seal. It must be in good condition and correctly seated (Chapter 3)
Inspect the PCV system hoses and connections for condition and security. Renew the PCV valve, except on California models (Chapter 3). (When fitting the new valve ensure that the large end fits downwards)
Check the charcoal canister for satisfactory operation (Chapter 3)
Check that the hoses are in good condition and securely connected
Inspect the evaporative emission control system hoses for condition and security (Chapter 3)

Suspension and steering

Check the wheel bearings for excessive wear (Chapter 10)
Lubricate the wheel bearings and the balljoint with grease (insert grease nipple in place of bottom screw plug to apply grease, then refit plug) (Chapter 10)
On IRS models, also lubricate the rear wheel bearings (Chapter 10)

Every 60 000 miles (90 000 km) or four years – whichever comes first

Cooling system

Drain the engine coolant and renew it using the correct antifreeze mixture (Chapter 2)
Check the cooling and heating system hoses for condition and security (Chapter 2)

Fuel system

Remove and renew the fuel filler cap seal (Chapter 3)
Remove and renew the fuel line filter (Chapter 3)
Check the emission control system hoses for condition and security
On California models, renew the PCV valve (when fitting the valve ensure that the large end fits downwards) (Chapter 3)

ADDITIONAL MAINTENANCE – VEHICLES USED IN SEVERE CONDITIONS

Where a vehicle is regularly used in severe operating conditions, some items will require more regular maintenance. To define the term 'severe conditions' the following is a guide.
Vehicle used regularly for:

(a) *Repeated short trips*
(b) *Pulling a trailer*
(c) *Driving on rough, muddy, dusty or mountainous roads*
(d) *Driving in very cold weather and in areas with salt on the roads*

When a vehicle is used under such conditions, the following items must be serviced at the mileage/time intervals specified below.

Engine oil and filter
Renew every 3750 miles (6000 km) or three months (Chapter 1)

Exhaust system and mountings
Check every 7500 miles (12 000 km) or six months (Chapter 3)

Air filter
Remove, inspect and blow clean every 3750 miles (6000 km) or three months (Chapter 3)
Renew every 30 000 miles (48 000 km) or two years (Chapter 3)

Ignition wiring
Clean and inspect every twelve months (Chapter 4)

Distributor cap
Clean and inspect every twelve months (Chapter 4)

Brake pads/discs and lining/drums
Inspect every 7500 miles (12 000 km) or six months (Chapter 9)

Steering/suspension balljoints and dust covers
Inspect every 7500 miles (12 000 km) or six months (Chapter 10)

Gearbox/transmission
Check oil level every 15 000 miles (24 000 km) or 12 months (Chapter 6)

Chassis and body
Clean and inspect for condition and security every 7500 miles (12 000 km) or six months

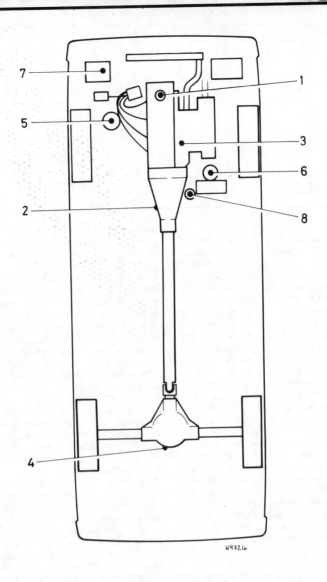

H9724

Recommended lubricants and fluids

Component or system	Lubricant type or specification
Engine (1)	Multigrade engine oil SAE 10W30 or 10W40 (see Chapter 1)
Manual gearbox (2)	SAE 75W-90 or SAE 90
Automatic gearbox (3)	ATF Dexron II
Differential (4)	SAE 90
Wheel bearings	Multi-purpose lithium based grease
Steering gear	Molybdenum disulphide grease
Power steering fluid (5)	ATF Dexron or Dexron II
Brake fluid (6)	SAE J 1703 or DOT 3
Cooling system (7)	Anti-corrosion type ethylene-glycol based antifreeze solution
Clutch fluid (8)	SAE J 1703 or DOT 3

Note: *The above are general recommendations only. Lubrication requirements vary from territory to territory and depend on vehicle usage. If in doubt, consult the operator's handbook supplied with the vehicle, or your nearest dealer.*

Fault diagnosis

Introduction

The vehicle owner who does his or her own maintenance according to the recommended schedules should not have to use this section of the manual very often. Modern component reliability is such that, provided those items subject to wear or deterioration are inspected or renewed at the specified intervals, sudden failure is comparatively rare. Faults do not usually just happen as a result of sudden failure, but develop over a period of time. Major mechanical failures in particular are usually preceded by characteristic symptoms over hundreds or even thousands of miles. Those components which do occasionally fail without warning are often small and easily carried in the vehicle.

With any fault finding, the first step is to decide where to begin investigations. Sometimes this is obvious, but on other occasions a little detective work will be necessary. The owner who makes half a dozen haphazard adjustments or replacements may be successful in curing a fault (or its symptoms), but he will be none the wiser if the fault recurs and he may well have spent more time and money than was necessary. A calm and logical approach will be found to be more satisfactory in the long run. Always take into account any warning signs or abnormalities that may have been noticed in the period preceding the fault – power loss, high or low gauge readings, unusual noises or smells, etc – and remember that failure of components such as fuses or spark plugs may only be pointers to some underlying fault.

The pages which follow here are intended to help in cases of failure to start or breakdown on the road. There is also a Fault Diagnosis Section at the end of each Chapter which should be consulted if the preliminary checks prove unfruitful. Whatever the fault, certain basic principles apply. These are as follows:

Verify the fault. This is simply a matter of being sure that you know what the symptoms are before starting work. This is particularly important if you are investigating a fault for someone else who may not have described it very accurately.

Don't overlook the obvious. For example, if the vehicle won't start, is there petrol in the tank? (Don't take anyone else's word on this particular point, and don't trust the fuel gauge either!) If an electrical fault is indicated, look for loose or broken wires before digging out the test gear.

Cure the disease, not the symptom. Substituting a flat battery with a fully charged one will get you off the hard shoulder, but if the underlying cause is not attended to, the new battery will go the same way. Similarly, changing oil-fouled spark plugs for a new set will get you moving again, but remember that the reason for the fouling (if it wasn't simply an incorrect grade of plug) will have to be established and corrected.

Don't take anything for granted. Particularly, don't forget that a 'new' component may itself be defective (especially if it's been rattling round in the boot for months), and don't leave components out of a fault diagnosis sequence just because they are new or recently fitted. When you do finally diagnose a difficult fault, you'll probably realise that all the evidence was there from the start.

Electrical faults

Electrical faults can be more puzzling than straightforward mechanical failures, but they are no less susceptible to logical analysis if the basic principles of operation are understood. Vehicle electrical wiring exists in extremely unfavourable conditions – heat, vibration and chemical attack – and the first things to look for are loose or corroded connections and broken or chafed wires, especially where the wires pass through holes in the bodywork or are subject to vibration.

All metal-bodied vehicles in current production have one pole of the battery 'earthed', ie connected to the vehicle bodywork, and in nearly all modern vehicles it is the negative (–) terminal. The various electrical components – motors, bulb holders etc – are also connected to earth, either by means of a lead or directly by their mountings. Electric current flows through the component and then back to the battery via the bodywork. If the component mounting is loose or corroded, or if a good path back to the battery is not available, the circuit will be incomplete and malfunction will result. The engine and/or gearbox are also earthed by means of flexible metal straps to the body or subframe; if these straps are loose or missing, starter motor, generator and ignition trouble may result.

Assuming the earth return to be satisfactory, electrical faults will be due either to component malfunction or to defects in the current supply. Individual components are dealt with in Chapter 12. If supply wires are broken or cracked internally this results in an open-circuit, and the easiest way to check for this is to bypass the suspect wire temporarily with a length of wire having a crocodile clip or suitable connector at each end. Alternatively, a 12V test lamp can be used to verify the presence of supply voltage at various points along the wire and the break can be thus isolated.

If a bare portion of a live wire touches the bodywork or other earthed metal part, the electricity will take the low-resistance path thus formed back to the battery: this is known as a short-circuit. Hopefully a short-circuit will blow a fuse, but otherwise it may cause burning of the insulation (and possibly further short-circuits) or even a fire. This is why it is inadvisable to bypass persistently blowing fuses with silver foil or wire.

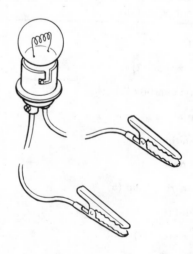

Simple test lamp is useful for tracing electrical faults

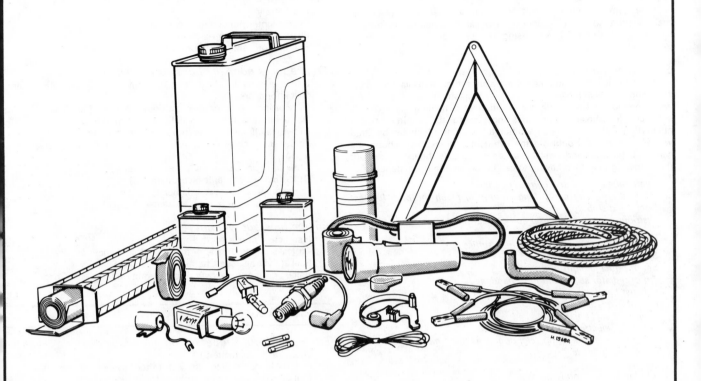

Carrying a few spares can save you a long walk!

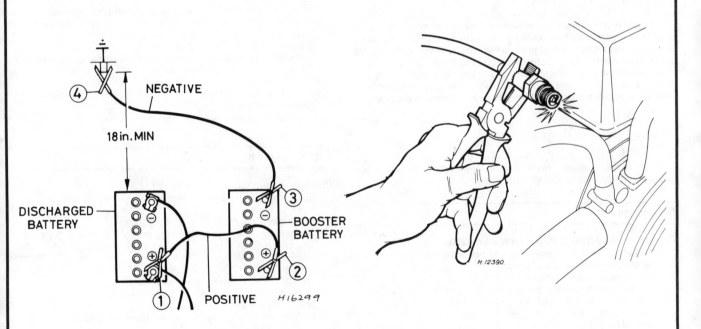

Jump start lead connections for negative earth vehicles – connect leads in order shown

Crank engine and check for a spark. Note use of insulated tool

EFI models

If an engine fault develops on a vehicle fitted with electronic fuel-injection, some fault diagnosis tests can be made by referring to Chapter 3, Section 33, and using the fault diagnosis system as described.

Spares and tool kit

Most vehicles are supplied only with sufficient tools for wheel changing; the *Maintenance and minor repair* tool kit detailed in *Tools and working facilities*, with the addition of a hammer, is probably sufficient for those repairs that most motorists would consider attempting at the roadside. In addition a few items which can be fitted without too much trouble in the event of a breakdown should be carried. Experience and available space will modify the list below, but the following may save having to call on professional assistance:

Spark plugs, clean and correctly gapped
HT lead and plug cap – long enough to reach the plug furthest from the distributor
Distributor rotor, condenser and contact breaker points (where applicable)
Drivebelt(s) – emergency type may suffice
Spare fuses
Set of principal light bulbs
Tin of radiator sealer and hose bandage
Exhaust bandage
Roll of insulating tape
Length of soft iron wire
Length of electrical flex
Torch or inspection lamp (can double as test lamp)
Battery jump leads
Tow-rope
Ignition waterproofing aerosol
Litre of engine oil
Sealed can of hydraulic fluid
Emergency windscreen
Worm drive clips
Tube of filler paste

If spare fuel is carried, a can designed for the purpose should be used to minimise risks of leakage and collision damage. A first aid kit and a warning triangle, whilst not at present compulsory in the UK, are obviously sensible items to carry in addition to the above.

When touring abroad it may be advisable to carry additional spares which, even if you cannot fit them yourself, could save having to wait while parts are obtained. The items below may be worth considering:

Throttle cable
Cylinder head gasket
Alternator brushes
Tyre valve core

One of the motoring organisations will be able to advise on availability of fuel etc in foreign countries.

Engine will not start

Engine fails to turn when starter operated

 Flat battery (recharge, use jump leads, or push start)
 Battery terminals loose or corroded
 Battery earth to body defective
 Engine earth strap loose or broken
 Starter motor (or solenoid) wiring loose or broken
 Automatic transmission selector in wrong position, or inhibitor switch faulty
 Ignition/starter switch faulty
 Major mechanical failure (seizure)
 Starter or solenoid internal fault (see Chapter 12)

Starter motor turns engine slowly

 Partially discharged battery (recharge, use jump leads, or push start)
 Battery terminals loose or corroded
 Battery earth to body defective
 Engine earth strap loose
 Starter motor (or solenoid) wiring loose
 Starter motor internal fault (see Chapter 12)

Starter motor spins without turning engine

 Flat battery
 Starter motor pinion sticking on sleeve
 Flywheel gear teeth damaged or worn
 Starter motor mounting bolts loose

Engine turns normally but fails to start

 Damp or dirty HT leads and distributor cap (crank engine and check for spark)
 Dirty or incorrectly gapped distributor points (if applicable)
 No fuel in tank (check for delivery at carburettor)
 Excessive choke (hot engine) or insufficient choke (cold engine)
 Fouled or incorrectly gapped spark plugs (remove, clean and regap)
 Other ignition system fault (see Chapter 4)
 Other fuel system fault (see Chapter 3)
 Poor compression (see Chapter 1, Section 20)
 Major mechanical failure (eg camshaft drive)

Engine fires but will not run

 Insufficient choke (cold engine)
 Air leaks at carburettor or inlet manifold (where applicable)
 Fuel starvation (see Chapter 3)
 Ballast resistor defective, or other ignition fault (see Chapter 4)

Engine cuts out and will not restart

Engine cuts out suddenly – ignition fault

 Loose or disconnected LT wires
 Wet HT leads or distributor cap (after traversing water splash)
 Coil or condenser failure (check for spark)
 Other ignition fault (see Chapter 4)

Engine misfires before cutting out – fuel fault

 Fuel tank empty
 Fuel pump defective or filter blocked (check for delivery)
 Fuel tank filler vent blocked (suction will be evident on releasing cap)
 Carburettor needle valve sticking (where applicable)
 Carburettor jets blocked (fuel contaminated) (where applicable)
 Other fuel system fault (see Chapter 3)

Engine cuts out – other causes

 Serious overheating
 Major mechanical failure (eg camshaft drive)

Engine overheats

Ignition (no-charge) warning light illuminated

 Slack or broken drivebelt – retension or renew (Chapter 2)

Ignition warning light not illuminated

 Coolant loss due to internal or external leakage (see Chapter 2)
 Thermostat defective
 Low oil level
 Brakes binding
 Radiator clogged externally or internally
 Cooling fan not operating correctly
 Engine waterways clogged
 Ignition timing incorrect or automatic advance malfunctioning
 Mixture too weak

Note: *Do not add cold water to an overheated engine or damage may result*

Low engine oil pressure

Gauge reads low or warning light illuminated with engine running

 Oil level low or incorrect grade
 Defective gauge or sender unit

Wire to sender unit earthed
Engine overheating
Oil filter clogged or bypass valve defective
Oil pressure relief valve defective
Oil pick-up strainer clogged
Oil pump worn or mountings loose
Worn main or big-end bearings

Note: *Low oil pressure in a high-mileage engine at tickover is not necessarily a cause for concern. Sudden pressure loss at speed is far more significant. In any event, check the gauge or warning light sender before condemning the engine.*

Engine noises

Pre-ignition (pinking) on acceleration
Incorrect grade of fuel
Ignition timing incorrect
Distributor faulty or worn
Worn or maladjusted carburettor (where applicable)
Excessive carbon build-up in engine

Whistling or wheezing noises
Leaking vacuum hose
Leaking carburettor, throttle body (EFI) or manifold gasket
Blowing head gasket

Tapping or rattling
Incorrect valve clearances
Worn valve gear
Worn timing chain
Broken piston ring (ticking noise)

Knocking or thumping
Unintentional mechanical contact (eg fan blades)
Worn drivebelt
Peripheral component fault (generator, water pump etc)
Worn big-end bearings (regular heavy knocking, perhaps less under load)
Worn main bearings (rumbling and knocking, perhaps worsening under load)
Piston slap (most noticeable when cold)

Chapter 1 Engine

Contents

Specifications

UK models

General

Type	Four-cylinder, in-line, water-cooled, single overhead camshaft, and five bearing cranskshaft
Engine code	21R
Capacity (displacement)	1972 cc
Bore	84 mm (3.31 in)
Stroke	89 mm (3.50 in)
Compression ratio	9.0 to 1 or 9.3 to 1*
	* 21R engine from August 1984

Compression pressure at 250 rpm:
  Standard .... 11.0 kgf/cm² (157 lbf/in²)
  Minimum .... 9.0 kgf/cm² (128 lbf/in²)
  Maximum difference between cylinders .... 1.0 kgf/cm² (14 lbf/in²)

Firing order 1-3-4-2

Valve clearances (hot)
  Inlet .... 0.20 mm (0.008 in)
  Exhaust .... 0.30 mm (0.012 in)

Cylinder head
Warpage limit .... 0.15 mm (0.0059 in)
Warpage limit on manifold face .... 0.20 mm (0.0079 in)
Valve seats:
  Contact surface angle .... 45°
  Contact width .... 1.2 to 1.6 mm (0.047 to 0.063 in)
  Refacing angles:
    Inlet .... 30°, 45°, 60°
    Exhaust .... 30°, 45°, 65°
Valve bushes:
  Inside diameter:
    Inlet .... 8.00 to 8.03 mm (0.3150 to 0.3161 in)
    Exhaust .... 8.01 to 8.03 mm (0.3154 to 0.3161 in)
  Outside diameter:
    Standard .... 13.040 to 13.051 mm (0.5134 to 0.5138 in)
    Oversize type 0.05 .... 13.090 to 13.101 mm (0.5154 to 0.5158 in)
  Replacement temperature .... Normal

Valves
Face angle .... 45°
Head edge thickness limit .... 0.6 mm (0.024 in)
Overall length:
  Inlet .... 115.5 mm (4.547 in)
  Exhaust .... 113.4 mm (4.465 in)
Valve stem end reface limit .... 0.5 mm (0.020 in)
Valve stem diameter (standard):
  Inlet .... 7.970 to 7.985 mm (0.3188 to 0.3145 in)
  Exhaust .... 7.965 to 7.980 mm (0.3136 to 0.3142 in)
Valve stem oil clearance (standard):
  Inlet .... 0.02 to 0.06 mm (0.0008 to 0.0024 in)
  Exhaust .... 0.03 to 0.07 mm (0.0012 to 0.0026 in)
Valve stem oil clearance limit:
  Inlet .... 0.08 mm (0.0031 in)
  Exhaust .... 0.10 mm (0.0039 in)
Valve springs:
  Free length .... 45.8 mm (1.803 in)
  Squareness .... 1.6 mm (0.063 in)
Valve rocker arm and shaft:
  Oil clearance (shaft to arm):
    Standard .... 0.01 to 0.05 mm (0.0004 to 0.0020 in)
    Limit .... 0.08 mm (0.0031 in)

Camshaft
Endfloat:
  Standard .... 0.08 to 0.18 mm (0.0031 to 0.0071 in)
  Limit .... 0.25 mm (0.0098 in)
Circular run-out limit .... 0.2 mm (0.008 in)
Cam lobe height (standard):
  Inlet .... 42.63 to 42.72 mm (1.6783 to 1.6819 in)
  Exhaust .... 42.69 to 42.78 mm (1.6807 to 1.6842 in)
Cam lobe height wear limit:
  Inlet .... 42.43 mm (1.6705 in)
  Exhaust .... 42.49 mm (1.6728 in)
Bearing oil clearance:
  Standard .... 0.01 to 0.05 mm (0.0004 to 0.0020 in)
  Wear limit .... 0.1 mm (0.004 in)
Journal diameter (standard) .... 32.98 to 33.00 mm (1.2984 to 1.2992 in)

Timing chain
Tensioner head thickness limit .... 11.0 mm (0.433 in)
No 1 damper thickness limit .... 5.0 mm (0.197 in)

No 2 damper thickness limit	4.5 mm (0.177 in)
Chain elongation limit at 17 links	147.0 mm (5.787 in)
Crankshaft sprocket wear limit	59.4 mm (2.339 in)
Crankshaft timing sprocket wear limit	113.8 mm (4.480 in)

Cylinder block

Bore diameter:	
Standard	84.00 to 84.03 mm (3.3071 to 3.3083 in)
Wear limit	0.2 mm (0.008 in)
Taper and ovality limit	0.01 mm (0.0004 in)
Face warpage limit	0.05 mm (0.0020 in)

Pistons and piston rings

Piston diameter:	
Standard	83.96 to 83.99 mm (3.3055 to 3.3067 in)
Oversize (0.50)	84.46 to 84.49 mm (3.3252 to 3.3264 in)
Oversize (1.00)	84.96 to 84.99 mm (3.3449 to 3.3461 in)
Cylinder-to-piston clearance	0.03 to 0.05 mm (0.0012 to 0.0020 in)
Piston ring end gap:	
Top compression	0.25 to 0.47 mm (0.0098 to 0.0185 in)
Second compression	0.15 to 0.42 mm (0.0059 to 0.0165 in)
Oil control	0.20 to 0.82 mm (0.0079 to 0.0323 in)
Compression ring-to-ring groove clearance	0.2 mm (0.008 in)
Gudgeon pin installation temperature	80°C (176°F)

Connecting rods and bearings

Thrust clearance:	
Standard	0.16 to 0.26 mm (0.0063 to 0.0102 in)
Wear limit	0.30 mm (0.0118 in)
Bearing oil clearance:	
Standard	0.025 to 0.055 mm (0.0010 to 0.0022 in)
Wear limit	0.1 mm (0.004 in)

Crankshaft

End float:	
Standard	0.02 to 0.22 mm (0.0008 to 0.0087 in)
Wear limit	0.3 mm (0.012 in)
Circular run-out limit	0.1 mm (0.004 in)
Main journal diameter:	
Standard	59.98 to 60.00 mm (2.3614 to 2.3622 in)
Undersize finish diameter (0.25)	59.70 to 59.71 mm (2.3504 to 2.3508 in)
Taper and ovality limit	0.01 mm (0.0004 in)
Main journal oil clearance:	
Standard	0.025 to 0.055 mm (0.0010 to 0.0022 in)
Limit	0.08 mm (0.0031 in)
Crankpin journal diameter:	
Standard	52.99 to 53.00 mm (2.0862 to 2.0866 in)
Undersize finished diameter (0.25)	52.70 to 52.71 mm (2.0748 to 2.0752 in)
Taper and ovality limit	0.01 mm (0.0004 in)
Oil clearance:	
Standard	0.025 to 0.055 mm (0.0010 to 0.0022 in)
Limit	0.08 mm (0.0031 in)
Thrust washer thickness:	
Standard	2.00 mm (0.0787 in)
Oversize (0.125)	2.06 mm (0.0811 in)
Oversize (0.250)	2.13 mm (0.0839 in)

Flywheel

Run-out limit	0.2 mm (0.008 in)

Lubrication system

Oil capacity:	
Dry refill with filter change	4.8 litre (8.4 Imp pints)
Drain and refill with filter change	4.3 litre (7.6 Imp pints)
Drain and refill without filter change	3.6 litre (6.4 Imp pints)
Lubricant:	
Viscosity rating (SAE):	
Temperatures above −23°C (−10°F)	10W30 or 10W40
Temperatures below −23°C (−10°F)	5W30
Oil pump:	
Relief valve operating pressure	4.5 kgf/cm² (64 lbf/in²)
Body clearance:	
Standard	0.09 to 0.15 mm (0.0035 to 0.0059 in)
Wear limit	0.02 mm (0.008 in)

Tip clearance:
  Driven gear-to-crescent (standard) .... 0.15 to 0.21 mm (0.0059 to 0.0083 in)
  Driven gear-to-crescent (wear limit) .... 0.3 mm (0.012 in)
  Drive gear-to-crescent (standard) .... 0.22 to 0.25 mm (0.0087 to 0.0098 in)
  Drive gear-to-crescent (wear limit) .... 0.3 mm (0.012 in)
Side clearance:
  Standard .... 0.03 to 0.09 mm (0.0012 to 0.0035 in)
  Wear limit .... 0.15 mm (0.0059 in)

Torque wrench settings

	kgf m	lbf ft
Cylinder head to block	7.2 to 8.8	53 to 63
Cylinder head-to-timing cover bolt	1.0 to 1.6	8 to 11
Timing cover to cylinder block	1.0 to 1.6	8 to 11
Inlet manifold to cylinder head:		
Bolt	1.8 to 2.6	14 to 18
Nut	1.5 to 2.2	11 to 15
Exhaust manifold to cylinder head	4.0 to 5.0	29 to 36
Main bearing caps	9.5 to 11.5	69 to 83
Connecting rod caps	5.4 to 6.6	40 to 47
Crankshaft pulley	14.0 to 18.0	102 to 130
Flywheel	10.0 to 12.0	73 to 86
Camshaft timing sprocket	7.0 to 9.0	51 to 65
Camshaft bearing cap	1.7 to 2.3	13 to 16
Chain tensioner	1.5 to 2.1	11 to 15
Chain damper	1.0 to 1.6	8 to 11
Sump	0.3 to 0.9	2 to 6
Sump drain plug	3.5 to 4.5	26 to 32
Spark plugs	1.5 to 2.1	11 to 15
Oil pump bolts (refer to Fig 1.41):		
(a)	2.5	18
(b)	2.0	14
(c)	1.3	9

USA models

General

Type .... Four-cylinder, in-line, water-cooled, single overhead camshaft, and five bearing crankshaft
Engine code .... 22R and 22RE
Capacity (displacement) .... 2366 cc (144.4 cu in)
Bore .... 92.0 mm (3.62 in)
Stroke .... 89.0 mm (3.50 in)
Compression ratio .... 9.0 to 1
Compression pressure at 250 rpm:
  Standard .... 12 kgf/cm² (171 lbf/in²)
  Minimum .... 10 kgf/cm² (142 lbf/in²)
  Maximum difference between cylinders .... 1.0 kgf/cm² (14 lbf/in²)

Firing order 1-3-4-2

Valve clearances (hot)

  Inlet .... 0.20 mm (0.008 in)
  Exhaust .... 0.30 mm (0.012 in)

Cylinder head

Warpage limit .... 0.15 mm (0.0059 in)
Valve seats:
  Contact surface angle .... 45°
  Contact width .... 1.2 to 1.6 mm (0.047 to 0.063 in)
  Refacing angles:
    Inlet .... 30°, 45°, 60°
    Exhaust .... 30°, 45°, 65°
Valve bushes:
  Inside diameter:
    Inlet .... 8.01 to 8.03 mm (0.3154 to 0.3161 in)
    Exhaust .... 8.01 to 8.03 mm (0.3154 to 0.3161 in)
  Outside diameter:
    Standard .... 13.040 to 13.051 mm (0.5134 to 0.5138 in)
    Oversize type 0.5 .... 13.090 to 13.101 mm (0.5154 to 0.5158 in)
  Protrusion from cylinder head .... 19 mm (0.75 in)
  Replacement temperature .... Normal

Valves

Face angle .... 44.5°
Head edge thickness limit .... 0.6 mm (0.024 in)

Overall length:
    Inlet .... 113.5 mm (4.468 in)
    Exhaust .... 112.4 mm (4.425 in)
Valve stem end reface limit .... 0.5 mm (0.020 in)
Valve stem diameter (standard):
    Inlet .... 7.970 to 7.985 mm (0.3138 to 0.3144 in)
    Exhaust .... 7.965 to 7.980 mm (0.3136 to 0.3142 in)
Valve stem oil clearance (standard):
    Inlet .... 0.02 to 0.06 mm (0.0008 to 0.0024 in)
    Exhaust .... 0.03 to 0.07 mm (0.0012 to 0.0028 in)
Valve stem oil clearance limit:
    Inlet .... 0.08 mm (0.0031 in)
    Exhaust .... 0.10 mm (0.0039 in)
Valve springs:
    Free length .... 45.8 mm (1.803 in)
    Squareness .... 1.6 mm (0.063 in)
Valve rocker arm and shaft:
    Oil clearance (shaft to arm):
        Standard .... 0.01 to 0.05 mm (0.0004 to 0.0020 in)
        Wear limit .... 0.08 mm (0.0031 in)

Camshaft

Endfloat:
    Standard .... 0.08 to 0.18 mm (0.0031 to 0.0071 in)
    Limit .... 0.25 mm (0.0098 in)
Circular run-out limit .... 0.2 mm (0.008 in)
Cam lobe height (minimum):
    Inlet .... 42.63 to 42.72 mm (1.6783 to 1.6819 in)
    Exhaust .... 42.69 to 42.78 mm (1.6807 to 1.6842 in)
Bearing oil clearance:
    Standard .... 0.01 to 0.05 mm (0.0004 to 0.0020 in)
    Wear limit .... 0.1 mm (0.004 in)

Timing chain

Tensioner head thickness limit .... 11.0 mm (0.433 in)
No 1 damper thickness limit .... 5.0 mm (0.197 in)
No 2 damper thickness limit .... 4.5 mm (0.177 in)
Crankshaft sprocket wear limit .... 59.4 mm (2.339 in)
Camshaft sprocket wear limit .... 113.8 mm (4.480 in)

Cylinder block

Bore diameter:
    Standard .... 92.00 to 92.03 mm (3.6220 to 3.6232 in)
    Wear limit .... 0.2 mm (0.008 in)
Taper and ovality limit .... 0.02 mm (0.0008 in)
Face warpage limit .... 0.05 mm (0.0020 in)

Pistons and piston rings

Piston diameter:
    Standard .... 91.938 to 91.968 mm (3.6196 to 3.6208 in)
    Oversize (0.50) .... 92.438 to 92.468 mm (3.6393 to 3.6405 in)
    Oversize (1.00) .... 92.938 to 92.968 mm (3.6590 to 3.6602 in)
Cylinder-to-piston clearance:
    Up to 1984 .... 0.052 to 0.072 mm (0.0020 to 0.0028 in)
    From 1985 .... 0.03 to 0.05 mm (0.0012 to 0.0020 in)
Piston ring end gap:
    Compression rings up to 1984 .... 0.18 to 0.36 mm (0.0071 to 0.0142 in)
    Compression rings from 1984:
        Top .... 0.24 to 0.39 mm (0.0094 to 0.0154 in)
        Second .... 0.18 to 0.42 mm (0.0071 to 0.0165 in)
    Oil control ring from 1984 .... 0.20 to 0.82 mm (0.0079 to 0.0323 in)
Compression ring-to-ring groove clearance .... 0.2 mm (0.008 in)
Gudgeon pin installation temperature .... 80°C (176°F)

Connecting rod and bearings

Thrust clearance:
    Standard .... 0.16 to 0.26 mm (0.0063 to 0.0102 in)
    Wear limit .... 0.30 mm (0.0118 in)
Bearing oil clearance:
    Standard .... 0.025 to 0.055 mm (0.0010 to 0.0022 in)
    Wear limit .... 0.10 mm (0.0039 in)
Gudgeon pin-to-bush oil clearance:
    Standard .... 0.05 to 0.011 mm (0.0002 to 0.0004 in)
    Wear limit .... 0.015 mm (0.0006 in)

Crankshaft

Endfloat:	
Standard	0.02 to 0.22 mm (0.0008 to 0.0087 in)
Wear limit	0.30 mm (0.0118 in)
Circular run-out limit	0.1 mm (0.004 in)
Main journal diameter:	
Standard	59.984 to 60.000 mm (2.3616 to 2.3622 in)
Undersize finish diameter (0.25)	59.70 to 59.71 mm (2.3504 to 2.3508 in)
Taper and ovality limit	0.01 mm (0.0004 in)
Main journal oil clearance:	
Standard	0.025 to 0.055 mm (0.0010 to 0.0022 in)
Wear limit	0.08 mm (0.0031 in)
Thrust washer thickness:	
Standard	2.00 mm (0.0787 in)
Oversize (0.125)	2.06 mm (0.0811 in)
Oversize (0.250)	2.13 mm (0.0839 in)

Flywheel

Run-out limit	0.02 mm (0.008 in)

Lubrication system

Oil capacity:	
Dry refill with filter change	4.8 litre (5.1 US qt)
Drain and refill with filter change	4.6 litre (4.9 US qt)
Drain and refill without filter change	3.8 litre (4.0 US qt)
Lubricant:	
Viscosity rating (SAE):	
Temperatures above –23°C (–10°F)	10W30 or 10W40
Temperatures below –23°C (–10°F)	5W30
Oil pump:	
Relief valve operating pressure	4.5 kgf/cm² (64 lbf/in²)
Body clearance:	
Standard	0.09 to 0.15 mm (0.0035 to 0.0059 in)
Wear limit	0.2 mm (0.008 in)
Tip clearance:	
Driven gear-to-crescent (standard)	0.15 to 0.21 mm (0.0059 to 0.0083 in)
Driven gear-to-crescent (wear limit)	0.3 mm (0.012 in)
Drive gear-to-crescent (standard)	0.22 to 0.25 mm (0.0087 to 0.0098 in)
Drive gear-to-crescent (wear limit)	0.3 mm (0.012 in)
Side clearance:	
Standard	0.03 to 0.09 mm (0.0012 to 0.0035 in)
Wear limit	0.15 mm (0.0059 in)
Oil pressure (at normal operating temperature):	
Minimum pressure at idle speed	0.3 kgf/cm² (4.3 lbf/in²)
Minimum pressure at 3000 rpm	2.5 to 5.0 kgf/cm² (36 to 71 lbf/in²)

Torque wrench settings

	kgf m	lbf ft
Cylinder head to block	8.0	58
Cylinder head-to-timing cover bolt	1.3	9
Timing cover bolts:		
8 mm	1.3	9
10 mm	4.0	29
Inlet manifold to cylinder head (EFI)	1.9	14
Inlet manifold to cylinder head (carburettor)	1.8 to 2.6	14 to 18
Exhaust manifold to cylinder head	4.5	33
Main bearing caps	10.5	76
Connecting rod caps	6.3	46
Crankshaft pulley	16.0	116
Flywheel	11.0	80
Camshaft bearing cap	2.0	14
Camshaft timing sprocket	8.0	58
Sump	0.6	4
Thermostatic valve	1.7 to 2.3	13 to 16
EGR valve	1.0 to 1.6	8 to 11
Oil pump bolts (refer to Fig. 1.41):		
(a)	2.5	18
(b)	2.0	14
(c)	1.3	9

1 General description

The engine fitted to all models is a four-cylinder, in-line, water-cooled, single overhead camshaft type. British market models are fitted with the 21R type engine of 1972 cc, whilst USA models are fitted with the 22R (carburettor) engine, or the 22 RE (EFI) engine of 2366 cc.

Mechanically all engine types are of similar design, but the associated fuel system, emission control system and ignition system will differ according to model and operating territory.

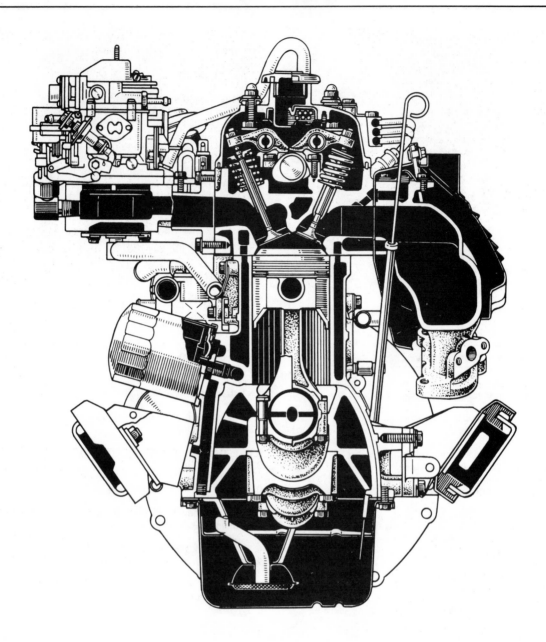

Fig. 1.1 21R Series engine – front section view (Sec 1)

2 Routine maintenance

The following routine maintenance procedures must be carried out at the specified intervals given at the front of this manual.

1 **Engine oil level check**: check the engine oil level with the car parked on level ground, preferably after allowing the engine to cool down. The oil level must be kept between the minimum and maximum markings on the dipstick. Top up the oil level through the filler neck in the rocker cover (photo).

2 **Engine oil change and filter renewal**: drain the old engine oil at the specified mileage intervals (photo) and at the same time renew the filter (see Section 4). Top up the engine oil level using oil of the specified grade.

3 Occasionally check the engine and associated components for signs of oil, coolant or fuel leakage.

4 Check and, if necessary, **adjust the valve clearances**, as described in Section 30, at the specified mileage intervals.

5 **Other associated engine checks** to be made are the drivebelts

and cooling system (Chapter 2), the fuel and emission control systems (Chapter 3), and the ignition system (Chapter 4).

3 Operations possible with engine in position and those requiring its removal

1 The majority of major overhaul operations can be carried out without removing the engine from the vehicle.

2 The only exceptions requiring its removal are the following:

   (a) Removal and refitting of the main bearing shells
   (b) Removal and refitting of the crankshaft
   (c) Attention to the flywheel, crankshaft rear oil seal can be given if the gearbox (or auto transmission) is first removed

3 On models fitted with air conditioning, the precautionary notes detailed in Section 8, paragraph 4 should be noted before disconnecting any part of the system.

2.1 Topping-up the engine oil level (21R engine)

2.2 Engine oil drain plug in sump

4 Oil filter – removal

1 The disposable type cartridge oil filter should be unscrewed from the engine using a strap or chain wrench. If such a tool is not available, drive a large screwdriver through the filter about 1 in (25 mm) from its outer end and use this to unscrew it (photo).

2 If the filter is being removed at a regular service interval and the vehicle has just come in from the road, be prepared for some loss of oil as the filter is unscrewed. Also the oil may be very hot.

3 The replacement filter should be of Toyota manufacture if possible since they are fitted with an integral valve which prevents oil loss from the filter when the engine is standing for long periods. This ensures that when the engine is restarted, a supply of filtered oil is instantly supplied to the bearings and journals, thus preventing the rattle sometimes heard when an engine is initially restarted.

4 Prior to fitting the new filter, thoroughly clean the mating surfaces of the filter and block.

5 When installing the oil filter during a routine service, smear the rubber seal ring of the filter with oil or grease and screw the filter home using only hand pressure. Do not use a wrench or tool to tighten the filter. Overtightening of the filter can not only distort the seal, but will

as many people find out, cause problems the next time the filter has to be removed. As a general guide, when the filter seal is in contact with the block surface, further tighten the filter approximately three quarters of a turn (photo).

6 When the engine is restarted check the filter joint for any signs of leaks.

5 Cylinder head and camshaft – removal

1 If the engine has been removed from the vehicle, proceed as described from paragraph 15.

2 Refer to Section 9 and, after observing the introductory note, proceed as described in paragraphs 4, 5 and 6.

3 Remove the air cleaner unit and hose, as described in Chapter 3.

4 Disconnect the top coolant hose from the thermostat housing, the two heater hoses from the cylinder head, and the coolant bypass hose from the inlet manifold.

5 Continue as described in Section 9, paragraphs 12 to 15 inclusive (as applicable).

4.1 Oil filter removal using a chain wrench

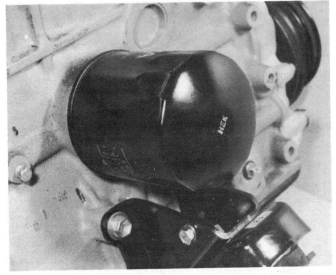

4.5 New oil filter in position

6 Disconnect the wiring from the cylinder head and associated components. Label the wires for identification on reassembly.

7 Continue as described in Section 9, paragraphs 17, 18 and 19 (as applicable).

8 Unbolt and remove the air compressor and its mounting bracket (where applicable).

9 Remove the fuel pump, as described in Chapter 3.

10 Remove the distributor and the spark plugs, as described in Chapter 4.

11 Remove the air-injection hoses (USA models) and suction hoses (as applicable).

12 If fitted, remove the power steering pump unit, complete with its mounting bracket, but leave the hoses connected. Place the pump to one side out of the way.

13 Unless the vehicle is on a ramp or over an inspection pit, raise it at the front end and support on safety stands.

14 Unbolt and detach the exhaust downpipe from the manifold.

15 Remove the cylinder head cover. This is secured by four nuts which rest on seals (photo). When the cover is removed, place a clean cloth over the oil hole in the head to prevent dirt entry.

16 Turn the engine over to set the No 1 cylinder piston at the TDC position on compression (both valves for that cylinder shut), and the timing indent mark on the crankshaft pulley aligned with the 0 timing mark on the timing plate (photo).

17 With the engine set at this position, make alignment marks across the front face of the camshaft sprocket and the timing chain, using a dab of quick-drying paint or with a spirit pen.

18 Remove the semi-circular plug from the top of the timing cover (photo), then unscrew and remove the camshaft sprocket retaining bolt. Insert a rod through the hole in the camshaft sprocket hub (photo) to prevent the camshaft from turning when the bolt is loosened. With the bolt removed, withdraw the distributor drivegear and the camshaft thrust plate (photo).

19 Lift the camshaft sprocket and chain from the camshaft, and support it on the vibration damper (Fig. 1.2).

20 Unscrew and remove the chain cover bolt (Fig. 1.3).

21 The cylinder head bolts, which also secure the rocker assemblies, can now be unscrewed and removed. Undo the bolts progressively in the order shown in Fig. 1.4. Progressive loosening of the bolts in the order shown ensures that the cylinder head does not crack or warp.

22 With all of the cylinder head bolts removed, lift the rocker gear assembly clear of the cylinder head. If stuck in position, prise at the front and rear ends to free it.

23 The cylinder head can now be lifted upwards and clear of the cylinder block and location dowels. If the head is stuck in position, prise it carefully free using a suitable screwdriver inserted between the projections in the joint face.

24 If the cylinder head is to be overhauled, remove any remaining associated components with reference to the relevant Chapters before

5.15 Unbolt the cylinder head cover

5.16 Set the engine at TDC

5.18A Remove the semi-circular plug

5.18B Unscrew the camshaft sprocket bolt. Note location of rod to prevent camshaft from turning (arrowed)

5.18C Withdraw the distributor drive gear and camshaft thrust plate

commencing to dismantle the cylinder head. Refer to Section 15 for overhaul details.
25 Before removing the camshaft from the cylinder head, measure its endfloat using feeler gauges inserted between the bearing and camshaft. If the clearance measured is outside the specified limit, the cylinder head must be renewed (photo).
26 Undo the bearing cap bolts, remove the caps and lift the camshaft clear.

6 Oil pump – removal

1 If the engine has been removed from the vehicle proceed from paragraph 4.
2 Toyota recommend that whenever the oil pump is removed for overhaul or renewal, the sump and oil pick-up tube are also removed and cleaned.
3 Refer to Section 7 and proceed as described in paragraphs 3 to 11 inclusive, but note that in paragraph 9 it is only necessary to loosen the drivebelts and disengage them from the crankshaft pulley.
4 Undo the five retaining bolts and remove the oil pump unit from the front face of the timing cover (Fig. 1.5).

5.25 Check the camshaft endfloat

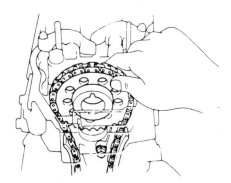

Fig. 1.2 Support chain and sprocket on vibration damper (Sec 5)

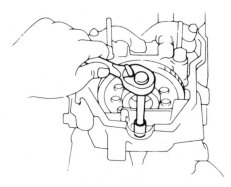

Fig. 1.3 Remove the chain cover bolt (Sec 5)

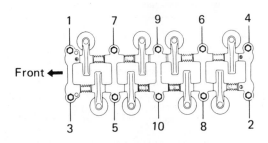

Fig. 1.4 Undo cylinder head bolts in sequence shown (Sec 5)

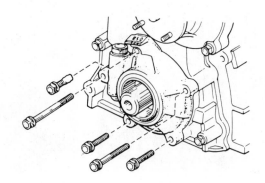

Fig. 1.5 Oil pump retaining bolts (Sec 6)

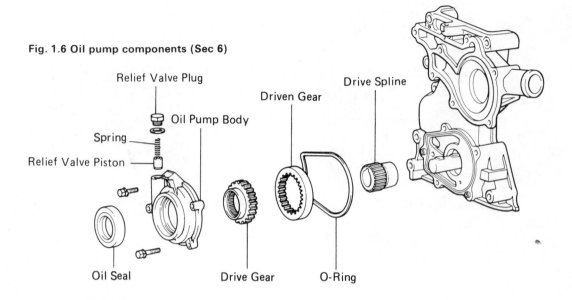

Fig. 1.6 Oil pump components (Sec 6)

Relief Valve Plug
Oil Pump Body
Spring
Relief Valve Piston
Oil Seal
Drive Gear
Driven Gear
O-Ring
Drive Spline

5   If required, withdraw the oil pump drive spline from the front end of the crankshaft (Fig. 1.6).
6   Undo the retaining plug and extract the relief valve spring and piston.
7   The oil pump housing O-ring seal and the relief valve retaining plug washer must be renewed, also the front oil seal (Section 23).
8   Clean the oil pump assembly and inspect it for wear, as described in Section 22.
9   Wash the sump and oil pick-up tube in fuel prior to reassembly. Clean all traces of sealant from the mating faces of the sump and cylinder block, and obtain a new oil/pick-up tube gasket ready for reassembly.

7   Timing cover, timing chain and sump – removal

1   Drain the cooling system and remove the radiator, as described in Chapter 2.
2   Remove the cylinder head, as described in Section 5.
3   Raise and support the vehicle on safety stands at the front and rear, so that there is sufficient room to work underneath at the front end.
4   Unbolt and remove the engine undercover.
5   Unscrew and remove the engine mounting bolts.
6   Position a jack under the transmission unit, and raise the engine approximately 25 mm (1.0 in). *A suitable piece of wood should be located between the jack saddle and the transmission to prevent damage.*

7   Unscrew the sump drain plug, and drain the engine oil into a suitable container (unless already drained).
8   Undo the sixteen bolts and two nuts which secure the sump, and lower the sump from the engine. Once removed, a certain amount of oil will drip from the engine, so cover the floor area underneath with old newspaper to prevent staining of the floor.
9   Refer to the relevant Chapter concerned, and remove the drivebelts and the following items which affect the removal of the timing case (as applicable):

Alternator – Chapter 12
Power steering pump – Chapter 10
Air pump (USA) – Chapter 3
Air conditioning compressor – Chapter 12

Where possible, leave the hoses and the unit concerned attached and swing them out of the way. The air conditioning hoses in particular must not be detached – see Section 8. If necessary, remove the alternator bottom mounting bracket to improve access.
10 Unscrew the crankshaft pulley bolt. Locate a suitable block of clean wood between the crankshaft and the inner crankcase wall to prevent the crankshaft from rotating (photo).
11 Withdraw the crankshaft pulley. It may pull straight out, but if necessary, remove it by carefully levering it free using two tyre levers behind it, or use a puller (there are two tapped holes in the pulley for this purpose – see Fig. 1.8).
12 Undo the three retaining bolts and remove the coolant bypass tube (Fig. 1.9).
13 Undo the three retaining bolts and remove the heater tube (photos).

7.10 Block of wood used to prevent the crankshaft from turning (sump removed)

7.13A Heater tube retaining bolts at front

7.13B Heater tube retaining bolt towards rear

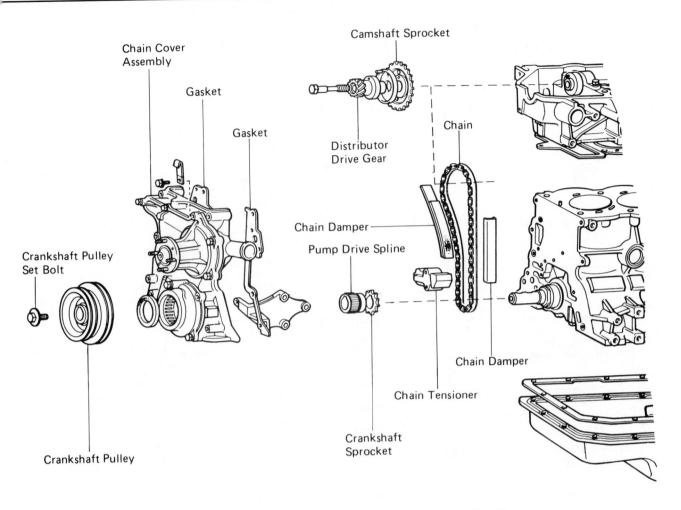

Fig. 1.7 Timing cover and chain assembly components (Sec 7)

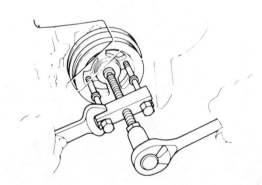

Fig. 1.8 Crankshaft pulley removal method (Sec 7)

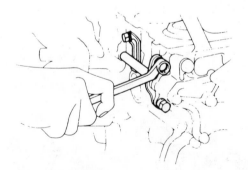

Fig. 1.9 Remove the coolant bypass tube (Sec 7)

14 If still attached, remove the alternator adjuster bracket from the timing cover.

15 Referring to Fig. 1.10, undo the timing cover retaining bolts from the positions indicated. Note that the large arrow indicates the position of the bolt which is removed from the rear face of the cover.

16 Remove the timing cover. It may be stuck, in which case tap it free using a plastic-faced hammer, but take care not to damage the cover.

Remove the old cover gasket.

17 Disengage the timing chain from the dampers and the crankshaft sprocket, and remove it keeping the camshaft sprocket engaged with it.

18 To inspect the timing chain, sprockets and associated components for wear, refer to Section 21.

19 If the oil pump drive and crankshaft sprocket are to be removed, withdraw them from the crankshaft using a suitable puller.

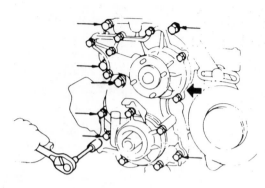

Fig. 1.10 Timing cover retaining bolts (arrowed) (Sec 7)

8 Engine – removal (general)

1   The engine may be removed with or without the transmission.
2   In the former case, consideration must be given to the additional weight and lifting angle required. Unless suitable heavy duty lifting equipment is available, the engine is best removed on its own. If required, removal of the gearbox/automatic transmission is described in Chapter 6.
3   Make sure that adequate lifting gear and, if possible, a trolley jack are available before attempting to remove the engine.
4   On models fitted with air conditioning equipment it is important not to disconnect any part of the system. The compressor and condenser can be unbolted and moved aside but only as far as their flexible hoses will permit. If insufficient room is provided to allow the engine to be removed, then the refrigerant must be discharged by your dealer or a competent refrigeration engineer.

9 Engine and transmission – removal

On models fitted with air conditioning equipment, refer to the precautionary notes in the previous Section before starting any engine removal procedures.
1   If the vehicle can be placed over an inspection pit or raised three or four inches on ramps or blocks of wood placed under the roadwheels

so much the better, as access to the exhaust mountings and rear engine mounting will be that much easier.
2   Unbolt and withdraw the engine undertray.
3   Remove the bonnet , as described in Chapter 11, and store it where it will not get damaged.
4   Disconnect the negative lead from the battery.
5   Drain the coolant from the engine cooling system, as described in Chapter 2. Retain the coolant for further use if it contains fairly fresh antifreeze.
6   Drain all the engine oil into a suitable container. Refit the drain plug.
7   Drain the gearbox oil or automatic transmission fluid, as applicable.
8   Undo the retaining nuts and remove the cooling fan and coupling from the water pump (Chapter 2).
9   Refer to Chapter 3 and remove the air cleaner unit and hose.
10 Disconnect the two heater hoses from the cylinder head (photo).
11 Remove the radiator, together with the fan shroud, as described in Chapter 2.
12 On carburettor models, disconnect the accelerator cable, and the automatic choke lead at its in-line connector.
13 On fuel-injection models, disconnect the accelerator cable from the support bracket on the engine.
14 On automatic transmission models, disconnect the throttle cable from the bracket on the valve cover and at the carburettor linkage, or from the support bracket on the engine on fuel-injection models (as applicable).
15 Disconnect the brake booster (servo) hose from the inlet manifold.
16 Disconnect the leads from the following components:

Starter motor, alternator, oil pressure switch (photo), coolant temperature sender, ignition coil (HT and LT leads).

Label the leads for identification where possible confusion may otherwise arise during reassembly.
17 On carburettor models, disconnect the fuel hoses at the fuel pump, noting their positions, and plug them to prevent fuel spillage and dirt ingress.
18 Disconnect the vacuum hoses and electrical leads from the emission control system (where applicable). It is important to mark these for identification to ensure correct refitting on reassembly. Refer to Chapter 3 for details.
19 Disconnect the wiring and hoses from the fuel-injection system, again marking them for identification to ensure correct refitting on reassembly. When disconnecting the fuel supply hoses, take care to allow for fuel leakage (possibly under pressure) – refer to Chapter 3 for details. Remove the air intake chamber and throttle body as described in Chapter 3.
20 On models fitted with power steering, remove the vane pump, together with its bracket, from the engine and position it out of the way, leaving its hoses attached.

9.10 Disconnect the heater hoses

9.16 Disconnect the oil pressure switch lead

9.21 Engine shock absorber top mounting

9.25 Engine shock absorber bottom mounting

21 Detach the top end of the engine shock absorber from the left-hand engine mounting (photo).
22 On air conditioned models, remove the compressor drivebelt, then unbolt the compressor and move it to one side, but leave the hoses attached.
23 On manual transmission models, release the gear lever gaiter (inside the vehicle), and pull it up the lever to give access to the lever mounting bolts. Undo the bolts and withdraw the lever.
24 Unless the vehicle is over an inspection pit, or has been previously raised, jack it up and support it on safety stands.
25 Undo the retaining bolts and detach the engine shock absorber at the bottom end (photo).
26 Unbolt and detach the exhaust pipe from the manifold, and the location bracket on the transmission. Where applicable, detach the exhaust pipe from the catalytic converter, referring to Chapter 3.
27 Unbolt and detach the clutch slave cylinder (manual transmission models), but leave the hydraulic hose attached to it. Tie the cylinder up out of the way (Fig. 1.11).
28 Undo the two steering gear coupling bolts shown in Fig. 1.12, and slide the coupling upwards to disengage it from the pinion shaft. As the coupling is withdrawn, check that the front roadwheels are in the straight-ahead position.
29 Disconnect the steering tie-rod end balljoints from the steering knuckle arm on each side, as described in Chapter 10.
30 Detach the power steering gear pressure line from the crossmember (where applicable), then unbolt and lower the steering gear unit,

and suspend it from the crossmember using cord or wire. On power steering models, leave the oil pipes connected, but check that, when suspended, the oil pipes are not stretched.
31 On automatic transmission models, disconnect the shift link rod from the shift lever (Fig. 1.14). Disconnect the oil cooler pipes.
32 Unscrew the knurled coupling collar and detach the speedometer cable from the gearbox/transmission, leaving the felt dust protector and washers in position (Fig. 1.15).

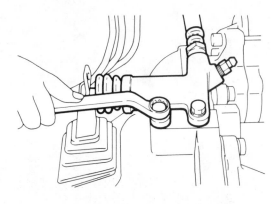

Fig. 1.11 Unbolt the clutch slave cylinder (Sec 9)

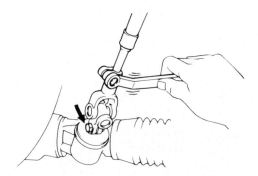

Fig. 1.12 Detach the steering gear-to-column coupling (Sec 9)

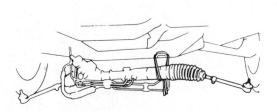

Fig. 1.13 Suspend the steering gear unit (Sec 9)

Fig. 1.14 Disconnect the shift rod link – automatic transmission (Sec 9)

Fig. 1.15 Disconnect the speedometer cable (Sec 9)

9.33 Unbolt the engine mountings

33 Unscrew and remove the engine mounting bolts on each side (photo).

34 Disconnect the following leads where still attached:

    (a) Earth leads from the gearbox and engine mounting
    (b) Reversing light switch lead and, on automatic transmission models, the neutral start switch wire.

35 Referring to Chapter 7, disconnect the intermediate propeller shaft at the centre bearing coupling, having made alignment marks across the flanges. Unbolt the centre bearing support, and withdraw the intermediate shaft from the gearbox/transmission. Plug the end of the gearbox/transmission to prevent oil/fluid leakage.

36 Position a jack under the gearbox/transmission, and raise it to support the weight. *Locate a suitable piece of wood between the jack saddle and the gearbox/transmission to prevent the possibility of damage.*

37 To avoid damaging the heater hose during the engine and gearbox/transmission removal, locate a suitable block of wood as a spacer between the cylinder head and the bulkhead cowl panel.

38 Check that the gearbox/transmission is securely supported by the jack, with the weight just taken off the mountings. Undo the eight bolts securing the rear mounting to the body and the gearbox/transmission, and remove the mounting (Fig. 1.16).

39 The engine and gearbox/transmission are now ready for removal from the vehicle. First check that all hoses, pipes and wires are disconnected and positioned clear of the power unit.

40 Fit a lifting sling to the engine lift brackets, and attach it to a hoist. Raise the hoist to take the weight of the engine.

41 An assistant will now be required to progressively lower the jack under the transmission as the engine is simultaneously lifted.

42 The angle of lift is quite steep, so get an assistant to help guide the engine and gearbox/transmission unit as it is withdrawn and also to support it once clear of the vehicle (photo).

9.42 Engine and gearbox removal

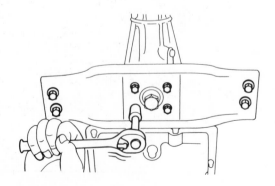

Fig. 1.16 Unbolt the gearbox/transmission mounting (Sec 9)

0 Engine – separation from manual gearbox

Remove the starter motor, as described in Chapter 12.
Unbolt and remove the two stiffener plates and the exhaust pipe bracket (photos).
3 Unscrew and remove the bolts securing the clutch bellhousing to the cylinder block (photo).
4 Pull the gearbox from the engine in a straight line, whilst supporting the gearbox so that its weight does not rest on the gearbox input shaft. Once the input shaft is clear of the clutch, the gearbox can be moved to one side out of the way (photo).

1 Engine – separation from automatic transmission

Remove the starter motor, as described in Chapter 12.

2 Prise free the rubber plug from the access hole in rear of the engine bottom cover, then unscrew and remove the engine driveplate-to-torque converter securing bolts. There are six bolts, and the crankshaft will need to be progressively turned to align each bolt in turn with the access hole to allow their removal. Mark the relative position of the driveplate and torque converter, using a spirit pen or a dab of quick-drying paint, so that during reassembly they can be fitted in their original relative positions.
3 Screw a guide pin into one of the torque convertor-to-driveplate holes. A pin can be made by using a bolt of suitable size with its head cut off. The guide pin will assist in retaining the converter in the transmission housing when separating the engine from the transmission.
4 Remove the transmission-to-engine mounting bolts.
5 Withdraw the automatic transmission unit from the engine in a straight line and supporting its weight during the operation. There may be some loss of fluid from the torque converter during the separation procedure, so be prepared to catch it in a suitable container. Do not separate the torque converter unit from the transmission.

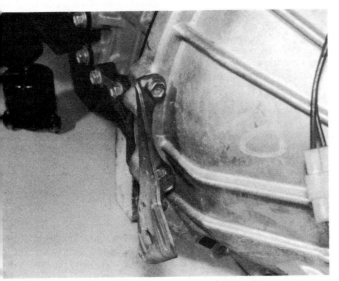

10.2A Left-hand stiffener plate

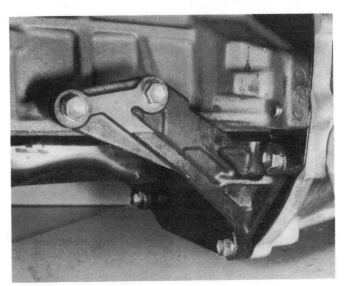

10.2B Right-hand stiffener plate

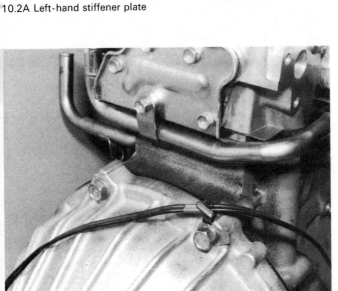

10.3 Bellhousing-to-engine bolts – note reverse light lead location clip position

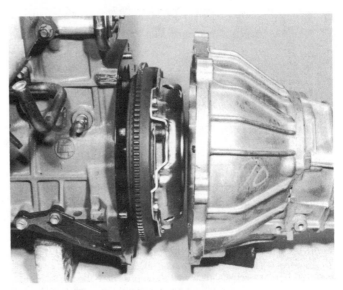

10.4 Separate the engine and gearbox

12 Engine dismantling – general

1   Keen home mechanics with previous engine dismantling experience may well have a stand on which to put the engine components, but most will make do with a work bench which should be large enough to spread around the inevitable bits and pieces and tools, and strong enough to support the engine weight. If the floor is the only place, try and ensure that the engine rests on a hard wood platform or similar rather than on concrete.

2   Spend some time on cleaning the unit. If you have been wise this will have been done before the engine was removed at a service bay. Good water soluble solvents will help to 'float off' caked dirt/grease under a water jet. Once the exterior is clean dismantling may begin. As parts are removed clean them in petrol/paraffin (do not immerse parts with oilways in paraffin – clean them with a petrol-soaked cloth and clean oilways with wire). If an air line is available use it for final cleaning off. Paraffin, which could possibly remain in oilways and would dilute the oil for initial lubrication after reassembly, must be blown out.

3   Always fit new gaskets and seals – but do not throw the old ones away until you have the new one to hand. A pattern is then available if they have to be made specially.

4   In general it is best to work from the top of the engine downwards. In all cases support the engine firmly so that it does not topple over when you are undoing stubborn nuts and bolts.

5   Always place nuts and bolts back with their components or place of attachment, if possible – it saves much confusion later. Otherwise put them in small, separate pots or jars so that their groups are easily identified.

6   If you have an area where parts can be laid out on sheets of paper, do so – putting the nuts and bolts with them. If you are able to look at all the components in this way it helps to avoid missing something on reassembly.

13 Engine ancillaries – removal

1   If you are stripping the engine completely or preparing to install a reconditioned unit, all the ancillaries must be removed first. If you are going to obtain a reconditioned 'short' motor (block, crankshaft, pistons and connecting rods) then obviously the cylinder head and associated parts will need retention for fitting to the new engine. It is advisable to check just what you will get with a reconditioned unit as changes are made from time to time.

2   The removal of all those items connected with fuel, ignition and charging systems are detailed in the respective Chapters but for clarity they are listed here:

>   *Distributor (Chapter 4)*
>   *Carburettor; can be removed together with inlet manifold (Chapter 3)*
>   *Air intake chamber and throttle body (EFI models) (Chapter 3)*
>   *Alternator*
>   *Fuel pump (where applicable)*
>   *Water pump (Chapter 2)*
>   *Thermostat (Chapter 2)*
>   *Exhaust manifold*
>   *Emission control equipment including, air pump, vacuum valves, connecting pipes etc*
>   *The clutch assembly (Chapter 5)*
>   *Oil filter (Chapter 1)*

14 Engine – dismantling

Cylinder head and rocker gear

1   Remove the cylinder head, as described in Section 5. If the engine has been removed, proceed from Section 5 paragraph 15 on.

Timing cover, timing chain and sump

2   Remove these items as described in Section 7. If the engine is removed from the vehicle, remove the sump, as described in Section 7, paragraphs 7 and 8, and unbolt and remove the oil pick-up tube and gasket. Remove the timing cover and chain, following the procedures described in Section 7 from paragraph 10.

Pistons and connecting rods

3   If the engine is still in the vehicle, first remove the cylinder head and sump, as previously described, then turn the crankshaft so that the pistons are all part way down their bores. Using a suitable scraper, carefully remove as much as possible of the carbon ring and wear ridge at the top of each bore, but take care not to damage or score the cylinder walls. This operation is essential to prevent the piston rings breaking as the pistons are withdrawn through the top of the cylinder bores.

4   Using a centre punch or quick-drying paint, mark each piston, connecting rod and big-end bearing cap numerically 1 to 4, from the front of the engine. Mark their positions relative to each other and to the crankcase, so that when the original assembly is refitted, it will be fitted in its exact, original position (Fig. 1.18).

5   Unbolt the big-end caps from the connecting rods, then push each piston/connecting rod assembly out through the top of the block, taking care not to score the cylinder bores with the big-end studs as they are withdrawn. If the bearing shells are to be used again, identify them in respect of exact original location.

Piston rings and gudgeon pins

6   The piston rings may be removed by opening each of them in turn, just enough to enable them to ride over the lands of the piston body. In order to prevent the lower rings dropping into an empty groove higher up the piston as they are removed, it is helpful to use two or three narrow strips of tin or old feeler blades inserted behind the ring at equidistant points and then to employ a twisting motion to slide the ring from the piston.

7   If the piston rings are likely to be re-used, identify them so that they can be refitted in their original positions.

8   To remove the gudgeon pin, first extract the circlips, (one at each end), then immerse the piston in hot water for a few minutes to heat it up to a temperature of about 80°C (176°F). The resultant piston expansion will allow the gudgeon pin to be pushed out of the piston and connecting rod using finger pressure.

9   If the gudgeon pins are to be re-used, mark each pin as it is removed (using masking tape), so that it is refitted in its original location on assembly. This is essential, as the piston and gudgeon pin are a matched set.

Flywheel (or drive-plate)

10   With the clutch assembly already removed, the bolts which secure the flywheel (or driveplate) should be unscrewed and removed. On some models, the flywheel bolts are secured with lockplates and these should be bent back first.

11   In order to prevent the flywheel (or driveplate) turning when attempting to unscrew the securing bolts, either place a block of wood between one of the webs of the crankshaft and the inside wall of the crankcase or jam the starter ring gear with a cold chisel or something similar.

12   Remove the flywheel (or driveplate) and then unbolt and remove the engine rear plate.

Crankshaft and main bearings

13   Before removing the crankshaft, check it for endfloat wear. Insert a screwdriver between one crankshaft web and main bearing cap, lever the crankshaft forwards and check the endfloat using feeler gauges. This should be as given in the Specifications. If excessive, new thrust washers or slightly oversize ones must be fitted.

14   Unbolt and remove the crankshaft rear oil seal retainer.

15   Undo and remove the ten bolts securing the main bearing caps to the cylinder block.

16   Make sure that the main bearing caps are numbered 1 to 5 on the front faces and also show an arrow towards the front of the engine.

17   Remove the main bearing caps and the bottom half of each bearing shell, taking care to keep the bearing shells in the right caps.

18   When removing the centre bearing cap, note the semi-circular halves of the thrust washers on either side of the main bearing. Lay them with the centre bearing along the correct side.

19   Slightly rotate the crankshaft to free the upper halves of the bearing shells and thrust washers which can be lifted away and placed over the correct bearing cap when the crankshaft has been lifted out.

20   Remove the crankshaft by lifting it away from the crankcase.

21   Lift away the bearing shells.

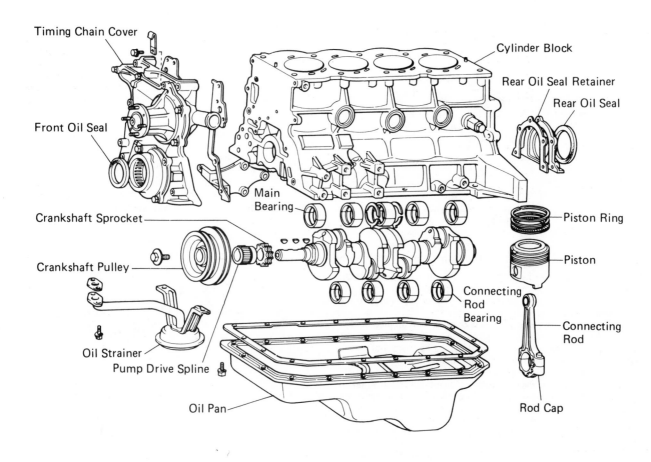

Fig. 1.17 Cylinder block and associated components (Sec 14)

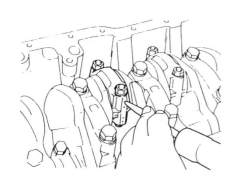

Fig. 1.18 Mark the main bearing and big-end caps numerically (Sec 14)

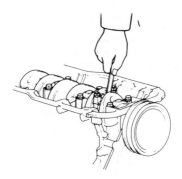

Fig. 1.19 Check the crankshaft endfloat before removing the bearing caps (Sec 14)

15 Cylinder head and valves – dismantling, overhaul and reassembly

Valve removal

1 With the cylinder head removed, it should be dismantled if the valve components are to be inspected and renovated or decarbonising carried out.

2 To remove a valve, a valve spring compressor will be required. Fit the compressor to the valve nearest the front of the cylinder head and compress the valve spring until the split collets which secure the spring retainer can be removed (Fig. 1.20).

3 Slowly release the compressor and then remove it. Extract the spring retainer, the valve spring, the valve stem oil seal and the spring seat.

4 Withdraw the valve from its cylinder head guide.

5 It is essential that all components of this and the other valves are kept together with their valves so that they will all be returned to their original locations. One method of doing this is to have a box with internal divisions numbered 1 to 8, ready before dismantling commences.

6 Repeat the foregoing operations on the remaining seven valves.

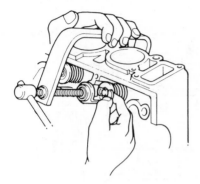

Fig. 1.20 Valve removal using valve spring compressor
(Sec 15)

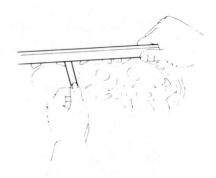

Fig. 1.21 Check cylinder head surface for warpage (Sec 15)

Cylinder head decarbonising and examination

7   When the cylinder head is removed either in the course of an
overhaul, or inspection of the bores or valve condition when the
engine is in the car, it is normal to remove all carbon deposits from the
piston crowns and cylinder head.

8   This is best done with a cup shaped wire brush and an electric drill
and is fairly straightforward when the engine is dismantled and the
pistons removed. Sometimes hard spots of carbon are not easily
removed except by a scraper. When cleaning the pistons with a scraper
take care not to damge the surface of the piston in any way.

9   When the engine is in the car certain precautions must be taken
when decarbonising the piston crowns in order to prevent dislodged
pieces of carbon falling into the interior of the engine which could
cause damage to the cylinder bores, piston and rings – or if allowed
into the water passages – damage to the water pump. Turn the engine
so that the piston being worked on is at the top of its stroke and then
mask off the adjacent cylinder bore and all surrounding water jacket
orifices with paper and adhesive tape. Press grease into the gap all
round by hand, carefully.

10 When completed, carefully clean out the grease round the rim of
the piston – bringing any carbon particles with it. Repeat the process
on the other three piston crowns.

11 Check that the cylinder head surfaces are within the specified
warpage limits using a straight-edge and feeler gauge. Renew the
cylinder head if warped beyond the specified limit. The cylinder head
must also be renewed if any cracks are present (Fig. 1.21).

12 Test each valve in its guide for wear. After a considerable mileage
the valve guide bore may wear elliptically and can be tested by rocking
the valve in the guide. The clearance between the valve guide and
valve stem (oil clearance) must not exceed that shown in the
Specifications.

13 To renew the valve guides, use a soft punch, and drive it against the
top of the valve guide, as shown in Fig. 1.22, to break off the top of the
guide. The cylinder head will then need to be heated up to about 90°C
(194°F), and the remaining guide section(s) driven out (Fig. 1.23).
Unless suitable heating equipment is available to heat the cylinder
head evenly entrust the valve guide replacement to a Toyota
dealer. Uneven heating could distort and ruin the cylinder head.

14 Drive the new valve guide(s) into position (with the cylinder head
at the previously mentioned temperature), until the snap-ring contacts
the cylinder head. The guide must now be reamed to obtain the
specified clearance.

Valve springs

15 Compare the face length of the valve springs with that given in the
Specifications. If the springs are permanently compressed much below
this length, renew them. In any event it is worth renewing the valve
springs if they have been in service for 35 000 miles (56 000 km) or
more.

Valves and valve seats

16 Examine the head for signs of cracking, burning away and pitting
of the edge where it seats in the port. The seats of the valve in the
cylinder head should also be examined for the same signs. Usually it is

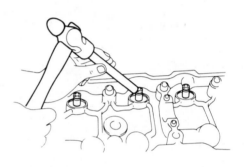

Fig. 1.22 Valve guide removal – break the top of the guide
(Sec 15)

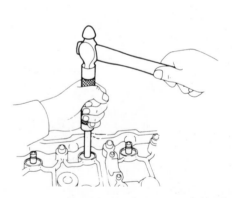

Fig. 1.23 Heat, then drive out the remaining portion of
guide (Sec 15)

the valve that deteriorates first but if a bad valve is not rectified the seat
will suffer and this is more difficult to repair.

17 If pitting on the valve and seat is very slight the marks can be
removed by grinding the seats and valves together with coarse and
then fine valve grinding paste.

18 Where bad pitting has occurred to the valve seats it will be
necessary either to recut the seats or, in severe cases, to fit new valve
seats. Grinding can be done if pitting on the valve and seat is only very
light or if as is usually the case, the valves only are badly burned then a
new set of valves can be ground into the seats.

19 Valve grinding is carried out as follows. Smear a trace of coarse
carborundum paste on the seat face and apply a suction grinder tool to
the valve head. With a semi-rotary motion, grind the valve head to its
seat, lifting the valve occasionally to redistribute the grinding paste.

When a dull matt even surface finish is produced on both the valve seat and the valve, wipe off the paste and repeat the process with fine carborundum paste, lifting and turning the valve to redistribute the paste as before. A light spring placed under the valve head will greatly ease this operation. When a smooth unbroken ring of light grey matt finish is produced, on both valve and valve seat faces, the grinding operation is completed.

20 Scrape away all carbon from the valve head and the valve stem. Carefully clean away every trace of grinding compound, taking care to leave none in the ports or in the valve guides. Clean the valves and valve seats with a paraffin-soaked rag, with a clean rag and finally, if an air line is available, blow the valves, valve guides and valve ports clean.

21 If it is found necessary to recut the valve seat faces then this is really a task best entrusted to an automotive engine workshop or your Toyota dealer. The valve seat face angles should be as shown in Fig. 1.24 and if the seats are to be refaced, it is important that cutters of the respective angles shown are used in the following manner:

Seating too high – use 30° then 45° cutters.
Seating too low – use 60° (inlet) or 65° (exhaust) then 45° cutters

22 When completed, the respective seat widths should comply with those given for the engine concerned in the Specifications. When the seats have been recut, the valves should be lapped in with grinding paste, as previously described.

23 If new valve seat inserts are needed, then this is definitely a job for your Toyota dealer who will have the necessary equipment for doing the work or will contract the job to a specialist engineering company.

24 On completion, wash the cylinder head and valve assembly components thoroughly with a suitable solution to remove all traces of carbon, swarf and grinding paste. Blow dry with compressed air to complete prior to reassembly of the valve assembly components.

Valves refitting

25 Refit the valves to their guides in their original sequence, or if new valves are being fitted, in their 'ground in' sequence. Start by inserting No 1 valve (nearest the front of the cylinder head) (photo).

26 Over the valve stem fit the plate washer, the valve stem oil seal, the valve spring, and the spring retainer (photos).

27 Compress the valve spring and drop in the split retaining collets (photo).

28 Gently release the compressor, making sure that the collets are secure in their valve stem cut-outs (photo).

29 Repeat the procedure on the remaining seven valves, then tap each valve in turn to ensure satisfactory assembly and valve movement.

30 Before refitting the cylinder head, examine the camshaft and rocker gear for excessive wear, as described in Section 24.

31 To refit the cylinder head, refer to Section 29.

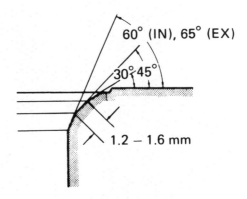

Fig. 1.24 Valve seat angles (Sec 15)

60° (IN), 65° (EX)
30° 45°
1.2 – 1.6 mm

15.25 Inserting the No 1 valve

15.26A Locate the valve stem oil seal ...

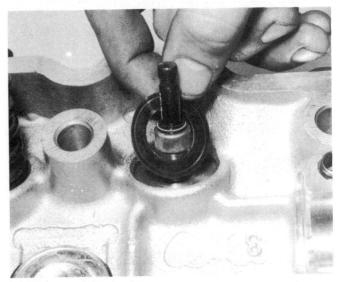

15.26B ... and plate washer over the guide and valve ...

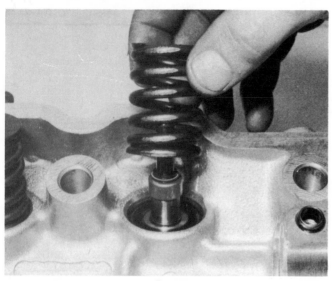

15.26C ... locate the spring ...

15.26D ... and retainer

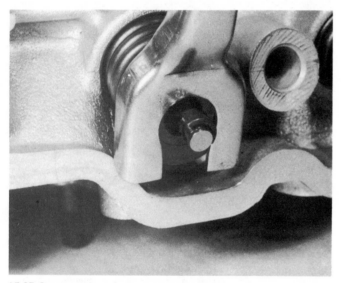

15.27 Compress the spring to insert the collets

15.28 Check that the collets are correctly engaged

16 Lubrication system – description

A forced feed lubrication system is used,. Oil is drawn from the sump through a pick-up tube, passes through the oil pump, which is located on the front of the timing cover, then on to the full-flow oil filter mounted on the side of the cylinder block. From the filter, the oil passes through the various oil galleries to the crankshaft and connecting rod bearings, the timing chain (lubricated via the tensioner), and up to the camshaft and rocker gear bearings.

An oil relief valve is located in the oil pump body. The relief valve is not adjustable.

17 Engine components – examination and renovation (general)

When the engine has been stripped down and all parts properly cleaned decisions have to be made as to what needs renewal and the following Sections tell the examiner what to look for. In any borderline case it is always best to decide in favour of a new part; even if a part may still be serviceable its life will have been reduced by wear and the degree of trouble needed to replace it in future must be taken into consideration.

18 Crankshaft, bearings and flywheel – examination and renovation

1   Look at the main bearing journals and the crankpins and if there are any scratches or score marks then the shaft will need regrinding. Such conditions will nearly always be accompanied by similar deterioration in the matching bearing shells.

2   Each bearing journal should also be round and can be checked with a micrometer or caliper gauge around the periphery at several points. If there is more than 0.01 mm (0.0004 in) of ovality or taper regrinding is necessary (Fig. 1.26).

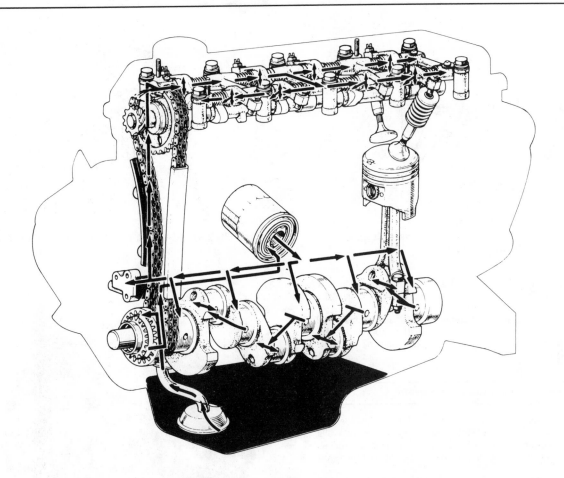

Fig. 1.25 Engine lubrication system – 21R engine (Sec 16)

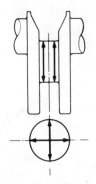

Fig. 1.26 Check the crankshaft bearing journals for excessive wear and ovality (Sec 18)

3 Your main Toyota dealer or motor engineering specialist will be able to decide to what extent regrinding is necessary and also supply the special under-size shell bearings to match whatever may need grinding off the journals.

4 Before taking the crankshaft for regrinding check also the cylinder bores and pistons as it will be more convenient to have the engineering operations performed at the same time by the same engineer.

5 With careful servicing and regular oil and filter changes bearings will last for a very long time but they can still fail for unforeseen reasons. With big-end bearings the indications are regular rhythmic loud knocking from the crankcase, the frequency depending on engine speed. It is particularly noticeable when the engine is under load. This symptom is accompanied by a fall in oil pressure although this is not normally noticeable unless an oil pressure gauge is fitted. Main bearing failure is usually indicated by serious vibration, particularly at higher engine revolutions, accompanied by a more significant drop in oil pressure and a rumbling noise.

6 Bearing shells in good condition have bearing surfaces with a smooth even, matt silver/grey colour all over. Worn bearings will show patches of a different colour where the bearing metal has worn away and exposed the underlay. Damaged bearings will be pitted or scored. It is nearly always well worthwhile fitting new shells as their cost is relatively low. If the crankshaft is in good condition it is merely a question of obtaining another set of standard size. A reground crankshaft will need new bearing shells as a matter of course.

7 Connecting rods are not normally subject to wear but in extreme cases such as engine seizure, they could be distorted. Such conditions may be visually apparent but where doubt exists their alignment must be checked and straightened if possible. If not they will have to be renewed. The bearing caps should also be examined for indications of filing down which may have been attempted in a mistaken idea that bearing slackness could be remedied in this way. If there are such signs then the connecting rods should be renewed.

8 Examine the spigot bearing in the centre of the crankshaft rear flange. If it is worn or noisy when rotated, renew it (Fig. 1.27).

9 The old bearing must be extracted using a suitable puller or, alternatively, apply heat to the bearing recess when it is usually possible to lever out the bearing (Fig. 1.28).

10 Drive in the new bearing applying pressure to the outer bearing track only (photo).

11 Examine the flywheel itself. If the clutch surface is scored or grooved, or there are lots of small cracks, visible (caused by overheating) then the flywheel must either be refinished or a new one obtained. Refinishing must be left to your dealer as the overall thickness of the flywheel must not be reduced beyond a specified limit.

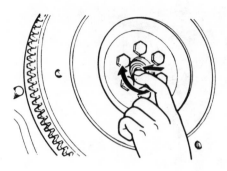

Fig. 1.27 Check the condition of the crankshaft spigot
bearing (Sec 18)

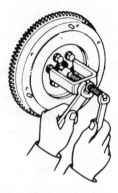

Fig. 1.28 Spigot bearing removal method (Sec 18)

12 If the flywheel starter ring gear teeth are worn or chipped, a new
ring gear should be fitted. In the case of a driveplate, renew the
driveplate complete.
13 Although a starter ring gear can be removed with a cold chisel and
a new one fitted after heating it in an oven or oil bath to 200°C (392°F),
it is recommended that this work is left to your dealer or specialist
engineering works.

19 Cylinder bores – examination and renovation

1 A new cylinder bore is perfectly round and the walls parallel
throughout its length. The action of the piston tends to wear the walls
at right angles to the gudgeon pin due to side thrust. This wear takes
place principally on that section of the cylinder swept by the piston
rings.
2 It is possible to get an indication of bore wear by removing the
cylinder head with the engine still in the car. With the piston down in
the bore first signs of wear can be seen and felt just below the top of
the bore where the piston ring reaches, and there will be a noticeable
lip. If there is no lip it is fairly reasonable to expect that bore wear is low
and any lack of compression or excessive oil consumption is due to
worn or broken piston rings or pistons or valves not seating correctly.
3 If it is possible to obtain a bore measuring micrometer, measure the
bore in the thrust plane just below the lip and again at the bottom of
the cylinder in the same plane. If the difference is more than 0.2 mm
(0.008 in), then a rebore is necessary. Similarly a difference of 0.2 mm
(0.008 in) or more across the bore diameter is a sign of ovality calling
for a rebore.
4 Any bore which is significantly scratched or scored will need
reboring. This symptom usually indicates that the piston or rings are
damaged in that cylinder. In the event of only one cylinder being in
need of reboring it will still be necessary for all four to be bored and
fitted with new oversize pistons and rings.
5 Your Toyota dealer or local engineering specialist will be able to
rebore and obtain the necessary matched pistons. If the crankshaft is
undergoing regrinding it is a good idea to let the same firm renovate
and reassemble the crankshaft and pistons to the block. A reputable
firm normally gives a guarantee for such work. In cases where engines
have been rebored already to their maximum, new cylinder liners are
available which may be fitted. In such cases the same reboring
processes have to be followed and the services of a specialist
engineering firm are required.
6 Apart from checking the cylinder bores, also check the cylinder
block for signs of damage or cracks. Renew any suspect core plugs
(photo).

20 Pistons, rings and connecting rods – examination and renovation

1 Worn pistons and rings can usually be diagnosed when the
symptoms of excessive oil consumption and low compression occur

18.10 Crankshaft spigot bearing

19.6 Cylinder block core plugs must be in good condition

nd are sometimes, though not always, associated with worn cylinder bores. Compression testers that fit into the spark plug holes are available and these can indicate where low compression is occurring. Wear usually accelerates the more it is left so when the symptoms occur, early action can possibly save the expense of a rebore.

2   Another symptom of piston wear is piston slap – a knocking noise from the crankcase not to be confused with big-end bearing failure. It can be heard clearly at low engine speed, when there is no load (idling for example) and the engine is cold, and is much less audible when the engine speed increases. Piston wear usually occurs in the skirt or lower end of the piston and is indicated by vertical streaks in the worn area which is always on the thrust side. It can be seen when the skirt thickness is different.

3   Piston ring wear can be checked by first removing the rings from the pistons, as described in Section 14. Then place the rings in the cylinder bores from the top, pushing them down about 38.1 mm (1.5 in) with the head of a piston (from which the rings have been removed) so that they rest squarely in the cylinder. Then measure the gap at the ends of the ring with a feeler gauge. If it exceeds 0.6 mm (0.02 in) then they will need renewal. (Fig. 1.29).

4   The grooves in which the rings locate in the piston can also become enlarged in use. The clearance between ring and piston, in the groove should not exceed the limits specified at the beginning of this Chapter.

5   However, it is rare that a piston is only worn in the ring grooves and the need to replace them for this fault alone is hardly ever encountered. Whenever the pistons are renewed, the weight of the four piston/ connecting rod assemblies should be kept within the limit variation of 8 gms (0.28 oz) to maintain engine balance.

6   The connecting rod and the gudgeon pin do not normally require renewal. If the pistons are being changed then the new pistons are usually supplied complete with gudgeon pins.

21 Timing sprockets, chain and tensioner – examination and renovation

1   Examine the teeth on both the crankshaft sprocket and the camshaft sprocket for wear. Each tooth forms an inverted V with the sprocket periphery, and if worn the side of each tooth under tension will be slightly concave in shape when compared with the other side of the tooth ie; one side of the inverted V will be concave when compared with the other. If any sign of wear is present the sprocket must be renewed.

2   Examine the links of the chain for side slackness and renew the chain if any slackness is noticeable when compared with a new chain. It is a sensible precaution to renew the chain at about 30 000 miles (48 000 km) and at a lesser mileage if the engine is stripped down for

Fig. 1.29 Measure the piston ring gaps (Sec 20)

major overhaul. The actual rollers on a very badly worn chain may be slightly grooved. The correct method for checking the chain for wear is shown in Figs. 1.30 and 1.31.

3   Attach the chain to a fixed point, and pull the chain as shown. The total chain length measured over seventeen links must not exceed 147.0 mm (5.787 in). Make this check with the chain fixed at three other positions selected at random. If the chain is stretched beyond the specified limit at any one place, renew the chain.

4   Referring to Fig. 1.31, wrap the chain around the camshaft sprocket as shown, and measure the outside diameter (outer sides of chain rollers). This should meet the minimum requirement of 113.8 mm (4.480 in).

5   Repeat the check in paragraph 4, this time with the crankshaft sprocket. This should meet the minimum requirement of 59.4 mm (2.339 in).

6   If either of the measurements taken in paragraphs 4 or 5 above is under the minimum specified limit, renew both sprockets and the chain.

7   Check the chain tensioner for wear as shown (photo). If the thickness measured is under 11.0 mm (0.433 in) the tensioner must be renewed.

8   Check the chain dampers for wear. Renew them if worn beyond the minimum thickness limit of 5.0 mm (0.020 in) for No 1 (curved) damper or 4.5 mm (0.177 in) for No 2 (straight) damper (photos).

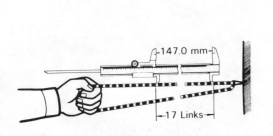

Fig. 1.30 Method used to check timing chain for excessive elongation (Sec 21)

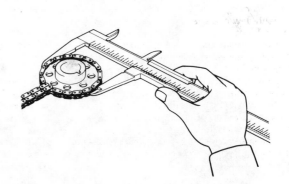

Fig. 1.31 Method used to check the chain and sprocket for wear (Sec 21)

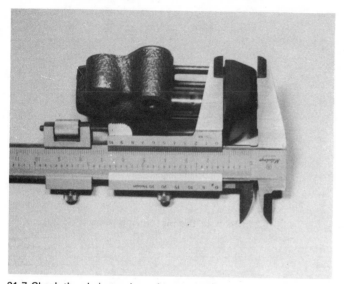

21.7 Check the chain tensioner for excessive wear

21.8A Check the No 1 chain damper (curved) for wear at point shown

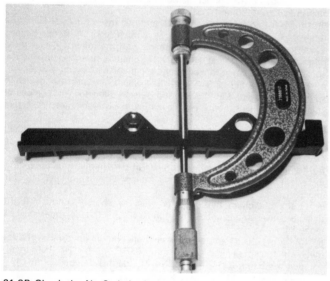

21.8B Check the No 2 chain damper (straight) for wear at point shown

22 Oil pump – examination and renovation

1   If the oil pump is worn it is best to purchase an exchange reconditioned unit as a good oil pump is at the very heart of long engine life. Generally speaking an exchange or overhauled pump should be fitted at a major engine reconditioning.

2   If it is wished to check the oil pump for wear, undo and remove the bolts securing the oil pump body to the timing cover, and withdraw the unit. The O-ring seal between the pump body and the timing cover must be removed from its groove and renewed.

3   Undo and remove the relief valve plug, and withdraw the spring and relief valve piston. The washer under the plug head must be renewed.

4   Wash the component parts of the pump in fuel, and dry them for inspection.

5   Check the clearance between the body and the driven gear using feeler gauges as shown (photo). The clearance should not exceed 0.2 mm (0.008 in).

6   Check the clearance between the tip of the gears and the crescent (photos). The clearance should not exceed 0.3 mm (0.012 in).

22.5 Oil pump body-to-driven gear clearance check

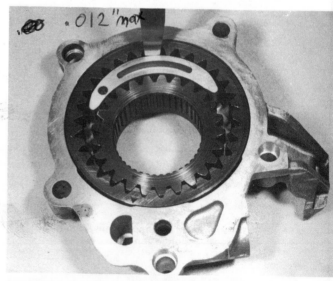

22.6A Oil pump driven gear-to-crescent clearance check

22.6B Oil pump drive gear-to-crescent clearance check

22.7 Oil pump body-to-gears side clearance check

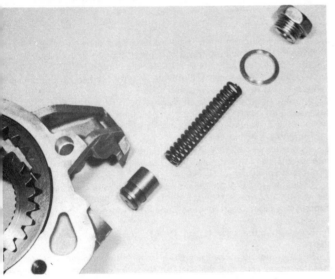

22.9 Oil pump relief valve, spring, washer and retaining plug

7   Lay a straight-edge across the face of the pump and check the side clearance as shown (photo). The clearance must not exceed 0.15 mm (0.006 in).
8   If wear in the pump components exceeds the specified limits, renew the pump unit complete.
9   Inspect the relief valve for pitting and the oil passages and sliding surfaces for damage in the form of score marks. Check that the spring is not damaged (photo).
10   Reassembly of the pump is the reverse sequence to dismantling.

23 Oil seals – renewal

1   At the time of major overhaul, always renew the oil seals as a matter of routine even though they may appear to be satisfactory.
2   The crankshaft front and rear seals are renewed simply by levering the old ones from the oil pump cover or rear oil seal retainer and tapping in the new ones, taking care to have the lips of the seals facing the correct way (photos).

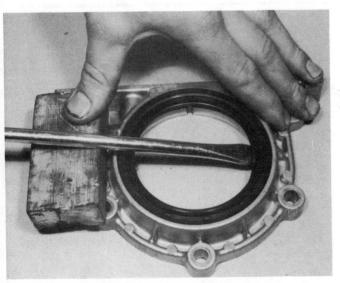

23.2A Oil seal removal method – crankshaft rear oil seal

23.2B New crankshaft rear oil seal in position in its retainer

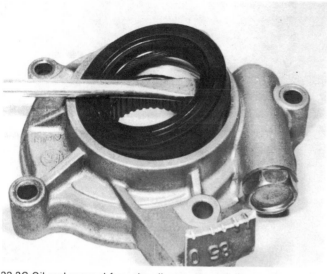

23.2C Oil seal removal from the oil pump cover (oil pump removed)

23.2D Drive the new oil seal into position using a tube drift

3   The oil pump cover oil seal can be renewed while the engine is still in the vehicle provided that the radiator and crankshaft pulley are removed first.

4   Draw out the old seal using a small claw type puller. Clean the oil seal recess and tap in the new seal using a piece of tubing of suitable diameter.

5   The crankshaft rear oil seal and its retainer are only accessible after removal of either the engine or if the engine is left in the vehicle, then the transmission must be withdrawn, followed by the clutch and flywheel (or driveplate).

24 Camshaft and rocker gear – examination and renovation

1   Check the camshaft journals for scoring or grooves, and then measure each journal at different points across the diameter to detect any taper or ovality.

2   Mount the camshaft in V-blocks at each end journal, then check it for run-out with a dial gauge on the centre bearing. If the run-out exceeds the maximum limit specified, renew the camshaft (Fig. 1.32).

3   Examine the camshaft lobes for signs of scoring or excessive wear. Measure the lobe height, as shown, using a micrometer (Fig. 1.33). If worn beyond the minimum allowable height specified on the inlet or exhaust lobes, renew the camshaft.

4   As mentioned previously in Section 5, if the camshaft endfloat is excessive and beyond the maximum specified, then the cylinder head will need to be renewed, as the camshaft runs directly in bearings and caps which are in-line bored.

5   To dismantle the rocker gear assembly, undo the three retaining screws and dismantle the various components, keeping them in order of removal (photo).

6   Check the rocker arms for excessive wear on the shafts. Also check the rocker arm contact pads on the valve stem and camshaft lobe contact faces for excessive wear. Renew the rocker arms and/or shaft if necessary (photo).

7   Check that the oilways are clear in the rocker gear stands and shafts.

8   Reassemble the rocker gear in the reverse order to removal, noting that the rocker arms are identical but the stands are not (photo).

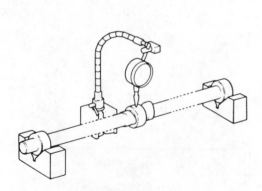

Fig. 1.32 Camshaft run-out check method (Sec 24)

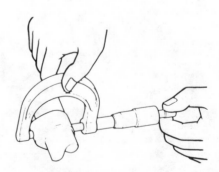

Fig. 1.33 Method used to check the camshaft lobe height (Sec 24)

24.5 Remove the retaining screws from the end stands to dismantle

24.6 Examine the rocker arm contact pads for excessive wear

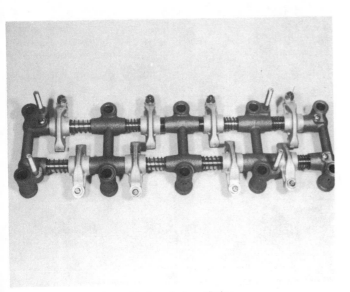

24.8 Rocker gear reassembled ready for refitting

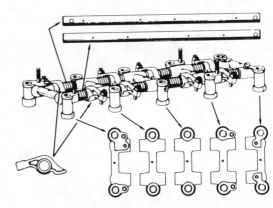

Fig. 1.34 Rocker gear shafts and stands showing orientation (Sec 24)

25 Engine reassembly – general

1   Prior to reassembling the engine, make sure that you have all the necessary gaskets ready, also a torque wrench and the correct range of socket and other spanners.
2   Always lubricate each component with fresh engine oil before reassembling or installing it.

26 Engine – reassembly

Crankshaft and main bearings

1   If new bearings are being fitted, carefully clean away all traces of the protective grease with which they are coated.
2   Fit the five upper halves of the main bearing shells to their location in the crankcase, after wiping the recess clean (photo).
3   Note that on the back of each bearing is a tab which engages in the locating grooves in either the crankcase or the main bearing cap housings (photo).
4   With the five upper bearing shells securely in place, wipe the lower bearing cap housings and fit the five lower bearing shells to their caps

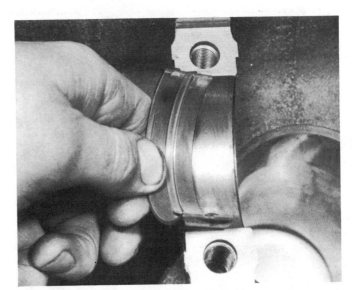

26.2 Fit the upper main bearing shells into position ...

26.3 ... ensuring that the tab engages in the slot

ensuring that the right shell goes into the right cap if the old bearings are being refitted.

5   Wipe the recesses either side of the centre main bearing which locate the upper halves of the thrust washers.

6   Smear a little grease onto the thrust washers and slip into position with their oil grooves facing outwards (photos).

7   Generously lubricate the crankshaft journals and the upper and lower main bearing shells and carefully lower the crankshaft into position. Make sure it is the right way round (photos).

8   Fit the main bearing caps in position ensuring that they locate properly. The mating surfaces must be spotlessly clean or the caps will not seat correctly. The arrow marking on each cap must point to the front of the engine when fitted (photos).

9   When locating the centre main bearing cap, ensure that the thrust washers, generously lubricated, are fitted with their oil grooves facing outwards and the locating tab of each washer is in the slot in the bearing cap (photo).

10   Insert the main bearing cap bolts and screw them up finger tight.

11   Test the crankshaft for freedom of rotation. Should it be very stiff to turn, or possess high spots a most careful inspection must be made, preferably by a skilled mechanic with a micrometer to trace the cause of the trouble. It is very seldom that any trouble of this nature will be experienced when fitting the crankshaft.

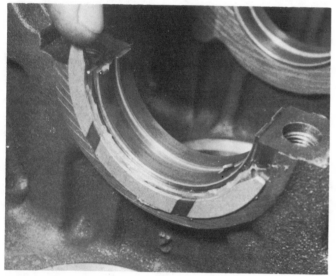

26.6A Locate the upper ...

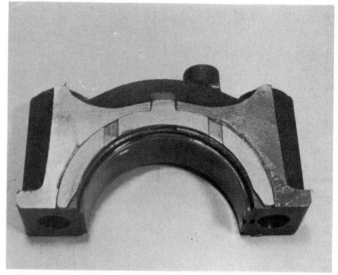

26.6B ... and lower thrust washers to the centre bearing and cap

26.7A Lubricate the bearings ...

26.7B ... then fit the crankshaft into position

26.8A The No 4 main bearing cap in position

26.8B Fitting the No 1 bearing cap

12 Tighten the main bearing cap bolts in the sequence shown in Fig. 1.35. Tighten the bolts a little at a time in progressive sequence up to the specified torque wrench setting (photo). Check the crankshaft for freedom of rotation again on completion.

13 Using a screwdriver between one crankshaft web and main bearing cap, lever the crankshaft forwards and check the endfloat using feeler gauges. This should be as given in the Specifications according to engine type. If excessive, new thrust washers or slightly oversize ones must be fitted (photo).

26.9 Centre main bearing cap fitted, together with half thrust washer each side

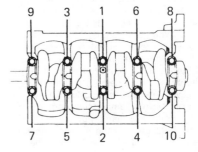

Fig. 1.35 Main bearing cap bolts tightening sequence (Sec 26)

26.12 Tightening the main bearing bolts to the specified torque

26.13 Check the crankshaft endfloat

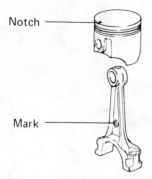

Notch

Mark

Fig. 1.36 Piston-to-connecting rod fitting position (Sec 26)

Fig. 1.37 Check that the ring-to-groove clearance is correct (Sec 26)

Pistons, rings and connecting rods

14 Using circlip pliers, insert a new circlip into the groove in one side of the gudgeon pin bore in the No 1 piston.

15 Immerse the piston in hot water, and heat it up to about 80°C (176°F). Locate the No 1 connecting rod in the piston, aligning the gudgeon pin bores of the piston and connecting rod. Check that the rod is the correct way round, with the notch on the piston aligned with the mark on the side of the rod (Fig. 1.36). Push the gudgeon pin into position, finger pressure being sufficient to push it home against the previously fitted circlip. Fit the second circlip, ensuring that it is well seated in its groove.

16 Repeat the above procedure and reassemble each remaining piston and its respective connecting rod in turn.

17 If new piston rings have been supplied, it is best to check the compression rings in the piston grooves for side clearance and then insert them into the cylinder bores to check the end gaps. Although the clearances and gaps should be correct, it could be disastrous if the rings are tight when compared with the clearances in the Specifications (Fig. 1.37). With used pistons, tightness of the piston rings in the grooves is most likely to be caused by carbon build up in the base and side walls of the groove. Unless this carbon is thoroughly cleaned out, the rings will not only be tight, but will not fully compress. This could prevent the pistons from being fitted into the cylinders, and at worst break the rings. Any carbon build up can be cleaned from the grooves using an old broken compression ring as a scraper, but take care not to damage or enlarge the ring grooves.

18 Fit the rings to the pistons over the crown of the piston by reversing the removal operations described in Section 14. The two upper piston rings are compression type while the lower one is an oil control ring.

19 Fit the oil control ring first. This requires a special technique for installation. First fit the bottom rail of the oil control ring to the piston and position it below the bottom groove. Refit the oil control expander into the bottom groove and move the bottom oil control ring rail up into the bottom groove. Fit the top oil control rail into the bottom groove.

20 Fit the second compression ring and then the top compression ring noting that the markings on the rings should face upwards (photo).

21 When all the rings are fitted, stagger their end gaps at equidistant points of a circle to prevent gas blow-by (Fig. 1.38).

22 Wipe the first cylinder bore clean and smear it with clean engine oil.

23 Install a piston ring compressor to the piston rings, first having lubricated the rings liberally. Compress the rings.

24 Lower the big-end of the connecting rod into the bore from above until the piston ring compressor is standing squarely on the top of the cylinder block and the piston crown notch is facing the front (timing cover) end of the engine. Rubber/nylon tubes fitted over the big-end studs will protect the bores during assembly (photos).

25 Place the wooden handle of a hammer on the crown of the piston and give the head of the hammer a sharp blow to drive the piston assembly into its bore. As this happens, the ring compressor will fly off (photo).

26 Wipe the connecting rod half of the big-end bearing location and the underside of the shell bearing clean, (as for the main bearing shells) and fit the shell bearing in position with its locating tongue engaged with the corresponding groove in the connecting rod. Always fit new shells.

26.20 Fitting the top compression ring

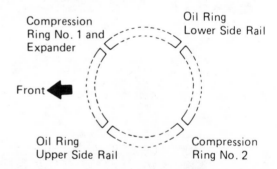

Compression
Ring No. 1 and
Expander

Oil Ring
Lower Side Rail

Front

Oil Ring
Upper Side Rail

Compression
Ring No. 2

Fig. 1.38 Arrange piston rings with gaps as shown (Sec 26)

27 Generously lubricate the crankpin journals with engine oil and turn the crankshaft so that the crankpin is in the most advantageous position for the connecting rod to be drawn onto it.

28 Fit the bearing shell to the connecting rod cap in the same way as with the connecting rod itself.

29 Generously lubricate the shell bearing and offer up the connecting rod bearing cap to the connecting rod. Fit the connecting rod retaining nuts (photos) and ensure that the rod and cap match marks are aligned.

30 Tighten the retaining nuts to the specified torque wrench setting in a progressive sequence (photo). Repeat the process on the remaining pistons.

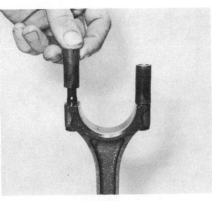

26.24A Fit rubber tubes temporarily onto studs to protect cylinder bores during assembly

26.24B Piston crown showing notch which must face the front when fitted

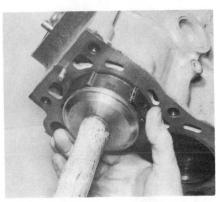

26.25 Fitting the piston and connecting rod

26.29A Fit the connecting rod cap ...

26.29B ... align the cap/rod match marks

26.30 Tighten the big-end bolts to the specified torque

31 Now check the crankshaft for rotation. There should be a certain amount of resistance, as the pistons and connecting rods are now fitted, but any severe effort required to rotate the crankshaft should be treated with suspicion and an inspection made to find the cause.
32 Finally, check the connecting rod big-ends for endfloat (thrust clearance), using a feeler gauge inserted between the side walls of the crankshaft and the connecting rod. If the clearance measured is beyond the maximum specified, the connecting rods must be renewed.

Crankshaft rear oil seal and flywheel (or driveplate)

33 Locate a new gasket in position on the rear face of the cylinder block, engaging it over the two location dowels (photo).
34 Lubricate the rear oil seal lips with grease, then fit the rear oil seal and retainer into position and tighten the retaining bolts (photo).

35 Fit the engine rear plate onto the rear face of the cylinder block and tighten the retaining bolts (photo).
36 Refit the flywheel (or driveplate), and tighten the retaining bolts to the specified torque (photo).

27 Timing cover, timing chain and sump – refitting

1 Position the crankshaft so that the sprocket keyways are at the top, and insert the Woodruff keys into their grooves.
2 Refit the timing chain dampers, and locate the timing cover gaskets (photo).
3 Refit the chain tensioner and tighten the retaining bolts (photos).

26.33 Locate the new gasket ...

26.34 ... then fit the rear oil seal retainer

26.35 Refit the engine rear plate

26.36 Refit the flywheel

27.2 Bolt the tensioners in position and locate the cover gaskets each side

27.3A Check that the mating surfaces of the chain tensioner are clean ...

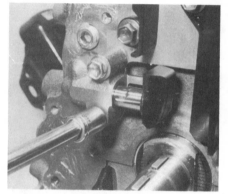

27.3B ... then fit it into position and secure

27.4 Slide the crankshaft sprocket into position

27.5 Align the chain bright link with the timing mark on the sprocket

27.6 Align the camshaft timing mark between the two bright links

27.7 Refit the timing cover ...

27.8 ... and tighten the bolts

4 Slide the crankshaft sprocket into position, aligning the keyway (photo).
5 Engage the timing chain over the crankshaft sprocket so that the single bright link is aligned with the timing mark on the front face of the sprocket (photo).
6 Engage the camshaft sprocket with the chain at the top end, so that the timing mark on the front face of the sprocket is between the two bright links (photo).
7 If the oil pump unit is already fitted to the timing cover, slide the oil pump drive spline into position on the crankshaft. Locate the chain between the dampers and tensioner then, supporting the camshaft sprocket, refit the timing lever, but check that the gaskets are still in their correct positions (photo).
8 Fit the timing cover bolts and tighten them to the specified torque setting – see Specifications (photo).

9 Tension the chain by turning the camshaft sprocket anti-clockwise, then rest the camshaft sprocket on the dampers.
10 Reconnect the water bypass tube to the rear face of the timing cover (photo).
11 Reconnect the heater tube to the rear face of the timing cover (on the left-hand side of the cylinder block).
12 Check that the mating faces of the sump and cylinder block are clean, then locate the pick-up tube gasket, and refit the oil pick-up tube (photos).
13 Apply sealant to the positions shown on the cylinder block mating face, locate a new sump gasket, and then refit the sump (Fig. 1.39 and photos).
14 Refit the alternator adjusting bracket (Fig. 1.40) and, if removed, the alternator bottom mounting bracket (photo).

27.10 Water bypass tube connection to timing cover

27.12A Locate gasket and oil pick-up tube ...

27.12B ... and tighten the retaining bolts

27.13A Locate the gasket and sump ...

27.13B ... and tighten the retaining bolts and nuts

27.14 Refit the alternator bottom mounting bracket

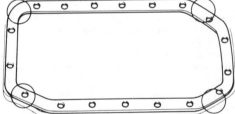

Fig. 1.39 Apply sealant to the encircled areas (Sec 27)

28 Oil pump – refitting

1 The oil seal in the front of the oil pump body must be renewed before refitting the pump unit, as must the large O-ring seal fitted between the pump and the timing cover. Refer to Section 23 to renew the oil seal.

2 Lubricate the oil pressure relief valve with clean engine oil, then insert it into position in the pump body, followed by the spring. Fit a new washer onto the relief valve plug, then screw the plug into position.

3 Lubricate the drive and driven gears with clean engine oil, then fit them into the pump body.

4 If removed, slide the oil pump drive spline onto the front end of the crankshaft, aligning the keyway (photo).

5 Locate a new oil ring seal into the groove in the front face of the timing cover, then refit the oil pump unit, engaging the drive gear with the drive spline (photos). Fit and tighten the retaining bolts to their respective torque settings. Note that the top bolt must have sealant applied (Fig. 1.41).

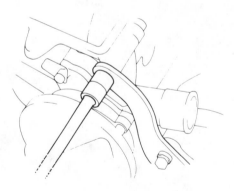

Fig. 1.40 Locate the alternator adjusting bracket when refitting the timing cover (Sec 27)

6 The crankshaft pulley can now be fitted onto the crankshaft, and the retaining bolt and washer screwed into position (photo). If the cylinder head is not in position, do not fully tighten the bolt until later, when the cylinder head is refitted and the camshaft sprocket is fitted onto the camshaft. When tightening the pulley bolt to the specified torque, jam the starter ring gear to prevent the engine from turning. On manual gearbox models, if the engine is in the vehicle, prevent the crankshaft from turning by placing the car in gear (1st or 2nd), and check that the handbrake is applied.

7 If the engine is in the vehicle, and the sump and oil pick-up tube have been removed for cleaning, the crankshaft can be prevented from turning with a block of wood. Refit the oil pick-up tube and sump, as described in Section 27 (paragraphs 12 and 13).

28.4 Fit the oil pump drive spline into position on the crankshaft

28.5A Grease and locate a new O-ring seal into the groove in the front face of the timing cover ...

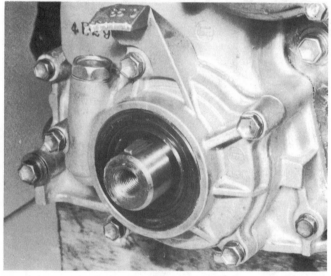

28.5B ... then refit the oil pump unit

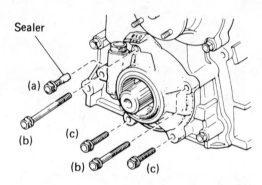

Fig. 1.41 Oil pump securing bolts – refer to Specifications for the tightening torques (Sec 28)

8   If the engine is in the vehicle, complete the operations by refitting the following items as applicable. Refer to the relevant Chapter concerned for details:

>   Air compressor (Chapter 12)
>   Air pump (Chapter 3)
>   Power steering pump (Chapter 10)
>   Alternator (Chapter 12)

9   Lower the engine and refit the mounting bolts.
10 Lower the vehicle, top up the engine oil, check for oil leaks, then refit the engine undercover.

29 Cylinder head and camshaft – refitting

1   Lubricate the camshaft bearing journals, then fit the camshaft into position on the cylinder head. Fit the bearing caps into position in their numerical order, with No 1 at the front (timing case end). The directional arrows on the caps must face the front (photos).
2   Fit the camshaft bearing cap bolts, and tighten them working from front to back to their specified torque settings. Check that the camshaft rotates freely (photo).
3   Apply some liquid sealant to each front corner of the cylinder block top face (photo).
4   Check that the cylinder head bolt holes are free of dirt and oil. Blow them out with compressed air to make certain. Check that the cylinder head location dowels are in position on the cylinder block top face.
5   Locate a new cylinder head gasket in position on top of the cylinder block; engaging it over the dowels (photo).

28.6 Refit the crankshaft pulley and bolt

9.1A Lubricate the bearing journals ...

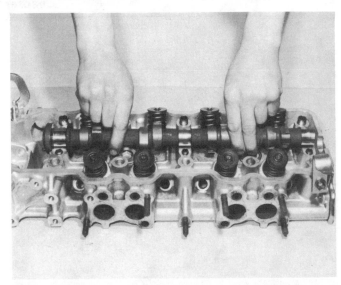

29.1B ... then fit the camshaft ...

29.1C ... and bearing caps in numerical order with arrows to the front

29.2 Tighten the bearing cap bolts to the specified torque

29.3 Apply liquid sealant to the front corners

29.5 Locate cylinder head gasket ...

29.7 ... and fit the cylinder head

29.8 Refit the rocker gear assembly ...

6   If the timing chain and cover assembly were not removed, but the camshaft sprocket was removed from the chain, refit it to the chain, aligning the marks made during the removal of the cylinder head. If the marks made on the camshaft sprocket and the chain are not aligned correctly, the timing will be incorrect.

7   Check that the cylinder head mating surface is clean, then lower the head down onto the gasket, and check that it engages over the location dowels (photo).

8   Locate the rocker assembly onto the cylinder head, and ensure that they engage over the location dowels in the top face of the cylinder head (photo).

9   Check that the cylinder head bolt threads are clean, then screw them into position finger tight (photo).

10 Tighten down the cylinder head bolts a half turn at a time, in a progressive sequence in the order shown in Fig. 1.42, to the specified torque setting (photo).

11 Tighten the cylinder head-to-timing chain cover top bolt to the specified torque setting.

12 Rotate the camshaft so that the dowel in the front end face is at the top. Grip the camshaft sprocket and chain, and turn the crankshaft over to bring the No 1 and No 4 cylinder pistons up to the top dead centre (TDC) position.

13 The camshaft sprocket can now be refitted to the camshaft, by engaging with the location dowel. It may be necessary to pull up on the sprocket and chain, whilst moving the camshaft back and forth to enable the sprocket to fit (Fig. 1.43).

14 Locate the distributor drive gear and the fuel pump drive cam onto the front end of the camshaft sprocket, then fit the retaining bolt and tighten to the specified torque setting. When tightening the bolt, prevent the camshaft from turning by engaging a suitable rod into the hole in the camshaft front end boss (behind the sprocket), as shown in Fig. 1.42.

29.9 ... and hand tighten the retaining bolts initially ...

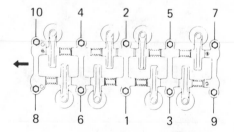

Fig. 1.42 Cylinder head bolt tightening sequence (Sec 29)

29.10 ... then in sequence to the specified torque

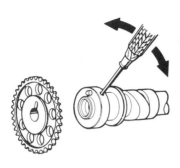

Fig. 1.43 Engage camshaft sprocket with the location dowel
– move camshaft to suit as shown (Sec 29)

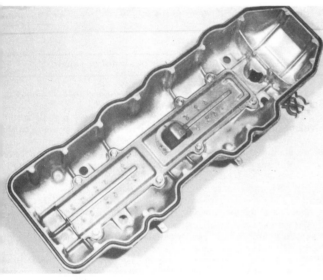

29.17 Locate a new seal into the cylinder head cover

29.18 Fit the gasket and thermostatic valve before locating the inlet
manifold

15 Refit the semi-circular plugs into the front and rear end of the cylinder head. Smear the mating surfaces with sealant before fitting.
16 Adjust the valve clearances, as described in Section 30.
17 Refit the cylinder head cover using a new seal (photo). Tighten the four retaining nuts (with seals). Do not overtighten.
18 If the engine is in the vehicle, reverse the removal procedures described in paragraphs 2 to 14 in Section 5, but note the following.

> (a) *Thermostatic valve: Locate the new inlet manifold gasket into position on the cylinder head, then fit the thermostatic valve before refitting the inlet manifold (photo). Tighten the bolts to the specified torque settings*
> (b) *Always use new gaskets/seals where applicable when refitting the various components, eg exhaust manifold, fuel pump etc*
> (c) *Tighten the retaining bolts/nuts to the specified settings where given. Do not overtighten fastenings*
> (d) *On completion, top up the engine oil and coolant levels*
> (e) *Refer to Section 32 before attempting to restart the engine*

19 Whenever the cylinder head has been refitted, the engine must be restarted and run up to its normal operating temperature, whilst checks are made for oil, fuel and cooling system leaks. After an initial running period, switch off the engine, remove the cylinder head cover, and retighten the cylinder head bolts as described in paragraphs 10 and 11. Check and adjust the valve clearances (Section 30) and the engine idle speed (Chapter 3). Recheck the engine oil and coolant levels and top up if required.

30 Valve clearances – adjustment

1 The valve clearances should be checked, and if necessary adjusted, when the engine is hot. Where checking and adjusting is made with the engine cold (eg during overhaul), the clearances will need to be rechecked after the engine has been run up to its normal operating temperature.
2 If the engine is in the vehicle, it will be necessary to remove first the cylinder head (rocker) cover. Take careful note of where any hoses and electrical connections are fitted. For information on removal of the air cleaner unit on carburettor models refer to Chapter 3.
3 Turn the crankshaft until No 1 piston is at TDC on its compression stroke. Turn the crankshaft by applying a ring spanner to the pulley nut. TDC can be determined by reference to the ignition timing marks. Also check that both No 1 cylinder valves are closed.
4 If you are at all doubtful about the position of No 1 piston, remove the spark plug and as you turn the crankshaft place a finger over the plug hole and feel the compression being generated. As soon as this is felt, refer to the ignition timing marks.
5 With the engine set at TDC on compression stroke, check and if necessary adjust the valves indicated in Fig. 1.44. Check the clearances using a feeler gauge of the specified clearance thickness, inserted between the rocker arm and the valve stem.
6 The appropriate feeler blade should be a stiff sliding fit between the end of the valve stem and the rocker arm. If it is not, release the adjuster screw locknut and turn the adjuster screw in or out as necessary to

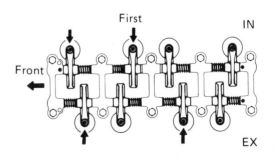

Fig. 1.44 First stage – check/adjust valves indicated (Sec 30)

achieve the gaps specified in the Specifications. Re-tighten the locknut (photo).

7 Turn the crankshaft through one complete turn (360°), then check the remaining valve clearances shown for the second stage, and adjust as necessary (Fig. 1.45).

8 Refit the rocker cover using a new seal where necessary. Fit new retaining nut seals where necessary. Do not overtighten the front retaining nuts.

9 If the engine is in the vehicle, refit the associated fittings. Restart the engine and check for oil leaks from the cylinder head cover.

30.6 Valve clearance adjustment

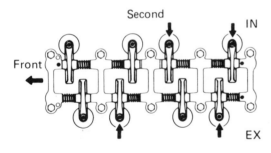

Fig. 1.45 Second stage – check/adjust valves indicated (Sec 30)

31 Engine and transmission – refitting

1 To reconnect the engine to the gearbox or automatic transmission where they are being refitted as a unit, reverse the separating details described in Section 10 or 11, as applicable.

2 When connecting the lifting sling, allow for the steep angle required for inserting the engine/gearbox into the vehicle. Ensure that the sling is securely located.

3 If the gearbox or automatic transmission have not been removed, lower the engine into position so that it is accurately aligned with the gearbox or automatic transmission, and reconnect the two as described in Chapter 6. On manual gearbox types, ensure that the clutch disc is centralised, as described in Chapter 5.

4 Once the engine/gearbox or automatic transmission mountings are secure, reconnect the ancillary items, reversing the removal procedures. If not yet fitted, fit the oil filter as described in Section 4.

5 Tighten all retaining nuts/bolts to the specified torque wrench settings (where given).

6 Ensure that all coolant, fuel and vacuum hoses are securely and correctly fitted as noted during removal.

7 Ensure that all wiring and earth leads are correctly and securely connected. Do not reconnect the battery until the engine is ready to be started, and if the battery was removed, reconnect the earth lead last.

8 Check that all tools and equipment are clear of the engine before attempting to restart it. Refer to the following Section when starting the engine.

32 Engine – initial start-up after overhaul or repair

1 Make sure that the battery is fully charged and that all lubricants, coolant and fuel are replenished.

2 If the fuel system has been dismantled, it will require several revolutions of the engine on the starter motor to pump petrol to the carburettor.

3 As soon as the engine fires and runs, keep it going at a fast tickover only (no faster) and bring it up to normal working temperature.

4 As the engine warms up, there will be odd smells and some smoke from parts getting hot and burning off oil deposits. Look for wear or oil leaks which will be obvious if serious. Check also the clamp connection of the exhaust pipe to the manifold as these do not always 'find' their exact gas tight position until the warmth and vibration have acted on them, and it is almost certain that they will need tightening further. This should be done of course with the engine stationary.

5 When the normal engine running temperature has been reached, adjust the idling speed as described in Chapter 3.

6 Stop the engine and wait a few minutes to see if any lubricant or coolant leaks.

7 If the cylinder head was removed and refitted, retighten the head bolts, as described in Section 29.

8 Road test the car to check that the timing is correct and giving the necessary smoothness and power. Do not race the engine. If new bearings and/or pistons and rings have been fitted, it should be treated as a new engine and run in at reduced revolutions for 500 miles (800 km).

3 Fault diagnosis – engine

Symptom	Reason(s)
Engine fails to turn over when starter operated	Discharged or defective battery Dirty or loose battery leads Defective starter solenoid or switch Engine earth strap disconnected Jammed starter motor drive pinion Defective starter mootor
Engine turns over but will not start	Ignition damp or wet Ignition system fault (see Chapter 4) Fuel system fault (see Chapter 3)
Engine stalls and will not start	Ignition system fault (see Chapter 4) Fuel system fault (see Chapter 3)
Engine misfires or runs unevenly	Battery leads loose on terminal Battery earth strap loose, or dirty connection Ignition system fault (see Chapter 4) Fuel system fault (see Chapter 3) Incorrect valve clearances
Engine lacks power	Burnt out or incorrectly adjusted valves Worn piston rings Ignition timing incorrect (see Chapter 4) Fuel system fault (see Chapter 3) Brakes sticking on (see Chapter 9)
Excessive oil consumption	Worn piston rings or cylinder bores Worn valve guides or defective stem seals Oil leak(s) from crankshaft rear oil seal, front oil seal in oil pump, sump gasket, timing cover or cylinder head cover seal
Excessive mechanical noises from engine	Valve/rocker clearances incorrect Worn camshaft bearings Slack or worn timing chain and sprockets Small ends, big ends or main bearings worn Worn cylinders (piston slap)

Chapter 2 Cooling system

Contents

Specifications

General
System type .... Pressurised, pump-assisted with thermostat and viscous-coupled fan
Blow-off pressure:
    Standard .... 0.75 to 1.05 bar (10.7 to 14.9 lbf/in²)
    Limit .... 0.6 bar (8.5 lbf/in²)

Coolant
Type .... Ethylene glycol based antifreeze and soft water
Capacity (total)
    UK models .... 7.5 litre (13.2 Imp pints)
    USA models .... 8.4 litre (8.9 US qt)

Thermostat
Opening commences:
    UK models:
        Low temperature type .... 80 to 84°C (176 to 183°F)
        High temperature type .... 86 to 90°C (187 to 194°F)
    USA models .... 86 to 90°C (187 to 194°F)
Fully open:
    UK models:
        Low temperature type .... 95°C (203°F)
        High temperature type .... 100°C (212°F)
    USA models .... 100°C (212°F)
Minimum opening travel (all models) .... 8 mm (0.31 in)

Drivebelt tensions (UK models)
All models as applicable:
    Alternator/water pump:

Deflection with 10 kg (22 lb) applied force

        New belt .... 5 to 7 mm (0.20 to 0.28 in)
        Used belt .... 7 to 10 mm (0.28 to 0.39 in)

Power steering:		
New belt	5 to 7 mm (0.20 to 0.28 in)	
Used belt	7 to 10 mm (0.28 to 0.39 in)	
Air pump:		
New belt	8 to 10 mm (0.31 to 0.39 in)	
Used belt	10 to 14 mm (0.39 to 0.55 in)	

Drivebelt tensions (USA models)

Using Burroughs tension gauge (No BT-33-73F):

All belts:		
New	45 to 68 kg (100 to 150 lb)	
Used	27 to 45 kg (60 to 100 lb)	

Torque wrench settings

	kgf m	lbf ft
Oil cooler (automatic transmission models):		
Cooler-to-radiator lower tank locknuts	2.25	16
Cooler pipes	1.50	11

General description

The cooling system is of pressurised type and the main components of the system are a front mounted radiator, a belt driven water pump and a thermostat. The cooling fan fitted is a viscous-coupled type attached to the water pump spindle flange.

The system functions as follows. With the engine running, cold water from the bottom of the radiator is drawn through the bottom radiator hose to the water pump. The water pump then forces the water through the cylinder block and water jackets to the cylinder head.

When the engine is cold and the thermostat is closed, the water passes through the bypass hose and is drawn into the water pump again; the water circulation is thus confined to the cylinder block and head. This assists rapid warming up.

The wax type thermostat is located in an outlet housing on the inlet manifold.

When the temperature of the coolant reaches the predetermined level, the thermostat opens and the water is forced through the top radiator hose to the radiator. The water is air cooled as it passes down through the radiator matrix and the cycle is then repeated.

The viscous-coupled fan is a variable speed type having a fluid coupling incorporated into its central hub. This allows the fan to operate at a reduced speed at higher engine speeds and thus reduces fan noise and power dissipation from the engine.

The coolant temperature is measured by a thermo-electric capsule located in the inlet manifold, just forward of the thermostat housing, and the reading is given on a gauge mounted on the instrument panel.

Drain cocks are provided on the cylinder block, and on the bottom of the radiator.

The heater unit is supplied with hot water from the engine cooling system, but the coolant flow through the heater is controlled by a valve manually operated by means of a cable connected to the heater control panel within the vehicle driving compartment. When the heater is off the valve is closed.

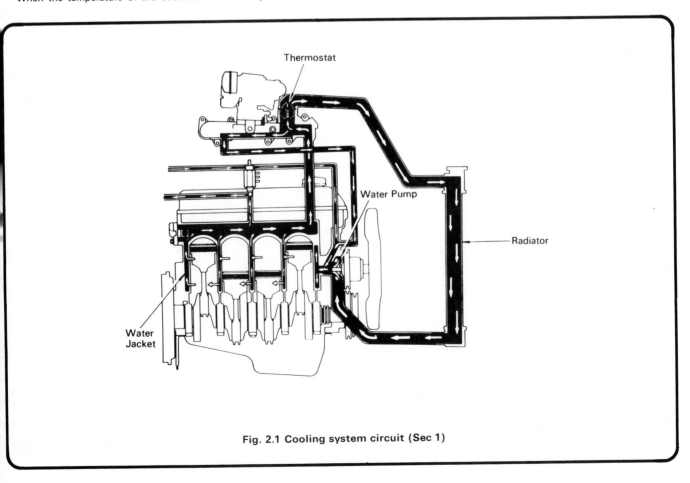

Fig. 2.1 Cooling system circuit (Sec 1)

2 Routine maintenance

1   At the intervals recommended in Routine Maintenance at the start of this manual, visually check the coolant level in the plastic coolant reservoir on the left-hand side of the radiator. If topping-up is required, use anti-freeze mixture of the same strength as the original coolant used for filling the system. Remove the filler cap from the coolant reservoir, and top up the level to the FULL mark. If topping-up the radiator is also necessary, refer to Section 3, paragraph 1 before removing the radiator cap. Top up the radiator and refill the system, as described in Section 6 (Fig. 2.2).
2   Frequent topping-up of the cooling system will indicate a leak, as under normal conditions the addition of coolant is a rare occurrence.
3   Regularly inspect all coolant hoses for security of clips, and for evidence of deterioration of the hoses.
4   At the specified intervals, check the condition and tension of the coolant pump/alternator drivebelt. Adjust if necessary as described in Section 7.
5   Occasionally make a check of the viscous coupling unit. It will need renewal if it shows any signs of oil leakage or malfunction.
6   On automatic transmission models, check the oil cooler hoses and connections at the base of the radiator for signs of leakage, or deterioration. Renew if necessary.

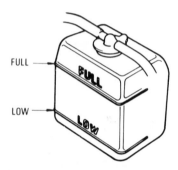

Fig. 2.2 Coolant reservoir showing level markings (Sec 2)

3 Cooling system – draining

1   With the car on level ground, drain the system as follows. If the engine is cold, remove the filler cap from the radiator by turning it anti-clockwise. If the engine is hot, then turn the filler cap very slightly

until the pressure in the system has had time to disperse. Use a rag over the cap to protect your hand from escaping steam. If, with the engine very hot, the cap is released suddenly, the drop in pressure can cause the water to boil. With the pressure released the cap can be removed.
2   If antifreeze is in the cooling system drain it into a clean bowl for re-use. A wide bowl will be necessary to catch all the coolant.
3   Open the radiator and cylinder block drain plugs/taps. The cylinder block drain plug is located on the left-hand side towards the rear (photos).
4   When the coolant has finished flowing, probe the plug holes or taps with a piece of wire to dislodge any particles of rust or sediment which may be causing a blockage and preventing all the coolant draining out.

4 Cooling system – flushing

1   With time the cooling system will gradually lose its efficiency as the radiator becomes choked with rust scale, deposits from the water and other sediment. To clean the system out, first drain it – leaving the drain plugs/taps open. Then remove the radiator cap and leave a hose running in the radiator cap orifice for ten to fifteen minutes.
2   In very bad cases the radiator should be reverse flushed. This can be done with the radiator in position. A hose must be arranged to feed water into the lower radiator outlet pipe. Water, under pressure, is then forced up through the radiator and out of the header tank filler orifice. *Take care not to allow water spray to splash onto the ignition leads and associated components and do not flush a hot engine with cold water.*
3   On completion, remove the hose and then flush through again in the normal manner inserting it through the radiator filler orifice.

5 Antifreeze solution

1   Apart from climatic considerations, antifreeze mixture should always be used in the engine cooling system to help combat rust and corrosion.
2   Standard solutions should be renewed every year while 'long life' products usually give protection for longer periods. Renew the coolant just before the winter season commences.
3   Before refilling the cooling system with antifreeze solution it is best to drain and flush the system, as described in Sections 3 and 4 of this Chapter.
4   Because antifreeze has a greater searching effect than water make sure that all hoses and joints are in good condition.
5   Ideally, a 50% solution of antifreeze with 50% soft water should be

3.3A Radiator coolant drain plug (arrowed)

3.3B Cylinder block coolant drain plug

used but where financial considerations dictate weaker mixtures, the table gives the protection to be expected from smaller percentages.

%	Complete protection	
25	–11°C	12.2°F
30	–14°C	6.8°F
35	–19°C	–2.2°F
40	–23°C	–9.4°F
45	–29°C	–20.2°F
50	–35°C	–31.0°F

5 Where the cooling system contains an antifreeze solution, any subsequent topping-up should be done with a solution of similar proportions to avoid dilution.

6 Cooling system – filling

1 Refit and tighten the radiator and cylinder block drain plugs.
2 Move the heater control lever to HOT.
3 Remove the radiator cap and pour antifreeze mixture slowly into the radiator until it is full to the brim.

4 Start the engine and let it run at a fast idle. The coolant level in the radiator will drop; make this up by adding more coolant until the level no longer falls (photo).
5 Switch off the engine, refit the radiator cap and then fill the expansion tank to the level mark halfway up its side.
6 When the engine is restarted and reaches its normal operating temperature, make a further check to ensure that the coolant level in the reservoir is correct and that the drain plugs and hoses show no signs of leaking.

7 Drivebelts – adjustment and renewal

1 The number of drivebelts fitted, and their arrangement, will depend upon the equipment fitted (water pump, emission control air pump, alternator, air conditioning compressor, power steering pump).
2 The respective drivebelt arrangements and their tension check-points are shown in the accompanying illustrations (Figs 2.3, 2.4 and 2.5). Refer to the Specifications for details on the belt adjustments.
3 Adjustment is carried out by slackening the mounting and adjustment link bolts of the driven component and pushing it in

6.4 Refill the cooling system initially via the radiator

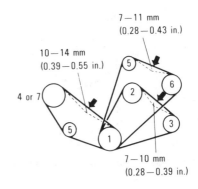

Fig. 2.3 Drivebelt arrangements showing tension check points. Note that the tensions given are for used belts – UK models (Sec 7)

1	Crank	5	Idler
2	Fan	6	Steering pump
3	Alternator	7	Air pump
4	Compressor		

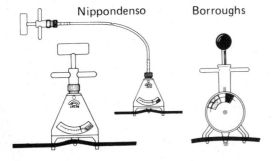

Fig. 2.4 Drivebelt tension checks can be made with deflector gauge if available. Typical types are shown (Sec 7)

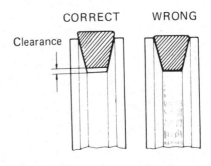

Fig. 2.5 View showing correct and incorrect fitting of drivebelt in a pulley when under the specified tension (Sec 7)

7.3A Drivebelt adjustment (power steering pump). Apply pressure to the belt ...

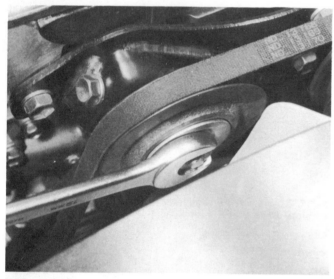

7.3B ... loosen the pulley locknut ...

7.3C ... turn the adjuster as required

towards or pulling it away from the engine. Where the drivebelt adjustment is made by an idler pulley, loosen the adjustment bolt and the control nut in the pulley to release the tension. Turn the adjustment bolt the required amount to set the belt tension, then tighten the idler pulley nut and adjusting bolt (photos).

4   On USA models fitted with an emission control air pump, the procedure differs according to type. On models without air conditioning, loosen the adjustment/support strap lockbolt, and prise the air pump in the required direction. But if using a lever, only prise against the rear cover of the pump, not the cast section, or damage may result. On models with air conditioning, loosen the lockbolt, then move the adjusting bolt to set the tension. See Fig. 2.6 for both types.

5   Retighten the adjuster lockbolt when the drivebelt tension is correct.

6   If a drivebelt requires renewal because of wear, cuts, fraying or breakage, always release the mountings and/or tensioner of the driven components and push it in towards the engine as far as possible so that the belt can be slipped over the pulley rims with the least strain.

7   With multiple belt arrangements, if a rear belt requires renewal then the ones nearer the front will of course have to be removed first.

8   With a new belt check the tension 250 miles (400 km) after fitting.

9   Periodic checking of the belt tension is necessary and there is no hard and fast rule as to the most suitable interval, because a drivebelt does not necessarily stretch or wear at a predetermined rate. Assuming most owners check their own oil and water levels regularly it is suggested as a good habit to check the belt tension every time the bonnet is opened.

8   Radiator – removal, servicing and refitting

1   Refer to Section 3 and drain the cooling system.

2   Slacken the clip which holds the top water hose to the radiator and carefully pull off the hose (photo).

3   Slacken the clip which holds the bottom water hose to the radiator bottom tank and carefully pull off the hose (photo).

4   On models fitted with the automatic transmission, wipe the area round the oil cooler pipe unions and then detach these pipes from the radiator. Plug the end to prevent dirt entering the pipes, and fluid loss.

5   Unclip and detach the hose from the radiator to the coolant reservoir (photo).

6   Unscrew and remove the radiator retaining bolts, then carefully lift the radiator, complete with fan shroud. On some models it may be necessary to remove the fan shroud from the radiator before lifting the radiator clear of the bottom mountings, and out of the vehicle (photos).

7   Clean out the inside of the radiator by flushing, as described in Section 3. When the radiator is out of the car it is well worthwhile to invert it for reverse flushing. Clean the exterior of the radiator by hosing down the matrix with a strong water jet to clean away embedded dirt and debris, which will impede the airflow. When an oil cooler is fitted (automatic transmission) make sure no water is allowed to enter. Note that if a high pressure cleaner is used to clean the matrix, care must be taken not to damage the core fins. The cleaner nozzle should be kept at a minimum distance of 20 inches from the radiator.

8   If it is thought that the radiator is partially blocked, a good proprietary chemical product should be used to clean it.

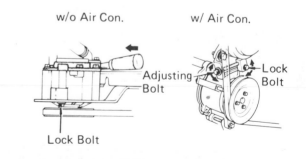

Fig. 2.6 Air pump drivebelt adjustment is according to type – 1982 USA model (Sec 7)

8.2 Disconnect the radiator top hose

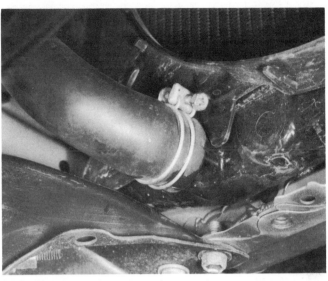

8.3 Radiator bottom hose connection

8.5 Coolant bypass hose

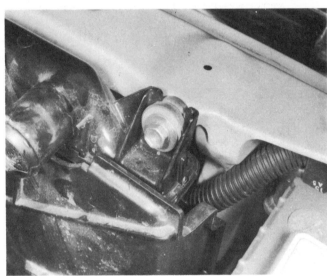

8.6A Radiator and retaining bolt

8.6B Radiator bottom mountings

9 If the radiator is leaking, a temporary repair may be made by plugging with a fibreglass type filler or by using a leak sealing product in the coolant. Permanent repairs should be left to your dealer or a radiator repair specialist. Localised heat has to be used to repair a radiator, obviously experience is necessary otherwise the problem could be made worse.

10 Although the construction of the radiator allows the upper and lower tank assemblies to be separated from the core by releasing the tank plate clips, this is not recommended. The reason for this is that a special Toyota service tool is required to release and refit the retaining clips. If the upper and/or lower O-ring seals are in need of replacement or, on automatic transmission models, the oil cooler pipe connection O-ring seals need renewing, entrust this task to your Toyota dealer (Fig. 2.7).

11 Inspect the radiator hoses for cracks, internal or external perishing and damage caused by the securing clips. Renew the hoses as necessary. Examine the radiator hose securing clips and renew them if they are rusted or distorted.

12 Refitting the radiator is the reverse sequence to removal. If automatic transmission is fitted check and top up its fluid level.

13 On completion check the radiator and its hose connections for any sign of leaks.

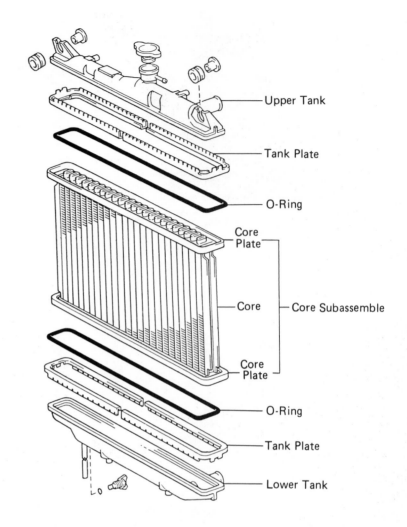

Upper Tank

Tank Plate

O-Ring

Core
Plate

Core — Core Subassemble

Core
Plate

O-Ring

Tank Plate

Lower Tank

Automatic Transmission only

Plate Washer
Spring Washer
Pipe
O-Ring
Nut
Oil Cooler
Lower Tank

Fig. 2.7 Exploded view of the radiator (Sec 8)

9 Thermostat – removal, testing and refitting

1 To remove the thermostat, partially drain the cooling system, as described in Section 3. The removal of 4 pints (2.27 litres) is usually enough.

2 Slacken the radiator top hose at the thermostat housing elbow and carefully draw it off the elbow.

3 Unscrew the two bolts securing the thermostat housing elbow (photo), and lift the housing and gasket away. If it has stuck because a sealing compound has been previously used, tap with a soft-faced hammer to break the seal.

4 Lift out the thermostat and observe if it is stuck open. If this is the case discard it (photo).

5 Suspend it by a piece of string, together with a thermometer, in a saucepan of cold water. Neither the thermostat nor the thermometer should touch the sides or bottom of the saucepan or a false reading could be obtained.

6 Heat the water, stirring it gently with the thermometer to ensure temperature uniformity, and note when the thermostat begins to open. Note the temperature and this should be comparable with the figure given in the Specifications at the beginning of this Chapter. For type identification, see the identifying mark on the thermostat body.

7 Continue heating the water until the thermostat is fully open. Now let it cool down naturally and check that it closes fully. If the thermostat does not fully open or close then it must be discarded and a new one obtained.

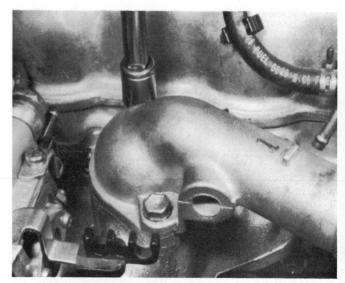

9.3 Undoing the thermostat housing bolts

9.4 Lift the thermostat out

9.8 Thermostat orientation when fitted

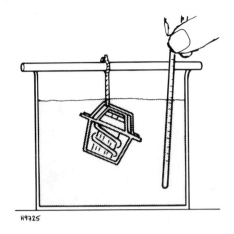

Fig. 2.8 Thermostat test method (Sec 9)

8 Refitting the thermostat is the reverse of the removal procedure. Always clean the mating faces thoroughly and use a new flange gasket (photo).
9 On completion, top up the cooling system, start the engine, and check for any signs of coolant leakage from the thermostat housing cover joint and the hose connection.

10 Water pump – removal and refitting

1 Refer to Section 3 and drain the cooling system.
2 Loosen the alternator pivot and adjustment bolts, then pivot the alternator inwards towards the engine so that the drivebelt is slack.
3 Unscrew and remove the four nuts securing the viscous-coupled cooling fan unit to the water pump pulley and drive flange. Withdraw the cooling fan unit, together with the water pump pulley and drivebelt (photo).
4 Undo the six bolts and three nuts which secure the water pump unit to the front of the engine, then withdraw the water pump unit and its gasket.
5 Refitting the water pump is the reverse sequence to removal, but the following additional points should be noted (photos).

   (a) Make sure the mating faces of the pump body and cylinder block are clean. Always use a new gasket

10.3 Viscous-coupled fan-to-water pump pulley showing retaining nuts (arrowed)

10.5A Locate a new gasket

10.5B Refit the pump unit

10.5C Tighten the retaining bolts

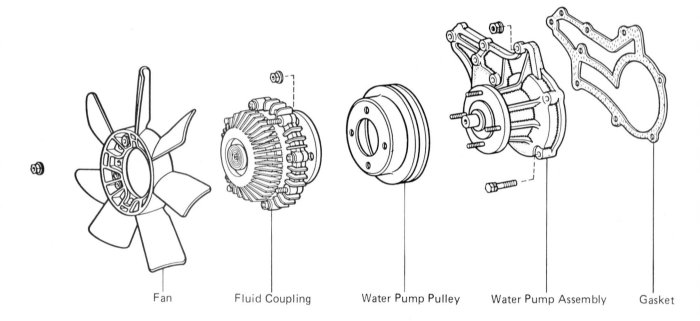

Fan   Fluid Coupling   Water Pump Pulley   Water Pump Assembly   Gasket

Fig. 2.9 Coolant pump components (Sec 10)

(b) Refer to Section 7 and adjust the drivebelt tension. If the belt is too tight undue strain will be placed on the water pump and alternator bearings. If the belt is too loose, it will slip and wear rapidly as well as giving rise to possible engine overheating and low alternator output.

(c) On completion top up the cooling system, run the engine and check for leaks around the water pump

11 Water pump – overhaul

1   If the water pump has been removed for inspection owing to noisy operation or possibly because it has developed a leak, overhaul is possible, but is not recommended. In the first place spare parts for the pump may not be readily available and secondly the cost of a factory reconditioned unit should not prove that expensive.

2   Where spare parts are available and it is preferred to overhaul the original pump unit first clean away all external dirt.

3   Support the underside of the pulley seat and, supporting the pump unit so that it does not fall and damage the housing, drive the shaft down through the pulley seat.

4   Heat up the pump unit in a bowl of hot water to a temperature of 85°C (185°F), then press or drift out the bearing and rotor assembly from the body.

5   Support the rotor on the underside of its inner flange (not on the blades) and press or drift the shaft from it to enable the seal assembly to be removed.

6   Renew any damaged or defective components. A new rotor and seal set must be fitted during reassembly.

7   Reassembly is the reversal of the dismantling procedure. Smear the seal surface in the pump body with sealant before inserting the new seal. Reheat the body to 85°C (185°F) before fitting the bearing which, when in position, should have its end face flush with the top surface of the body.

8   Press the pulley seat home so that its clearance from the body is as shown in the illustrations.

9   The rotor to body clearance must be set at 6.1 mm (0.240 in) see Fig. 2.10.

10 The pulley seat depth must be as shown in Fig. 2.11.

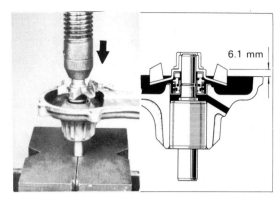

Fig. 2.10 Press rotor into position to give the specified clearance indicated (Sec 11)

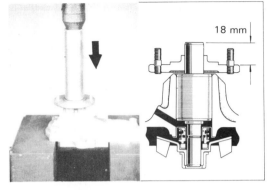

Fig. 2.11 Press the pulley seat home to depth shown (Sec 11)

12 Viscous-coupled cooling fan – removal, inspection and refitting

1   To remove the viscous-coupled cooling fan unit, refer to Section 10, paragraphs 1 to 3 inclusive.
2   To separate the fan from the coupling unit, undo the securing nuts in the front face of the fan.
3   Check the coupling unit for signs of damage or leakage of silicone oil. Do not dismantle the unit or apply pressure to the bi-metal spring. If the unit is defective or suspected of malfunction, renew it. It cannot be repaired.
4   Refitting is a reversal of the removal procedure. Refer to Section 7 when adjusting the drivebelt tension.

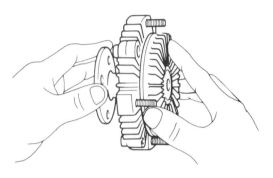

Fig. 2.12 Check the fluid coupling for damage or leakage (Sec 12)

13 Fault diagnosis – cooling system

Symptom	Reason(s)
Engine overheats	Insufficient water in cooling system
	Drivebelt slipping (accompanied by a shrieking noise on rapid engine acceleration)
	Radiator core blocked or radiator grille restricted
	Bottom water hose collapsed, impeding flow
	Thermostat not opening properly
	Ignition advance and retard incorrectly set (accompanied by loss of power and perhaps, misfiring) (see Chapter 4)
	Carburettor incorrectly adjusted (mixture too weak) (see Chapter 3)
	Exhaust system partially blocked (see Chapter 3)
	Oil level in sump too low (see Chapter 7)
	Blown cylinder head gasket (water/steam being forced down the radiator overflow pipe under pressure)
	Viscous-coupled fan defective
	Engine not yet run-in
	Brakes binding (see Chapter 9)
Engine being overcooled	Thermostat jammed open
	Incorrect grade of thermostat fitted allowing premature opening of valve
	Thermostat missing
Leaks in system	Loose clips on water hoses
	Top or bottom water hoses perished and leaking
	Radiator core leaking
	Thermostat gasket leaking
	Pressure cap spring worn or seal ineffective
	Blown cylinder head gasket (pressure in system forcing water/steam down overflow pipe)
	Cylinder wall or head cracked (see Chapter 1)

Chapter 3
Fuel, exhaust and emission control systems

Contents

Specifications

Part A: Carburettor and associated fuel system components
Air cleaner type .... Renewable paper element with automatic air temperature control

Fuel pump
UK models .... Mechanical diaphragm
USA models up to 1983 .... Mechanical diaphragm

Fuel tank
Location .... Under body at rear
Capacity .... 61 litre (13.4 Imp gal; 16.1 US gal)

Fuel type (octane rating)
UK models .... 98 octane (4-star)
USA models .... Unleaded, Research Octane No 91 (octane rating 87) or higher

Carburettor – UK models

	Primary	Secondary
Type .... Aisan twin choke downdraught		
Acceleration pump stroke .... 4.1 mm (0.161 in)		
Float level:		
Raised – float top to air horn .... 10.5 mm (0.413 in)		
Lowered – float bottom to air horn .... 48.0 mm (1.89 in)		
Throttle valve angles (from horizontal)	Primary	Secondary
Valve fully open	90°	90°
Valve fully closed	9°	20°
Fast idle angle .... 21°		
Unloader angle .... 49°		
Throttle positioner angle .... 17°		
Choke breaker opening angle .... 38°		
Dashpot return time to idle position (approx) .... 3 seconds		
Outer vent control valve resistance at 20°C (68°F) ...... 63 to 73 ohm		
Choke coil resistance at 20°C (68°F) .... 16 to 20 ohm		
Idle mixture screw presetting .... Screw out 2¹/₂ turns		
Idle mixture speed:		
Manual transmission .... 740 rpm		
Automatic transmission .... 790 rpm		
Idle speed:		
Manual transmission .... 700 rpm		
Automatic transmission .... 750 rpm		
Fast idle speed .... 2600 rpm		

Carburettor – USA 1982 models

	Primary	Secondary
Type .... Aisan twin choke downdraught		
Float level:		
Raised – float top to air horn .... 10.5 mm (0.413 in)		
Lowered – float bottom to air horn .... 48 mm (1.89 in)		
Float lip clearance (float lowered) .... 1.0 mm (0.04 in)		
Throttle valve angles (from horizontal)	Primary	Secondary
Valve fully open	90°	90°
Valve fully closed	9°	20°
Secondary touch angle .... 59°		
Fast idle angle .... 24°		
Unloader angle .... 45°		
Choke breaker opening angle .... 38°		
Idle-up angle .... 16°		
Idle mixture adjuster screw presetting .... Screw out 2¹/₂ turns		
Idle mixture speed:		
Manual transmission .... 740 rpm		
Automatic transmission .... 790 rpm		
Fast idle speed .... 2600 rpm		

Carburettor – USA 1983 models

	Primary	Secondary
Type .... Aisan twin choke downdraught		
Float level:		
Raised – float top to air horn .... 10.5 mm (0.413 in)		
Lowered – float bottom to air horn .... 48 mm (1.89 in)		
Float lip clearance (float lowered) .... 1.0 mm (0.04 in)		
Throttle valve angles (from horizontal)	Primary	Secondary
Valve fully open	90°	90°
Valve fully closed	9°	20°
Secondary touch angle .... 59°		
Fast idle angle .... 22°		
Unloader angle .... 50°		
Choke breaker opening angle .... 42°		
Idle-up angle .... 16.5°		
Idle mixture adjuster screw presetting .... Screw out 4 turns		
Idle mixture speed .... 740 rpm		
Fast idle speed .... 2600 rpm		

Torque wrench settings

	kgf m	lbf ft
Exhaust manifold	4.50	33
Inlet manifold	1.95	14
Fuel tank mounting bolts	2.20	16
Fuel tank drain plug	1.25	9

Part B: Electronic fuel-injection and associated fuel system

Air cleaner type .... Renewable paper element

Fuel pump .... Electric, located within fuel tank

Fuel tank
Location .... Under body at rear
Capacity .... 61 litres (13.4 Imp gal; 16.1 US gal)

Fuel type (octane rating) .... Unleaded. Research Octane No 91 (octane rating 87) or higher

Fuel supply system .... Electronic fuel-injection (EFI)

Torque wrench settings

	kgf m	lbf ft
Exhaust manifold	4.50	33
Inlet manifold	1.95	14
Pressure regulator locknut	3.00	22
Injector bolts	1.95	14
Pulsation damper	4.50	33
Fuel hose to delivery pipe (at manifold)	4.50	33
Fuel line connections	3.00	22
Flare nut/bolt	3.00	22
Fuel tank mounting bolts	2.20	16
Fuel tank drain plug	1.25	9

PART A: CARBURETTOR AND ASSOCIATED FUEL SYSTEM COMPONENTS

1 General description

All carburettor engine models are fitted with a rear mounted fuel tank, a mechanically operated fuel pump and an Aisan downdraught carburettor of twin choke design.

The carburettor model fitted is dependent on the engine and market to which it has been supplied.

The air cleaner is a renewable paper element type, and the air cleaner unit incorporates an automatic temperature control within the air intake duct.

Numerous emission control system components are used in conjunction with the fuel and exhaust system. The extent of emission control equipment used is dependent on model and operating territory but is dealt with from Section 34 onwards.

2 Routine maintenance – fuel and exhaust system (carburettor models)

The following routine maintenance procedures must be undertaken at the specified intervals given at the start of this manual. When making any checks and adjustments to the fuel system it is essential that the ignition system components must be in good condition, with the ignition timing correctly adjusted. Refer to Chapter 4 concerning the ignition system requirements.

1   **Air cleaner:** Remove the air cleaner element, and clean or renew it as required. Refer to Section 3 for details.

2   **Fuel filter:** Renew the in-line fuel filter unit. Detach the hoses and remove the old unit. When refitting the new unit, the inlet and outlet hoses must be correctly connected, as indicated by the arrow(s) on top of the unit (Fig. 3.1).

3   **Engine idle and fast idle speed:** Check and if necessary adjust the idle and fast idle speed settings, as described in Sections 11 and 12 respectively.

4   **Automatic choke:** This unit must be checked for satisfactory operation. The air cleaner unit must be removed for access. Push the choke valve down, then release it and check that it returns fully and without hesitation. Start the engine (cold) and run it, checking that the choke valve progressively opens as the engine warms up. Feel the choke housing with your fingers. It should feel hot to the touch. If required, the auto-choke can be adjusted by loosening the retaining screws and rotating the housing in the required direction (clockwise to weaken or anti-clockwise to richen the mixture). Retighten the screws on completion and refit the air cleaner.

5   **Fuel filler cap:** The cap gasket must be inspected occasionally and renewed at the specified intervals. The gasket is secured by four screws and a retainer (Fig. 3.2).

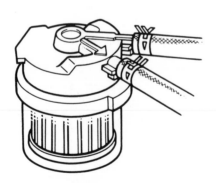

Fig. 3.1 Fuel filter and hose connections. Outlet hose is indicated by arrow (Sec 2)

Fig. 3.2 Fuel filler cap showing gasket location and orientation (Sec 2)

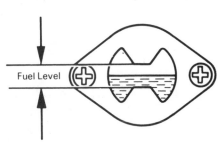

Fig. 3.3 Carburettor float chamber fuel level to be as shown (Sec 2)

Fuel system general: Periodically check the system hoses and connections for condition and security. Check that the fuel level in the carburettor float chamber is level with the index mark in the window (Fig. 3.3).

Exhaust system: Check the exhaust system for security and general condition. A leaky or severely corroded system must be repaired or renewed, as described in Section 17.

Air cleaner – servicing

Unscrew and remove the wing nut, release the toggle clips, and lift the cover from the air cleaner unit. Withdraw the element (photos).

2 If the element is only dirty in one spot, move the element round to present a new surface to the air intake aperture. If the element is only moderately dusty it can be cleaned by blowing it clean from the inside out with compressed air (Fig. 3.4). The element must not be washed or immersed in oil.

3 If the element is very dirty it must be renewed.

4 Wipe out the air cleaner casing and fit a new element into the casing. Do not run the engine rapidly or for extended periods with the element or filter cover or casing removed, as a backfire could cause a fire under the bonnet.

5 Refit the lid, moderately tighten the wing nut (overtightening may damage the carburettor), and reconnect the toggle clips around the rim. Note that the lid must be positioned so that its arrow mark aligns with the corresponding mark on the intake spout (Fig. 3.5).

6 If the air cleaner unit complete is to be removed from the engine, remove the cover wing nut and the two mounting bracket nuts (photo). Lift the cleaner unit clear of the carburettor stud, then disengage the intake spout from the ducting and the hoses from their connections. Note positions, or make identification marks on the hoses to ensure correct reassembly.

7 Refitting is a reversal of the removal procedure. Renew any hoses which are in poor condition, and ensure that they are securely located.

8 To verify that the automatic temperature control in the air cleaner is functioning correctly, detach the ducting from the intake spout, and hold a mirror at the end of the spout. With the engine cold and running, check that the valve plate is closed against cold air. Allow the engine to warm up, and again check to see that the valve plate is now open to allow the entry of cold air (photo).

9 If necessary the valve unit can be removed for inspection by detaching the vacuum hose and undoing the retaining screw. Partially lift the valve unit, and disengage the cranked operating arm from the valve, then remove it (photo).

10 Refit in the reverse order to removal.

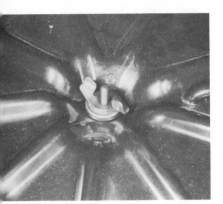

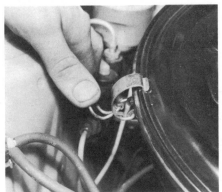

3.1A Carburettor air cleaner cover wing nut ...

3.1B ... and retaining clips

3.1C Air cleaner element removal

Fig. 3.4 Air cleaner element – cleaning with compressed air (Sec 3)

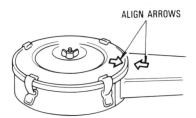

Fig. 3.5 Align the arrow marks as indicated (Sec 3)

3.6 Air cleaner unit retaining nut on cylinder head cover (arrowed). Note that it also retains a hose clip

3.8 Air cleaner intake ducting (A) and automatic temperature control unit (B)

4 Fuel filter – renewal

1   A disposable type fuel filter is fitted in the line to the fuel pump (photo).
2   At the specified intervals, disconnect the fuel lines from the filter and discard the filter.
3   Fit the new filter making sure that the directional arrow on the outside of the unit is pointing in the direction of fuel flow to the pump.
4   Check that the hose connections are secure and on changing the filter recheck for any sign of fuel leaks when the engine is restarted.

5 Fuel pump – testing in vehicle

1   Where lack of fuel is evident at the carburettor (level visible through float chamber sight glass), first check that there is fuel in the tank and that the in-line filter is not choked through not being renewed at the specified mileage.
2   Disconnect the fuel inlet pipe from the carburettor and place its open end in a container.
3   Disconnect the HT lead from the coil to prevent the engine firing and turn the ignition on. Let the starter motor turn the engine over for several revolutions when regular spurts of fuel should be seen being ejected from the open end of the fuel pipe.
4   If no fuel is observed then the pump must be faulty, there is a break in the fuel line or tank union allowing air instead of fuel to be drawn in.

6 Fuel pump – removal, testing and refitting

1   Unclip and detach the fuel supply hose to the fuel pump, the return hose from the pump, and the feed hose at the pump (to the carburettor). Plug the respective hoses to prevent fuel leakage and the ingress of dirt (photo).
2   Undo the two retaining bolts and remove the fuel pump, together with its gasket.
3   Clean the pump external surfaces. To check the pump for malfunction, first inject some fuel into the pump to make sure that the check valves are tightly sealed (a dry valve may not fully seal). Leaving the respective pipe connections clear, actuate the pump lever to assess the amount of force required to operate the pump, and also note the amount of operating arm movement. During the following checks apply the same amount of force and movement to the operating lever.

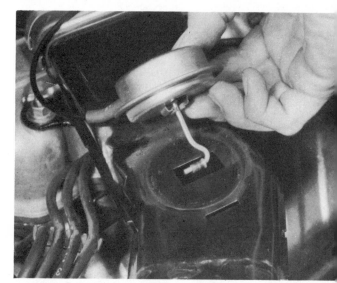

3.9 Automatic temperature control unit removal

4.1 The in-line fuel filter location and hose connections

TYPE I

TYPE II

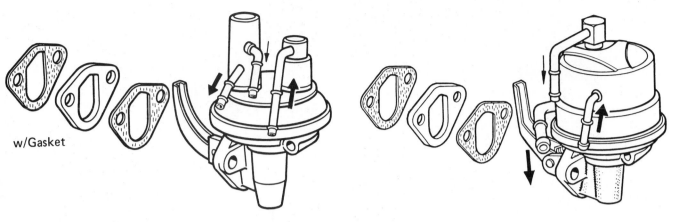

w/Gasket

Fig. 3.6 Fuel pump types used (Sec 6)

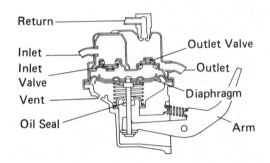

Return
Inlet
Inlet
Valve
Vent
Oil Seal
Outlet Valve
Outlet
Diaphragm
Arm

Fig. 3.7 Fuel pump components and hose connections
(Sec 6)

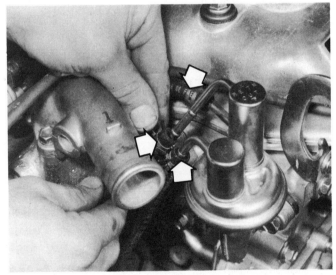

6.1 Detach the hoses (arrowed) from the fuel pump

4 **Inlet valve check:** Plug the outlet and return pipes, then check that the operating lever has additional free play and that it moves without tension (Fig. 3.8).

5 **Outlet valve check:** Plug the intake pipe and check that the operating arm is locked, but do not use any more force than that applied initially in paragraph 3 (Fig. 3.9).

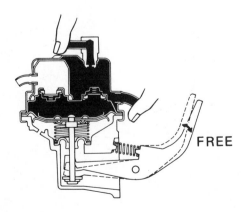

FREE

Fig. 3.8 Fuel pump inlet valve check (Sec 6)

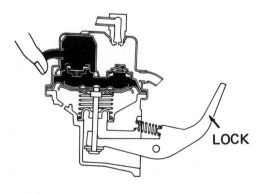

LOCK

Fig. 3.9 Fuel pump outlet valve check (Sec 6)

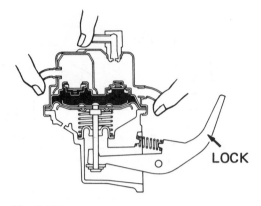

Fig. 3.10 Fuel pump diaphragm check (Sec 6)

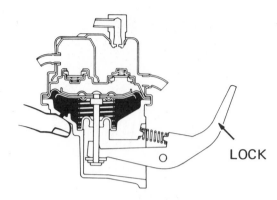

Fig. 3.11 Fuel pump oil seal check (Sec 6)

6 **Diaphragm check:** Plug off the intake, outlet and return pipes, and check that the operating lever is locked (Fig. 3.10). Again do not apply more force than that applied in paragraph 3.
7 If any of the three checks made prove a malfunction, then the upper body-to-lower body seal is defective, and the pump must be renewed as it cannot be overhauled.
8 **Oil seal check:** Referring to Fig. 3.11, plug off the vent hole in the base of the lower body, and check that the operating arm is locked. If this proves defective, again the pump must be renewed.
9 To refit the fuel pump, reverse the removal procedure but use a new gasket. Ensure that the hose connections are correctly made (photos).
10 When the engine is restarted, check that there are no signs of fuel leaks from the pump connections.

7 Fuel tank – removal and refitting

1 At all times during fuel tank draining, removal and refitting, exercise extreme caution with regard to fire risk. Disconnect the battery earth lead before starting removal.
2 Removal of the fuel tank is not a difficult task, but to improve access when working underneath the vehicle, raise and support it at the rear end (or use ramps if available).
3 The tank should first be drained of any fuel into a suitable container for storage and subsequent use. If a drain plug is not fitted, the fuel will have to be syphoned out.
4 Lift the floor covering in the luggage compartment out of the way, and remove the cover from the access aperture to the fuel tank sender unit (photo). Detach the lead connector.
5 Disconnect the fuel filler pipe (photo).
6 Disconnect the fuel outlet pipe, return pipe, emission, and where applicable the expansion tank pipes, noting their respective connections.
7 Disconnect all breather or fuel evaporative system hoses according to type.
8 Disconnect the tank mounting straps or withdraw the mounting bolts and withdraw the tank from the vehicle (photos).
9 If a leak is detected in a fuel tank, a temporary repair may be made with fibreglass or similar material but never attempt to weld or solder a leak. Renew the tank complete or take it for professional repair.
10 The fuel contents sender unit can be removed by undoing the retaining screws and withdrawing the unit from the tank.
11 Water and sediment often collect at the base of the tank, this can be removed using two or three changes of clean paraffin with a final rinse of fuel. Shake the tank and tip out the flushing solvent, but remove the sender unit first.
12 Refitting is a reversal of removal. Use a new seal gasket for the sender unit. Also use a new gasket when refitting the fuel filler pipe to the tank. Renew the rubber protectors on the top face of the tank, and also those which are located between the tank and the securing straps.
13 Renew any defective or suspect hoses. The hose and pipe connections must be in good condition and secure.

6.9A Locate a new gasket ...

6.9B ... and refit the fuel pump

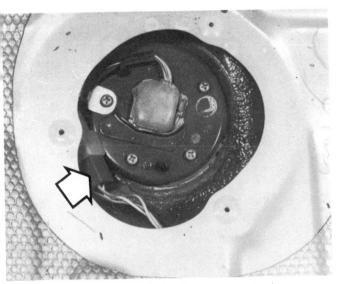

7.4 Fuel tank gauge sender unit showing wiring connection (arrowed)

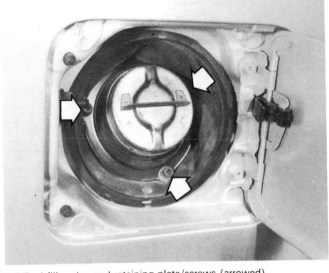

7.5 Fuel filler pipe and retaining plate/screws (arrowed)

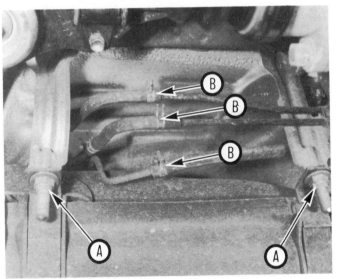

7.8A Fuel tank retaining strap securing nuts (A) and fuel line connections (B)

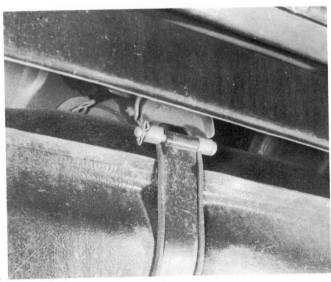

7.8B Fuel tank retaining strap pivots at the rear

14 Tighten the mounting strap retaining nuts and the drain plug to the specified torque settings.
15 Reconnect the fuel level sender unit wiring before reconnecting the battery earth lead.
16 Refill the fuel tank, and check for any signs of leaks from the tank or its pipe/hose connections.

8 Fuel gauge and sender unit – testing

1 Should a fault develop in the fuel gauge reading, first check that the gauge fuse has not blown. If it has, check the reason, a short in the wiring being the most likely cause.
2 Check the security and condition of the leads to the gauge and the sender unit in the fuel tank.
3 Disconnect the lead which runs from the fuel gauge to the sender unit from the back of the fuel gauge.
4 From this terminal on the gauge, run a lead to a good earth incorporating a 3.4W bulb in the lead. Turn the ignition switch on, the test bulb should light and then start to flash after a few seconds. The

gauge needle should also deflect. If this test proves satisfactory then the gauge is in good condition and the sender unit is probably at fault.
5 To check the sender unit, remove it from the fuel tank, as described in the preceding Section.

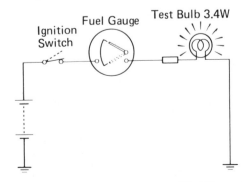

Fig. 3.12 Fuel gauge test (Sec 8)

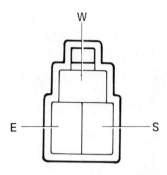

Fig. 3.13 Fuel gauge sender unit terminal connections (Sec 8)

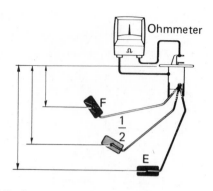

Fig. 3.14 Fuel gauge sender unit resistance check (Sec 8)

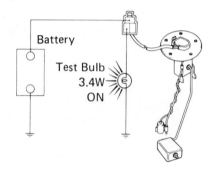

Fig. 3.15 Fuel level warning switch operation check (Sec 8)

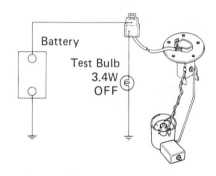

Fig. 3.16 Fuel level warning switch operation check – switch submerged (Sec 8)

6   Using a circuit tester, measure the resistance between the S terminal on the sender unit and earth. Move the float arm smoothly and compare the readings obtained with those shown in the following table (Figs. 3.13 and 3.14).

Float position	Resistance
FULL	3 ± 2.1 ohm
1/2 FULL	32.5 ± 4.8 ohm
EMPTY	110 ± 7.7 ohm

7   The fuel level warning light is actuated by a level switch mounted on the sender unit. When 5.0 litre (1.1 Imp gal; 1.3 US gal) of fuel remains in the tank the light comes on as a reminder to re-fuel.
8   To check the warning light switch operation, first ensure that the wiring connections are clean and securely made, then connect up a test light between the wiring connector and earth (Fig. 3.15). The bulb should light. Now submerge the switch in a bowl of water or fuel. The bulb should go out (Fig. 3.16).
9   When refitting the sender unit to the fuel tank, use a new gasket and ensure that the wiring connections are clean and secure.

9   Accelerator linkage – removal and refitting

Accelerator cable
1   Disconnect the accelerator cable from the throttle control quadrant or linkage connector at the carburettor/throttle body. Loosen the securing nuts, and detach the outer cable from the support bracket (photo).
2   Release the inner cable from the accelerator pedal within the car (photo).
3   Withdraw the cable through the bulkhead and grommet(s), and remove it from the car.
4   Refitting is a reversal of the removal procedure. On completion, check that the throttle operation is satisfactory through its full range by fully depressing then releasing the accelerator pedal. Start the engine and check the idle speed settings.

Accelerator pedal
5   Release the accelerator cable from the pedal, undo the pivot/mounting bracket bolts, and remove the pedal and bracket (photo).
6   If the pedal is removed from the bracket, note how the return spring is located.
7   Refit in the reverse order of removal and check for satisfactory operation on completion. Lubricate the pedal pivot.

9.1 Accelerator cable-to-throttle linkage connection – outer cable securing nuts arrowed

.2 Accelerator cable-to-pedal connection (arrowed)

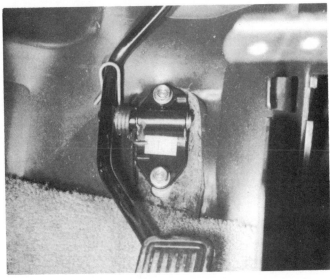

9.5 Accelerator pedal and pivot/mounting bracket

0 Carburettor – description

1 The carburettor fitted is of twin choke downdraught type, fitted with a thermo-electric choke. The carburettor types used differ according to model and operating territory, the main differences being dictated by the complexity of the emission control features fitted (Figs. 3.17 and 3.18).

2 The carburettor design gives correct and efficient performance under all operating conditions so giving a good engine performance

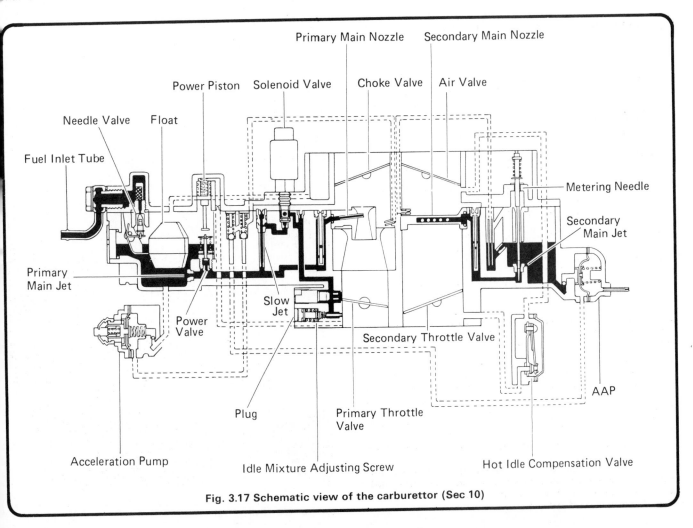

Fig. 3.17 Schematic view of the carburettor (Sec 10)

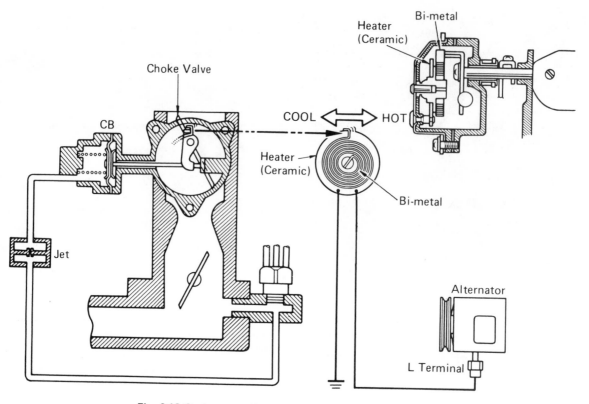

Fig. 3.18 Carburettor thermo-electric choke system (Sec 10)

whilst maintaining an acceptable fuel economy. It is similar to two single barrel carburettors but built into one body.

3   The primary circuit is designed to supply the correct air/fuel ratio for normal operation. The primary circuit incorporates a power valve which supplements the fuel supplied by the main jet when the throttle valve is opened quickly.

4   The carburettor also incorporates an accelerator pump which discharges fuel into the primary barrel.

5   When the throttle valve is fully open as for fast motoring or acceleration, or a fully laden car, the secondary system also operates to supply an additional air/fuel mixture together with the primary circuit. The throttle valves of both the primary and secondary circuits are operated by a linkage which is interlocked so enabling both the throttle valves to open fully simultaneously.

6   The fuel cut solenoid is operated by the ignition circuit. With the ignition on, the solenoid is energised and the valve opens the idling circuit. When the ignition is switched off, the valve shuts and prevents the engine running-on.

11 Carburettor – idle speed and mixture adjustments

Note: *Carburettor adjustments should only be made with the aid of a tachometer and vacuum gauge as detailed in this Section. On some models a plastic cap is fitted on the idle mixture screw; this must be removed for any adjustment, but note that it may be necessary to use the Toyota tool No. 09243-00010 to turn the screw.*

1   Initially check the fuel level is up to the centre of the window in the float chamber (Fig. 3.3).

2   Ensure that the valve clearances are correctly set, that the air cleaner element is clean and that the ignition system is correctly adjusted (eg spark plugs, ignition timing).

3   Run the engine up to the normal operating temperature, then connect a tachometer in accordance with the manufacturer's instructions. Note that some tachometers may not be compatible with the ignition system fitted. If in doubt, check with your Toyota dealer before

connecting up. Do not let the tachometer terminal go to earth, or damage to the igniter and/or ignition coil could result.

4   Check that all accessories are switched off. On automatic transmission models, the selector must be in the N position.

Idle speed adjustment

5   If an idle limiter cap is fitted on the idle adjustment screw break it free using a suitable pair of pliers (Fig. 3.19).

6   With the engine running, turn the idle adjustment screw to obtain the idle speed given for your model (see Specifications at the beginning of this Chapter) (photo).

7   If adjustments to the fast idle speed and mixture are required, leave the tachometer attached.

Idle mixture adjustment

8   The idle mixture setting is preset during manufacture and normally does not require further adjustment. The idle mixture screw is covered by a tamperproof metal plug, and therefore if adjustment is to be made, this plug must be removed.

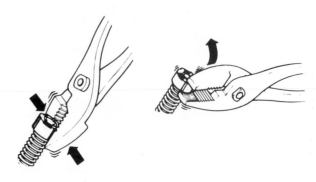

Fig. 3.19 Limiter cap removal method (Sec 11)

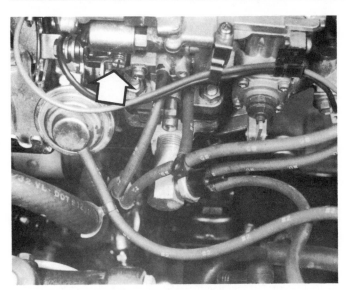

11.6 Carburettor idle adjustment screw (arrowed)

9   To remove the plug, first centre punch it, then drill a 6.5 mm (0.256 in) hole through it, but take care not to allow the drill to contact the head of the mixture screw. The clearance between the plug and screw head is 1 mm (0.04 in), so care is needed. Insert a screwdriver through the hole made in the plug, and screw it in to its limit (but don't overtighten it). Extract the plug using a 7.5 mm (0.295 in) diameter drill. Blow the hole clean of steel drilling particles. If the screw head has been damaged, renew it (Figs. 3.20 and 3.21).

10 Before making adjustments, check that the conditions outlined in paragraphs 1 to 4 are complied with, and that the mixture screw is tightened to its limit (not overtightened). Undo the screw two and a half turns (UK and 1982 USA models), or four turns (1983 USA models).

11 Start the engine, then unscrew the mixture screw to give the maximum possible engine speed then, leaving the mixture screw at this setting, adjust the idle speed screw to give the correct mixture speed setting specified for the carburettor type (Fig. 3.22).

12 Continue the adjustment outlined in the previous paragraph to give the highest speed possible irrespective of further adjustment with the idle mixture screw.

13 Screw the idle mixture adjusting screw in to set the idle speed at that specified for your model.

14 On completion, carefully drive a new tamperproof plug into the mixture screw recess so that it is level with the flange face.

15 If fitted, press a new limit cap onto the idle speed screw.

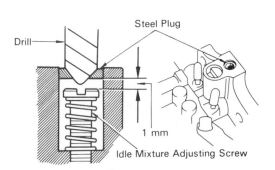

Fig. 3.20 Idle mixture screw tamperproof plug removal method (Sec 11)

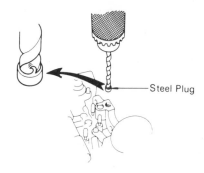

Fig. 3.21 Tamperproof plug withdrawal method (Sec 11)

Fig. 3.22 Carburettor idle mixture adjusting screw (Sec 11)

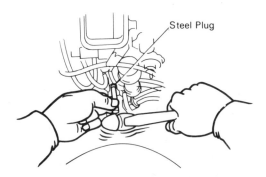

Fig. 3.23 Fitting a new tamperproof plug (Sec 11)

12 Carburettor fast idle speed – on-car adjustment

USA models

1   Adjust the idle speed, as described in Section 11, paragraphs 1 to 7 inclusive, then switch the engine off.
2   Remove the air cleaner unit (Section 3).
3   Disconnect and plug the HAI and MC hose connections (Fig. 3.24).
4   Disconnect the choke opener diaphragm hose, and plug the hose to shut off the choke opener system (Fig. 3.25).
5   On 1981 models, detach the hoses from the distributor sub-diaphragm and main diaphragm, and plug the hoses.
6   Detach the EGR valve hose, and plug the hose.
7   To set the fast idle cam, pivot the throttle valve so that it is slightly open, and press the choke valve shut with a finger. Hold the choke valve closed and release the throttle valve, allowing it to close (Fig. 3.26).
8   Restart the engine but do not touch the throttle pedal.
9   If required, adjust the fast idle speed setting screw to set the fast idle at the specified speed (Fig. 3.27).
10 Switch the engine off, reattach the vacuum hoses, remove the tachometer and refit the air cleaner unit.

UK models

11 Proceed as described in paragraphs 1 and 2 above.
12 Detach the vacuum hose from the FICB diaphragm, and plug the hose (Fig. 3.28).
13 Proceed as described in paragraphs 7 to 9 inclusive, to check and if necessary adjust the fast idle speed.

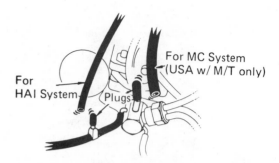

Fig. 3.24 Detach and plug the hoses shown – USA models (Sec 12)

14 On completion, plug and reconnect the FICB hose, then check that the FICB lever moves. Also check that the fast idle cam is released onto the third step or beyond.
15 Refit the air cleaner unit to complete.

13 Carburettor – removal and refitting

1   Disconnect the battery earth lead.
2   Remove the air cleaner, as described in Section 3.

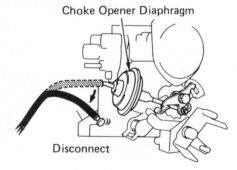

Fig. 3.25 Detach the choke opener diaphragm hose and plug it (Sec 12)

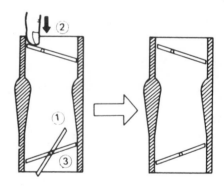

Fig. 3.26 Open the throttle valve (1), close the choke valve (2), release the throttle valve (3) (Sec 12)

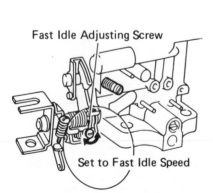

Fig. 3.27 Fast idle adjustment screw (Sec 12)

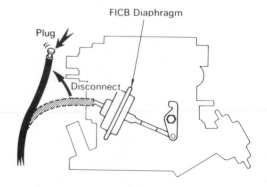

Fig. 3.28 FICB diaphragm – UK models (Sec 12)

13.4 Disconnect the fuel supply hose from the carburettor

13.5 Carburettor hose connections – manifold side (UK models)

13.7 Removing the carburettor

13.8 Carburettor-to-manifold joint gaskets and spacer – note spacer orientation mark (UP)

3   Detach the wires at their connections to the carburettor, noting their locations.
4   Disconnect the fuel supply hose to the carburettor. Plug the hose to prevent fuel loss and the ingress of dirt (photo).
5   Disconnect the emission control hoses at the carburettor. To avoid confusion during reassembly, mark or label the hoses and their connections. Diagrams of the various emission control hoses and circuitry are shown later in this Chapter, and can be referred to for identification if required (photo).
6   Disconnect the accelerator linkage or cable at the carburettor (see Section 9).
7   Check that the hoses, electrical leads and control cables/rods are detached from the carburettor. Then unscrew and remove the carburettor-to-manifold retaining nuts. Carefully lift the carburettor clear, trying not to damage the joint gasket to the manifold (photo).
8   Refitting is the reverse of the removal procedure, but make sure that the flange surfaces are clean, and that a new gasket is used (photo). After refitting, where original settings may have been altered, set the idle mixture screw to the specified initial setting, then carry out all the idle adjustments.

14   Carburettor – overhaul (general)

1   The carburettor should not be dismantled unnecessarily. In fact, removal of the air horn in order to clean out the float chamber is usually sufficient and this can be done without removing the unit from the manifold.
2   If considerable wear has occurred, it is often more economical to purchase a new or rebuilt unit rather than to obtain individual spare parts as even then the bushes and bearing surfaces within the carburettor body may be worn out and this wear cannot be rectified.
3   Complete dismantling instructions are given, but only carry out those operations which are needed to give access to a particular worn component or to correct a fault.
4   If complete dismantling is being carried out, always purchase a repair kit in advance. This will contain all the necessary gaskets and other renewable items required.
5   Remove the carburettor from the inlet manifold as previously described and clean away all external dirt.

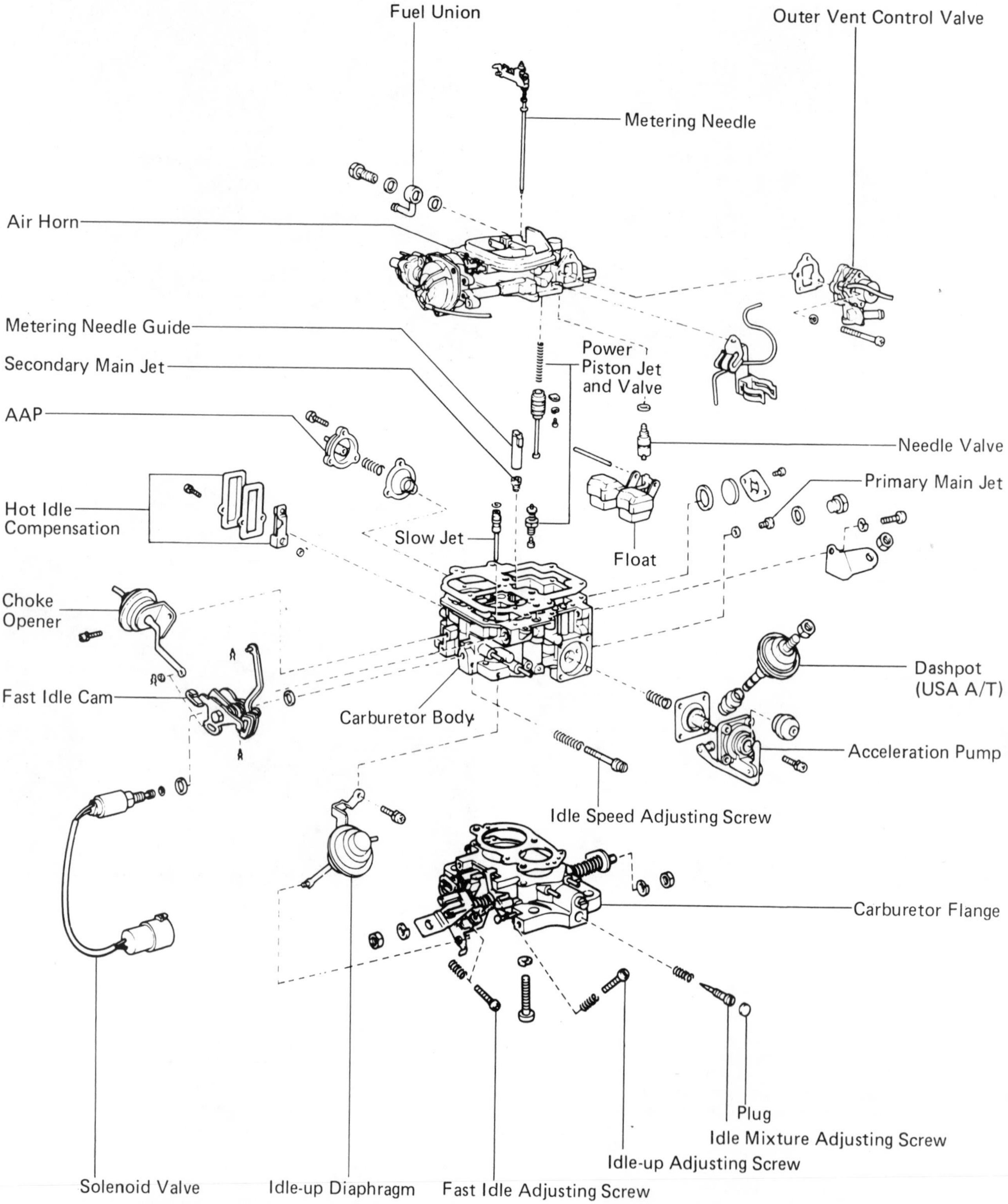

Fuel Union

Outer Vent Control Valve

Metering Needle

Air Horn

Metering Needle Guide

Secondary Main Jet

Power Piston Jet and Valve

AAP

Needle Valve

Primary Main Jet

Hot Idle Compensation

Slow Jet

Float

Choke Opener

Dashpot (USA A/T)

Fast Idle Cam

Acceleration Pump

Carburetor Body

Idle Speed Adjusting Screw

Carburetor Flange

Plug

Idle Mixture Adjusting Screw

Idle-up Adjusting Screw

Solenoid Valve

Idle-up Diaphragm

Fast Idle Adjusting Screw

Fig. 3.29 Exploded view of the carburettor (Sec 15)

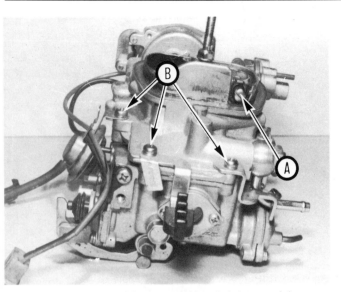

15.1 Metering needle retaining screw (A) and air horn retaining screws (B)

15.2 Fast idle linkage (A) and air valve connecting rod (B)

15 Carburettor – overhaul

1   Undo the retaining screw and remove the metering needle (photo).
2   Detach the fast idle linkage and the air valve connecting rod (photo).
3   Unscrew and remove the five screws securing the air horn (top section) to the carburettor main body, then carefully lift the air horn clear. Try not to break the air horn-to-main body gasket as the horn is lifted clear.
4   Do not dismantle beyond this unless absolutely essential.
5   The float and needle valve can be removed for inspection and cleaning by withdrawing the pivot pin, and then removing the float and needle valve. If necessary, unscrew and remove the needle valve seat and washer (Fig. 3.30). Take care not to damage the needle valve seat when unscrewing it.
6   Press the power piston down under finger pressure and check for a smooth movement. If required, remove the power piston by undoing the retainer screw, then hold the piston and turn the retainer. Remove

the piston, together with its spring (Fig. 3.31).
7   Loosen the solenoid valve, then remove it by turning the body anti-clockwise.
8   Undo the three retaining screws and remove the outer vent control valve.
9   Clean and inspect the carburettor main body, and remove the following items as necessary for inspection and/or renewal.
10   The jets can be unscrewed and removed from the main body. Take particular care not to damage them in removal. Note their respective positions and keep any washers with the primary and secondary main jets when they are removed.
11   The acceleration pump can be withdrawn after removal of the four retaining screws. Withdraw the pump housing complete with diaphragm and spring. Take care not to damage the diaphragm.
12   Remove the auxiliary acceleration pump (AAP) in a similar manner. This is secured by three screws.
13   To remove the idle-up diaphragm, withdraw the retaining clip using a pair of needle-nosed pliers, then disconnect the linkage (Fig. 3.32).

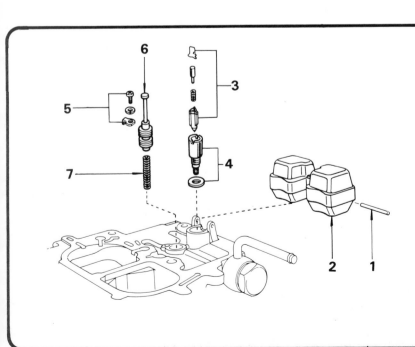

Fig. 3.30 Float, needle valve and power piston assemblies (Sec 15)

1   Pivot pin
2   Float
3   Needle valve
4   Needle valve seat
5   Power piston retainer
6   Power piston
7   Spring

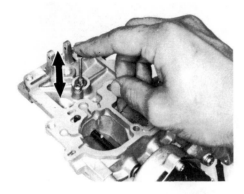

Fig. 3.31 Checking the power piston (Sec 15)

Fig. 3.32 Idle-up diaphragm removal (Sec 15)

14 To remove the choke opener, extract the retaining clip using a pair of needle-nosed pliers, then remove the choke opener (Fig. 3.33).

15 If required, the main body can be removed from the lower flange by undoing the three retaining screws recessed in the top face.

16 With the carburettor dismantled, clean all components in fuel and examine for wear. Clean out jets with air from a tyre pump, never probe them with wire for their calibration will be ruined. Renew any defective or suspect components as required. In particular check the float and its pivot pin for wear or distortion and the float for leaks.

17 Check the float needle valve and seat, the choke valve pivot shaft, the throttle valve pivot shafts and the idle mixture adjusting screw tapered tip for wear. Check for excessive wear in the float pivot pin holes. The strainer on the valve seat must be in good condition.

18 Check the power piston, spring and bore for wear or damage.

19 Check the outer vent control valve and seats for wear or damage. The valve rod should move smoothly. If an ohmmeter is available, check the resistance between the solenoid body and the terminal, referring to Fig. 3.34.

20 To check the choke breaker diaphragm, apply vacuum to its hose connection, and check that the vacuum drop is progressive rather than immediate. When vacuum is applied, the choke valve should open a fraction.

21 The choke heater can be checked using an ohmmeter connected between the housing and the terminal to check its resistance (Fig. 3.35).

22 To check the solenoid (fuel cut-off) valve, connect up a 12 volt supply to its lead terminals. The solenoid should be heard to click on. When the supply is disconnected it should click off. Check that the O-ring seal is in good condition.

23 Check that the choke opener diaphragm functions correctly by repeating the test procedure given for the choke breaker in paragraph 20. When vacuum is applied, the link should be seen to move. The idle-up diaphragm can be checked in the same manner.

24 Renew any defective parts, or parts which are worn or suspect. During reassembly use new gaskets and seals.

25 Reassembly is a reversal of the dismantling procedure. Ensure that all parts are clean before fitting, and take care not to overtighten fastenings and jets. The following special points should be noted, and adjustments made where applicable.

26 If the idle mixture adjustment screw was removed, temporarily locate it before reassembling the main body to the lower flange.

27 Refit the jets and power valve to the main body in the sequence shown in Fig. 3.36.

28 Refit the AAP and the acceleration pump in the sequences shown in Figs. 3.37 and 3.38.

29 When refitting the power piston, locate the spring and piston into the bore in the body, then push on the piston and rotate the retainer over it. The retainer is then secured by a screw.

30 Reassemble the float chamber components by first inserting the valve seat with its new gasket into the fuel inlet port, then locate the needle valve onto the seat. Engage the float lip under the needle valve wire, and insert the pivot pin. Check and adjust the float level as follows.

31 Let the float hang down under its own weight, and check the distance from the top of the float to the air horn face (without a gasket). This should be as specified for the 'raised' position (refer to the Specifications for your carburettor type). If necessary, bend the float arm (at A in Fig. 3.39) to adjust.

32 Check the float in the lowered position as shown in Fig. 3.40, using a depth gauge or vernier calipers, by lifting the float and measuring the

Fig. 3.33 Choke opener removal (Sec 15)

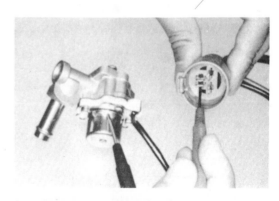

Fig. 3.34 Outer vent control valve check. Resistance between solenoid body and terminal should be 63 to 73 ohm at 20°C (Sec 15)

Fig. 3.35 Choke heater check. Heater housing to terminal resistance should be 19 to 23 ohm at 20°C (Sec 15)

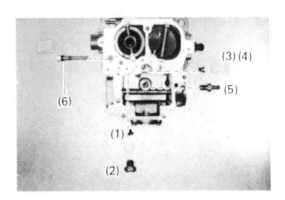

Fig. 3.36 Jets and power valve locations (Sec 15)

1 Primary main jet (with new gasket)
2 Plug (with new gasket)
3 Secondary main jet
4 Metering needle guide
5 Power valve and jet
6 O-ring and slow jet

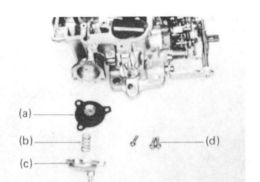

Fig. 3.37 AAP assembly (Sec 15)

a Diaphragm   c Cover
b Spring   d Screws

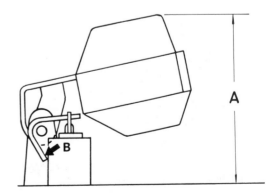

Fig. 3.38 Acceleration pump assembly (Sec 15)

a Spring   d Boot
b Diaphragm and outer gasket   e Screws
c Cover

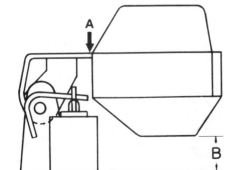

Fig. 3.39 Float top to air horn adjustment (Sec 15)

A Adjustment point   B Clearance to be as specified

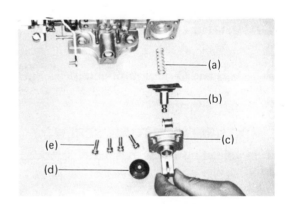

Fig. 3.40 Float lip to air horn check (Sec 15)

A Clearance as specified   B Adjustment point

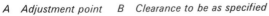

distance from the float lower face to the air horn flange face (A). This must be as specified for your carburettor type. If necessary, adjust by bending the float arm tag (B).
33 When refitting the metering needle, locate it with its collar, and hook the spring end into the hole. Retain with the screw and washer.
34 If the choke coil cover was removed, locate a new gasket, and refit the housing so that the choke lever engages with the outer end of the bi-metal spring. Align the index mark on the cover with the central index mark on the housing, and tighten the retaining screws (photo). On completion, check that the choke valve action is satisfactory, and then stake the air valve screw and valve shaft screw.
35 The carburettor is now reassembled, but before refitting to the car, it is advisable to make the adjustment checks described in the following Section.

16 Carburettor – off-car adjustments

The following adjustment checks can only be made with the carburettor removed from the car. Some checks will require the use of a suitable angle measuring gauge.

Throttle valve opening
1 Operate the throttle linkage, and check that both the primary and secondary throttle valves fully open. When fully open they should be at 90° from the horizontal plane (surface flange). If necessary, adjust by bending the throttle arm levers accordingly (photo).

Secondary touch angle
2 Open the primary throttle valve to the point where the secondary throttle valve just starts to open. Hold the primary throttle valve in this position, and check that its angle is 59° from the horizontal. This cannot be adjusted.

Fast idle setting
3 Move the throttle shaft lever and set it at the first step position of the fast idle cam (Fig. 3.41). Check that the choke valve is fully shut, then measure the angle of the primary throttle valve. If the angle measured does not correspond with the specified fast idle angle, adjust by turning the fast idle screw in the required direction.

Unloader
4 Open the primary throttle valve fully, then check the choke valve angle. If the angle measured does not correspond with the specified unloader angle, bend the primary throttle arm to suit.

Choke opener
5 Apply a vacuum to the choke opener diaphragm. With vacuum applied, the fast idle cam should be released to the fourth step. If adjustment is necessary, bend the choke opener lever (photo).
6 Release the vacuum, and shut off the choke valve. Set the fast idle lever on the first step, and then check that a clearance exists between the fast idle cam and the choke opener lever (Fig. 3.42).

Idle-up (throttle positioner) – USA models
7 Apply a vacuum to the idle-up diaphragm, then measure the throttle valve opening angle. If the angle does not correspond to that specified, turn the adjustment screw to correct.

Choke breaker
8 Apply a vacuum to the choke breaker diaphragm, and shut the choke valve by hand. Check that the choke valve opening angle corresponds with that specified.

Air valve and metering needle
9 Check that the metering needle and the air valve move smoothly together, then with the primary throttle valve angle in the idle position, measure the opening angle of the air valve. Check that when the primary throttle valve is fully open, a clearance exists between the connector rod and stopper.

Acceleration pump
10 Check that the pump lever and diaphragm rod move smoothly when the throttle shaft is rotated.

15.34 Alignment of the choke cover index mark

16.1 Invert the carburettor to check the throttle valves

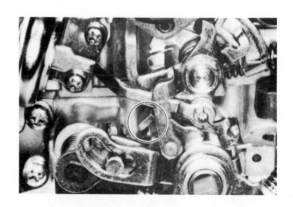
Fig. 3.41 Throttle shaft lever at first step position (Sec 16)

16.5 Choke opener adjustment. Bend opener lever indicated

Secondary throttle valve lock system

11 Hold the throttle valve open a fraction, and simultaneously push the choke valve shut. Hold the choke valve shut and release the throttle valve (Fig. 3.43). Now, referring to Fig. 3.44, check that lever A holds lever B locked.

12 Check that lever A can move smoothly at the 2nd or 3rd fast idle cam step position. If necessary, adjust lever A by bending it at the top.
13 Repeat the procedure in paragraph 11, but instead of checking that lever A holds lever B, rotate lever B to the point where it contacts lever A, then measure the clearance between the secondary valve and bore. This should be as shown (Fig. 3.45). If required, bend lever A at the top end to adjust.
14 Open the choke valve beyond 52°, and check that lever A releases as the throttle valve opens.
15 Again hold the throttle valve open a fraction, and simultaneously push the choke valve shut, then release the throttle valve. Apply a vacuum to the choke opener, and ensure that lever A withdraws and lever B releases.

Dashpot (USA models with automatic transmission) – where fitted

16 Open the choke valve fully and release the fast idle cam to the fourth step. Now fully open and then close the throttle valve, and check that the throttle valve returns to the idle position in three seconds. If adjustment is required, turn the dashpot adjustment nut in the required direction.

Idle mixture adjustment screw

17 If the idle mixture adjustment screw was removed, initially preset it by screwing it fully into position (but do not overtighten it), then unscrew it by the following amount:

UK models	–	$2^1/2$ turns
1982 USA models	–	$2^1/2$ turns
1983 USA models	–	4 turns

This is an initial adjustment only. Further adjustment may be required after the carburettor has been refitted and the engine is restarted. For details refer to Section 11.

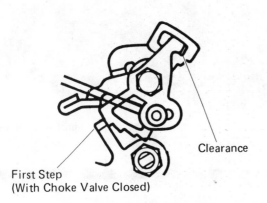

Fig. 3.42 Check for 1 mm (0.04 in) clearance between lever and fast idle cam (Sec 16)

First Step
(With Choke Valve Closed)

Clearance

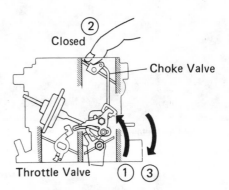

Fig. 3.43 Secondary throttle valve lock system check sequence (Sec 16)

Closed

Choke Valve

Throttle Valve

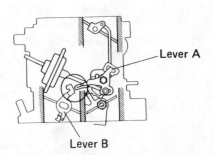

Fig. 3.44 Lever A to hold lever B locked (Sec 16)

Lever A

Lever B

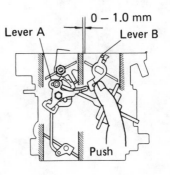

Fig. 3.45 Clearance requirement between bore and secondary valve (Sec 16)

0 – 1.0 mm

Lever A

Lever B

Push

17 Manifolds and exhaust system

1   On all engine types the inlet and exhaust manifolds can be removed and refitted individually, the inlet manifold together with the carburettor if required (photos).

2   The layout of the exhaust system is similar on all models although the individual components may vary in detail design. Some variants have a catalytic converter incorporated into the exhaust system which is part of the emission control system, the description of which is given in Section 43.

3   The exhaust system is supported on flexible mountings and incorporates a main silencer and expansion box (photo).

4   Examination of the exhaust pipe and silencers at regular intervals is worthwhile as small defects may be repairable. If left, they will almost certainly require renewal of one of the sections of the system. Also, any leaks, apart from the noise factor, may cause poisonous exhaust gases to get inside the car which can be unpleasant, to say the least, even in mild concentrations. Prolonged inhalation could cause sickness and giddiness.

5   Sleeve connections and clamps are usually very difficult to separate and it is quicker and easier in the long run to remove the complete system from the car when renewing a section. It can be expensive if another section is damaged when trying to separate a bad section from it. Bolted flange connections are easier to detach (photo).

6   To remove the system, jack up the car at front and rear and support it on safety stands.

7   Disconnect the front downpipe from the exhaust manifold and the gearbox location bracket.

8   Disconnect all flexible mountings, and then lower and withdraw the complete system from the rear of the vehicle.

9   Unbolt and separate the pipe sections to facilitate repair or renewal of a section.

10 When reassembling the pipe sections, ensure that the mating faces are clean. Use new gaskets where applicable, and smear the surfaces with a suitable exhaust sealant before assembling. Renew any defective mounting straps.

11 Push the complete system under the vehicle and jack it up so that the front pipe can be bolted to the manifold and the rear tail pipe

17.1A Inlet manifold and retaining bolts (arrowed) (carburettor removed)

17.1B Inlet manifold removed showing the upper side (UK models)

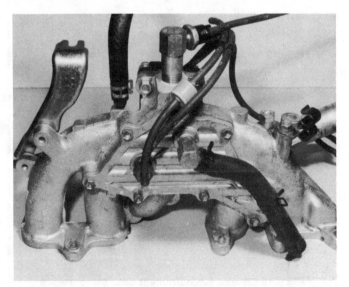

17.1C Inlet manifold showing lower side and associated fittings (UK models)

17.1D Always use a new gasket before refitting the manifolds. Note: Refit the gasket and thermostatic valve before the manifold (see Chapter 1)

17.1E Remove the exhaust manifold preheat cowl ...

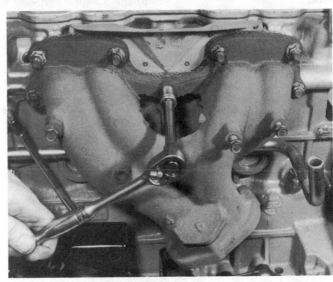

17.1F ... then the exhaust manifold ...

17.1G ... and its gasket

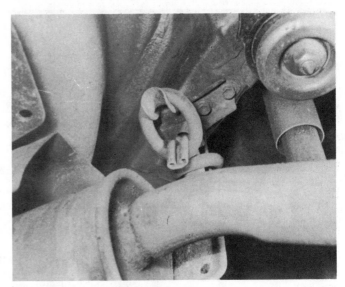

17.3 Exhaust system flexible mountings

17.5 Exhaust system flange connection joint

mounting connected. Use a new gasket between the manifold and downpipe.

12 When the system is in position and fully located, restart the engine and check for any signs of leaks, particularly from the joints.

PART B: ELECTRONIC FUEL-INJECTION (EFI)

18 General description

An electronic fuel-injection system is fitted to all USA models from December 1983 on, and comprises a fuel supply system, an air induction system and an electronic control system. The system circuits are shown in Figs. 3.46 and 3.47.

The fuel is supplied by an electric pump located within the fuel tank. The pump supplies the required amount of fuel under a constant pressure to the EFI injectors. On early models, a rotor type fuel pump is used, whilst models produced from December 1983 have a turbine type electric pump. The turbine type pump has the advantage of being quieter in operation, and gives less fuel pulsation.

The fuel injectors supply the required amount of fuel to the intake manifold in accordance with the signals from the EFI computer or, on models produced from 1985, the ECU unit (electronic control unit). Each injector operates simultaneously, to supply the correct fuel requirement to give the most efficient mixture during each revolution of the engine.

The air induction system operates via the airflow meter, the operation of which is also controlled by the EFI computer (or ECU), to ensure the correct air to fuel ratio in accordance with the engine operating conditions.

The EFI computer (or ECU) is located behind the glovebox. The computer determines the air/fuel ratio requirement in accordance with the operating conditions, from the signals transmitted by the various sensors.

On later models, an Electronic Spark Advance (ESA) system is fitted, and the ECU triggers the spark at the exact moment in accordance with the engine operating conditions (see Chapter 4).

Should a fault develop in the system, the 'check engine' warning light on the instrument panel is illuminated, and in this instance, a back-up circuit provides a basic fuel supply as a temporary measure, until the fault in the main system is repaired.

Before working on any part of the EFI system, note the precautions listed in Section 19.

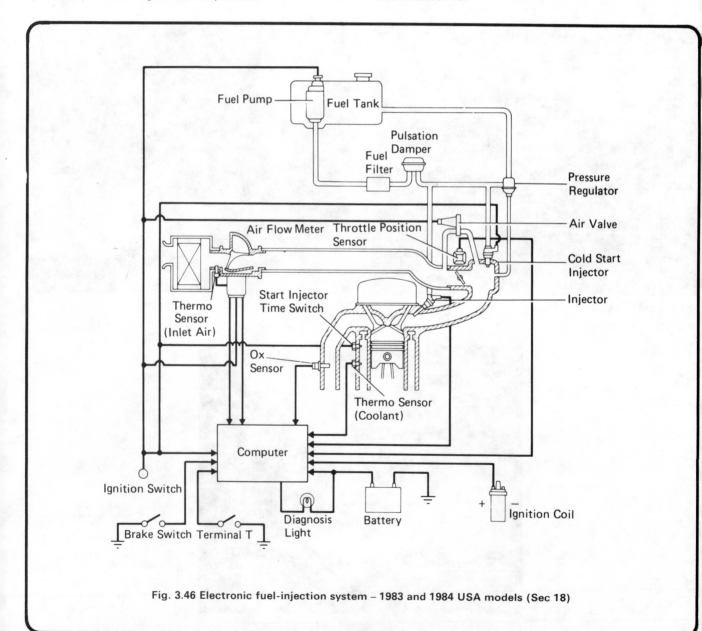

Fig. 3.46 Electronic fuel-injection system – 1983 and 1984 USA models (Sec 18)

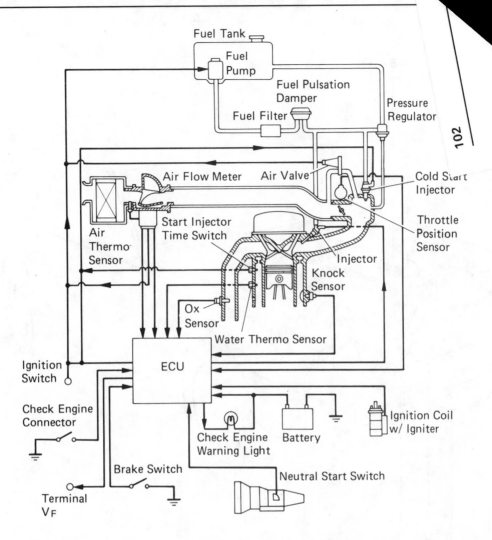

Fig. 3.47 Electronic fuel-injection system – 1985 models (USA) (Sec 18)

19 EFI system – precautions

The following precautions should be noted and adhered to whenever any part of the EFI system is to be worked on.

1 Before disconnecting or working on any part of the EFI system, the battery must be disconnected by detaching the earth (negative) lead from its battery terminal.

2 Whenever the battery leads are disconnected, the diagnosis code in the computer will be cleared. Any diagnosis checks to be made must therefore be read before disconnecting the battery.

3 Whenever any part of the fuel system is to be disconnected and/or worked on, fire precautions must be taken (no smoking etc).

4 Do not allow fuel to spill onto rubber or leather parts.

5 When any part of the system is disconnected for any reason, particular care must be taken to ensure that no dirt is allowed to enter the system.

6 The system is normally pressurised, and care must therefore be taken when disconnecting fuel lines. Note the following:

  a) *Before loosening a high pressure connection, put a container under it in which to catch spilt fuel. Loosen the connection slowly. Plug detached pipes*

  b) *When reconnecting the high pressure pipe union, locate a new washer each side of the flare nut/bolt and lubricate the flare with a thin coat of oil. Tighten to the specified torque*

  c) *Always renew system O-ring seals. Lubricate them with a thin coat of oil before assembly*

7 When using a tachometer for engine tuning it must be connected to the ignition coil service connector as shown in Fig. 3.48. The battery must be used as the power source for the tachometer, timing light etc.

8 When cleaning the engine compartment with water, take care not to let water enter the fuel system. The electrical systems must also be protected.

9 If a mobile radio (such as CB) is to be used, consult your Toyota dealer for confirmation on suitability. Although the EFI computer or

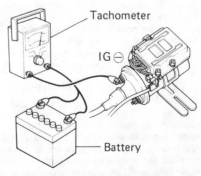

Fig. 3.48 Tachometer used for engine tuning must be connected as shown (Sec 19)

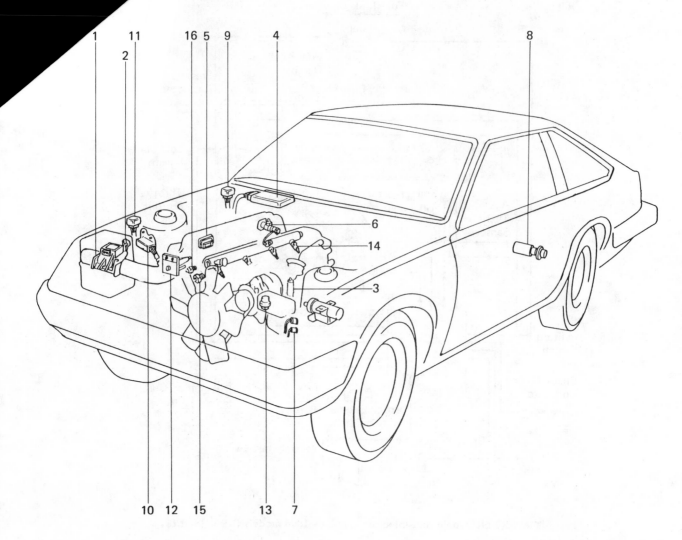

Fig. 3.49 Location of the electrical components associated with the EFI system – 1983 and 1984 USA models (Sec 19)

1	Airflow meter	5	Throttle position sensor
2	Fuel pump check connector	6	Cold start injector
3	Oxygen sensor	7	Service connector
4	Computer	8	Fuel pump

9	Circuit opening relay	13	No 1 main relay
10	Resistor	14	Injector
11	No 2 main relay	15	Water thermo-sensor
12	Air valve	16	Cold start injector time switch

ECU unit should not be affected by outside interference, such radio equipment may upset the operation of these items, particularly if the antenna and feeder are in close proximity. Your Toyota dealer will advise on suitability and the best fitting location for such equipment.

10 Care must be taken when checking and testing electrical circuits. Incorrectly connected wires can damage the transistor circuits and cause further problems within the computer. The computer cover must not be removed.

11 The location and identification of the EFI system electrical components is shown in the accompanying figures (Figs. 3.49 and 3.50).

12 In most instances, fault diagnosis and checking of the electrical system components is not recommended for the home mechanic. Incorrect test procedures could not only cause damage to the components concerned, but could also damage the computer and this is an expensive item to replace! Except where indicated in this Chapter, testing and fault diagnosis of the EFI system electrical components should be entrusted to a Toyota dealer.

20 Routine maintenance – fuel and exhaust system (EFI models)

The following routine maintenance procedures must be undertaken at the specified intervals given at the start of this manual. It is essential that the ignition system components are in good condition and the ignition timing correctly adjusted (as described in Chapter 4) prior to making any adjustments to the fuel system.

1 **Air cleaner:** Remove the air cleaner element and clean or renew it as required. Refer to Section 21 for details.

2 **Fuel lines and connections:** Check the fuel line pipes and hoses for condition and security.

3 **Engine idle speed:** Check the engine idle speed, as described in Section 22.

4 **Fuel filler cap gasket:** Prise free the ring gasket from the fuel filler cap and renew it (Fig. 3.51).

5 **Exhaust system:** Refer to Section 2, paragraph 7.

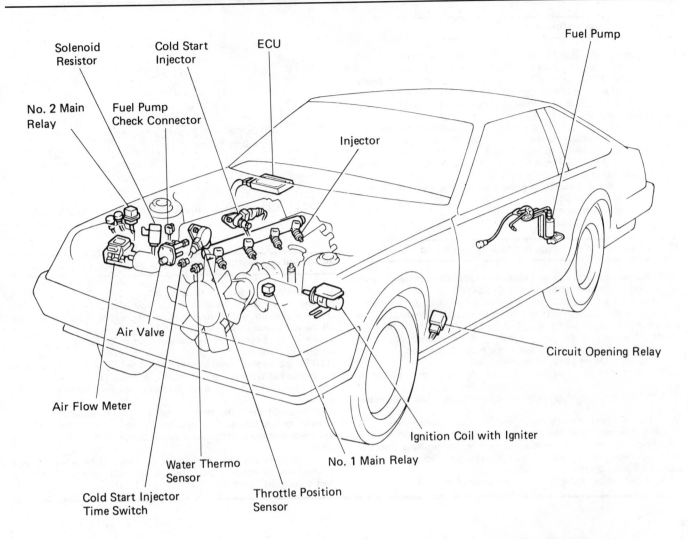

Fig. 3.50 Location of the electrical components associated with the EFI system – 1985 models (Sec 19)

Fig. 3.51 Renew the fuel filler cap gasket at the specified intervals – EFI models (Sec 20)

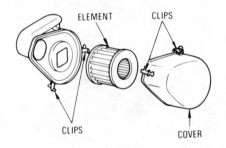

Fig. 3.52 Air cleaner components – EFI models (Sec 21)

21 Air cleaner – servicing

1   Release the filter cover retaining clips, then withdraw the cover, together with the element, by lifting it straight up.
2   Extract the element from the cover. If the outer surface of the element is very dirty it must be renewed. If it is only moderately dirty, it can be cleaned by blowing through it from the inside out with compressed air. The element must not be washed or immersed in oil.

3   Wipe out the cover and fit a new element, ensuring that it is correctly seated in the case. Do not run the engine rapidly or for extended periods with the element or filter cover removed, as a backfire could cause a fire under the hood.
4   Refit the element and cover, and secure the retaining clips.
5   To remove the air cleaner unit complete, detach it from the intake duct and mountings and lift it clear.
6   Refit the air cleaner unit in the reverse order of removal.

22 Idle speed – adjustment

1   The idle speed adjustment must be made with the air cleaner unit fitted, and the engine must be at its normal operating temperature. All emission control and vacuum hoses must be in good condition and securely attached. The EFI wiring must also be fully connected.
2   Connect up a tachometer in accordance with the manufacturer's instructions (see Fig. 3.48).
3   Check that all electrical accessories are switched off and, on automatic transmission models, check that the handbrake is fully applied and the transmission selector lever is in the N position.
4   Run the engine at 2500 rpm for a period of two minutes, then allow it to idle and check the engine speed.
5   To adjust the idle speed, turn the adjuster screw on the throttle body as required (Fig. 3.53).
6   Disconnect the tachometer to complete.

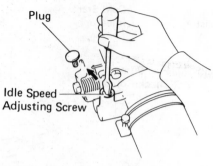

Fig. 3.53 Idle speed adjustment – EFI models (Sec 22)

23 Airflow meter – testing, removal and refitting

1   The airflow meter is located between the air cleaner unit and the air intake duct to the throttle housing (Fig. 3.54).
2   To test the airflow meter, you will require the use of an ohmmeter. Unplug the wiring connector from the meter unit, then connect up the ohmmeter to the terminals specified in Fig. 3.55. Check that the resistance values are as given. If any of the resistance values are outside those specified, the airflow meter must be renewed.
3   Disconnect the air hoses to the meter unit.
4   If attached, unplug and detach the wiring connector to the meter unit.
5   Undo the three retaining nuts and the single bolt, and remove the meter unit.
6   A further check can be made of the airflow meter when it is removed. Connect up an ohmmeter between the terminals indicated in Fig. 3.56, and check the measuring plate openings. Note that the resistance between terminals E2 and V5 will change according to the measuring plate opening.
7   Refit the airflow meter in the reverse order of removal.

24 Air valve – testing, removal and refitting

1   The air valve allows additional air into the air intake chamber when the engine is cool, to assist in regulating the air/fuel mixture. As the engine warms up to its normal operating temperature, the valve closes off the additional air supply (Fig. 3.57).
2   An initial check of the air valve can be made by pinching the air supply pipe. When the engine coolant temperature is below 60°C (140°F), the engine speed should drop as the hose is pinched. When the engine has warmed up to its normal operating temperature and the hose is pinched, the engine speed should not drop by more than 50 rpm.
3   If an ohmmeter is available, detach the wiring connector from the air valve, connect the ohmmeter to the air valve terminals (E1 and Ep), and check that the heat coil resistance is between 39 and 59 ohm (Fig. 3.59).
4   To remove the air valve, clamp together the coolant hose connections (or partially drain the cooling system – see Chapter 2), then detach the hoses.

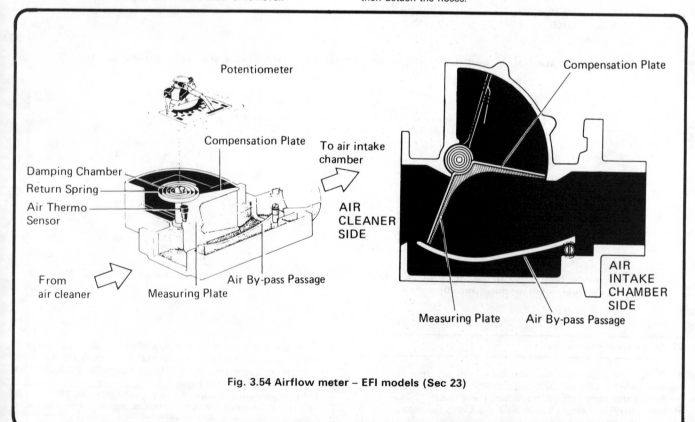

Fig. 3.54 Airflow meter – EFI models (Sec 23)

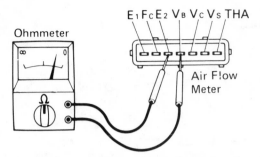

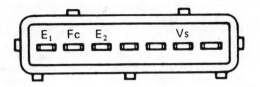

Fig. 3.55 Airflow meter test – check resistance between terminals (Sec 23)

E2 to Vs – 20 to 100 ohm
E2 to Vc – 100 to 300 ohm
E2 to Vb – 200 to 400 ohm
E2 to THA – 10 to 20 K ohm (at 20°C)
E1 to Fc – infinity

AT LOW TEMPERATURE

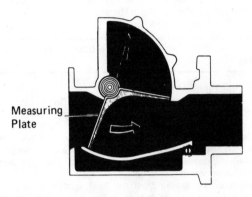

Fig. 3.56 Check resistance readings with measuring plate as follows (Sec 23)

E1 to Fc – fully closed (infinity)
E1 to Fc – opened (zero)
E2 to Vs – fully closed (20 to 400 ohm)
E2 to Vs – fully closed to open (20 to 1000 ohm)

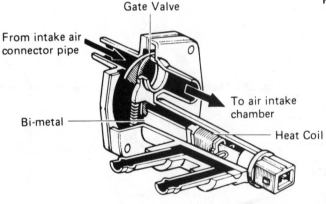

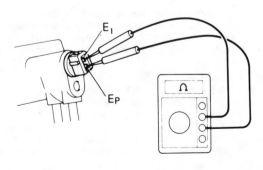

Fig. 3.58 Air valve initial check – pinch air pipe (Sec 24)

AFTER WARM-UP

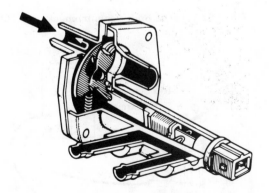

Fig. 3.57 Air valve operation in accordance with temperature (Sec 24)

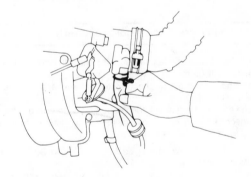

Fig. 3.59 Air valve heater coil check (Sec 24)

5   Disconnect the inlet and outlet air hoses from the valve unit, and if still attached, the wiring connector.
6   Undo the two retaining bolts, and remove the air valve, together with its gasket.
7   A further check can be made on the airflow meter when it is removed by checking the valve opening. At an ambient temperature of 20°C (68°F) the valve should be slightly open. An adjuster screw on the outer body of the valve unit allows a certain amount of adjustment if the previous tests show that the valve is otherwise in good condition. Otherwise the valve must be renewed.
8   Refit in the reverse order to removal. Use a new gasket when fitting the valve. Check that the hose connections are secure, and on completion top up the cooling system.

25 Air intake chamber and throttle body – removal and refitting

1   Disconnect the battery negative lead.
2   Drain the engine coolant with reference to Chapter 2.
3   Disconnect the accelerator cable and, on automatic transmission models, the transmission throttle cable.
4   Disconnect the various emission control and fuel-injection system hoses which affect the removal of the air intake chamber and throttle body. Mark or identify the respective hoses as they are detached to avoid confusion when reassembling.
5   Disconnect the wiring from the cold start injector, the throttle position sensor, and where applicable the air valve.
6   Unscrew and remove the EGR valve-to-intake chamber retaining bolt. Detach the chamber and stay.
7   Undo the bolts and nuts, and remove the intake chamber and throttle body from the intake manifold.
8   Refitting is a reversal of the removal procedure. Use a new gasket when refitting the chamber and throttle body to the intake manifold. Ensure that the hose connections are correctly and securely made.

26 Throttle body – testing, removal and refitting

1   The following on-vehicle checks of the throttle body can be made. An ohmmeter will be required for some checks.
2   Inspect the condition of the throttle linkage and ensure that it moves freely (Fig. 3.61).
3   Start the engine, then check the vacuum at each port on the throttle body by disconnecting each hose in turn. The vacuum requirements are described below. Refer to Fig. 3.62.

Port	At idle speed	At 3000 rpm
1983/1984 models		
8/S	Vacuum	No vacuum
6/E	No vacuum	Vacuum
*/A	No vacuum	Vacuum
I/P	No vacuum	Vacuum
1985 models		
E, R and P	No vacuum	Vacuum

4   To check the throttle position sensor, detach the wiring connector and insert a feeler gauge between the throttle stop lever and stop screw to measure the clearance. Connect an ohmmeter to the terminals and check for continuity as shown below. Refer to Fig. 3.63 or Fig. 3.64 as applicable.

1983 and 1984 models

Terminals	0.5 mm (0.0197 in) clearance	0.7 mm (0.0276 in) clearance	Fully open
IDL–TL	Continuity	No continuity	No continuity
Psw–TL	No continuity	No continuity	Continuity
IDL–Psw	No continuity	No continuity	No continuity

1985 models

Terminals	Clearance	Resistance
VTA–E$_2$	0 mm (0 in)	0.2 to 0.8 Kohm
IDL–E$_2$	0.57 mm (0.0224 in)	0 to 100 ohm
IDL–E$_2$	0.85 mm (0.0335 in)	Infinity
VTA–E$_2$	Fully open	3.3 to 10 Kohm
Vcc–E$_2$		3 to 7 Kohm

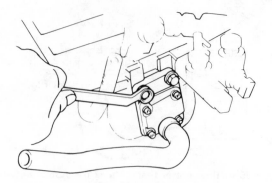

Fig. 3.60 Air valve removal (Sec 24)

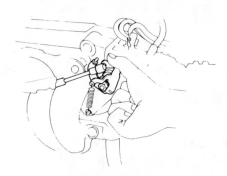

Fig. 3.61 Check that the throttle linkage movement is satisfactory (Sec 26)

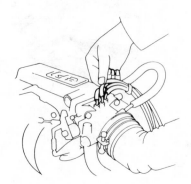

Fig. 3.62 Throttle body vacuum check (Sec 26)

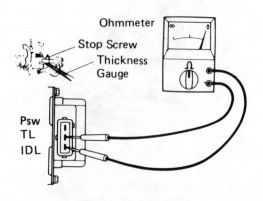

Fig. 3.63 Throttle position sensor check – 1983 and 1984 models (Sec 26)

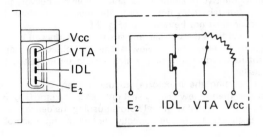

Fig. 3.64 Throttle position sensor check – 1985 models (Sec 26)

5   To remove the throttle body, undo the air intake hose clip and detach the hose from the body.

6   Detach the PCV hose from the throttle body.

7   The emission control hoses should be marked for identification and fitting position, then detached from the throttle body.

8   Clamp the coolant bypass hoses, or partially drain the engine coolant (see Chapter 2), then detach these hoses from the throttle body.

9   If attached, disconnect the throttle sensor wiring connector.

10 Disconnect the throttle linkage.

11 Unscrew the four retaining bolts and remove the throttle body and gasket (Fig. 3.65).

12 With the throttle body removed, it can be cleaned with a suitable solvent and blown dry. To avoid damage, the throttle position sensor should not be cleaned.

13 Check the following items on the throttle valve:

   (a) *With the throttle valve fully shut, check that there is no clearance between the stop screw and lever*

   (b) *With the throttle valve fully shut, check that the advancer port is on the air cleaner side as shown (Fig. 3.66).*

14 If required, the throttle closing angle can be adjusted, but this, together with further checks and adjustments of the throttle position sensor (off the vehicle), are best entrusted to a Toyota dealer.

15 Refit the throttle body in reverse order of removal. Use new gaskets and ensure that the various hoses are correctly and securely attached.

16 Top up the engine cooling system on completion (see Chapter 2).

---

27 Injectors – cleaning (on vehicle)

---

1   If a malfunction of the injectors is suspected, the most probable cause, particularly after a high mileage has been covered, will be a build up of deposits in the injector nozzles. Faults which indicate this are an erratic idle speed, hesitation, and/or possibly backfiring.

2   Basic checks can be made on the injectors by referring to paragraphs 1 to 3 inclusive in Section 28. If the resistance check made in paragraph 3 is satisfactory, but paragraphs 1 and 2 confirm a malfunction in any of the injectors, it is possible that the injector nozzles have become blocked.

3   An injection cleaner has been developed to clean the injector nozzles during engine operation, therefore avoiding having to remove them. Before obtaining the cleaning solution, it is advisable to further check the problems with your Toyota dealer. A diagnosis check may be required to confirm the cause.

4   The cleansing solution is added to the fuel in the fuel tank, but it is important that the ratio of cleaner used is relative to the amount of fuel in the tank. The cleaner solution is supplied in a 150 cc container, and this is sufficient for a half tank of fuel. Therefore if the tank is only one quarter full, half the container contents (75 cc) will be required. The correct ratio of cleaner to fuel is of utmost importance. The excessive use of the cleaning solution will have a harmful effect on the fuel system (Fig. 3.67). Prior to using the cleaner, note the following additional precautions.

   (a) *Use in a well ventilated area*

   (b) *Do not use or store the cleaner near heat or a flame*

Fig. 3.65 Unbolting the throttle body (Sec 26)

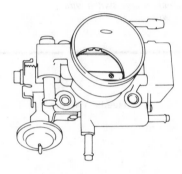

Fig. 3.66 Vacuum advance port on air cleaner side with valve shut (Sec 26)

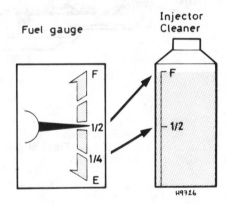

Fig. 3.67 Injector cleaner ratio requirement in accordance with fuel tank contents (Sec 27)

   (c) *If cleaner is spilled onto the paintwork, wipe it clean without delay*

   (d) *Keep out of reach of children. If swallowed, vomiting must not be induced, but medical treatment should be sought without delay*

5   Pour the exact amount of cleaner solution into the fuel tank in accordance with the ratio requirement, preferably to a quarter or half full tank. The vehicle can now be driven in a normal manner. After about one hour of driving, the injector nozzles should be clear of deposits. Do not top up with fuel again until the tank is nearly empty, but note that this must be within one week of applying the cleaner. Any prolonged use of the cleaner will harm the fuel system.

28 Injectors – testing, removal and refitting

1   If any of the injectors are suspected of malfunction, a simple initial test can be made by starting or cranking the engine over, and using a sound scope with the probe pressed against each injector in turn. Listen and check that the injection noise is normal and proportional to the engine speed. A long screwdriver can be used as a sound scope.

2   Another method of checking the injectors is to hold each injector in turn with your fingers and feel the injection flow pulses. Where no sound or an unusual sound is heard from one or more injectors, check that the wiring connections are in good condition and securely made.

3   Measure the resistance of a suspect injector by detaching its wiring connector, then connect up an ohmmeter across the injector wiring terminals, and test the resistance, which should be between 1.5 and 3.0 ohm.

4   To remove the injector(s), the air intake chamber and associated components must first be removed. Refer to Section 25 for details.

5   Detach the wiring connectors from the following items:

(a) Temperature sensor wire
(b) Coolant temperature sender unit wire
(c) Overdrive thermo-switch (automatic transmission)
(d) Start injection time switch wire
(e) Injector wires

6   Remove the pulsation damper, then unscrew the bolt securing the fuel hose to the delivery pipe, and detach the hose.

7   Unscrew the two retaining bolts, and remove the delivery pipe and injector(s), but take care not to drop the injector(s). Note that the injector cover must not be removed (Fig. 3.69).

8   On removal from the vehicle, any suspect injectors can be checked for injection efficiency, but in view of the specialised procedure and equipment required, it is a task which should be entrusted to your Toyota dealer.

9   Before refitting the injector(s) to the delivery pipe(s), locate a grommet and then a new O-ring seal onto each injector (Fig. 3.70).

10 Coat the O-ring seal with fuel before pushing the delivery pipe into position. Ensure that they are correctly aligned during assembly (Fig. 3.71).

11 Insert the four insulators into position in each injector hole in the intake manifold, then refit the injectors with delivery pipes. Before fitting the retaining bolts, ensure that the injectors can rotate smoothly. If they do not, the O-rings are probably distorted, in which case withdraw the injector and renew the O-ring. Align the injector retaining bolt holes, insert the bolts, and tighten them to the specified torque.

12 Reconnect the fuel hose to the delivery pipe, then fit the pulsation damper (with new gaskets). Tighten the damper to the specified torque.

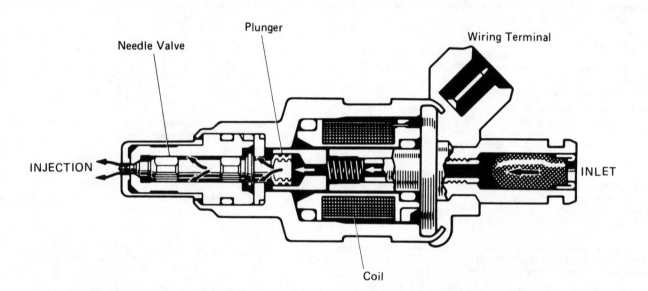

Fig. 3.68 Sectional view of an injector (Sec 28)

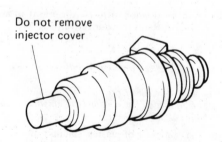

Fig. 3.69 Injector cover location (Sec 28)

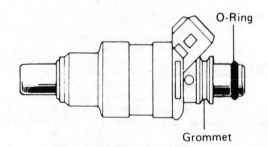

Fig. 3.70 Injector O-ring and grommet location (Sec 28)

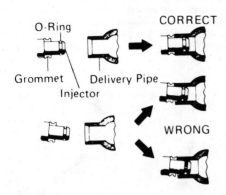

Fig. 3.71 Delivery pipe must be correctly located (Sec 28)

13 Reconnect the wires to the items listed in paragraph 5.
14 Refit the air intake chamber and associated components, referring to Section 25. Reconnect the battery negative lead.
15 On completion, make a check to ensure that there is no fuel leakage

from the injectors and associated components. To do this, remove the plug from the fuel pump check wire connector, then bridge the terminals in the connector using a short length of wire (with the ignition switched on). Any leaks must be repaired. Remove the bridging wire and refit the plug to the fuel pump check wire connector (Fig. 3.72).

29 Cold start injector – removal, testing and refitting

1 Disconnect the battery negative lead.
2 Disconnect the wiring connector from the cold start injector (Fig. 3.73).
3 Unscrew the union bolt, and remove the cold start injector fuel delivery pipe. Remove the union gaskets.
4 Locate a cloth or suitable container under the delivery pipe at the rear end to catch any leaking fuel.
5 Unbolt and remove the cold start injector unit.
6 The cold start injector is best tested by your Toyota dealer, as special service tools are required. If an ohmmeter is available, an initial check of the cold start injector can be made by connecting the ohmmeter to the injector wiring terminals, and checking that the resistance value is between 2 to 4 ohm (Fig. 3.75).
7 Refitting is a reversal of the removal procedure. New gaskets must be used and care must be taken not to get dirt into the fuel line.

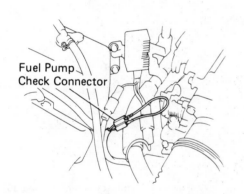

Fig. 3.72 Refit plug to the fuel pump check connector (Sec 28)

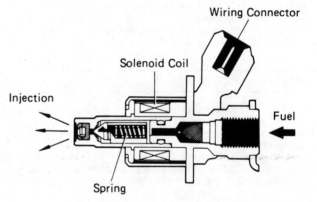

Fig. 3.73 Sectional view of the cold start injector (Sec 29)

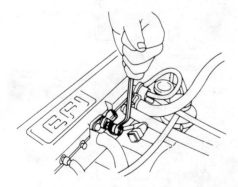

Fig. 3.74 Cold start injector removal (Sec 29)

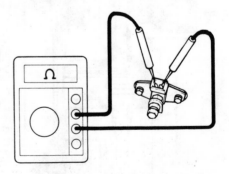

Fig. 3.75 Cold start injector check (Sec 29)

30 Pressure regulator – removal and refitting

1 If the pressure regulator is suspected of malfunction, before removing it have the fuel pressure checked by your Toyota dealer. If the pressure regulator is at fault, it can be renewed as follows.

2 Disconnect the battery negative lead.

3 Locate a cloth or suitable container under the pressure regulator to catch fuel spillage, then detach the fuel hose from the regulator and the No 2 fuel pipe (1982/3 models only).

4 Detach the vacuum hose from the regulator unit.

5 Unscrew the locknut and remove the pressure regulator unit (Fig. 3.77).

6 Refitting is a reversal of the removal procedure. Ensure that the hose and vacuum connections are clean, and tighten the regulator locknut to the specified torque. On 1982/83 models, use new gaskets when reconnecting the No 2 fuel pipe.

31 Fuel pump – testing on vehicle

1 Turn the ignition switch on, but do not start the engine. Use a short length of wire and bridge the fuel pump check connector terminals as shown (Fig. 3.79). It should be possible to hear fuel return noise in the pressure regulator (Fig. 3.80).

2 Detach the wires from the check connector and refit the rubber cap. Turn off the ignition switch. If the check proves that there is no return pressure, inspect the condition of the fusible link, fuses EF1 15A and 1GN 7.5A, the circuit opening relay, system wiring connections, and the fuel pump and line connections.

3 A further check which can be made concerning the fuel pump before removing it is a fuel pressure check. This requires the use of a special Toyota service tool, and in view of the procedures involved, this task is best entrusted to your Toyota dealer.

32 Fuel pump – removal and refitting

1 Disconnect the battery negative lead.

2 Remove the fuel tank, as described in Section 7.

3 Undo the fuel pump unit retaining screws, and withdraw the pump unit from the fuel tank.

4 Disconnect the wires to the fuel pump.

5 Swing the pump unit outwards from the bracket at the bottom end, then loosen the hose retaining clip and pull the pump clear (Fig. 3.81).

6 To remove the fuel pump filter from the pump, detach the rubber cushion, remove the clip, and withdraw the filter (Fig. 3.82).

7 Refitting is a reversal of the removal procedure. Renew the fuel filter, the outlet hose, and retaining clips as necessary. Always use a new gasket when installing the pump to the fuel tank, and ensure that the mating surfaces are clean.

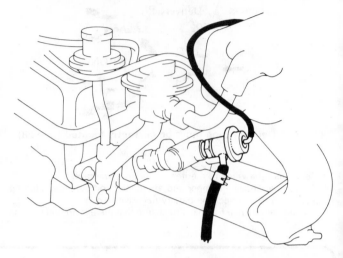

Fig. 3.76 EFI system pressure regulator location (Sec 30)

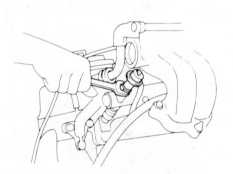

Fig. 3.77 Pressure regulator removal (Sec 30)

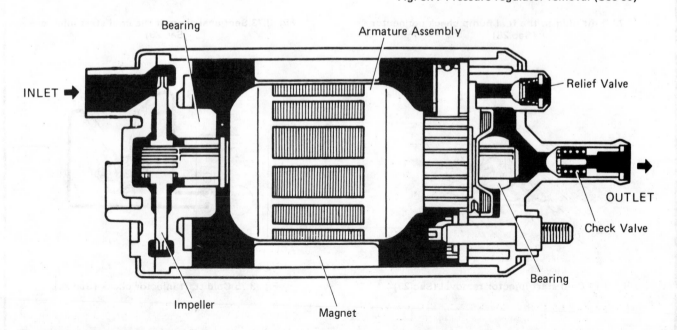

Fig. 3.78 Sectional view of the turbine type fuel pump fitted to 1984/85 models (Sec 31)

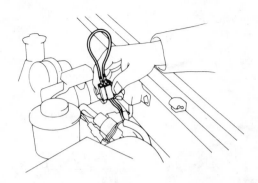

Fig. 3.79 Bridge the fuel pump check connector as shown (Sec 31)

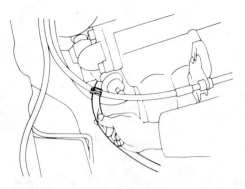

Fig. 3.80 Check for pressure in hose to cold start injector (Sec 31)

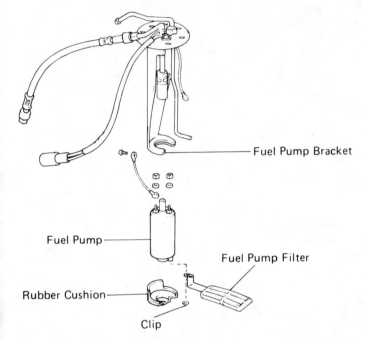

Fuel Pump Bracket

Fuel Pump

Fuel Pump Filter

Rubber Cushion

Clip

Fig. 3.81 Fuel pump and associated components (Sec 32)

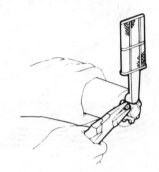

Fig. 3.82 Fuel pump filter removal (Sec 32)

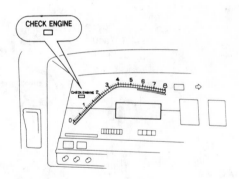

CHECK ENGINE

Fig. 3.83 'Check engine' warning light (Sec 33)

8   When the fuel tank is refitted to the vehicle and the engine is restarted, check for any signs of fuel leaks from the hose and pipe connections.

33 Diagnosis system (EFI) – checking

1   The EFI system computer contains a fault diagnosis analyser. Should a fault develop in the engine electrical system, the 'Check Engine' warning light will illuminate (Fig. 3.83).
2   Whilst it is normal for the 'Check Engine' warning light to illuminate initially when the ignition is switched on, when the engine has started the light should go out.
3   If the warning light does not go out when the engine has started, or it illuminates whilst driving, this indicates a fault in the EFI system.
4   If a fault is indicated, an initial check should be made to ensure that all of the system wiring connections and hoses are clean, secure, and in good condition. Any problem found should be rectified, and the system re-checked.
5   If a fault still exists, the system is designed so that it can be used to diagnose a fault by means of diagnostic codes given by the warning light during a system check.
6   This system is designed for use by Toyota trained mechanics, and if

a fault in the EFI system is suspected, the diagnosis is best referred to a Toyota dealer, who will have the necessary test equipment and technical expertise.
7   Whenever a fault in the EFI system has been traced or repaired, it is important that the diagnostic code retained in the EFI computer memory is cancelled. Again, this is best left to a Toyota dealer.

PART C: EMISSION CONTROL

34 General description

To prevent pollution of the atmosphere, a number of (fume) emission control systems are fitted to all vehicles. Their complexity depends upon the operating territory but as a general rule vehicles destined for North America have the most comprehensive and sophisticated systems. All vehicles have a Positive Crankcase Ventilation (PCV) System.

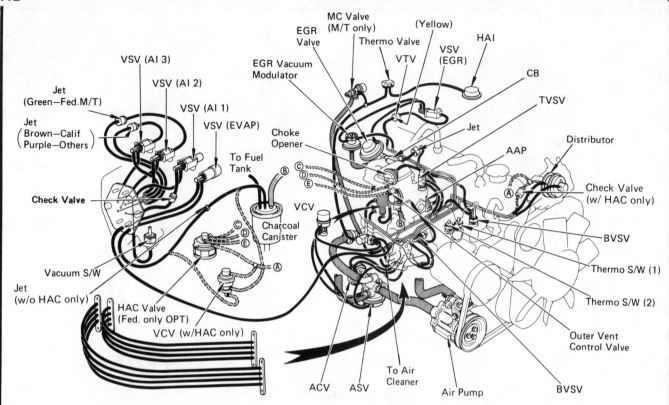

VSV (AI 3)

Jet
(Green—Fed.M/T)

VSV (AI 2)

Jet
(Brown—Calif
Purple—Others)

VSV (AI 1)

VSV (EVAP)

MC Valve
(M/T only)

EGR
Valve

Thermo Valve

(Yellow)

VTV

VSV
(EGR)

HAI

EGR Vacuum
Modulator

CB

TVSV

Choke
Opener

Jet

AAP

Distributor

Check Valve

VCV

To Fuel
Tank

Charcoal
Canister

Check Valve
(w/ HAC only)

BVSV

Thermo S/W (1)

Thermo S/W (2)

Vacuum S/W

Jet
(w/o HAC only)

HAC Valve
(Fed. only OPT)

VCV (w/HAC only)

Outer Vent
Control Valve

BVSV

ACV

ASV

To Air
Cleaner

Air Pump

Fig. 3.84 Emission control system components – 1982 USA models (Sec 35)

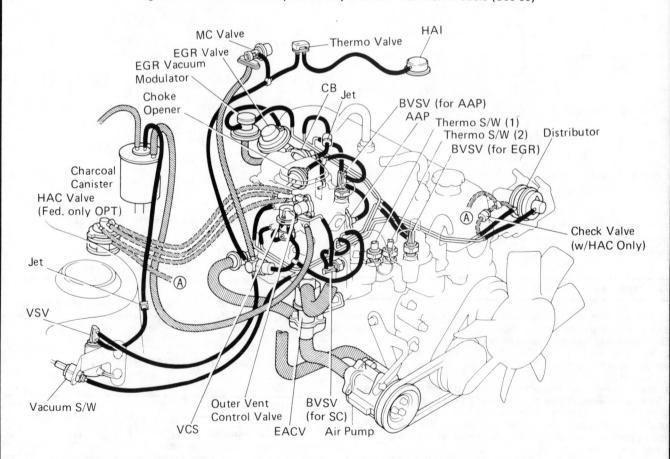

MC Valve

Thermo Valve

HAI

EGR Valve

EGR Vacuum
Modulator

Choke
Opener

CB

Jet

BVSV (for AAP)

AAP

Thermo S/W (1)

Thermo S/W (2)

BVSV (for EGR)

Distributor

Charcoal
Canister

HAC Valve
(Fed. only OPT)

Check Valve
(w/HAC Only)

Jet

VSV

Vacuum S/W

Outer Vent
Control Valve

VCS

EACV

BVSV
(for SC)

Air Pump

Fig. 3.85 Emission control system components – 1983 USA models with carburettor engine (Sec 35)

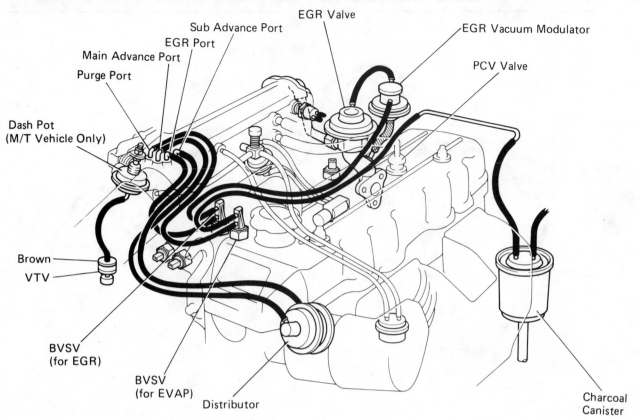

Fig. 3.86 Emission control system components – 1983 USA models with EFI (Sec 35)

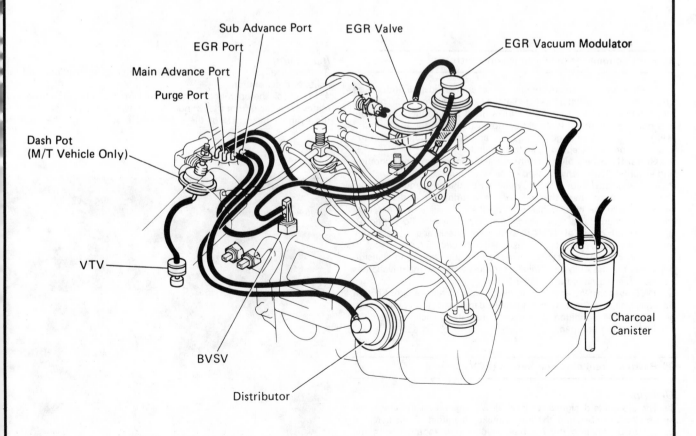

Fig. 3.87 Emission control system components – 1984 USA models with EFI (Sec 35)

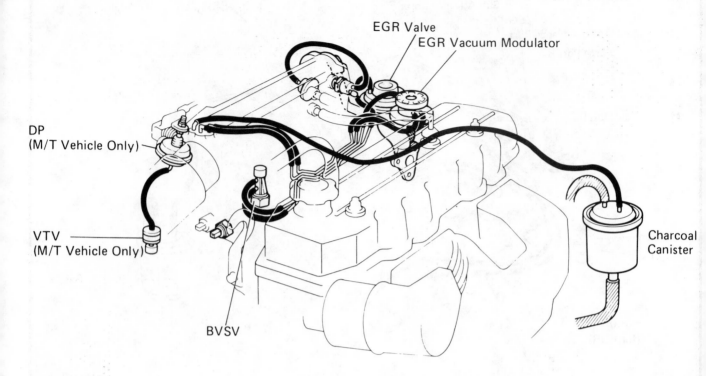

Fig. 3.88 Emission control system components – 1985 USA models (Sec 35)

35 Routine maintenance – emission control

The following routine maintenance procedures must be undertaken on the emission control items listed at the start of this manual. The type and extent of emission control features fitted is dependent on model and operating territory. It should be noted that both the ignition and fuel systems must be in good condition and correctly adjusted for the emission control system to operate efficiently.

1   **General:** Inspect all system hoses and connections for condition and security. Renew any cracked or perished hoses.

2   **PCV system:** Renew the PCV valve. Pull the hose and valve from the cylinder head cover, then release the securing clip and withdraw the valve from the hose. When refitting the new valve, it is essential that its larger end faces downwards to give the correct airflow (photo).

3   **Charcoal canister (EVAP system):** Check and if necessary renew the charcoal canister, as described in Section 37.

4   **Drivebelt (AI system):** Inspect the condition and tension adjustment of the AI system drivebelt. Adjust or renew the drivebelt as necessary, as described in Chapter 2.

5   **TWC system:** When checking the exhaust system, refer to Section 43 concerning the maximum allowable damage to the catalyst, and also check the condition of the heat insulator panel between the catalyst and the floorpan.

36 Positive crankcase ventilation (PCV) system

Description

1   The system is designed to draw blow-by gas from the crankcase and rocker chamber into the inlet (intake) manifold. From here the gases are drawn into the combustion chambers together with the fuel/air mixture, and are burnt off in the combustion process.

2   The system is simple, comprising of rubber hoses and a PCV valve (Figs. 3.89 or 3.90).

Inspection

3   Periodically inspect the hoses for security of connections and for splits or deterioration.

4   To check the operation of the PCV valve, disconnect the hose and remove the valve from the cylinder head cover. Attach a clean hose to the cylinder head side of the valve, and blow through the hose to

35.2 PCV valve location in the cylinder head cover (21R engine)

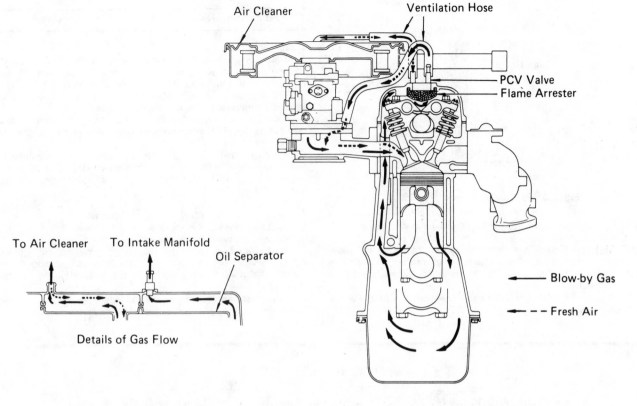

Fig. 3.89 PCV system layout – USA models with carburettor engine (Sec 36)

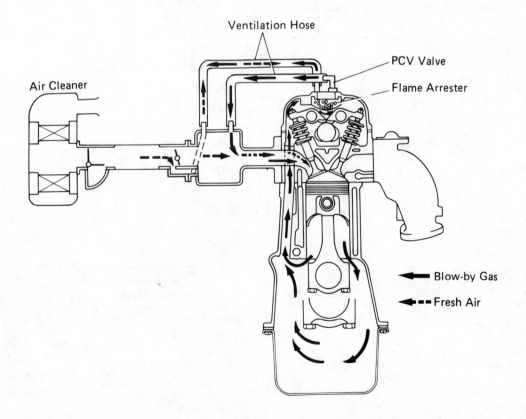

Fig. 3.90 PCV system layout – USA models with EFI engine (Sec 36)

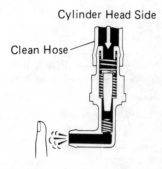

Fig. 3.91 PCV valve check (Sec 36)

ensure that air passes through the valve without restriction. Remove the hose (Fig. 3.91).
5   Fit the clean hose to the manifold side of the valve, and blow through it. From this direction the passage of air through the valve should be noticeably restricted. Remove the hose. **Note:** *do not suck through the valve.*
6   If defective or suspect, the valve must be renewed. Also renew any defective hoses.

37 Fuel evaporative emission control (EVAP) system

Description

1   The system is designed to reduce the emission of fuel vapour to the atmosphere by directing the vapour from the fuel tank through a non-return valve into an absorbent charcoal-filled canister.
2   The system layout will differ according to model, but the basic system diagrams are shown in Figs. 3.92 and 3.93.
3   Although normally sealed, the fuel filler cap incorporates a valve to admit air when partial vacuum conditions are created within the system or fuel tank.
4   At certain road speeds, a vacuum switching valve is actuated and the vapour stored in the canister is then drawn into the intake manifold where it is burned as a controlled fuel/air mixture within the engine combustion chambers.

Inspection (carburettor and EFI models)

5   **System hoses:** Check the system hoses for security and condition. Renew where necessary.
6   **Fuel filler cap:** Undo the four retaining screws and remove the cap and retainer. Renew the gasket if it is distorted or damaged. Renew the cap if damaged or suspect. Refit in the reverse order to removal (Fig. 3.94).
7   **Charcoal canister:** Remove and inspect the charcoal canister. If damaged, or cracks are visible, it must be renewed.

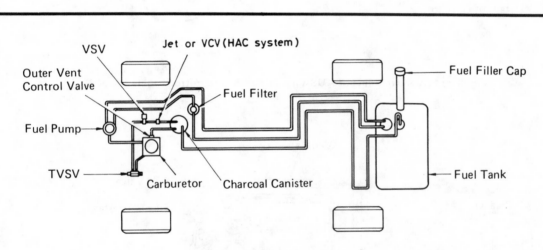

Fig. 3.92 EVAP system – USA models with carburettor engine (Sec 37)

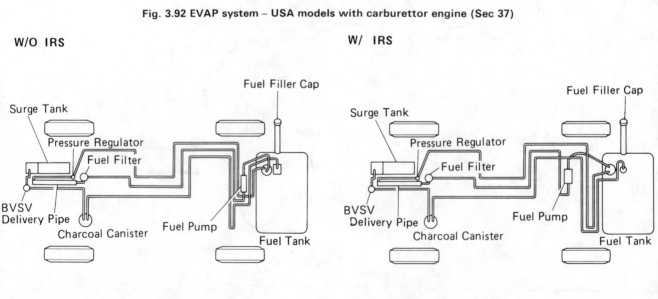

Fig. 3.93 EVAP system – USA models with EFI engine (Sec 37)

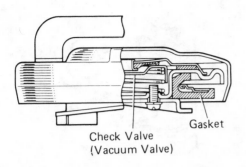

Fig. 3.94 EVAP system fuel filler cap (Sec 37)

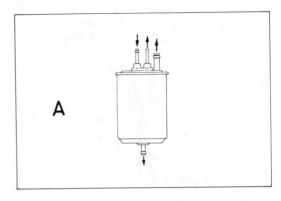

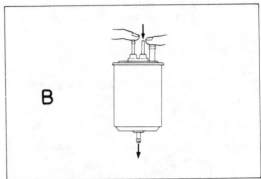

Fig. 3.95 Charcoal canister (carburettor models) (Sec 37)

A Clogged filter and stuck check valve check
B Cleaning method

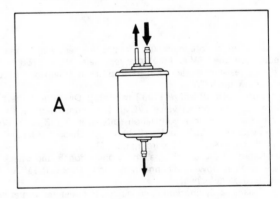

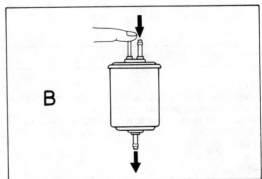

Fig. 3.96 Charcoal canister (EFI models) (Sec 37)

A Clogged filter and stuck check valve check
B Cleaning method

8 Apply low pressure compressed air to the pipe connections as indicated. With air applied to the tank pipe, air should flow freely from the other pipes.
9 Apply air to the purge pipe. On carburettor models air should flow freely from the other pipes, but on EFI models, no air should flow through the other pipes (Figs. 3.95 and 3.96).
10 The canister is cleaned by applying an air pressure of 3 kgf/cm² (43 lbf/in²) to the purge pipe whilst simultaneously plugging the adjacent pipe(s). No activated carbon should come out of the canister. Note that the canister must not be cleaned by any other method.

Inspection – carburettor models only
11 **Outer vent control valve:** Detach the outer control vent valve hose from the carburettor, then blow air into the outer vent pipe. The valve should be open (Fig. 3.97).
12 Start the engine and run it at idle speed. Blow air into the outer vent pipe again, but this time check that the vent valve is closed.
13 Detach the wiring connector from the vent control valve solenoid, then connect up an ohmmeter. At a temperature of 20°C (68°F) the resistance between the positive terminal and the solenoid body should be 63 to 73 ohm.
14 **Thermo-switch (1983 models):** Drain the cooling system, as described in Chapter 2, then disconnect the wire and unscrew the thermo-switch from the inlet manifold.
15 Immerse the switch probe into cold water so that its temperature drops below 43°C (109°F), then connect up an ohmmeter to the switch and check that there is continuity.
16 Repeat the above check, this time in hot water, so that the switch temperature rises above 55°C (131°F), and check that there is no continuity.
17 Renew the thermo-switch if it is found to be defective. When refitting the switch, smear the threads with sealant. Top up the cooling system on completion.
18 **Thermostatic vacuum switching valve (TVSV) (1982 models):** Disconnect the hoses, then with the coolant temperature below 60°C (140°F), blow air into the middle pipe (J). Air should exit from the top pipe (L) (Fig. 3.98).
19 Run the engine up to its normal operating temperature, then again blow air into the middle pipe (J). This time air should exit from the lower pipe (K).
20 **Speed sensor to vacuum switching valve (VSV):** This check can only be made using specialised equipment, therefore entrust it to your Toyota dealer. This also applies if the speed sensor is to be checked.
21 **Vacuum switching valve (VSV):** Disconnect the wiring connector at the vacuum switching valve, also the two vacuum hoses. Using suitable leads, connect them to the battery terminals and the VSV wiring connector as shown in Fig. 3.99. Connect a suitable length of clean pipe to the inner vacuum hose connection on the VSV, and blow into the pipe. Air should be felt to exit from the outer pipe on the VSV, proving that the VSV is open.
22 Disconnect the lead from the battery positive terminal (to the VSV), blow into the pipe again and check that this time the valve is closed. Disconnect the negative lead to the VSV.
23 Connect up an ohmmeter between the positive terminal of the lead connector and the VSV body. There should be no continuity. If a short circuit is evident, the VSV must be renewed (Fig. 3.100).

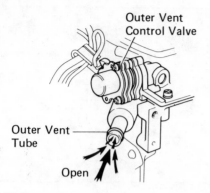

Fig. 3.97 Outer vent control valve check (carburettor models) – engine switched off (Sec 37)

Fig. 3.98 TVSV check (1982 models) – stage 1 check (Sec 37)

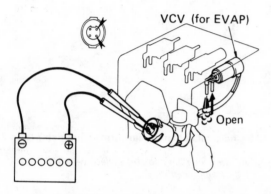

Fig. 3.99 VSV open check method (Sec 37)

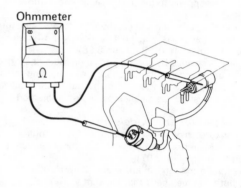

Fig. 3.100 VSV check for short circuit (Sec 37)

24 Connect up an ohmmeter to the positive terminal of the lead connector from the VSV and the other terminals. At 20°C (68°F) there should be a resistance reading of 51 to 57 ohm. If an open circuit is evident renew the VSV.

25 **Vacuum control valve (1982 models):** Disconnect the hoses from the vacuum control valve (VCV), then connect up a vacuum supply to the upper hose connection (pipe B in Fig. 3.101). With a minimum vacuum of 250 mm Hg (9.84 in Hg), check that air is drawn into middle pipe (A) and exits from pipe (B).

26 Disconnect the vacuum pipe from connection B and check that there is a small air flow from connection A to C. Renew the VCV unit if it is found to be defective.

27 **Jet:** This is easily checked by detaching the inlet and outlet hoses from the jet, then blowing through the jet from each side. The jet should be free of any blockage (Fig. 3.102).

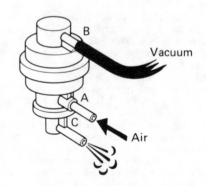

Fig. 3.101 VCV check (1982 models) (Sec 37)

38 Mixture control (MC) system

Description

1 This system is fitted to 1982 and 1983 USA models fitted with a carburettor and manual gearbox (Fig. 3.103).

2 Its purpose is to permit fresh air to enter the inlet manifold at time of sudden deceleration in order to improve combustion and reduce the emission of hydrocarbons.

Inspection

3 General maintenance consists of checking the hoses and connections.

4 In the event of a suspected fault, remove the air cleaner cover and lift out the element. Start the engine, disconnect the vacuum sensing hose from the valve, and block the hose. Now place the hand over the air intake of the valve, no vacuum should be felt.

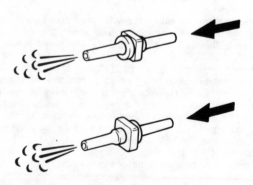

Fig. 3.102 Jet check method (Sec 37)

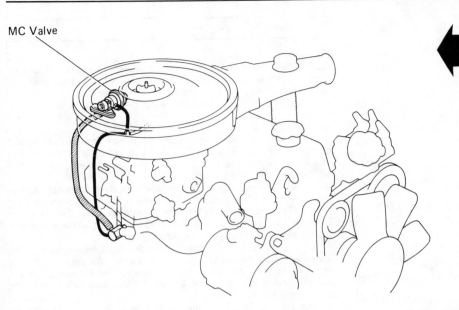

MC Valve

Fig. 3.103 Mixture control (MC) system – 1982 and 1983 USA models with carburettor engine (Sec 38)

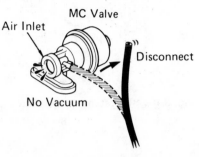

Air Inlet   MC Valve

Disconnect

No Vacuum

Fig. 3.104 MC valve check – hose disconnected (Sec 38)

5   Reconnect the hose and as it is connected, vacuum should be felt momentarily, together with rough idle condition.
6   If the valve does not operate as described, renew it as a sealed unit.

39 Spark control (SC) system

Description
1   This system is designed to delay the distributor vacuum advance of the ignition timing when the engine is cold, to quicken the warming up of the engine and the three-way catalyst (TWC). This reduces the formation of noxious gases which would otherwise be produced during the warm-up period by lengthening the combustion time. When the coolant temperature rises above 44°C (111°F), the bi-metal vacuum switching valve (BVSV) opens to allow normal distributor advance.

Inspection
2   Maintenance consists of periodically inspecting the condition of the connecting hoses.
3   Tests on this system can only be made if you have a vacuum gauge and a tachometer. Proceed as follows to make checks on the various components.
4   Detach the distributor diaphragm unit vacuum supply hose. Run the engine at idle speed (engine cold) and check that the gauge registers zero vacuum (throttle open or closed) (Fig. 3.106).

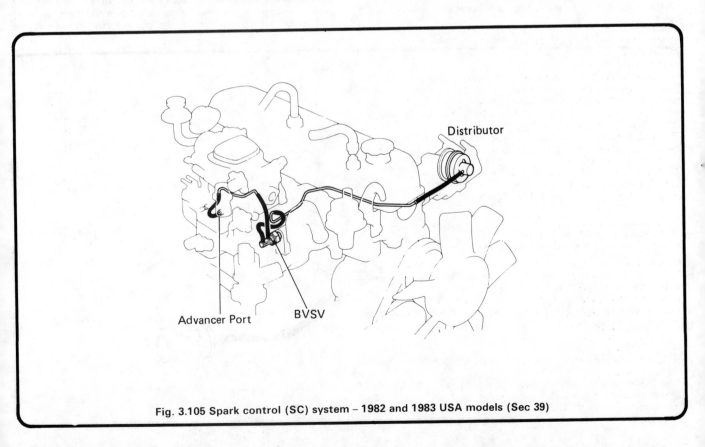

Distributor

Advancer Port   BVSV

Fig. 3.105 Spark control (SC) system – 1982 and 1983 USA models (Sec 39)

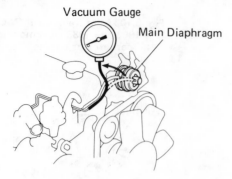

Fig. 3.106 SC system check using vacuum gauge (Sec 39)

5   Run the engine up to its normal operating temperature, then repeat the test in paragraph 4. When the throttle is opened and closed, the vacuum reading should change quickly.
6   If the BVSV is suspect (as proved by the previous checks) it must be removed for further inspection. To do this leave the hoses detached, drain the engine coolant (Chapter 2), and unscrew the BVSV unit.
7   With the BVSV removed, partially immerse it in cold water below 30°C (86°F), blow through the top hose connector, and check that no air passes out of the bottom connector.
8   Heat the water up to a minimum temperature of 44°C (111°F) and repeat the check in paragraph 7. This time the valve should be open and air should pass freely from the top connector through the unit and out of the lower connector.
9   Renew the BVSV if it is found to be defective.
10 When refitting the BVSV unit, apply sealant to the threads, and on completion top up the cooling system.
11 Now check the distributor vacuum advance by first removing the distributor cap followed by the rotor and dust cover. Apply vacuum to the diaphragm and check that the vacuum advancer is seen to operate in accordance with the applied vacuum.
12 If this test is satisfactory, refit the dust cover, rotor and distributor cap.

40 Dashpot (DP) system

Description
1   The DP system is fitted to USA models fitted with EFI and on manual gearbox. The dashpot ensures complete burning of the air/fuel mixture when the engine is decelerating. To do this it opens the throttle valve slightly more than when at normal idle speed (Fig. 3.107).

Inspection
2   To check the system operation, run the engine until its normal operating temperature is reached, then connect up a tachometer and check that the engine idle speed is as specified (see Section 11 if adjustment is required).
3   Increase the engine speed up to 2500 rpm, then whilst holding it at this speed, pinch the vacuum hose between the vacuum transmitting valve (VTV) and the DP. Release the throttle valve and check that the DP is set, and the idle speed is now 2000 rpm. To adjust the speed, turn the DP adjustment screw as necessary (Fig. 3.108).
4   VTV check: With the DP speed set as described in paragraphs 2 and 3 above, release the pinch on the hose and check that the engine speed drops to the normal idle speed within one second (approx). If this is not the case inspect the VTV. Disconnect the hose and remove the valve and filter (Fig. 3.109).
5   Remove the filter from the valve. If dirty it can be cleaned by blowing through with compressed air. Renew the filter if it is too contaminated to clean properly or is damaged.
6   Check the valve for satisfactory operation by blowing through it from the B (black) side. Air should pass through the valve quite freely. Now reverse the direction of blow, and check that when blowing from the A (white) side of the valve a considerable resistance is felt. If the valve is faulty it must be renewed.

41 Exhaust gas recirculation (EGR) system

Description
1   This system is designed to re-introduce small amounts of exhaust gas into the combustion cycle to reduce the generation of oxides of nitrogen by the reduction of combustion temperatures. The amount of gas re-introduced is governed by engine vacuum and temperature.
2   The EGR valve is connected to the inlet and exhaust manifold; the

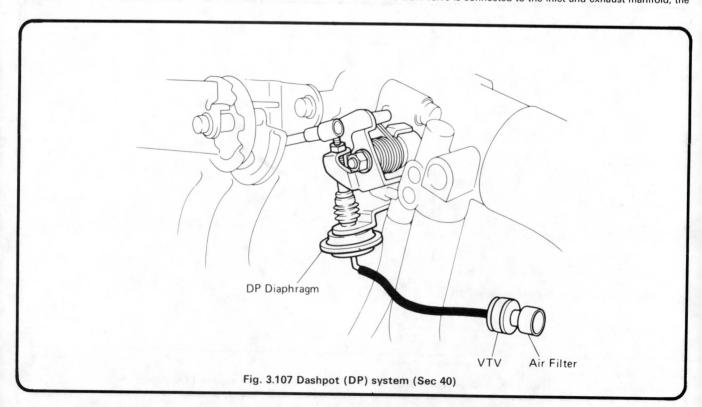

Fig. 3.107 Dashpot (DP) system (Sec 40)

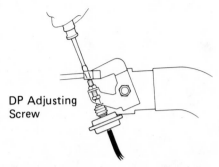

Fig. 3.108 Dashpot adjustment (1983/4 models). Use a hexagon wrench on 1985 models (Sec 40)

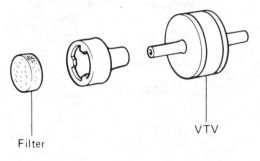

Fig. 3.109 Dashpot system VTV filter (Sec 40)

internal spring-tensioned diaphragm is operated by inlet manifold vacuum and is controlled by a thermal valve (BVSV). The system layout differs according to model (Figs. 3.110, 3.111, 3.112 and 3.113).

Inspection
3 Periodically check the system hoses and connections for security and condition, renew if necessary.
4 The EGR vacuum modulator contains a filter, and this must periodically be removed for cleaning by blowing through with compressed air. If the filter is damaged or contaminated with dirt which cannot be removed, the filter must be renewed (Fig. 3.114).
5 If any part of the EGR system is suspect, the individual items of the system can be checked as follows. A vacuum gauge with a three-way hose connector will be required for some checks.
6 **EGR valve:** Disconnect the hose from the EGR valve and apply a direct vacuum to the EGR valve with the engine idling. A vacuum supply can be made by detaching the hose at the EGR port at the intake manifold and connecting up a suitable length of vacuum hose from the EGR port direct to the EGR valve.
7 The engine should idle erratically or stop.
8 If necessary, further check the EGR valve by removing it and

inspecting it for heavy carbon deposits and/or a sticky action. Renew the valve if necessary. When refitting the EGR valve, use a new gasket and reconnect the hoses.
9 **BVSV unit:** For the initial check on this unit, the engine must be cold. Disconnect the hoses between the following:

(a) *EGR valve and VSV unit (1982 models)*
(b) *EGR valve and EGR vacuum modulator (1983 models)*
(c) *EGR valve and EGR vacuum modulator (1984 models)*
(d) *EGR valve and BVSV unit (1985 models)*

Connect up a vacuum gauge with a three-way connector between the EGR valve and the appropriate item disconnected (as applicable), then start the engine and run it at the following speed according to year; 2000 rpm (1982), 3000 rpm (1983 carburettor models), 4000 rpm (1983 EFI models and 1984 models) or 3500 rpm (1985 models). At the specified engine speed check that there is zero vacuum registered on the gauge. Leave the vacuum gauge connected.
10 Run the engine up to its normal operating temperature, then repeat the check in paragraph 9. With the engine hot a low vacuum reading should be given.
11 On 1985 models, further check by detaching the hose from the R port on the EGR vacuum modulator, then using a suitable length of spare vacuum hose, connect the R port direct to the intake manifold

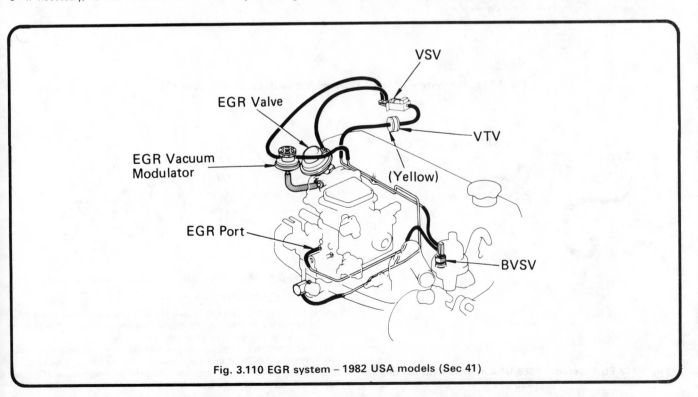

Fig. 3.110 EGR system – 1982 USA models (Sec 41)

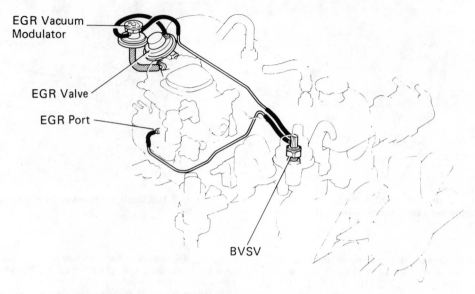

Fig. 3.111 EGR system – 1983 USA models with carburettor engine (Sec 41)

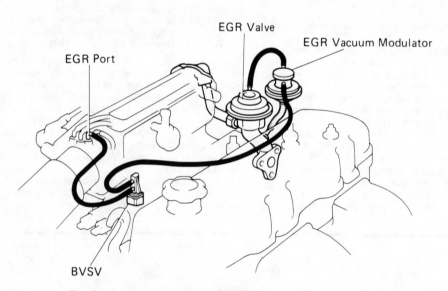

Fig. 3.112 EGR system – 1983/4 USA models with EFI engine (Sec 41)

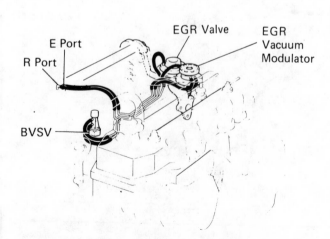

Fig. 3.113 EGR system – 1985 USA models with EFI engine (Sec 41)

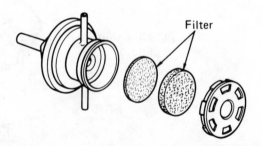

Fig. 3.114 EGR vacuum modulator filter (Sec 41)

vacuum connector. Run the engine at 3500 rpm and check that a high vacuum reading is given on the gauge. The engine may misfire slightly due to a large induction of EGR gas.

12 Disconnect the vacuum gauge. If these tests indicate a possible malfunction, the BVSV unit must be removed for further checking.

13 To remove the BVSV unit, first drain the engine coolant (Chapter 2), then unscrew and remove the unit.

14 Check the BVSV unit as described in Section 39, paragraphs 7 to 10 inclusive.

15 **EGR vacuum modulator (1982 to 1984 models):** Disconnect the vacuum hoses each side of the vacuum modulator unit, plug one pipe connector with a finger and blow through the other connector (inlet side). The applied air flow should be felt to pass freely through the modulator unit to the air filter side (Fig. 1.115).

16 Now start the engine and run it at 2000 rpm. Repeat the above test – an air flow resistance should be felt.

17 If the EGR vacuum modulator is found to be defective it must be removed and renewed.

18 **EGR vacuum modulator (1985 models):** Detach the vacuum hoses from the modulator ports. Refer to Fig. 3.116, plug ports P and R with your fingers, and blow air into the Q port. Air should pass freely through to the filter side.

19 Start the engine and run it at 3000 rpm, then repeat the above check. This time there should be a resistance to airflow through the unit. Renew the unit if defective. Reconnect the hoses.

20 **VSV (for EGR) (1982 models):** This can be checked in the same manner as that described for the VSV unit for the EVAP system in Section 37, paragraphs 21 to 24 inclusive, but refer to Fig. 3.117 and note the following differences when checking for continuity.

21 With battery connected, blow into the E port and check that air exits from the F port. With the battery disconnected, check that air exits from the G port.

22 **VTV unit (for EGR) (1982 models):** Disconnect the vacuum hoses, then blow through the B port (black side) and check that air passes freely through the unit and exits from the A port (white side). Now blow from A to B and check that a resistance is felt. Renew the valve if defective (Fig. 3.118).

---

42 Air injection (AI) with feedback system

Description

1 This system is fitted to 1982 and 1983 USA models fitted with a carburettor engine. The system assists in reducing harmful emissions by regulating the air/fuel ratio of the inlet gases for the three-way catalyst (TWC). The system directs air drawn from a belt-driven air compressor pump into the exhaust ports or the air cleaner unit as required, and in accordance with the oxygen content within the exhaust manifold. The system layout differs according to year of manufacture as shown in Figs. 3.119 and 3.120.

Inspection

2 Maintenance consists of checking the tension of the air compressor pump drivebelt for condition and tension, and keeping the connecting hoses secure and in good condition. To adjust the tension of the drivebelt refer to Chapter 2.

3 The following periodic checks should be made to ensure that the AI system is functioning correctly. Prepare for the checks by detaching the air bypass hose from the air cleaner unit. On models fitted with a HAC system (see Section 44), detach the vacuum hose from the lower connection on the HAC valve, and plug the end of the hose.

4 First check the air switching valve (ASV) on 1982 models, or the Electronic air control valve (EACV) on 1983 models, as applicable. The engine must be cold, with the coolant temperature below 6°C (43°F). Start the engine and check that there is a discharge of air from the air bypass hose.

5 Run the engine and warm up the coolant to a temperature between 18°C (64°F) and 43°C (109°F). Leave the engine idling, and check that there is no air flowing from the air bypass hose.

6 **Check valve (1982 models):** Detach the vacuum hose between the valve and pipe on the check valve side. Plug the end of the hose and check the air bypass hose to ensure that air is still not discharged. Unplug the hose to the check valve and reconnect (Fig. 3.121).

7 **EACV unit (1983 models):** Run the engine up to its normal operating temperature, then increase its speed and hold it at 2000 rpm. At this speed, air should be intermittently discharged from the air bypass hose.

8 **ACV and VSV's (1982 models):** With the engine at its normal operating temperature, run the engine at 2000 rpm and simultaneously check that there is an intermittent discharge of air from the air bypass hose.

9 **VCV (1982) and VCS (1983):** Accelerate the engine, then

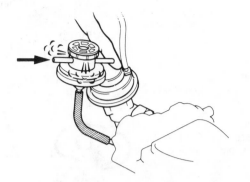

Fig. 3.115 EGR vacuum modulator check – 1982 to 1984 models (Sec 41)

Engine Stopped

Fig. 3.116 EGR vacuum modulator check – 1985 models (Sec 41)

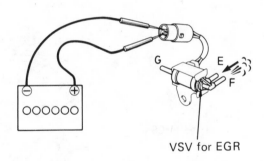

VSV for EGR

Fig. 3.117 EGR system VSV check – 1982 models (Sec 41)

Fig. 3.118 EGR system VTV check – 1982 models (Sec 41)

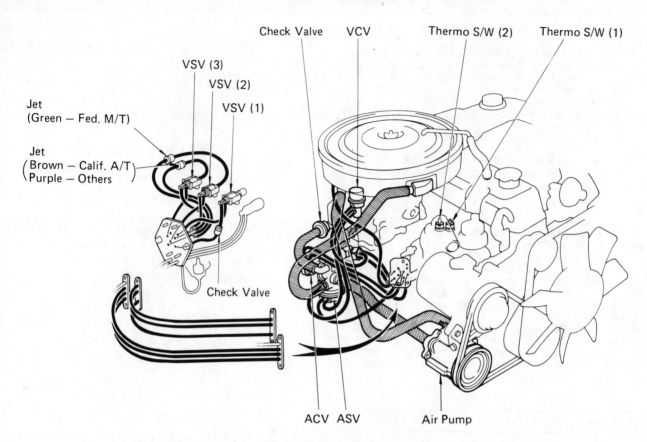

Jet
(Green — Fed. M/T)

Jet
(Brown — Calif. A/T
Purple — Others)

VSV (3)

VSV (2)

VSV (1)

Check Valve

Check Valve

VCV

Thermo S/W (2)

Thermo S/W (1)

ACV ASV

Air Pump

Fig. 3.119 Air injection with feedback system – 1982 USA models (Sec 42)

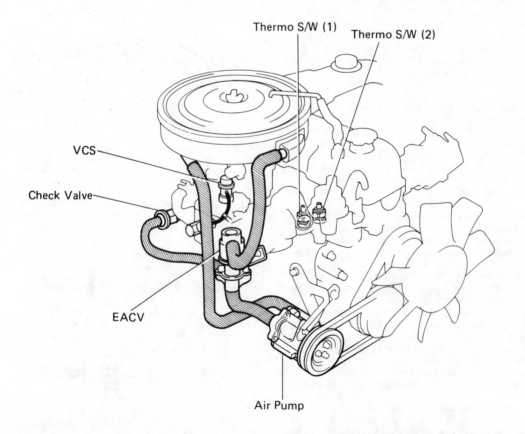

Thermo S/W (1)

Thermo S/W (2)

VCS

Check Valve

EACV

Air Pump

Fig. 3.120 Air injection with feedback system – 1983 USA models (Sec 42)

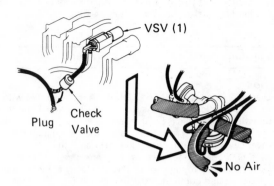

Fig. 3.121 AI system check valve inspection – 1982 USA models (Sec 42)

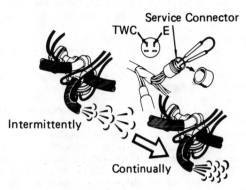

Fig. 3.122 TWC thermo-sensor to VSV (1) check – 1982 USA models (Sec 42)

quickly decelerate and check that there is a momentary discharge of air from the air bypass hose.

10 **TWC Thermo-sensor to VSV(s) (1982) or EACV (1983):** Unplug the service connector which is located behind the battery on the right-hand wing. Run the engine at idle speed and connect a length of wire to the TWC terminal, and the E terminal on the service connector. The intermittent discharge of air from the air bypass hose should change to a continuous discharge (Fig. 3.122 or 3.123, as applicable).

11 On completion of this check, detach the service wire from the service connector and refit the cap. Refit the air bypass hose to the air cleaner, and if applicable the vacuum hose to the HAC valve.

12 If any of the previous checks prove a malfunction, it will be necessary to have a Toyota dealer carry out a complete check on the system to find and rectify the fault.

13 **Air pump:** If the air pump is suspected of malfunction, have it checked by a Toyota dealer. Leave it on the vehicle for this check.

14 To remove the air pump, loosen the drivebelt tensioner lockbolt and the adjusting bolt, and remove the drivebelt. Detach the pump hoses, undo the mounting bolts and remove the unit.

15 Refit in the reverse order of removal. Adjust the drivebelt tension, as described in Chapter 2.

43 Three-way catalyst (TWC) system

Description

1 This device is fitted to USA models only and is an integral part of the exhaust system. As the exhaust gases pass through the system they are oxidized and converted to nitrogen, carbon dioxide and water. The system is shown in Fig. 3.124.

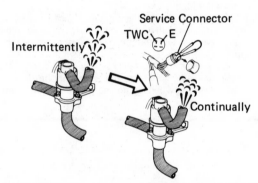

Fig. 3.123 TWC thermo-sensor to EACV check – 1983 USA models (Sec 42)

2 As the exhaust gases pass through the system, their oxidation and reduction causes an increase in their temperature. To avoid overheating on carburettor models, a thermo-sensor is fitted to the second catalyst. This switches off the air induction into the exhaust system should the temperature in the catalyst rise above 785°C (1445°F).

Inspection

3 When checking the exhaust system during the routine maintenance at the specified mileage intervals the following additional checks on the TWC system should be made when the system is cool.

4 Check the respective system connections and components for signs of damage or excessive deterioration. Make a careful inspection

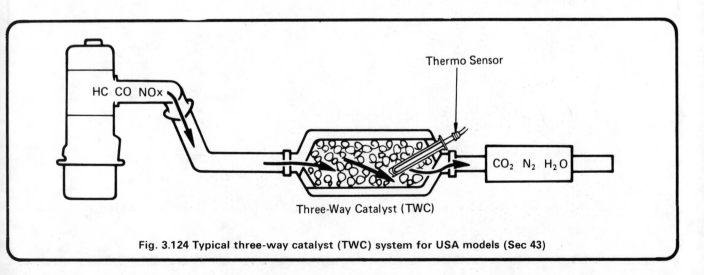

Fig. 3.124 Typical three-way catalyst (TWC) system for USA models (Sec 43)

of the number two catalyst for damage or dents. Any dent beyond a depth of 20 mm (0.8 in) necessitates renewal of the catalyst. The catalyst should also be shaken to see if it rattles. If it does rattle then it must be renewed.

5   Check that the heat insulator above the catalyst is in good condition and that a suitable clearance exists between the catalyst and the insulator (Fig. 3.126).

6   The thermo-sensor should be checked periodically by unplugging the thermo-sensor lead connection (under the driver's seat) and the resistance between the two connector terminals tested using an ohmmeter with the engine idling. Only insert the ohmmeter probes on the rear side of the connector (Fig. 3.127). There should be a resistance reading of 2 to 200 ohm. At the same time check that the sensor wiring is in good condition and the connections are secure.

7   If the number two catalyst and/or the thermo-sensor are to be removed, disconnect the wiring connector to the sensor within the vehicle then raise and support the vehicle. Unbolt and detach the catalyst at the front and rear from the exhaust pipe and withdraw the catalyst and gaskets from the joint flanges. Only remove the catalyst when it is cool.

8   To remove the thermo-sensor, support the catalyst so that the sensor is uppermost then unbolt and withdraw the sensor from the catalyst. Remove the joint gasket.

9   When fitting a service replacement catalyst, insert the sensor into the plastic guide supplied with it and use the new gasket supplied (Fig. 3.128). Keep the catalyst with the sensor aperture upwards whilst the sensor is removed.

10 Refitting of the sensor and catalyst is otherwise a reversal of the removal procedure. Where applicable the delta mark on the converter must be facing the front when fitting the converter. On completion

ensure that the sensor wire is routed correctly and not in contact with the exhaust system at any point. Check for leaks on completion around the catalyst joints and also the thermo-sensor joints.

44 High altitude compensation (HAC) system

Description

1   This system is fitted to 1982 and 1983 USA models fitted with the carburettor engine. Its function is to supply additional air to the carburettor when the vehicle is being operated at high altitudes (above 1198 m/3930 feet). This is necessary as the fuel/air mixture becomes richer when operating at higher altitudes, and the HAC system overcomes this problem and ensures the correct ratio. The ignition timing is also advanced to improve engine efficiency at high altitudes. The system circuit and components are shown in Fig. 3.129.

Inspection

2   The only maintenance normally required is to check the system hoses and their connections periodically to ensure that they are satisfactory. Inspect and clean the HAC valve filter when required (Fig. 3.130).

3   The HAC valve can be checked for position by blowing into any one of the three valve connector ports on the top of the valve when the engine is idling. If in its normal setting position no air flow should be felt underneath the unit. If an air flow can be felt then the passage is open and in the high altitude position (Fig. 3.131).

4   To test the check valve, disconnect it and apply an air flow through the orange pipe to the black pipe. The air should flow freely through

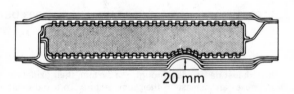

Fig. 3.125 Dents in catalyst must not exceed 20 mm (Sec 43)

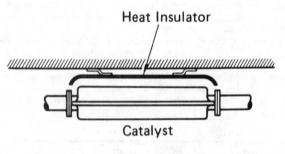

Fig. 3.126 Check heat insulator clearance and condition (Sec 43)

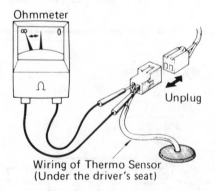

Fig. 3.127 Thermo-sensor check (Sec 43)

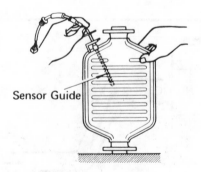

Fig. 3.128 Inserting sensor into plastic guide (Sec 43)

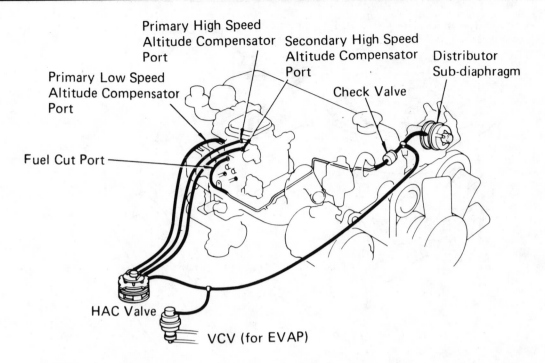

Fig. 3.129 High altitude compensation (HAC) system – 1983 USA models do not have the EVAP VCV unit fitted (Sec 44)

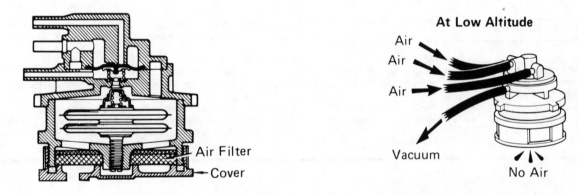

Fig. 3.130 HAC valve showing filter and cover location (Sec 44)

Fig. 3.131 HAC valve check for high altitude operation (Sec 44)

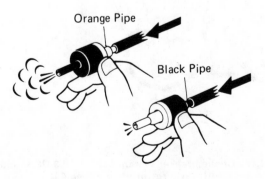

Fig. 3.132 HAC system check valve testing (Sec 44)

the valve and be felt to exit on the black side. When air is applied through the black side it should not flow freely to the orange side (Fig. 3.132). Renew the valve if found to be defective.

45 Hot air intake (HAI) system

Description and checking

1   This is an auxiliary system fitted to all carburettor engine models. The system is designed to improve cold weather driveability. It does this by leading warmed air directly to the carburettor. This helps the carburettor to warm up and prevent the carburettor from icing in extremely cold weather (Fig. 3.133).

2   The components which make up this system do not require routine maintenance and require only a periodic check normally performed at the same time a tune-up is done.

3   For details on checking refer to Section 3, paragraphs 8, 9 and 10.

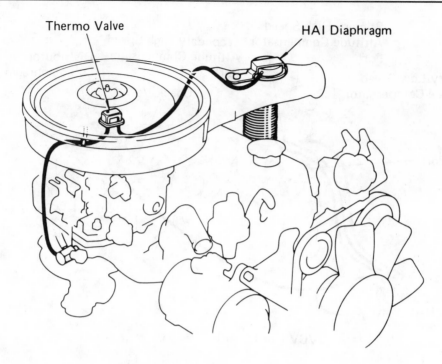

Fig. 3.133 Automatic hot air intake system (HAI) (Sec 45)

46 Choke breaker (CB) system

Description
1   The function of this system is to hold the carburettor choke valve slightly open when the engine is started from cold to prevent an over rich mixture (Figs. 3.134 and 3.135).
2   When the engine is started and idles with the throttle valve closed, vacuum from the engine side of the throttle valve operates a diaphragm which in turn opens the choke valve.

3   When the throttle valve is opened the vacuum to the diaphragm is reduced and the choke valve closes to enrich the fuel/air mixture.

Inspection
4   Maintenance is confined to checking the system hoses periodically for security and condition. Renew the hoses when necessary.
5   To check the choke breaker linkage and diaphragm, the engine must be cold and the air cleaner removed (Section 3).
6   Open the throttle slightly and push the choke valve shut. Hold the choke valve in the closed position and release the throttle (Fig. 3.26).

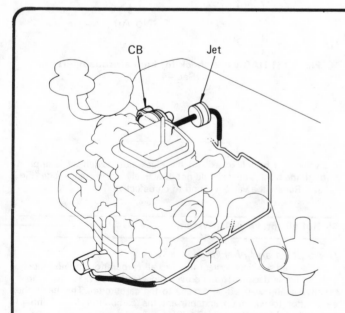

Fig. 3.134 Choke breaker system (CB) – 1982 USA models with carburettor engine (Sec 46)

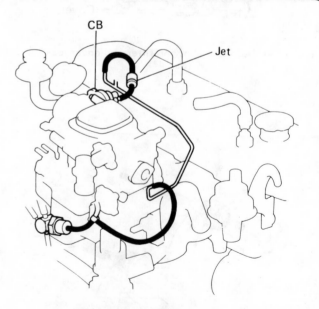

Fig. 3.135 Choke breaker system (CB) – 1983 USA models with carburettor engine (Sec 46)

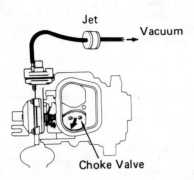

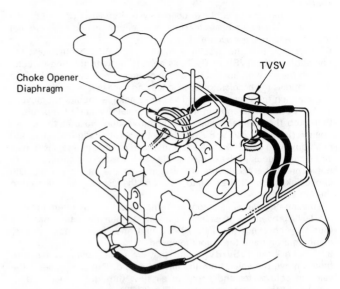

Fig. 3.136 CB system check – choke valve should be slightly open (Sec 46)

Detach the vacuum hose at the restrictor jet and apply a vacuum on the jet side and check that the choke valve opens slightly (Fig. 3.136).
7   If defective, renew the CB diaphragm. Refit the air cleaner unit and reconnect the vacuum hose to the jet to complete.

47 Choke opener system

Fig. 3.137 Choke opener system – 1982 USA models with carburettor engine (Sec 47)

Description
1   As with the CB system, the choke opener system reduces unnecessary emission of noxious gases when the automatic choke is in operation by forcibly holding the choke valve open. The choke opener system layout is shown in Figs. 3.137 and 3.138.
2   The choke valve is actuated in accordance with the engine temperature and is actuated by the TVSV (thermostatic vacuum switching valve) or the BVSV (bi-metal vacuum switching valve) as applicable.

3   When the engine coolant temperature is low the TVSV or BVSV (as applicable) is closed, the choke opener diaphragm is released under spring tension, the choke valve closed by the automatic choke and the fast idle cam will be set at the 1st or 2nd cam position giving a high idle speed.
4   When the engine temperature rises the TVSV (or BVSV) opens, the choke opener diaphragm is actuated under manifold vacuum, the choke valve opened and the fast idle cam set at the 3rd position which reduces the engine idle speed.

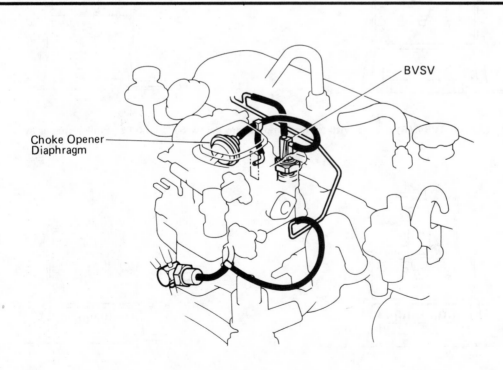

Fig. 3.138 Choke opener system – 1983 USA models with carburettor engine (Sec 47)

Inspection

5   Maintenance of the choke opener system consists of periodically checking the vacuum hoses for signs of deterioration and ensuring that their connections are secure.

6   To check that the system is functioning correctly, first test the operation of the TVSV or BVSV as applicable, with the engine cold. Detach the vacuum hose at the choke opener (from the TVSV/BVSV), then depress the accelerator pedal once and release it. Start the engine and reattach the vacuum hose. The choke linkage should not move.

7   Start the engine and run it up to its normal operating temperature, then stop the engine. Again, detach the vacuum hose at the choke opener (from the TVSV/BVSV). Hold the throttle slightly open and push down on the choke valve to shut it and retain it in this position as you simultaneously release the throttle valve. Restart the engine but do not depress the accelerator. Now reconnect the vacuum hose. The choke linkage should be seen to move and the fast idle cam released to the 4th step.

8   If each test was satisfactory, then the system is fully operational. If the tests proved the existence of a defect, then the cause must be found by checking the TVSV/BVSV unit and/or the choke opener diaphragm unit and the culprit renewed.

9   To check the TVSV/BVSV unit, first drain the cooling system and then remove the valve from the inlet manifold. Partially immerse the valve in cold water and apply an air flow through connector J. It should exit through connection L (Fig. 3.139).

10   To check the valve when hot, heat up the water to or above the temperature indicated in Fig. 3.140, and then inject air through the same connector J and note if this time the air exits through the third connector K.

11   If the valve unit is found to be defective it must be renewed. When refitting the valve, smear the threads with a suitable liquid sealant. Top up the cooling system and check for leaks on completion.

12   The choke opener diaphragm can be checked by observing if its linkage moves according to vacuum. If it does not then it must be renewed.

48 Auxiliary acceleration pump (AAP) system

Description

1   This system supplements the main accelerating pump when the engine coolant is cold, and thus the quantity of fuel required for acceleration is increased (Figs. 3.141 or 3.142).

2   A thermal valve is employed to connect the inlet manifold depression to a diaphragm on the acceleration chamber and, when the throttle valve is closed, the high vacuum acts on the diaphragm to draw fuel into the chamber.

3   When the throttle valve is opened for acceleration, the inlet manifold depression drops and spring pressure acts on the diaphragm to inject additional fuel into the carburettor venturi.

4   The system only operates when the engine coolant temperature is below 60°C (140°F).

Inspection

5   Maintenance of this system is confined to checking the system hoses periodically for condition and security.

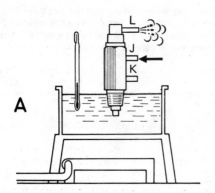
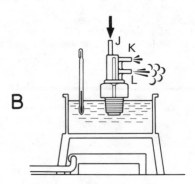

Fig. 3.139 TVSV (A) and BVSV (B) checks with water temperature below 60°C (140°F) – choke opener system (Sec 47)

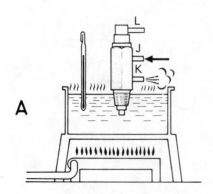
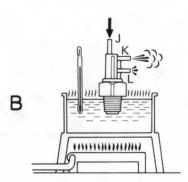

Fig. 3.140 TVSV (A) and BVSV (B) checks with water temperature above 75°C (167°F) – choke opener system (Sec 47)

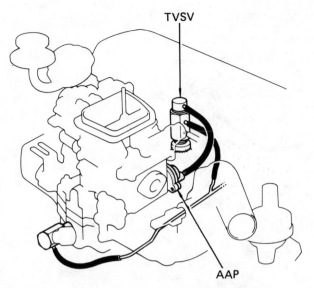

Fig. 3.141 Auxiliary acceleration pump (AAP) system – 1982 USA models with carburettor engine (Sec 48)

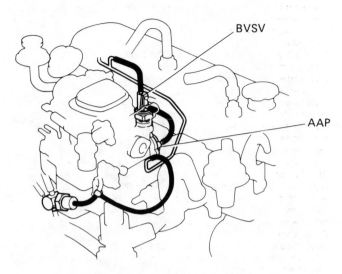

Fig. 3.142 Auxiliary acceleration pump (AAP) system – 1983 USA models with carburettor (Sec 48)

6   The AAP system can be checked for satisfactory operation in the following manner. The engine must be cold (coolant temperature under 60°C [140°F]) and the air cleaner unit cover removed.
7   Start the engine then pinch the AAP hose and stop the engine. When the hose is released fuel should eject from the acceleration nozzle.
8   Repeat this test with the engine at its normal operating temperature. This time no fuel should be ejected from the nozzle.
9   If the above tests prove a defect in the system check the AAP diaphragm unit by detaching the AAP hose from the TVSV/BVSV unit (as applicable) and then apply and release vacuum to the diaphragm unit while the engine is idling. The engine speed should be observed to change as the vacuum is released. Renew the unit if found to be defective.
10 To check the TVSV/BVSV unit proceed as described in paragraph 9 in the previous Section.

49 Deceleration fuel cut system

Description
1   This system effectively controls the idle circuit of the carburettor. When the engine speed or vacuum in the carburettor is below a certain limit, the fuel cut solenoid valve is energised and the idle circuit is opened (Fig. 3.143).
2   In addition to providing the normal idle function, the system reduces overheating and afterburn in the exhaust system during periods of protracted deceleration.

Inspection
3   Maintenance consists of checking the security and condition of the vacuum hoses and electrical wiring.
4   Should the system be suspected of being defective it is recommended that it be checked by your local Toyota dealer.

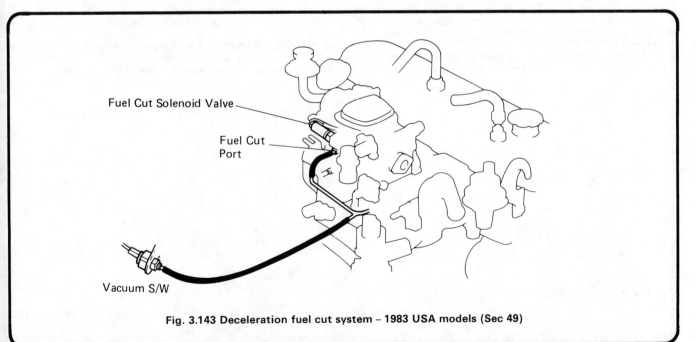

Fig. 3.143 Deceleration fuel cut system – 1983 USA models (Sec 49)

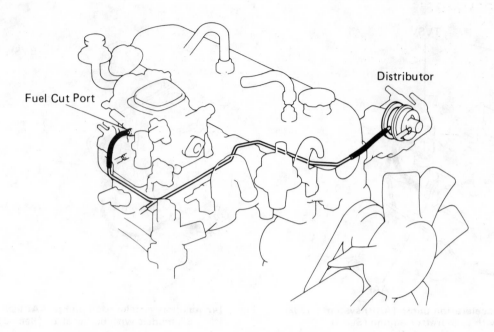

Fuel Cut Port

Distributor

Fig. 3.144 Idle advance system – 1982/83 USA models with carburettor engine (Sec 50)

50 Idle advance system (non HAC system models)

Description
1   Fitted to 1982 and 1983 USA carburettor engine models, this system is designed to increase fuel economy at idle speed by advancing the ignition timing (plus 7°) in accordance with the vacuum received at the fuel cut port on the carburettor (Fig. 3.144).

Inspection
2   Maintenance consists of checking the security and condition of the system vacuum hoses.
3   To check the system for correct operation, run the engine up to its normal operating temperature, allow it to idle and check that the ignition timing is advanced 7° beyond that specified for your model (see Chapter 4), but with the vacuum advance hose attached. When the hose is detached, the ignition timing should drop 7° to comply with that specified.
4   If the vacuum advancer unit is suspect, detach the hoses and remove the distributor cap and rotor. Apply vacuum to the advancer

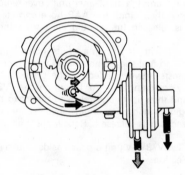

Fig. 3.145 Distributor vacuum advancer check – idle advance system (Sec 50)

connections, and check that the advancer arm moves in accordance with the vacuum applied (Fig. 3.145).
5   Renew the vacuum advancer unit or distributor if faulty.

PART D: FAULT DIAGNOSIS

Note: *Irrespective of engine type, the efficiency of the fuel system and emission control system is dependent on the correct setting and adjustment of all other engine components. These include ignition, cooling and lubrication systems, the valve clearances and general condition of the engine. Refer to the appropriate Sections and Chapters of this manual for the specification requirements and service procedures*

51 Carburettor models

Symptom	Reason(s)
Engine will not start	No fuel supply to carburettor Choke system fault Fuel cut solenoid valve fault Float chamber flooding or needle valve sticking Vacuum hose detached or faulty
Engine runs erratically or stalls	Incorrect idle speed setting Slow jet blocked Idle mixture incorrect Fast idle speed setting incorrect (cold engine) Choke system fault Fuel cut solenoid fault
Engine hesitates/poor acceleration	Air cleaner blocked Fuel line blocked Float level too low Power valve faulty Acceleration pump faulty Choke system faulty
Engine dieseling (continues running after ignition switch is turned off)	Carburettor problems: Linkage sticking Idle speed or fast idle speed out of adjustment TP (Throttle positioner) system faulty Fuel cut solenoid faulty

Poor petrol mileage	Fuel leak
	Air cleaner clogged
	Carburettor problems:
	    Choke faulty
	    Idle speed too high
	    Incorrect float level setting

52 EFI system models

Models fitted with the electronic fuel-injection system have an integral fault diagnosis device operated by the computer. It is not recommended that owners use this system as it is designed for use by Toyota dealers. Refer to Section 33 for further information concerning the diagnostic system

Symptom	Reason(s)
Engine difficult to start	Fuel pump faulty or filter blocked Fuel line fault Fuel pressure regulator fault Air leak between airflow meter and throttle body Airflow meter fault Injector(s) faulty Cold start injector fault Start injector time switch fault Air valve or hoses faulty System electrical fault
Engine stalls	Air filter element needs cleaning or renewal Incorrect idle speed adjustment Cold start injector or start injector time switch faulty Air valve or hoses faulty Fuel pump fault or filter blocked Fuel line fault Pressure regulator faulty Injector(s) faulty System electrical fault

EFI system models (continued)

Symptom	Reason(s)
Continuous high engine idle speed	Accelerator linkage fault Air valve stuck open Leak in air valve for air conditioning Leak in VSV for air conditioning Fuel pressure regulator fault Leak at start injector Leak at injector(s) System electrical fault
Engine back-fires	Weak fuel mixture Cold start injector fault Cold start injector time switch fault Fuel pump faulty or filter blocked Injectors blocked System electrical fault
Muffler explosion (after-fire)	Incorrect fuel mixture (too rich) Cold start injector fault Cold start injector timeswitch fault Leak at injector(s) System electrical fault
Engine hesitates and/or poor acceleration	Air filter element needs cleaning or renewal Fuel pump faulty or filter blocked Fuel pressure regulator faulty Faulty injector(s) System electrical fault

53 Emission control system

Where a malfunction is suspected in the emission control system, first check that the various system hoses and connections are in good condition and secure. If these are in order, check the following items in accordance with the symptom and system fitted

Symptom	Reason(s)
Engine idle speed erratic or stalls	HAI system fault EGR system fault MC system fault
Engine hesitates/poor acceleration	HAI system fault APP system fault EGR system fault HAC system fault
Engine dieseling (continues running on after ignition is switched off)	EGR system fault
Exhaust back-fires on deceleration	AI system fault AS system fault MC system fault Deceleration fuel cut system permanently off Exhaust system leak
Exhaust back-fires all the time	Choke system fault
Excessive fuel consumption	SC system fault EGR system fault
Excessive oil consumption	PCV line blocked

Chapter 4 Ignition system

Contents

Specifications

Type
Early UK models .... Battery, coil, conventional distributor (with contact breaker points)
Later UK and all USA models .... Battery, coil, transistorized distributor

Firing order .... 1-3-4-2 (No 1 at front)

Spark plugs
21R engine (UK models) .... Nippondenso W16 EXR-U
NGK BPR 6 EY
22R and 22RE engines (USA models) .... Nippondenso W16 EXR-U
NGK BPR 5 EA or BPR 5 EY
Electrode gap (all models) .... 0.8 mm (0.031 in)
HT leads resistance limit (max) .... 21 Kohm (per lead)

Distributor (contact breaker points type)
Rubbing block gap .... 0.45 mm (0.0177 in)
Damping spring gap .... 0.1 to 0.4 mm (0.004 to 0.016 in)
Dwell angle .... 52°

Distributor (transistorized)
Air gap .... 0.2 to 0.4 mm (0.008 to 0.016 in)

Ignition timing (at idle speed with vacuum advance hose attached)
21R engine .... 8° BTDC
22R engine (up to 1983) .... 8° BTDC
22R and 22RE engines (1983 and 1984 models) .... 5° BTDC
22RE engine (1985 model)* .... 5° BTDC
* Non-vacuum advance type (ESA system used)

Ignition coil
21R engine:
    Primary coil resistance .... 1.2 to 1.5 ohm
    Secondary coil resistance .... 8.5 to 11.5 Kohm
    External resistor resistance .... 1.3 to 1.5 ohm
22R and 22RE engines (up to 1984):
    Primary coil resistance .... 0.8 to 1.1 ohm
    Secondary coil resistance .... 10.7 to 14.5 Kohm
    Insulation resistance (minimum) .... 10 M ohm
22RE engine (1985):
    Primary coil resistance .... 0.5 to 0.7 ohm
    Secondary coil resistance .... 11.4 to 15.6 Kohm
    Insulation resistance (minimum) .... 10 M ohm

Torque wrench settings

	kgf m	lbf ft
Distributor retaining bolt	1.8 to 2.6	13 to 19
Spark plugs	1.5 to 2.1	11 to 15

1   General description

Different types of ignition system are used on the models covered by this manual. These are the conventional contact breaker type ignition and the transistorized ignition system.

The contact breaker type system was used on an initial number of early UK models only. All USA and later UK models are fitted with the transistorized ignition system.

Conventional (contact breaker) system

The ignition system consists of several components, the battery, the ignition/starter switch, the coil, the distributor and the spark plugs. Low and high tension wires connect the various components.

The coil acts as a transformer to step up the 12 volt battery voltage to many thousands of volts, sufficient to jump the spark plug gaps.

The distributor consists of a contact breaker, condenser, rotor arm, distributor cap with brush, and centrifugal and vacuum advance and retard mechanism, and is driven by the oil pump driveshaft or camshaft at half crankshaft speed.

The spark plugs ignite the compressed mixture in the combustion chambers.

When the ignition is switched on, a current flows from the battery to the ignition switch, through the coil primary winding to the moving contact breaker inside the distributor cap and to earth when the contact breaker points are in the closed position. During this period of points closure, the current flows through the primary winding of the coil and magnetises the laminated iron core which in turn creates a magnetic field through the coil primary and secondary windings.

Each time the points open due to the rotation of the distributor cam, the current flow through the primary winding of the coil is interrupted. This causes the induction of a very high voltage (25 000 volts) in the coil secondary winding. This HT (high tension) current is distributed to the spark plugs in correct firing order sequence by the rotor arm and by means of the cap brush and HT leads.

A condenser is fitted to the distributor, and is connected between the moving contact breaker and earth. It prevents excessive arcing and pitting of the contact breaker points, and also assists in the rapid breakdown of the coil magnetic field.

The actual point of ignition of the fuel/air mixture which occurs a few degrees before TDC is determined by correct static setting of the ignition timing, as described in Section 12. The ignition is advanced to meet varying operating conditions by the centrifugal counterweights fitted in the base of the distributor body and by vacuum from the inlet manifold operating through a capsule linked to the movable distributor baseplate.

Transistorized ignition system

The transistorized ignition system functions in a similar manner to that of the conventional type, but instead of having contact breaker points fitted to the distributor, a signal generator is used and this operates in conjunction with a device known as an igniter.

The low tension (primary) circuit consists of the battery, lead to the ignition switch, lead from the ignition switch to the low tension or primary coil windings (terminal +), and the lead from the low tension coil windings (coil terminal −), to the igniter, through the signal generator (pick-up coil), through a resistor and back to the igniter.

The high tension circuit consists of the high tension or secondary coil windings, the heavy ignition lead from the centre of the coil to the centre of the distributor cap, the rotor arm, and the spark plug leads and spark plugs.

The system functions in the following manner. Low tension voltage is changed in the coil into high tension voltage breaking a magnetic field in the low tension circuit. High tension voltage is then fed via the carbon brush in the centre of the distributor cap to the rotor arm of the distributor. Each time the rotor arm comes in line with one of the four metal segments in the cap, which are connected to the spark plug leads, breaking a magnetic field causes the high tension voltage to build up, jump the gap from the rotor arm to the appropriate metal segment and so via the spark plug lead to the spark plug where it finally jumps the spark plug gap before going to earth.

The advantages of the transistorized system are that there is no contact breaker to adjust or maintain, low speed performance is improved and cold starting under adverse weather conditions is less likely to be affected.

With the exception of the 1985 USA models, a mechanical and vacuum advance system is used, but on some models a dual vacuum

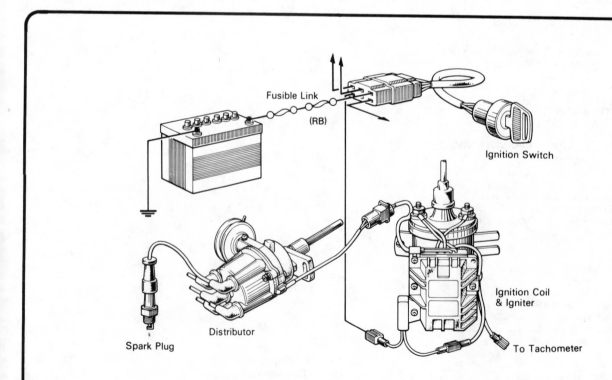

Fig. 4.1 Ignition system circuit – transistorized type (Sec 1)

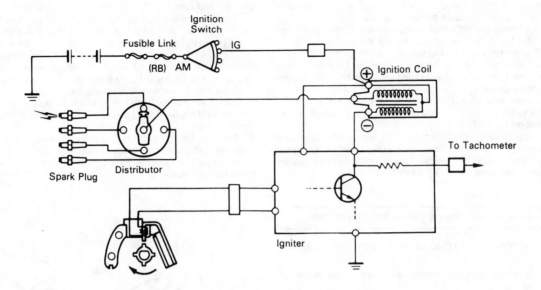

Fig. 4.2 Ignition system wiring diagram – transistorized type (Sec 1)

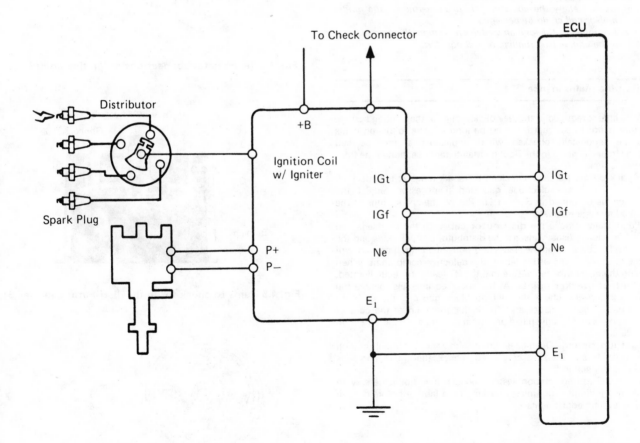

Fig. 4.3 Electronic Spark Advance (ESA) ignition system as fitted to 1985 USA models (Sec 1)

unit is fitted. The dual vacuum unit comprises a main diaphragm which operates in the normal manner and sub-diaphragm which is used in conjunction with certain emission control systems.

The ignition timing on 1985 USA models differs from earlier types in that the ignition timing is controlled by an Electronic Spark Advance (ESA) system via the Electronic Control Unit (ECU). The ECU is an integral part of the Toyota Computer Control System (TCCS) which also controls the Electronic Fuel Injection (EFI) system and the Diagnosis Systems.

Engine sensors monitor the varying engine operating conditions such as engine speed, loading, coolant temperature and air intake, and supply information to the ECU.

The data programmed in the ECU then regulates the ESA to control the ignition timing as required. This eliminates the need for a vacuum control on the distributor. The dynamic timing method differs slightly with this system (see from paragraph 14 in Section 12).

2 Precautionary notes – transistorized ignition system

Certain precautions must be observed with a transistorized ignition system.

(a) *Do not disconnect the battery leads when the engine is running*
(b) *Make sure that the igniter is always well earthed*
(c) *Keep water away from the igniter and distributor*
(d) *If a tachometer is to be connected to the engine, always connect the tachometer (+) terminal to the ignition coil (–) terminal; never to the distributor*
(e) *Do not allow the coil terminals to be earthed – the igniter and/or coil could be damaged*
(f) *Do not leave the ignition switch on for more than ten minutes if the engine isn't running or will not start*

3 Routine maintenance

Very little is required in the way of servicing for the ignition system, but that is not to say that it should be ignored. The following items must be periodically checked, where applicable, at the specified mileage intervals given in the Routine Maintenance section at the front of this manual.

1 **Spark plugs:** Remove and clean the spark plugs at the specified intervals. Check the electrode gap and if necessary adjust the clearance, as described in Section 15. Renew the spark plugs at the specified mileage intervals.

2 Periodically remove the **distributor cap** with the HT leads and wipe them clean. Visually inspect the distributor cap, HT leads and the rotor arm for signs of hairline cracks and signs of arcing. If any signs of cracks or damage are visible renew the defective component. When refitting the distributor cap ensure that the HT leads are securely fitted.

3 **Contact breaker points:** At the specified intervals remove the distributor cap and check the rubbing block gap and the damping spring gap. Adjust if necessary. Check the condition of the contact breaker points and if badly pitted or worn renew them. Refer to Section 5 for details.

4 **Ignition timing:** On models fitted with a conventional ignition system (with contact breaker points), check the dwell angle as described in Section 6.

5 On transistorized ignition system models, it is not necessary to check the ignition timing unless checking for a fault or before making any fuel system adjustments.

4 Contact breaker points – inspection and adjustment

1 To check the condition and adjustment of the contact breaker points, remove the distributor cap and lift off the rotor arm and dust cover.

2 Prise the contact breaker points open and examine the condition of their faces. If they are rough, pitted or dirty it will be necessary to remove them for refacing or a replacement set to be fitted.

3 Presuming that the points are satisfactory, or that they have been cleaned and refitted, they must be adjusted as follows.

4 Turn the engine over by hand to position the rubbing block of the moving contact at the midway point between two cams on the rotor shaft (points closed). Use feeler gauges to check the rubbing block gap (Fig. 4.6). It should be as specified. If adjustment is necessary, slacken the fixed contact breaker securing screw and move the contact as required to set the rubbing block gap, then retighten the screw.

5 Now check the damping spring gap in the same manner as that described for the rubbing block. If the clearance is not as specified, loosen the damping spring screw and adjust as required. Retighten the screw.

6 On completion, refit the dust cover, the rotor arm and distributor cap. This adjustment must be regarded as an initial setting and the dwell angle should now be checked and if necessary adjusted, as described in Section 6.

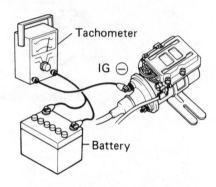

Fig. 4.4 Tachometer connections to ignition coil (Sec 2)

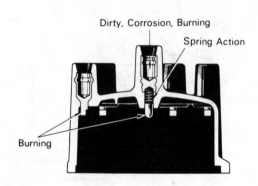

Fig. 4.5 Items to check for in the distributor cap (Sec 3)

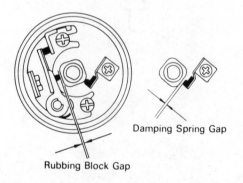

Fig. 4.6 Check the rubbing block gap then the damping spring gap – contact breaker points distributor (Sec 4)

5 Contact breaker points – renewal

1 If the contact breaker points are burned, pitted or badly worn they must be removed and renewed.
2 With the distributor cap removed, lift off the rotor arm by pulling it straight up from the spindle. Also remove the dust cover.
3 Detach the contact breaker points lead from the LT terminal on the side of the distributor body. Release the terminal nuts to do this.
4 Extract the two securing screws which hold the contact breaker arm to the distributor baseplate. Note that an earth lead is retained by one of these screws.
5 Lift the contact breaker set from the distributor.
6 If the contact points are only lightly pitted or burned they can be cleaned up using fine abrasive paper and used again. Severe burning or pitting will mean renewal of the contact breaker assembly.
7 Consistent severe burning or pitting of the points may mean that the condenser is faulty (see Section 7) or that one of the engine earth bonds is loose or that one of the distributor baseplate or earth lead screws requires tightening.
8 Refitting is a reversal of removal, set the rubbing block gap and damper spring gap as described in the previous Section. Check the dwell angle, as described in Section 6.

6 Dwell angle – checking (conventional system only)

1 On modern engines, setting the distributor contact breaker gap with feeler blades must only be considered an initial step to get the engine running. For optimum engine performance, the dwell angle must always be checked as soon as possible.
2 The dwell angle is the number of degrees through which the distributor cam turns between the closure and opening of the contact breaker points. It can only be checked using a dwell meter.
3 Connect the dwell meter in accordance with the maker's instructions (usually between the negative LT terminal on the coil and a good earth) and with the engine running at the specified idling speed, check the dwell angle on the meter.
4 If the dwell angle is larger than that specified, switch off the engine and increase the rubbing block gap, if it is too much, decrease the gap. Recheck the dwell angle.

7 Condenser (conventional system only) – removal, testing and refitting

1 The purpose of the condenser (sometimes known as a capacitor) is to ensure that when the contact breaker points open there is no sparking across them which would waste voltage and cause wear.
2 The condenser is fitted in parallel with the contact breaker points. If it develops a short circuit, it will cause ignition failure as the points will be prevented from interrupting the low tension circuit.
3 If the engine becomes very difficult to start or begins to misfire after

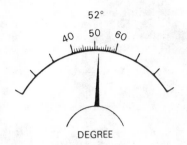

Fig. 4.7 Dwell angle check – contact breaker points distributor (Sec 6)

several miles running and the contact breaker points show signs of excessive burning, then the condition of the condenser must be suspect. A further test can be made by separating the points by hand with the ignition switched on. If this is accompanied by a flash it is indicative that the condenser has failed.
4 Without special test equipment the only sure way to diagnose condenser trouble is to replace a suspected unit with a new one and note if there is any improvement.
5 To remove a condenser from the distributor take off the distributor cap to give better access.
6 Detach the condenser lead from the terminal block.
7 Undo and remove the screw and washer securing the condenser to the distributor body. Lift away the condenser and lead.
8 Refitting the condenser is the reverse sequence to removal.

8 Signal generator air gap (transistorized ignition) – checking and adjustment

1 Remove the two retaining screws and withdraw the distributor cap from the distributor body (photo).
2 Lift off the rotor arm (photo).
3 Align one of the signal rotor teeth with the projection on the pick-up coil by turning the crankshaft.
4 Measure the air gap between the signal rotor tooth and the projection on the pick-up coil using feeler gauges. The air gap should be as given in the Specifications (photo).
5 If the gap is not as specified, loosen the two retaining screws and move the signal generator as required to correct the air gap setting, then retighten the screws. Recheck the gap when the screws are retightened.
6 Before refitting the rotor arm and distributor cap, clean and inspect them for signs of damage. It is unlikely that the four segments within

8.1 Remove the distributor cap ...

8.2 ... withdraw the rotor arm

8.4 Measure the air gap

8.6 Check the distributor cap

9.4 Align the pulley/ignition timing marks

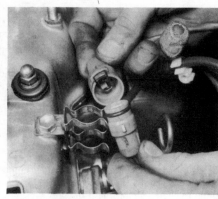

9.6 Disconnecting the signal generator wire socket

the cap will be badly burned or scored but if they are, or the cap and/or rotor are damaged in any way, they must be renewed. The contact in the centre of the distributor cap must also be in good condition (photo).

9 Distributor – removal and refitting

1 Disconnect the vacuum tube(s) from the distributor advance diaphragm (where applicable).
2 Undo the retaining screws and remove the distributor cap.
3 Remove the No 1 spark plug and position a finger over the plug hole to feel the compression being generated as the engine is rotated by means of a spanner on the crankshaft pulley bolt.
4 Rotate the crankshaft in its normal direction of rotation until compression is felt through the plug hole, indicating that the No 1 piston is rising on its compression stroke. Continue turning the crankshaft until the timing notch in the pulley is aligned with the timing mark on the timing cover (photo). This will be 5° or 8° as applicable (not the 0/TDC mark).
5 Mark the rim of the distributor body at the point opposite the centre of the contact end of the rotor arm. This is equivalent to alignment with the No 1 contact segment in the distributor cap. Also mark the installed position of the distributor body for reference.
6 Disconnect the LT wire or signal generator wire at the socket attached to the cylinder head and withdraw the socket from the clip (photo).

7 Undo the retaining bolt and withdraw the distributor. As it is withdrawn, note the position of the rotor arm as the distributor driven gear disengages from the drivegear.
8 The distributor cap can be removed if the HT leads are disconnected from the spark plugs and the centre lead from the ignition coil.
9 If the engine is turned with the distributor removed, reset the crankshaft pulley position opposite the ignition timing mark as previously described before refitting the distributor.
10 Refitting the distributor is a reversal of the removal procedure. Check that the timing notch on the crankshaft pulley is aligned with the ignition timing mark. Align the rotor at the point noted when withdrawing the distributor then, as the distributor is pushed into its housing, the driven gear should mesh with the drivegear. When the distributor is fully fitted the rotor should be aligned with the mark on the distributor body rim.
11 On a contact breaker type distributor turn the ignition on and carefully rotate the distributor until a spark jumps the points gap. On transistorized ignition models turn the distributor to align the signal rotor tooth with the projection on the signal generator (Fig. 4.10).
12 Smear the retaining bolt threads with sealant then fit the bolt and tighten it to the specified torque setting.
13 Refit the distributor cap, leads and vacuum pipe(s).
14 Check and further adjust the ignition timing, as described in Section 12 and, on contact breaker distributor types, check the dwell angle, as described in Section 6.

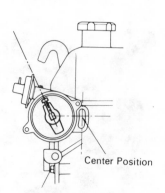

Fig. 4.8 Distributor and rotor alignment prior to inserting the distributor (Sec 9)

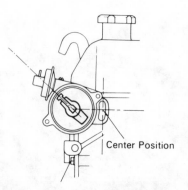

Fig. 4.9 Rotor position when distributor is fully fitted (Sec 9)

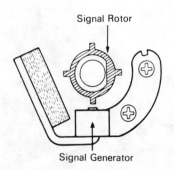

Fig. 4.10 Align signal rotor tooth with signal generator projection – transistorized type (Sec 9)

10 Distributor (contact breaker type) – dismantling and overhaul

1 With the distributor removed, withdraw the rotor arm and remove the dust cover.
2 Remove the contact breaker points, as described in Section 5.
3 Remove the seal gasket from the top face of the distributor body.
4 Remove the condenser, as described in Section 7.
5 Undo the retaining screw and remove the damping spring.
6 Prise free the spring clip and remove the vacuum advance arm from the location/pivot pin. Remove the vacuum advance unit.
7 Remove the retaining screws and lift out the breaker plate, noting its fitted position.

8 Prise free the lubrication pad out of the top of the cam spindle, undo the retaining screw and lift the cam clear.
9 Using a pair of pliers, carefully disconnect and lift away the two centrifugal weight springs, noting their respective positions.
10 Carefully remove the circlips and lift away the centrifugal weights.
11 Using a suitable diameter parallel pin punch carefully tap out the pin securing the spiral gear to the spindle. It may be found that the pin ends are peened over. If so it will be necessary to file flat before attempting to drift out the pin. The gear may now be removed from the spindle.
12 The spindle may now be drawn upwards from the distributor body. Recover the thrust washers and bearing, the spring and upper thrust washer. Keep them in order of fitting.
13 Wash all parts and wipe dry with a clean non-fluffy rag. Check the contact breaker points for wear. Inspect the distributor cap for signs of tracking (indicated by a thin black line between the segments). Also

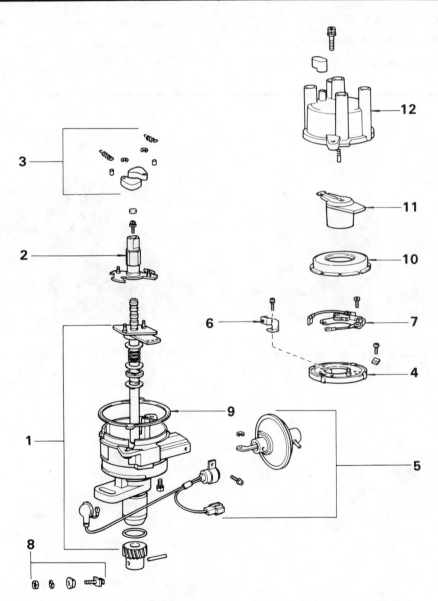

Fig. 4.11 Contact breaker points distributor components (Sec 10)

1 Governor shaft and housing assembly	4 Breaker plate	7 Breaker points	10 Dust cover
2 Cam	5 Vacuum advancer and condenser	8 Terminal	11 Rotor
3 Governor weight and spring	6 Damping spring	9 Gasket	12 Distributor cap

look at the segments for signs of excessive corrosion. Renew the cap if necessary.

14 If the metal portion of the rotor arm is badly burned or loose renew the arm. If only slightly burned, clean the end with a fine abrasive paper.

15 Check that the contact in the centre of the distributor cap is in good order.

16 Examine the centrifugal weights and pivots for wear and the advance springs for slackness. These can be best checked by comparing with new parts. If they are slack their bearings can be renewed.

17 Check the points assembly for fit on the breaker plate, and the cam follower for wear.

18 Examine the fit of the spindle in the distributor body. If there is excessive side movement it will be necessary to obtain a new distributor body and spindle, or spindle bearing.

19 Check the resistance of the breaker plate sliding part, it should rotate smoothly (Fig. 4.12).

20 Check the cam-to-spindle fit. If it is slack new parts will be necessary.

21 Check the spindle bearing and thrust bearings for signs of excessive wear and renew if necessary. The spindle bearing is secured by a circlip. Check that the thrust spring is in good condition and not distorted.

22 Commence reassembly by lubricating the governor shaft with engine oil and locate the upper bearing, circlip, washer, coil spring and thrust bearing assembly onto the shaft (Fig. 4.15).

23 Locate the governor shaft in the distributor body, then fit the driven gear. Align the pin holes and supporting the gear/shaft assembly, drive the new pin into position. Take care not to damage the gear teeth, peen or stake the pin ends to secure.

24 Fit the centrifugal weights onto the cam, fit the cam over the governor shaft. Fit the E-ring clips to secure the weights then locate the springs. Align the cam match mark with the stopper, fit the retaining screw and lubrication pad.

25 Lightly lubricate the centrifugal weight pivot points also the cam pad.

26 Refit the breaker plate and damping spring. Leave the damping spring screw hand tight at this stage as it has to be adjusted later.

27 Refit the vacuum advance unit. Ensure that the retaining clip is fully engaged when fitted. Refit the condenser.

28 Refit the contact breaker points then adjust the rubbing block gap and damper spring clearance, as described in Section 4.

29 Check that the governor shaft rotates freely then, before refitting the rotor arm and dust cover, do the following:

    (a) Lubricate the distributor cam by smearing liberally with petroleum jelly

    (b) Apply two drops of engine oil into the recess in the top of the cam spindle (rotor removed). This then runs down the spindle when the engine is hot and lubricates the bearings

Fig. 4.12 Check the breaker plate sliding resistance (Sec 10)

Fig. 4.13 Check the spindle bearing for wear (Sec 10)

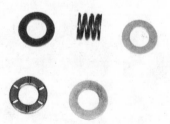

Fig. 4.14 Examine the thrust needle roller bearing, spring and thrust washer (Sec 10)

Fig. 4.15 Thrust washers, spring and bearing assemblies, showing order of fitting (Sec 10)

(c) To lubricate the automatic timing control allow a few drops of engine oil to pass through the hole in the contact breaker baseplate through which the four sided cam emerges. Apply not more than one drop of oil to the moving contact pivot post and remove any excess

(d) Wipe clean any excess oil or petroleum jelly so that when operating none may be dispersed onto the contact breaker points to cause burning and/or misfiring

(e) Check that the vacuum advancer operates in a satisfactory manner by applying a vacuum to the diaphragm hose connector. The advancer should move in accordance with the amount of vacuum applied (see Fig. 4.23).

Fig. 4.16 Align the match mark with the stopper (Sec 10)

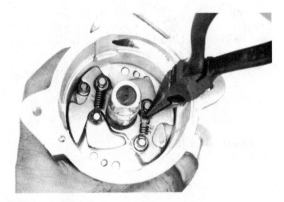

Fig. 4.17 Refit the centrifugal advance springs (Sec 10)

11 Distributor (transistorized) – dismantling and overhaul

1   With the distributor removed, as previously described in Section 9, withdraw the rotor arm and remove the plastic dust cover (photo).
2   Remove the seal ring from the rim of the distributor body.
3   Undo the two retaining screws and remove the signal generator unit complete with wiring.
4   To remove the vacuum advancer unit, undo the retaining screw on the outside and prise free the advancer arm to pivot pin retaining clip on the inside. Take care not to distort or lose the clip. Withdraw the vacuum advance unit.
5   Undo the two retaining screws and withdraw the breaker plate.
6   Mark one of the governor springs and its pivot with paint for identification then release and remove the springs.
7   To remove the signal rotor, prise free the grease stopper from the recess in the top of the rotor, undo the retaining screw in the recess and withdraw the rotor.

8   Prise free the snap-rings and remove the governor weights; noting their orientation.
9   Clean the respective parts for inspection. Inspect and renew any parts which are excessively worn, cracked or distorted. Rotate the breaker plate and check that a slight resistance is felt. Renew it if there is a strong resistance or it binds.
10 If there is excessive wear in the drivegear or governor shaft, grind or file the peened face end of the retaining pin then supporting the shaft/gear assembly, drive out the pin. Remove the gear then undo the two bolts at the base of the distributor housing and drive out the governor shaft using a soft-faced hammer (Fig. 4.19).
11 To reassemble the drivegear and governor, align the holes of the bearing retainer and housing, insert the governor shaft and fit the two retaining bolts.
12 Align the pin hole in the shaft and gear and drive a new retaining pin into position, taking care not to damage the gear. Squeeze the ends of the pin in a vice to peen over the ends for security. Note that the punch mark on the gear and the notch on the signal rotor must align when fitted.
13 Smear the governor shaft with a light coating of oil then fit the signal rotor on the shaft and align the 10.5 mark with the stopper (Fig. 4.21).
14 Fit the governor weights with bearings, as noted during dismantling, and secure using new snap-rings. Locate the springs as noted during reassembly.
15 Locate and tighten the rotor retaining screw, then lubricate the stopper with grease and insert it.
16 Locate the four clips onto the breaker plate in the slots in the housing then fit the hold-down clips and screws.
17 Refit the vacuum advancer using a new gasket and a new retaining clip to secure the arm on the pivot pin. Check that the clip engages in the groove in the pin.
18 Refit the signal generator into position but do not fully tighten the securing screws until after the air gap has been adjusted. To set the air gap, align a rotor tooth with the pick-up coil then insert a feeler gauge of the thickness specified for the air gap. Move the breaker plate to set the air gap clearance then tighten the retaining screws.
19 Refit the dust cover, locate the sealing ring and fit the rotor arm.
20 Check that the O-ring seal is in its groove on its lower end of the distributor before fitting it to the engine.
21 Check that the vacuum advancer operates in a satisfactory manner by applying a vacuum to the diaphragm hose connector(s). The advancer should be seen to move in accordance with the amount of vacuum applied (Fig. 4.23).

11.1 Transistorized distributor
A   Plastic dust cover
B   Seal ring
C   Advancer arm pivot

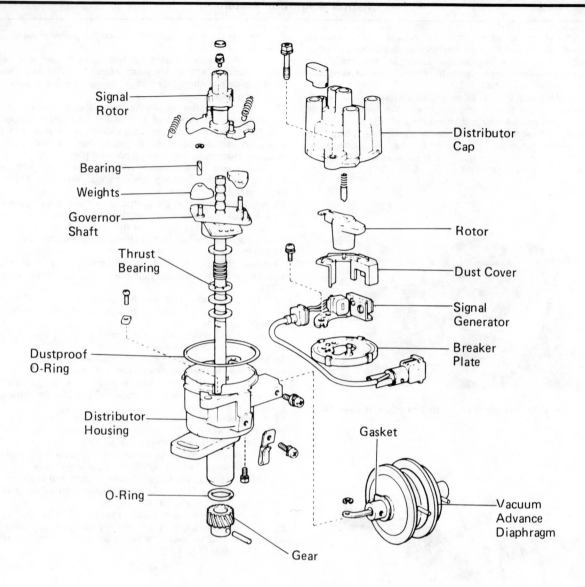

Fig. 4.18 Exploded view of the transistorized distributor (Sec 11)

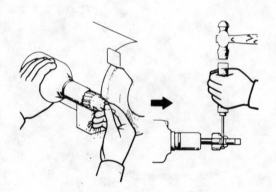

Fig. 4.19 Distributor driven gear removal method (Sec 11)

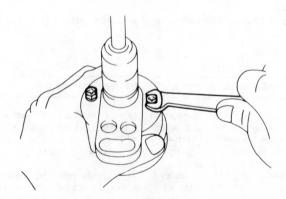

Fig. 4.20 Refit the retaining bolts (Sec 11)

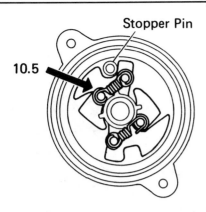

Fig. 4.21 Align the 10.5 mark with the stopper pin (Sec 11)

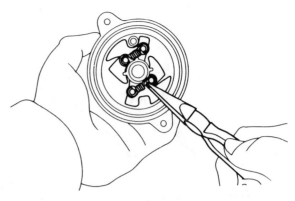

Fig. 4.22 Refit the centrifugal advance springs (Sec 11)

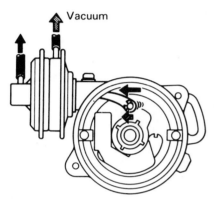

Fig. 4.23 Vacuum advance check (Sec 11)

12 Ignition timing – checking and adjustment

1 To set the ignition timing statically, such as when the distributor is being refitted, refer to Section 9. This describes the initial setting procedure so that the engine can be restarted and the timing checked dynamically.

2 A dynamic timing check must be made whenever the engine is being tuned (prior to fuel system adjustments), whenever any part of the ignition system has been repaired or renewed, or after reassembling the engine after an overhaul.

3 To check the ignition timing dynamically, the engine must be warmed up to its normal operating temperature and running at its normal idle speed.

All UK models, and USA models up to 1984

4 Pull off the vacuum advance pipe from the distributor diaphragm and plug the pipe(s).

5 Connect a stroboscope in accordance with the manufacturer's instructions (usually between No 1 spark plug and the end of No 1 spark plug lead).

6 Point the stroboscope at the timing cover scale when the notch in the crankshaft pulley and the appropriate (BTDC) mark on the scale will appear stationary. Any difficulty in observing these marks clearly can be overcome by painting them with quick drying white paint.

7 If the timing is correct, the notch should appear to be in alignment with the specified BTDC mark on the scale. If it is out of alignment then loosen the distributor clamp bolt and turn the distributor body one way or the other. Retighten the clamp bolt when adjustment is correct. Gross errors in ignition timing will be due to incorrect installation of the distributor. Refer to Section 9.

8 While the stroboscope is connected, it is useful to check the efficiency of the centrifugal and vacuum advance mechanisms of the distributor.

9 With the vacuum pipe(s) still disconnected and plugged, speed up the engine. The timing marks which were in alignment at idling will move apart, proving that the centrifugal advance mechanism is operating.

10 Now reconnect the vacuum pipe(s) to the distributor and again speed up the engine. The timing marks will move apart a much greater distance for the same relative engine speed. This proves that both the centrifugal and vacuum advance mechanisms of the distributor are functioning.

HAC system models

11 Some USA models will be fitted with a high altitude compensation (HAC) system, the function of which is described in Chapter 3, Section 44.

12 On these models the ignition timing is checked dynamically in the same manner as that for other models using the stroboscope method. When checking at low or high altitude with the vacuum hose disconnected from the distributor sub-diaphragm (the inner diaphragm), the ignition timing should be as specified (Fig. 4.25).

13 A second check should then be made but this time with the vacuum hose reconnected to the sub-diaphragm. With the hose reconnected the ignition timing should then be advanced a further 7° at idle speed. As an example: if the specified ignition timing is 5° (with the vacuum hose detached) it should then be 12° BTDC (with the vacuum hose reconnected) at either high or low altitude.

Dynamic timing – 1985 USA models

14 On these models the ignition timing is controlled by an Electronic Spark Advance (ESA) system, the basic details of which are described in Section 1. With this system, the dynamic timing method differs slightly to that described for earlier models.

15 Proceed as described in paragraphs 3 and 5.

16 Remove the plug from the engine check connector and connect a short length of wire between the T and E1 terminals in the connector. Now check and if necessary adjust the timing as described in paragraphs 6 and 7. It should be set at 5° BTDC.

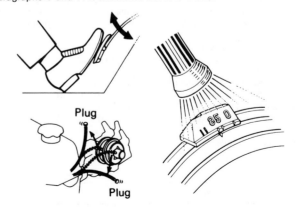

Fig. 4.24 Ignition timing check (Sec 12)

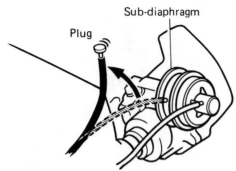
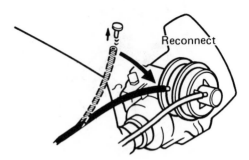

Fig. 4.25 Ignition timing check for USA models with HAC system – 1st stage check, detach sub-diaphragm hose only (Sec 12)

Fig. 4.26 Second stage ignition timing check (USA models with HAC system) – reconnect sub-diaphragm hose (Sec 12)

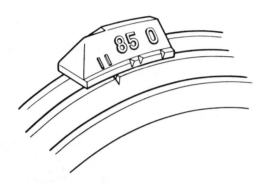
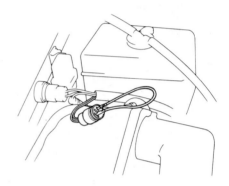

Fig. 4.27 Ignition timing advanced to 12° BTDC – USA models with HAC system (Sec 12)

Fig. 4.28 Ignition timing check method (1985 USA models). Bridge terminals T and E1 (Sec 12)

17 Disconnect the wire from the T and E1 terminals, and recheck the timing. It should now be 12° BTDC at idle speed.
18 Refit the engine check connector plug and disconnect the stroboscope to complete.

13 Ignition coil – checking, removal and refitting

1 The ignition coil requires no maintenance apart from periodic checks to ensure that the wiring connections are in good condition and secure.
2 If the coil is suspected of malfunction it can be checked using an ohmmeter.
3 Detach the high tension lead from the centre of the coil (photo) then connect up an ohmmeter between the positive and negative low tension terminals as shown (Fig. 4.29) to check the primary coil resistance.
4 To check the secondary coil resistance measure the resistance between the high tension terminal and the positive low tension terminal (Fig. 4.30).
5 If the ignition coil is defective it must be renewed.
6 To remove the coil, first detach the battery earth lead, then disconnect the low and high tension leads from the coil.
7 Unbolt and remove the coil, then detach the ignition igniter unit from it.
8 Refit in the reverse order of removal. Ensure that the wiring connections are correctly and securely made.

14 Igniter unit – checking

1 The igniter can be tested if a voltmeter is available. Turn on the ignition then connect the positive probe of the voltmeter to the positive

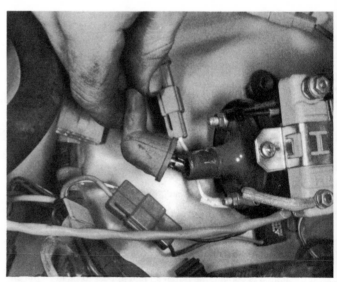

13.3 Disconnecting the HT lead from the ignition coil

terminal on the ignition coil. Earth the negative probe and check that there is a 12 volt reading (Fig. 4.31).
2 Now connect the positive probe of the voltmeter to the negative terminal of the ignition coil. Earth the negative probe. Again there should be a 12 volt reading (photo).
3 Disconnect the low tension lead connector to the distributor then, using a 1.5 volt dry cell battery, connect a length of wire between the

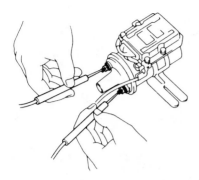

Fig. 4.29 Coil primary resistance check method (Sec 13)

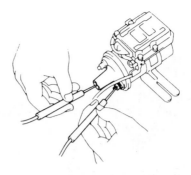

Fig. 4.30 Coil secondary resistance check method (Sec 13)

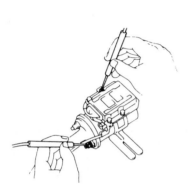

Fig. 4.31 Igniter power source line voltage check method (Sec 14)

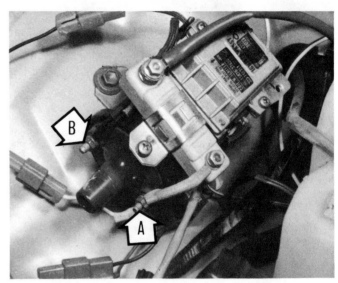

14.2 View of ignition coil and igniter unit
A   Coil positive terminal
B   Coil negative terminal

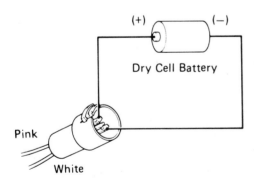

Fig. 4.32 Connect low tension leads to 1.5 dry cell battery as shown (Sec 14)

Note: *do not leave connected longer than five seconds*

positive pole of the battery and the pink wire terminal in the LT connector (Fig. 4.32). Connect a second length of wire between the battery negative pole and the white wire terminal in the LT connector. **Note:** *These wires must not be left connected for a period exceeding 5 seconds or the power transistor in the igniter will be damaged. The voltage applied is for test purposes only.*
4   Connect the voltmeter, as described in paragraph 2, and check that the voltage reading is 5 to 8 volts. Disconnect the probe wires and the wires to the LT connector. Turn off the ignition.
5   The igniter must be renewed if found to be defective.

15 Spark plugs and HT leads

1   The correct functioning of the spark plugs is vital for the correct running and efficiency of the engine. The plugs fitted as standard are listed in the Specifications page.
2   At specified intervals, the plugs should be removed, examined, cleaned and, if worn excessively, renewed. The condition of the spark plug will also tell much about the overall condition of the engine.
3   When detaching the spark plug leads grip and pull on the rubber insulator sleeve, not on the lead itself (photo). To unscrew the spark plug(s), use the plug spanner supplied in the vehicle tool kit or a suitable extension socket to reach the plug body hexagon section which is recessed within the cylinder head (photo). Take care not to tilt the socket during plug removal and refitting or you may break the ceramic insulator. On removal of a plug inspect the insulator nose of the plug before cleaning it since it is this which is the guide to the efficiency of combustion.
4   If the insulator nose of the spark plug is clean and white, with no deposits, this is indicative of a weak mixture, or too hot a plug.
5   If the top and insulator nose is covered with hard black looking deposits, then this is indicative that the mixture is too rich. Should the plug be black and oily, then it is likely that the engine is fairly worn, as well as the mixture being too rich.
6   If the insulator nose is covered with light tan to greyish brown deposits, then the mixture is correct and it is likely that the engine is in good condition.

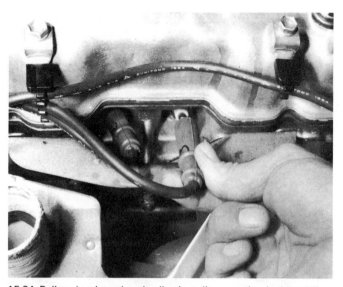

15.3A Pull on insulator (not lead) when disconnecting ignition HT leads

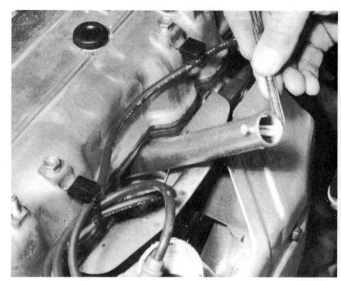

15.3B Plug removal using spanner supplied with vehicle

7   If there are any traces of long brown tapering stains on the outside of the white portion of the plug, then the plug will have to be renewed, as this shows that there is a faulty joint between the plug body and the insulator, and compression is being allowed to leak away.

8   Plugs should be cleaned by a sand blasting machine, which will free them from carbon more thoroughly than cleaning by hand. The machine will also test the condition of the plugs under compression. Any plug that fails to spark at the recommended pressure should be renewed.

9   The spark plug gap is of considerable importance, as if it is too large or too small the size of the spark and its efficiency will be seriously impaired. The spark plug should be set to the specified clearance.

10   To set it, measure the gap with a feeler gauge, and then bend open, or close the outer plug electrode until the correct gap is achieved. The centre electrode should never be bent as this may crack the insulation and cause plug failure.

11   The HT leads to the coil and spark plugs may be of internal resistance, carbon core type. They are used in the interest of eliminating interference caused by the ignition system. They are much more easily damaged than copper cored cable and they should be pulled from the spark plug terminals by gripping the metal end fitting at the end of the cable. Occasionally wipe the external surfaces of the leads free from oil and dirt using a fuel moistened cloth.

12   Always check the connection of the HT leads to the spark plugs (and distributor cap) is in correct firing order sequence 1-3-4-2.

13   If it is necessary to detach the HT leads from the distributor cap at any time, do not pull on the leads, but grip the rubber insulators and pull on them. Note the sequence of the leads for correct refitting.

16 Fault diagnosis – ignition system

Symptom	Reason(s)
Engine turns over normally on starter but will not fire	Damp HT leads or moisture inside distributor cap Faulty condenser/igniter (as applicable) Oil on contact breaker points/signal generator (as applicable) Disconnected lead at distributor, ignition switch or coil
Engine runs but misfires	Faulty spark plug Faulty HT lead Contact breaker gap too close, too wide or pitted points Signal generator air gap too close or too wide Crack in rotor arm Crack in distributor cap Faulty coil
Engine overheats or lacks power	Faulty distributor condenser/or igniter (as applicable) Seized centrifugal advance weights or cam on shaft Perforated vacuum pipe from vacuum diaphragm unit Incorrectly timed ignition
Engine 'pinks' (pre-detonation) under load	Ignition timing too advanced Centrifugal advance mechanism stuck in advance position Broken centrifugal advance spring Octane rating of fuel too low

Measuring plug gap. A feeler gauge of the correct size (see ignition system specifications) should have a slight 'drag' when slid between the electrodes. Adjust gap if necessary

Adjusting plug gap. The plug gap is adjusted by bending the earth electrode inwards, or outwards, as necessary until the correct clearance is obtained. Note the use of the correct tool

Normal. Grey-brown deposits, lightly coated core nose. Gap increasing by around 0.001 in (0.025 mm) per 1000 miles (1600 km). Plugs ideally suited to engine, and engine in good condition

Carbon fouling. Dry, black, sooty deposits. Will cause weak spark and eventually misfire. Fault: over-rich fuel mixture. Check: carburettor mixture settings, float level and jet sizes; choke operation and cleanliness of air filter. Plugs can be re-used after cleaning

Oil fouling. Wet, oily deposits. Will cause weak spark and eventually misfire. Fault: worn bores/piston rings or valve guides; sometimes occurs (temporarily) during running-in period. Plugs can be re-used after thorough cleaning

Overheating. Electrodes have glazed appearance, core nose very white – few deposits. Fault: plug overheating. Check: plug value, ignition timing, fuel octane rating (too low) and fuel mixture (too weak). Discard plugs and cure fault immediately

Electrode damage. Electrodes burned away; core nose has burned, glazed appearance. Fault: pre-ignition. Check: as for 'Overheating' but may be more severe. Discard plugs and remedy fault before piston or valve damage occurs

Split core nose (may appear initially as a crack). Damage is self-evident, but cracks will only show after cleaning. Fault: pre-ignition or wrong gap-setting technique. Check: ignition timing, cooling system, fuel octane rating (too low) and fuel mixture (too weak). Discard plugs, rectify fault immediately

Chapter 5 Clutch

Contents

Specifications

Type	Single dry plate, diaphragm spring. Hydraulic actuation

Pedal
Free play:
UK models	13 to 23 mm (0.51 to 0.91 in)
1982 and 1983 USA models	13 to 23 mm (0.51 to 0.91 in)
1983 on USA models (with turn over type)	5 to 15 mm (0.20 to 0.59 in)
Pushrod play at pedal	1.0 to 1.5 mm (0.04 to 0.20 in)
Pedal height	154 to 164 mm (6.06 to 6.46 in)

Clutch disc
Run-out (maximum)	0.8 mm (0.031 in)
Rivet depth (minimum)	0.3 mm (0.012 in)

Diaphragm spring
Wear limit – depth	0.6 mm (0.024 in)
Wear limit – width	5.0 mm (0.197 in)

Torque wrench settings

	kgf m	lbf ft
Clutch master cylinder bolt/nut:		
UK models, and USA models up to 1983	2.0 to 3.0	14 to 22
USA models – 1984	2.5	18
USA models – 1985	1.3	9
Clutch housing to engine:		
UK models, and USA models up to 1983	5.0 to 8.0	36 to 58
USA models – 1984	6.5	47
USA models – 1985	7.3	53
Clutch cover to flywheel	1.8	13
Release fork support to clutch housing	4.0	29

1 General description

The clutch consists of a steel cover which is bolted and dowelled to the rear face of the flywheel and contains the pressure plate and clutch disc (driven plate).

The pressure plate and diaphragm spring are attached to the clutch assembly cover.

The clutch disc is free to slide along the splined gearbox input shaft and is held in position between the flywheel and pressure plate by the pressure of the diaphragm spring.

Friction lining material is riveted to the clutch disc which has a cushioned hub to absorb transmission shocks and to help ensure a smooth take off.

With the hydraulically operated clutch system the pendant clutch pedal is connected to the clutch master cylinder and hydraulic fluid reservoir by a short pushrod. The master cylinder and fluid reservoir are mounted on the engine side of the bulkhead in front of the driver.

Depressing the clutch pedal moves the piston in the master cylinder forwards, so forcing hydraulic fluid through to the slave cylinder. The piston in the slave cylinder moves rearwards on the entry of the fluid and actuates the clutch release arm, via a short pushrod. The opposite end of the release arm is forked and carries the release bearing assembly.

As the pivoted clutch release arm moves rearwards it pushes the release bearing forwards to bear against the diaphragm spring and pushes forwards so moving the pressure plate backwards and disengaging the pressure plate from the clutch disc.

When the clutch pedal is released the pressure plate is forced into contact with the high friction bearings on the clutch disc and at the same time pushes the clutch disc a fraction of an inch forwards on its splines so engaging the clutch disc with the flywheel. The clutch disc is now firmly sandwiched between the pressure plate and the flywheel so the drive is taken up.

2 Routine maintenance – clutch

1 **Hydraulic fluid level:** Check the level of the hydraulic fluid in the clutch master cylinder reservoir at regular intervals. The fluid must be kept within 10 mm (0.4 in) beneath the MAX mark on the reservoir body. If topping-up is necessary, only use the specified fluid type, do not overfill and take care not to spill fluid onto the bodywork. Also ensure that no dirt is allowed to enter the hydraulic system (photo).
2 The need for regular topping-up indicates a fault in the hydraulic system and this should be traced and repaired without delay.
3 **Clutch pedal height and free play:** Periodically check the clutch pedal height setting and free play, as described in Section 3. If the vehicle is used in heavy traffic on a regular basis, the check should be made at regular intervals of say three months, depending on mileage and conditions.

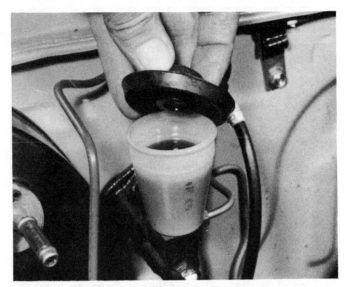

2.1 Fluid level check – clutch master cylinder

3 Clutch pedal – adjustment

Pedal height
1 Measure the distance from the floor to the clutch pedal and check the pedal height. The pedal should be in its fully retracted position when making the measurement. If the pedal height is not within the margin specified adjust as follows.
2 Loosen the adjustment bolt locknut and then turn the bolt to set the height within the range specified. Retighten the locknut. The clutch pedal free play must now be checked.

Pedal free play
3 The clutch pedal free play is the distance through which the pedal can be depressed with the fingers until firm resistance is met. Measure the free play and check it against the specified free play requirement.
4 If adjustment is required, loosen the pushrod locknut and then rotate the pushrod in the direction required to set the free play requirement. Tighten the locknut to secure the pushrod, then recheck the pedal height.

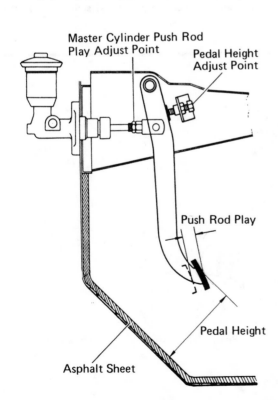

Fig. 5.1 Clutch pedal height and free play check points (Sec 3)

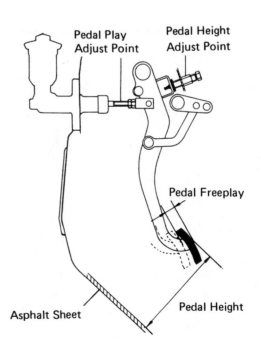

Fig. 5.2 Clutch pedal height and free play check points – turn-over type (Sec 3)

4 Clutch hydraulic system – bleeding

1   Gather together a clean jar, a length of rubber/plastic tubing which fits tightly over the bleed nipple on the slave cylinder, and a tin of hydraulic brake fluid. You will also need the help of an assistant.
2   Check that the master cylinder reservoir is full. If it is not, fill it and also fill the bottom two inches of the jar with hydraulic fluid.
3   Remove the rubber dust cap from the bleed nipple on the slave cylinder, and with a suitable spanner open the bleed nipple approximately three-quarters of a turn.
4   Place one end of the tube over the nipple and insert the other end in the jar so that the tube orifice is below the level of the fluid.
5   The assistant should now depress the pedal and hold it down at the end of its stroke. Allow the pedal to return to its normal position.
6   Continue this series of operations until clean hydraulic fluid without any traces of air bubbles emerges from the end of the tubing. Be sure that the reservoir is checked frequently to ensure that the hydraulic fluid does not drop too far, thus letting air into the system.
7   When no more air bubbles appear tighten the bleed nipple during a downstroke.
8   Refit the rubber dust cap over the bleed nipple.
9   Wipe away any hydraulic fluid that may have spilt onto the bodywork of the vehicle as the fluid is harmful to paintwork.

5.3 Clutch slave cylinder

5 Clutch slave cylinder – removal and refitting

1   Wipe the top of the clutch master cylinder, unscrew the cap and place a piece of polythene sheet over the top to create a partial vacuum and to stop hydraulic fluid syphoning out when the slave cylinder is removed. Refit the cap.
2   Wipe the area around the union on the slave cylinder and unscrew the union. Tape the end of the pipe to stop dirt entering.
3   Undo and remove the two cylinder retaining bolts and then withdraw the cylinder from the clutch housing, simultaneously disengaging the pushrod from the release arm (photo).
4   Refitting the clutch slave cylinder is the reverse sequence to removal. It will be necessary to bleed the hydraulic system, as decribed in Section 4.

6 Clutch release cylinder – overhaul

1   Clean the exterior of the slave cylinder using a dry non-fluffy rag.
2   Carefully ease back the dust cover from the end of the slave cylinder and lift away, together with the pushrod.
3   The piston and seal assembly should be ejected by the force of the spring. If for any reason they are stuck in the cylinder, try shaking them out. If a low pressure air line is available (a foot pump may suffice), apply a jet of air into the hydraulic line connection port but place a rag over the open end to catch the piston and spring with as they are ejected.

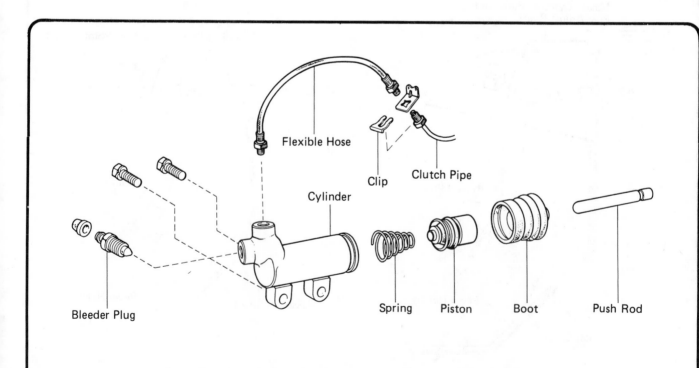

Fig. 5.3 Clutch slave cylinder components (Sec 6)

Lithium Soap Base Glycol Grease

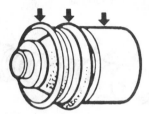

Fig. 5.4 Lubricate the slave cylinder piston and seals before refitting (Sec 6)

4   Thoroughly clean the piston and cylinder bore.
5   Carefully prise free the seals from the piston noting their orientation. Do not scratch the piston surfaces during removal of the seals.
6   Inspect the inside of the cylinder for score marks caused by any impurities in the hydraulic fluid. If any are found then the slave cylinder unit complete must be renewed.
7   The old rubber seals must be renewed irrespective of condition.
8   Smear the new seals with hydraulic fluid and fit into position on the piston. Use only the fingers to manipulate the seals into position.
9   To reassemble, first insert the spring into the cylinder with its wide taper leading. Lubricate the piston and seals with lithium soap base glycol grease or hydraulic fluid, then carefully insert the piston into the cylinder. Gently edge the leading edge of the seal into the bore so that it does not distort.
10 Refit the dust cover boot over the end of the cylinder, then insert the pushrod. The clutch release cylinder is now ready for refitting.

7 Clutch master cylinder – removal and refitting

1   Drain the fluid from the clutch master cylinder reservoir by attaching a rubber or plastic tube to the slave cylinder bleed nipple. Undo the nipple by approximately three-quarters of a turn and then pump the fluid out into a suitable container by operating the clutch pedal repeatedly until the fluid reservoir is empty.
2   Place a rag under the master cylinder to catch any hydraulic fluid that may be spilt. Unscrew the union nut from the end of the metal pipe

7.2 Clutch master cylinder showing mounting nut and hydraulic pipe connection

where it enters the clutch master cylinder and gently pull the pipe clear (photo).
3   Withdraw the split pin that retains the pushrod yoke to the pedal clevis pin and remove the clevis pin.
4   Undo and remove the nut (engine side) and bolt (inside) that secure the master cylinder to the bulkhead. Lift away the master cylinder, taking care not to allow hydraulic fluid to come into contact with the paintwork.
5   Refitting the master cylinder is the reverse sequence to removal. Bleed the system, as described in Section 4 and finally adjust the clutch pedal height and free play, as described in Section 3.

8 Clutch master cylinder – overhaul

1   Clean the exterior of the master cylinder using a non-fluffy rag.
2   Peel back the flexible boot from the end of the master cylinder to expose the circlip. Extract the snap-ring so that the pushrod and piston stop plate can be withdrawn (Fig. 5.5).

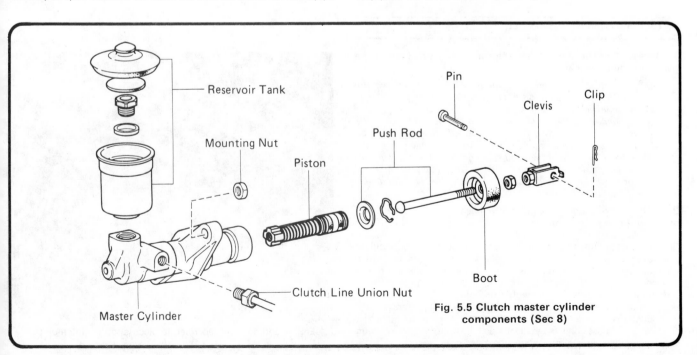

Fig. 5.5 Clutch master cylinder components (Sec 8)

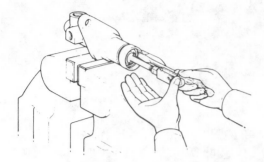

Fig. 5.6 Withdrawing the clutch master cylinder pushrod (Sec 8)

Rubber Grease

Fig. 5.7 Lubricate the clutch master cylinder piston seals before fitting (Sec 8)

3   Remove the piston/seal assembly by either tapping the end of the master cylinder on a block of hardwood or by applying air pressure at the fluid outlet port.

4   Examine the bore of the cylinder carefully for any signs of scores or ridges and, if this is found to be smooth all over, new seals can be fitted. If there is any doubt of the condition of the bore then a new cylinder must be fitted complete.

5   If examination of the seals shows them to be apparently oversize or swollen, or very loose on the piston, suspect oil contamination in the system. Ordinary lubricating oil will swell these rubber seals, and if one is found to be swollen it is reasonable to assume that all seals in the clutch hydraulic system will need attention. Fit them using the fingers only to manipulate them into position.

6   Thoroughly clean all parts in either fresh hydraulic fluid or methylated spirit. Ensure that the bypass parts are clean.

7   All components should be assembled wetted with clean hydraulic fluid, or lithium soap based glycol grease.

8   Check that the master cylinder bore is clean and smear with clean hydraulic fluid. With the piston suitably wetted with hydraulic fluid, carefully insert the assembly into the bore – valve end first. Ease the lip of the piston seal carefully into the bore.

9   Refit the pushrod and refit the snap-ring into the groove in the cylinder bore. Smear the sealing areas of the dust cover with a little rubber grease and pack the cover with the rubber grease so as to act as a dust trap. Fit the cover to the master cylinder body. The master cylinder is now ready for refitting to the car.

5   It is important that no oil or grease gets on the clutch disc friction linings, or the pressure plate and flywheel faces. It is advisable to handle the parts with clean hands and to wipe down the pressure plate and flywheel faces with a clean dry rag before inspection or refitting commences.

6   In the normal course of events clutch dismantling and reassembly is the term for simply fitting a new clutch pressure plate and disc. Under no circumstances should the pressure plate assembly be dismantled. If a fault develops in the assembly an exchange replacement must be fitted.

7   If a new clutch disc is being fitted it is false economy not to renew the release bearing at the same time. This will preclude having to replace it at a later time when wear on the clutch linings is very slight, see Section 10.

8   Examine the clutch disc friction linings for wear or loose rivets and the disc for rim distortion, cracks and worn splines.

9   Renew the clutch disc complete, do not attempt to reline this component yourself.

10 Check the machine faces of the flywheel and the pressure plate. If either is badly grooved it should be machined until smooth, or replaced with a new item. If the pressure plate is cracked or split it must be renewed.

11 Examine the hub splines for wear and make sure that the centre hub is not loose.

12 Check the pilot bearing in the crankshaft rear face and renew it if it shows any signs of advanced wear (see Chapter 1, photo 18.10).

9   Clutch – removal and inspection

1   Access to the clutch unit and the clutch release mechanism can be gained in one of three ways:

(a)   *By removing the gearbox leaving the engine in position in the vehicle, as described in Chapter 6*

(b)   *By removing the engine*

(c)   *By removing the engine and gearbox. Method (a) is the easiest, whilst method (b) is advisable if other work is to be undertaken on the engine. Method (c) is normally only used if a major overhaul of the engine and gearbox are also required. With method (c), the engine and gearbox must be separated for access to the clutch (photo). Refer to Chapter 1 for details of methods (b) and (c)*

2   With a centre punch, mark the relative position of the clutch cover and flywheel to ensure correct refitting if the original parts are to be reused.

3   Remove the clutch assembly by unscrewing the six bolts holding the cover to the rear face of the flywheel. Unscrew the bolts in a diagonal sequence half a turn at a time to prevent distortion of the cover flange, also to prevent an accident caused by the cover flange binding on the dowels and suddenly flying off.

4   With the bolts removed, lift the assembly off the locating dowels. The clutch disc will fall out at this stage, as it is not attached to either the clutch cover assembly or flywheel. Carefully note which way round the disc is fitted (greater projecting side away from flywheel).

9.1 Engine and gearbox separated for access to the clutch unit

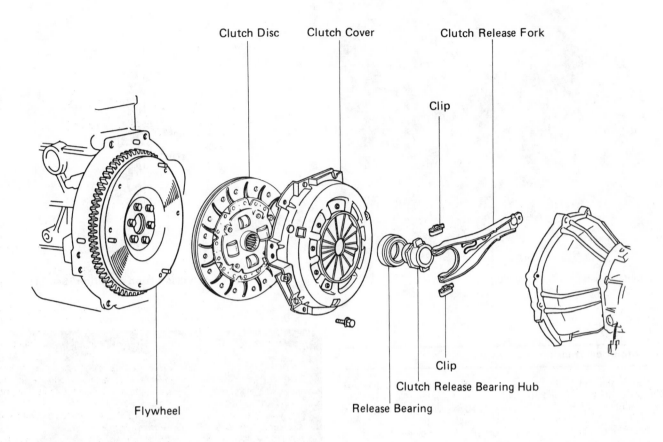

Fig. 5.8 Clutch unit components (Sec 9)

10 Clutch release bearing – removal and refitting

1   To gain access to the clutch release bearing refer to paragraph 1 in the previous Section.
2   Detach the spring clips from the release bearing carrier and release fork. Draw the release bearing carrier from the flat bearing retainer (photo).
3   Check the bearing for signs of overheating, wear or roughness, and, if evident, the old bearing should be removed by pressing or drifting it from the carrier. Note which way round the bearing is fitted.
4   Using a bench vice and suitable packing, press a new bearing onto the carrier (Fig. 5.9).
5   Apply some high melting-point grease to the contact surfaces of the release lever and pivot assembly, and bearing carrier. Pack some grease into the inner recess of the bearing carrier (photo).
6   Refitting the bearing and carrier is the reverse sequence to removal.

10.2 Clutch release bearing and spring clip to release arm location

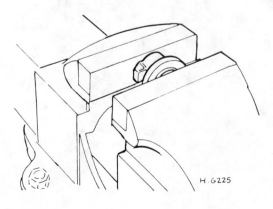

Fig. 5.9 Pressing a new clutch release bearing into the carrier (Sec 10)

10.5 Clutch release arm – grease the pivot

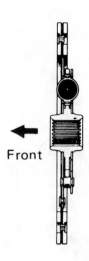

Fig. 5.10 Clutch disc fitting direction (Sec 11)

11 Clutch – centralising and refitting

1   To refit the clutch plate, place the clutch disc against the flywheel with the larger end of the hub away from the flywheel (Fig. 5.10). On no account should the clutch disc be refitted the wrong way round as it will be found impossible to operate the clutch (photo).

2   Refit the clutch cover assembly loosely on the dowels. Locate the six bolts and tighten them finger tight so that the clutch disc is gripped but can still be moved.

3   The clutch disc must now be centralised so that when the engine and gearbox are mated, the gearbox input shaft splines will pass through the splines in the centre of the hub.

4   Centralisation can be carried out quite easily by inserting a round bar or long screwdriver through the hole in the centre of the clutch, so that the end of the bar rests in the small hole in the crankshaft containing the input shaft bearing bush. Moving the bar sideways or up and down will move the clutch disc in whichever direction is necessary to achieve centralisation (photo).

11.1 Refitting the clutch disc

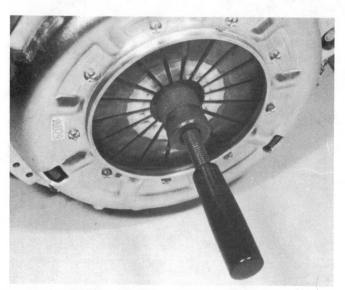

11.4 Centralising the clutch disc

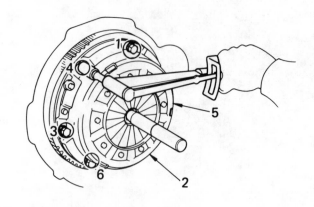

Fig. 5.11 Clutch cover bolts to be tightened in sequence shown (Sec 11)

11.6 Tighten the retaining bolts to the specified torque

12.3 General view of clutch pedal assembly showing return spring and retaining clip through the clevis pin

5   Centralisation is easily judged by removing the bar or screwdriver and viewing the driveplate hub in relation to the hole in the centre of the diaphragm spring. When the hub is exactly in the centre of the release bearing hole, all is correct. Alternatively, if an old input shaft can be borrowed this will eliminate all the guesswork as it will fit the bearing and centre of the clutch hub exactly, obviating the need for visual alignment.
6   Tighten the clutch bolts firmly in sequence (Fig. 5.11) to ensure that the cover plate is pulled down evenly and without distortion of the flange. Tighten the bolts to the specified torque setting (photo).

12 Clutch pedal – removal and refitting

1   Remove the lower trim panel on the driver's side for access.
2   Disconnect the return spring.
3   Prise free the retaining clip and withdraw the clevis pin (photo).
4   Undo the pivot bolt nut, withdraw the bolt and remove the pedal.
5   Inspect and renew any worn components as necessary.
6   Refitting is a reversal of the removal procedure. Lubricate the pivot with grease during assembly. On completion check and if necessary adjust the clutch pedal, as described in Section 3.

13 Fault diagnosis – clutch

Symptom	Reason(s)
Judder when taking up drive	Loose engine or gearbox mountings Clutch disc linings worn or contaminated with oil Worn splines in clutch disc hub or on input shaft of gearbox Worn flywheel centre spigot bearing
Clutch spin (failure to disengage completely so that gears cannot be meshed)	Incorrect clutch pedal free movement Air in clutch hydraulic system Damaged or misaligned pressure plate assembly
Clutch slip (increase in engine speed does not result in vehicle speed increasing – particularly on uphill gradients)	Incorrect pedal free movement Clutch disc friction linings worn out or oil contaminated
Noise evident on depressing clutch pedal	Faulty or worn release bearing Insufficient pedal free movement
Noise evident as clutch pedal released	Distorted clutch disc Weak driven plate torsion shock absorbers in hub Insufficient pedal free movement Weak or broken pedal or release lever return spring Distorted or worn input shaft Release bearing loose on retainer hub

Chapter 6
Manual gearbox and automatic transmission

Contents

Specifications

Manual gearbox
General

Type	Five-speed, all synchromesh
Application:	
UK models	W55 and W57
USA models	W58

Ratios

	W55 and W57	W58
1st	3.28 to 1	3.29 to 1
2nd	1.89 to 1	1.89 to 1
3rd	1.27 to 1	1.28 to 1
4th	1.00 to 1	1.00 to 1
5th	0.86 to 1	0.79 to 1
Reverse	3.48 to 1	3.47 to 1

Lubrication

Capacity:	
UK models	2.4 litre (4.2 Imp pints)
USA models	2.4 litre (2.5 US qt)

Tolerances (all models)

Output shaft (wear limits):	
2nd gear journal diameter	42.85 mm (1.6870 in)
3rd gear journal diameter	37.80 mm (1.4882 in)
Flange thickness	5.60 mm (0.2205 in)
Run-out	0.06 mm (0.0024 in)
1st gear inner race flange thickness	4.70 mm (0.1850 in)
1st gear inner race outside diameter	42.85 mm (1.6870 in)
1st/2nd gear inside diameter	49.15 mm (1.9350 in)
3rd gear inside diameter	38.15 mm (1.5020 in)
5th counter gear inside diameter	33.15 mm (1.3051 in)
Reverse idler gear inside diameter	20.2 mm (0.795 in)
Counter gear:	
Centre bearing journal outside diameter	29.90 mm (1.1772 in)
5th gear journal outside diameter	26.85 mm (1.0571 in)

Reverse idler gear shaft outside diameter .... 19.9 mm (0.783 in)
Reverse shift arm shoe-to-idler gear groove clearance .... 0.90 mm (0.035 in)

Gear thrust clearance:

    1st, 2nd and 3rd:

        Standard .... 0.10 to 0.25 mm (0.0039 to 0.0098 in)

        Limit .... 0.30 mm (0.0118 in)

    5th counter gear:

        Standard .... 0.10 to 0.41 mm (0.0039 to 0.0161 in)

        Limit .... 0.46 mm (0.0181 in)

Gear oil clearances:

    1st and 2nd:

        Standard .... 0.009 to 0.060 mm (0.0004 to 0.0024 in)

        Limit .... 0.15 mm (0.0059 in)

    3rd gear:

        Standard .... 0.060 to 0.103 mm (0.0024 to 0.0041 in)

        Limit .... 0.20 mm (0.0079 in)

    5th counter gear:

        Standard .... 0.009 to 0.062 mm (0.0004 to 0.0024 in)

        Limit .... 0.15 mm (0.0059 in)

Shift fork-to-hub sleeve clearance:

    Limit .... 1.0 mm (0.039 in)

Synchroniser ring to gear:

    Standard .... 0.7 to 1.7 mm (0.028 to 0.067 in)

    Limit .... 0.5 mm (0.020 in)

Input shaft snap-ring thickness .... 2.05 to 2.10 mm (0.0807 to 0.0827 in)
2.10 to 2.15 mm (0.0827 to 0.0846 in)
2.15 to 2.20 mm (0.0846 to 0.0866 in)
2.20 to 2.25 mm (0.0866 to 0.0886 in)
2.25 to 2.30 mm (0.0886 to 0.0906 in)
2.30 to 2.35 mm (0.0906 to 0.0925 in)
2.35 to 2.40 mm (0.0925 to 0.0945 in)

Output shaft snap-ring thickness:

    Front .... 1.80 to 1.85 mm (0.0709 to 0.0728 in)
1.86 to 1.91 mm (0.0732 to 0.0752 in)
1.92 to 1.97 mm (0.0756 to 0.0776 in)
1.98 to 2.03 mm (0.0780 to 0.0799 in)
2.04 to 2.09 mm (0.0803 to 0.0823 in)
2.10 to 2.15 mm (0.0827 to 0.0846 in)

    Rear .... 2.31 to 2.36 mm (0.0909 to 0.0929 in)
2.37 to 2.42 mm (0.0933 to 0.0953 in)
2.43 to 2.48 mm (0.0957 to 0.0976 in)
2.49 to 2.54 mm (0.0980 to 0.1000 in)
2.55 to 2.60 mm (0.1004 to 0.1024 in)
2.61 to 2.66 mm (0.1028 to 0.1047 in)
2.68 to 2.73 mm (0.1055 to 0.1075 in)
2.74 to 2.79 mm (0.1079 to 0.1098 in)

    Reverse gear .... 2.25 to 2.30 mm (0.0886 to 0.0906 in)
2.30 to 2.35 mm (0.0906 to 0.0925 in)
2.35 to 2.40 mm (0.0925 to 0.0945 in)
2.40 to 2.45 mm (0.0945 to 0.0965 in)
2.45 to 2.50 mm (0.0965 to 0.0984 in)
2.50 to 2.55 mm (0.0984 to 0.1004 in)
2.55 to 2.60 mm (0.1004 to 0.1024 in)
2.61 to 2.66 mm (0.1028 to 0.1047 in)
2.67 to 2.72 mm (0.1051 to 0.1071 in)
2.73 to 2.78 mm (0.1075 to 0.1094 in)
2.79 to 2.84 mm (0.1098 to 0.1118 in)
2.85 to 2.90 mm (0.1122 to 0.1142 in)
2.91 to 2.96 mm (0.1146 to 0.1165 in)
2.97 to 3.02 mm (0.1169 to 0.1189 in)

Countergear snap-ring thickness:

    Front .... 2.05 to 2.10 mm (0.0807 to 0.0827 in)
2.10 to 2.15 mm (0.0827 to 0.0846 in)
2.15 to 2.20 mm (0.0846 to 0.0866 in)
2.20 to 2.25 mm (0.0866 to 0.0886 in)
2.25 to 2.30 mm (0.0886 to 0.0906 in)
2.30 to 2.35 mm (0.0906 to 0.0925 in)
2.35 to 2.40 mm (0.0925 to 0.0945 in)

    Rear .... 1.90 to 1.95 mm (0.0748 to 0.0768 in)
1.96 to 2.01 mm (0.0772 to 0.0791 in)
2.02 to 2.07 mm (0.0795 to 0.0815 in)
2.08 to 2.13 mm (0.0819 to 0.0839 in)
2.14 to 2.19 mm (0.0843 to 0.0862 in)
2.20 to 2.25 mm (0.0866 to 0.0886 in)
2.26 to 2.31 mm (0.0890 to 0.0909 in)

Clutch hub No 3 .... 2.06 to 2.11 mm (0.0811 to 0.0831 in)
2.12 to 2.17 mm (0.0835 to 0.0854 in)
2.18 to 2.23 mm (0.0858 to 0.0878 in)
2.24 to 2.29 mm (0.0882 to 0.0902 in)

Torque wrench settings

	kgf m	lbf ft
Shift fork set bolt	1.25	9
Straight screw plug	2.50	18
Idler shaft stopper bolt	2.50	18
Reserve restrictor pin	2.50	18
Front bearing retainer set bolt	2.50	18
Extension housing/intermediate plate	3.75	27
Restrictor pin	4.10	30
Shift lever housing/shift and selector lever	4.00	29
Shift lever retainer/extension housing	1.85	13
Drain and filler plugs	4.10	30
Reversing light switch	4.10	30
Clutch housing to transmission case	3.75	27
Output shaft centre bearing plate	1.30	9

Automatic transmission
General

Type .... Three-speed and overdrive, Type A40 D
Ratios:
    1st .... 2.450 to 1
    2nd .... 1.450 to 1
    3rd .... 1.000 to 1
    4th (overdrive) .... 0.689 to 1
    Reverse .... 2.222 to 1

Lubrication

Capacity:
    Drain and refill .... Up to 2.4 litre (4.2 Imp pints; 2.5 US qt)
    Dry fill .... 6.3 litre (11.0 Imp pints; 6.7 US qt)
Torque converter fluid capacity .... 2.0 litre (3.6 Imp pints; 2.1 US qt)

Tolerances

Driveplate run-out (maximum) .... 0.20 mm (0.0079 in)
Torque converter sleeve run-out (maximum) .... 0.30 mm (0.0118 in)

Torque wrench settings

	kfg m	lbf ft
Engine to transmission	6.50	47
Transmission housing:		
10 mm	3.45	25
12 mm	5.80	42
Extension housing	3.45	25
Rear support member	4.25	31
Driveplate	8.50	61
Torque converter	1.85	13
Centre support	2.60	25
Oil pan	0.45	3
Cooler pipe union nut	3.50	25
Parking lock pawl bracket	0.75	5
Neutral starter switch (bolt)	0.55	4
Neutral starter switch (nut)	0.70	5

1 General description – manual gearbox

The gearbox fitted to all models is of five forward gears and one reverse gear type. The gearbox is mounted in line at the rear of the engine, and drive is transmitted by a propeller shaft to the rear axle unit.

The gearbox comprises four sub-assemblies: the clutch housing, the main gearcase, the intermediate plate with gear assemblies, and the extension housing.

The reverse and fifth gear assemblies are positioned at the rear of the intermediate plate whilst the remaining forward gears are positioned on the front side. All forward gears have synchromesh. The intermediate plate also carries the selector rods whilst the main gear selector rod and change lever are carried in the extension housing.

2 Routine maintenance – manual gearbox

1 The only maintenance required is to check and top up, if necessary, the gearbox oil level or renew it at the intervals specified in the Routine Maintenance at the beginning of this manual.

2 Ideally the oil level check or renewal (as applicable) should be made with the vehicle over an inspection pit or on ramps. Failing this it will need to be raised and supported on axle stands but it must be level.

3 A combined oil level/filler plug is fitted in the side of the gearcasing. Unscrew and remove this plug (photo).

4 The oil level is correct when it is level with the bottom of the plug hole. Top up the level if necessary through the hole using only the specified grade of oil. Regular topping-up should not be necessary and

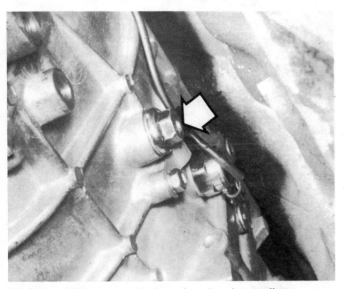

2.3 Oil level/filler plug on side face of gearbox (arrowed)

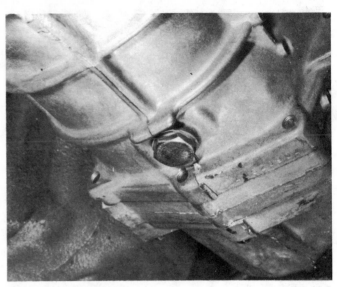

2.5 Gearbox oil drain plug

if persistent oil loss is noticed a front or rear oil seal are probably at fault and must be replaced. Refit the filler plug on completion.

5 At the specified intervals, remove the drain plug in the base of the gearcase and drain the oil into a suitable container for disposal. Refit and tighten the drain plug to the specified torque then top up the oil level using the specified grade. Refit the filler plug on completion (photo).

3 Manual gearbox – removal and refitting

1 If the engine is being removed at the same time, refer to Chapter 1 for removal procedure.
2 If the gearbox is to be removed on its own, carry out the following operations, having first drained the gearbox oil.
3 If an inspection pit is not available, run the rear roadwheels up on ramps or jack up the rear of the vehicle and secure on stands so that there is a clearance below the gearbox at least equal to the diameter of the clutch bellhousing to enable the gearbox to be removed from below, and to the rear of, the vehicle.
4 Disconnect the lead from the battery negative terminal.

5 Pull free the gear lever gaiter, undo the four retaining screws and withdraw the gaiter and plate (photos). Removal of the ashtray will give improved access to the forward screws.
6 Pull free the lower gaiter, undo the four retaining screws and remove the gear lever unit (photos).
7 You will now need to work underneath the vehicle.
8 Disconnect and remove propeller shaft, as described in Chapter 7.
9 Detach the exhaust pipe from the location plate on the clutch housing.
10 Disconnect the speedometer cable and the reverse light lead from the gearbox (photo).
11 Unbolt and remove the clutch slave cylinder from the clutch bellhousing. Support the cylinder out of the way leaving the hydraulic line attached to it. Take care not to dislodge the rubber end cover, or the pushrod piston assembly will be ejected under spring tension (together with hydraulic fluid). Also leave the operating rod in position in the unit.
12 Disconnect the leads from the starter motor, then unbolt and withdraw the starter motor.
13 On some models fitted with power steering it may be necessary to lower the steering gear unit to allow sufficient clearance when

3.5A Pull the upper gaiter free from the console

3.5B Remove the main gaiter and plate

3.6A Prise back the lower gaiter ...

3.6B ... undo the retaining bolts ...

3.6C ... and remove the gear lever

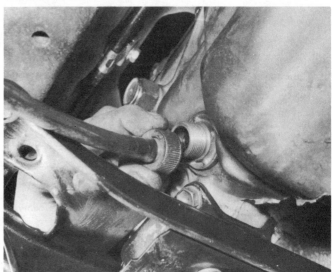

3.10 Detach the speedometer cable at the gearbox

withdrawing the gearbox from the engine. In such instances, refer to Chapter 10 and detach the tie-rod outer balljoints each side then undo the steering gear unit retaining bolts. Lower the steering gear unit complete without disconnecting the feed (pressure) and return hydraulic lines. Support the weight of the steering gear using a length of cord attached to the subframe crossmember.

14 Position a jack under the engine and support its weight. *Fit a suitable piece of flat wood between the jack saddle and the sump to prevent possible damage.*

15 Now position a second jack under the gearbox to support its weight. If possible use a trolley jack as this is more practical during the actual withdrawal of the gearbox.

16 Unscrew and remove the four bolts (two each side) securing the gearbox support member to the floorpan. Note that one of the bolts also secures an earth strap (photo).

17 Unscrew and remove the engine-to-transmission securing bolts. Note the position of the exhaust support bracket and remove it. Also note that the reversing light switch lead is located in a clip attached by the upper right-hand securing bolt. At the bottom end, the stiffener brackets can be left attached to the engine on each side.

18 The gearbox is now ready for removal. An assistant should be at hand to help in supporting the weight of the gearbox as it is withdrawn and lowered from beneath the vehicle.

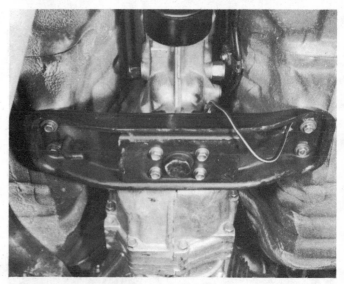

3.16 Rear mounting, showing earth lead location

19 Remove the gearbox by carefully pulling it rearwards whilst simultaneously moving the support jack at the rear and supporting the weight of the gearbox under the clutch housing. When the gearbox input shaft is clear of the clutch unit lower the gearbox and remove it from underneath the vehicle. During the initial withdrawal from the engine, do not allow the weight of the gearbox to be taken by the input shaft while the latter is still engaged in the splines of the clutch disc.

20 Refitting is a reversal of the removal procedure but note the following special points:

(a) If the clutch mechanism has been disturbed, make sure that the clutch disc has been centralised before refitting the gearbox (see Chapter 5)

(b) Apply a small amount of molybdenum disulphide lithium based grease to the input shaft splines

(c) When fitting the gearbox, engage a gear to lock the input shaft and prevent it from turning when engaging it with the splines of the clutch disc. The engine flywheel can be turned to align the splines and allow engagement

(d) When the engine and gearbox are fully coupled together support the gearbox with a jack at the rear and locate two upper set bolts to secure initially the two assemblies together

(e) Fit the respective retaining bolts and tighten them to the specified torque wrench settings (this Chapter and Chapter 5)

(f) Refer to Chapter 7 when refitting the propeller shaft

(g) On completion check that the gearbox drain plug is secure then top up the gearbox oil level (Section 2)

4 Manual gearbox – dismantling (general)

1 Complete dismantling of the manual gearbox and gear assemblies will necessitate the use of some special tools in addition to a normal range of tools.

2 A set of Torx keys will be required.

3 To withdraw (and later refit) certain bearing and gear and bearing assemblies it will be necessary to use the Toyota special service tools, but failing this a comprehensive range of pullers will suffice.

4 A micrometer or vernier caliper will be required to measure the selective snap-ring thicknesses during inspection and reassembly.

5 Unless these tools are available, the dismantling, overhaul and reassembly of the gearbox must be entrusted to a Toyota dealer or gearbox specialist.

6 When dismantling the gear assemblies, it is important to keep the respective components in order and direction of fitting. Selective snap-rings are used to set the endfloat tolerances and where a single item or, for example, the synchronizer rings only are to be replaced, label to identify each snap-ring and avoid the possibility of confusion over fitting positions during reassembly. The endfloat tolerances should in any case be checked during reassembly to ensure the specified tolerances are met.

5 Manual gearbox – dismantling

1 Clean the external surfaces of the gearbox using a suitable water soluble solvent and wipe dry.

2 Refer to Chapter 5 and remove the clutch release lever and bearing assembly.

3 Unscrew the reversing light switch and detach the lead from the retaining clip (photo).

4 Undo the retaining bolt and remove the speedometer driven gear unit from underneath the extension housing on the right-hand side (photo).

5 Undo the six retaining bolts and remove the gear shift retainer from the top of the extension housing (photos).

6 Unscrew and remove the selector restricter pins from the extension housing (photo).

7 Undo the nine retaining bolts and remove the clutch housing. Tap it free using a soft-headed hammer (photo).

8 Undo the nine retaining bolts and remove the extension housing.

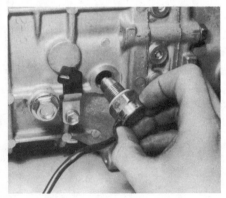
5.3 Remove the reversing light switch

5.4 Remove speedometer driven gear

5.5A Remove gear shaft cover ...

5.5B ... and gasket

5.6 Remove the restrict pins

5.7 View showing the clutch housing bolts and the front bearing retainer

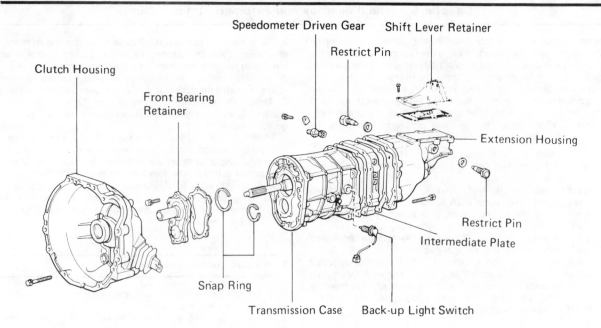

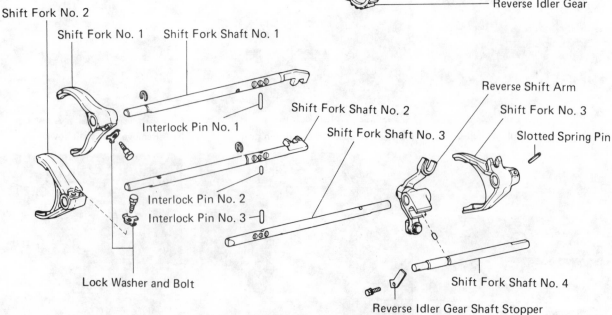

Fig. 6.1 Exploded view of the manual gearbox (Sec 5)

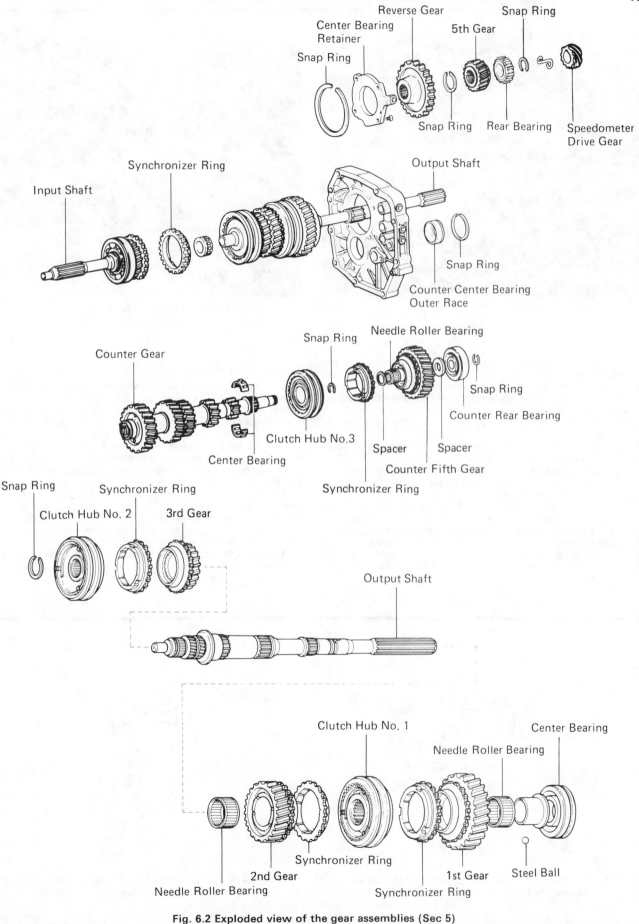

Fig. 6.2 Exploded view of the gear assemblies (Sec 5)

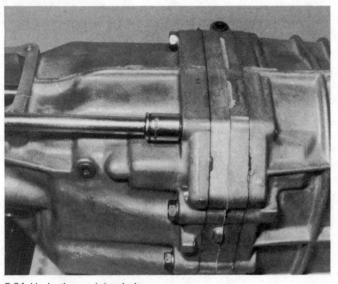

5.8A Undo the retaining bolts ...

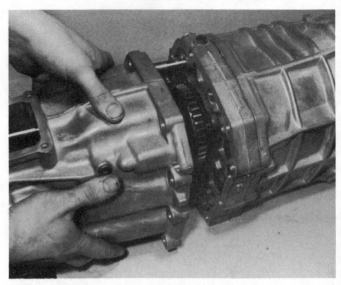

5.8B ... and withdraw the extension housing

Tap the housing free using a soft-headed hammer then rotate the housing clockwise (looking from the rear) whilst pulling upwards, and rearwards. Leave the gasket attached to the intermediate plate. As the housing is withdrawn, guide the selector lever clear of the fifth gear on the output shaft (photos).
9 Undo the seven retaining bolts and remove the front bearing retainer and gasket.
10 Prise free and remove the snap-rings from the front bearing outer races of the input shaft and the counter gear.
11 The transmission case can now be separated from the intermediate plate. Support the intermediate plate and tap the transmission case free using a soft-headed hammer.
12 With the transmission case removed, an initial inspection of the gear assemblies can be made. If extensive wear or damage to the gears and/or the associated components is visually obvious it is advisable to reassemble the dismantled items and exchange the complete unit for a new or reconditioned transmission unit. The cost of renewing numerous individual items will almost certainly cost more than an exchange unit.

Gear selector assemblies
13 To remove and dismantle the gear asemblies from the intermediate plate it is advisable to mount and secure the assembly in a vice, as shown in Fig. 6.3. Do not clamp the vice jaws directly onto the intermediate plate, but insert two long clutch housing bolts with plate washers and nuts as shown (inset). Use sufficient washers so that when tightened to the intermediate plate the nut is flush to the end of the bolt, then fit the assembly into the vice and clamp onto the bolt heads on one side and the nuts on the other. Check when in position that the assembly is secure.
14 Unscrew and remove the interlock plugs from the outer face of the intermediate plate. Extract the interlock springs and balls noting that the 1st/2nd plug and spring are shorter than the others. NB The plugs are removed using a Torx key, but a 6 mm Allen key may suffice, but take care not to damage the plug.
15 Bend back the locktabs and unscrew and remove the retaining bolt from the 1st/2nd (No 1) and 3rd/4th (No 2) shift forks. Remove the snap-rings from the No 1 and 2 shift rods.

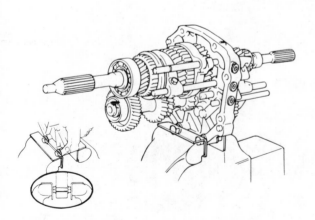

Fig. 6.3 Mount the intermediate plate as shown to dismantle the gear assemblies (Sec 5)

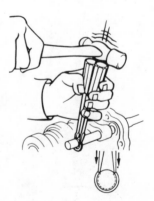

Fig. 6.4 Snap-ring removal method from the selector shafts using two screwdrivers (Sec 5)

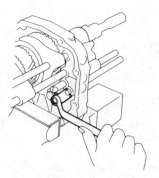

Fig. 6.5 Reverse idler gear shaft stopper removal (Sec 5)

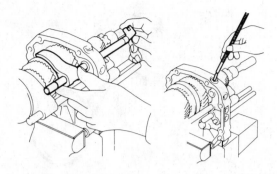

Fig. 6.6 Remove No 1 shift fork, shaft and interlock pin (Sec 5)

16 Undo the retaining bolt and remove the reverse idler shaft stopper plate (Fig. 6.5).

17 Withdraw the No 1 shift fork and shaft (Fig. 6.6).

18 Extract the interlock pin (No 1 and 2) using a magnetic finger probe (or a rod with greased end).

19 Withdraw the No 2 shift shaft and fork then extract the No 3 interlock pin. Rotate the shaft to free it for withdrawal. Note the locations and difference in sizes of the interlock pins.

20 Remove the reverse idler gear and shaft. Note that the gear selector groove is positioned to the front.

21 Drive out the No 3 shift fork-to-shaft roll pin. Support the shaft when driving out the pin. Withdraw the shaft and remove the fork. Keep them together.

22 Withdraw the No 4 shift fork shaft and the reverse shift arm and pin.

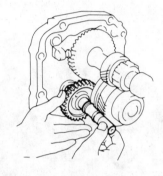

Fig. 6.7 Reverse idler gear and shaft removal (Sec 5)

Gear assemblies

23 Prise free the speedometer drivegear retaining clip and withdraw the drivegear from the rear end of the output shaft.

24 Measure and take note of the clearance between the 5th gear and bearing on the countergear shaft using feeler gauges, then remove the snap-ring retaining the bearing.

25 Fit a puller into position and withdraw the rear bearing, spacer, 5th gear and bearing from the rear of the countergear shaft. As they are withdrawn care must be taken not to catch the 5th gear on the output shaft rear bearing roller. Remove the spacer.

26 Remove the snap-ring securing the No 3 clutch hub (synchro unit for 5th gear). Fit a puller into position and withdraw the No 3 clutch hub unit. Care must be taken when fitting the puller not to damage the shift key retainer plate on the front face of the clutch hub unit (see Fig. 6.11). If possible, use Toyota special service tool No 09950-20014.

27 Remove the snap-ring securing the rear bearing roller on the output shaft, then fit a puller into position and withdraw the 5th gear and bearing roller from the output shaft. If available use Toyota special

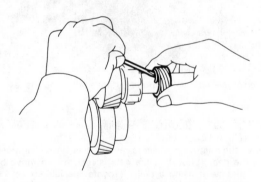

Fig. 6.8 Releasing the speedometer drivegear retaining clip (Sec 5)

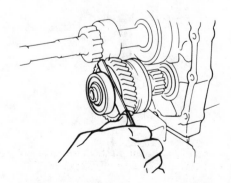

Fig. 6.9 Measure the 5th gear thrust clearance (Sec 5)

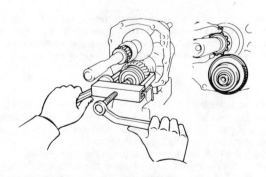

Fig. 6.10 Remove 5th gear, spacer and rear bearing assembly from the countergear shaft (Sec 5)

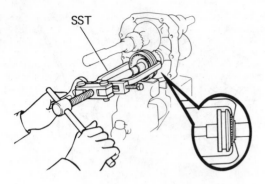

Fig. 6.11 No 3 clutch hub unit removal (Sec 5)

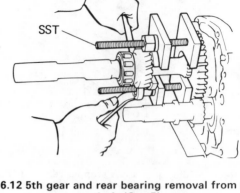

Fig. 6.12 5th gear and rear bearing removal from output shaft (Sec 5)

5.28 Reverse gear removal from the output shaft using the lever method

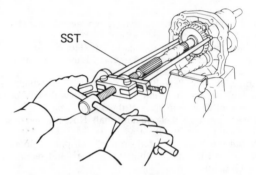

Fig. 6.13 Reverse gear removal from the output shaft using a suitable puller (Sec 5)

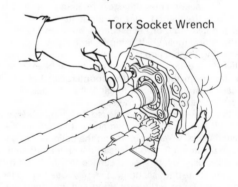

Fig. 6.14 Centre bearing retainer removal (Sec 5)

Fig. 6.15 Centre bearing and 1st gear removal from output shaft (Sec 5)

service tool No 09312-20010 or a suitable alternative puller with a 230 mm reach (Fig. 6.12).

28 Remove the snap-ring securing reverse gear on the output shaft, lever free the gear (photo). If the gear is reluctant to move by this method, withdraw it using a puller (Toyota special service tool No 09950-20014 if possible). Note the orientation of the gear as it is withdrawn.

29 Use a Torx key and undo the four screws which secure the centre bearing retainer. Remove the retainer from the intermediate plate (Fig. 6.14).

30 Remove the snap-ring from the groove in the outer races of the output shaft centre bearing and countergear shaft centre bearing.

31 The output shaft, input shaft and countergear assemblies can now be withdrawn from the intermediate plate (as a complete unit) then separated.

Output shaft

32 Remove the centre bearing and 1st gear from the output shaft. Support 1st gear and press or drive the output shaft through the bearing and gear. The gear is removed, together with the needle roller bearing, inner race and the synchroniser ring.

33 Extract the lock ball from its recess in the output shaft.

34 Support 2nd gear and press or drive the output shaft through it. Remove the 2nd gear, complete with the No 1 clutch hub unit and needle roller bearing as a unit.

35 Remove the No 2 clutch hub unit and 3rd gear from the front end of

the output shaft by first removing the snap-ring then pressing or driving the gear and hub unit from the shaft. If preferred, a suitable puller could be used to withdraw the clutch hub and 3rd gear.

6 Manual gearbox – inspection

General

1   It is assumed that the gearbox has been dismantled for reasons of excessive noise, lack of synchromesh action on certain gears or for failure to stay in gear. If anything more drastic than this (total failure, seizure or main casing cracked) it would be better to leave well alone and look for a replacement, either secondhand or an exhange unit.
2   Examine all gears for excessively worn, chipped or damaged teeth. Any such gears should be renewed.

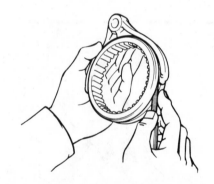

Fig. 6.16 Check the synchro-rings for excessive wear (Sec 6)

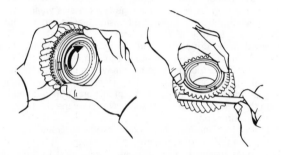

Fig. 6.17 Check shift fork-to-hub sleeve clearance (Sec 6)

6.8 Input shaft bearing and selective snap-ring

Synchromesh units

3   Check all synchromesh rings for wear on the bearing surfaces, which normally have clear machined oil reservoir lines in them. If these are smooth or obviously uneven, replacement is essential. Also when the rings are fitted to their gears – as they would be in operation – there should be no rock. This would signify ovality or lack of concentricity.
4   Push the ring against the gearwheel cone and simultaneously rotate it. A firm braking action should be felt. Further check for wear by measuring the synchro ring-to-gear clearance as shown (Fig. 6.16) using feeler gauges. Renew the rings if worn down to the minimum allowable clearance specified.
5   It is not normally necessary to dismantle the synchromesh clutch units but if they are, note the relative positions of the hub and sleeve, also the retaining springs each side and the keys. Mark them so that they are reassembled in the same positions and orientation.
6   Slot the respective shift forks into their hub sleeves and check the side clearance using feeler gauges. If worn beyond the maximum specified clearance, renew as necessary (Fig. 6.17).

Bearings

7   All ball race bearings should be checked for chatter and roughness after they have been washed out. It is advisable to renew these any way even though they may not appear too badly worn.
8   If the input shaft bearing is in need of renewal, first remove the snap-ring which secures it then support the bearing and press the shaft through it to remove it. If a press is not available a suitable puller can be used to withdraw it from the shaft (photo).
9   Press or drive the new bearing into position on the shaft so that the snap-ring groove in the bearing outer race is offset towards the front (away from the gear). If driving the bearing into position use a tube drift of suitable diameter which will only apply pressure onto the side of the bearing inner race. When the bearing is in position select a snap-ring of suitable thickness to allow the minimum axial play when fitted. A list of the snap-ring thicknesses available is given in the Specifications at the start of this Chapter.
10 If the countergear front bearing is in need of renewal, the procedure is similar to that described for the input shaft ball-bearing replacement. When the bearing is removed, check the side race for wear or damage. If necessary remove it using a suitable puller, but if this fails to withdraw it, carefully grind part of the side race away then cut it off using a chisel as shown (Fig. 6.18), but take care not to damage the countergear or shaft. A suitable socket can be used to press or drive the new bearing, side race and inner race into position.
11 When the countergear front bearing is renewed, select a snap-ring of suitable thickness which when fitted will allow the minimum amount of axial play (see Specifications for snap-ring thickness available.
12 To remove the countergear centre roller bearing, prise it apart at the joint and separate the two halves of the roller cage. Drive the roller outer race from the intermediate plate using a suitable tube drift. If renewing this bearing, the roller cage unit and outer race must be renewed as a set. Fit the new roller cages into position on the countergear journal, but leave filling the outer race until later during transmission reassembly.

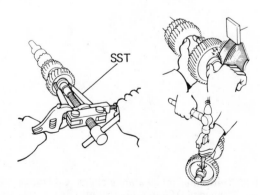

Fig. 6.18 Countergear front bearing side race removal methods (Sec 6)

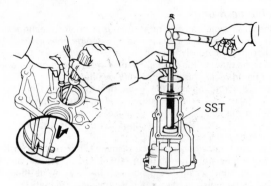

Fig. 6.19 Output shaft rear bearing race removal methods (Sec 6)

13 If the output shaft rear bearing is worn or damaged this must be renewed as a set (roller assembly and outer race). To remove the outer race from the extension housing first prise free the snap-ring which retains it, using screwdrivers as shown in Fig. 6.19. Drive out the bearing outer race using a suitable tube drift.

14 Drive the new outer race into position then insert the snap-ring to secure it. If the snap-ring was distorted on removal this should be renewed also. Check that the snap-ring is fully engaged when refitted.

Output shaft and inner bearing races

15 Check the output shaft and the corresponding inner races for signs of excessive wear or damage. Measure for wear using a vernier caliper or micrometer where applicable and check against the respective wear limits given in the Specifications. Renew as necessary.

Gear oil clearances

16 A dial indicator will be required to check the gear oil clearances. Refer to the accompanying illustrations for the method required to check the clearances and the Specifications for the respective wear limits allowable (Fig. 6.20, 6.21 and 6.22).

Front bearing retainer

17 Examine the front bearing retainer for any signs of damage. The oil seal should be renewed (photo). Prise out the old seal noting its fitting direction. Drive the new seal into position using a suitable tube drift to a fitted depth (from the retainer end) of 11.4 to 12.0 mm (0.449 to 0.472 in).

Extension housing

18 Inspect the extension housing for signs of damage. The oil seal should be renewed (photo). Remove the old seal using a puller or drift out from the inside. Before inserting the new oil seal check the bush within the housing for signs of damage or excessive wear. If the bush needs renewing, heat the extension housing rear end to a temperature of 80 to 100°C (176 to 212°F) by immersing it in hot water. The old bush can then be drifted out and the new replacement drifted into position. Drive the new oil seal into position in its housing (Fig. 6.23).

19 If the reverse restrict pin is to be renewed proceed as follows. First unscrew the plug from the side of the extension housing then, using a suitable punch inserted through the plug hole, drift out the roll pin securing the lever housing to the shaft. Withdraw the shaft and remove the lever housing (photos).

20 Refit the shaft and lever housing in reverse order and align the roll pin holes. Use a new roll pin and drift it into position to secure them. Apply a liquid sealant to the plug before refitting it to the extension housing. Tighten it to the specified torque setting given for the 'straight screw plug'.

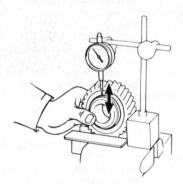

Fig. 6.20 First gear oil clearance check. Clearance must not exceed 0.15 mm (0.0059 in) (Sec 6)

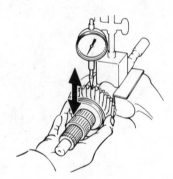

Fig. 6.21 Fifth gear oil clearance check. Clearance not to exceed 0.15 mm (0.0059 in) (Sec 6)

Fig. 6.22 Third gear oil clearance check. Clearance not to exceed 0.20 mm (0.0079 in) (Sec 6)

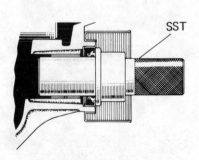

Fig. 6.23 New extension housing oil seal pressed into housing (Sec 6)

6.17 Front bearing retainer oil seal should be removed

6.18 Extension housing and rear oil seal

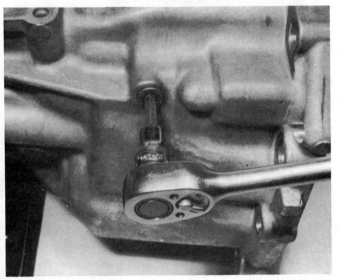

6.19A Remove the plug ...

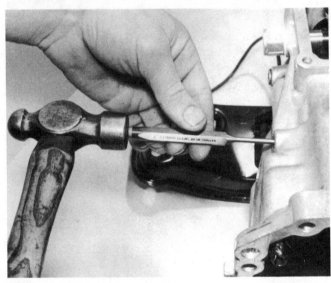

6.19B ... and drive out the roll pin ...

6.19C ... securing the reverse restrict pin

7 Manual gearbox – reassembly

1   Check that all parts are cleaned and ready for reassembly. Reference to Figs. 6.1 and 6.2, as well as the accompanying figures and photos for this Section, will assist during reassembly.

2   If dismantled, reassemble the synchromesh clutch hubs and sleeves together with the shift keys. Engage the key springs underneath the shift keys, but ensure that the key spring and gaps are not aligned with each other when fitted (photo).

3   Lubricate the output third gear journal with oil, then fit the third gear with the number two synchro unit. The synchro unit must be fitted so that the inner hub large boss faces rearwards. The hub will need to be drawn onto the shaft using a suitable puller or supported and the shaft pressed through it (photos).

4   Fit a selective snap-ring into position in the shaft groove to take up as much play as possible (photo).

5   Using feeler gauges as shown, check the 3rd gear thrust clearance. It must be as specified (photo).

7.2 Clutch hub and sleeve alignment

7.3A Refit 3rd gear ...

7.3B ... the synchro ring ...

7.3C ... and the clutch hub assembly. This shows the puller requirement

7.4 Fit a selective snap-ring

7.5 Check the 3rd gear thrust clearance

7.6A 2nd gear and No 1 clutch hub assembly fitment using a puller

7.6B 2nd gear and the No 1 clutch hub in position

7.7 Fit 1st gear synchro ring

7.8 Fit the ball-bearing

7.9 1st gear and needle bearing assembly

6   Lubricate the shaft journal then fit the 2nd gear, together with the No 1 clutch hub, onto the shaft. The needle roller bearing in the 2nd gear must also be well lubricated. A suitable puller or press will be required to draw the syncho unit into position. Ensure that the synchro ring slots align with the shift keys as they are assembled (photos).
7   Locate the 1st gear synchro ring (photo).

8   Locate the ball-bearing into the shaft (photo).
9   Assemble 1st gear, needle bearing and bush (photo).
10 Slide the 1st gear, with the needle roller bearing, into the shaft, aligning the slot in the bearing bush with the ball bearing on the shaft (photos).
11 Locate the centre bearing onto the shaft so that the snap-ring

7.10A Align the bush slot so that when fitting ...

7.10B ... it engages over the ball-bearing in the shaft

7.11A Output shaft centre bearing

7.11B Using a puller to draw the output shaft centre bearing into position. Take care that 1st gear needle bearing inner bush does not become dislodged

groove in its outer race is offset to the rear (photo). Press or use a draw puller to fit the bearing into position on the shaft (against 1st gear bearing bush) (photo).

12 Check that the 1st-to-2nd gear thrust clearance is as specified (photo).

13 Fit the intermediate plate into position over the bearing as shown (photo).

14 Fit the countergear/shaft unit, together with the input shaft unit. Before fitting the countergear unit check that the half race roller bearings are assembled in position on their shaft journal (photos). Before fitting the input shaft ensure that the pilot bearing is in position (photo). Locate the countergear through the intermediate plate, then engage the input shaft into the end of the output shaft. Mesh the assemblies as shown (photos).

15 Fit the countergear centre bearing outer race, taking care not to damage the bearing rollers. This should push into position by hand (photo).

16 Locate the snap-rings into the countergear and output shaft centre bearing outer race grooves (photo).

7.12 Check 1st/2nd gear thrust clearance

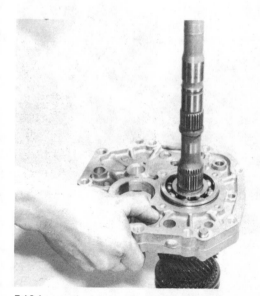

7.13 Locate the intermediate plate with recessed side forwards

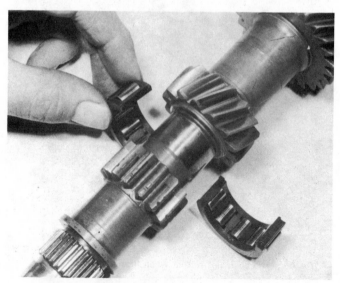

7.14A Countergear centre bearing is fitted ...

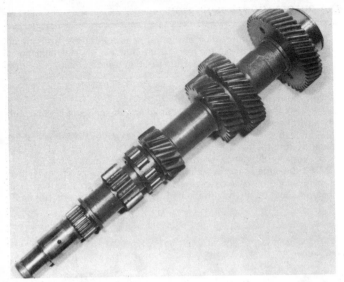

7.14B ... onto the counter gear ...

7.14C Locate the input shaft pilot bearing

7.14D Fit the countergear into the intermediate plate ...

7.14E ... and the input shaft into engagement with the output and countergear shafts

7.15 Fit the countershaft centre bearing outer race

7.16 Locate the bearing snap-rings

17 Refit the output shaft centre bearing retaining plate. Tighten the retaining screws to the specified torque wrench setting (photo).

18 Fit the output shaft reverse gear into position with its large boss offset to the front (photos). Press or drift the gear into position on the splines (photo).

19 Fit a selective snap-ring to give the minimum axial play possible (photos).

20 Fit the 5th gear and the rear bearing onto the output shaft. The gear must be positioned as shown (photo). Drive the gear and bearing into position on the shaft, then secure with a selective snap-ring to provide the minimum play possible (photos). Note that the bearing is fitted with the open side of the retainer cage facing rearwards.

21 If dismantled, reassemble the No 3 synchro clutch hub and sleeve, engaging the shift key springs under the keys. When assembled, the spring and gaps must not be in line. Refer to Fig. 6.24 for orientation.

22 Support the countergear at the front end and fit the No 3 clutch hub onto the shaft from the rear. Ensure that it is correctly aligned as shown in Fig. 6.25, then drive it into position using a suitable tube drift (photo).

23 Select a snap-ring of suitable thickness to take up the play then fit it into position (photos).

24 Check that the synchro ring is fitted and the ring slot aligned with the shift keys (photo).

25 Slide the small spacer onto the shaft followed by the 5th gear roller bearing (photos).

26 Lubricate the needle bearing, then fit the 5th gear (photo).

27 Fit the large spacer washer against the rear face of 5th gear, then locate and drive the countergear rear bearing onto the shaft. The bearing must be fitted with the ball shield facing rearwards (photos).

7.17 Tighten the bearing retainer plate Torx screws

7.18A Fit the reverse gear ...

7.18B ... with its boss to the front ...

7.18C ... and drive into position

7.19A Select a snap-ring ...

7.19B ... and fit it to secure reverse gear

7.20A 5th gear must be fitted as shown (large shoulder to rear)

7.20B Select a snap-ring to take up the play ...

7.20C ... then fit it to secure the bearing and gear

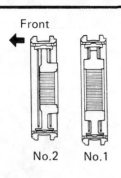
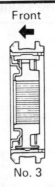

Front   Front

No.2   No.1   No. 3

Fig. 6.24 Clutch hub and sleeves must be orientated as shown (Sec 7)

Fig. 6.25 No 3 synchro clutch hub orientation (Sec 7)

7.22 Locate the No 3 clutch hub onto the rear of the countergear shaft

7.23A Select a suitable snap-ring ...

7.23B ... and fit it into position

7.24 Align the synchro-ring slot with the shift key

7.25A Slide the spacer onto the shaft ...

7.25B ... then the needle roller bearing

7.26 Refit the 5th gear onto the countergear shaft

7.27A Locate the large spacer ...

7.27B ... and drive the bearing into position

28 Select a snap-ring which gives the minimum amount of play, then fit it into position (photos).
29 Refit the speedometer drivegear onto the output shaft and secure it with the clip (photos).
30 Fit the reverse idler gear and shaft to the intermediate plate. Ensure that the gear is fitted with its offset hub boss towards the intermediate plate (photo).

Gear selector assemblies

31 Locate the reverse shift arm and the No 3 shift fork as shown, then slide the shift fork shaft No 3 into position through them so that the roll pin hole aligns (photos).
32 Locate the interlock plunger into the reverse shift arm (the groove in the shaft must also align), then slide the No 4 shift fork shaft into position. Drive the No 3 shift fork roll pin into position (photos).
33 Lubricate the No 3 interlock pin (middle size) with grease, then insert it into the intermediate plate (photo).
34 Locate the No 2 shift fork shaft into the intermediate plate, engage the No 2 shift fork over the 3rd/4th gear clutch hub, and insert the No 2 interlock pin into the shaft. Slide the shaft through the intermediate plate and into the No 2 shift fork, aligning the retaining bolt hole (photos).

7.28A Select a snap-ring ...

7.28B ... fit it to secure the bearing

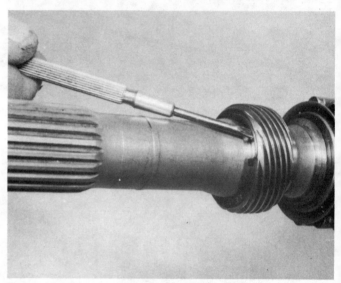

7.29A Refit the speedometer drivegear and retaining clip

7.29B Check that the clip is fully located

7.30 Fit the reverse gear and shaft

7.31A Locate the reverse shift arm ...

7.31B ... the No 3 shift fork ...

7.31C ... and the shift fork shaft

7.32A Locate the interlock plunger ...

7.32B ... fit the No 4 shaft and drive home the No 3 shift fork roll pin

7.33 Locate the No 3 interlock pin

7.34A Insert the interlock pin into the No 2 shift fork shaft ...

7.34B ... slide the shaft through the No 2 shift fork

7.35 Fit the snap-ring to the No 2 shaft

7.36 Insert the No 1 interlock pin

7.37A Insert the No 1 shift rod ...

7.37B ... and fit the snap-ring

35 Fit the snap-ring into its groove on the No 2 shaft (photo).
36 Lubricate the No 1 interlock pin (large) with grease then insert it into position in the interlock plate (photo).
37 Engage the 1st/2nd (No 1) shift fork into the clutch hub groove then pass the No 1 shaft through the intermediate plate and the shift fork. Fit the snap-ring into its groove at the front end of the shaft (photos).
38 Align the shift fork and shaft bolt holes, then insert the securing bolts with lock washers. Tighten the bolts to the specified torque then bend up the locktabs to secure (photo).
39 Insert the lock balls and springs into the intermediate plate, smear the plug threads with sealant, then fit and tighten the four plugs to the specified torque setting (photos). Note that the short spring and plug are fitted to the 1st/2nd shaft detent hole.
40 Fit the reverse idler gear shaft stopper plate and secure the retaining bolt to the specified torque (photo).
41 With the gear selector assemblies refitted, check that they are fully secured and that they operate in a satisfactory manner (photos). Clean the intermediate plate and gearcase and extension housing mating faces.

7.38 Fit the shift fork to shaft lockbolts and washers

7.39A Insert the ball and spring ...

7.39B ... tighten the retaining plugs to the specified torque

7.40 Reverse idler gear shaft stopper plate and retaining bolt

7.41A General view showing the reasembled gears and selectors – gearcase side

7.41B General view showing the reassembled gears and selectors – extension housing side

Gear casings – refitting

42 Locate the transmission case-to-intermediate plate gasket. Lubricate the gasket with grease to secure it in position on the plate face. Lubricate the selector shafts with grease, then fit the transmission case into position (photo). As it is fitted align it with the selector shafts and the bearing outer races before lightly tapping it fully into position, flush against the intermediate plate.

43 Fit the snap-rings into the grooves in the countergear and output shaft front bearings (photo).

44 The front bearing retainer can now be fitted. Check that the mating faces are clean, locate a new gasket, apply liquid sealant to the retaining bolt threads. Fit the retainer into position and tighten the securing bolts to the specified torque (photos).

45 Clean the mating faces, locate a new extension housing gasket (smeared with grease) then refit the extension housing. As it is fitted engage the shift and selector lever in the extension housing to the shift fork shaft (Fig. 6.26). Fit the extension housing into position and tighten the bolts to the specified torque (photos). If it was removed, the shift lever housing must be fitted onto the shaft as the housing is fitted (photo).

46 With the extension housing refitted, check that the input and output shafts rotate freely and also ensure that the gear selections are satisfactory.

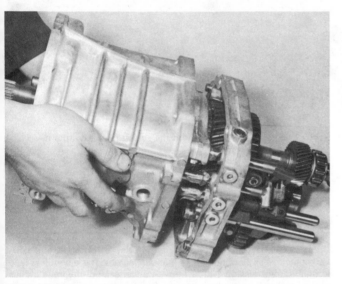

7.42 Refit the transmission case

7.43 Fit the snap-rings to the front bearings

7.44A Locate the gasket ...

7.44B ... and fit the front bearing retainer

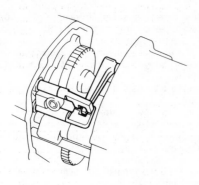

Fig. 6.26 Engage selector lever
with the shift fork (Sec 7)

7.45A Fit a new extension housing gasket

7.45B Selector lever in the extension
housing

7.45C Fit and secure the shift lever housing
on the shaft

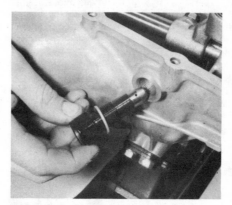

7.47 Refit the restrict pins with new
washers

7.48 Refit the selector cover with a new
gasket

47 Refit the restrict pins to the extension housing. Use new washers
and note that the black pin is fitted to the reverse/5th gear side.
Tighten to the specified torque (photo).
48 Locate a new gasket and refit the selector cover (photo).
49 Check that the speedometer driven gear has a new O-ring seal
fitted then insert it into position, locate the retainer plate and bolt to
secure (photos).
50 Refit the reversing light switch, tighten to the specified torque and
retain the wire in the clip (photo).
51 Refit the clutch housing and tighten the retaining bolts to the
specified torque setting.
52 Refit the clutch release fork and bearing (Chapter 5).

8 Automatic transmission – description and precautions

The A40 D automatic transmission is fitted to both UK and USA
market models as an option to the manual gearbox. It is a bandless type
automatic transmission with a torque converter and integral clutches
and multi-disc brakes which actuate the planetary gears. An oil pump
supplies pressure to actuate the clutches and brakes.
The only external adjustments possible are to the transmission
throttle cable and shift linkage.
Due to the complexities of the overhaul procedures on the

7.49A Locate a new O-ring seal on the
speedometer driven gear

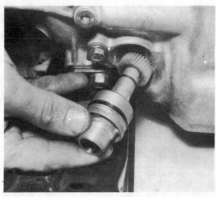

7.49B Refit the speedometer driven gear

7.50 Refit the reversing light switch

automatic transmission, the operations described in this Chapter are limited to maintenance, adjustment, and removal and refitting.

Precautions

In the event of a breakdown, the vehicle must not be towed in excess of 30 mph (45 kph) or further than 50 miles (80 km) unless the propeller shaft is removed. Failure to observe this precaution will damage the automatic transmission due to lack of lubrication.

Whenever making adjustments to the engine or external adjustments to the transmission, it is essential that the handbrake is fully applied, the front roadwheels should be chocked, N (neutral) or P (park) engaged and, where applicable, an assistant should fully apply the footbrake.

9 Routine maintenance – automatic transmission

1 **Fluid level check:** This check should be made when the transmission fluid has warmed up to its normal operating temperature, that is, after driving the vehicle for a minimum distance of 10 miles (16 km), or 15 miles (24 km) in frigid conditions. The vehicle must be parked on level ground.

2 It should be noted that a fluid level check should not be made directly after driving the vehicle for an extended period at high speed, after pulling a trailer, in hot weather or after driving in congested traffic conditions, since under these circumstances an accurate fluid level check cannot be made. Therefore allow the vehicle to stand for about thirty minutes before checking the level.

3 To check the fluid level, leave the engine running at idle speed and fully apply the handbrake. Depress the brake pedal then move the selector lever from P through the range and back to P. Now withdraw the dipstick, wipe it clean and reinsert it fully. Withdraw the dipstick and observe the fluid level. Under the conditions described the level should be within the HOT range. When making the fluid check take care to keep hands and clothing away from the cooling fan and drivebelt. Also the exhaust system.

4 Top up with fluid of the specified grade only when necessary. Do not overfill. Top up the fluid level through the dipstick guide tube then, on completion, refit the dipstick.

5 The fluid level can be provisionally checked before running the vehicle to warm it up, but in this instance the level should be in the COLD range. Recheck the level after the vehicle has been driven the appropriate distance to warm up the fluid to its normal operating temperature.

6 Keep the external surfaces of the transmission unit clean and free from mud and grease to prevent overheating. An oil cooler is fitted, make sure that the connecting pipes are secure and in good condition.

7 **Fluid renewal:** the automatic transmission fluid normally only requires changing at the specified intervals (see Routine Maintenance), but if the oil on the dipstick appears burned or discoloured or if particularly arduous or dusty operating conditions prevail, the fluid should be drained and renewed at more frequent intervals.

8 Unscrew the transmission drain plug and drain the fluid into a suitable container for disposal (take care when draining the fluid when hot). Refit the drain plug then top up the fluid level with 2 litre (3.5 Imp pints: 2.1 US qt), of the specified ATF through the dipstick guide tube.

9 Check that the handbrake is fully applied, depress the footbrake then restart the engine and run at idle speed. Move the selector lever from P through the gear ranges and back to P. Leaving the engine running at idle speed, check the fluid level on the dipstick as previously described in paragraph 3, but note that the fluid should be up to the COLD level mark on the dipstick. Add further fluid to bring it up to this mark (do not overfill).

10 Recheck the fluid level again after the vehicle has been used and the fluid warmed up, as described in paragraphs 1 to 4.

10 Automatic transmission – adjustments

The following adjustments are not part of the routine servicing procedures and should only be made when wear in the components or faulty operation of the transmission is experienced.

Floor shift linkage adjustment

1 Raise and support the vehicle on safety stands.

2 Working from underneath the vehicle, loosen the shift linkage nut (Fig. 6.29). Move the manual selector lever fully forwards (to P) then back three notches to the N (neutral) position.

3 With the shift selector in N, but held lightly towards R (reverse), tighten the shift linkage nut.

Transmission throttle cable

4 On carburettor models, refer to Chapter 3 and remove the air cleaner unit.

5 Fully depress the accelerator pedal and check that the throttle valve opens fully. If it doesn't then adjustment is necessary to the cable.

6 Referring to Fig. 6.30, loosen the cable adjustment nuts then, with the accelerator pedal fully depressed, adjust as necessary to set the clearance between the cable boot and the inner cable stopper at 0 to 1.0 mm (0 to 0.04 in). Retighten the adjustment nuts and then recheck the adjustment.

7 On carburettor models, refit the air cleaner unit.

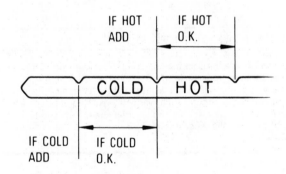

Fig. 6.27 Automatic transmission dipstick fluid level markings (Sec 9)

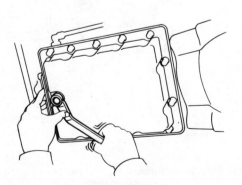

Fig. 6.28 Drain plug removal – automatic transmission (Sec 9)

Fig. 6.29 Loosening the shift linkage nut (Sec 10)

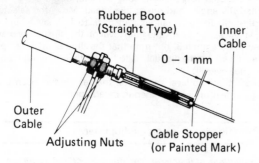

Fig. 6.30 Automatic transmission throttle cable and adjustment nuts (Sec 10)

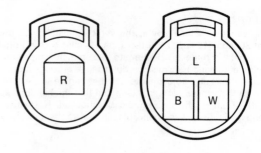

Fig. 6.31 Neutral start switch terminals (Sec 10)

Neutral start switch adjustment

8   Move the shift lever through the various function positions and check for correct operation as follows:

(a) *In positions N or P only – engine should start. The engine should not start with the lever in any other position*

(b) *Reversing lights should come on when lever is moved to R*

9   If the above checks showed a malfunction in the selection, then adjust the neutral starter switch as follows with the engine off and the selector lever in N.

10 Detach the wiring connector to the neutral starter switch, then connect up an ohmmeter between terminals B and W (see Fig. 6.31). Loosen the neutral starter switch bolt and adjust the position of the switch to give continuity between the B and W terminals (Fig. 6.32), then retighten the switch bolt to the specified torque setting. Check that there is continuity between the L and R terminals on the switch with the selector moved to R then reconnect the wiring connector.

---

11 Extension housing oil seal – renewal

---

1   Renewal of the oil seal may be carried out with the transmission unit in position in the vehicle.

2   Remove the propeller shaft, as described in Chapter 7.

3   Knock off the dust deflector towards the rear and prise out the dust seal. Using a suitable extractor and levering against the end face of the mainshaft, extract the oil seal (Fig. 6.33).

4   Drive in the new oil seal with a tubular drift, fit a new dust seal and refit the dust deflector.

5   Refit the propeller shaft after first greasing the front sliding sleeve both internally and externally. Make sure that the propeller shaft and pinion driving flanges have their mating marks aligned.

6   On completion check and top up the transmission fluid level as necessary, as described in Section 9.

---

12 Overdrive relay and solenoid – checking

---

1   These items need only be checked if they are suspected of malfunction. An ohmmeter will be necessary to check the units separately. Refer to Fig. 6.34 or 6.35 as applicable for the automatic transmission wiring diagram.

2   An initial check of the units can be made as follows. Turn the ignition switch and the overdrive main switch on.

3   Detach the wiring connector from the coolant thermo switch then, using a suitable length of insulated wire attached to the wire side of the connector, repeatedly earth the wire. The solenoid and transmission relay should be heard to operate.

4   If they are not heard to operate, check them individually and if necessary renew.

Overdrive relay unit

5   Detach and remove the relay unit from the pedal bracket.

6   Connect up an ohmmeter between terminals 1 and 2 and check that there is continuity between these two terminals (Fig. 6.37).

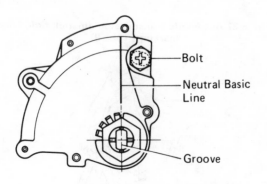

Fig. 6.32 Neutral start switch adjustment (Sec 10)

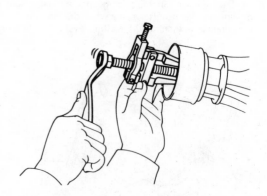

Fig. 6.33 Extension housing oil seal removal – automatic transmission (Sec 11)

7 On UK models, and USA models up to 1984, connect the ohmmeter between terminals 1 and 3 and check that a resistance of 80 ohm is given.

8 Connect terminals 1 and 3 or, on USA models from 1985, terminals 2 and 4, to a 12 volt battery as shown (Fig. 6.38) then, with the ohmmeter connected to terminals 1 and 2, check that there is no continuity between them. Renew the relay unit if it is found to be defective.

Overdrive solenoid unit

9 You will need to work underneath the vehicle for this check so raise and support it on safety stands.

10 Detach the wiring from the solenoid unit and apply a 12 volt battery voltage to the solenoid terminal. The solenoid should be heard to operate.

11 Connect an ohmmeter to the solenoid and check that its coil resistance is 13 ohm. If found to be defective the solenoid will need to be renewed.

Thermo-switch

12 Detach the wire from the thermo-switch and connect up an ohmmeter as shown (Fig. 6.39). The resistance measured between the thermo-switch terminal and earth should be as given. If found to be defective, the thermo-switch will need to be renewed. Partially drain the cooling system before removal.

Overdrive main switch

13 Access to the overdrive main switch wiring connector must be obtained. On some models this is accessible after removing the ashtray, whilst on other models it will be necessary to remove the central console.

14 On all UK models (and USA models up to 1984) connect up an ohmmeter and check for continuity between the switch positions in accordance with Fig. 6.40.

15 On USA models from 1985, measure the resistance between terminals 1 and 3 using an ohmmeter; referring to Fig. 6.41. With the main switch on, there should be an infinite ohm resistance. With the main switch off there should be 0 ohm resistance.

16 Renew the switch if found to be defective.

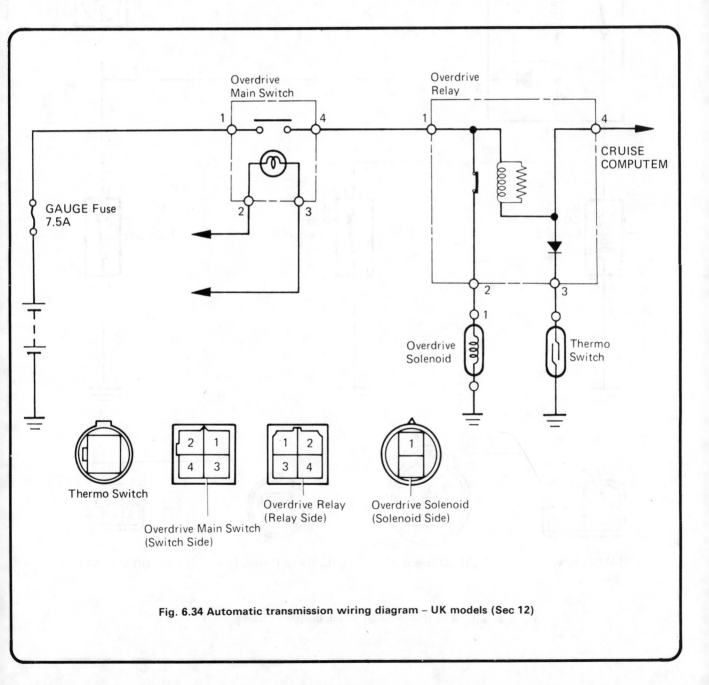

Fig. 6.34 Automatic transmission wiring diagram – UK models (Sec 12)

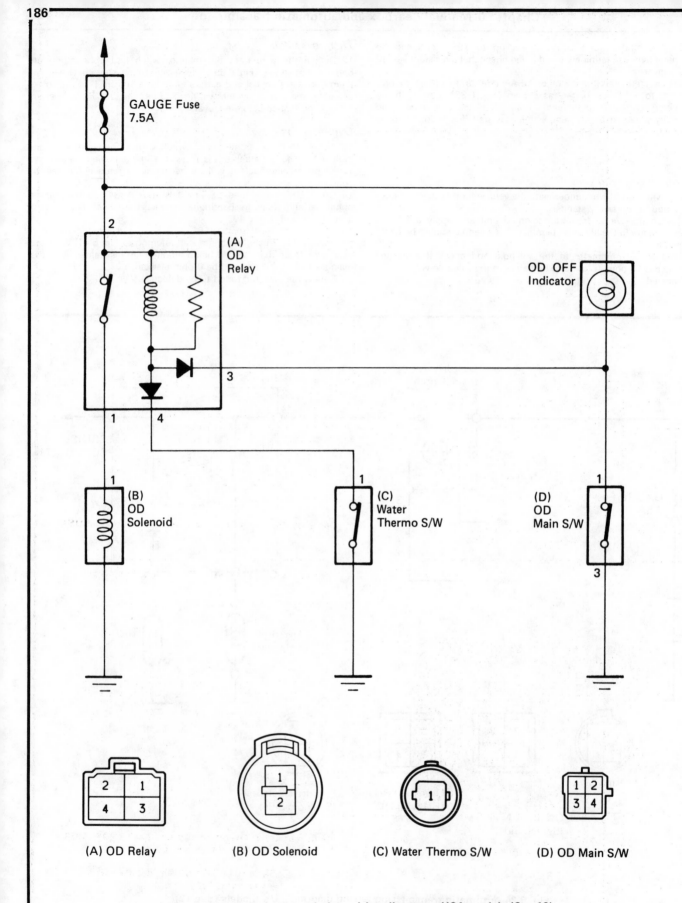

Fig. 6.35 Automatic transmission wiring diagram – USA models (Sec 12)

187

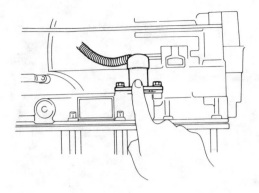

Fig. 6.36 Automatic transmission overdrive solenoid –
1985 USA model shown (Sec 12)

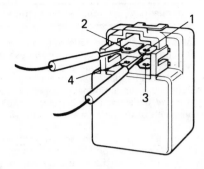

Fig. 6.37 Automatic transmission overdrive relay
terminals – 1985 USA model shown (Sec 12)

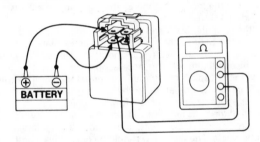

Fig. 6.38 Overdrive relay continuity check method – 1985
USA model shown (Sec 12)

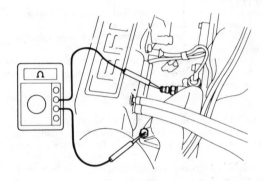

Fig. 6.39 Thermoswitch resistance check – 1985 USA
model shown (Sec 12)

Below 43°C (109°F) – 0 ohm (closed)
Above 55°C (131°F) – infinite ohm (open)

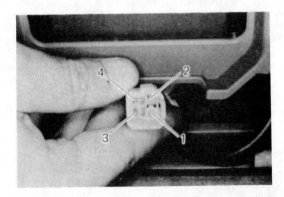

Fig. 6.40 Overdrive main switch check – UK models, and
USA models up to 1984 (Sec 12)

Switch on – continuity between 1 and 4 and 2 and 3
Switch off – continuity between 2 and 3 only

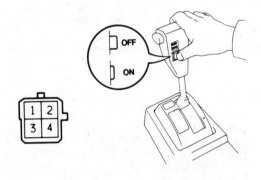

Fig. 6.41 Overdrive main switch check – 1985 USA
models (Sec 12)

Switch on – infinite ohm resistance
Switch off – 0 ohm resistance

13 Automatic transmission – removal and refitting

1   It must be realised that the automatic transmission unit is of considerable weight and adequate assistance or the use of a trolley jack will be required for the following operations.

2   Disconnect the lead from the battery negative terminal.

3   Drain the cooling system and disconnect the radiator top hose.

4   Refer to Chapter 3 and, according to model, detach and remove the carburettor air cleaner unit or the air intake connector (fuel-injection models).

5   On carburettor models, loosen the adjustment nuts for the transmission throttle cable at the support bracket on the top face of the cylinder head cover. Then prise free the inner cable retaining clip from the pin and detach the inner cable from the carburettor linkage.

6   On fuel-injection models, loosen the transmission throttle cable adjustment nuts from the support bracket and detach the cable from the throttle housing and bracket and throttle linkage.

7   On carburettor models, unscrew and remove the upper mounting nut on the starter.

8   Unless the vehicle is over an inspection pit, raise it and support on safety stands, ensuring that it is level and there is sufficient clearance underneath to remove and withdraw the transmission unit. Drain the transmission (Section 9).

9   Disconnect and remove the propeller shaft or intermediate shaft and central bearing (see Chapter 7 for details).

10 Disconnect the lead connectors from the reverse light switch and the neutral starter switch on the transmission.

11 On carburettor models, remove the starter motor (see Chapter 12).

12 Unscrew the knurled retaining nut and disconnect the speedometer cable from the transmission.

13 Detach the manual shift linkage at the rear pivot connector (Fig. 6.45).

14 Unscrew the union nuts and detach the oil cooler pipes at their connection to the transmission. Be prepared for oil spillage and plug the pipe ends to prevent the ingress of dirt. Position the pipes out of the way.

15 Unbolt and detach the exhaust pipe location bracket from the transmission. On fuel-injection models detach and remove the front exhaust pipe (Chapter 3).

16 Unbolt and remove the engine/transmission stiffener plate brackets each side (Fig. 6.46).

17 Unbolt and detach the steering column sliding yoke from the steering gear housing (see Chapter 10).

18 Detach the steering tie-rod outer joints and then unbolt and lower the power steering gear unit from the support member. Support the steering gear unit by suspending it from the crossmember with a length of suitable cord. Where applicable also disconnect the oil cooler pipe location clamp from the left-hand side of the engine and the power steering pressure lines clamp.

19 Locate a jack (trolley type if available) under the transmission unit and raise it to take the weight of the transmission unit. *Locate a piece*

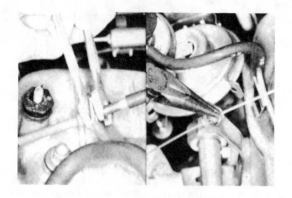

Fig. 6.42 Detach the transmission throttle cable – carburettor models (Sec 13)

of wood between the transmission oil pan and the jack saddle to prevent damaging the oil pan.

20 Unbolt and remove the transmission rear support member. Where applicable note the location of the earth strap and the exhaust rubber hanger. (Fig. 6.47).

21 Undo the retaining bolts and remove the engine under cover.

22 Prise free the two rubber plugs from the cover plate on the lower front face of the torque converter housing. Using a socket and extension inserted through the access hole, unscrew the six bolts which hold the driveplate and torque converter together. The bolts can be brought into view one at a time by rotating the crankshaft with a ring spanner applied to the crackshaft pulley bolt.

23 When all of the bolts are removed, screw a guide pin (which can be fabricated from an old bolt with the head cut off) into a torque converter bolt hole. The guide pin should be of suitable length so that, when fitted, its front end will protrude beyond the rear plate inspection hole and will provide a leverage point when separating the transmission from the engine and driveplate. Make an alignment mark on the driveplate adjacent to the guide pin to ensure correct realignment of the converter with the driveplate during refitting.

24 Place a jack under the engine sump (use a block of wood to protect it) and remove the bolts which secure the torque converter housing to the engine.

25 Lower both jacks progressively until the transmission unit will clear the lower edge of the engine rear bulkhead.

26 The aid of an assistant will be needed at this point to steady the transmission as it is withdrawn. Use a suitable lever and prise against the end of the guide pin as shown (Fig. 6.50), and simultaneously withdraw the transmission unit, complete with the torque converter,

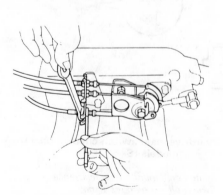

Fig. 6.43 Detach the transmission throttle cable – EFI models (Sec 13)

Fig. 6.44 Disconnect the speedometer cable (Sec 13)

Fig. 6.45 Disconnect the manual shift linkage (Sec 13)

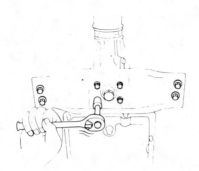

Fig. 6.46 Unbolt and remove the stiffener plate (Sec 13)

Fig. 6.47 Transmission support member and retaining bolts (Sec 13)

Fig. 6.48 Undo the driveplate-to-torque converter bolts (Sec 13)

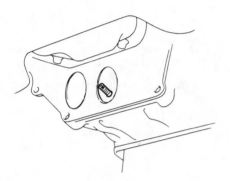

Fig. 6.49 Insert a guide pin (Sec 13)

Fig. 6.50 Lever against the guide pin to ease transmission withdrawal (Sec 13)

Fig. 6.51 Torque converter run-out check (Sec 13)

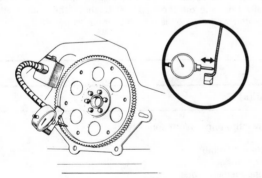

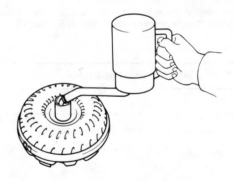

Fig. 6.52 Driveplate run-out check (Sec 13)

Fig. 6.53 Topping-up the torque converter fluid level before refitting (Sec 13)

away from the engine. Catch the fluid which will run from the torque converter during this operation. **On no account should levers be placed between the driveplate and the torque converter as damage or distortion will result.** As the transmission moves away from the engine, the driveplate will remain bolted to the rear flange of the crankshaft. Take care not to snag the transmission on the throttle cable or neutral starter switch. Keep the transmission upright (oil pan down).

27 The torque converter should be kept in position in its housing whilst the transmission is removed. To do this bolt a temporary plate and spacer across the front face of the housing with a suitable spacer to retain the converter unit.

28 If the torque converter is removed for any reason it is advisable to check its run-out before refitting it. Temporarily bolt it in position on

the driveplate and, using a dial gauge as shown, check the run-out of the hub sleeve (Fig. 6.51). If the run-out exceeds the specified maximum allowed, reposition the converter on the driveplate. When set in a position which complies with the specified tolerance mark the relative positions of the driveplate and converter before removing the bolts to ensure correct installation when refitting the transmission.

29 If it is found impossible to correct excessive run-out, remove the torque converter and check the run-out of the driveplate. Renew the torque converter and/or the driveplate as necessary (Fig. 6.52).

30 Before refitting the torque converter to the transmission, it will have to be refilled with new ATF of the specified type. Check that the old fluid is completely drained then top up as shown in Fig. 6.53, using the specified quantity and type of automatic transmission fluid. Lubricate the central hub and the driveplate pilot hole with grease.

Fig. 6.54 Lubricate the centre hub and driveplate pilot hole (Sec 13)

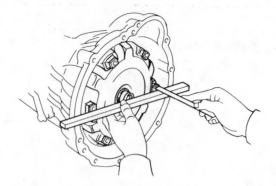

Fig. 6.55 Torque converter installation depth check (Sec 13)

31 When the converter is refitted, check that the clearance between the installed surface (on the front face) and the transmission housing front face is 26 mm (1.02 in) – see Fig. 6.55. Use a straight-edge and calipers for this check.

32 Refitting of the transmission is a reversal of the removal procedure, but the following points should be noted.

33 When the transmission is being manoeuvred into position take care that the torque converter does not slip forward. Align the driveplate hole with the guide pin in the torque converter for ease of engagement. Locate the guide pin at the bottom of the converter for convenience and check that the relative alignment marks between the converter and driveplate correspond.

34 When the transmission is in position, reconnect the reversing light switch and check that the wiring from it is correctly routed over the transmission, particularly in the area above the starter motor. The wiring loom must not be positioned so that it will chafe against the steering column. Secure it in such a position to prevent this.

35 On completion, top up the transmission fluid level, as decribed in Section 9, top up the cooling system, with reference to Chapter 2, and check that all fastenings are secure. All bolts should be retightened to the specified torque settings where given.

36 Check and if necessary adjust the floor shift linkage and the transmission throttle cable, as described in Section 10.

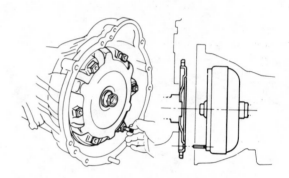

Fig. 6.56 Insert guide stud, check that it aligns with hole in driveplate (Sec 13)

37 Road test the vehicle and then check for any signs of fluid leaks, especially from the oil cooler pipes. Recheck the fluid level of the transmission when the oil is hot and top up as necessary.

14 Fault diagnosis – manual gearbox

Symptom	Reason(s)
Ineffective synchromesh on one or more gears	Worn synchro rings. Worn shift keys
Jumps out of one or more gears	Weak detent springs Worn shift forks Worn engagement dogs Worn clutch hubs
Whining, roughness, vibration allied to other faults	Bearing failure and/or overall wear
Noisy and difficult gear engagement	Clutch not operating correctly
Sloppy and impositive gear selection	Overall wear throughout the selector mechanism

15 Fault diagnosis – automatic transmission

Symptom	Reason(s)
Oil on dipstick discoloured or burnt	Contaminated fluid Faulty torque converter Faulty transmission Transmission misused (eg overweight towing or wheel spinning in mud or snow)
No vehicle movement in forward range, or reverse	Incorrectly adjusted selector linkage Faulty torque converter Broken driveplate Park pawl faulty Transmission fault
Incorrect shift lever position	Linkage needs adjustment Manual valve and lever faulty Transmission fault
Harsh engagement when any drive range selected	Throttle cable out of adjustment Transmission fault
Delayed upshifts or downshifts and/or downshift too quick when coasting	Throttle cable needs adjustment Throttle cable and/or cam faulty Transmission fault
Kickdown fault	Throttle cable needs adjustment Transmission fault
Slip on upshifts, downshifts squawk or shudder on take off	Manual linkage needs adjustment Throttle cable needs adjustment Transmission fault
Vehicle will not hold parked in P	Incorrectly adjusted selector linkage

Before carrying out any of the foregoing diagnosis checks always verify that the transmission fluid is at its correct level. Where an internal transmission fault is suspected, have it checked out by a Toyota dealer without delay.

Chapter 7 Propeller shaft

Contents

Specifications

General

Type	Tubular, two section, three universal joints and centre bearing. Front sliding sleeve
Universal joints	Greased, sealed for life, needle roller bearings
Spider axial play allowance	Zero
Propeller and intermediate shaft run-out limit	0.8 mm (0.031 in)

Torque wrench settings

	kgf m	lbf ft
UJ flange yoke to companion flange:		
UK models and 1982/1983 USA models	3.0 to 4.0	22 to 28
1984/1985 USA models	4.3	31
Centre bearing flange to UJ yoke flange:		
UK models and 1982/1983 USA models	3.0 to 4.0	22 to 28
1984/1985 USA models	4.3	31
Centre bearing bracket to body:		
UK models and 1982/1983 USA models	3.0 to 4.5	22 to 32
1984/1985 USA models	4.1	30
Intermediate shaft/centre bearing/joint flange:		
UK models and 1982/1983/1984 USA models:		
1st	17.0 to 20.0	123 to 144
2nd	Loosen nut	
3rd	2.5 to 3.5	19 to 25
1985 USA models:		
1st	18.5	134
2nd	Loosen nut	
3rd	7.0	51

1 General description

The drive from the gearbox to the rear axle is transmitted by the tubular propeller shaft. Due to the variety of angles caused by the up and down motion of the rear axle in relation to the gearbox, universal joints are fitted to each end of the shaft to convey the drive through the constantly varying angles. As the movement also increases and decreases the distance between the rear axle and the gearbox, the forward end of the propeller shaft is a splined sleeve which is a sliding fit over the rear of the gearbox splined mainshaft.

The propeller shaft fitted is a two section type (intermediate shaft and propeller shaft), with a central steady bearing mounted to the body. The universal joints are not of the serviceable type and therefore, when the joints become worn, the universal joint unit and shaft must be renewed.

The universal joints each consist of a four-way trunnion, or spider – each leg of which runs in a needle roller bearing race – preloaded with grease and fitted in the bearing journal yokes of the sliding sleeve and the propeller shaft and flange.

The splined sleeve runs in an oil seal in the gearbox rear extension housing and is supported with the mainshaft on the gearbox rear bearing. The splines are lubricated by oil in the rear extension housing which comes from the gearbox.

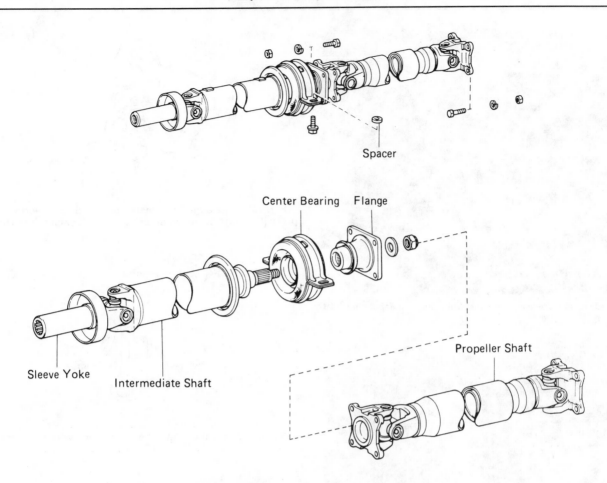

Spacer

Center Bearing   Flange

Propeller Shaft

Sleeve Yoke   Intermediate Shaft

Fig. 7.1 Intermediate and propeller shaft assemblies (Sec 1)

2   Routine maintenance – propeller shaft

No maintenance is required except for occasionally checking the tightness of the propeller shaft rear flange bolts, the intermediate shaft flange bolts and central bearing mounting bolts. At the same time check the condition of the universal joints, as described in the next Section.

3   Universal joints – inspection (on-vehicle)

1   Wear in the needle roller bearings is characterised by vibration in the transmission, 'clonks' on taking up the drive and in extreme cases of lack of lubrication, metallic squeaking, and ultimately grating and shrieking sounds as the bearings break up.
2   It is easy to check if the needle roller bearings are worn, with the propeller shaft in position, by trying to turn the shaft with one hand, the other hand holding the rear axle flange. Any movement between the propeller shaft and the flange is indicative of considerable wear. The front needle roller bearings should be tested for wear using the same principle as described in paragraph 2.
3   The front needle roller bearings should be tested for wear using the same principle as described in paragraph 2.
4   To test the splined coupling for wear, lift the end of the shaft and note any movement in the splines.
5   Check the splined coupling dust cover for signs of damage or looseness on the shaft.
6   If renewal or repairs are necessary to any part(s) of the propeller shaft and/or intermediate shaft then the propeller shaft assembly, complete, must be removed from the vehicle, as described in the next Section.

4   Propeller shaft – removal and refitting

1   Jack up the rear of the car and support on firmly based safety stands.
2   The rear of the propeller shaft is connected to the rear axle pinion by a flange held by four nuts and bolts. Mark the position of both flanges relative to each other, and then undo and remove the nuts and bolts (photo).
3   Remove the centre bearing securing strap bolts, lower the strap and centre bearing assembly and note the position of the strap bolt washers (photo).
4   Support the propeller shaft and withdraw it from the rear of the gearbox, then lower and remove the shaft assembly complete from underneath the car.
5   Place a container under the gearbox rear extension housing to catch any oil which may come out. Refitting the propeller shaft is the reverse sequence to removal but the following additional points should be noted:

(a)   Ensure that the mating marks on the propeller shaft and differential pinion flanges are lined up
(b)   If originally fitted, locate the height spacer between the centre bearing support and the body. Hand tighten the central bearing support bolts initially then, when the pinion joint is reconnected, check to make sure that the bearing support bracket is at right-angles to the propeller shaft. When the central bearing is secure the bearing should be positioned as shown with the centre line of the bracket and bearing in alignment (Fig. 7.4)
(c)   Tighten all bolts to the specified torque wrench setting
(d)   Don't forget to check the gearbox oil level and top-up if necessary

4.2 Propeller shaft-to-rear axle universal joint – independent rear suspension (IRS) type

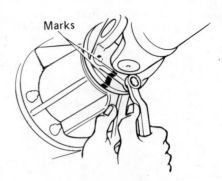

Fig. 7.2 Make alignment marks before disconnecting the propeller shaft or intermediate shaft universal joints (Sec 4)

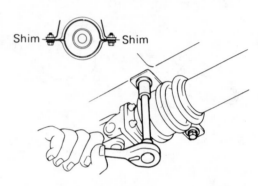

Fig. 7.3 Locate the centre bearing shims where applicable (Sec 4)

4.3 Propeller shaft centre bearing and mounting bolts

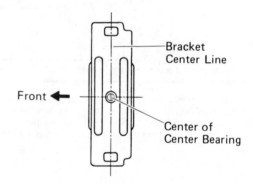

5 Propeller shaft – dismantling and assembly

1   Scribe or paint an alignment mark across the joint faces of the propeller shaft and intermediate shaft flanges.
2   Unscrew and remove the four attachment bolts and nuts, then separate the two assemblies.
3   To remove the centre bearing unit from the intermediate shaft, support the shaft securely in a vice as shown (Fig. 7.6) then, using a suitable chisel, relieve the staking on the nut. Unscrew the nut and remove it.
4   Make an alignment mark on the end of the shaft and flange. The intermediate shaft can then be withdrawn through the bearing, but should it prove tight, support the flange in a vice and use a soft metal drift to drive the shaft through.
5   Inspect the centre bearing for wear or damage and renew it as a unit if necessary. The central bearing should turn freely.
6   Check the universal joints of each shaft for wear and if necessary renew the shaft(s) and joints complete.

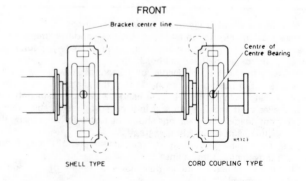

Fig. 7.4 Centre line of bracket and bearing must correspond. Bearing orientation is according to type (Sec 4)

7   If the propeller shaft run-out is checked and is found to be beyond the specified maximum limit, then the shaft will have to be renewed.

8   Reassembly is a reversal of the dismantling procedure, but note the following points:

    (a)   Lubricate the intermediate shaft splines with a medium grease before fitting. Align the match marks

    (b)   Tighten the intermediate shaft flange retaining nut to the initial specified torque setting. Then, having pressed the bearing into position, loosen the nut and retighten it to its final torque wrench setting (see Specifications), then stake lock the nut

    (c)   Align the flange marks made during dismantling and fit and tighten the four attachment nuts and bolts to the specified torque wrench setting

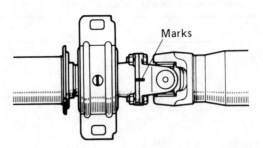

Fig. 7.5 Propeller shaft-to-intermediate shaft joint flange must be marked (Sec 5)

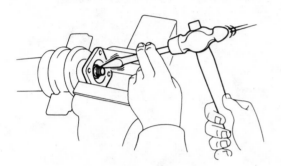

Fig. 7.6 Relieve the nut retainer staking using a suitable chisel (Sec 5)

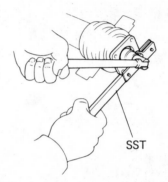

Fig. 7.7 Centre bearing nut removal method. Bar (SST) prevents shaft from turning (Sec 5)

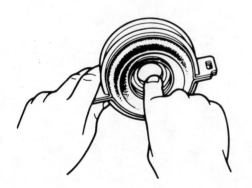

Fig. 7.8 Check centre bearing for excessive wear or damage (Sec 5)

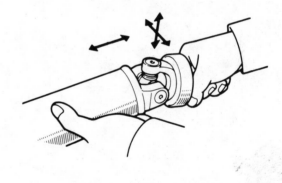

Fig. 7.9 Check universal joints for excessive wear or damage (Sec 5)

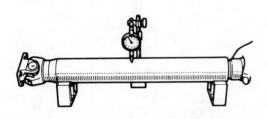

Fig. 7.10 Check shaft(s) for excessive run-out (Sec 5)

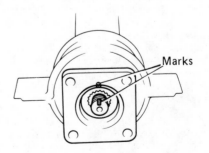

Fig. 7.11 Align the shaft-to-flange match marks (Sec 5)

6 Fault diagnosis – propeller shaft and universal joints

Symptom	Reason(s)
Propeller shaft vibration	Universal joint spider bearing worn or damaged Bent propeller shaft Propeller shaft out of balance Worn gearbox extension housing bush Universal joint mounting loose Worn central bearing (where applicable)
Noisy starting or while coasting	Universal joint spider bearing worn or damaged Slackness in the spider bearings Universal joint mounting loose No preload of the differential drive pinion bearing Worn splines of drive pinion companion flange Worn splines of universal joint sleeve yoke Incorrect installation of splined coupling dust cover

Chapter 8 Rear axle

Contents

Specifications

General

Type .... Hypoid bevel differential fitted to rigid axle (four link suspension models) or swing axle (independent rear suspension models)

Ratios .... 3.909 to 1 or 3.42 to 1 (depending on model)

Oil capacity

UK models:
FLS axle .... 1.3 litre (2.3 pints)
IRS axle (6.7 in) .... 1.0 litre (1.8 Imp pints)
IRS axle (7.5 in) .... 1.3 litre (2.3 Imp pints)

USA models:
1982 models with unitized axle .... 1.2 litre (1.3 US qt)
1982 models with conventional axle .... 1.3 litre (1.4 US qt)
1983 and 1984 models with IRS .... 1.0 litre (1.1 US qt)
1983 and 1984 models with FLS .... 1.3 litre (1.4 US qt)
1985 models with IRS and manual gearbox .... 1.2 litre (1.3 US qt)
1985 models with IRS and automatic gearbox .... 1.0 litre (1.1 US qt)
1985 models with FLS .... 1.3 litre (1.4 US qt)

Independent rear suspension (IRS) axle details

Rear axleshaft:
Oil seal drive in depth:
Inner – all models .... 31 mm (1.22 in)
Outer – UK models .... 5.5 mm (0.217 in)
Outer – USA models .... 6.0 mm (0.346 in)
Flange runout limit (maximum) .... 0.1 mm (0.004 in)
Bearing preload (add oil seal rotation resistance) at starting .... 0.01 to 0.04 kgf m (0.07 to 0.29 lbf ft)

Rear driveshaft:
Installed length (flange to flange):
NTN Type – UK models .... 441.0 to 443.0 mm (17.36 to 17.44 in)
NTN Type – USA models .... 416.5 to 419.5 mm (16.40 to 16.52 in)
Toyota type – UK models .... 436.0 to 438.0 mm (17.17 to 17.24 in)
Toyota type – USA models .... 415.5 mm (16.36 in)

Differential:
Crownwheel-to-pinion backlash .... 0.13 to 0.18 mm (0.005 to 0.007 in)
Pinion-to-side gear backlash .... 0.05 to 0.20 mm (0.002 to 0.008 in)

RIng gear run-out limit .... 0.07 mm (0.003 in)
Companion flange run-out limit (maximum) .... 0.10 mm (0.004 in)
Drive pinion oil seal drive in depth:
    UK models with 6.7 in differential .... 4.0 mm (0.157 in)
    UK models with 7.5 in differential .... 1.5 mm (0.059 in)
    1983 and 1984 USA models .... 2.0 mm (0.08 in)
    1985 USA models with 6.7 in differential .... 2.0 mm (0.08 in)
    1985 USA models with 7.5 in differential .... 1.5 mm (0.06 in)
Side gear oil seal drive in depth .... Flush with carrier end face
Side gear shaft run-out limit (maximum) .... 0.2 mm (0.008 in)

Pinion bearing preload – at starting:	kgf m	lbf ft
New bearing (6.7 in differential)	0.10 to 0.16	0.72 to 1.16
New bearing (7.5 in differential)	0.12 to 0.19	0.87 to 1.37
Used bearing (6.7 in differential)	0.05 to 0.08	0.36 to 0.58
Used bearing (7.5 in differential)	0.06 to 0.10	0.43 to 0.72

Four link suspension (FLS) axle details

Rear axle:
    Axleshaft run-out limit (maximum):
        UK and 1982/1983 USA models .... 2.0 mm (0.079 in)
        1984 and 1985 USA models .... 1.5 mm (0.059 in)
    Axleshaft flange runout limit (maximum):
        UK and 1982/1983 USA models .... 0.2 mm (0.008 in)
        1984 and 1985 USA models .... 0.1 mm (0.004 in)
Differential:
    Crownwheel-to-pinion backlash .... 0.13 to 0.18 mm (0.005 to 0.007 in)
    Pinion gear-to-side gear backlash:
        UK models .... 0.13 to 0.18 mm (0.005 to 0.007 in)
        USA models .... 0.5 to 0.20 mm (0.002 to 0.008 in)
    Ring gear (crownwheel) run-out limit .... 0.07 mm (0.0028 in)
    Companion flange run-out .... 0.10 mm (0.0039 in)
    Oil seal drive in depth:
        UK models and USA models (conventional axle types) .... 4.0 mm (0.157 in)
        1982 USA models with unitized axle .... 2.0 mm (0.079 in)

Pinion bearing preload – at starting:	kgf m	lbf ft
New bearing	0.10 to 0.16	7.2 to 1.16
Used bearing	0.05 to 0.08	0.36 to 0.58
Total preload at starting	Pinion bearing preload plus 0.03 to 0.05 kgf m (0.22 to 0.36 lbf ft)	

Torque wrench settings

	kgf m	lbf ft
IRS axle		
Driveshaft to rear axleshaft	7.0	51
Driveshaft to differential	7.0	51
Axleshaft to flange (see text for procedure):		
Stage 1	4.0	29
Stage 2	8.0	58
Stage 3 (if required) up to maximum of	20.0	145
Propeller shaft to companion flange:		
UK and 1983 USA models	3.5	25
1984 and 1985 USA models	4.3	31
Carrier cover bolts	2.2	16
Driveshaft to side gear shaft	7.0	51
Pinion/companion flange nut (see text for details):		
Initial tightening of flange nut	11.0	80.0
Further tightening to preload requirement in increments of	1.3	9
Maximum allowable tightening of nut	24.0	174
Ring gear to differential	9.8	71
Side bearing cap	8.0	58
Differential carrier to support	8.5	61
Carrier support to suspension member	8.5	61
FLS axle		
Bearing retainer to backing plate	6.7	4.8
Propeller shaft to companion flange:		
UK and 1982/1983 USA models	2.0 to 4.0	14 to 28
1984 and 1985 USA models	4.3	31
Pinion/companion flange nut (see text for details):		
Initial tightening of flange nut	11.0	80.0
Further tightening to preload requirement in increments of	1.3	9
Maximum tightening of flange nut	24.0	174
Ring gear to differential case	9.8	71
Side bearing cap to differential carrier	8.0	58
Side bearing adjusting nut lock	1.3	9
Differential carrier to axle housing (conventional)	3.1	22
Unitized differential carrier cover bolts	2.5	18

1 General description

The rear axle type used is dependent on the model and the rear suspension system fitted. The axle types used are the swing axle type, fitted to models with the independent rear suspension (IRS) system, or fixed beam axle type, used on models with the four link suspension (FLS) system.

With the IRS type, the differential carrier unit is centrally mounted to the rear suspension member and external drive shafts. CV joints transmit the drive to the axleshafts and rear wheels.

With the FLS type, the differential unit and axleshafts are housed in a common beam axle of traditional design.

On all models, the differential unit is of hypoid bevel type.

The 1982 USA models with FLS differ in that a unitized differential unit is fitted. This is described in Section 13 and differs from other models with FLS, which have a conventional differential carrier unit.

Operations on the rear axle should be limited to those described in this Chapter. Overhaul of the differential unit is not considered to be within the scope of the home mechanic due to the specialised procedures involved.

The axle types are identified in the Section headings as IRS or FLS.

2 Routine maintenance – rear axle

1 **Axle oil level:** Check the oil level in the differential housing at the intervals specified in the Routine Maintenance section at the start of this manual.

2 The vehicle must be parked on level ground and the handbrake fully applied. Unscrew the filler level plug from the differential housing and check that the oil level is up to the bottom of the plug hole (photo). Top up if required using the correct grade of oil, but do not overfill. Refit the plug. The need for regular topping-up with oil indicates a leak and its source must be found and repaired. The most likely will be a defective oil seal.

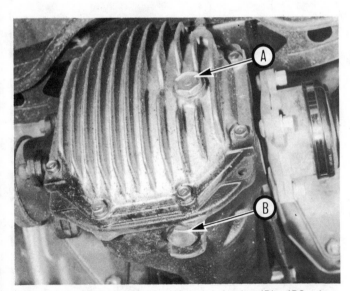

2.2 Rear axle oil filler/level plug (A) and drain plug (B) – IRS axle

3 Where the vehicle is, or has been, used in severe operating conditions, the differential oil must be drained and renewed at the specified intervals (see Routine Maintenance Section at start of manual). Remove the drain plug from the base of the differential housing and drain the old oil into a suitable container for disposal. Refit the drain plug then remove the filler/level plug and top up the oil level with the correct grade and quantity of oil. Refit the filler level plug.

4 **Driveshafts (IRS models):** Periodically check the driveshaft CV gaiters (boots) for signs of cracks, damage or leaks. Repair or renew as necessary.

3 Axleshaft bearings and oil seals (IRS) – removal and refitting

Special note: Some stages of the removal and refitting procedures require the use of Toyota special service tools (SST), in particular tool No 09557-22022. Unless these tools are available, this task must be entrusted to a Toyota dealer.

1 Raise the vehicle at the rear so that the roadwheel(s) are clear of the ground. Support the vehicle on safety stands. Remove the roadwheel(s).

2 Make an alignment mark across the outer faces of the rear axleshaft flange and the driveshaft flange, then unscrew the securing nuts and disconnect the driveshaft.

3 Apply the handbrake fully. Release the lock stake of the axle flange nut then unscrew and remove the nut and washer.

4 The axle flange can now be withdrawn using SST 09557-22022 (Fig. 8.4). Remove the axle flange washer.

5 Refer to Chapter 9 and remove the rear brake disc or disc drum (as applicable) on the side concerned.

6 Withdraw the rear axleshaft using SST 09520-00031, or an alternative puller or slide hammer. Withdraw the axleshaft, complete with the outer oil seal, bearing and spacer (Fig. 8.5).

7 Withdraw the inner oil seal from the axle housing using a puller, then remove the inner bearing cup by drifting it out from the outside in. Use a soft metal drift or a tube of suitable diameter.

8 Remove the outer bearing cone and oil seal from the axleshaft. Using a suitable chisel or metal wedge, drive it between the hub and bearing to provide a clearance between the hub and bearing. Engage a puller behind the bearing and withdraw it. Take care not to damage the hub and, if it is to be used again, the bearing (Figs. 8.7 and 8.8).

9 Remove the oil seal.

10 Remove the bearing outer race in the same manner as that described for the inner bearing (para 7).

11 Clean and examine the dismantled components and renew if damaged or excessively worn. The oil seals, spacer and axleshaft flange retaining nut must always be renewed. Renew the bearings as a set (cup and cone race).

12 Commence reassembly by refitting the inner bearing cup into position in the housing using a suitable tube drift. Lubricate the rollers in the bearing cone with grease and install the bearing.

13 Smear the oil seal inner lip with grease, then drift the seal into the housing so that its fitted depth is 31 mm (1.22 in). The seal cavity must face the bearing.

14 Drive the outer bearing race into position in the outside end of the housing using a tube drift.

15 Coat the area within the housing between the bearings, and the new spacer with grease then insert the spacer between the bearings.

16 Thoroughly lubricate the bearing rollers with grease and install the bearing.

17 Lubricate the inner oil seal lip with grease, then drift the seal into position so that its full fitted depth is 5.5 to 6.0 mm (0.22 to 0.24 in).

18 Smear the inner bore of the axleshaft flange with a thin coating of grease, insert the axleshaft into the housing, then locate the flange and washer on the inner side of the housing. The assemblies are assembled together using Toyota SST No. 09557-22022 and a spacer (see Fig. 8.13). With the tool in position, draw the two assemblies into position to the point where the shaft deflector tip and flange are in alignment. Do not get grease on the threads of the shaft.

19 Fit the new axleshaft flange nut. This must be tightened to the initial specified torque wrench setting to set the bearing preload. Prevent the shaft from turning when tightening the nut by using SST No 09520-00031. When tightened to the specified torque range, it is essential that the axleshaft has horizontal play.

20 Rotate the axleshaft in each direction to seat the bearings, then refit the torque wrench onto the nut and measure the initial resistance required (rotational torque) to turn the axleshaft when turning the axle shaft one turn per six seconds.

21 Now tighten the nut to the Stage 2 torque setting and recheck the rotational torque of the axleshaft. Compare this with the rotational torque requirement specified and if required, further tighten the nut in

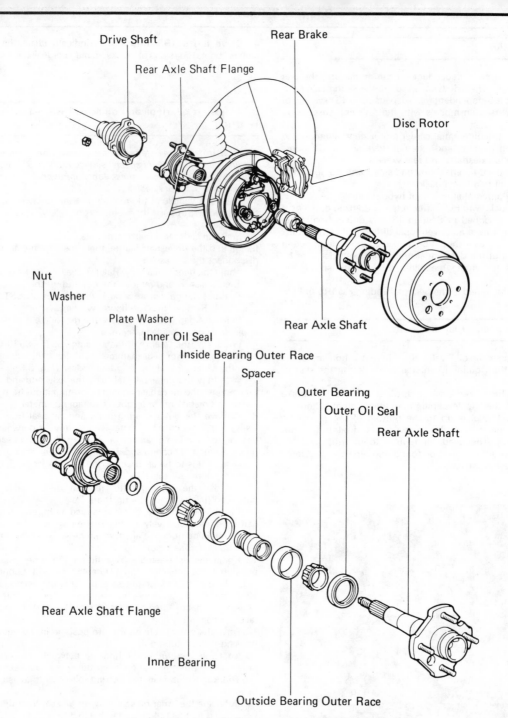

Drive Shaft

Rear Brake

Rear Axle Shaft Flange

Disc Rotor

Rear Axle Shaft

Nut

Washer

Plate Washer

Inner Oil Seal

Inside Bearing Outer Race

Spacer

Outer Bearing

Outer Oil Seal

Rear Axle Shaft

Rear Axle Shaft Flange

Inner Bearing

Outside Bearing Outer Race

Fig. 8.1 Rear axleshaft components – IRS Type (Sec 3)

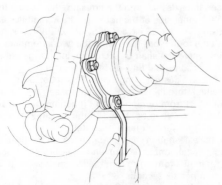

Fig. 8.2 Remove the driveshaft flange bolts – IRS Type
(Sec 3)

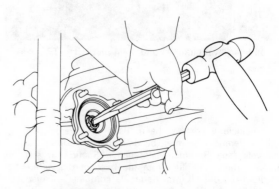

Fig. 8.3 Relieve the lock stake on the axle flange nut –
IRS Type (Sec 3)

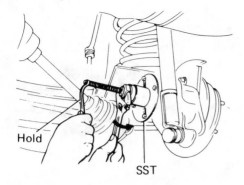

Fig. 8.4 Axle flange removal using special tool – IRS Type (Sec 3)

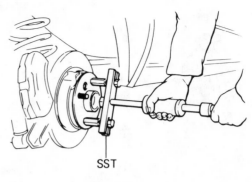

Fig. 8.5 Axleshaft removal using special tool – IRS Type (Sec 3)

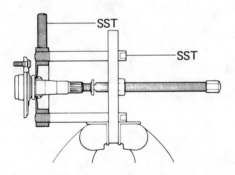

Fig. 8.6 Axle inner bearing cup removal – IRS Type (Sec 3)

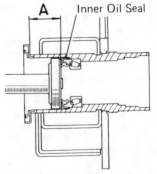

Fig. 8.7 Move outer bearing cone away from the hub – IRS Type (Sec 3)

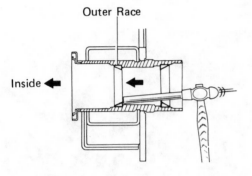

Fig. 8.8 Withdraw outer bearing cone with puller – IRS Type (Sec 3)

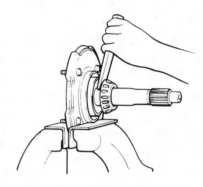

Fig. 8.9 Inner oil seal fitting depth (A) – IRS Type (Sec 3)

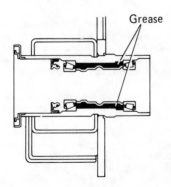

Fig. 8.10 Lubricate with grease – IRS Type (Sec 3)

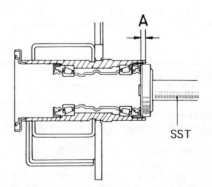

Fig. 8.11 Outer oil seal fitting depth (A) – IRS Type (Sec 3)

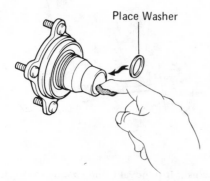

Place Washer

Fig. 8.12 Lubricate the flange prior to fitting – IRS Type
(Sec 3)

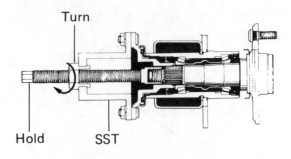

Turn

Hold   SST

Fig. 8.13 Axleshaft and flange installation using Toyota
special tool – IRS Type (Sec 3)

increments of 5 to 10° to meet the specified requirement, but do not
exceed the maximum allowable tightening torque for the nut.
22 If the maximum allowable nut tightening torque is exceeded, or
excessive preload persists, dismantle the unit and fit a new spacer, then
reassemble and adjust the preload.
23 With the preload correctly set, stake punch the nut to secure it in
the set position.
24 Refit the rear brake assembly, as described in Chapter 9.
25 Reconnect the driveshaft, ensuring that the match marks made
during dismantling are in alignment. Tighten the nuts to the specified
torque.
26 Refit the roadwheel and lower the vehicle.

4 Driveshaft (IRS) – removal, inspection and refitting

1   Raise the vehicle at the rear and support on safety stands.
2   Make an alignment index mark across the faces of the driveshaft-
to-differential unit flange and the driveshaft-to-axleshaft flange.
3   Undo the four retaining bolts and detach the driveshaft from the
differential unit flange. Support the driveshaft and take care not to
damage the joint gaiters (photo).
4   Undo the four retaining bolts and detach the driveshaft from the
axleshaft flange. Withdraw the driveshaft.
5   Clean the driveshaft externally, then inspect the gaiters. If the
gaiters are perished or split, they must be removed and renewed.
6   Secure the shaft in a vice then check that the outer joint slides
smoothly in both directions of thrust. Check the inboard and outboard
joint for excessive radial play. If the joints are damaged or excessively
worn they must be overhauled.
7   When renewing or repairing driveshafts it should be noted that two
types have been fitted, being either a Toyota type, which has a
triangular shaped outboard joint or an NTN type which has a circular
outboard joint.
8   Refitting is a reversal of the removal procedure. Align the flange
index marks when locating the driveshaft and tighten the retaining
nuts to the specified torque setting.

5 NTN type driveshaft (IRS) – overhaul

1   Remove the driveshaft, as described in the previous Section.
2   Clean away the external dirt and grease, release the boot retaining
clips and slide the gaiters inwards towards the centre of the shaft; clear
of the joints.
3   Wipe away the grease from the joints before dismantling them.
4   Remove the snap-ring from its location in the outer race.
5   Paint a match mark on the end face of the driveshaft and the outer
race (do not punch mark them), then withdraw the outer race from the
shaft.
6   The end cover must be renewed if damaged or excessively worn.
7   Lightly tap the end of the ball cage on its outer circumference in the
axial direction of the shaft with a soft-faced hammer. Remove the balls.

4.3 Driveshaft-to-differential flange

8   Remove the snap-ring securing the outboard joint inner race on the
shaft then press or drive the outboard joint inner race from the
driveshaft. Remove the inner snap-ring.
9   Withdraw the outboard and inboard joint boots from the shaft.
10 Prise free the endplate from the end of the inboard joint using a
screwdriver.
11 Paint match marks on the inner end of the driveshaft and the
inboard joint, remove the snap-ring and then press or pull the inboard
joint from the shaft.
12 Clean the respective components then inspect them for signs of
excessive wear, damage or cracks. Renew as necessary.
13 Commence reassembly by winding some vinyl insulation tape over
the splined end sections of the shaft, then slide the new clamps and the
inboard and outboard boots onto the shaft. Remove the protective tape
from the splined sections.
14 Locate a new snap-ring onto the inner groove on the shaft, then
position the outboard ball cage over the end of the shaft with its larger
diameter facing out.
15 Align the match marks made during dismantling and fit the inner
race onto the shaft. It will need to be pressed or driven into position
using a 27 mm socket bearing on the inner race. Check that the
alignment marks correspond and then fit the outer snap-ring to secure.
16 Smear the balls, inner race and cage with some grease from the
repair pack supplied, then tap the balls into position using a light
pressure with a soft-faced hammer.
17 Align the match marks made during dismantling and press the
inboard joint into position on the shaft. Use a 26 mm socket to bear on

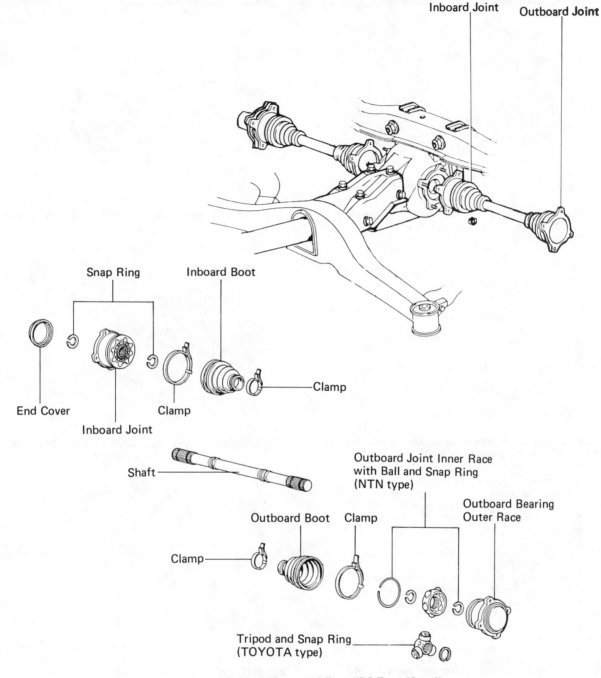

Fig. 8.14 Driveshaft assemblies – IRS Type (Sec 4)

Fig. 8.15 Driveshaft checks – IRS Type (Sec 4)

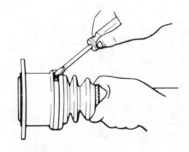

Fig. 8.16 Release the driveshaft boot clips – IRS Type (Sec 4)

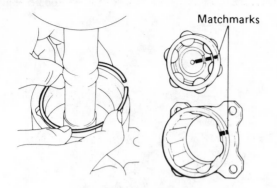

Fig. 8.17 Remove snap-ring and make match marks (NTN driveshaft) – IRS Type (Sec 5)

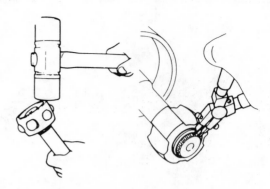

Fig. 8.18 NTN type joint dismantling – IRS Type (Sec 5)

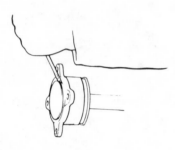

Fig. 8.19 End cover removal from inboard joint – IRS Type (Sec 5)

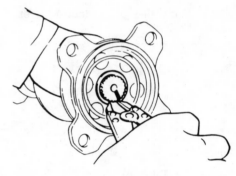

Fig. 8.20 Remove snap-ring securing the inboard joint – IRS Type (Sec 5)

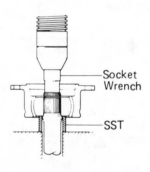

Fig. 8.21 Inboard joint removal from driveshaft – IRS Type (Sec 5)

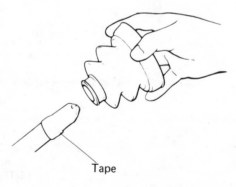

Fig. 8.22 Wind tape over splines to protect boots when fitting (Sec 5)

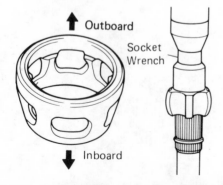

Fig. 8.23 NTN outboard joint inner race reassembly – IRS Type (Sec 5)

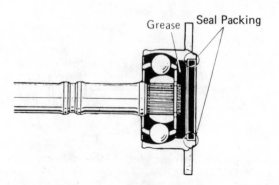

Fig. 8.24 Inboard joint lubrication points – IRS Type (Sec 5)

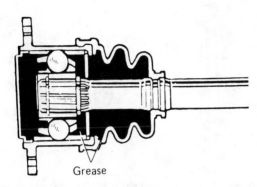

Fig. 8.25 Outboard joint must be packed with specified grease (Sec 5)

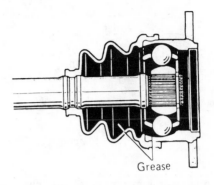

Fig. 8.26 Pack inboard joint with specified grease, also its gaiter (Sec 5)

the inboard joint for protection. Fit a new snap-ring into its groove on the shaft to secure.

18 Pack the inboard joints with 60 g (0.13 lb) of grease from the repair kit supplied, then apply the seal packing No 5 (also supplied) around the inboard face of the end plate. Carefully tap the endplate into position, taking care not to distort it.

19 The inboard and outboard joint boots can now be refitted. Each boot should be packed with 60 g (0.13 lb) of grease from the repair kit and the same amount applied to the inboard joint and the outboard outer race. Install the snap-ring into position in the outer race of the outboard joint.

20 Locate the boots over the joints with the shaft length set as specified (Fig. 8.27) according to model.

21 Position the clamp locks between the bolt holes in the flanges, then secure them. Turn each joint to stretch the boot and ensure that it doesn't deform.

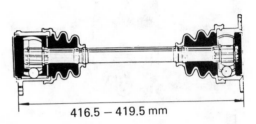

416.5 – 419.5 mm

Fig. 8.27 Driveshaft boots must be clamped to set the shaft at the required installed length – see Specifications (Sec 5)

6 Toyota type driveshaft (IRS) – overhaul

1   Remove the driveshaft, as described in Section 4.

2   Clean away the external dirt and grease, release the boot retaining clips and slide the boots inwards towards the centre of the shaft to clear the joints.

3   Wipe away the grease from the joints before dismantling them.

4   Paint a match mark on the end face of the driveshaft and the outer race (do not punch mark them), then remove the outer race from the shaft.

5   The end cover must be renewed if damaged or excessively worn.

6   Paint match marks across the end face of the driveshaft and the tripod joint, then remove the snap-ring and press or drive the tripod joint free from the shaft. Use a tube drift to bear on the hub of the tripod joint. Do not put any pressure on the rollers.

7   Withdraw the outboard and inboard joint boots from the driveshaft.

8   The procedure for dismantling the inboard joint is the same as that described for the NTN type in Section 5, paragraph 10.

9   Clean the respective components then inspect them for signs of excessive wear, damage or cracks. Renew as necessary.

10 Commence reassembly by winding some vinyl insulation tape over the splines and sections of the driveshaft, then slide the new clamps and inboard and outboard boots on the shaft. It should be noted that Toyota manufactured boots are designed to fit only the inboard or outboard side so it is important that they are identified and fitted correctly. Locate the clamps so that the strap is bent in the opposite direction of rotation.

11 Refit the outboard tripod joint onto the shaft so that the match marks made during dismantling correspond. This is not applicable if a new joint is being fitted, but ensure that the joint is fitted with the chamfer inwards (Fig. 8.30). Press or drift the tripod joint onto the shaft using a socket or metal tube of suitable diameter to bear on the hub of the tripod joint (not on the rollers).

12 With the tripod joint in position, fit a new snap-ring into the groove in the shaft to secure the joint.

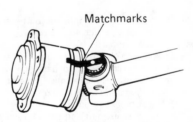

Fig. 8.28 Make alignment marks on the outer joint race and shaft (Toyota driveshaft) – IRS Type (Sec 6)

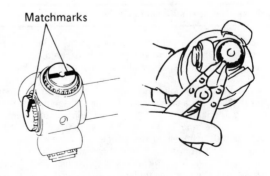

Fig. 8.29 Tripod joint removal (Toyota driveshaft) – IRS Type (Sec 6)

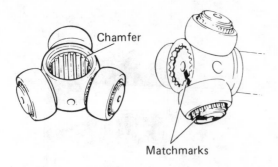

Chamfer

Matchmarks

Fig. 8.30 Align match marks and fit with chamfer inwards (Toyota driveshaft) – IRS Type (Sec 6)

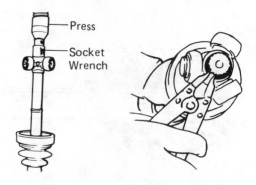

Press

Socket Wrench

Fig. 8.31 Tripod to driveshaft fitting method (Toyota driveshaft) – IRS Type (Sec 6)

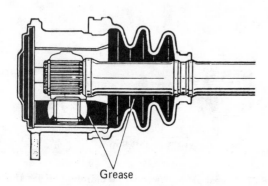

Grease

Fig. 8.32 Pack specified quantity of grease to areas shown (Toyota driveshaft) – IRS Type (Sec 6)

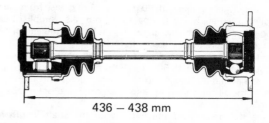

436 – 438 mm

Fig. 8.33 Set driveshaft to installed length setting (see specifications) – IRS Type (Sec 6)

13 The procedure for assembling the inboard joint is the same as that described for the NTN joint. Refer to Section 5 and proceed as described in paragraphs 17 and 18.
14 Using the grease supplied with the joint repair kit, apply 90 g (0.20 lb) of grease to the outer joint race and pack the same amount of grease into the outer boot. Also smear some grease on the tripod.
15 Lubricate the inboard joint and boot with grease from the repair kit, packing 70 g (0.15 lb) of grease to each.
16 Assemble each boot over its joint and set the total shaft length to the specified length (according to model) – see Fig. 8.33. With the shaft set at the specified length, fit and fasten the boot clamps, positioning the clamp lock between the flange retaining bolts holes.
17 Turn each joint to stretch the boot and ensure that it doesn't deform.

7 Differential unit side seals (IRS) – renewal

1 Unscrew the drain plug from the base of the differential housing and drain the oil into a suitable container. Refit the drain plug.
2 Disconnect the driveshaft on the side concerned, as described in Section 4.
3 Undo the retaining bolts and remove the differential carrier cover and gasket. Allow for a small amount of oil spillage as it is removed.
4 On models fitted with the 6.7 inch differential, remove the snap-ring from the inner end of the side gear shaft (Fig. 8.35).
5 Attach a slide hammer to the flange of the side gear shaft and withdraw the shaft from the differential carrier.
6 Extract the oil seal from the side gear carrier using a suitable puller or, if available, Toyota service tool No. 09520-22010/1.
7 Smear the lip of the new oil seal with grease then locate and drive the new seal into position using a suitable tube drift. When in position the seal must be flush with the end face of the carrier.

Bending Direction

Revolving

Fig. 8.34 Boot clamp locks must be positioned between flange bolt holes (Sec 6)

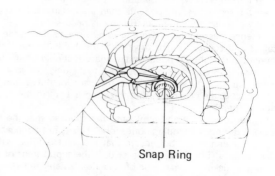

Snap Ring

Fig. 8.35 Remove side gear snap-ring (Sec 7)

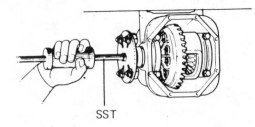

Fig. 8.36 Side gear shaft removal using slide hammer (Sec 7)

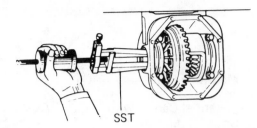

Fig. 8.37 Side gear shaft oil seal removal using special tool (Sec 7)

8 Locate the side gear shaft into the differential carrier and carefully drive it home using a soft-headed mallet. Drive the shaft in so that it makes contact with the pinion shaft, at which point the sound made when tapping it should change.
9 On models fitted with the 6.7 inch differential, refit the snap-ring into the groove on the inner end of the shaft. Check that the snap-ring is fully engaged.
10 If a dial gauge indicator is available, check the side gear shaft run-out. The maximum permissible run-out is 0.20 mm (0.0079 in). If this figure is exceeded, the side gear shaft must be renewed.
11 Check that the mating faces are clean, locate the gasket and refit the carrier cover.
12 Reconnect the driveshaft, as described in Section 4.
13 Check that the drain plug is secured, then top up the differential oil level with the specified type and quantity of oil. Refit the filler plug to complete.

8 Pinion oil seal (IRS) – renewal

1 To remove and renew the pinion oil seal, pinion bearing and/or bearing spacer on independent rear suspension models, follow the procedures described for the four link type in Section 11. Note the following differences.

2 During reassembly, reference must be made to the IRS Specifications at the start of this Chapter for the following setting details (according to model).

   (a) Pinion oil seal fitting depth
   (b) Pinion bearing preload requirement

9 Differential unit (IRS) – removal and refitting

1 Drain the oil from the differential unit into a suitable container then refit the drain plug.
2 Disconnect the rear driveshaft each side, as described in Section 4.
3 Refer to Chapter 7 and disconnect the propeller shaft from the pinion companion flange. Tie the propeller shaft up out of the way.
4 Referring to Fig. 8.39, undo the retaining nuts and remove the differential support member No 1 mounting bolt.
5 Support the weight of the differential unit with a jack (trolley type if available).
6 Unscrew and remove the bolts securing the differential carrier/ suspension member to the pinion housing (photo).
7 Slowly lower the jack and remove the differential unit from under the car. Get an assistant to provide additional support for the differential unit on the jack as it is lowered and removed to prevent it from falling off the jack.
8 Apart from the renewal of the pinion oil seal and the side gear oil

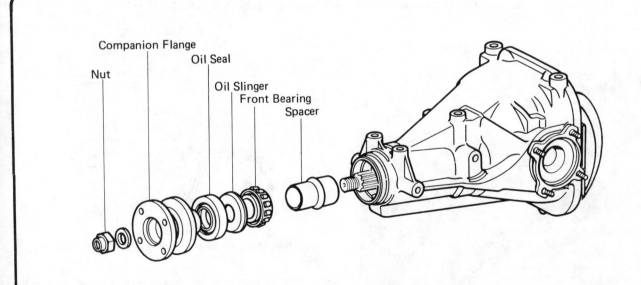

Companion Flange
Oil Seal
Nut
Oil Slinger
Front Bearing
Spacer

Fig. 8.38 Front oil seal and associated components – IRS Type (Sec 8)

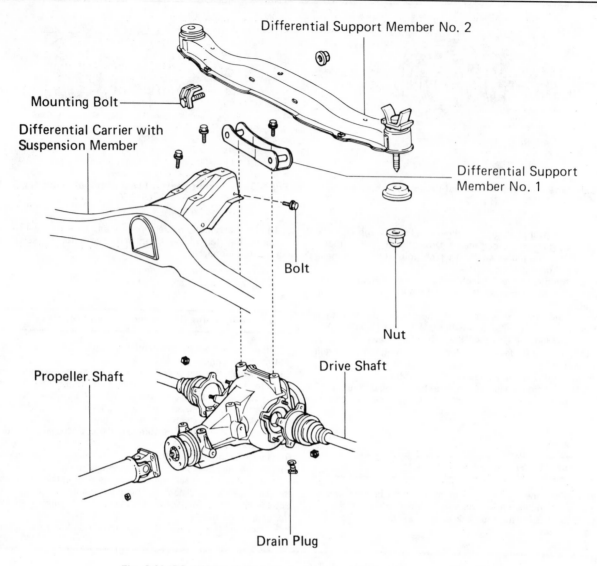

Fig. 8.39 IRS differential housing and associated components (Sec 9)

9.6 Differential carrier-to-suspension member bolts – IRS axle

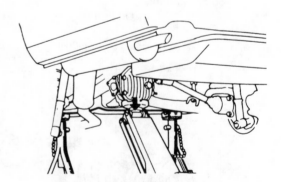

Fig. 8.40 IRS differential carrier unit removal (Sec 9)

seals, covered elsewhere in this Chapter, any checks and repairs to the crownwheel and pinion assemblies or the differential carrier should be entrusted to a Toyota dealer.

9   Refitting is in general a reversal of the removal procedure. Tighten all retaining bolts to their specified torque settings. Ensure that the match marks of the rear driveshafts and the propeller shaft align with the corresponding marks on their mating flanges.

10 On completion, top up the oil level in the differential with the specified grade and quantity of oil. Check that the drain and filler plugs are secure.

10 Axleshaft, bearing and oil seal (FLS) – removal and refitting

1   Jack up the rear axle and support it securely on safety stands.
2   Remove the rear roadwheel.
3   Remove the brake drum (referring to Chapter 9 if necessary).
4   Insert a socket and extension through one of the holes in the axleshaft flange and unscrew the four nuts which secure the brake backing plate to the axle casing.
5   A slide hammer will now be required to extract the axleshaft from the axle casing. A slide hammer can easily be made up or, if this is not possible, try bolting an old roadwheel onto the axle flange studs and striking two opposite points on the inner rim simultaneously to drive the axleshaft out of the axle casing. It is pointless just to try and pull the shaft out, you will only succeed in pulling the vehicle off the stands.
6   With the axleshaft removed, if it is only the oil seal that is leaking, lever the old one from the axle casing and drive a new one in using a distance piece of tubing as a drift. Make sure that the lips of the seal are facing inwards and that the end face of the oil seal is the specified distance below the end of the axle casing flange.
7   Refer to Fig. 8.44 for axleshaft oil seal fitting depth.
8   If the axleshaft bearing is rough or noisy when turned, it must be renewed.
9   To remove the old bearing, first grind a flat on one side of the bearing retaining collar and then split it with a sharp cold chisel. Take care not to damage the axleshaft.
10   Remove the bearing from the shaft either by supporting the bearing and pressing the axleshaft from it or by drawing it off if a suitable extending leg extractor can be obtained.
11   The new bearing should be pressed onto the shaft but don't forget

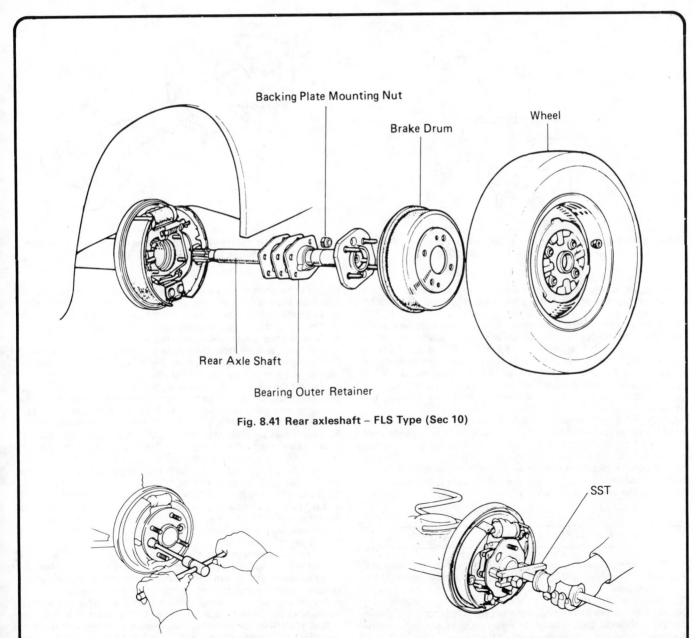

Fig. 8.41 Rear axleshaft – FLS Type (Sec 10)

Backing Plate Mounting Nut

Brake Drum

Wheel

Rear Axle Shaft

Bearing Outer Retainer

SST

Fig. 8.42 Undo the brake backing plate bolts – FLS Type (Sec 10)

Fig. 8.43 Axleshaft removal using slide hammer – FLS type (Sec 10)

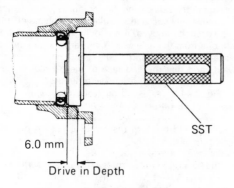

Fig. 8.44 Fit oil seal to depth shown – FLS Type (Sec 10)

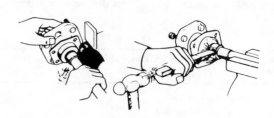

Fig. 8.45 Bearing inner retainer removal method – FLS Type (Sec 10)

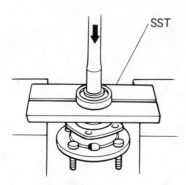

Fig. 8.46 Support bearing underneath then press or drive the shaft through it – FLS Type (Sec 10)

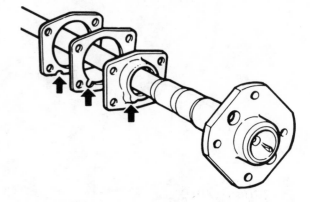

Fig. 8.47 Refit axleshaft with retainer/gaskets and ensure that notches face down – FLS Type (Sec 10)

to apply pressure to the bearing track only and make sure that the spacer bearing retainer plate and gaskets are in position on the shaft first.

12 With the bearing fitted, the bearing retaining collar must be pressed onto the shaft. Before pressing the collar onto the shaft it should be heated in an oven to between 140 and 160°C (284 and 320°F). Note that the non-bevelled side of the inner retainer must face towards the bearing. Keep the axleshaft and retainer free of oil and grease.

13 Before refitting the axleshaft, smear the oil seal lip with a medium grade grease. Allow the collar to fully cool off before inserting the axleshaft.

14 Pass the assembled axleshaft into the casing taking care not to damage the oil seal. Hold the shaft quite level and turn it gently until the splines on its inner end can be felt to pick up those in the differential side gears then push the shaft fully home.

15 Refit the backplate bolts, the brake drum and the roadwheel. Check that the roadwheel rotates freely and the brakes are operational.

16 Lower the vehicle to the ground.

11 Pinion oil seal (FLS) – renewal

1   The pinion oil seal may be renewed with the differential carrier still in position on the rear axle casing and the casing still attached to the rear suspension.

2   Jack up the rear of the vehicle and support on safety stands.

3   Mark the edges of the propeller shaft rear flange and the pinion companion flange, then remove the retaining bolts and separate the flanges. Tie the propeller shaft up out of the way.

4   Ensure that the handbrake is fully off and then attach a spring balance to a length of cord wound round the companion flange. Give an even pull and read off the bearing preload on the spring balance. Note the figure for later comparison.

5   Mark the companion flange in relation to the pinion splines and knock back the staking on the pinion nut with a drift or narrow chisel.

6   Hold the companion flange quite still by bolting a length of flat steel to two of the flange holes and then unscrew the pinion nut. A ring spanner of good length will be required for this.

7   Remove the lever from the flange and withdraw the companion flange. If it is tight, use a two or three-legged puller, but on no account attempt to knock it from the splined pinion.

8   Extract the oil seal using a two-legged puller.

9   Grease the new oil seal lip then fit it into the axle housing. The lips of the oil seal must face inwards. Using a piece of brass or copper tubing of suitable diameter, carefully drive the new oil seal into the axle housing recess until the face of the seal is at the specified insertion depth (drive-in depth) – see Fig. 8.51. Take particular care not to drive the seal beyond the specified depth.

10 Refit the companion flange onto the pinion splines aligning the notch marks made when removing it.

11 Smear the threads of the new pinion nut with grease. Fit the nut and prevent the companion flange from turning with the lever used during removal. Tighten the nut until the pinion endfloat only just disappears. Do not overtighten. The torque wrench setting should not exceed the specified limit.

12 Rotate the pinion to settle the bearings and then check the preload using the cord and spring balance method previously described. By slight adjustment of the nut and rotation of the pinion, obtain a spring preload figure to match that which applied before dismantling. Do not overtighten the nut as it cannot be backed off without having to renew the internal compressible spacer. Access to the spacer, if it has to be removed, is gained by removing the oil seal, oil slinger and the taper roller bearing located behind it. You will need a suitable puller for bearing removal, as shown in Fig. 8.52.

13 When preload tightening the nut after refitting a new bearing or bearing spacer, tighten the nut to the specified torque, then using a suitable spring balance as previously described, or a torque wrench set

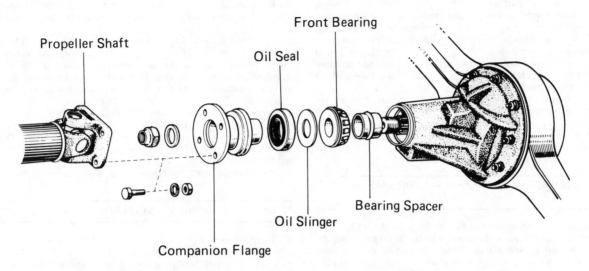

Fig. 8.48 Conventional axle showing drive pinion oil seal components – FLS Type (Sec 11)

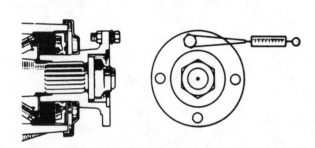

Fig. 8.49 Axle pinion bearing preload test method using spring balance (Sec 11)

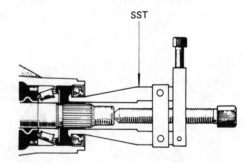

Fig. 8.50 Oil seal removal using special puller (Sec 11)

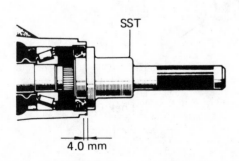

Fig. 8.51 Insert new oil seal to its 'drive in' depth (Sec 11)

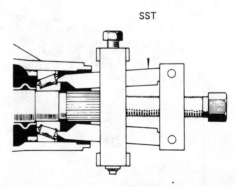

Fig. 8.52 Pinion front bearing removal method using special puller (Sec 11)

to the bearing preload requirement, check the preload between the ring gear and drive pinion. The preload should be as specified.

14 If the preload measured exceeds the specification, the bearing spacer must be renewed. If the preload measured is less than that specified, continue tightening the nut in increments of 1.3 kgf m (9.0 lbf ft) until the specified preloading is reached, but the maximum torque applied should not exceed 24.0 kgf m (174.0 lbf ft). The pinion nut must not be loosened to reduce the preload. If it is found necessary to exceed the maximum torque allowable in order to meet the preload requirement, the spacer must be renewed.

15 On completion, stake the drive pinion nut to secure it in the set position, then reconnect the propeller shaft, making sure to align the mating marks.

16 Lower the vehicle and check the oil level in the axle.

12 Conventional differential unit (FLS) – removal and refitting

1 Drain the oil from the differential by removing the drain plug.

2 Jack up the car at the rear and support it each side on safety stands.

3 Refer to Section 10 and withdraw the axleshaft on each side far enough to allow the inner end of each shaft to disengage from the differential side gears.

4 Make an alignment mark across the faces of the propeller shaft and pinion coupling flanges and then unbolt and separate the two. If it is

not necessary to remove the propeller shaft completely, rest it to one side out of the way.

5 Undo the nuts and washers holding the differential carrier to the casing. The whole unit can be drawn forward off the studs and taken out.

6 The differential unit can now be cleaned and inspected for signs of excessive wear or damage, which if evident, will necessitate a complete or at least partial dismantling and overhaul of the unit. This is a task to be entrusted to your Toyota dealer or a qualified automotive engineer since special tools and setting procedures are required during reassembly.

7 When refitting the differential carrier assembly, ensure that the mating faces are perfectly clean and free from burrs. A new gasket coated with sealing compound should also be used. Otherwise refitting is a reversal of the removal operation. Tighten the nuts to the specified torque.

8 Refill the unit with the correct grade and quantity of oil.

13 Unitized differential unit (FLS)

1 This type of axle unit was fitted to the 1982 USA models. It differs from the conventional type axle fitted to other models fitted with the FLS system in that the differential carrier is an integral part of the rear axle casing. Unlike the conventional type, the carrier cannot be withdrawn forward from the axle casing with the pinion assembly and differential unit.

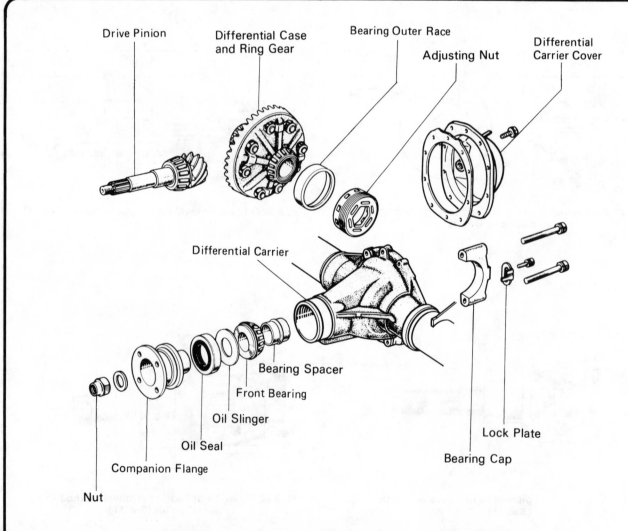

Fig. 8.53 Unitized differential unit components – FLS Type (Sec 13)

2 When required, the differential unit and pinion assembly must be withdrawn and refitted through the rear of the axle banjo housing.

3 The differential is secured in position by bearing caps and the side bearing preload, together with the crownwheel and pinion mesh adjustment is set by circular adjusting nuts, one on the ring gear side and one on the drive pinion side.

4 Although the differentail unit and pinion assembly can be removed without difficulty or the need for special tools, the refitting procedures are critical as they simultaneously adjust the crownwheel and pinion adjustment. These procedures are usually outside the scope of the average home mechanic. If incorrectly fitted or adjusted, substantial damage could result and for this reason it is advisable to have any malfunctions in the differential unit checked, and if necessary repaired, by your Toyota dealer.

5 If required the following items can be removed to undertake repairs:

(a) Rear axleshaft, bearing and oil seal – see Section 10
(b) Pinion oil seal – see Section 11. Note that the drive pinion oil seal drive in depth differs from that specified for the conventional axle pinion oil seal

6 If required, the differential unit can be visually inspected by removing the carrier cover (after draining the axle oil).

7 To remove the rear axle unit complete refer to Section 14.

14 Rear axle (FLS) – removal and refitting

1 Jack up the rear of the vehicle, place safety stands under the rear body frame members and securely chock the front wheels. Place the jack under the differential and take its weight.

2 Remove the roadwheels and disconnect the propeller shaft at the rear axle pinion coupling flange. Remember to mark the edges of the flange before disconnecting them so that they will be refitted in their original positions. Move the rear end of the propeller shaft to one side and support it.

3 Refer to Chapter 9 and disconnect the handbrake cable and the hydraulic line to each rear brake unit. Plug the hydraulic line connections to prevent loss of fluid and the ingress of dirt. Check that the cable and lines are clear of the axle.

4 Unbolt and disconnect the rear shock absorbers each side.

5 Remove the retaining nut and disconnect the lateral control rod from the axle casing. Refer to Chapter 10 for suspension details and illustrations.

6 Unbolt and detach the stabilizer bar from the brackets on the underside of the axle casing and then pivot the bar downwards out of the way.

7 Disconnect the upper and lower control arms from their axle or body mountings (as required). Check that the jack is securely positioned under the axle before disconnecting the arms.

8 As the axle is now only supported by the jack, get a couple of assistants to support and steady the axle each side at the wheel hubs, then slowly lower the jack under the differential.

9 When the tension of each coil spring is fully released they can be removed together with their respective seatings.

10 The axle unit can now be withdrawn from under the car.

11 Refitting is a reversal of the removal process, but when attaching the various associated suspension components refer to the refitting details given in the appropriate Sections in Chapter 10. Tighten the respective fastenings to the specified torque wrench settings, as given in that Chapter, only when they are fully connected and with the jack raised under the axle so that the body is clear of the safety stands.

12 Reconnect the brake components and bleed the hydraulic system, as given in Chapter 9, to complete.

15 Fault diagnosis – rear axle

Symptom	Reason(s)
Rear axle noisy	Lack of oil or wrong grade Worn gears or bearings Damaged gears or bearings Incorrect adjustment of crownwheel and pinion
Oil leak – rear axle	Excessively worn or damaged oil seals Axle housing cracked Bearing retainer loose Cover/carrier gasket defective
Oil leak – pinion shaft	Oil level too high or incorrect grade Oil seal worn or damaged Companion flange loose or damaged
Oil leak – side gear shaft (IRS) type	Oil level too high or incorrect grade Oil seal worn or damaged Loose or damaged side gear shaft
Vibration from rear axle	Worn or damaged driveshaft joints (IRS type) Driveshafts loose (IRS type) Propeller shaft coupling flange loose Pinion companion flange loose

Chapter 9 Braking system

Contents

Specifications

Type .... Four wheel hydraulic with mechanically operated handbrake on the rear wheels only. Front disc brakes. Self-adjusting rear drum brakes or combination disc (foot)/drum (hand) brakes. Vacuum servo booster unit and dual hydraulic system on all models

Front disc brakes

	Standard	Limit
Disc thickness:		
TA type	12.5 mm (0.49 in)	11.5 mm (0.45 in)
RA type	20.0 mm (0.79 in)	19.0 mm (0.75 in)
Disc run-out limit	0.15 mm (0.0059 in)	
Pad thickness limit (minimum):		
UK models	1.0 mm (0.039 in)	
USA models	3.0 mm (0.118 in)	

Rear disc brakes

Disc thickness:	
Standard	18.0 mm (0.709 in)
Limit	17.0 mm (0.669 in)
Pad thickness limit (minimum):	
UK models	1.0 mm (0.039 in)
USA models	3.0 mm (0.118 in)
Disc run-out limit	0.15 mm (0.0059 in)

Rear drum brake (foot)

Drum inner diameter:	
Standard	228.6 mm (9.000 in)
Limit	230.6 mm (9.079 in)
Lining thickness limit (minimum)	1.0 mm (0.039 in)

Handbrake

Lever travel at 20 kg (44.1 lb):	
With rear brake drum	4 to 7 clicks
With rear brake disc	5 to 8 clicks

Rear shoe-to-lever clearance	0.0 to 0.35 mm (0.0 to 0.0138 in)
Drum inner diameter:	
Standard	167.0 mm (6.57 in)
Limit	168.0 mm (6.61 in)
Lining thickness limit	1.0 mm (0.039 in)
Adjustment shim thickness available:	
With rear drum brake	0.2 mm (0.008 in)
	0.3 mm (0.012 in)
	0.6 mm (0.024 in)
	0.9 mm (0.036 in)
With rear disc	0.3 mm (0.012 in)
	0.6 mm (0.024 in)
	0.9 mm (0.036 in)

Pedal

Brake pedal height (from floor)	154 to 164 mm (6.06 to 6.46 in)
Brake pedal free play	3 to 6 mm (0.12 to 0.24 in)
Brake pedal reserve distance at 50 kg (110 lb)	75 mm (2.95 in) (minimum)

Brake booster (servo)

Pushrod-to-piston clearance:	
At idle vacuum	0.10 to 0.50 mm (0.004 to 0.020 in)
At no vacuum	0.60 to 0.65 mm (0.024 to 0.026 in)

Torque wrench settings

	kgf m	lbf ft
Brake booster clevis locknut	2.5	18
Master cylinder to brake booster (servo)	1.3	9
Brake booster to pedal bracket	1.3	9
Master cylinder reservoir union	2.5	18
Master cylinder outlet plugs (check valves)	4.5	33
Master cylinder piston stopper bolt	1.0	7
Booster band (Aisin type)	1.0	7
Front brake caliper to knuckle	9.25	67
Front brake disc cover to knuckle	1.85	13
Front brake cylinder bolt	2.0	14
Flexible hoses	2.3	17
Brake tube flare nut	1.5	11
Bleed plugs	0.85	6
Front disc to hub	6.5	47
Drum backing plate to rear axle housing	6.3	46
Drum backing plate to rear suspension arm	4.5	33
Rear wheel cylinder	1.0	7
Handbrake lever to floor	1.3	9
Handbrake No 1 cable locknut	0.55	4
Handbrake cable clamp	0.55	4
Vacuum tube to cowl panel	0.90	7
P and B valve to bracket	0.90	7
P and B valve to dash panel	0.90	7
Rear disc caliper to suspension arm	4.75	34
Rear disc brake cylinder bolt	2.0	14
Handbrake backing plate to suspension arm	1.85	13
Handbrake backplate anchor pin to suspension arm	14.5	105
Rear disc torque plate	4.75	34

1 General description

All models have a four wheel hydraulically operated braking system with a mechanically operated handbrake on the rear wheels only.

All models are fitted with front disc brakes but the rear brakes are drum or disc/drum type, dependent on model. The rear drum brake is of conventional design. With the disc/drum type rear brake unit, the foot brake operates on the disc via a conventional caliper whilst the handbrake operates the drum brake. With both types the handbrake is operated by a central lever and cable system. The foot brake is actuated by a dual circuit hydraulic system and a vacuum servo booster.

A fluid level warning switch is fitted to the master cylinder reservoir and, in the event of the fluid dropping below the minimum level, the switch actuates a warning light to advise the driver.

A pressure regulating valve is fitted into the hydraulic circuit and its function is to prevent the rear wheels locking during severe braking application.

2 Routine maintenance – braking system

1 **Brake fluid level**: At weekly intervals check the fluid in the translucent reservoir on the master cylinder. The fluid will drop very slowly indeed over a period of time to compensate for lining wear, but any sudden drop in level or the need for frequent topping-up should be investigated immediately.

2 Always top up with hydraulic fluid which meets the specified standard and has been left in an airtight container. Hydraulic fluid is hygroscopic (absorbs moisture from the atmosphere) and must not be stored in an open container. **Do not** shake the tin prior to topping-up. Fluids of different makes can be intermixed provided they all meet the specification.

3 **Brake pedal**: Periodically check the brake pedal for smooth operation. Check its height, free play and reserve distance, as described in Section 3.

4 **Handbrake**: Check that the handbrake lever has the correct

amount of travel, as described in Section 21. Check that the handbrake operates efficiently.

5   **Brake pads and linings:** Inspect the thickness of the friction linings on the disc pads and brake shoes, as described in the following Sections, at the intervals specified in Routine Maintenance.

6   **Hydraulic system:** The rigid and flexible hydraulic pipes and hoses should be inspected for leaks or damage regularly. Although the rigid lines are plastic coated to preserve them against corrosion, check for damage which may have occurred through flying stones, careless jacking or the traversing of rough ground.

7   Bend the hydraulic flexible hoses sharply with the fingers and examine the surface of the hose for signs of cracking or perishing of the rubber. Renew if evident.

8   **Renew the brake fluid:** Renew the brake fluid at the specified intervals and examine all rubber components (including master cylinder and piston seals) with a critical eye, renewing where necessary.

Fig. 9.1 Master cylinder fluid level must be maintained (Sec 2)

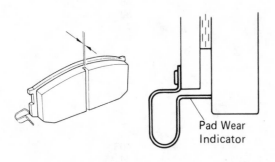

Fig. 9.2 Inspect the disc pads for excessive wear – pad wear indicator fitted to some models (Sec 2)

Pad Wear Indicator

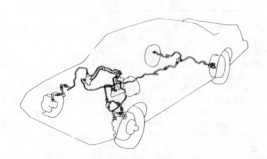

Fig. 9.3 Examine the brake lines and hoses for corrosion and security (Sec 2)

3   Brake pedal – height adjustment

1   Refer to Fig. 9.4 and measure the height from the brake pedal rubber to the floor (with the carpet folded back). Check the measured height against the specified height.

2   If pedal height adjustment is necessary, loosen the stop-light switch securing nut and then detach the switch leads.

3   Loosen the pushrod locknut and then adjust the pushrod to give the correct pedal height. You may need to unscrew the stop-light switch assembly to allow an increase in the height.

4   With the correct pedal height adjustment made, tighten the pushrod locknut and then adjust the stop-light switch unit so that it is lightly touching the pedal stopper. Retighten the locknut to secure the switch in this position and then reconnect the switch wires. Check the stop-light switch operation is satisfactory.

5   The pedal free play should now be checked. The engine must be switched off for this check and vacuum remaining in the servo booster expelled by pressing down on the pedal a few times.

6   To make the check, press the pedal down by hand until the initial increase in pressure is felt. This is the total of the pedal free play travel and when measured it should be within the pedal free play tolerance limits given in the Specifications.

7   If the free play measured is not within the specified limits then further adjustment of the pushrod is necessary. Adjustment should be made so that the pedal height specified is also complied with, as given previously.

8   Finally recheck the pedal with the engine running, the handbrake released and with the servo boost vacuum applied, but note that the pedal free play during this check is not measured from the time that the servo booster piston is actuated. Check that the pedal reserve travel distance is as specified (Fig. 9.5).

4   Front brake disc pads – inspection and renewal

1   No adjustment is required to the front disc brakes, the pads being kept in contact with the disc through the flexible characteristic of the cylinder boot and piston seal.

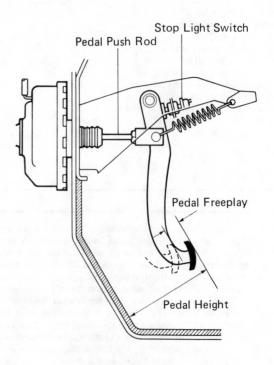

Stop Light Switch

Pedal Push Rod

Pedal Freeplay

Pedal Height

Fig. 9.4 Brake pedal height and freeplay adjustments must be as specified (Sec 3)

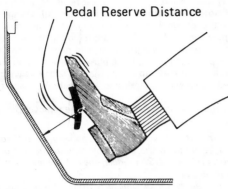

Fig. 9.5 Footbrake pedal reserve distance (Sec 3)

2 Jack up and support the front of the vehice with safety stands, then remove the roadwheels.

3 With the wheel(s) removed, the brake pad thicknesses can be checked through the inspection aperture in the caliper unit (photo). If the pads are worn down to or beyond the specified wear limit they must be removed and renewed as a set, (renew the pads of both front brake caliper units). Some models have a pad wear indicator (Fig. 9.2).

4 To remove the pads, use a pair of spanners, one to retain the bushing head and the other to unscrew and remove the cylinder unit retaining bolt. The cylinder can then be pivoted upwards and retained in this position to allow pad removal by inserting the retainer bolt or rod into the torque plate hole. It is not necessary to disconnect the brake hose or the cylinder from the torque plate, but do not strain the flexible hose (photos).

5 Withdraw the inner pad and then the outer pad with its anti-squeal shim. On UK models note that the shim type differs in accordance with the brake type (photo). All USA models use the 14 inch type shown (Fig. 9.6).

6 Note their locations and how they are fitted, then remove the anti-rattle spring, the pad guide plate and the pad support plate. These

4.3 Front brake unit pad wear inspection aperture (arrowed)

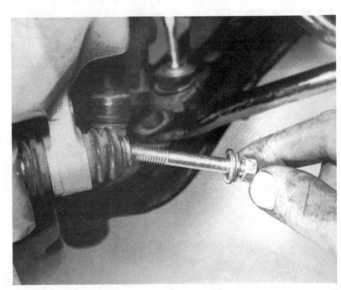

4.4A Remove the brake cylinder retaining bolt ...

4.4B ... lift the cylinder up ...

4.4C ... and support with bolt or rod

4.5 Outer pad removal with anti-squeal shim (13 in disc wheel)

items are supplied with the new pad kit and must be renewed (Fig. 9.7).

7   Brush any dust or dirt from the caliper recesses, the housing, and springs. **Do not inhale the dust** as it is harmful. Using a piece of wood, press the piston into the caliper to accommodate the new linings. Keep an eye on the brake fluid level in the reservoir during this operation and, if necessary, syphon some to prevent it overflowing.

8   Whilst the pads are removed, the brake disc should be checked for condition, wear and run-out to ensure that the specified wear limits are not exceeded. Removal and refitting of the brake disc is given in Section 6.

9   Fitting of the new pads is a reversal of the removal procedure but the following points must be observed.

    (a)   With the 13 inch disc brake (UK models) the anti-squeal shim must be fitted to the outer pad (photo), whilst on 14 inch models (UK and USA models) the anti-squeal shim is fitted to the inner pad

    (b)   Do not allow oil or grease to touch the disc/pad contact surfaces. Brake grease can be smeared on the piston contact face of the inner pad

    (c)   On models with a pad wear indicator, fit the outer pad so that the indicator is at the top

    (d)   When lowering the cylinder back into position take care not to wedge or damage the rubber protection boot

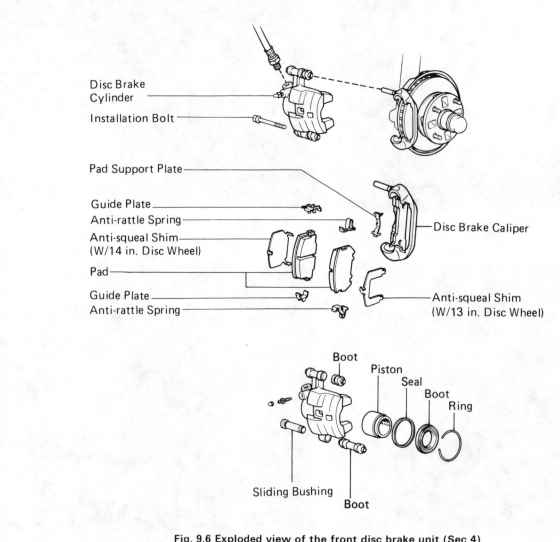

Fig. 9.6 Exploded view of the front disc brake unit (Sec 4)

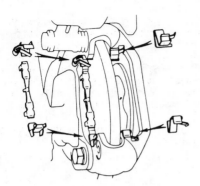

Fig. 9.7 Location of pad support plate, anti-rattle springs and guides (Sec 4)

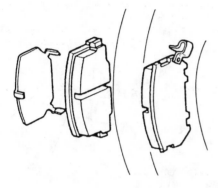

Fig. 9.8 Anti-squeal shim (14 in Type) and outer pad with wear indicator (must be at top) (Sec 4)

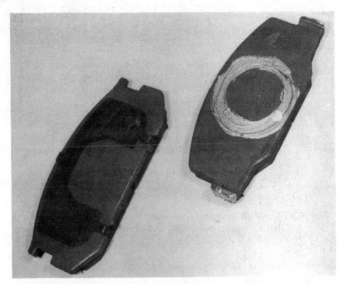

4.9 Anti-squeal shim location on outer pad. Note brake grease applied to piston contact face on inner pad

(e) Hold the bush hexagons while tightening the caliper retaining bolts to the specified torque. If this precaution is not taken, uneven pad wear may occur

(f) With the disc pads fitted, depress the footbrake pedal several times, and if necessary top-up the master cylinder fluid level

2 To prevent loss of hydraulic fluid during subsequent operations, either seal the master cylinder at the vent hole and round the rim of the cap with adhesive tape, or clamp the flexible hose with a suitable clamp, being careful not to damage the hose.

3 Unscrew the cylinder retaining bolt and withdraw it. Secure the bushing with a spanner when undoing the bolt to prevent it from turning.

4 Withdraw the cylinder unit from the pivot pin and support it to prevent straining the hose then loosen the flexible hose union at the caliper and unscrew the caliper from the hose. Retain the sealing washer (if fitted) and plug the end of the hose to prevent entry of foreign matter.

5 Remove the brake pad assemblies, as described in the previous Section.

6 Clean the external surfaces of the caliper unit then, using a suitable screwdriver, prise free the sliding bush and pin boot. To remove the main pin boot chisel it free (Fig. 9.9).

7 Prise free the protector boot set ring and remove the boot from the cylinder bore.

8 Remove the piston from the caliper leg, applying air pressure to the inlet port with a foot pump. Take care not to damage the piston.

9 Extract the piston seal from the cylinder bore with a small screwdriver, taking care not to damage or scratch the bore surface (Fig. 9.10).

5 Front brake disc caliper – removal, overhaul and refitting

1 Loosen the front roadwheel bolts, then raise and support the vehicle at the front end on safety stands. Remove the front roadwheel(s).

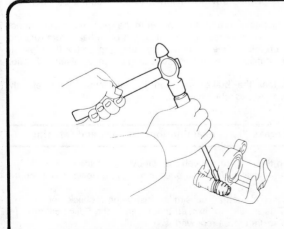

Fig. 9.9 Main pin boot removal (Sec 5)

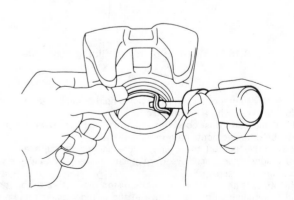

Fig. 9.10 Piston seal removal (Sec 5)

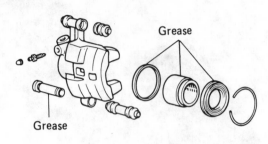

Fig. 9.11 Lubricate items indicated with rubber grease or lithium soap based glycol grease (Sec 5)

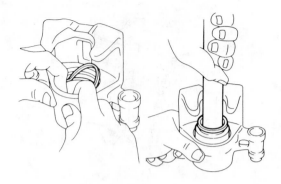

Fig. 9.12 Locate the seal and insert the piston (Sec 5)

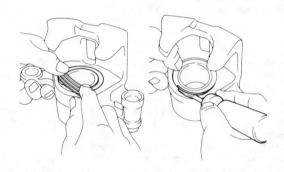

Fig. 9.13 Refit the dust boot and set ring (Sec 5)

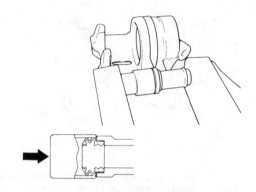

Fig. 9.14 Press the main boot into position using a 21 mm socket (Sec 5)

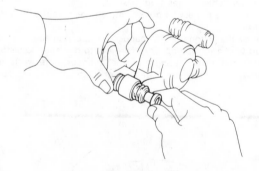

Fig. 9.15 Fit the dust boot and sliding bush (Sec 5)

10 Wash all components in clean brake fluid or methylated spirits and wipe them dry with a lint-free cloth.
11 All seals and dust covers must be renewed so a service repair kit must be obtained containing these items.
12 Carefully inspect the cylinder bore and piston surfaces. If they show signs of advanced wear or damage then a new caliper cylinder unit must be fitted.
13 To reassemble, first lubricate the piston seal with a rubber grease and manipulate it into its groove in the cylinder using fingers only. Check that it is correctly seated and not distorted.
14 Smear the piston with rubber grease and then insert it into position in the cylinder bore.

15 Smear the rubber boot with rubber grease and locate it into position and secure with the set ring (Fig. 9.13).
16 Lubricate the main pin boot and press it into position using a 21 mm socket and vice as shown in Fig. 9.14. Do not re-use the old boot.
17 Lubricate the dust boot and slide bush with rubber grease and locate them, but ensure that the seal is not distorted.
18 Refit the brake pad assemblies, with reference to Section 4.
19 Fit the cylinder unit onto the main pin, taking care not to wedge the boot as it is pivoted down to align with the securing bolt hole and bushing.
20 Insert the retaining bolt, and tighten to the specified torque wrench setting whilst simultaneously preventing the bush head from rotating.
21 Re-attach the flexible hydraulic hose then top up the fluid level in the master cylinder reservoir and bleed the system, as given in Section 18.
22 Check that the brake operation is satisfactory, then refit the roadwheel and lower the vehicle.

6 Front brake disc – examination, removal and refitting

1 Jack up the front of the vehicle, remove the roadwheel.
2 Inspect the disc surfaces for deep scoring or grooves. Light scoring is normal.
3 Using a dial gauge or similar instrument, check for run-out (buckle). This should not exceed that given in the Specifications; if it does the disc should be renewed.
4 The disc thickness should not be reduced below the minimum specified, either by normal wear or by grinding to remove scoring.

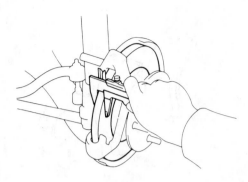

Fig. 9.16 Check that the disc is not worn beyond the minimum allowable thickness (Sec 6)

5   To remove the disc/hub assembly, refer to the procedure given in Chapter 10.
6   Unscrew the disc-to-hub bolts, and separate the two parts.
7   Refitting is the reverse of the removal procedure. Adjust the disc/hub, as described in Chapter 10.

7   Rear brake disc pads – inspection and renewal

1   No adjustment is required to the rear disc brakes, the pads being kept in contact with the disc through the flexible characteristics of the cylinder boot and piston seal.
2   To inspect the rear brakes, raise the vehicle at the rear and support on safety stands.
3   Remove the roadwheel(s). On some models, this is not necessary for an initial examination of the pads for wear as there is an inspection hole in the caliper backplate.
4   If the pads are worn down to or beyond the specified wear limit they must be removed and renewed as a set (renew the pads of both rear brake caliper units). Some models have a pad wear indicator fitted to the outer pad (Fig. 9.18).
5   To renew the pads, refer to Section 4 and follow the procedures described in paragraphs 5 on, but note the following differences:

> (a)   The anti-squeal shim is the same type on all models
> (b)   The anti-squeal shim is fitted to the outer pad (Fig. 9.19)
> (c)   Where applicable, the wear indicator on the outer pad is positioned at the bottom
> (d)   Ensure that the pad support plate, guide plates and anti-rattle springs are located as shown (Fig. 9.20)

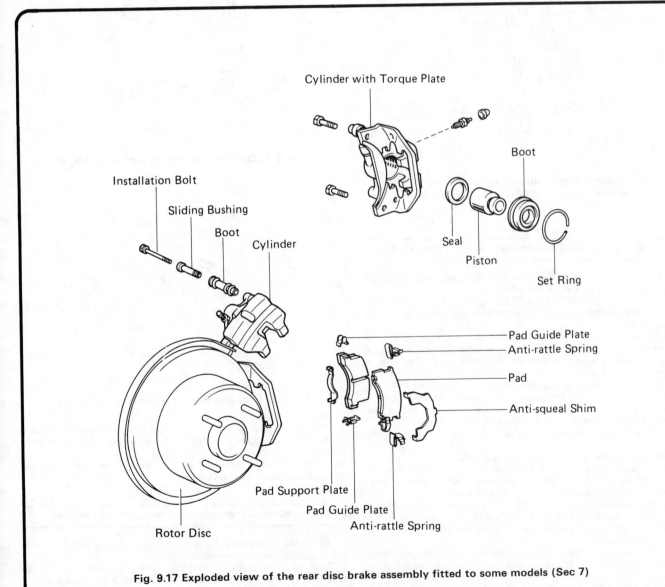

Fig. 9.17 Exploded view of the rear disc brake assembly fitted to some models (Sec 7)

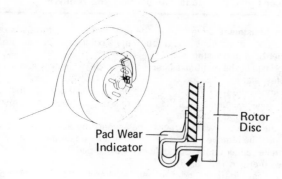

Fig. 9.18 Brake pad wear indicator – rear disc brakes (Sec 7)

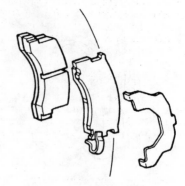

Fig. 9.19 Rear disc brake pad anti-squeal shim (Sec 7)

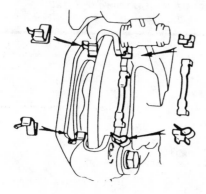

Fig. 9.20 Location of pad support plate, guide plates and anti-rattle springs on the disc rear brakes (Sec 7)

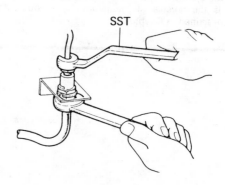

Fig. 9.21 Detach the brake caliper hose (Sec 8)

8 Rear brake disc caliper – removal, overhaul and refitting

1 Chock the front wheels. Raise the vehicle at the rear and support on safety stands. Remove the rear roadwheel(s).

2 To prevent the loss of brake fluid during subsequent operations, seal the master cylinder reservoir filler cap hole and the rim of the cap with adhesive tape.

3 Disconnect the caliper brake hose from the rigid line tube connector at the support bracket. Use a special service tool or a brake spanner to loosen the union nut (Fig. 9.21). Catch any fluid spillage in a container for disposal and plug the end of the pipe.

4 Release the hose retaining clip and detach the hose from the support bracket. The hose can now be unscrewed from the caliper.

5 Unscrew the caliper retaining bolt and withdraw it. Secure the bushing with a second spanner to prevent it from turning.

6 Pivot the cylinder outwards and push it free from the torque plate pin.

7 Remove the brake pad assembly from the caliper (Section 7).

8 Clean the external surfaces of the caliper then proceed as described in Section 5, paragraphs 6 to 17 inclusive to overhaul the cylinder unit.

9 Refit the brake pad assembly, referring to Section 7.

10 To refit the caliper cylinder unit, engage it onto the main pin groove, then insert the installation bolt through the cylinder body. Fit the cylinder body over the brake pads. Tighten the installation bolt to the specified torque.

11 Check that the connections are clean and unplugged, then reconnect the brake hose to the cylinder and tighten it to the specified torque.

12 Relocate the brake hose to the support bracket then engage and tighten the brake rigid line connector.

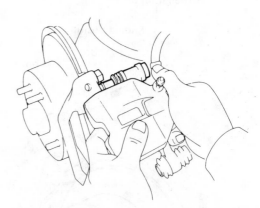

Fig. 9.22 Rear disc brake caliper removal (Sec 8)

13 Remove the sealing tape from the master cylinder reservoir cap, top up the hydraulic fluid level and bleed the system with reference to Section 18.

14 Check that the brake operation is satisfactory, then refit the roadwheel(s) and lower the vehicle.

9 Rear brake disc – examination, removal and refitting

1 Chock the front wheels. Raise the vehicle at the rear and support on safety stands. Remove the roadwheel(s).

2 The rear brake discs are examined in the same manner as that described for the front brake disc (see Section 6 paragraphs 2 to 4 inclusive).

3 To remove the disc, first remove the caliper unit, as described in the

previous Section, but note that the hydraulic line can be left attached
to the caliper. Support the caliper unit to prevent distorting the hose.
4   Unbolt and detach the torque plate from the rear axle.
5   Locate two wheel nuts diagonally opposite onto the hub studs and
tighten against the disc/drum. Insert a screwdriver through the
inspection hole and contract the handbrake shoes by turning the
adjuster (Fig. 9.23). Undo the nuts and withdraw the disc/drum.
6   If fitting a new disc/drum, polish the contact surfaces of the disc
and drum with sandpaper prior to fitting.
7   Locate the disc/drum so that the service hole is aligned with the
groove in the rear axleshaft flange. Fit the two nuts as previously and
adjust the brake shoe clearance (see Section 10, paragraph 16).
8   Refit the torque plate and caliper (Section 8).

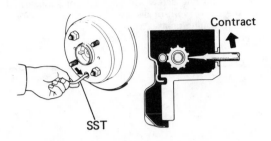

Fig. 9.23 Contract the handbrake shoes as shown (Sec 9)

10 Rear disc/drum handbrake shoes – inspection and renewal

1   Remove the rear brake disc/drum as described in the previous
Section.
2   Brush away any accumulated dust **taking care not to inhale it**,
and inspect the linings. If the linings are worn below the specified limit
renew the shoes as a complete axle set. If the linings are in good
condition, clean and refit the disc/drum (see paragraphs 15 and 16).
3   To remove the shoes, disconnect and remove the return springs
then remove the shoe strut and spring. Note how they are located.
4   Depress the shoe hold-down springs with a pair of pliers and turn
them through 90° to release them from the pins. Align the slot in the
hub for access.

5   Remove the front brake shoe, together with the adjuster screw set
and the tension spring.
6   Detach the handbrake cable from the rear shoe and withdraw the
rear shoe (Fig. 9.26).
7   Using feeler gauges, check the clearance between the handbrake
shoe and the lever. If the clearance exceeds the specified maximum
amount, release the lever retaining clip, remove the lever and shim. Fit a
shim of suitable thickness to take up the excessive clearance. Shims are
available in thicknesses of 0.3, 0.6 and 0.9 mm. Refit the lever and use
a new clip to secure it (Figs. 9.27 and 9.28).

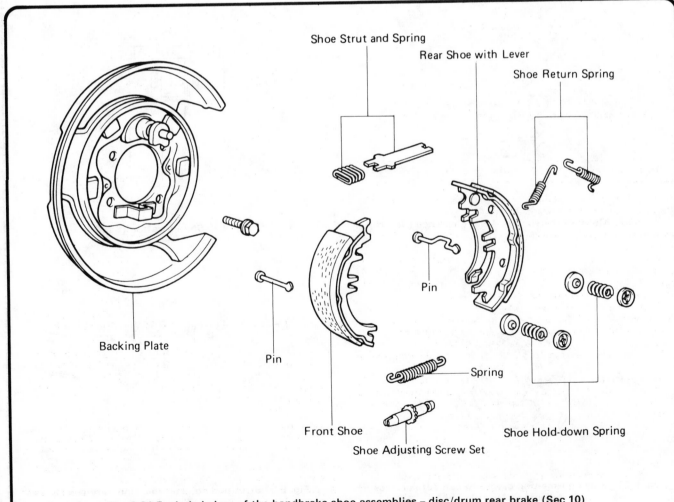

Fig. 9.24 Exploded view of the handbrake shoe assemblies – disc/drum rear brake (Sec 10)

8   Clean the brake backplate prior to assembly and smear the contact surfaces with a non-melting grease (Fig. 9.29).

9   Renew the adjusting screw set, strut and/or springs if they are damaged, excessively worn or distorted. Lubricate the shoe adjuster screw with non-melting grease.

10 Commence reassembly by refitting the rear brake shoe first.

Reconnect the handbrake cable and position the shoe on the backing plate. Engage the shoe with its hold-down spring. The hold-down spring pin must be horizontal, the slot in the cup washer vertical. The rear spring is painted blue.

11 To refit the front shoe, locate the strut and adjuster screw between the shoes; engaging as shown (Fig. 9.30).

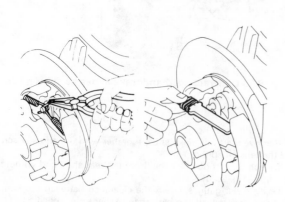

Fig. 9.25 Detach the return springs and remove the strut and spring (Sec 10)

Fig. 9.26 Unhook the cable and remove the rear shoe (Sec 10)

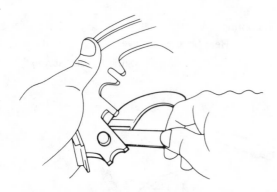

Fig. 9.27 Measure the shoe-to-lever clearance (Sec 10)

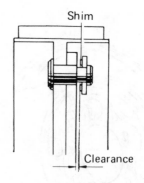

Fig. 9.28 Shim location (Sec 10)

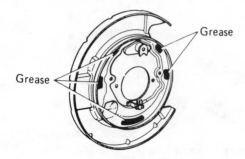

Fig. 9.29 Apply non-melting grease to contact surfaces indicated (Sec 10)

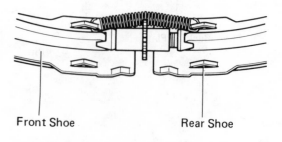

Fig. 9.30 Strut and adjuster location between shoes (Sec 10)

12 With the front shoe in position, fit the hold-down spring. The front spring is identified with white paint. Align the hold-down spring pin and washer, as described for the rear shoe.

13 Refit the front shoe return spring then the rear return spring.

14 Before refitting the brake disc/drum, check that the brake assembly is as shown in Fig. 9.31.

15 If fitting a new disc/drum, polish the contact surfaces of the disc and drum with sandpaper prior to refitting. Locate the disc/drum so that the service hole is aligned with the hub groove. Fit two nuts onto diagonally opposite studs and tighten against the disc/drum.

16 Insert a screwdriver blade through the service hole in the disc/drum and engage it onto the brake shoe adjuster. Turn the adjuster to take up the drum-to-shoes clearance. When the shoes are expanded against the drum and preventing it from turning, back off the adjustment eight notches. The shoe clearance is now adjusted. Before removing the two nuts from the hub/wheel studs, check that the handbrake lever travel is satisfactory. Refer to Section 21 for details.

17 Refit the brake caliper unit, referring to Section 8 for details.

18 Refit the roadwheel then check the hand and footbrake for satisfactory operation before lowering the vehicle.

19 When the vehicle is lowered, the handbrake shoes and drum should be bedded in. To do this drive the vehicle at a speed of about 30 mph on a level road then push the handbrake lever release button in and pull on the lever, applying 9 kg (20 lb) of force to it. Continue applying this force whilst driving at the specified speed for a distance of 400 metres (1/4 mile).

20 Repeat the above procedure two or three times to bed the handbrake in fully, then recheck the satisfactory operation of the handbrake and the handbrake lever travel to complete.

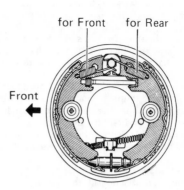

Fig. 9.31 General view of a reassembled brake unit, showing the return spring positions (Sec 10)

11 Rear drum brake shoes – inspection and renewal

1 Securely chock the front wheels, jack-up the rear of the car and remove the roadwheels. Fully release the handbrake lever. Support the car with safety stands.

2 Withdraw the brake drum from the wheel studs. If this proves difficult, extract the rubber plug from the brake backplate (four-link suspension models) or brake drum (independent rear suspension

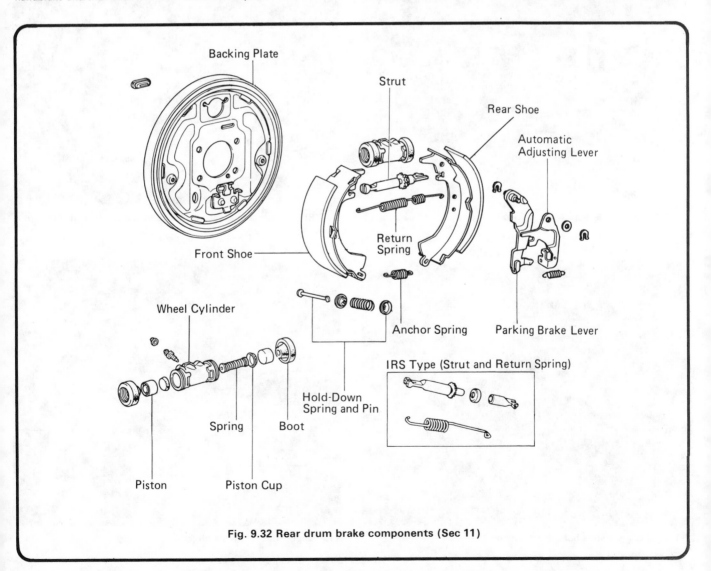

Fig. 9.32 Rear drum brake components (Sec 11)

models), and use two screwdrivers to secure the adjusting lever away from the adjustment bolt, simultaneously release the adjuster bolt turning it clockwise (Fig. 9.33). If the drum is still difficult to remove, insert two bolts into the threaded holes in the drum and tighten them evenly in a progressive sequence to withdraw the drum (photo). As it is withdrawn note that the inspection hole in the drum aligns with the hole in the hub.

3   Brush away any accumulated dust, **taking care not to inhale it,** and inspect the linings. If the friction material is worn below the specified limit, renew the shoes as a complete axle set. If the linings are in good condition, clean and refit the drum (photo).

4   To renew the shoes, first depress the shoe hold-down springs with a pair of pliers and turn them through 90° to release them from the pins (photo).

5   Disconnect the upper shoe return spring and expand the shoes over the lower anchor. Disconnect the lower shoe return spring (photo).

6   Disconnect the handbrake cable (photo).

7   Remove the brake shoes and clean them for inspection.

8   Disconnect the short spring and extract the C-washer. The

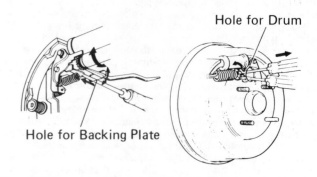

Fig. 9.33 Releasing the brake shoe adjustment (according to type) (Sec 11)

11.2 Brake drum withdrawal using two bolts

11.3 Brake shoes and associated components can be inspected with drum removed

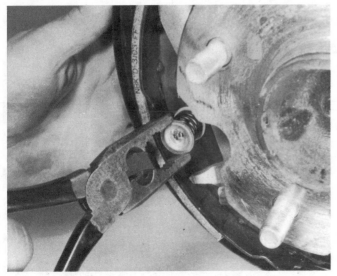

11.4 Release the shoe hold-down springs

11.5 Upper shoe return spring location

11.6 Disconnect the handbrake cable

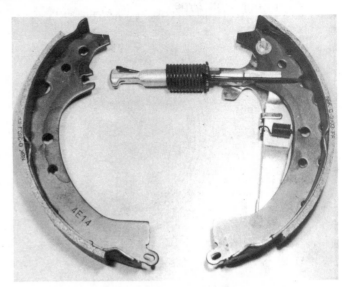

11.10 Brake shoes and associated components

handbrake lever and automatic adjuster lever can now be transferred to the new shoe. If necessary, separate the two levers after extracting the retaining C-washer. Turn the toothed wheel on the adjuster strut so that the strut is fully retracted.

9 After high mileages the brake drums should also be examined for deterioration and wear. If excessive scoring is evident, the drum must either be renewed or ground by an engineering works. If the drum is to be ground, the specified maximum internal diameter must not be exceeded.

10 Inspect the springs, levers and strut for wear, and renew them as necessary (photos).

11 Using a feeler gauge, check the clearance between the trailing shoe web and the automatic adjuster lever. If necessary, fit a shim between the C-washer and the shoe web to obtain the specified clearance (photos).

12 Clean the brake backplate and check for oil leakage (see Chapter 8 for axleshaft seal renewal), or a leaking wheel cylinder. If evident, the fault should be rectified before proceeding.

13 Refer to Fig. 9.34 and note the position of the brake shoes in relation to the front of the car. The shoes must be assembled as shown.

14 Smear a little brake grease on the rubbing surfaces of the backplate and on the shoe web ends (Fig. 9.35).

15 Fit the strut and spring to the trailing shoe, locate it on the backplate, then locate the leading shoe on the backplate. Make sure that both shoes are engaged correctly on the lower anchor (photos).

16 Connect the handbrake cable to the lever on the trailing shoe with the short return spring disconnected, then fit the spring (photo).

17 Fit the upper return spring to the trailing shoe, making sure that the strut is located correctly and the shoe webs are engaged in the wheel cylinder piston grooves.

18 Fit the two shoe hold-down springs to the pins with the open ends facing upwards.

19 Centralise the brake shoes so that the lining contour matches that of the backplate. Now expand the shoes by turning the toothed adjuster wheel until the point is reached where the brake drum will just slide over them and any further rotation of the adjuster wheel would obstruct the fitting of the drum (photo).

20 Refit the brake drum aligning the inspection holes in the drum with the hub. Refit the plug into the inspection hole in the drum or backplate as applicable, then fit the roadwheel.

21 Repeat the procedure on the remaining rear brake, then operate the handbrake lever several times. With the lever applied, both rear wheels should be locked, and with it fully released both wheels should be free. If necessary adjust the handbrake, as described in Section 21.

22 Lower the car to the ground.

11.11A Check clearance between web and lever

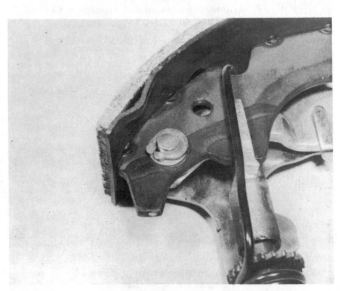

11.11B Close-up view showing C-washer and shim

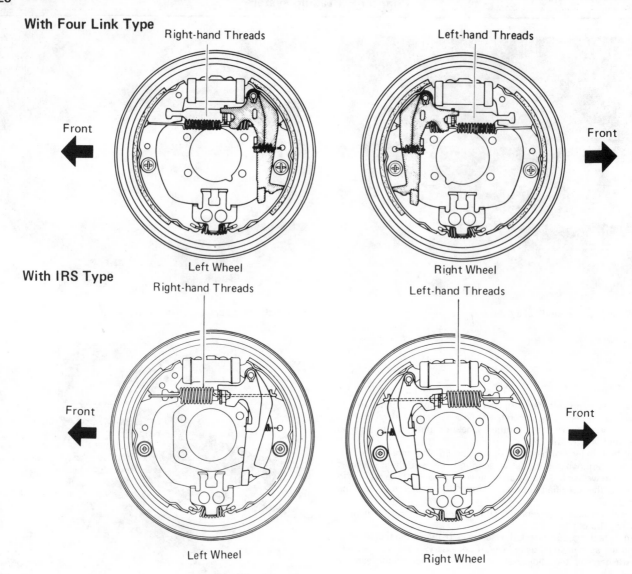

With Four Link Type

Right-hand Threads

Left-hand Threads

Front

Front

Left Wheel

Right Wheel

With IRS Type

Right-hand Threads

Left-hand Threads

Front

Front

Left Wheel

Right Wheel

Fig. 9.34 Brakes must be assembled according to type and side (Sec 11)

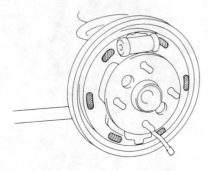

Fig. 9.35 Apply non-melting brake grease to the shaded contact surfaces (Sec 11)

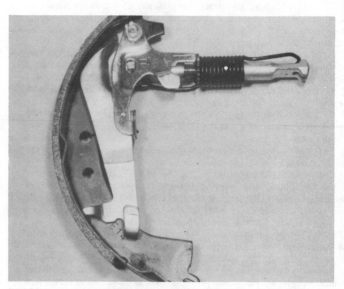

11.15A Locate the strut and adjusting lever onto the trailing shoe

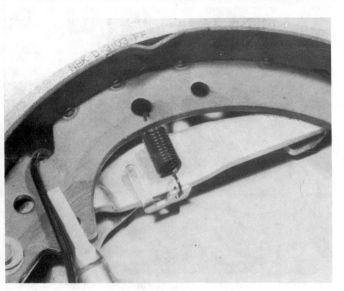

11.15B Adjusting lever spring location

11.16 Brake shoes refitted showing anchor spring and handbrake cable location

11.19 Adjust shoes to allow drum to be refitted

12 Rear drum brake wheel cylinder – removal, servicing and refitting

1   Chock the front wheels, jack up the rear of the car and support it on safety stands. Remove the roadwheel.
2   Remove the rear brake shoes, as described in Section 11.
3   To prevent unnecessary loss of hydraulic fluid in subsequent operations, seal the master cylinder reservoir cap or vent with adhesive tape to create a vacuum.
4   Prise the rubber boots from each end of the wheel cylinder (photo).
5   Extract the pistons from the wheel cylinder bore.
6   Remove the internal spring.
7   Prise the rubber seals from the pistons and discard them. Obtain a wheel cylinder repair kit.
8   Clean all components with fresh hydraulic fluid or methylated spirit. Inspect the surfaces of the pistons and cylinder bore; if any scoring or bright wear areas are evident, renew the complete assembly.
9   To remove the cylinder, disconnect the hydraulic line and unbolt the wheel cylinder from the backplate. Plug the line to prevent entry of foreign matter. Remove the bleed screw.
10   Before reassembly, ensure that all parts are perfectly clean.
11   Dip the pistons in clean hydraulic fluid and fit the new seals, using the fingers only to manipulate them into position. Make sure that the seal lips are facing the correct way.

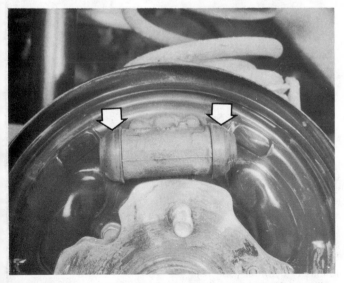

12.4 Rear drum brake wheel cylinder showing and boots (arrowed)

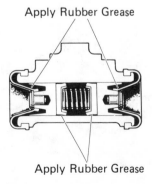

Apply Rubber Grease

Apply Rubber Grease

Fig. 9.36 Sectional view of the wheel cylinder unit (drum brake), showing parts to lubricate when assembling (Sec 12)

12 Refitting is a reversal of removal, but the following points must be observed.

> (a) *Take care not to cross thread the hydraulic line when reconnecting to the cylinder*
> (b) *Refit the brake shoes, as described in Section 11*
> (c) *Remove the adhesive tape from the master cylinder reservoir and bleed the hydraulic system, as described in Section 18*

13 Master cylinder – removal, servicing and refitting

1   The master cylinder is of tandem type and is mounted on the front face of the servo unit. The fluid level reservoir filler cap incorporates a fluid level warning float (photo).
2   Disconnect the fluid level wiring at the plug.
3   Remove the reservoir cap and float and syphon out the hydraulic fluid. Take care not to spill any fluid onto the paintwork.
4   Disconnect the brake pipes from the master cylinder and wipe away any surplus fluid.
5   Wash off any spilled fluid with water immediately.
6   Unscrew the retaining nuts and withdraw the master cylinder and gasket.
7   Clean the master cylinder and reservoir externally before dismantling.
8   Disconnect the elbow pipe between the reservoir and the master cylinder body then, reaching down into the reservoir with a suitable socket and extension, unscrew and remove the reservoir retaining union. Extract the union and washer and lift the reservoir clear of the cylinder body. Release the snap-ring and lift out the elbow.
9   Prise free the dust cover from the rear end of the cylinder then use a pair of circlip pliers to compress and extract the circlip (Fig. 9.39).
10 Press the pistons into the cylinder and remove the stopper bolt (Fig. 9.40). The pistons can then be extracted from the cylinder bore by shaking them out or by applying compressed air into the cylinder outlet aperture at the front.

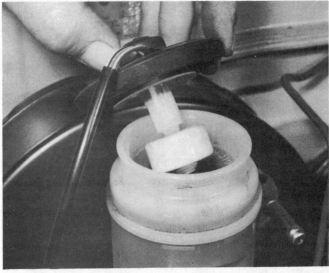

13.1 Master cylinder reservoir filler cap and low level warning float

11 Clean the pistons, springs and cylinder bore for inspection by washing them in hydraulic fluid or methylated spirits.
12 Examine the pistons and cylinder bore surfaces for scoring or bright wear areas. Where these are evident, renew the complete master cylinder. If the surfaces are good discard the seals and obtain a master cylinder repair kit. Dip all components in fresh hydraulic fluid before reassembling to lubricate them.
13 Fit the new seals to the pistons with reference to Fig. 9.41 using the fingers only to manipulate them into position.

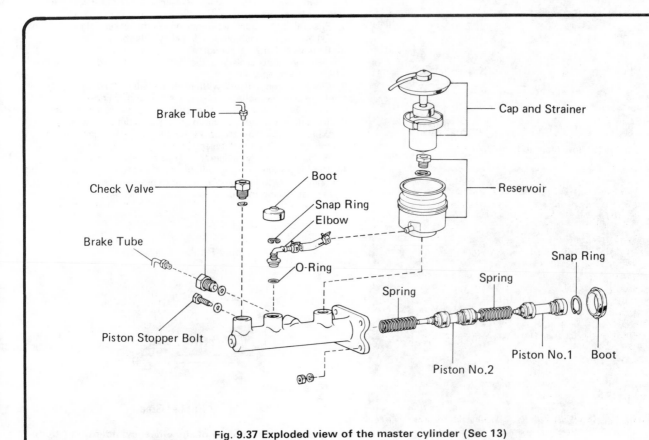

Fig. 9.37 Exploded view of the master cylinder (Sec 13)

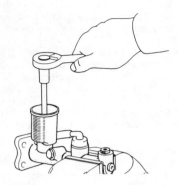

Fig. 9.38 Unbolt and remove the master cylinder reservoir (Sec 13)

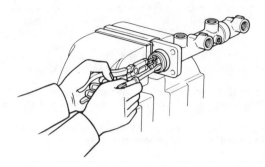

Fig. 9.39 Remove the piston securing circlip (Sec 13)

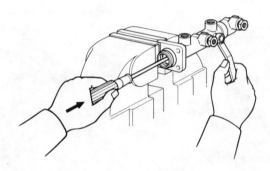

Fig. 9.40 Undo the stopper bolt (Sec 13)

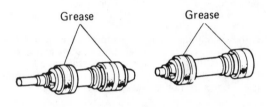

Fig. 9.41 Lubricate and locate the piston seals (Sec 13)

14 Refit the pistons to the master cylinder body by reversing the removal procedure and similarly reassemble the remaining components. As the pistons are inserted, ensure that the seals seat correctly in the bore and do not distort.

15 When the pistons and springs are all in position, press them fully into the cylinder and then insert the stop bolt in the side of the cylinder.

16 Insert the circlip into the end of the cylinder bore to secure the piston assemblies. Check that the boot location groove on the rear end of the master cylinder body is clean, then fit the new rubber dust boot into position so that the UP mark on the boot is at the top (Fig. 9.42).

17 Refit the check valves and tighten them to the specified torque.

18 Insert the elbow with a new O-ring seal into its port and secure with a snap-ring. Fit a new dust boot onto the end of the elbow pipe and reconnect the pipe to the elbow and press the boot down over the boss.

19 Relocate and secure the master cylinder reservoir. The MAX level marking must face the front. Use a new washer and tighten the retaining union to the specified torque.

20 Reconnect the elbow pipe to the master cylinder reservoir.

21 Before refitting the master cylinder, check the adjustment of the booster (servo) pushrod. The clearance between the pushrod and the master cylinder piston must be as specified. Screw the pushrod in or out as necessary to set the clearance required when the master cylinder is fitted. Do not forget to allow for the thickness of the new gasket fitted between the master cylinder and the booster.

22 Refit the master cylinder with its new gasket and tighten the retaining nuts to the specified torque.

23 Reconnect the brake pipes to the master cylinder. Ensure that the unions are clean and take care not to cross-thread the nuts as they are fitted.

24 Top up the fluid level in the reservoir then bleed the brake hydraulic system, as described in Section 18.

25 Finally check and if necessary adjust the brake pedal adjustment, as described in Section 3.

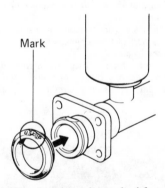

Fig. 9.42 Rubber dust boot is marked for orientation (Sec 13)

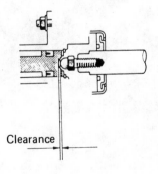

Fig. 9.43 Adjust booster pushrod to give specified pushrod-to-piston clearance (Sec 13)

14 Pressure regulating valve

1   This valve is incorporated in the hydraulic circlip close to the master cylinder. It varies the hydraulic pressure between the front and rear circuits in order to prevent the rear wheels locking during heavy brake applications.

2   The valve cannot be adjusted or repaired and in the event of the valve leaking or a tendency for the rear wheels to lock, renew the valve complete.

3   Disconnect the fluid pipes from the valve body by unscrewing the unions and then remove the valve securing bolts and lift the valve away.

4   Installation of the new valve is a reversal of removal, but bleed the hydraulic system, as described in Section 18.

15 Brake fluid level warning switch – description and testing

1   The switch is an integral part of the master cylinder reservoir cap. Should the fluid level drop below the minimum limit, the switch contacts will operate the warning light on the instrument panel (photo).

2   To test the switch, disconnect the supply wires at the plug and remove the cap. Connect a 12 volt test lamp, battery and leads to the two wires; with the float at the bottom of its stroke the lamp should glow, but with the float at the top of its stroke the lamp should be extinguished. If this is not the case, renew the cap and switch assembly.

16 Rigid brake lines – inspection, removal and refitting

1   At regular intervals wipe the steel pipes clean and examine them for signs of rust or denting caused by flying stones.

2   Examine the securing clips. Bend the tongues of the clips if necessary to ensure that they hold the brake pipes securely without letting them rattle or vibrate.

3   Check that the pipes are not touching any adjacent components or rubbing against any part of the vehicle. Where this is observed, bend the pipe gently away to clear.

4   Any section of pipe which is rusty or chafed should be renewed.

5   Before disconnecting any brake lines, clean the area around the union joints to be detached using a wire brush. Apply a small amount

of penetrating oil to the rigid line and union to ease removal. Whenever possible use brake type spanners to avoid damaging the union nuts.

6   Where a rigid line is connected to a flexible hose, hold the flexible hose connector with a spanner to prevent it from turning then unscrew the rigid line nut (photo).

7   Brake pipes are available to the correct length and fitted with end unions from most Toyota dealers and can be made to pattern by many accessory suppliers. When fitting the new pipes use the old pipes as a guide to bending and do not make any bends sharper than is necessary.

8   The hydraulic system will of course have to be bled when the circuit has been reconnected (Section 18).

17 Flexible hoses – inspection, removal and refitting

1   Regularly inspect the condition of the flexible hydraulic hoses. If they are perished, chafed, or swollen they must be renewed (photo).

2   To remove a flexible hose, first disconnect the rigid brake line

15.1 The brake fluid level warning switch in the reservoir cap

16.6 Rigid brake line-to-flexible hose connection

17.1 Flexible hose connection and bracket showing retaining clip

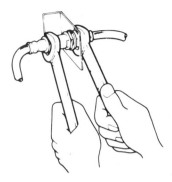

Fig. 9.44 Disconnecting two flexible hoses (Sec 17)

unions while holding the hose stationary (see previous Section, paragraphs 5 and 6).

3   Extract the retaining clip(s) from the bracket(s) and withdraw the flexible hose.

4   Refitting is a reversal of removal, but take care to enter the union threads correctly and make sure that when fitted, the hose is not twisted and has sufficient clearance from surrounding components. Tighten the unions to the specified torque. Bleed the hydraulic system, as described in Section 18.

18 Hydraulic system – bleeding

1   Removal of all the air from the hydraulic system is essential to the correct operation of the braking system. Before undertaking this, examine the fluid reservoir cap to ensure that the vent hole is clear. Check the level of fluid in the reservoir and top-up as required.

2   Check all brake line unions and connections for possible leakage, and at the same time check the condition of the flexible hoses.

3   If the condition of the caliper or wheel cylinders is in doubt, check for possible signs of fluid leakage.

4   If there is any possibility that incorrect fluid has been used in the system, drain all the fluid out and flush through with hydraulic fluid. Renew all piston seals and cups since they will be contaminated and could possibly fail under pressure.

5   One advantage of a dual line braking system is that if work is done to either the front or rear part of the system it will only be necessary to bleed half the system provided that the level of fluid in the reservoir has not fallen below half full.

6   Gather together a clean glass jar, a 305 mm (12 inch) length of tubing which fits tightly over the bleed screws and a tin of the correct brake fluid.

7   To bleed the system, clean the area around the rear right-hand or left-hand wheel bleed screw (whichever is the further away from the master cylinder) and remove the dust cap (photo).

8   Place one end of the tube in the clean jar, which should contain sufficient fluid to keep the end of the tube underneath during the operation, and the other end over the bleed nipple.

9   Open the bleed screw 1/4 turn with the right sized spanner and have an assistant depress the brake pedal. When the brake pedal reaches the floor close the bleed screw and slowly return the pedal.

10 Open the bleed screw and continue the sequence in paragraph 9 until air ceases to flow from the end of the pipe. At intervals make certain that the reservoir is kept topped-up, otherwise air will enter at this point.

11 Finally press the pedal down fully and hold it there whilst the bleed screw is tightened.

12 Repeat this operation on the opposite rear brake, and then the right and left front wheels.

13 Wheels completed, check the level of the fluid in the reservoir and then check the feel of the brake pedal, which should be firm and free from any 'spongy' action – which is normally associated with air in the system.

14 Always discard fluid which has been expelled from the hydraulic system, and always top up the level with fresh fluid which has remained unshaken for the previous 24 hours and has been stored in an airtight container.

19 Brake booster (vacuum servo) air filter – renewal

1   Withdraw the R-clip and disengage the return spring from the brake pedal-to-pushrod clevis pin. Extract the pin.

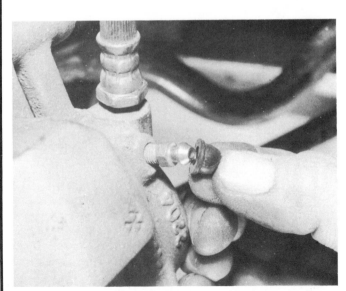

18.7 Bleed screw and dust cap

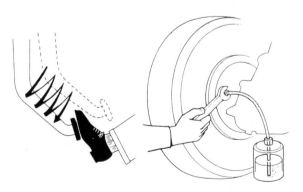

Fig. 9.45 Pump pedal slowly until air free fluid exits from the bleed screw (Sec 18)

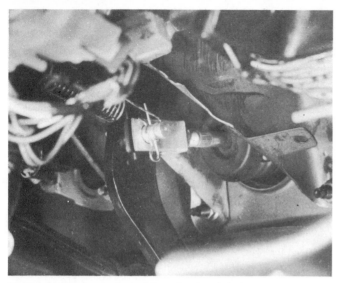

19.2 View showing brake pedal, pushrod and clevis

2   Disengage the clevis from the pedal then loosen the locknut and unscrew the clevis. Unscrew the locknut from the pushrod (photo).
3   Withdraw the dust boot, remove the retainer and remove the air filter element assembly from the pushrod.
4   Refitting is a reversal of the removal procedure. On completion adjust the brake pedal, as described in Section 3.

20 Brake booster (vacuum servo) unit – removal and refitting

1   Use up any vacuum remaining in the unit by making repeated applications of the brake pedal (with the engine stationary).
2   Remove the master cylinder unit, as described in Section 13, and the pressure regulating valve (Section 14).
3   Disconnect the vacuum hose from the booster unit body.
4   Working inside the vehicle, disconnect the brake pedal return spring and then disconnect the pushrod from the pedal arm by extracting the split pin and clevis pin.
5   Unscrew the four retaining nuts from the inner face of the bulkhead (pedal side) and withdraw the booster unit from the engine compartment side.
6   It is not recommended that the booster is dismantled but if faulty renew it with a new or rebuilt unit. Several different makes and size of booster are used according to model so make sure that the correct type for your vehicle is ordered. Renewal of the servo filter can be carried out (see Section 19).
7   Refitting is a reversal of removal, but before assembling the master cylinder to the booster, check that the specified clearance exists between the end of the servo unit pushrod and the end of the master cylinder piston (see Section 13) also refit the pressure regulating valve.
8   When installation is complete, bleed the hydraulic system (Section 18) and check and adjust the brake pedal height and free play settings, as described in Section 3.
9   On completion check the vacuum unit operation by depressing the brake pedal a few times with the engine switched off. There should be no change in the pedal reserve distance.
10 With the brake pedal depressed, start the engine. The operation is normal if the pedal is felt to go down slightly.
11 To check the unit for air tightness proceed as follows. Run the engine for about two minutes then switch it off. Slowly depress the brake pedal a few times and check that the pedal goes further down the

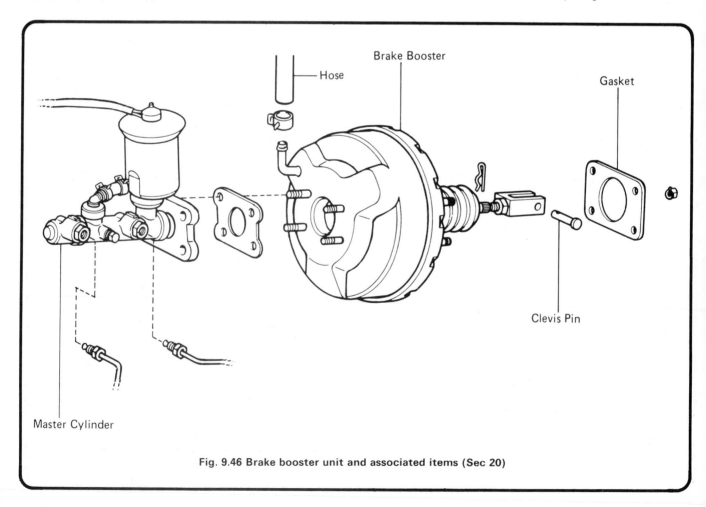

Fig. 9.46 Brake booster unit and associated items (Sec 20)

first time but then progressively rises the second and third time. Restart the engine, depress the brake pedal and hold it down. Switch the engine off with the pedal held down for thirty seconds, the pedal reserve travel should remain the same.

12 If the booster fails the above checks it must be checked, removed and repaired or renewed as necessary.

21 Handbrake – adjustment

1 The handbrake is normally adjusted automatically by the action of the self-adjusting rear brake mechanism. However, due to cable stretch or when fitting a new cable, adjustment will be required to make sure that the handbrake is fully applied with the lever within the specified number of notches from the released position.

2 To check the handbrake for correct adjustment, pull the lever up as far as possible and count the number of clicks. The number of clicks registered should comply with the number specified according to rear brake type.

3 If adjustment is needed, it is first necessary to check that the rear brake shoe-to-drum clearance is correct. To do this raise the car at the rear and support on safety stands.

4 On disc/drum brake models set the clearance as described in Section 9, paragraph 16.

5 On rear drum brake models, remove the brake drum as described in Section 11. Using vernier calipers, measure the inside diameter of the drum and then adjust the brake shoes by turning the adjustment bolt so that their outside diameter is 0.6 mm (0.024 in) under that measured for the inside diameter of the brake drum. Refit the brake drum and roadwheel.

6 Remove the rear console box and lift it clear of the handbrake lever.

7 Loosen the cable locknut then turn the adjuster nut as required to adjust the handbrake. Retighten the locknut (photo).

8 Refit the console box, check that the rear brakes prevent the rear roadwheels from turning when the lever is applied the specified amount. Release the lever and check that the roadwheels rotate freely.

9 Apply the handbrake, then lower the car at the rear.

22 Handbrake lever – removal and refitting

1 Chock the front and rear wheels and fully relese the handbrake lever.

2 Detach and remove the rear console box from the handbrake lever.

3 Unscrew and remove the cable locknut and adjustment nut.

4 Unscrew the mounting bolts and withdraw the handbrake lever. Note the location of the handbrake warning switch.

21.7 Handbrake lever and cable showing adjuster and locknuts. The warning switch is also shown

5 Refitting is a reversal of removal, but it will be necessary to adjust the handbrake, as described in Section 21.

23 Handbrake cable – renewal

1 The handbrake cable is in three sections, any of which can if necessary be removed separately.

2 Remove the handbrake lever, as described in Section 22.

3 With the front wheels chocked, jack up the rear of the car and support it on safety stands.

4 Reach over the propeller shaft and disconnect the front cable from the equaliser by turning the cable stop plate through 90°. Withdraw the cable through the handbrake lever baseplate.

5 Prise the guide grommets at the front of the rear cables from the underframe brackets, then disconnect the equaliser.

6 Remove the rear brake shoes as described in Section 10 or 11, as applicable.

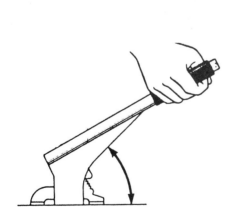

Fig. 9.47 Handbrake adjustment check (Sec 21)

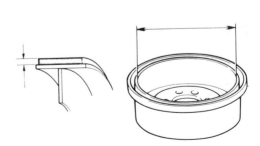

Fig. 9.48 Handbrake adjustment in accordance with shoe lining wear and inside diameter of brake drum – rear drum brake models (Sec 21)

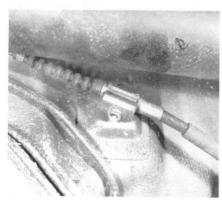

23.7A Handbrake cable-to-body location bracket

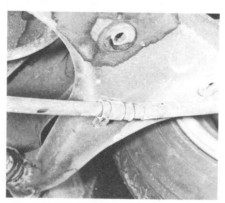

23.7B Handbrake cable-to-rear suspension arm location bracket

23.8 Handbrake cable securing clip on backplate

7   Disconnect the rear cable(s) from the location clamps between the equaliser and the rear brake unit(s) (photos).

8   Compress the spread clips securing the cable to the outer face of the brake backplate and then pass the cable through the hole in the backplate and remove it from underneath the car (photo).

9   Refitting is a reversal of removal, but it will be necessary to refit the brake shoes as described, in Section 10 or 11 as applicable, and also to adjust the handbrake, as described in Section 21.

24 Brake pedal – removal and refitting

1   Remove the lower trim panel on the driver's side.

2   Disconnect the return spring from the outer groove in the pushrod clevis pin.

3   Withdraw the R-clip and extract the clevis pin.

4   Unscrew the pivot bolt nut, withdraw the bolt and remove the pedal.

5   Refit in the reverse order of removal. Lubricate the pivot with grease. Check and·adjust the brake pedal on completion, as described in Section 3.

25 Brake stop-light switch – removal, refitting and adjustment

1   Disconnect the battery negative lead.

2   Remove the lower trim panel on the driver's side.

3   Detach the switch wiring, undo the locknut and unscrew the switch from the pedal bracket.

4   Refit in the reverse order of removal. Adjust the switch position so that it lightly contacts the pedal stopper and then tighten the locknut.

5   Check for satisfactory operation on completion.

26 Fault diagnosis – braking system

Symptom	Reason(s)
Pedal travels almost to floor before brakes operate	Brake fluid too low Caliper leaking Master cylinder leaking (bubbles in master cylinder fluid) Brake flexible hose leaking Brake line fractured Brake system unions loose Rear brakes badly out of adjustment (automatic adjusters seized)
Brake pedal feels springy	New linings not yet bedded-in Brake discs or drums badly worn or cracked Master cylinder securing nuts loose
Brake pedal feels 'spongy' and 'soggy'	Caliper or wheel cylinder leaking Master cylinder leaking (bubbles in master cylinder fluid) Brake pipe line or flexible hose leaking Unions in brake system loose
Excessive effort required to brake car	Faulty vacuum servo unit Pad or shoe linings badly worn New pads or shoes recently fitted – not yet bedded-in Harder linings fitted than standard causing increase in pedal pressure Linings and brake drums contaminated with oil, grease or hydraulic fluid
Brake uneven and pulling to one side	Linings and discs or drums contaminated with oil, grease or hydraulic fluid Tyre pressures unequal Brake caliper loose or seized Brake pad or shoes fitted incorrectly Different type of linings fitted at each wheel Anchorage for front suspension or rear suspension loose Brake discs or drums badly worn, cracked or distorted
Brakes tend to bind, drag or lock-on	Faulty pressure regulating valve Air in system Handbrake cable over-tightened Wheel cylinder or caliper pistons seized
Brake warning light stays on	Leak in front or rear hydraulic circuits Faulty handbrake switch Faulty master cylinder fluid level switch

Chapter 10 Suspension and steering

Contents

Specifications

General

Front suspension	Independent, MacPherson struts, coil springs and stabilizer bar
Steering	Rack and pinion, power-assisted on some models
Rear suspension	Four link type with coil springs and double acting shock absorbers. Stabilizer bar or independent rear suspension with semi-trailing arms, coil springs and double-acting shock absorbers. Stabilizer bar

Steering angles

	Inspection	Adjustment
Toe-in (all models):		
With power steering	5 ± 4 mm (0.20 ± 0.16 in)	5 ± 1 mm (0.20 ± 0.04 in)
Without power steering	4 ± 4 mm (0.16 ± 0.16 in)	4 ± 1 mm (0.16 ± 0.04 in)
Camber:		
With 14 inch wheels	55' ± 45'	55' ± 30'
Left to right error	30'	30'
Steering axis inclination:		
With 14 inch wheel	9°20 ± 45'	9°20' ± 30'
Left to right error	30'	30'
Castor:		
With 14 inch wheel	3°20 ± 45'	3°20 ± 30'
Left to right error	30'	30'

Side slip (maximum) .... 3.0 mm per m (0.118 in per 3.3 ft)
Roadwheel lateral run-out (maximum) .... 1.2 mm (0.047 in)
Hub axial play (maximum) .... 0.05 mm (0.0020 in)
Balljoint vertical play (maximum) .... 2.5 mm (0.098 in)
Wheel angle:
    UK models, and USA models up to 1984:
        Inside wheel .... 37° + 0°/–4°
        Outside wheel .... 32° (reference)

Wheel bearing preload

Front wheel bearing (turning load at hub bolt):
    UK models, and USA models up to 1983:
        With new oil seal .... 350 to 875 g (0.8 to 1.91 lb)
        With used oil seal .... 50 to 500 g (0.1 to 1.11 lb)
    USA models from 1984 .... 0 to 1050 g (0 to 2.3 lb)
Rear wheel bearing – all IRS models .... 1.0 to 4.0 kgf m (8 to 28 lbf ft)

Rear wheel alignment (IRS models)

	Inspection	Adjustment
Toe-in	0 ± 4 mm (0 ± 0.016 in)	0 ± 2 mm (0 ± 0.08 in)
Camber:		
UK models	6′ ± 45′	6′ ± 45′
USA models	–10′ ± 45′	–10′ ± 45′
Left to right error	30′	30′
Side slip limit	3.0 mm per metre (0.118 in per 3.3 ft)	
Roadwheel lateral run-out (maximum)	1.2 mm (0.047 in)	

Vehicle height

	Front	Rear
With 165 SR 14 tyres:		
Coupe	228.0 mm (8.976 in)	260.0 mm (10.236 in)
Liftback	228.0 mm (8.976 in)	264.5 mm (10.413 in)
With 185/70 SR 14 tyres:		
Coupe	230.0 mm (9.055 in)	262.0 mm (10.315 in)
Liftback	230.0 mm (9.055 in)	266.5 mm (10.492 in)
With 225/60 HR 14 tyres (USA models):		
Coupe	231.0 mm (9.094 in)	263.0 mm (10.354 in)
Liftback	231.0 mm (9.094 in)	267.5 mm (10.531 in)

Steering

Steering wheel free play (maximum) .... 30 mm (1.18 in)
Steering rack run-out (maximum) .... 0.3 mm (0.12 in)
Pinion bearing preload (at turning) .... 2.3 to 3.3 kgf cm (2.0 to 2.9 lbf in)
Pinion total preload (at turning) .... 10 to 13 kgf m (8.7 to 11.3 lbf in)
Balljoint vertical play (maximum) .... 2.5 mm (0.098 in)
Power steering:
    Maximum oil rise .... 5 mm (0.20 in)

	New belt	Used belt
Drivebelt tension (UK models):		
Deflection with 10 kg (22 lb) applied force	5 to 7 mm (0.20 to 28 in)	7 to 10 mm (0.28 to 0.39 in)
Drivebelt tension (USA models):	New belt	Used belt
Using Burroughs tension gauge (No BT-33-73F)	45 to 68 kg (100 to 150 lb)	27 to 45 kg (60 to 100 lb)

    Steering effort at steering wheel (maximum) .... 4 kg (8.8 lb)
    Fluid type .... ATF Dexron or Dexron II
Tilt steering:
    No 1 collar – outer diameters available .... 17.989 to 17.996 mm (0.7085 to 0.7088 in)
          18.003 to 18.010 mm (0.7088 to 0.7091 in)
          18.010 to 18.017 mm (0.7091 to 0.7093 in)
          18.017 to 18.024 mm (0.7093 to 0.7096 in)
    No 2 collar – outer diameters available .... 17.982 to 18.000 mm (0.7080 to 0.7087 in)
          18.000 to 18.018 mm (0.7087 to 0.7094 in)
    Support shim – thicknesses available .... 0.2 mm (0.008 in)
          0.5 mm (0.020 in)
          0.8 mm (0.031 in)
          1.4 mm (0.055 in)
          1.8 mm (0.071 in)

Roadwheels and tyres

Wheel type .... Pressed steel or alloy
Wheels/tyre sizes:
    UK models .... 5.5 J : 165 SR 14
          185/70 HR 14
          185/80 VR 14
    USA models .... 5.5 J x 14: 175 SR 14
          5.5 JJ x 14 : 185/70 R 14
          5.5 J x 14 or 5.5 JJ x 14: 185/70 SR 14
          7 JJ x 14 : 225/60 HR 14
    USA models – compact spare .... 4 T x 15 : T 135/70 D 15
          5.5 J x 14 : 185/70 R 14

Inflation pressures (cold)

	Front	Rear
UK models:		
165 SR 14 tyres	1.8 kg/cm² (26 lb/in²)	2.0 kg/cm² (28 lbf/in²)
185/70 HR 14 and 185/70 VR 14 tyres	1.8 kg/cm² (26 lbf/in²)	1.8 kg/cm² (26 lb/in²)
USA models:		
All roadwheels (front and rear)	1.9 kg/cm² (27 lb/in²)	
Compact spare:		
T 135/70 D 15	4.2 kg/cm² (60 lb/in²)	
185/70 R 14	2.8 kg/cm² (40 lb/in²)	

For sustained speeds over 75 mph (120 kph), inflate 0.3 kg/cm² (4 lb/in²) higher than standard inflation pressures given above. Tyre pressures may differ slightly according to size and type. Check with your dealer for the exact recommended settings.

Torque wrench settings

	kgf m	lbf ft
Front axle and suspension		
Shock absorber-to-suspension support nut	4.75	34
Lower arm to crossmember	8.00	58
Lower balljoint to steering knuckle arm	8.00	58
Strut bar to strut bar bracket	9.25	67
Steering knuckle arm to tie-rod	6.00	43
Strut bar to lower arm	6.70	48
Strut bar bracket to body	4.25	31
Stabilizer bar to lower arm	1.80	13
Stabilizer bar bracket to strut bar bracket	1.85	13
Suspension support to wing apron	3.75	27
Shock absorber to knuckle arm	10.00	72
Suspension member to body	11.00	80
Disc brake unit to dust cover	7.00	51
Wheel nuts (front and rear)	10.50	76
Disc brake unit to steering knuckle	10.00	72
Hub nut (initial setting)	3.00	22
Rear suspension (FLS)		
Shock absorber to body	2.50	18
Shock absorber to rear axle	3.75	27
Lateral control rod to axle	5.90	43
Lateral control rod to body	8.00	58
Upper control arm to axle	12.50	90
Upper control arm to body	14.50	105
Lower control arm to axle	12.50	90
Lower control arm to body	14.50	105
Stabilizer bracket to axle	1.85	13
Stabilizer link to stabilizer bar	3.10	22
Rear suspension (IRS)		
Shock absorber to body	2.50	18
Shock absorber to suspension arm	3.75	27
Stabilizer link to suspension arm	1.80	13
Stabilizer bar end to stabilizer link	3.10	22
Stabilizer bar bracket to member	1.85	13
Suspension arm to body (UK models)	10.00 to 13.50	73 to 97
Differential support member to body	12.00	87
Suspension arm to body (USA models):		
Inside	13.25	96
Outside	11.75	85
Steering		
Steering wheel nut	3.50	25
Column tube to column hole cover	1.30	9
Breakaway bracket to instrument panel	2.50	18
Manual steering housing:		
Intermediate shaft/universal joint/steering worm shaft	3.50	25
Pinion bearing adjustment screw locknut to rack housing	11.50	83
Rack guide spring cap locknut to rack housing	7.00	51
Steering rack end to rack	10.50	76
Tie-rod end to steering rack end	1.75	13
Steering gear housing to body	4.75	34
Knuckle arm to tie-rod	6.00	43
Power steering housing:		
Rack housing to cylinder	1.85	13
Rack end to steering rack	10.50	76
Control valve housing to rack housing	1.85	13
Pinion bearing adjustment screw locknut to rack housing	7.00	51
Rack guide spring locknut	7.00	51
Return pressure	3.00	22
Pressure line to rack housing	3.90	28
Steering gear housing to body	4.75	34
Steering tilt mechanism:		
Pawl set bolt	1.85	13
Tilt lever retainer	1.85	13

Torque wrench settings (continued)

	kgf m	lbf ft
Support-to-breakaway bracket (castle) nut	1.85	13
Support stopper bolt	1.00	7
Breakaway bracket to column	1.85	13
Mainshaft to intermediate shaft	2.50	18
Upper bracket to tilt steering support	0.75	5
Support reinforcement to tilt steering support	0.75	5

1 General description

The front suspension fitted to all models is of MacPherson strut type. The struts are secured at their upper ends to reinforced areas under the wings and attached at their lower ends to the steering knuckle arms.

A strut bar is fitted between the lower suspension arm and the bodyframe and a stabilizer bar is also fitted to ensure good handling characteristics.

The rear suspension fitted will be one of two systems, there being a four link system (FLS) or independent rear suspension (IRS).

The four link system has coil springs, double-acting telescopic shock absorbers and upper and lower control arms mounted between the body and the axle. Longitudinal movement of the rear axle is controlled by the lower control arm, and side to side movement by the upper arms. The telescopic shock absorbers are attached to brackets on the axle tube at their lower ends, and to the body underframe at their upper ends. A lateral control rod and stabilizer bar are also fitted to improve handling.

The independent rear suspension system also has coil springs and double-acting telescopic shock absorbers. These are connected to the semi-trailing arms which pivot obliquely to the car's centre line via a chassis crossmember. A stabilizer bar is also fitted to improve handling.

On all models the steering is of rack and pinion type; some models being fitted with power-assisted steering. A tilt mechanism at the top of the steering column allows the steering wheel to be adjusted for rake.

2 Routine maintenance – suspension and steering

Refer to the Routine Maintenance section at the front of the manual and carry out the checks and lubrication operations, together with the general checks listed below, at the specified intervals.

1 **Wheels and tyres:** Check these at regular intervals, as described in Section 26. In particular look for excessive and/or uneven tyre wear, the latter being indicative of steering or suspension misalignment.

2 **Steering wheel free play:** With the vehicle parked and the roadwheels in the straight-ahead position, gently rock the steering wheel back and forth under a light finger pressure and check that the free play does not exceed that specified. If excessive free play exists, check the steering system components for excessive wear or damage and repair as necessary.

3 **Steering linkages:** Check the tie-rod ends for excessive play and at the same time inspect the steering rack gaiters for signs of leakage or damage. On power steering models check for signs of fluid leakage from the system hoses and line connections.

4 **Power steering:** Check the fluid level in the power steering fluid reservoir, as described in Section 12. Check the condition and tension of the power steering pump drivebelt and renew or adjust the belt if necessary, as described in Section 13.

5 **Steering knuckle balljoint:** Check the steering balljoints by jacking up the front of the vehicle and positioning a 7.5 inch thick block under the roadwheel. Lower the jack to give a half loading on the front coil springs. Fit safety stands as shown (Fig. 10.2) and then use a lever to move the lower arm up and down whilst checking the balljoint for excessive wear. Measure the amount of play and compare it with the specified maximum amount allowable. The joints will have to be renewed if worn beyond the specified figure. Inspect the steering knuckle balljoint dust cover for signs of deterioration or damage. Renew the cover if necessary.

6 **Front wheel hub:** With the vehicle jacked up at the front end and the roadwheels clear of the ground, grip the roadwheels top and bottom and attempt to rock them. Any movement may indicate incorrectly adjusted or excessively worn hub bearings.

7 **Front and rear wheel bearings:** At the specified intervals, remove the hub and clean and lubricate the wheel bearings, as described in Section 3.

8 **Front and rear suspension:** Check the front and rear suspension components for signs of excessive wear or damage, in particular the various pivot bushes, the shock absorbers and the coil springs. Check that the suspension-to-body mountings are secure (Figs. 10.5 and 10.6). Also check the wheel nuts for security.

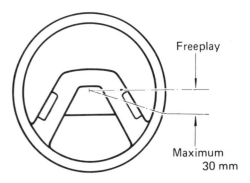

Fig. 10.1 Check the steering wheel free play (Sec 2)

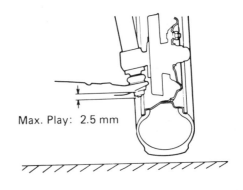

Fig. 10.3 Steering balljoint vertical play must not exceed specified limit (Sec 2)

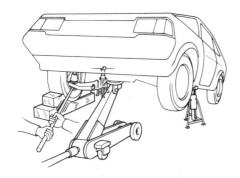

Fig. 10.2 Steering balljoint check method (Sec 2)

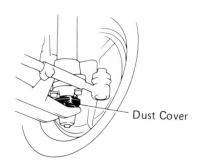

Fig. 10.4 Check the steering balljoint dust cover (Sec 2)

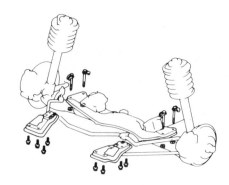

Fig. 10.5 Check the front suspension/body mounting bolts and nuts for security (Sec 2)

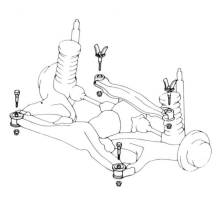

Fig. 10.6 Check the rear suspension/body mounting bolts and nuts for security – IRS shown (Sec 2)

3 Front hubs – removal, servicing, refitting and adjustment

1   Chock the rear wheels, raise the vehicle at the front and support it on safety stands. Remove the front roadwheel(s).
2   Remove the brake caliper unit, as described in Chapter 9. There is no need to disconnect the hydraulic hose but simply tie the caliper assembly to the front suspension strut using a piece of wire.
3   Prise off the grease cap and extract the split pin (photos).
4   Remove the nut retainer then unscrew and remove the nut and thrust washer (photo).
5   Pull the hub assembly from the steering knuckle, complete with brake disc.
6   Extract the outer bearing race from the hub.
7   Extract the oil seal, which must be renewed, and then extract the inner bearing race (Fig. 10.8).
8   Wash out all old grease from the bearings and hub using petrol or a suitable grease solvent. Check the bearings and their tracks for wear, damage or scoring.

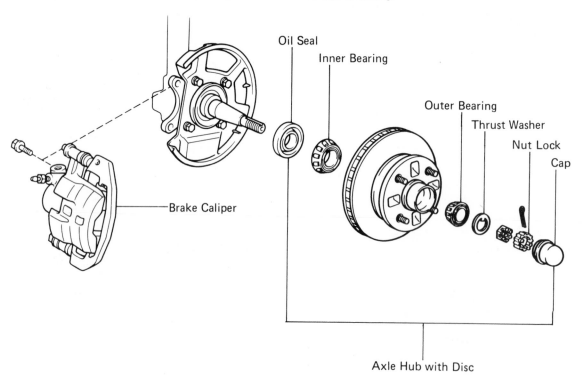

Fig. 10.7 Front brake disc/hub components (Sec 3)

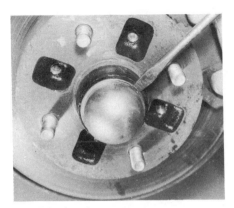

3.3A Prise free the grease cap ...

3.3B ... remove the split pin and nut retainer ...

3.4 ... undo the nut

9   If they are found to be in a serviceable condition, repack the inside of the hub with grease and proceed from paragraph 14.

10 If either the inner or outer bearings require renewal, drive out the old tracks with a brass drift and then press in the new bearing tracks, ensuring that they are housed correctly.

11 Where both front hubs are being serviced at the same time, do not mix the bearing components as the races and tracks are matched in production.

12 The disc should not be removed from the hub unless it is to be refaced or renewed.

13 Reassembly is a reversal of the removal procedure. Drive the new oil seal carefully into position and smear it with grease.

14 Thoroughly lubricate the inner bearing race with multi-purpose grease and insert it into the hub. Pack the inner hub with grease, then relocate the hub/disc onto the steering knuckle, but take care not to get grease onto the disc contact surface. Refit the outer bearing race, again thoroughly lubricated with grease, locate the thrust washer and then adjust the bearings for preload as follows.

15 Fit and tighten the hub nut to the specified initial torque setting whilst simultaneously rotating the hub. Now loosen the nut then retighten it hand tight only, and check the bearing preload.

16 To do this attach a spring balance to one of the roadwheel studs and observe the pull effort which is required to rotate the hub. This should be as specified (Fig. 10.11).

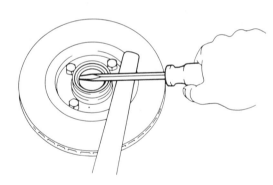

Fig. 10.8 Oil seal removal from hub (Sec 3)

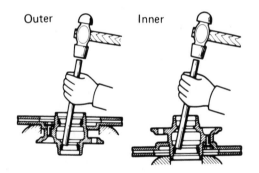

Fig. 10.9 Bearing cup removal from hub (Sec 3)

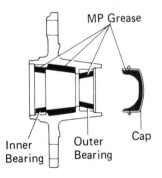

Fig. 10.10 Lubricate areas shown (Sec 3)

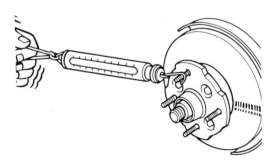

Fig. 10.11 Check the hub bearing preload (Sec 3)

17 Tighten or loosen the nut to adjust as necessary then when the adjustment is correct, refit the adjuster cap and insert a new split pin to secure in the set position.
18 Fill the grease cap about $1/3$rd full with grease and knock it into position (photo).
19 Refit the brake caliper unit, as described in Chapter 9.
20 Refit the roadwheel(s) to complete and lower the vehicle.

4   Front strut unit – removal, inspection and refitting

1   Chock the rear roadwheels then raise the front of the vehicle and support on safety stands. Remove the roadwheel on the side concerned.
2   The front shock absorbers are removed as a unit, together with the coil spring and steering knuckle assembly.
3   Disconnect the front brake flexible hose-to-rigid hose connection at the mounting bracket on the wing inner panel. To prevent excess fluid leakage from the brake line when disconnected, seal off the reservoir filler neck with a sheet of clean polythene stretched across the filler neck and secured with an elastic band. Plug the exposed pipe ends when separated to prevent the ingress of dirt.
4   Unscrew and remove the three securing nuts at the top of the shock absorber at the wing mounting within the engine compartment (photo).
5   Unscrew and remove the two bolts securing the shock absorber to the steering knuckle arm (photo).
6   The front shock absorber, axle hub and brake caliper unit can now be withdrawn. Push downwards on the suspension lower arm so that the shock absorber clears the collars, which protrude from the knuckle bolt holes by 5 mm (0.20 in) (Fig. 10.13).
7   If required, the brake caliper can be removed, as described in Chapter 9, and also the front hub unit, as described in Section 3 of this Chapter.
8   To remove the coil spring from the strut assembly you will need a suitable coil spring compressor to retain the spring tension during subsequent dismantling operations, and also for reassembly. Do not proceed further unless you have such a tool.
9   Locate the spring compressor into position and check that it is fully engaged on the spring.
10 Prise free the rubber bung from the top of the unit to expose the nut and bearing. Unscrew the nut whilst gripping the spring seat to prevent it rotating, (if available, use the special Toyota service tool number 09729-22031).

3.18 Apply grease to the cap before fitting

11 With the nut removed, withdraw the suspension support, release the spring compressor and remove the coil spring with seat and dust cover; noting how each is located.
12 Clean and inspect the components for signs of excessive wear or damage.
13 Check the spring for signs of deformity and if possible check its length against a new one. If necessary, renew it, and also the opposing front suspension coil spring. To renew one spring only could cause adverse handling characteristics.
14 Check the bearing in the spring seat, and the seat itself, for signs of wear or damage and renew as necessary. The bearing inner race should rotate freely.
15 Renew the spring bumper, dust seal and also the bearing dust cover if decayed or damaged.

4.4 Shock absorber (strut) top mounting nuts

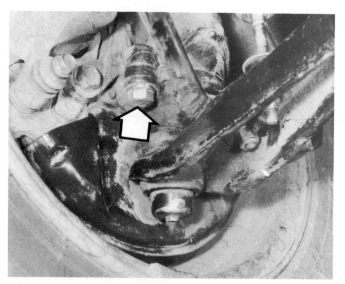

4.5 Shock absorber-to-steering knuckle arm bolt (arrowed)

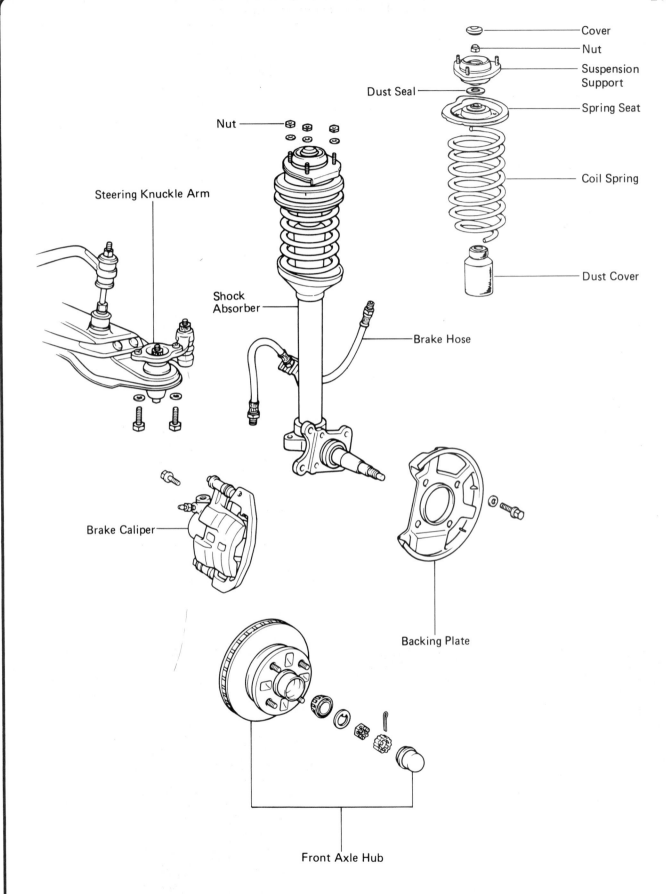

Cover

Nut

Suspension Support

Dust Seal

Spring Seat

Coil Spring

Dust Cover

Nut

Steering Knuckle Arm

Shock Absorber

Brake Hose

Brake Caliper

Backing Plate

Front Axle Hub

Fig. 10.12 Front strut unit and associated components (Sec 4)

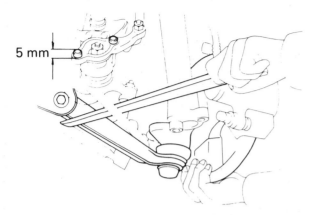

Fig. 10.13 Lever the suspension arm down to provide necessary clearance (Sec 4)

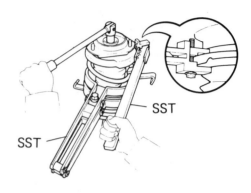

Fig. 10.14 Coil spring removal requires the use of special tools (Sec 4)

16 Check the operation of the shock absorber by withdrawing and then pushing the piston rod back into the cylinder. Its action should be smooth whilst offering some resistance. If the shock absorber has been leaking it will have to be dismantled for inspection and the oil seal renewed. This is a test best entrusted to your Toyota dealer who will dismantle the unit and check its serviceability.

17 If the shock absorber is to be renewed or dismantled you will need to remove the wheel hub and disc assembly, as described in Section 3. The backplate must also be removed.

18 To reassemble the strut unit, recompress the coil spring sufficiently to allow refitting of the various components.

19 Reassemble in the reverse order to removal, fitting the spring bumper, the spring and seat, which should be aligned with the piston rod. Align the coil spring lower end with the seat dent.

20 Align the spring seat with the piston rod when fitting and locate the dust seal.

21 Relocate the top support and fit a new nut to secure it. Tighten the nut to the specified torque wrench setting whilst simultaneously gripping the support to prevent it from rotating.

22 Pack the support bearing and cavity with grease and refit the rubber bung. Remove the spring compressor.

23 If applicable, refit the backing plate and front hub to the steering knuckle and preload the bearings, as described in Section 3.

24 If applicable, refit the brake caliper, as described in Chapter 9.

25 Relocate the assembled strut unit into position on the steering knuckle arm, check that it is fully seated and correctly aligned then insert the retaining bolts and tighten them to the specified torque.

26 Locate the three studs at the top of the strut unit through the holes in the wing mounting, then fit and tighten the retaining nuts to the specified torque.

27 Reconnect the brake hydraulic lines. Top up and bleed the brakes, as described in Chapter 9.

28 Refit the roadwheel and on completion have the front wheel alignment checked by your Toyota dealer. A provisional alignment check can be made as given in Section 16.

5 Front suspension lower arm – removal, inspection and refitting

1 Chock the rear wheels, then raise and support the vehicle at the front end on safety stands. Remove the roadwheel on the side concerned.

2 Unscrew and remove the two bolts securing the knuckle arm to the bottom end of the shock absorber. Press down on the lower suspension arm to disengage the shock absorber from the knuckle arm.

3 Disconnect the tie-rod balljoint from the knuckle arm, as described in Section 15.

4 Unscrew the retaining nut and disconnect the stabilizer bar from the lower arm.

5 Unscrew the retaining nuts and disconnect the strut bar from the lower arm.

6 Unscrew the nut from the pivot bolt at the inboard end of the lower arm. Support the weight of the lower arm, withdraw the pivot bolt and remove the lower arm from the crossmember.

7 If the bushes are worn at the inner end of the arm, they can be removed and new ones fitted either using a press or a long bolt, nuts, washers and distance pieces of suitable diameter.

8 If the lower suspension arm balljoint is worn excessively, it can only be renewed as part of a new lower suspension arm assembly. The balljoint dust cover, however, can be renewed. To do this separate the knuckle arm from the lower arm as follows:

9 Extract the cotter pin and unscrew the nut securing the knuckle arm to the balljoint. Support the underside of the knuckle arm each side of the balljoint and, using a press or soft-headed hammer, drive or press the balljoint stud down through the knuckle arm to separate. Take care not to damage the stud threads.

10 Prise free the dust cover retaining wire, then remove the cover.

11 Clean the stud and the cover seat on the joint. Lubricate the new cover with grease where indicated in Fig. 10.20, then fit the dust cover over the stud and onto the joint seat so that the escape valve (C) is facing rearwards relative to its fitting position on the car.

12 Wind the new securing wire two full turns around the dust cover and, with the ends at the front, twist them together to make the wire secure. Do not overtighten the wire. Trim off the excess wire ends with snips and bend the wire knot downwards.

13 Unscrew the plug from the base of the balljoint, insert a grease nipple and lubricate the joint with molybdenum disulphide lithium based grease. Remove the nipple and refit the plug.

14 Refit the knuckle arm to the lower arm balljoint, fit and tighten the nut to the specified torque and insert a new cotter pin to secure.

15 To refit the lower arm, align it with the pivot bolt holes in the crossmember on the inboard end, insert a pivot bolt (from front to rear) and hand tighten the nut.

16 Reconnect the stabilizer bar and strut bar to the lower arm and tighten their retaining nuts to the specified torque settings.

17 Reconnect the tie-rod balljoint to the knuckle arm, tighten the nut to the specified torque and insert a new cotter pin to secure.

18 Reconnect the knuckle arm to the bottom end of the shock absorber unit and tighten the two bolts to the specified torque.

19 Refit the roadwheel and lower the vehicle to the ground.

20 Bounce the front end of the vehicle up and down a few times to ensure that the suspension is settled in its normal position then tighten the lower arm inner pivot bolt and nut to the specified torque.

21 On completion have the front wheel alignment checked by your Toyota dealer. An initial alignment check can be made by referring to Section 16.

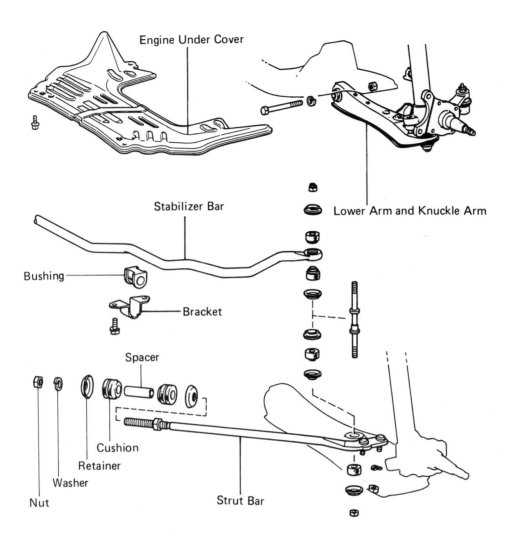

Engine Under Cover

Stabilizer Bar

Lower Arm and Knuckle Arm

Bushing

Bracket

Spacer

Cushion

Retainer

Washer

Nut

Strut Bar

Fig. 10.15 Front suspension components (Sec 5)

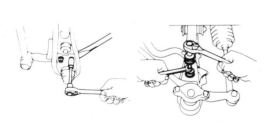

Fig. 10.16 Disconnect the stabilizer bar and the strut bar (Sec 5)

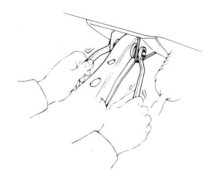

Fig. 10.17 Unbolt the suspension arm inner pivot (Sec 5)

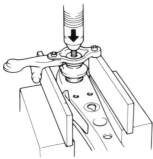

Fig. 10.18 Detaching the knuckle arm from the lower arm (Sec 5)

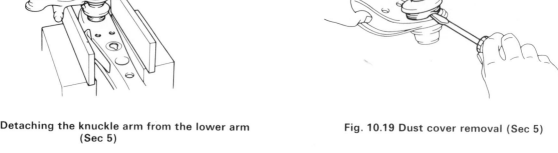

Fig. 10.19 Dust cover removal (Sec 5)

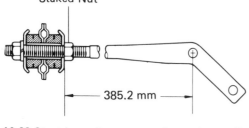

Fig. 10.20 Balljoint dust cover renewal. Apply grease to A and B. Escape valve C must face rearwards (Sec 5)

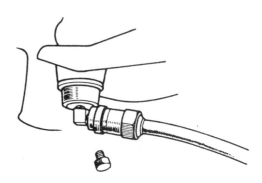

Fig. 10.21 Remove plug, and insert grease nipple to lubricate the steering balljoint (Sec 5)

Staked Nut

385.2 mm

Fig. 10.22 Strut bar adjustment to be as shown. Do not adjust unless absolutely necessary (Sec 6)

6 Strut bar – removal and refitting

1   Chock the rear wheels, raise the vehicle at the front and support it on safety stands.
2   Unbolt the bar from the lower arm and from the bodyframe attachment bracket. The backing nut at the bracket is staked in position and should not be removed, or the castor angle will be altered. However, where a new bar is to be fitted, tighten the nuts at the bracket end in accordance with the appropriate diagram to the specified torque settings, and then stake the new backing nut (photo) (Fig. 10.22).
3   Refit the roadwheel and lower the vehicle.
4   On completion the front wheel alignment must be checked. Refer to Section 16 for details.

7 Front suspension stabilizer bar – removal and refitting

1   Chock the rear wheels, raise the vehicle at the front and support it on safety stands.

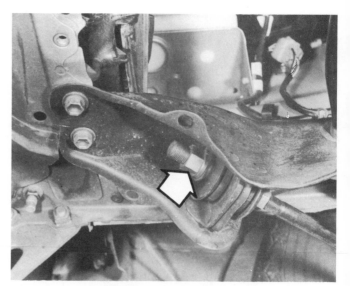

6.2 Strut bar-to-body frame bracket mounting. Unscrew the nut indicated (not the inner nut)

2   Unbolt and remove the engine under shield.
3   Unbolt and remove the stabilizer bar brackets from the strut bar bracket. Move the strut bar with bracket to one side by detaching it from the lower arm and removing the four bracket bolts.
4   The stabilizer bar can now be withdrawn by pulling it through the strut bar bracket hole.
5   Clean and inspect the stabilizer bar, bushes and through-bolts. Renew any damaged or worn components (Fig. 10.25).

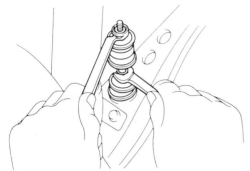

Fig. 10.23 Unbolt stabilizer bar from the lower arm (Sec 7)

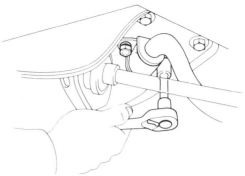

Fig. 10.24 Remove stabilizer bar brackets (Sec 7)

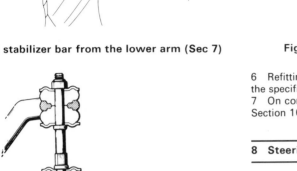

Fig. 10.25 Stabilizer bar bushes arrangement (Sec 7)

6   Refitting is a reversal of removal, but tighten all nuts and bolts to the specified torque wrench settings.
7   On completion the front wheel alignment should be checked. See Section 16 for details.

8   Steering column – removal and refitting

1   The steering column is removed complete with the tilt mechanism. First remove the steering wheel as described in Section 17. Also remove the upper column cover (shroud).
2   Remove the lower trim panel and the air duct on the driver's side.
3   Remove the combination switch unit referring to Chapter 12 for details.

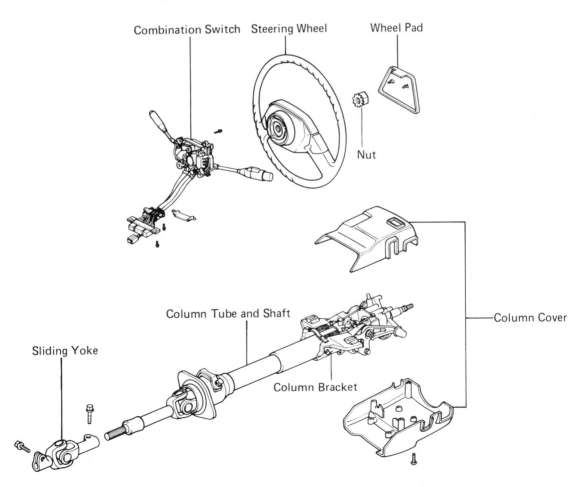

Fig. 10.26 Steering column and associated components (Sec 8)

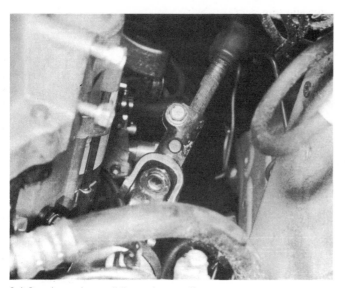

8.4 Steering column sliding yoke coupling

8.5 Steering column-to-bulkhead cover

4   On the engine compartment side, unscrew and remove the sliding yoke set bolts (photo).
5   Undo the column mounting bolts from the bulkhead cover plate (photo).
6   At the top end, remove the two column mounting bracket nuts.
7   Rotate the column in a clockwise direction and withdraw the column from inside the vehicle. As it is withdrawn get an assistant to disengage the sliding yoke unit from the bottom end of the column (Fig. 10.27).
8   Refitting is a reversal of the removal procedure. Ensure that the alignment is correct when reconnecting the shaft to the yoke.
9   Tighten the mounting and yoke bolts to their specified torque settings.
10 Refit the combination switches, as described in Chapter 12. Ensure that all wiring connections are correctly and securely made.
11 Refit the steering wheel with reference to Section 17.
12 On completion, check the steering action for satisfactory operation also the column lock and ignition and combination switch functions.

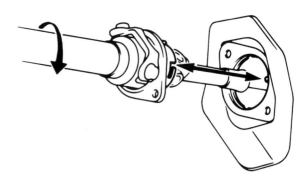

Fig. 10.27 Steering column tube and shaft removal (Sec 8)

9   Steering column and tilt mechanism – dismantling, inspection and reassembly

1   Remove the ignition/lock cylinder from the column, with reference to Chapter 12, Section 25.
2   Tilt the mainshaft up fully then detach the springs and cords (Fig. 10.29).
3   Make alignment marks across the faces of the intermediate shaft and the universal joint, undo one of the joint bolts and the four bracket bolts. Separate the intermediate shaft from the main shaft (Fig. 10.30).
4   Unbolt and remove the support reinforcement. Where necessary remove the taper head bolt by tapping its head with a punch and remove the bracket bolts. Remove the bracket from the support.
5   Extract the circlip securing the upper bracket on the mainshaft, then withdraw the mainshaft from the bracket (photo).
6   Remove the retainer from the tilt mechanism. This is secured by a bolt and two nuts.
7   Remove the reclining release pin and collar. Release the coil spring and remove the reclining pawl (Fig. 10.31).
8   Undo the guide pin bolt and the support bolt and shim (where fitted).
9   Drive out the serrated bolt and remove the tilt lever. Temporarily fit a nut onto the end of the bolt to protect the threads when driving it out initially then remove the nut (Fig. 10.32).
10 If the bearings in the mainshaft are in need of replacement, drive or press them from the shaft and upper bracket using suitable tube drifts.

Pack the new bearing(s) with grease and press or drive them into position. Ensure that they are fully located.
11 Inspect and renew any other column and tilt mechanism components which are excessively worn.
12 Note that during reassembly some items are selected components, these being the No 1 and 2 collars and the shim which fits against the No 2 collar. Refer to Specifications for availability.
13 Smear all rubber parts with MP grease prior to fitting.
14 Refit the pawl set bolt and tighten it to the specified torque.
15 Fit the tilt lever to the support and fit a No 1 collar of suitable thickness to take up all play (Fig. 10.33).
16 Fit a No 2 collar to the support, again selected to take up any play, then drive the serrated bolt into position in the support (Fig. 10.34).
17 Fit the reclining pawl, the return spring and release pin (Fig. 10.35).
18 Locate the collar onto the pin and fit the lever retainer.
19 Locate a selective shim which, when fitted, is a snug fit by hand, then fit the bolt, washer and castle nut. Tighten the nut to the specified torque and insert a new cotter pin to secure (Figs. 10.36 and 10.37).
20 Fit the support stopper bolt with bracket, locate the washer and tighten the nut to the specified torque. Hold the bracket by hand when tightening the nut (Fig. 10.38).
21 Fit the collar and spring onto the mainshaft and locate them in the upper bracket. Press the shaft into the housing so that the snap-ring

Column Tube and Intermediate Shaft

Fig. 10.28 Steering column components (Sec 9)

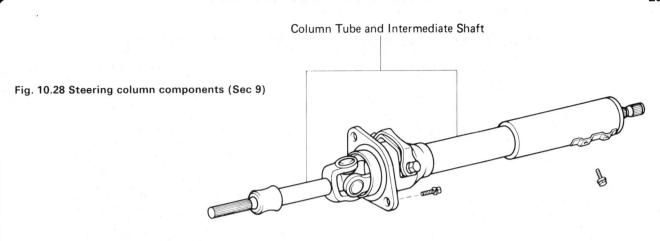

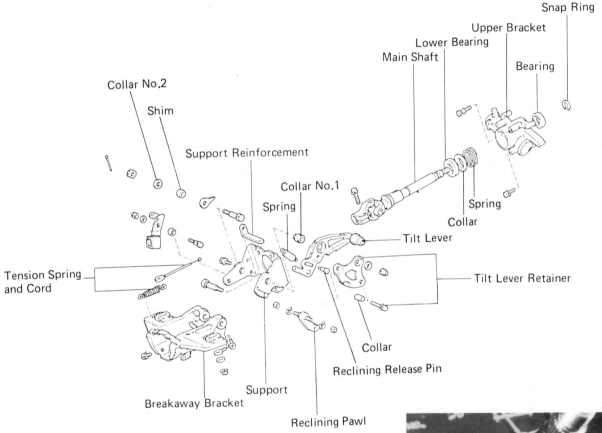

Snap Ring

Upper Bracket

Lower Bearing

Bearing

Main Shaft

Collar No.2

Shim

Support Reinforcement

Collar No.1

Spring

Spring

Collar

Tilt Lever

Tension Spring and Cord

Tilt Lever Retainer

Collar

Reclining Release Pin

Breakaway Bracket

Support

Reclining Pawl

Fig. 10.29 Disconnect the tension springs and cords (Sec 9)

Fig. 10.30 Detach the intermediate shaft and mainshaft (Sec 9)

9.5 Steering column upper bracket snap-ring (arrowed)

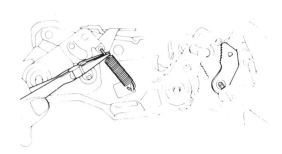

Fig. 10.31 Remove tension spring and pawl (Sec 9)

Fig. 10.32 Serrated bolt removal (Sec 9)

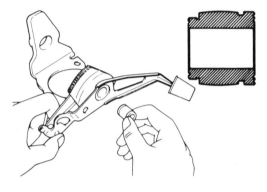

Fig. 10.33 Select a No 1 collar to take up the play (Sec 9)

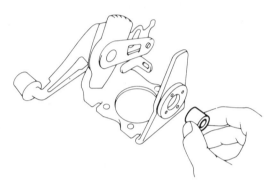

Fig. 10.34 Select a No 2 collar to take up the play (Sec 9)

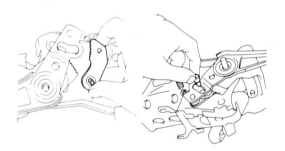

Fig. 10.35 Fit the tilt pawl, spring and release pin (Sec 9)

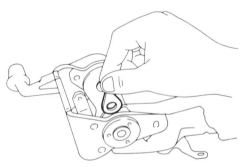

Fig. 10.36 Inserert the selective shim (Sec 9)

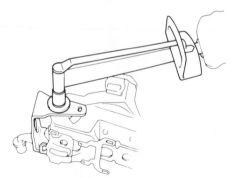

Fig. 10.37 Tighten castle nut to the specified torque (Sec 9)

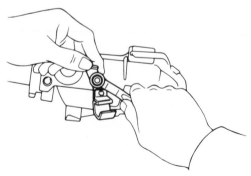

Fig. 10.38 Hold the bracket when tightening the support stopper bolt (Sec 9)

groove in the shaft is visible and fit a new snap-ring to secure the assembly.

22 Fit the upper bracket to the support and insert the two retaining bolts, the lower of which also secures a wiring clip. The third bolt is a taper head shear-bolt which is tightened to the point where the head breaks off. The other two bolts must be tightened to the specified torque setting.

23 Fit the support reinforcement and tighten its securing bolts to the specified torque.

24 Fit the breakaway bracket over the column tube and tighten the bolts to the specified torque.

25 Reconnect the mainshaft and intermediate shaft, aligning the index marks made during dismantling. Tighten the retaining bolt to the specified torque.

26 Refit the two springs and cords, hooking the springs to the hanger and hook the cord into the engagement slots in the support and guides.

27 With the main reassembly procedures complete, check for any signs of axial play at the end of the mainshaft and also that the shaft locks in all six tilt positions.

28 Refit the ignition switch/lock to complete (Chapter 12).

10 Steering gear unit (manual) – removal, overhaul and refitting

1 Jack up the front of the car and support it on stands. Remove the roadwheels.

2 Unscrew and remove the intermediate steering shaft-to-pinion yoke clamp bolts. Pull the yoke upwards along the splines of the intermediate shaft to disengage the yoke at the bottom end from the pinion.

3 Disconnect the tie-rod ends from the steering knuckle arm. Refer to Section 15.

4 Unscrew and remove the steering gear mounting clamp bolts and remove the clamps.

5 Lift the steering gear from the front crossmember and withdraw it from beneath the car. Take care not to damage the rubber rack boots.

6 Clean the exterior of the steering gear and grip it in a soft-jawed vice around the grooved mounting, but do not overtighten the vice.

7 Mark the position of the tie-rod ends on the rack ends, and also mark each tie-rod end for location. Loosen the pinch-bolts and unscrew the tie-rod ends (Fig. 10.41).

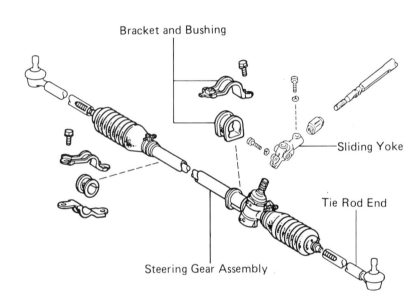

Bracket and Bushing

Sliding Yoke

Tie Rod End

Steering Gear Assembly

Fig. 10.39 Rack and pinion steering gear unit and associated components – manual (Sec 10)

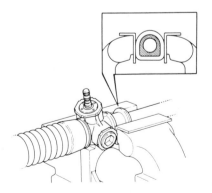

Fig. 10.40 Clamp steering gear unit as shown (Sec 10)

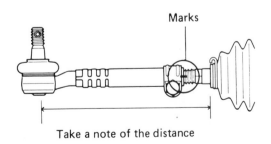

Marks

Take a note of the distance

Fig. 10.41 Tie-rod removal (Sec 10)

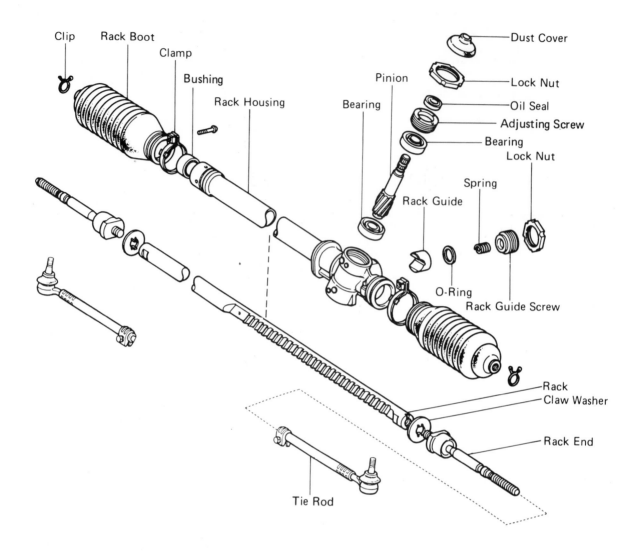

Fig. 10.42 Exploded view of the rack and pinion components (Sec 10)

8 Remove the spring and hose clips from the rubber bellows. Withdraw the bellows from the rack ends and mark the bellows left-hand and right-hand sides as they are different.

9 Bend up the tab (claw) washers and mark the rack ends left-hand and right-hand sides.

10 Hold the rack steady, then unscrew and remove the rack ends and tab (claw) washers. Take care not to damage the surface of the rack when supporting with spanner. Mark each rack end right- and left-hand for identification.

11 Unscrew and remove the rack guide thrust bearing locknut and the spring cap, using a hexagon key for the latter.

12 Extract the spring and rack guide and O-ring.

13 Prise the dust cover from the pinion and unscrew the adjusting screw locknut.

14 Unscrew the pinion bearing adjusting screw, using the special tool (if available) or a suitable pin wrench. The tool incorporates two pegs for locating in the screw, and if necessary one can easily be made out of flat steel and two bolts of suitable diameter.

15 Pull the rack from the pinion end of the steering gear until the pinion is located in the recess and is not in mesh with the teeth.

16 Withdraw the pinion and bearing. If they will not pull out of the rack housing by hand, grip the yoke bolt groove in the pinion shaft with a pair of needle-nosed pliers and tap the underside of the pliers with a hammer to ease the pinion out, but take care not to damage the splines.

17 Withdraw the rack from the pinion end of the steering gear. Do not rotate the rack as it is withdrawn.

18 Using a screwdriver, lever the oil seal from the pinion bearing adjusting screw.

19 Using a suitable puller, remove the upper bearing from the pinion. Alternatively support the bearing in a vice and drive the pinion through it. Recover the spacer and note its location for correct reassembly.

20 Heat the pinion end of the steering gear in boiling water then tap it on a piece of wood to release the lower pinion bearing. Note the direction of fitting.

21 Wash all components in paraffin and wipe them dry with lint-free cloth. Examine the components for wear and deterioration and renew them as necessary. If the bush in the end of the steering gear housing requires renewal, it can be driven out using a length of metal rod. Fully drive in the new bush using a suitable tubular drift.

22 Commence reassembly by fitting the pinion lower bearing into the housing after having heated the housing in boiling water. Make sure that the bearing is located the correct way round.

23 Wipe away any traces of water, then pack the pinion lower bearing and housing with a lithium based grease. Smear grease also on the housing bush. The housing should be approximately half full of grease.

24 Grease the rack teeth and insert it into the pinion end of the housing until the recess is in line with the pinion aperture.

25 Using suitable tubing, drive the pinion bearing into position with its seal face downwards.

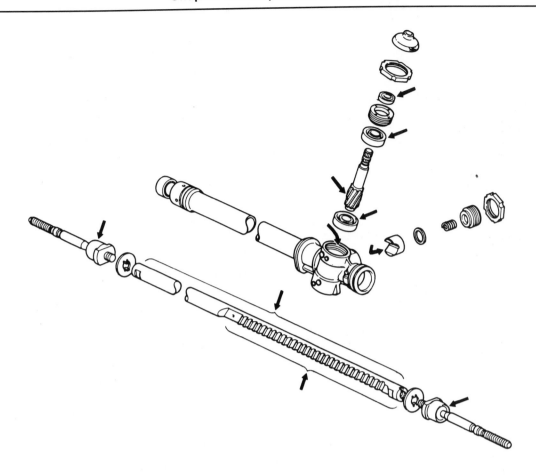

Fig. 10.43 Lubricate items indicated with molybdenum disulphide lithium based grease during reassembly (Sec 10)

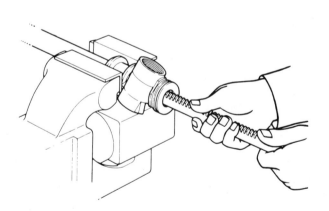

Fig. 10.44 Insert the rack into the gear housing (Sec 10)

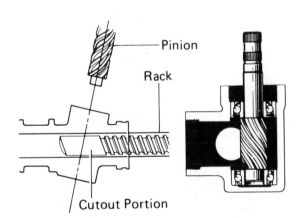

Pinion

Rack

Cutout Portion

Fig. 10.45 Align pinion with rack (Sec 10)

26 Grease the pinion teeth and bearing. Tap the pinion and bearing into the housing (Fig. 10.45).
27 Drive the new oil seal into the pinion adjusting screw, leaving it protruding by 0.5 mm (0.02 in).
28 Grease the oil seal lip, then insert and tighten the adjusting screw until the pinion turning torque is 3.7 kgf cm (3.2 lbf in) measured with a torque wrench. A special adaptor will be required to check the torque. Now loosen the screw until the specified preload (without rack) of 2.3 to 3.3 kgf cm (2.0 to 2.9 lbf in) is obtained (Fig. 10.46).

29 Smear some liquid sealer on the base of the locknut, then tighten it onto the adjusting screw to the specified torque, holding the adjusting screw with the pin wrench. Check that the pinion turning torque is now reduced to within the specified limits.
30 Push the rack into its normal central position and at the same time mesh it with the pinion.
31 Lubricate the rack guide then fit it, together with its new O-ring.
32 Insert the rack guide spring then coat the guide screw threads with sealant and insert the screw. Tighten the screw to a torque of 2.5 kgf m

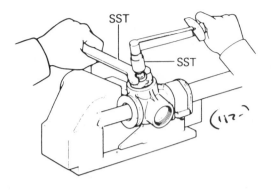

Fig. 10.46 Pinion bearing preload adjustment using special tools (Sec 10)

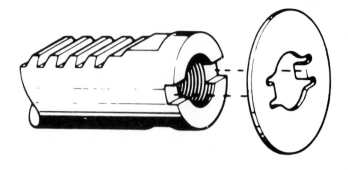

Fig. 10.47 Align tab washers with rack and grooves (Sec 10)

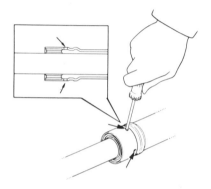

Fig. 10.48 Pressure transfer holes must be clear (Sec 10)

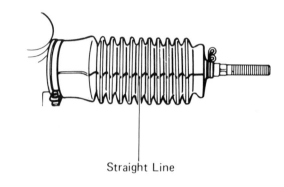

Straight Line

Fig. 10.49 Rack boots must not be twisted (Sec 10)

(18 lbf ft). From the tightened position, loosen the screw a quarter turn (90°), then measure the pinion pre-load. This should be between 10 to 13 kgf cm (8.7 to 11.3 lbf in). Adjust if necessary to meet this requirement.

33 Smear the locknut threads and the contact surface on the housing with sealant, then fit the locknut onto the guide screw and tighten it to the specified torque whilst retaining the screw in the set position.

34 Recheck the pinion turning torque to ensure that it is still within the specified limits.

35 Fit the rubber dust cover.

36 Grease the rack end balljoints, locate the tab (claw) washers, and screw the rack ends into the rack. With the tab washers located in the rack grooves, tighten the rack ends to the specified torque and bend over the tab washers. A special adaptor will be needed for the torque wrench.

37 Check that the pressure transfer holes in the housing are unobstructed (Fig. 10.48).

38 Refit the rubber bellows (rack boots) taking care not to twist them when fitting and also ensure that each is fitted to its correct side.

39 Fit the bellow clamps and tighten as shown (Fig. 10.50).

40 Locate the rack boot securing clips as shown with the ends facing out (Fig. 10.51).

41 Turn the pinion and check that the rack moves freely without binding in each direction.

42 Refit the steering gear to the front crossmember, locate the clamps, and tighten the retaining bolts.

43 Insert the tie-rod ends into the steering knuckle arms. Tighten the nuts to the specified torque and fit the split-pins.

44 With the steering wheels in the straight-ahead position, refit the intermediate steering shaft and tighten the clamp bolts to the specified torque.

45 Refit the roadwheels and lower the car to the ground.

46 Adjust the front wheel alignment, as described in Section 16.

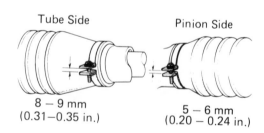

Tube Side   Pinion Side

8 – 9 mm
(0.31–0.35 in.)

5 – 6 mm
(0.20 – 0.24 in.)

Fig. 10.50 Tighten boot clamps as shown (Sec 10)

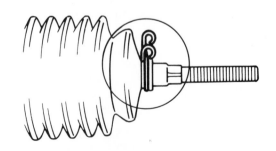

Fig. 10.51 Boot clips must fit with ends facing out (Sec 10)

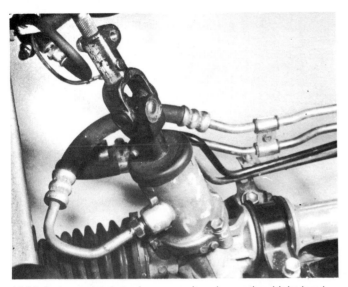

11.1A Power-assisted steering gear unit and mounting (right-hand drive, viewed from top)

11.1B Power-assisted steering gear unit mounting on passenger side (RHD)

11 Steering gear unit (power-assisted) – removal, overhaul and refitting

1   The steering gear unit is removed in the same manner as that described for manual models in Section 10, paragraphs 1 to 5. In addition to those items mentioned, also disconnect the pressure and return line hoses from the steering gear unit. Allow for fluid spillage as they are detached (photos).
2   Clean the exterior of the steering gear unit and grip it in a soft-jawed vice around the grooved mounting, but do not overtighten the vice.
3   Disconnect and remove the hydraulic return pressure tubes. Remove the union seats and keep them with the tubes in a clean storage area or container (photo).
4   Remove the tie-rod ends and rack boots and the rack guide assembly, as described in paragraphs 7 to 12 inclusive in Section 10. Note that, on power steering models, the rack guide also incorporates a seat.
5   Remove the dust cover from the control valve housing. Undo the three retaining bolts and remove the control valve housing and O-ring.
6   Unscrew the pinion adjusting screw locknut, then unscrew and remove the pinion adjusting screw. If available, use the special Toyota service tools, if not you will need to fabricate a suitable tool with two pegs for locating in the screw.
7   Bend up the tabs on the claw washers at the rack ends. Mark the rack ends left and right-hand sides.
8   Hold the rack steady, then unscrew and remove the rack ends on the left-hand and right-hand side. Take care not to damage the rack with the supporting spanner. Mark each rack end right- and left-hand for identification.
9   Bend up the locking tab from the cylinder end stopper nut then unscrew and remove the nut.
10 Undo the four retaining bolts and remove the rack housing and O-ring.
11 Remove the spacer and seat from the housing.
12 Withdraw the steering rack, complete with stopper, O-ring, wave washer and rack end guide. To ease withdrawal, and to protect the oil seal within the housing (although this should be renewed), slide a suitable thin tube along the rack up to the seal as shown. If the special service tool is available use this (Fig. 10.54).
13 Remove the respective items from the rack, noting their order of fitting and orientation (fig. 10.55).
14 Clean and inspect the various components.
15 To inspect the control valve, remove it, with the pinion, from the housing.
16 To remove the oil seal from the rack housing, prise it out using a

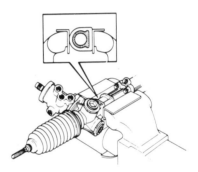

Fig. 10.52 Support power steering gear unit as shown (Sec 11)

11.3 Power-assisted steering hydraulic return pressure tube connections to the steering gear unit

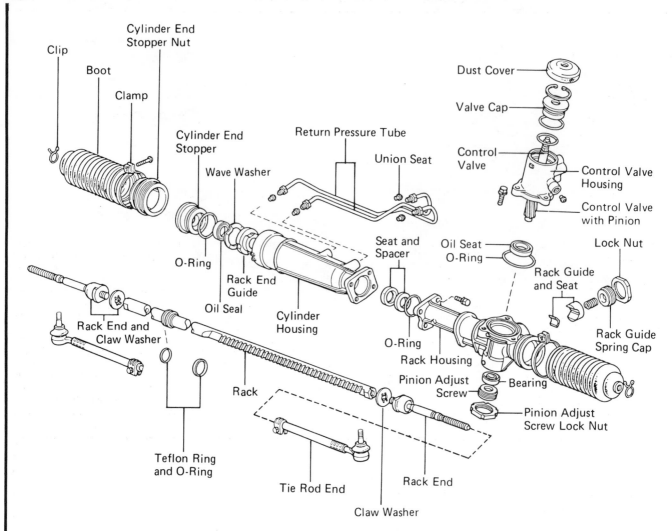

Fig. 10.53 Exploded view of the power steering gear unit (Sec 11)

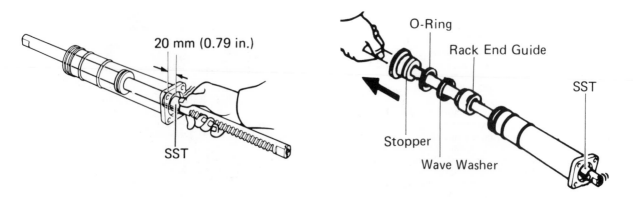

20 mm (0.79 in.)

SST

Fig. 10.54 Steering rack removal using special tool fitted to depth indicated (Sec 11)

O-Ring

Rack End Guide

SST

Stopper

Wave Washer

Fig. 10.55 Steering rack and components removal using special tool (Sec 11)

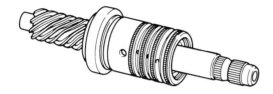

Fig. 10.56 Remove the control valve and pinion (Sec 11)

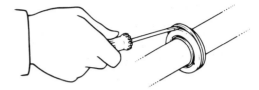

Fig. 10.57 Teflon ring and O-ring removal (Sec 11)

suitable screwdriver, but take care not to damage the housing. Note the orientation and depth of the seal before removal.

17 The oil seal in the cylinder housing can be driven out using a suitable tube drift. Again note the orientation and depth of the seal prior to removal.

18 To remove the oil seal and bearing in the control valve housing, extract the circlip and drift out the bearing and seal using a suitable tube drift (note fitting position and orientation of each).

19 The pinion lower bearing can be removed by driving out with a suitable drift.

20 Prise free the Teflon ring from the rack as shown (Fig. 10.57).

21 Renew any components which are excessively worn or damaged. During reassembly, lubricate the items shown in Fig. 10.58 with grease or power steering fluid, as applicable.

22 Insert the new oil seals into their respective positions, ensuring that they are correctly orientated and fitted to the depth originally noted during removal. Drive them into position using suitable tube drifts. With the control valve housing, also fit the new bearing and secure with a new circlip.

23 When fitting the new Teflon ring onto the rack, use a tapered guide tube or shim to prevent distorting or twisting the ring as it is fitted into its location groove. Coat the ring with power steering fluid and ensure that it is fully engaged in its groove when fitted.

24 Fit the seat spacer and O-ring. To protect the oil seal lip and the Teflon ring from damage when inserting the rack unit, Toyota recommend the use of special service tool guide tubes. However, a sheet of suitable shim material furled over to suit may be used for this purpose, then removed afterwards. Alternatively, take the rack and housing to your Toyota dealer and have him assemble the rack.

25 Insert the rack into the cylinder housing, passing it through

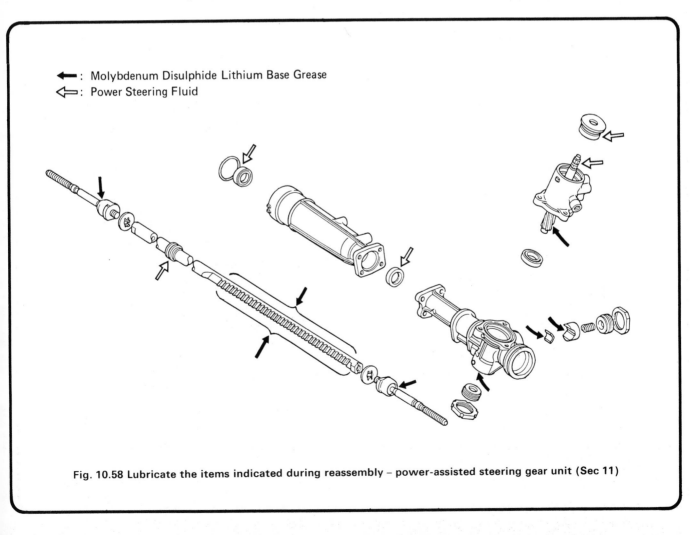

← : Molybdenum Disulphide Lithium Base Grease
⇐ : Power Steering Fluid

Fig. 10.58 Lubricate the items indicated during reassembly – power-assisted steering gear unit (Sec 11)

towards the rack housing end. When it emerges at the rack housing end, remove the special guide tubes or shim as applicable.

26 Refit the wave washer and rack end guide into the end of the cylinder housing. The oil groove in the guide must be positioned horizontally when fitted (Fig. 10.59).

27 Refit the cylinder end stopper and O-ring. Protect the O-ring from damage during assembly using the special service tool guides or shim method as previously described. Remove the guide/shim when the end stopper is in position.

28 With the O-ring, spacer and seal in position between the rack housing and the cylinder, fit the two assemblies together and tighten the four retaining bolts to the specified torque setting.

29 Smear the threads of the end stopper nut with sealant, then fit and tighten the nut to the specified torque. Carefully stake punch the cylinder housing flange to secure.

30 Align the inner tabs of the claw washers at the rack ends with the grooves of the rack ends then refit the rack ends and tighten to the specified torque setting. Bend the tab washer over to secure, but take care not to damage the rack.

31 Refit the control valve/pinion.

32 Insert the screw valve spring seat and compression spring, then fit the control valve housing with O-ring seal. Smear the securing bolt threads with sealant and tighten them to the specified torque.

33 Smear the pinion adjusting screw threads with sealant, then fit and tighten the screw to a torque of 1.5 kgf m (11.0 lbf ft). From this point, undo the adjustment screw 10° and then measure the control valve preload using a torque wrench. This should be between 4.5 to 6.5 kgf cm (3.9 to 5.6 lbf in). Further adjust the screw if required to achieve this preload setting (Fig. 10.60).

34 Smear the pinion screw locknut threads with sealant also the gear housing contact surface, then fit the locknut and tighten it to the specified torque whilst retaining the adjustment screw at the previous setting. Recheck the control valve shaft preload.

35 Insert the rack guide with seat followed by the guide spring and cap. Smear the threads of the cap with sealant before fitting. Tighten the cap to a torque of 2.5 kgf m (18 lbf ft), then from this point unscrew the cap a quarter of a turn (90°). Measure the turning preload which should be between 9 to 12 kgf cm (7.8 to 10.4 lbf in). Readjust the cap setting if necessary to achieve this preload.

36 Smear sealant onto the rack guide spring locknut threads and the contact surface on the gear housing. Fit the locknut and tighten to the specified torque. Check that the total turning preload is as specified in the previous paragraph and, if necessary, readjust the locknut to suit. Refit the dust cover.

37 Refit the rack boots and clips as described in Section 10, paragraphs 37 to 40 inclusive.

38 Turn the pinion and check that the rack moves freely without binding in each direction.

39 Refit the steering gear unit to the car following the instructions given in Section 10, paragraphs 42 on. In addition, insert the union seats and reconnect the hydraulic pressure and return lines.

40 On completion top up the power steering fluid level, as described in Section 12, and bleed the system.

41 Finally, check the operation of the steering, check for any signs of fluid leaks from the cylinder, and pressure hoses, then check the front wheel alignment (Section 16).

12 Power steering – fluid level check and system bleeding

1 This check must be made with the vehicle on level ground, the engine idling at the normal operating temperature and ideally after a run so that the fluid temperature is between 40 and 80°C (104 and 176°F).

2 Turn the steering wheel from lock to lock a few times then make the level check by removing the reservoir cap to which a dipstick is attached. If the fluid level is below the specified minimum level mark on the dipstick top up the level with some of the specified fluid, then refit the cap, and switch off the engine (photo).

3 To bleed the power steering system, check that the fluid level is up to the mark, then jack up the car at the front and support with axle stands.

4 Turn the steering wheel through full lock in each direction a few times and then recheck the reservoir fluid level. Top up if necessary.

5 Start and run the engine at 1000 rpm or less and turn the steering wheel from lock to lock a few times then return it to its central position.

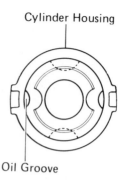

Fig. 10.59 Oil groove in rack and guide to be horizontal (Sec 11)

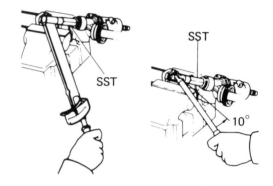

Fig. 10.60 Control valve shaft preload adjustment (Sec 11)

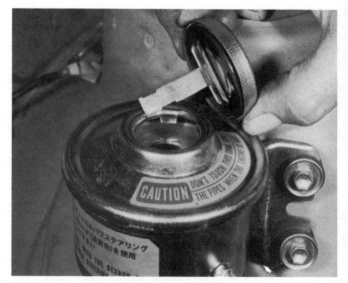

12.2 Power steering reservoir fluid level check

6 Check the condition of the fluid in the reservoir which should not be cloudy or foaming. The fluid should not be above the maximum level mark with the engine stopped. When the engine is stopped the fluid level may rise initially by a maximum permissible amount of 5 mm (0.2 in). Any rise above that is not permissible and a fault probably exists in the vane pump which should be repaired as necessary.

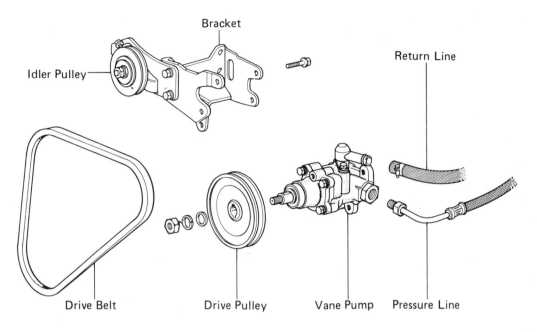

Fig. 10.61 Power steering pump and associated components
(Sec 13)

13 Power steering pump and drivebelt – removal and refitting

1   Where applicable, loosen the securing clips and detach the air control valve hoses. As a safety measure, detach the distributor HT leads.
2   Disconnect the fluid return hose from the reservoir tank and drain the power steering fluid from the reservoir into a suitable container for disposal (photo).
3   Disconnect the hydraulic fluid return and supply pressure hoses from the power steering pump.
4   Push on the power steering pump drivebelt by hand to increase its tension and unscrew the pulley set nut.

5   Loosen the drivebelt adjuster bolt and remove the drivebelt.
6   Undo the mounting bolts and remove the power steering pump unit.
7   If the power steering pump unit is suspected of malfunction, have it checked out and overhauled by a Toyota dealer.
8   Refit in the reverse order to removal, tightening the fastenings to the specified torque settings where applicable. Adjust the drivebelt tension to that specified. When fitting a new drivebelt recheck the tension after an initial mileage and take up any possible stretch which may have occurred (photo).
9   Top up the fluid level in the reservoir and bleed the system, as given in Section 12. Check for fluid leaks from the hose connections on completion.

13.2 Power steering pump return hose (A) and pressure tube (B) connections

13.8 General view of power steering pump, hose connections and drivebelt

Fig. 10.62 Drain the fluid from the reservoir into a container (Sec 14)

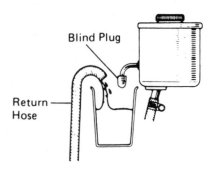

Fig. 10.63 Stop engine when fluid discharges from fluid return hose (Sec 14)

14 Power steering fluid – draining and renewal

1   Raise the front of the vehicle and support on safety stands.
2   Disconnect the fluid return hose from the power steering fluid reservoir (see Fig. 10.62) and drain the reservoir fluid into a container for disposal.
3   Start the engine and run it at idle speed and continue draining the fluid from the system into the container whilst turning the steering wheel from lock to lock. When draining is complete stop the engine and plug off the reservoir return pipe.
4   Top up the reservoir fluid level using fluid of the specified type.
5   Restart the engine and run it at a speed of 1000 rpm, but simultaneously keep watching the return hose. After a brief period of 1 to 2 seconds fluid should start to discharge from the hose at which point, stop the engine (Fig. 10.63).
6   Top up the fluid level in the reservoir and repeat the process described in the previous paragraph. Repeat this procedure five or six times then connect the return hose to the reservoir.
7   Bleed the system to complete, as described in Section 12, then lower the car.

15 Tie-rod ends – testing and renewal

1   The tie-rod end balljoints should be examined for deterioration and

excessive wear at the intervals specified in the Routine Maintenance section at the front of this manual.
2   Grip the tie-rod near the balljoint and attempt to move it back and forth in a horizontal plane. Renew the tie-rod end if any movement is evident.
3   Raise the front of the vehicle and support it on safety stands. Remove the front roadwheels.
4   Clean the tie-rod end-to-steering knuckle arm joint nut using a wire brush, then extract the cotter pin. If necessary apply some penetrating fluid to ease its removal.
5   Loosen but do not fully remove the nut yet. Use a balljoint separator and free the tie-rod end from the knuckle arm, then remove the nut and separator (photo).
6   Using a wire brush, clean the area at the inner end of the inboard end of the tie-rod where it is clamped to the rack end. Measure or mark the exposed length of rack end thread. This is important during reassembly when the new tie-rod end can be set at the same position and will give an initial adjustment to the steering angle and alignment (photo).
7   Loosen the clamp bolt and unscrew the tie-rod end from the steering rack whilst holding the steering rack with a pair of suitable grips. Take care not to damage the rack end gaiter.
8   Refitting is a reversal of the removal procedure. Screw the tie-rod end onto the rack end to the point where the index mark was made during removal.
9   Before tightening the tie-rod inboard end clamp. check that the rod length each side is equal and then check the steering angle and alignments, as described in Section 16. Further adjustment may be necessary before tightening the clamp bolt.

15.5 Use a balljoint separator to detach the tie-rod ends

15.6 Clean and measure the threaded portion exposed on the inner end of the tie-rod

16 Steering angles and front wheel alignment

1   Accurate front wheel alignment is necessary to ensure slow tyre wear, good steering and handling characteristics. Heavy steering and uneven tyre wear are the most obvious symptoms of misalignment.

2   The steering angles should be checked whenever a new suspension or steering component has been fitted, where part of the steering or suspension system has been disconnected and refitted for any reason, when misalignment is suspected or when specified during routine maintenance.

3   Before making any checks and adjustments, ensure that the tyres are correctly inflated, the front hub bearings are correctly adjusted, the front wheels are balanced and not buckled, the strut shock absorbers are serviceable, and that the tie-rod ends are not worn.

4   The vehicle height settings must also be as specified. To check the height setting the vehicle must be standing on firm, level ground and the tyres must be correctly inflated to the specified pressures. The height must be measured from the centre line of the suspension arm pivot point at the body to the ground (See Figs. 10.64, 10.65 and 10.66).

5   If the heights measured are not as specified bounce the vehicle at each end to settle the suspension then recheck. If the height is still incorrect, check the suspension components for excessive wear, damage or looseness. The coil springs are the most likely culprits, even though they may look to be in good condition. If the vehicle height settings are correct the wheel alignment can be checked.

6   Wheel alignment consists of four main factors:

(a) Camber, the angle at which the front wheels are set from the vertical when viewed from the front of the car
(b) Castor, the angle at which the steering axis is set from the vertical when viewed from the side of the car

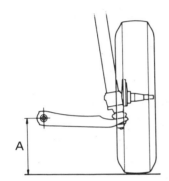

Fig. 10.64 Vehicle height check point (A) – front (Sec 16)

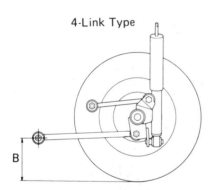

Fig. 10.65 Vehicle height check point (B) – rear (FLS type) (Sec 16)

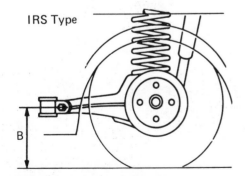

Fig. 10.66 Vehicle height check point (B) – rear (IRS type) (Sec 16)

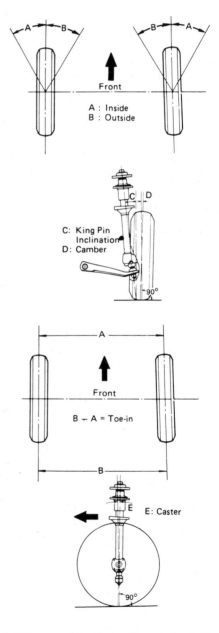

Fig. 10.67 Diagram to show various wheel alignment angles and checks (Sec 16)

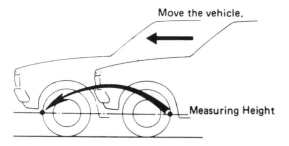

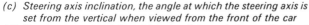

Fig. 10.68 Measuring height on wheel for toe-in adjustment
check (Sec 16)

Fig. 10.69 Position trammel bar as shown to check toe-in
(Sec 16)

(c) *Steering axis inclination, the angle at which the steering axis is
set from the vertical when viewed from the front of the car*
(d) *Toe-in, the amount by which the distance between the front
edges of the roadwheels (measured at hub height) is less than
the corresponding distance between the rear edges of the
front roadwheels*

7   Camber and steering axis inclination are not adjustable. Castor can
be adjusted. Toe-in can be adjusted by repositioning the track-rod
ends on the rack ends.
8   Accurate checking of steering angles and wheel alignment is only
possible with expensive equipment and is therefore best entrusted to
your Toyota dealer. However, reasonable adjustment of toe-in is
possible by using a home made adjustable trammel bar.
9   Drive the car onto level ground and adjust the trammel bar between
the centres of the tyre tread on the rear of the front tyres. Mark the tyres
with a small dot at the point where the trammel bar touches the tyres.
10 Move the car forwards so that the marks are now at hub height on
the front of the tyres (wheel turned through 180°). Move the trammel
bar to the front of the car without altering the adjustment. The distance
between the two dots should now be less than the first distance by the
specified amount of toe-in.
11 To adjust the toe-in, loosen the rack boot clip at the outer end
(each side), loosen the tie-rod clamp bolts then push the rock boot
inwards. Turn the left and right-hand tie-rod ends an equal amount to
adjust the toe-in.
12 Check that the tie-rod lengths are equal, tighten the clamp bolts
and refit the rack boot clips.
13 If the castor angle is suspect, it can only be checked using
specialised alignment equipment and therefore this must be entrusted

to your Toyota dealer. The castor angle is set in accordance with the
length of the strut bar.
14 The roadwheel angles are adjustable by altering the setting of the
steering knuckle stopper bolts, but again, specialised equipment is
required to check·the angles. Any checks and adjustments to the
roadwheel angles must therefore be entrusted to your Toyota dealer.

17 Steering wheel – removal and refitting

1   Disconnect the battery negative lead.
2   Set the front roadwheels in the straight-ahead position.
3   Prise free the pad from the centre of the steering wheel. On some
models the pad is detached by removing the lower column cover and
undoing the two retaining screws from the underside of the steering
wheel (photo).
4   Unscrew and remove the steering wheel retaining nut with a socket
or box spanner (photo).
5   Mark the relative position of the wheel to the steering shaft by dot
punching the end faces.
6   Pull the steering wheel from the shaft splines; do not attempt to jar
it off as this may damage the shaft shear pins. If it is very tight, a puller
will have to be used.
7   Refitting is a reversal of removal, but make sure that the steering
wheel engages the direction indicator cancelling cam and that the
previously made marks are aligned. Tighten the retaining nut to the
specified torque.

17.3 Steering wheel centre pad removal

17.4 Steering wheel retaining nut

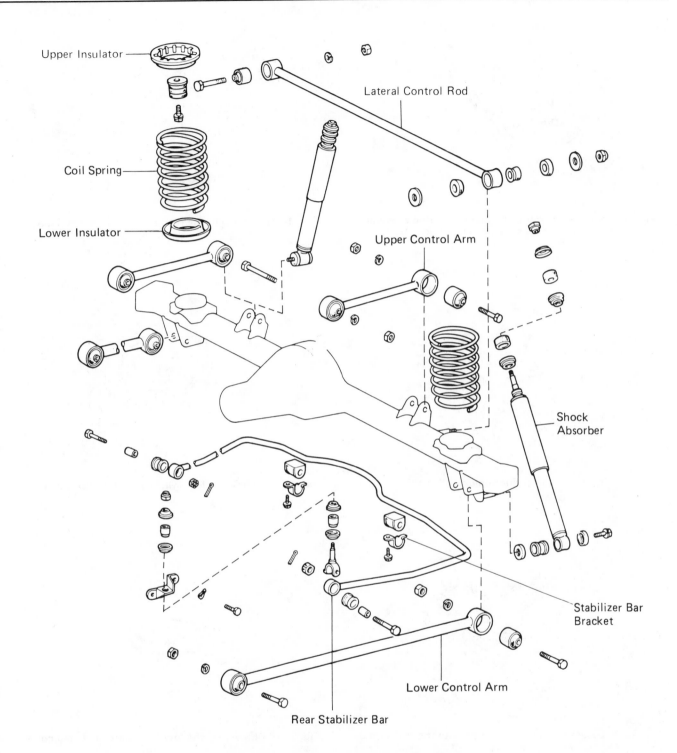

Upper Insulator

Lateral Control Rod

Coil Spring

Upper Control Arm

Lower Insulator

Shock
Absorber

Stabilizer Bar
Bracket

Lower Control Arm

Rear Stabilizer Bar

**Fig. 10.70 Exploded view of the four link suspension
(Sec 18)**

**18 Rear shock absorber and coil spring (FLS) – removal and
refitting**

1   Position a jack under the rear axle banjo housing, raise the vehicle
at the rear and support it on safety stands – located each side under the
body side-members forward of the rear wheel arches. Leave the jack
supporting the weight of the axle.
2   Unscrew and remove the bolt securing the shock absorber to the
rear axle.

3   If the shock absorber is being renewed, remove the trim cover from
its top mounting in the luggage compartment for access to the top
mounting. Undo the retaining nut whilst preventing the shaft from
turning with a screwdriver and remove the shock absorber from
underneath the vehicle.
4   Undo the bolts from the stabilizer bar bush brackets and remove the
brackets from the axle.
5   Undo the bolt securing the lateral control rod to the axle and detach
the rod.
6   Slowly lower the jack under the axle. As it is lowered, take care not

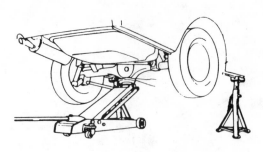

Fig. 10.71 Rear shock absorber and coil spring removal –
support vehicle as shown – FLS (Sec 18)

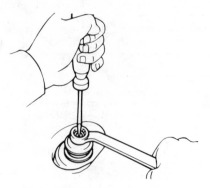

Fig. 10.72 Loosening the rear shock absorber top mounting
(Sec 18)

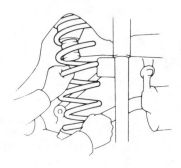

Fig. 10.73 Coil spring removal (Sec 18)

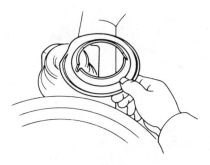

Fig. 10.74 Locate the lower insulator onto the axle (Sec 18)

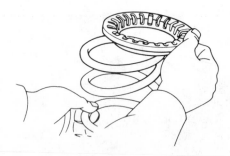

Fig. 10.75 Locate the upper insulator onto the coil spring
(Sec 18)

Fig. 10.76 Check that the lower insulator is fitted correctly
(Sec 18)

to stretch the hydraulic brake lines or the handbrake cable. Lower the
jack to the point where the tension is removed from the coil spring and
it can be removed, together with the upper and lower insulators. Do
not allow the jack to be lowered any further.
7   Refit the coil spring by first locating the lower insulator into
position on the axle. Locate the upper insulator onto the coil spring
and then fit the spring into position.
8   Raise the jack under the axle and check that the lower insulator is
correctly fitted, if not lower the jack and reposition the insulator (Fig.
10.76).

9   Refit the lateral control rod washer, bush, spacer, rod bush, washer
and nut in that order to the axle, but do not fully tighten the nut yet.
10 Refit the shock absorber in the reverse order to removal. Tighten
the upper nut and lower bolt to the specified torque settings. When
tightening the upper end nut, prevent the shaft from turning with a
screwdriver.
11 Reconnect the stabilizer bar to the axle and tighten the bracket
bolts to the specified torque.
12 Raise the jack so that the body is clear of the safety stands, remove
the stands then lower the vehicle so that it is free-standing.

13 Bounce the vehicle at the rear end to stabilize the rear suspension, then jack the vehicle up under the rear axle and tighten the lateral control rod to the specified torque.
14 Lower the jack and remove it to complete.

19 Lateral control rod (FLS) – removal and refitting

1 Position a jack under the rear axle banjo housing, raise the jack to lift the vehicle so that the rear wheels are clear of the ground. Locate a safety stand under the axle each side of the jack and lower the axle onto the stands for support (Fig. 10.77). Remove the roadwheels at the rear.
2 Unscrew the retaining nut securing the lateral control rod to the rear axle and detach the control rod from it.
3 Unscrew the retaining nut and remove the lateral control rod from the body mounting then from underneath the vehicle.
4 If the old bushes are worn or decayed they must be removed by pressing out and new bushes pressed in. If the rod is damaged it must be renewed. Do not use any form of lubricant when fitting the bushes.
5 To refit the lateral control rod, lift the axle clear of the stands then fit the control rod to the body mounting.
6 Reconnect the control rod to the axle, fitting the washer, bush, spacer, control rod, bush washer and nut in that order, but do not fully tighten the nut yet. Refit the roadwheels.
7 Remove the stands from under the car, also the jack. With the vehicle free-standing, bounce the vehicle at the rear end to stabilize the suspension then jack up the axle and tighten the lateral control rod fixing nuts to the specified torque settings.
8 Lower the vehicle to complete.

20 Upper and lower control arms (FLS) – removal and refitting

1 Jack up the rear of the vehicle and support the body each side forward of the rear wheel arches. Retain the jack in position under the axle housing for support.
2 The upper and lower control arms are removed in the same manner. Undo the retaining bolt at each end and remove the control arm.
3 If the control arm is damaged or bent it must be renewed.
4 The bushes can be renewed if necessary. Support the arm and press out the old bush, pressing from the chamfered side. Press or draw the new bush into position, also from the chamfered side.
5 Refitting is a reversal of the removal procedure but do not fully

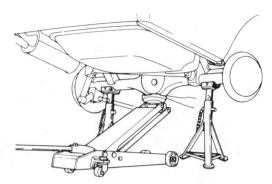
Fig. 10.77 Support as shown for lateral control rod removal – FLS (Sec 19)

tighten the retaining bolts until the vehicle has been lowered to the ground and bounced at the rear to settle the rear suspension.

21 Rear stabilizer bar (FLS) – removal and refitting

1 Position the car over an inspection pit, onto ramps at the rear or jack up and support with safety stands.
2 Unbolt and detach the two stabilizer bar location brackets.
3 Unbolt and detach the stabilizer bar at each end mounting and withdraw it from under the car.
4 Renew any worn or defective bushes or associated components.
5 Refit in the reverse order to removal. When reassembling the body mounting link bushes, they must be fitted as shown in Figs. 10.78 and 10.79.

22 Rear shock absorber and coil spring (IRS) – removal and refitting

1 Position a jack under the differential carrier unit and raise the vehicle at the rear so that the roadwheels are clear of the ground. Position safety stands under the rear suspension member for support.

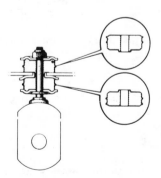
Fig. 10.78 Rear stabilizer bar bush orientation – FLS (Sec 21)

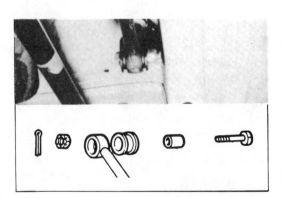
Fig. 10.79 Rear stabilizer bar-to-bracket bush assembly – FLS (Sec 21)

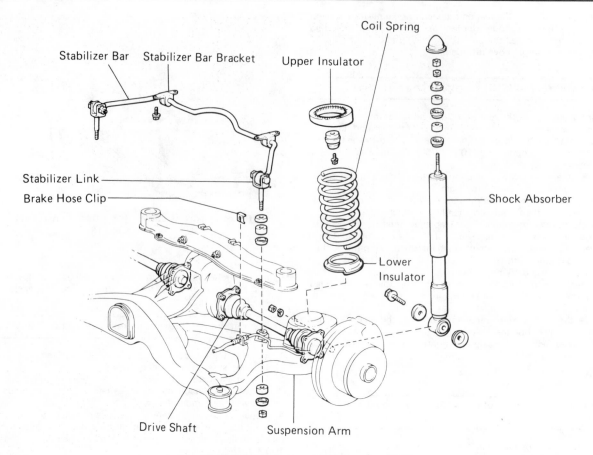

Fig. 10.80 Independent rear suspension (IRS) components (Sec 22)

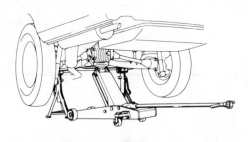

Fig. 10.81 Support as shown to remove rear shock absorber and coil spring on IRS models (Sec 22)

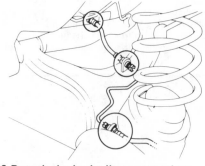

Fig. 10.82 Detach the brake line connections – encircled (Sec 22)

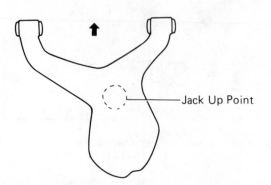

Fig. 10.83 Support suspension arm at point indicated (Sec 22)

2   Release the brake hose to location bracket retaining clips on the suspension arm (Fig. 10.82).
3   Undo the retaining nut, remove the cushion and retainer and detach the stabilizer bar link from the suspension arm.
4   Position a suitable jack under the suspension arm to support it at the point shown (Fig. 10.83).
5   Remove the retaining nuts and separate the driveshaft from the axle shaft (make alignment marks across the flanges if the axle is to be turned) (photo).
6   Unbolt and detach the shock absorber from the rear suspension arm.
7   If renewing the shock absorber, remove the trim cover in the luggage compartment for access to the shock absorber top mounting

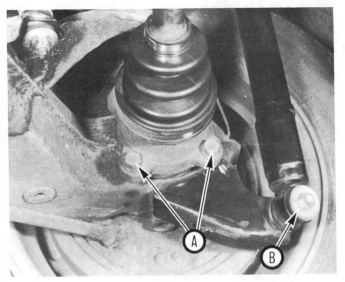

22.5 Driveshaft-to-axle shaft bolts (A) and shock absorber lower retaining bolt (B)

22.7 Shock absorber upper mounting and cover

(photo). Unscrew the retaining nut whilst holding the shaft with a screwdriver to prevent it from turning. Remove the shock absorber.

8   Slowly lower the jack under the suspension arm, taking care not to allow the brake hydraulic line and handbrake cable to stretch. Lower the suspension arm to the point where the coil spring can be removed, together with the upper and lower insulators. Do not allow the suspension arm to be lowered any further.

9   Refit the coil spring by first locating the lower insulator into position on the suspension arm, then fit the spring with top insulator into position (see Figs. 10.73, 10.74 and 10.75).

10   Raise the jack under the suspension arm and check that the lower insulator is correctly fitted, if not lower the jack and reposition the insulator.

11   Refit the driveshaft and tighten the securing nuts to the specified torque (see Chapter 8).

12   Refit the shock absorber in the reverse order of removal. Tighten the upper nut and the lower bolt to the specified torque. When tightening the upper nut, prevent the shaft from turning with a screwdriver.

13   Reconnect the stabilizer bar to the rear suspension, referring to Section 24 for details.

14   Reconnect the brake hoses to their location brackets and fit the retaining clips.

15   Remove the safety stands and jacks, then with the vehicle free-standing bounce the vehicle at the rear to settle the suspension.

23 Rear suspension arm (IRS) – removal and refitting

The following procedure describes the removal and refitting of the rear suspension arm, complete with the rear brake unit, and with the axle shaft unit in position. If the rear axleshaft is to be removed from the suspension arm reference must be made to Chapter 8, Section 3 where full details, together with the Toyota special service tools required for the removal of the axleshaft, are given. To remove the rear brake assembly components refer to Chapter 9.

1   Disconnect the rear stabilizer bar from the suspension arm, as described in Section 24.

2   Make an alignment index mark across the axleshaft to driveshaft flanges, then unbolt and detach the driveshaft from the axleshaft.

3   Disconnect the brake hydraulic line and the handbrake cable from the rear brake unit and the suspension arm, with reference to Chapter 9 for details.

4   Unbolt and detach the shock absorber from the suspension arm and remove the coil spring, as described in Section 22.

5   With the weight of the suspension arm supported by a jack, unscrew and remove the pivot bolt retaining nuts. Note that the inner pivot bolt incorporates a toe-in adjusting cam (photos). Note or mark

23.5A Suspension arm inner pivot showing the toe-in adjustment cam

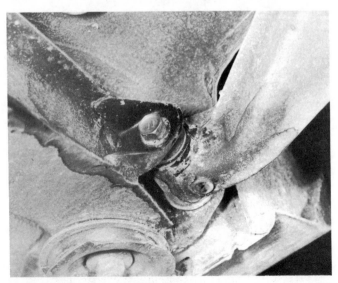

23.5B Suspension arm outer pivot

the position of the cam with the index alignment mark. Remove the pivot bolts and the camber adjusting cam, then lower and withdraw the suspension arm. Remember that with the brake and axleshaft unit in position in the suspension arm, the complete unit will be imbalanced, so take care to support it accordingly during removal.

6 If the suspension arm pivot bushes are excessively worn, cracked or in generally poor condition they must be renewed.

7 If the suspension arm is distorted, cracked or damaged in any way this must be renewed.

8 To renew the bushes, cut the exposed end flange faces of the bushes as shown (Fig. 10.84) then bend the remaining sections inwards using a chisel, but take care not to damage the flange (Fig. 10.85).

9 Bend the flange tips in using pliers and pull the flange off. The remaining flange section must be bent so that it does not interfere with the press or drift tool during bush removal.

10 Support the inner flange face of the suspension bush eye with a steel tube having an inside diameter sufficient to allow the bush to pass through it and just longer than the bush in length.

11 Press the bush through the eye and into the support tube using a socket wrench 19 to 24 mm in diameter (Fig. 10.88). The outer and inner arm bushes are removed in a similar manner.

12 Refitting is a reversal of the removal. Do not lubricate the bushes with oil or grease. Press the bushes in from the opposing outer faces of the arm, and when fitted ensure that the flanges are in contact with the flange faces of the suspension arm eyes.

13 Refitting the suspension arm is a reversal of the removal procedure but note the following.

(a) When fitting the inner pivot bolt align the index and toe-in cam alignment mark as noted during removal. Do not fully tighten the pivot bolts and nuts at this stage

(b) Reassemble the brake unit (if applicable) and reconnect the brake lines and the handbrake cable, as described in Chapter 9

(c) Refit the coil spring and shock absorber, as described in Section 22. Do not fully tighten the shock absorber lower mounting bolt at this stage

(d) Refit the rear axleshaft and driveshaft, referring to Chapter 8 for details

(e) With the roadwheel(s) refitted, lower the vehicle to the ground and bounce the vehicle at the rear a few times to settle the suspension, then tighten the suspension arm pivot bolts and the shock absorber lower mounting bolt to their specified torque settings

(f) Reconnect the stabilizer bar, referring to Section 24

(g) Bleed the brake hydraulic circuit (Chapter 9)

(h) On completion, have the rear wheel alignment checked by a Toyota dealer

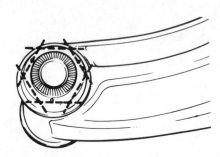

Fig. 10.84 Rear suspension arm bush removal – cut old bush flange as indicated – IRS models (Sec 23)

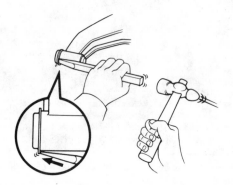

Fig. 10.85 Bend the remaining portions over as shown – IRS models (Sec 23)

Fig. 10.86 Bend the flange tips inwards – IRS models (Sec 23)

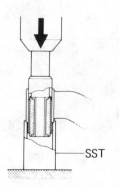

Fig. 10.87 Outer bush removal from suspension arm – IRS models (Sec 23)

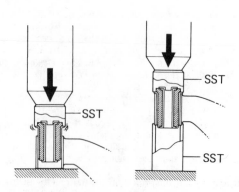

Fig. 10.88 Suspension arm inner bush fitting using special press tool 3 (Sec 23)
Support on spacer to allow full bush refitting – IRS models

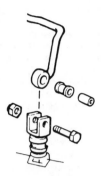

Fig. 10.89 Rear stabilizer bar-to-link assembly – IRS models (Sec 24)

24.1 Rear stabilizer bar and link mounting

24 Rear stabilizer bar (IRS) – removal and refitting

1   The procedure for removing and refitting the rear stabilizer bar on IRS models closely follows that described for the FLS models in Section 21 (photo). During reassembly, ensure that the bar to link and link arm bushes are located as shown in Figs. 10.78 and 10.79.

25 Rear wheel alignment (IRS)

It is normally only necessary to check the rear wheel alignment when the rear tyres are wearing unevenly or after refitting the rear suspension arm(s) if they were removed for any reason. As with the front roadwheels, accurate checking of the alignment can only be made using specialized equipment and is therefore best entrusted to a Toyota dealer. The following provisional checks can be made.
1   First check that the tyres are in good condition and correctly inflated.
2   Jack up the rear of the car and support on safety stands. Release the handbrake and engage neutral.
3   Check the rear wheel bearings for signs of excessive play or wear. Also check that the roadwheel run-out is within the specified limits.
4   Check that the respective rear suspension components are in good condition and secure.
5   Lower the vehicle to the ground then bounce it at the rear to settle the suspension and check at the same time that the shock absorbers are operating efficiently (the car should not continue to bounce after it is released).

6   Measure the vehicle height at the rear and the front, as described in Section 16.
7   The camber angle can only be measured using specialised equipment, but this must be as specified. If the rear suspension components were found to be in good condition during the initial check in paragraph 4, then the angle should be correct.
8   To check the toe-in of the rear wheels, measure the distance between the roadwheel inner rim and the differential carrier bolt each side (Fig. 10.90). The distance should be equal on both sides. If the distances measured are different for each side but are within 5 mm (0.20 in) they can be equalized by adjusting the toe-in cam setting after loosening the securing bolt located on the inner arm pivot point (to the crossmember) each side (Fig. 10.91). After adjustment has been made, check the toe-in in the same manner as that described for the front roadwheels in Section 16 using an adjustable trammel bar. The toe-in should be as specified for the rear wheels.
9   If further adjustment is required, the toe-in cam setting bolt each side must be moved in equal amounts to the left or right as required. Each graduation on the cam is equal to approximately 1 mm (0.04 in) difference in toe-in.
10 After making any adjustments, retighten the toe-in cam securing bolt.

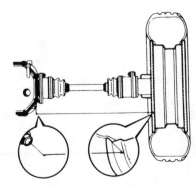

Fig. 10.90 Rear wheel toe-in check (IRS models): measuring points at wheel inner rim and differential carrier (Sec 25)

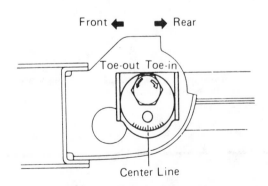

Fig. 10.91 Rear wheel toe-in adjustment (IRS models) is made at inner arm pivot (Sec 25)

26 Wheels and tyres – general care and maintenance

Wheels and tyres should give no real problems in use provided that a close eye is kept on them with regard to excessive wear or damage. To this end, the following points should be noted.

Ensure that tyre pressures are checked regularly and maintained correctly. Checking should be carried out with the tyres cold and not immediately after the vehicle has been in use. If the pressures are checked with the tyres hot, an apparently high reading will be obtained owing to heat expansion. Under no circumstances should an attempt be made to reduce the pressures to the quoted cold reading in this instance, or effective underinflation will result.

Underinflation will cause overheating of the tyre owing to excessive flexing of the casing, and the tread will not sit correctly on the road surface. This will cause a consequent loss of adhesion and excessive wear, not to mention the danger of sudden tyre failure due to heat build-up.

Overinflation will cause rapid wear of the centre part of the tyre tread coupled with reduced adhesion, harsher ride, and the danger of shock damage occurring in the tyre casing.

Regularly check the tyres for damage in the form of cuts or bulges, especially in the sidewalls. Remove any nails or stones embedded in the tread before they penetrate the tyre to cause deflation. If removal of a nail *does* reveal that the tyre has been punctured, refit the nail so that its point of penetration is marked. Then immediately change the wheel and have the tyre repaired by a tyre dealer. Do *not* drive on a tyre in such a condition. In many cases a puncture can be simply repaired by the use of an inner tube of the correct size and type. If in any doubt as to the possible consequences of any damage found, consult your local tyre dealer for advice.

Where a compact spare tyre is fitted it should be noted that the tyre pressure for this differs to the other roadwheel tyres. Although the specified pressure is higher, care must be taken when adding pressure to the compact spare as it gains pressure very quickly due to its size. The compact spare tyre must not be used on any other wheel. For other precautionary notes regarding the compact spare refer to the manufacturer's handbook supplied with the vehicle.

Periodically remove the wheels and clean any dirt or mud from the inside and outside surfaces. Examine the wheel rims for signs of rusting, corrosion or other damage. Light alloy wheels are easily damaged by 'kerbing' whilst parking, and similarly steel wheels may become dented or buckled. Renewal of the wheel is very often the only course of remedial action possible.

The balance of each wheel and tyre assembly should be maintained to avoid excessive wear, not only to the tyres but also to the steering and suspension components. Wheel imbalance is normally signified by vibration through the vehicle's bodyshell, although in many cases it is particularly noticeable through the steering wheel. Conversely, it should be noted that wear or damage in suspension or steering components may cause excessive tyre wear. Out-of-round or out-of-true tyres, damaged wheels and wheel bearing wear/maladjustment also fall into this category. Balancing will not usually cure vibration caused by such wear.

Wheel balancing may be carried out with the wheel either on or off the vehicle. If balanced on the vehicle, ensure that the wheel-to-hub relationship is marked in some way prior to subsequent wheel removal so that it may be refitted in its original position.

General tyre wear is influenced to a large degree by driving style – harsh braking and acceleration or fast cornering will all produce more rapid tyre wear. Interchanging of tyres may result in more even wear, but this should only be carried out where there is no mix of tyre types on the vehicle. However, it is worth bearing in mind that if this is completely effective, the added expense of replacing a complete set of tyres simultaneously is incurred, which may prove financially restrictive for many owners.

Front tyres (and rear tyres on IRS models) may wear unevenly as a result of wheel misalignment. The wheels should always be correctly aligned according to the settings specified by the vehicle manufacturer.

Legal restrictions apply to the mixing of tyre types on a vehicle. Basically this means that a vehicle must not have tyres of differing construction on the same axle. Although it is not recommended to mix tyre types between front axle and rear axle, the only legally permissible combination is crossply at the front and radial at the rear. When mixing radial ply tyres, textile braced radials must always go on the front axle, with steel braced radials at the rear. An obvious disadvantage of such mixing is the necessity to carry two spare tyres to avoid contravening the law in the event of a puncture.

In the UK, the Motor Vehicles Construction and Use Regulations apply to many aspects of tyre fitting and usage. It is suggested that a copy of these regulations is obtained from your local police if in doubt as to the current legal requirements with regard to tyre condition, minimum tread depth, etc.

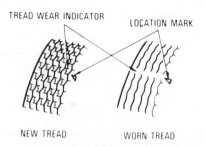

Fig. 10.92 Typical tyre tread wear indicators warn when tyres should be renewed (Sec 26)

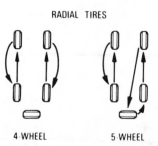

Fig. 10.93 The manufacturer's recommend rotating the wheel/tyre positions every 10 000 km (6000 miles) (Sec 26)

4 wheel diagram is for models fitted with a compact spare

27 Fault diagnosis – suspension and steering

Symptom	Reason(s)
Lost motion at steering wheel	Worn rack and pinion or steering box Worn tie-rod end balljoints Worn suspension arm balljoints
Steering wander	Worn steering gear Worn tie-rod end or suspension arm balljoints Incorrect front wheel alignment Incorrectly adjusted front hub bearings Tyre pressures incorrect
Heavy or stiff steering	Dry or distorted steering rack Incorrect front wheel alignment Incorrect tyre pressures Seized suspension strut upper bearing
Wheel wobble and vibration	Roadwheels out of balance or buckled Weak shock absorbers Worn tie-rod end or suspension arm balljoints
Excessive pitching or rolling	Weak shock absorbers Weak or broken coil spring

Chapter 11 Bodywork and fittings

Contents

1 General description and precautions

1 The body and underframe are of unitary, all-steel welded construction.

2 The Celica is produced in two body styles; the Coupé and Liftback. Both models have two side doors; the Coupé has a boot lid, whilst the Liftback has a tailgate (back door). On both models the rear seats fold forward to provide additional luggage area if required.

3 The bumpers are of urethane construction with metal reinforcements. Some body mouldings are also urethane in construction. **Caution:** If welding or applying a heat source in the vicinity of urethane bumpers or mouldings particular care must be taken against fire and/or distortion of such parts. Similar care must also be taken when applying heat to the underbody panels or components, particularly around the fuel tank, fuel lines and floor panels which have carpets or upholstery on the inner face.

4 It should be noted that the repainting of urethane body parts, including the bumpers, is not recommended to the home mechanic, as special preparations and materials are required. The repainting process of such items is critical and should therefore be entrusted to a Toyota dealer.

2 Maintenance – bodywork and underframe

The general condition of a vehicle's bodywork is the one thing that significantly affects its value. Maintenance is easy but needs to be regular. Neglect, particularly after minor damage, can lead quickly to further deterioration and costly repair bills. It is important also to keep watch on those parts of the vehicle not immediately visible, for instance the underside, inside all the wheel arches and the lower part of the engine compartment.

The basic maintenance routine for the bodywork is washing – preferably with a lot of water, from a hose. This will remove all the loose solids which may have stuck to the vehicle. It is important to flush these off in such a way as to prevent grit from scratching the finish. The wheel arches and underframe need washing in the same way to remove any accumulated mud which will retain moisture and tend to encourage rust. Paradoxically enough, the best time to clean the underframe and wheel arches is in wet weather when the mud is thoroughly wet and soft. In very wet weather the underframe is usually cleaned of large accumulations automatically and this is a good time for inspection.

Periodically, except on vehicles with a wax-based underbody protective coating, it is a good idea to have the whole of the underframe of the vehicle steam cleaned, engine compartment included, so that a thorough inspection can be carried out to see what minor repairs and renovations are necessary. Steam cleaning is available at many garages and is necessary for removal of the accumulation of oily grime which sometimes is allowed to become thick in certain areas. If steam cleaning facilities are not available, there are one or two excellent grease solvents available which can be brush applied. The dirt can then be simply hosed off. Note that these methods should not be used on vehicles with wax-based underbody protective coating or the coating will be removed. Such vehicles should be inspected annually, preferably just prior to winter, when the underbody should be washed down and any damage to the wax coating repaired. Ideally, a completely fresh coat should be applied. It would also be worth considering the use of such wax-based protection for injection into door panels, sills, box sections, etc, as an additional safeguard against rust damage where such protection is not provided by the vehicle manufacturer.

After washing paintwork, wipe off with a chamois leather to give an unspotted clear finish. A coat of clear protective wax polish will give added protection against chemical pollutants in the air. If the paintwork sheen has dulled or oxidised, use a cleaner/polisher combination to restore the brilliance of the shine. This requires a little effort, but such dulling is usually caused because regular washing has been neglected. Care needs to be taken with metallic paintwork, as special non-abrasive cleaner/polisher is required to avoid damage to the finish. Always check that the door and ventilator opening drain holes and pipes are completely clear so that water can be drained out (photos). Bright work should be treated in the same way as paint work. Windscreens and windows can be kept clear of the smeary film which often appears by the use of a proprietary glass cleaner. Never use any form of wax or other body or chromium polish on glass.

2.4A Check that the body drain holes are clear

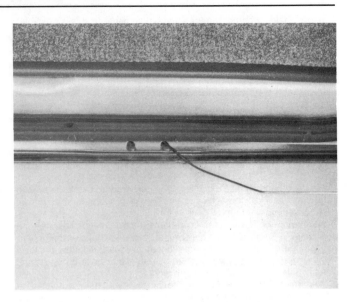

2.4B Check that the door drain/ventilation holes are clear

3 Maintenance – upholstery and carpets

Mats and carpets should be brushed or vacuum cleaned regularly to keep them free of grit. If they are badly stained remove them from the vehicle for scrubbing or sponging and make quite sure they are dry before refitting. Seats and interior trim panels can be kept clean by wiping with a damp cloth. If they do become stained (which can be more apparent on light coloured upholstery) use a little liquid detergent and a soft nail brush to scour the grime out of the grain of the material. Do not forget to keep the headlining clean in the same way as the upholstery. When using liquid cleaners inside the vehicle do not over-wet the surfaces being cleaned. Excessive damp could get into the seams and padded interior causing stains, offensive odours or even rot. If the inside of the vehicle gets wet accidentally it is worthwhile taking some trouble to dry it out properly, particularly where carpets are involved. *Do not leave oil or electric heaters inside the vehicle for this purpose.*

4 Minor body damage – repair

The photographic sequences on pages 282 and 283 illustrate the operations detailed in the following sub-sections.
Note: *For more detailed information about bodywork repair, the Haynes Publishing Group publish a book by Lindsay Porter called The Car Bodywork Repair Manual. This incorporates information on such aspects as rust treatment, painting and glass fibre repairs, as well as details on more ambitious repairs involving welding and panel beating.*

Repair of minor scratches in bodywork

If the scratch is very superficial, and does not penetrate to the metal of the bodywork, repair is very simple. Lightly rub the area of the scratch with a paintwork renovator, or a very fine cutting paste, to remove loose paint from the scratch and to clear the surrounding bodywork of wax polish. Rinse the area with clean water.

Apply touch-up paint to the scratch using a fine paint brush; continue to apply fine layers of paint until the surface of the paint in the scratch is level with the surrounding paintwork. Allow the new paint at least two weeks to harden: then blend it into the surrounding paintwork by rubbing the scratch area with a paintwork renovator or a very fine cutting paste. Finally, apply wax polish.

Where the scratch has penetrated right through to the metal of the bodywork, causing the metal to rust, a different repair technique is required. Remove any loose rust from the bottom of the scratch with a penknife, then apply rust inhibiting paint to prevent the formation of rust in the future. Using a rubber or nylon applicator fill the scratch

with bodystopper paste. If required, this paste can be mixed with cellulose thinners to provide a very thin paste which is ideal for filling narrow scratches. Before the stopper-paste in the scratch hardens, wrap a piece of smooth cotton rag around the top of a finger. Dip the finger in cellulose thinners and then quickly sweep it across the surface of the stopper-paste in the scratch; this will ensure that the surface of the stopper-paste is slightly hollowed. The scratch can now be painted over as described earlier in this Section.

Repair of dents in bodywork

When deep denting of the vehicle's bodywork has taken place, the first task is to pull the dent out, until the affected bodywork almost attains its original shape. There is little point in trying to restore the original shape completely, as the metal in the damaged area will have stretched on impact and cannot be reshaped fully to its original contour. It is better to bring the level of the dent up to a point which is about ⅛ in (3 mm) below the level of the surrounding bodywork. In cases where the dent is very shallow anyway, it is not worth trying to pull it out at all. If the underside of the dent is accessible, it can be hammered out gently from behind, using a mallet with a wooden or plastic head. Whilst doing this, hold a suitable block of wood firmly against the outside of the panel to absorb the impact from the hammer blows and thus prevent a large area of the bodywork from being 'belled-out'.

Should the dent be in a section of the bodywork which has a double skin or some other factor making it inaccessible from behind, a different technique is called for. Drill several small holes through the metal inside the area – particularly in the deeper section. Then screw long self-tapping screws into the holes just sufficiently for them to gain a good purchase in the metal. Now the dent can be pulled out by pulling on the protruding heads of the screws with a pair of pliers.

The next stage of the repair is the removal of the paint from the damaged area, and from an inch or so of the surrounding 'sound' bodywork. This is accomplished most easily by using a wire brush or abrasive pad on a power drill, although it can be done just as effectively by hand using sheets of abrasive paper. To complete the preparation for filling, score the surface of the bare metal with a screwdriver or the tang of a file, or alternatively, drill small holes in the affected area. This will provide a really good 'key' for the filler paste.

To complete the repair see the Section on filling and re-spraying.

Repair of rust holes or gashes in bodywork

Remove all paint from the affected area and from an inch or so of the surrounding 'sound' bodywork, using an abrasive pad or a wire brush on a power drill. If these are not available a few sheets of abrasive paper will do the job just as effectively. With the paint removed you will be able to gauge the severity of the corrosion and therefore decide whether to renew the whole panel (if this is possible) or to repair the affected area. New body panels are not as expensive as most people think and it is often quicker and more satisfactory to fit a new panel than to attempt to repair large areas of corrosion.

Remove all fittings from the affected area except those which will act as a guide to the original shape of the damaged bodywork (eg headlamp shells etc). Then, using tin snips or a hacksaw blade, remove all loose metal and any other metal badly affected by corrosion. Hammer the edges of the hole inwards in order to create a slight depression for the filler paste.

Wire brush the affected area to remove the powdery rust from the surface of the remaining metal. Paint the affected area with rust inhibiting paint; if the back of the rusted area is accessible treat this also.

Before filling can take place it will be necessary to block the hole in some way. This can be achieved by the use of aluminium or plastic mesh, or aluminium tape.

Aluminium or plastic mesh is probably the best material to use for a large hole. Cut a piece to the approximate size and shape of the hole to be filled, then position it in the hole so that its edges are below the level of the surrounding bodywork. It can be retained in position by several blobs of filler paste around its periphery.

Aluminium tape should be used for small or very narrow holes. Pull a piece off the roll and trim it to the approximate size and shape required, then pull off the backing paper (if used) and stick the tape over the hole; it can be overlapped if the thickness of one piece is insufficient. Burnish down the edges of the tape with the handle of a screwdriver or similar, to ensure that the tape is securely attached to the metal underneath.

Bodywork repairs – filling and re-spraying

Before using this Section, see the Sections on dent, deep scratch, rust holes and gash repairs.

Many types of bodyfiller are available, but generally speaking those proprietary kits which contain a tin of filler paste and a tube of resin hardener are best for this type of repair. A wide, flexible plastic or nylon applicator will be found invaluable for imparting a smooth and well contoured finish to the surface of the filler.

Mix up a little filler on a clean piece of card or board – measure the hardener carefully (follow the maker's instructions on the pack) otherwise the filler will set too rapidly or too slowly.   Using the applicator apply the filler paste to the prepared area; draw the applicator across the surface of the filler to achieve the correct contour and to level the filler surface. As soon as a contour that approximates to the correct one is achieved, stop working the paste – if you carry on too long the paste will become sticky and begin to 'pick up' on the applicator. Continue to add thin layers of filler paste at twenty-minute intervals until the level of the filler is just proud of the surrounding bodywork.

Once the filler has hardened, excess can be removed using a metal plane or file. From then on, progressively finer grades of abrasive paper should be used, starting with a 40 grade production paper and finishing with 400 grade wet-and-dry paper. Always wrap the abrasive paper around a flat rubber, cork, or wooden block – otherwise the surface of the filler will not be completely flat. During the smoothing of the filler surface the wet-and-dry paper should be periodically rinsed in water. This will ensure that a very smooth finish is imparted to the filler at the final stage.

At this stage the 'dent' should be surrounded by a ring of bare metal, which in turn should be encircled by the finely 'feathered' edge of the good paintwork. Rinse the repair area with clean water, until all of the dust produced by the rubbing-down operation has gone.

Spray the whole repair area with a light coat of primer – this will show up any imperfections in the surface of the filler. Repair these imperfections with fresh filler paste or bodystopper, and once more smooth the surface with abrasive paper. If bodystopper is used, it can be mixed with cellulose thinners to form a really thin paste which is ideal for filling small holes. Repeat this spray and repair procedure until you are satisfied that the surface of the filler, and the feathered edge of the paintwork are perfect. Clean the repair area with clean water and allow to dry fully.

The repair area is now ready for final spraying. Paint spraying must be carried out in a warm, dry, windless and dust free atmosphere. This condition can be created artificially if you have access to a large indoor working area, but if you are forced to work in the open, you will have to pick your day very carefully. If you are working indoors, dousing the

floor in the work area with water will help to settle the dust which would otherwise be in the atmosphere. If the repair area is confined to one body panel, mask off the surrounding panels; this will help to minimise the effects of a slight mis-match in paint colours. Bodywork fittings (eg chrome strips, door handles etc) will also need to be masked off. Use genuine masking tape and several thicknesses of newspaper for the masking operations.

Before commencing to spray, agitate the aerosol can thoroughly, then spray a test area (an old tin, or similar) until the technique is mastered. Cover the repair area with a thick coat of primer; the thickness should be built up using several thin layers of paint rather than one thick one. Using 400 grade wet-and-dry paper, rub down the surface of the primer until it is really smooth. While doing this, the work area should be thoroughly doused with water, and the wet-and-dry paper periodically rinsed in water. Allow to dry before spraying on more paint.

Spray on the top coat, again building up the thickness by using several thin layers of paint. Start spraying in the centre of the repair area and then, using a circular motion, work outwards until the whole repair area and about 2 inches of the surrounding original paintwork is covered. Remove all masking material 10 to 15 minutes after spraying on the final coat of paint.

Allow the new paint at least two weeks to harden, then, using a paintwork renovator or a very fine cutting paste, blend the edges of the paint into the existing paintwork. Finally, apply wax polish.

Plastic components

With the use of more and more plastic body components by the vehicle manufacturers (eg bumpers, spoilers, and in some cases major body panels), rectification of damage to such items has become a matter of either entrusting repair work to a specialist in this field, or renewing complete components. Repair by the DIY owner is not really feasible owing to the cost of the equipment and materials required for effecting such repairs. The basic technique involves making a groove along the line of the crack in the plastic using a rotary burr in a power drill. The damaged part is then welded back together by using a hot air gun to heat up and fuse a plastic filler rod into the groove. Any excess plastic is then removed and the area rubbed down to a smooth finish. It is important that a filler rod of the correct plastic is used, as body components can be made of a variety of different types (eg polycarbonate, ABS, polypropylene).

If the owner is renewing a complete component himself, he will be left with the problem of finding a suitable paint for finishing which is compatible with the type of plastic used. At one time the use of a universal paint was not possible owing to the complex range of plastics encountered in body component applications. Standard paints, generally speaking, will not bond to plastic or rubber satisfactorily. However, it is now possible to obtain a plastic body parts finishing kit which consists of a pre-primer treatment, a primer and coloured top coat. Full instructions are normally supplied with a kit, but basically the method of use is first to apply the pre-primer to the component concerned and allow it to dry for up to 30 minutes. Then the primer is applied and left to dry for about an hour before finally applying the special coloured top coat. The result is a correctly coloured component where the paint will flex with the plastic or rubber, a property that standard paint does not normally possess.

5 Major body damage – repair

Where serious damage has occurred, or large areas of the body need renewal due to rusting; it means certainly that complete new sections or panels will need welding in and this is best left to the professionals. If the damage is due to impact it will also be necessary to check the alignment of the body shell structure completely. Due to the principle of construction the strength and shape of the whole car can be affected by damage to a relatively small area. In such instances the services of a Toyota garage with specialist jigs are essential. If a body is left misaligned it is first of all dangerous as the car will not handle properly, and secondly, uneven stresses will be imposed on the steering, engine and transmission, causing abnormal wear or complete failure. Tyre wear may also be excessive.

6 Seat belts – checking and maintenance

1 Periodically check the belts for fraying or other damage. If evident, renew the belt.
2 If the belts become dirty, wipe them with a damp cloth using a little liquid detergent only.
3 Check the tightness of the anchor bolts and, if they are ever disconnected, make quite sure that the original sequence of fitting of washers, bushes and anchor plate is retained (photo).
4 **Never** modify the belt or alter its attachment point to the body.

7 Maintenance – hinges, door catches and locks

1 Oil the hinges of the bonnet, boot and doors with a drop or two of light oil periodically. A good time is after the car has been washed.
2 Oil the bonnet safety catch thrust pin periodically.
3 Do not over-lubricate door latches and strikers. Normally one or two drops regularly applied is better than a lot at one go.

8 Doors – tracing rattles and their rectification

1 Check first that the door is not loose at the hinges and that the latch is holding the door firmly in position. Check also that the door lines up with the aperture in the body.
2 If the hinges are loose or the door is out of alignment it will be necessary to reset the hinge position, as described in Section 9.
3 If the latch is holding the door properly it should hold the door tightly when fully latched and the door should line up with the body. If it is out of alignment it needs adjustment, as described in Section 10. If loose, some part of the mechanism must be worn out and requiring renewal.
4 Other rattles from the door would be caused by wear or looseness in the window winder, the glass channels and sill strips or the door buttons and interior latch release mechanism. All these are dealt with in subsequent Sections.

9 Door alignment – hinge adjustment

1 The hinges are adjustable both on the door and pillar mountings. Access to some of the bolts will require removal of trim and the use of a spanner.
2 When re-aligning is necessary, first slacken the bolts holding the hinge to the door and reposition the door as required and make sure

the bolts are thoroughly tightened up again. If the amount of movement on the door half of the hinge is insufficient it may be adjusted at the door pillar.
3 If the hinges themselves are worn at the hinge pin the door should be detached from the hinges, the hinges removed and new ones fitted.

10 Door latch striker – alignment

1 Assuming that the door hinges are correctly aligned but the trailing edge of the door is not flush with the body when the door is fully latched, then the striker plate needs adjusting.
2 Slacken the two cross-head screws holding the striker plate to the door pillar just enough to hold the striker plate in position and then push the plate to the inner limit of its position. Try and shut the door, moving the striker plate outwards until the latch is able to engage fully (photo).
3 Without pulling on the release handle, but working inside the car, push the door outwards until it is flush with the bodywork. This will move the striker plate along with the latch.
4 Release the latch very carefully so as not to disturb the striker plate and open the door. Tighten down the striker plate securing screws.

11 Door trim panel – removal and refitting

1 Disconnect the battery earth lead.
2 Undo the two retaining screws and withdraw the door courtesy light lens and body from the trim panel. Detach the leads at the connector to the unit (photo).
3 Prise free the plugs from the armrest, undo the four retaining screws and remove the armrest. The two lower screws are accessible by hinging down the lower armrest trim (photo).
4 On models with a manual window regulator, remove the regulator handle by inserting a clean cloth between the handle and the panel (photo), then disengage the retaining clip. The clip will spring free so be prepared to catch it. Withdraw the handle and the nylon protector washer (photo).
5 Unscrew and remove the retaining screw from the door lock release handle bezel and remove the bezel (photo).
6 Carefully prise free the panel around its periphery to release the retaining clips and withdraw the panel.
7 Carefully peel back the plastic insulation panel for access to the inner door fittings.
8 Refitting is a reversal of the removal procedure. Check the panel alignment as it is being refitted and press home the retainer clips. Feed the door courtesy light wire through the light unit aperture in the panel as it is being fitted. Position the retaining clip on the regulator handle, and push the handle on.

6.3 Check the seatbelt anchor bolts for security

10.2 Door striker plate

11.2 Remove the door courtesy light

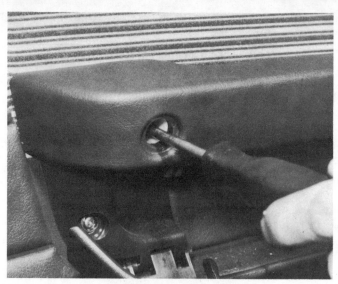

11.3 Remove the armrest/door pull

11.4A Release the regulator retaining clip

11.4B Window regulator removed showing clip and nylon washer

11.5 Remove the door release handle bezel

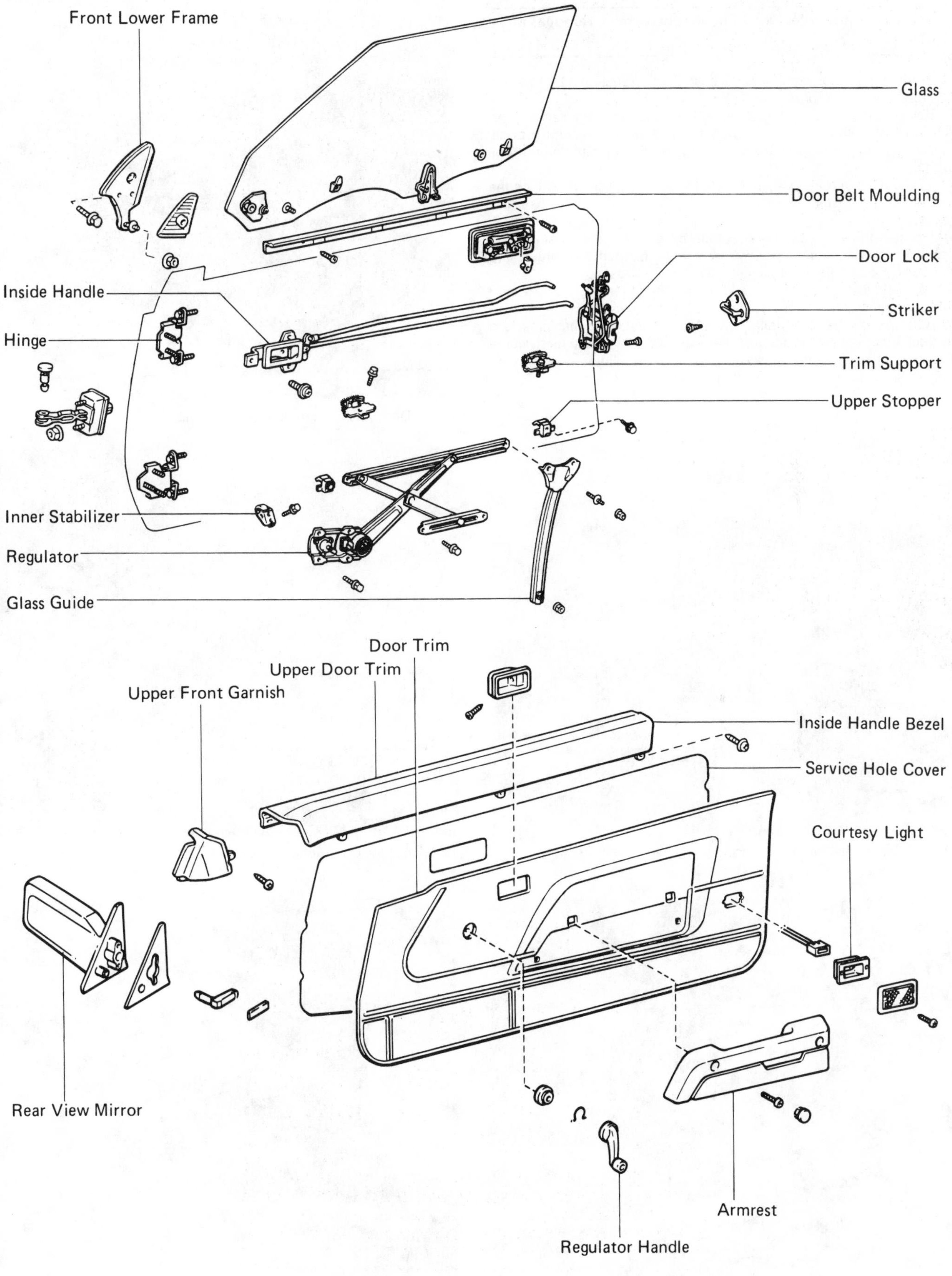

Fig. 11.1 Exploded view of the door components (Sec 11)

Front Lower Frame

Glass

Door Belt Moulding

Door Lock

Striker

Inside Handle

Hinge

Trim Support

Upper Stopper

Inner Stabilizer

Regulator

Glass Guide

Door Trim

Upper Door Trim

Upper Front Garnish

Inside Handle Bezel

Service Hole Cover

Courtesy Light

Rear View Mirror

Armrest

Regulator Handle

12 Door lock and release handle mechanisms – removal and refitting

1   Remove the door trim panel, as described in Section 11.
2   Fully raise the door glass.
3   Remove the inside release handle by detaching the connecting rods from the door lock unit, undo the two handle retaining bolts, release the rods from the guide clips and remove the handle and rods (photos).
4   To remove the door lock unit, undo the retaining screws, detach the connecting rods and remove the lock unit from within the door (photo).
5   Remove the outside release handle by detaching the connecting rods from the handle and lock cylinder, undo the retaining screws and withdraw the handle and lock cylinder unit (photos).
6   To remove the cylinder lock, undo the retaining screws and withdraw the cylinder from the outside release handle.
7   Refitting of the door lock and release handle mechanisms is a reversal of the removal procedure. Renew the nylon clips which secure the connecting rods if necessary. Lubricate the sliding and moving contact surfaces with grease as they are assembled.

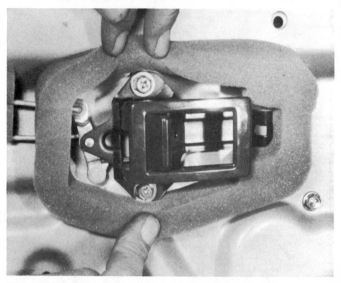

12.3A Door release handle retaining bolts

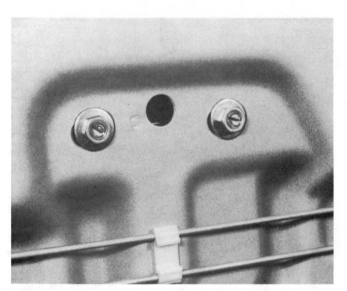

12.3B Door release handle connecting rods and location clips

12.4 Door lock unit retaining screws

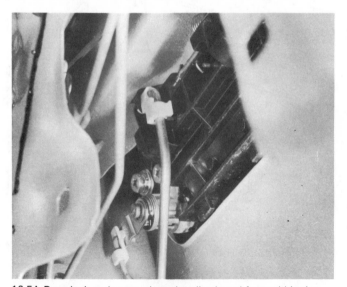

12.5A Door lock and outer release handle viewed from within the door, showing connecting rods and lock cylinder

12.5B Outer door handle retaining screw

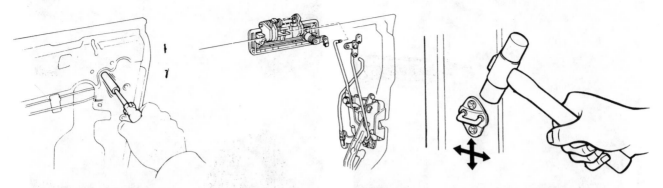

Fig. 11.2 Door inside lock adjustment (Sec 12)

Fig. 11.3 Door outside handle adjustment (Sec 12)

Fig. 11.4 Door lock striker adjustment (Sec 12)

8   Before refitting the trim panel, make the following adjustments where necessary.
9   **Inside handle adjustment:** Loosen the retaining screws and push the door handle forwards to the point where a positive resistance is felt, then move the handle rearwards 0.5 to 1.0 mm (0.020 to 0.039 in) and tighten the retaining bolts.
10 **Inside lock adjustment:** Loosen the adjustment bolt and push the bolt upwards to the point where a positive resistance is felt, then move the bolt downwards 0.5 to 1.0 mm (0.020 to 0.039 in) and tighten it (Fig. 11.2).
11 **Outside door handle:** With the control link detached, lift the handle 0.5 to 1.0 mm (0.020 to 0.039 in) from the rest position then turn the adjuster and locate the pin in the hole (Fig. 11.3).
12 **Door lock striker adjustment:** The door lock striker position can be adjusted by loosening the retaining screws and moving it laterally or longitudinally to suit. This adjustment is of the trial and error type and when correctly set, the door should close securely and be aligned with the adjacent panels (Fig. 11.4).
13 Refit the trim panel with reference to Section 11.

13 Door mirror – removal and refitting

1   Remove the door trim panel, as described in Section 11.
2   Undo the three retaining screws and remove the upper trim bezel from the door (photo).
3   Undo the retaining screw and remove the front upper garnish.
4   Undo the retaining screw and remove the knob (photo) or detach the wiring connector (as applicable).

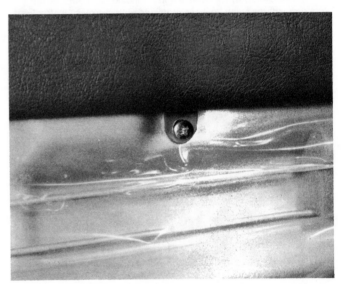

13.2 Upper trim bezel retaining screw

5   Prise free and remove the cover. It may be necessary to remove a retaining screw as well on some models (photo).
6   Remove the three retaining screws and withdraw the mirror from the door (photo).
7   Refitting is a reversal of the removal procedure.

13.4 Door mirror adjuster knob screw is on inner face

13.5 Remove the cover

13.6 Door mirror retaining screws

This sequence of photographs deals with the repair of the dent and paintwork damage shown in this photo. The procedure will be similar for the repair of a hole. It should be noted that the procedures given here are simplified — more explicit instructions will be found in the text .

In the case of a dent the first job — after removing surrounding trim — is to hammer out the dent where access is possible. This will minimise filling. Here, the large dent having been hammered out, the damaged area is being made slightly concave

Now all paint must be removed from the damaged area, by rubbing with coarse abrasive paper. Alternatively, a wire brush or abrasive pad can be used in a power drill. Where the repair area meets good paintwork, the edge of the paintwork should be 'feathered', using a finer grade of abrasive paper

In the case of a hole caused by rusting, all damaged sheet-metal should be cut away before proceeding to this stage. Here, the damaged area is being treated with rust remover and inhibitor before being filled

Mix the body filler according to its manufacturer's instructions. In the case of corrosion damage, it will be necessary to block off any large holes before filling — this can be done with aluminium or plastic mesh, or aluminium tape. Make sure the area is absolutely clean before ...

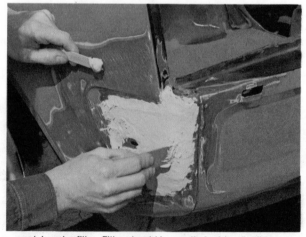

... applying the filler. Filler should be applied with a flexible applicator, as shown, for best results; the wooden spatula being used for confined areas. Apply thin layers of filler at 20-minute intervals, until the surface of the filler is slightly proud of the surrounding bodywork

Initial shaping can be done with a Surform plane or Dreadnought file. Then, using progressively finer grades of wet-and-dry paper, wrapped around a sanding block, and copious amounts of clean water, rub down the filler until really smooth and flat. Again, feather the edges of adjoining paintwork

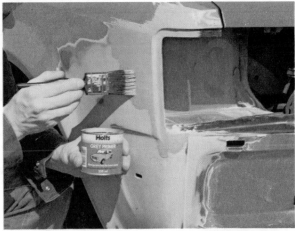

The whole repair area can now be sprayed or brush-painted with primer. If spraying, ensure adjoining areas are protected from over-spray. Note that at least one inch of the surrounding sound paintwork should be coated with primer. Primer has a 'thick' consistency, so will find small imperfections

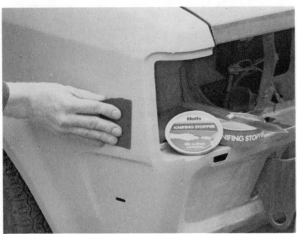

Again, using plenty of water, rub down the primer with a fine grade wet-and-dry paper (400 grade is probably best) until it is really smooth and well blended into the surrounding paintwork. Any remaining imperfections can now be filled by carefully applied knifing stopper paste

When the stopper has hardened, rub down the repair area again before applying the final coat of primer. Before rubbing down this last coat of primer, ensure the repair area is blemish-free — use more stopper if necessary. To ensure that the surface of the primer is really smooth use some finishing compound

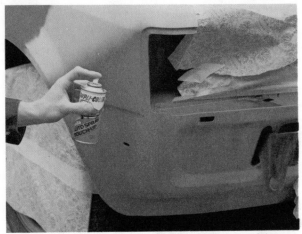

The top coat can now be applied. When working out of doors, pick a dry, warm and wind-free day. Ensure surrounding areas are protected from over-spray. Agitate the aerosol thoroughly, then spray the centre of the repair area, working outwards with a circular motion. Apply the paint as several thin coats

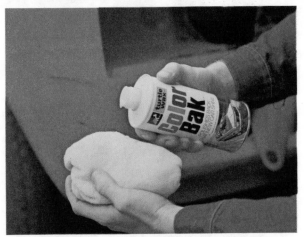

After a period of about two weeks, which the paint needs to harden fully, the surface of the repaired area can be 'cut' with a mild cutting compound prior to wax polishing. When carrying out bodywork repairs, remember that the quality of the finished job is proportional to the time and effort expended

14 Door glass and regulator – removal and refitting

1   Remove the door trim panel, as described in Section 11.
2   Undo the three retaining screws and remove the upper trim bezel from the door. Wind the door glass fully down.
3   Remove the door mirror, as described in Section 13.
4   Remove the glass weatherstrip each side then remove the two screws and carefully prise free the belt moulding using a suitable flat tool. Wind tape around the blade of the tool to protect the paintwork (Fig. 11.5).
5   Undo the retaining screws and remove the upper stopper, the trim support and the inner stabilizer (Fig. 11.6 and photos).
6   Lift the glass 20 to 40 mm (0.80 to 1.56 in) and undo the two guide setting bolts and remove them (photos).

7   Pull the glass upwards out of the door and remove the glass guide and the front lower frame.
8   To remove the glass regulator unit, detach the wiring connector (where applicable), undo the regulator retaining bolts and withdraw the regulator unit from the door (photo).
9   If the glass is to be renewed, remove the items shown in Fig. 11.7 and fit them to the new glass.
10 Before installing the regulator and glass, smear the sliding surfaces of the regulator and the spring and gears with grease (Fig. 11.8).
11 Refitting is a reversal of the removal procedure. When refitting the belt moulding tap it down carefully by hand (Fig. 11.9)
12 Before refitting the trim panel check the door glass for satisfactory operation and if necessary adjust it as follows.
13 Prior to making any adjustments first check that the door to body alignment and fitting position is satisfactory.

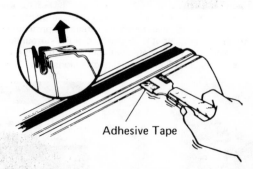

Fig. 11.5 Use tool as shown to remove weatherstrip from door (Sec 14)

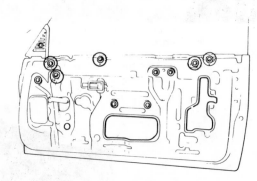

Fig. 11.6 Upper stopper, trim support and inner stabilizer positions (Sec 14)

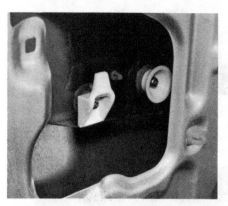

14.5A Door glass stabilizer and stopper

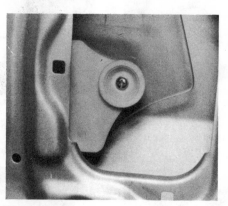

14.5B Door glass plate and stopper

14.6A Door glass guide setting bolt (front) is accessible through inspection aperture

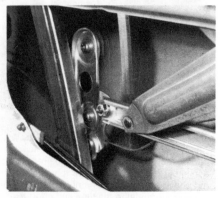

14.6B Door glass guide setting bolt (rear)

14.8 Door glass regulator bolts (manual)

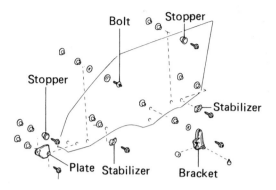

Fig. 11.7 Door glass and fittings (Sec 14)

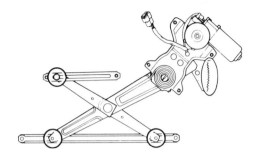

Fig. 11.8 Lubricate the regulator sliding parts encircled (Sec 14)

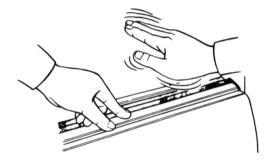

Fig. 11.9 Tap the belt moulding into position by hand (Sec 14)

14 Refer to Fig. 11.10. First check the glass-to-belt moulding contact. If necessary adjust by repositioning the trim support(s) as required. (a).

15 Move the glass backwards and forwards and if necessary adjust the forward and rear positions for the upper glass guide tip (b).

16 The tilt angle of the glass can be adjusted by repositioning the equalizer (c).

17 The upper glass contact can be adjusted by setting the two glass guide tip adjuster bolts as required (d).

18 Move the front and rear upper stoppers as required to adjust the upper position of the glass (e).

19 When fully raised, the roller of the inner stabilizer should make a light contact with the glass. If required adjust the position of the glass plate to achieve this. (Fig. 11.11).

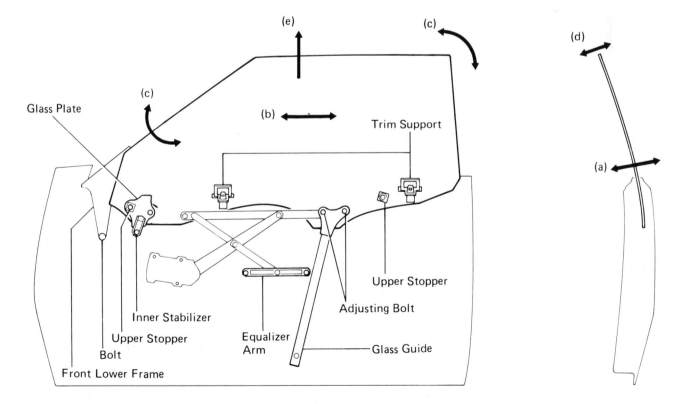

Fig. 11.10 Door glass adjustment and items which affect it (Sec 14)

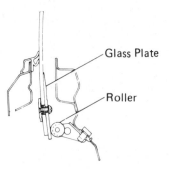

Fig. 11.11 Roller-to-glass contact is adjusted with glass plate (Sec 14)

15.5 Door check strap

15 Door – removal and refitting

1   Remove the door trim panel, as described in Section 11. Fully raise the door glass.
2   Detach any wiring connection within the door.
3   Open the door fully and support it on a suitable jack or blocks, but take care not to damage the paintwork.
4   Make an alignment mark with a pencil or felt tip pen around the hinge on the door.
5   Extract the door check strap hinge pin (photo).
6   Undo the retaining bolts and detach the door from the hinges. Get an assistant to help support the door as these bolts are removed. Remove the door (photo).
7   Refit in the reverse order of removal. Align the hinges with the outline marks made during removal. On completion check the door alignment when closed before refitting the trim panel. If necessary adjust by loosening the hinge bolts and realigning the door. Tighten the bolts and recheck the alignment with the adjacent panels around the periphery of the door. If necessary readjust the lock striker position (Section 10).

16 Bonnet – removal and refitting

1   Open and support the bonnet. Use a felt tip pen or pencil and mark the outline position of each hinge on the bonnet. This will act as an alignment guide when refitting.
2   Detach the windscreen washer nozzle hoses.
3   Where applicable disconnect the bonnet stay rods.
4   Get an assistant to support the bonnet and undo the hinge bolts. Lift the bonnet clear (photo).
5   Do not attempt to dismantle the stays. Renew them if necessary.
6   Refit in the reverse order of removal, aligning the hinges with the marks made during removal before fully tightening the bolts.
7   Lower the bonnet and check it for alignment. Adjust if required as follows.
8   To adjust the bonnet in a forward or rearward direction, loosen the hinge bolts and move the bonnet as necessary, then retighten the bolts.
9   To adjust the bonnet height along its front edge, loosen the locknut and turn the cushion in the required direction to raise or lower the closed bonnet position. Retighten the locknut when adjustment is satisfactory (Fig. 11.12).
10 To adjust the bonnet height along its rear edge, loosen the hinge-to-body retaining bolts and add or subtract the spacer shims as required. Retighten the bolts.
11 On completion, check that the bonnet closes securely.

15.6 Door hinge

17 Bonnet release cable and catch – removal and refitting

1   Raise and support the bonnet.
2   To remove the cable, pull back the release and undo the retaining screw. Withdraw the release and detach the cable from it (photos).

16.4 Undoing the bonnet hinge bolts

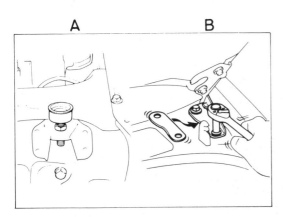

Fig. 11.12 Bonnet adjustment points (Sec 16)

A   *Bonnet height at leading edge – adjust cushion position*
B   *Bonnet height at rear edge – change the shim setting(s)*

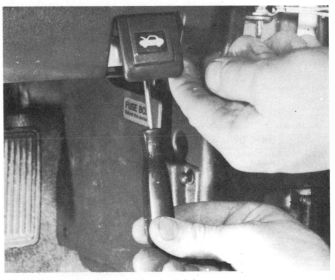

17.2A Remove the bonnet release retaining screw ...

17.2B ... withdraw the release ...

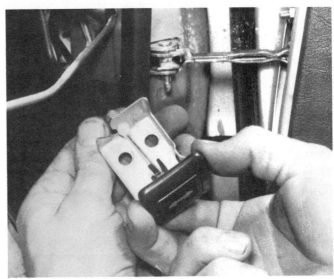

17.2C ... and detach the cable from it

17.4 Bonnet release/lock unit

3   Detach the cable from the bonnet lock at the front end and withdraw the cable.
4   To remove the bonnet lock unit, detach the cable and undo the three retaining bolts. Remove the lock (photo).
5   Refitting of both the cable and lock are a reversal of the removal procedure. Before fully closing the bonnet check that the lock release mechanism operates in a satisfactory manner, that the safety catch engages (the auxiliary catch release tab needs to be lifted before the bonnet can be opened) and then, when fully closed, the bonnet is securely held.

18   Back door (tailgate), – removal and refitting

1   Open the door fully and disconnect the leads from the heating element, wiper motor and the tubing from the washer jet.
2   Disconnect the stays.
3   Have an assistant support the door and disconnect the hinges from it. Lift the door from the vehicle (Fig. 11.13).
4   On no account attempt to dismantle the gas-filled stays. Renew them if they are faulty.
5   Refitting is a reversal of removal, adjust if necessary by loosening

the hinge bolts and moving the back door in the required direction. To adjust the vertical alignment of the door at the front edge, add or subtract the number of hinge spacer washers. Tighten the bolts when the adjustment is correct. The lock-to-striker adjustment can be made by loosening the striker bolts and moving the striker in the required direction, then tighten the bolts.

6   The back door lock is attached to the tailgate by three bolts and its removal and refitting details are similar to those given for the boot lid lock.

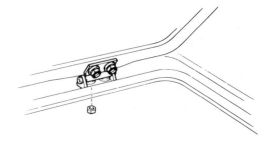

Fig. 11.13 Back door (tailgate) hinge nuts – Liftback (Sec 18)

19 Boot lid (Coupe) – removal and refitting

1   With the boot lid open, mark the fitted position of the hinge relative to the boot lid.
2   An assistant should now support the weight of the boot lid. Undo and remove the four bolts and washers securing the boot lid to the hinges (photo).
3   Lift away the boot lid and recover the hinge spacers.
4   If necessary the torsion bar may be removed by detaching at one end to release the tension and then lifting away (Fig. 11.15).
5   To remove the lock cylinder, release the spring retainer with a pair of pliers, detach the pullrod and lift away the lock cylinder.
6   To remove the lock from the boot lid, undo and remove the securing bolts and washers (photo).
7   Reassembly and refitting of the boot lid, lock and hinges is the reverse sequence to removal.
8   The following adjustments may be required if the hinge-to-body bolts have been disturbed or new components fitted.
9   Adjustment of the boot lid in the aperture is effected by slackening the boot lid-to-hinge securing bolts and repositioning the boot lid in the aperture.
10   To lift or lower the hinge end of the boot lid fit or remove hinge spacers as necessary.
11   To adjust the lock, slacken the lock striker securing bolts and move the striker as necessary. Tighten the securing bolts.

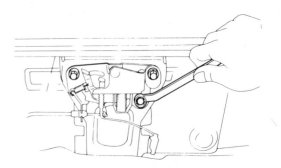

Fig. 11.14 Back door lock removal (Sec 18)

3   If dismantling the impact absorbing type bumper assemblies the multi-component construction of the bumper unit should be noted.
4   Refitting is a reversal of the removal procedure. Check the bumper for alignment before fully tightening the retaining bolts.

20 Front grille – removal and refitting

1   Unscrew and remove the three retaining screws at the top (photo).
2   Compress the three recessed securing clips at the bottom of the grille to release them and remove the grille.
3   Refit in the reverse order of removal.

22 Fuel filler cap door and lock – removal and refitting

1   To remove the door, open it, undo the hinge-to-body screws and remove the door.
2   To remove the lock unit, prise free the retainer clip on the inside and withdraw the lock unit (photo).
3   Refitting of the lock and door is a reversal of removal.

21 Bumpers – removal and refitting

1   Bumper removal is dependent on model and market, but all types are mounted by means of support stay brackets to the main body. USA and Canada models have impact absorbing type bumper assemblies fitted to the front and rear.
2   The bumpers can be removed by unbolting them from the stay brackets or by unbolting the stay brackets from the bodyframe, and withdrawing the complete assembly.

23 Sunroof – checking and adjustment

1   To check the sunroof for satisfactory operation, start the engine and open the panel. It should take five seconds to fully open from the closed position and the same time to close from the fully opened

19.2 Boot lid hinge bolts – Coupe

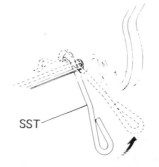

Fig. 11.15 Boot lid torsion bar removal (Sec 19)
SST Special tool

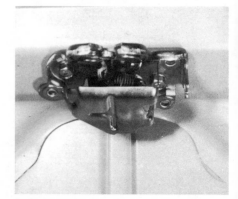

19.6 Boot lid lock unit – Coupe

20.1 Front grille retaining screw removal

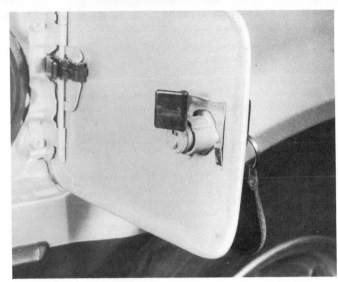

22.2 Fuel filler cap door showing lock retaining clip

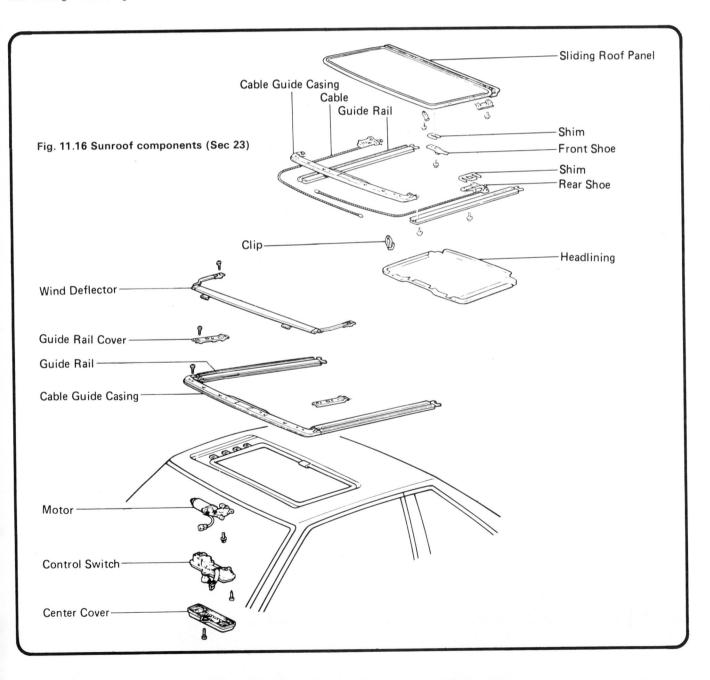

Fig. 11.16 Sunroof components (Sec 23)

Sliding Roof Panel

Cable Guide Casing
Cable
Guide Rail

Shim
Front Shoe
Shim
Rear Shoe

Clip

Headlining

Wind Deflector

Guide Rail Cover

Guide Rail

Cable Guide Casing

Motor

Control Switch

Center Cover

position. Any abnormal noises or binding when opening or closing the panel indicate a malfunction and it should be checked for correct adjustment.

2   Should the sunroof fail to operate, it can be manually operated by removing the control box cover, undoing the screw and then inserting the screwdriver through the screw hole and turning the drive shaft (Fig. 11.17).

3   To check that the sunroof alignment is correct when closed, check the level difference between the roof panel and the sliding panel. It should be as follows:

> *Front edge 0 ± 1.5 mm (0 ± 0.059 in)*
> *Rear edge 0 ± 2.0 mm (0 ± 0.079 in)*

If necessary adjustments can be made as follows.

4   Open the roof to its halfway position and carefully prise free the headlining from the roof sliding panel at its leading edge. When the retaining clips are free, slide the headlining rearwards. During each adjustment check, reconnect the headlining to the sliding panel prior to moving the panel (Fig. 11.18).

5   **Vertical adjustment (front and/or rear edge):** Loosen the retainer screws and add or subtract the shoe spacers as required. Retighten the screws and check the alignment. Further adjustment may be necessary. If the front edge is still too high even without any spacers fitted, ensure that the front shoes are contacting the stoppers (Fig. 11.19).

6   **Front to rear adjustment:** Loosen the retaining screws and move the front shoe each side as required, then tighten the screws. Check the alignment in the fully closed position and ensure that the front shoe contacts the stopper (Figs. 11.20 and 11.21).

7   **Left to right adjustment:** Loosen the rear shoe nuts then slide the roof panel forwards and rearwards. The panel will automatically adjust itself.

8   **Tilted roof adjustment (right to left front edge clearance);** If the difference is approximately 2 mm (0.08 in), detach the drive motor and move the operating cable one notch on the large clearance side. Refit the motor (Fig. 11.22).

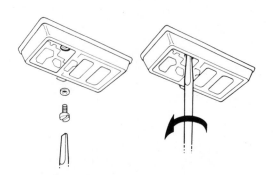

Fig. 11.17 Remove control box centre cover for access to manual operation of sunroof (Sec 23)

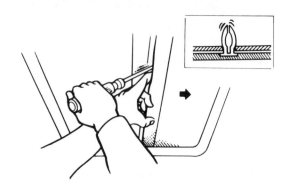

Fig. 11.18 Prise clips free and move sunroof headlining to rear for adjustment (Sec 23)

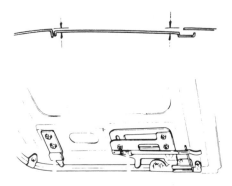

Fig. 11.19 Sunroof vertical alignment checks at front and rear edges (Sec 23)

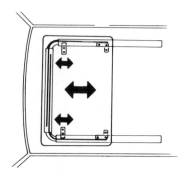

Fig. 11.20 Sunroof front to rear adjustment by moving shoes each side (Sec 23)

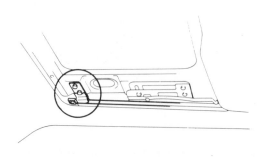

Fig. 11.21 Check that front shoe contacts stopper when roof is fully shut (Sec 23)

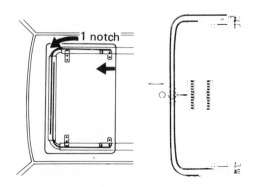

Fig. 11.22 Roof panel tilt adjustment for difference of about 2 mm (0.08 in) (Sec 23)

9 If the difference is approximately 1 mm (0.04 in), slacken off the rear shoe bolts and move the roof panel to correct the adjustment. Retighten the bolts.

24 Sunroof sliding panel – removal and refitting

1 To remove the sliding panel on its own, half open the panel then carefully prise free the panel headlining from the retaining clips along the front edge. Push the headlining rearwards.
2 Unscrew and remove the front and rear shoe nuts.
3 Carefully lift out the sliding panel (Fig. 11.23).
4 Refitting is a reversal of the removal procedure. On completion check the sunroof operation and adjustment, as described in Section 23.

25 Sunroof unit (complete) – removal and refitting

1 Disconnect the battery earth lead.
2 Remove the sunroof control switch and motor, as described in Chapter 12.
3 Undo the retaining screws and remove the wind deflector.

4 Undo the retaining screws and remove the guide rail cover each side.
5 To protect the body paintwork when removing the sunroof unit, stick some masking tape around the aperture edges.
6 Remove the sunroof unit by pulling it, together with the guide rail, upwards and forwards and withdraw it.
7 Refitting is a reversal of the removal procedure. Refer to Chapter 12 when refitting the sunroof motor. On completion, check the sunroof operation and adjustment, as described in Section 23 (Fig. 11.24).

26 Sunroof unit – dismantling and reassembly

1 With the sunroof unit removed, as described in the previous Section, dismantle it on a clean workbench. Take particular care not to damage the paintwork during dismantling and reassembly. Lay a protective padded cover on the bench.
2 Detach the headlining retaining clips on the front edge of the panel and pull the headlining rearwards to remove it.
3 Slacken the retaining screws and pull the guide rail rearwards to remove it (Fig. 11.25).
4 Pull the guide casing for the cable forwards and remove it.
5 Undo the retaining shoe screws, note the number of spacer shims (front and rear) then remove the front shoe, the drive cable with rear shoe, and the drive cables from the guide casing (Fig. 11.26).

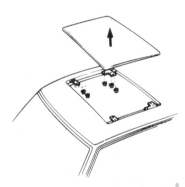

Fig. 11.23 Undo front and rear shoe nuts to lift panel clear (Sec 24)

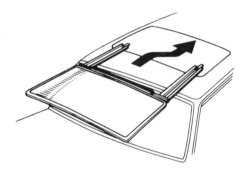

Fig. 11.24 Refit the sunroof unit (complete) with the guide rail (Sec 25)

Fig. 11.25 Guide rail removal (Sec 26)

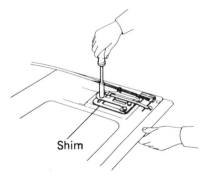

Shim

Fig. 11.26 Note spacer shims fitted when removing the retainer shoes (Sec 26)

6   Renew any excessively worn or damaged component.

7   Reassembly is a reversal of the dismantling procedure. Smear the drive cable with grease prior to fitting to the guide casing. Apply some protective tape to cover the cut section of the weatherstrip at the guide rail-to-case connection. Take care not to damage the headlining during reassembly (Fig. 11.27).

27 Windscreen, rear window and quarter windows

The removal and refitting of the windscreen, rear window and quarter windows on the models covered by this manual is a task best entrusted to a Toyota dealer. This is because of the specialised nature of the job. Special tools and techniques are required, together with a specific range of primers and sealants.

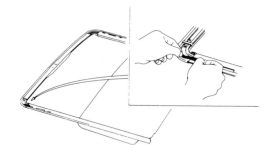

Fig. 11.27 Protect weatherstrip cut section with tape (Sec 26)

Chapter 12 Electrical system

Contents

Specifications

General

System type	12 volt, negative earth
Battery	12 volt, 60 amp hour

Alternator

Output current	55 or 60A	
Rotor coil resistance	2.8 to 3.0 ohm	
Brushes:	**Exposed length (standard)**	**Exposed length (limit)**
UK models	12.5 mm (0.492 in)	5.5 mm (0.217 in)
USA:		
1982/1983 models	16.5 mm (0.650 in)	5.5 mm (0.217 in)
1984 models	12.5 mm (0.492 in)	5.5 mm (0.217 in)
1985 models	10.5 mm (0.413 in)	4.5 mm (0.177 in)
Regulating voltage (at 20°C):		
UK models	14.0 to 14.7 V	
USA:		
1982/1983/1984 models	13.8 to 14.4 V	
1985 models	13.5 to 15.1 V	

Starter motor

Type:
UK models .... Direct drive or reduction gear type
USA models .... Reduction gear type
Rating and output power:
Direct drive type .... 12 volt, 0.8 kW or 1.0 kW
Reduction gear type .... 12 volt, 1.0 kW or 1.4 kW

Direct drive starter motor details:	**0.8 kW**	**1.0 kW**
No load characteristic at 11 volts	50 amp maximum at minimum of 5000 rpm	50 amp maximum at minimum of 5000 rpm
Armature shaft:		
Bearing-to-shaft clearance:		
Standard	0.035 to 0.077 mm (0.0014 to 0.0030 in)	0.035 to 0.077 mm (0.0014 to 0.0030 in)
Limit	0.2 mm (0.008 in)	0.2 mm (0.008 in)
Thrust clearance:		
Standard	0.05 to 1.0 mm (0.0020 to 0.0394 in)	0.05 to 1.0 mm (0.0020 to 0.0394 in)
Limit	1.0 mm (0.039 in)	1.0 mm (0.039 in)
Commutator outside diameter:		
Standard	28.0 mm (1.102 in)	32.7 mm (1.287 in)
Limit	27.0 mm (1.06 in)	31.0 mm (1.22 in)
Run-out:		
Standard (maximum)	0.1 mm (0.004 in)	0.1 mm (0.004 in)
Limit	0.3 mm (0.012 in)	0.3 mm (0.012 in)
Mica depth (standard)	0.04 to 0.08 mm (0.016 to 0.031 in)	0.04 to 0.08 mm (0.016 to 0.031 in)
Brush length:		
Standard	16.0 mm (0.63 in)	19.0 mm (0.75 in)
Limit	10.0 mm (0.39 in)	10.0 mm (0.39 in)
Pinion end-to-stop collar clearance	0.1 to 4.0 mm (0.004 to 0.157 in)	0.1 to 4.0 mm (0.004 to 0.157 in)
Moving stud length	34 mm (1.34 in)	34 mm (1.34 in)

Reduction drive starter motor details:	**1.0 kW**	**1.4 kW**
No load characteristic at 11.5 Volts	90 amp maximum at 3000 rpm minimum	90 amp maximum at 3500 rpm minimum
Brush length:		
Standard	13.5 mm (0.531 in)	14.5 mm (0.571 in)
Limit	10.0 mm (0.39 in)	10.0 mm (0.39 in)
Commutator:		
Outer diameter:		
Standard	30 mm (1.18 in)	
Limit	29 mm (1.14 in)	
Mica depth limit	0.2 mm (0.008 in)	
Run out limit:		
UK and 1982 USA models	0.2 mm (0.008 in)	
USA models (1983 on)	0.5 mm (0.0020 in)	

Fuses – UK models

Fuse holder	Rating	Protected circuits
1	7.5A	Reversing lights, brake system warning light, choke button reminder light, coolant temperature gauge, engine electrical system warning light, oil pressure warning light and gauge, handbrake reminder light, seat belt reminder light/buzzer, speed warning, tachometer, voltmeter
2	7.5A	Clock, courtesy lights, start up light, interior light, luggage compartment light, door open warning light, personal light, power antenna, step light
3	7.5A	Radio, stereo cassette tape player
4	15A	Cigarette lighter
5	7.5A	Turn signal lights
6	7.5A	Ignition main relay, discharge warning light, EFI main relay
7	10A	Air conditioner
8	7.5A	Carburettor choke heater, discharge warning light
9	15A	EFI control system
10	15A	Alternator (IG terminal), emission control system
11	20A	Headlight cleaner relay, rear window wiper/washer, windscreen wiper/washer
12	15A	Emergency (hazard) flashers, horns, retractable headlight system
13	15A	Stop (brake) lights
14	10A	Glove box light, inspection light, instrument panel lights, RH parking light, RH tail lights
15	10A	LH parking light, LH tail lights
16	15A	RH headlight (high beam)

Fuse holder	Rating		Protected circuits
17	15A	....	RH headlight (low beam)
18	15A	....	LH headlight (high beam)
19	15A	....	LH headlight (low beam)
20	15A	....	Glovebox light, inspection light, instrument panel lights, licence plate lights, parking lights, tail lights
21	15A	....	RH headlight
22	15A	....	LH headlight
Fuse locations:			
1 to 6		....	Driver's side kick panel
7		....	Passenger side kick panel
8 to 22		....	Engine compartment

Fuses – USA models

Fuse holder	Rating		Protected circuits
1	7.5A	....	Back-up lights, brake system warning light, engine temperature gauge, fuel gauge, heater main relay coil, low fuel level warning light, low oil pressure/gauge, parking brake reminder light, rear window defogger indicator light, tachometer, voltmeter, automatic transmission overdrive solenoid Additional (1984 and 1985 models): Engine electrical system warning light, seat belt reminder light and buzzer
2	7.5A	....	Interior light, key reminder buzzer, luggage compartment light, open door warning light, personal lights, illuminated start up light, door courtesy lights, automatic shoulder belt control system (where applicable) Additional (1984 and 1985 models): Clock, step light, power antenna
3	7.5A	....	Radio, stereo cassette tape player
4	15A	....	Cigarette lighter, clock (1982 and 1983 models), outer rear view mirror
5	15A	....	Cruise control system
6 ('82 to '84)	7.5A	....	Retractable headlight system
6 (1985)	7.5A	....	Turn signal lights
7 ('82 to '84)	7.5A	....	Turn signal lights and indicator lights
7 (1985)	7.5A	....	Discharge warning light, EFI main relay, ignition main relay
8 ('82 to '83)	7.5A	....	Discharge warning light, ignition main relay coil
8 (1984)	7.5A	....	Discharge warning light, EFI main relay, ignition main relay
8 (1985)	10A	....	Air conditioner
9 ('82 to '83)	7.5A	....	Discharge warning light relay
9 (1984)	10A	....	Air conditioner
9 (1985)	7.5A	....	Discharge warning light
10 ('82 to '83)	15A	....	Alternator (1G terminal), emission control system
10 (1984)	7.5A	....	Discharge warning light
10 (1985)	15A	....	EFI control system
11 ('82 to '83)	20A	....	Windscreen wipers/washer, rear window wiper/washer
11 (1984)	15A	....	EFI control system
11 (1985)	15A	....	Alternator (1G terminal), emission control system
12 ('82 to '83)	15A	....	Emergency (hazard) flashers and indicator light, horns, radio (with electronic tuner)
12 (1984)	15A	....	Alternator (IG terminal), emission control system
12 (1985)	20A	....	Windscreen wipers/washer, rear window wiper/washer
13 ('82 to '83)	15A	....	Stop (brake) lights
13 (1984)	20A	....	Windscreen wiper/washer, rear window wiper/washer
13 (1985)	15A	....	Emergency (hazard) flasher and indicator lights, horn, retractable headlights system
14 ('82 to '83)	15A	....	Automatic transmission shift indicator light, clock (digital), front side marker lights, glovebox light, instrument panel lights, licence plate lights, rear side marker lights, tail lights
14 (1984)	15A	....	Emergency (hazard) flasher lights, horn
14 (1985)	15A	....	Stop (brake) lights
15 ('82 to '83)	15A	....	High beam indicator light, RH headlight (high beam)
15 (1984)	15A	....	Stop (brake) lights
15 (1985)	15A	....	Front side marker lights, glovebox light, instrument panel lights, licence plate lights, rear side marker lights, tail lights
16 ('82 to '83)	15A	....	RH headlight (low beam)
16 (1984)	15A		Front side marker lights, glovebox lights, instrument panel lights, licence plate lights, parking lights, rear side marker lights, tail lights
16 (1985)	15A	....	RH headlight
17 ('82 to '83)	15A	....	LH headlight (high beam)
17 (1984)	15A	....	RH headlight
17 (1985)	15A	....	LH headlight
18 ('82 to '83)	15A	....	LH headlight (low beam)
18 (1984)	15A	....	LH headlight
19 ('82 to '84)	10A	....	Air conditioner main relay coil

Bulbs

	Wattage (UK)	Wattage (USA)
Parking lights	5	8
Front indicator lights	21	27
Front side marker lights	5	3.8 or 8
Rear indicator lights	21	27
Stop/tail lights	21/5	27/8
Back-up (reversing) lights	21	27
Rear fog lights	21	
Licence plate lights (on bumper)	5	7.5
Licence plate lights (on lower rear panel)	10	7.5
Interior light	10	10
Personal light(s)	10	10
Glovebox light	1.2	1.2 or 5
Door courtesy lights	5	5
Step light	1.4	1.4
Inspection light	7.5	
Luggage compartment light	5	5

Torque wrench settings

	kgf m	lbf ft
Alternator pulley nut	5 to 6	36 to 43
Starter motor lower bolt	6.5	47

1 General description

A 12 volt negative earth system is used on all models. The main components of the electrical system consist of a battery, an alternator with voltage regulator, and a pre-engaged starter motor.

The battery supplies a steady amount of current for the ignition, lighting, and other electrical circuits and provides a reserve of electricity when the current consumed by the electrical equipment exceeds that being produced by the alternator.

All electrical circuits are protected by fuses and the main power cable from the battery incorporates a fusible link.

USA models fitted with electronic fuel-injection have a Toyota computer control system. The details and special precautions regarding this are described in Chapter 3.

2 Routine maintenance – electrical system

1 **Alternator drivebelt:** Check the condition and tension of the alternator drivebelt at the specified intervals. If necessary renew/adjust it as described in Chapter 2, Section 7.
2 **Battery:** Check the battery, as described in Section 3, at the specified intervals.
3 **General checks:** Make a periodic inspection of the lights, horns, windscreen/back window wiper and warning devices for satisfactory operation. Check that the wiper blades are in good condition, top up the fluid level in the washer reservoir(s) and check the washer for satisfactory operation.
4 **On air conditioned models** check the compressor drivebelt for tension and condition. Renew/adjust if necessary as described in Chapter 2, Section 7. Check the air conditioning system hoses and connections for condition and security. Before working on any part of the air conditioning system note the precautions and general information given in Section 52.
5 Periodically check the electrical system wiring for condition and security. Renew or repair as necessary.

3 Battery – maintenance

1 Once a week, check the level of electrolyte in the battery cells and top up if necessary with distilled or purified water.
2 Various types of battery may be encountered but of the two most popular types, one has a translucent case where the electrolyte level should be maintained between the two marks on the casing (Fig. 12.1).
3 Where a non-translucent battery case is used, the electrolyte level should be maintained at the bottom of the filler tubes.
4 The acid in a battery does not evaporate, it is only the water which requires replenishment. Acid is used in the electrolyte when the battery

is first filled and charged and no acid should be needed throughout the life of the unit.
5 Periodically clean the top of the battery, check the tightness of the battery leads and apply petroleum jelly to the terminals to prevent corrosion (photo).
6 If corrosion is evident (white fluffy deposits) on the battery tray or clamp, the battery should be removed and the corrosion removed by wire brushing and by applying household ammonia. Paint the cleaned components with anti-corrosive paint.
7 To check the state of charge of the battery, use a hydrometer to draw up electrolyte from each of the cells in turn. The specific reading

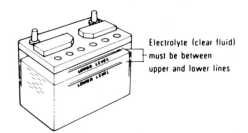

Electrolyte (clear fluid) must be between upper and lower lines

Fig. 12.1 Battery refill levels to be as shown (Sec 3)

3.5 Check the battery terminals and lead connections

on the hydrometer should be in accordance with the following at an ambient temperature 20°C (68°F).

Fully charged	1.260
Half charged	1.160
Discharged	1.060

8   Any variation in reading in excess of 0.025 between the cells will indicate an internal failure and battery renewal should be anticipated.

4   Battery charging

1   In winter time when heavy demand is placed upon the battery, such as when starting from cold, and much electrical equipment is continually in use, it is a good idea to have the battery fully charged occasionally from an external source at the rate of 3.5 or 4 amps.
2   Continue to charge the battery at this rate until no further rise in specific gravity is noted over a four hour period.
3   Alternatively, a trickle charger charging at the rate of 1.5 amps can be safely used overnight.
4   Specially rapid 'boost' charges which are claimed to restore the power of the battery in 1 to 2 hours are not recommended as they can cause serious damage to the battery plates.
5   Before charging the battery from an external source always disconnect the battery leads to prevent damage to the alternator.

5   Battery – removal and refitting

1   The battery is located at the front right or left-hand corner within the engine compartment.
2   Disconnect the leads from the battery terminals.
3   Unbolt the battery hold down clamp and lift the battery from the battery support tray.
4   Refitting is a reversal of removal. If any corrosive deposits have been noticed on the battery terminals and connectors, they must be cleaned using hot water or ammonia and then smeared with petroleum jelly before reconnection.

6   Alternator – general description, maintenance and precautions

1   The alternator generates three-phase alternating current which is rectified into direct current by three positive and three negative silicone diode rectifiers installed within the end frame of the alternator. The in-built characteristics of the unit obviate the need for a cut-out or current stabiliser.
2   A voltage regulator unit is incorporated in the charging circuit to control the exciting current and the current applied to the voltage coil.
3   Check the drivebelt tension at the intervals specified in Routine Maintenance and adjust, as described in Chapter 2, by loosening the mounting bolts. Pull the alternator body away from the engine block; do not use a lever as it will distort the alternator casing.
4   No lubrication is required as the bearings are grease sealed for life.
5   Take extreme care when making circuit connections to a vehicle fitted with an alternator and observe the following.

> When making connections to the alternator from a battery always match correct polarity
> Before using electric-arc welding equipment to repair any part of the vehicle, disconnect the connector from the alternator and disconnect the battery
> Never start the car with a battery charger connected
> Always disconnect the battery leads before using a mains charger
> If boosting from another battery, always connect in parallel using heavy cable

7   Alternator – testing in vehicle

1   In the event of failure of the normal performance of the alternator, carry out the following test procedure paying particular attention to the possibility of damaging the charging and electrical system unless the notes (a) to (c) are observed.

> *(a)   The alternator output B terminal must be connected to the battery at all times. When the ignition switch is operated, the F terminal is also at battery voltage.*
> *(b)   Never connect the battery leads incorrectly or the rectifiers and flasher unit will be damaged.*
> *(c)   Never run the engine at high revs with the alternator B terminal disconnected otherwise the voltage at the N terminal will rise abnormally and damage to the voltage relay will result*

2   Check the security of the alternator mountings, the terminal leads and the drivebelt tension (Chapter 2).
3   Check the ignition fuse, the charge fuse and the engine fuse and renew them if they are blown.
4   Check that all of the alternator and charge circuit wiring connectors are secure and that the wiring is in good condition (Fig. 12.2).

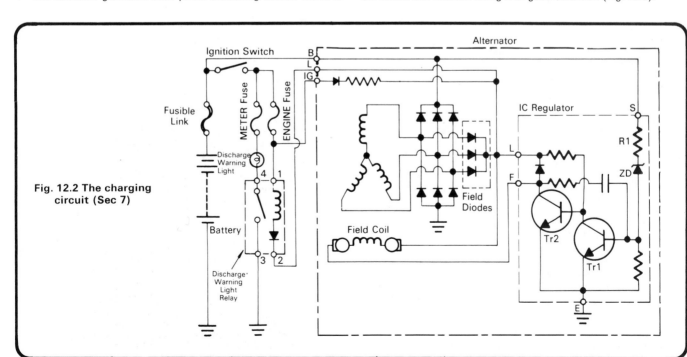

Fig. 12.2 The charging circuit (Sec 7)

5 If the alternator is making abnormal noises when the engine is running then an internal malfunction is indicated. It should be removed, as described in the following Section, and dismantled for inspection, as described in Section 9 or 10.

6 To check the charge circuit you will need a voltmeter and an ammeter. Connect them as follows, referring to Fig. 12.3.

7 Disconnect the terminal B wire from the alternator and connect it to the ammeter negative terminal. The ammeter positive lead is then connected to the terminal B on the alternator as is the positive voltmeter test lead. The negative lead of the voltmeter must be earthed. To test the circuits proceed as follows.

8 Run the engine at a speed of 2000 rpm and check the readings of the ammeter and voltmeter. Compare them with the following specified amperage readings according to type. Under 10 amps, between 13.8 and 14.4 volts (or 13.5 to 15.1 on 1985 USA models). If the reading is outside the specified range check the unit in the following way. Earth terminal F and then start the engine and check the terminal B voltage. A voltage reading above that specified necessitates renewal of the IC regulator whilst a lower reading indicates an alternator fault.

9 The charge circuits should also be checked under load conditions. Start the engine and run it at 2000 rpm, then turn on the headlight main beams and the heater fan to the HI position. The minimum ammeter reading should be 30 amps although if the battery is in a fully charged state, it may cause the reading to drop below the specified minimum figure. The test should therefore be rechecked with the battery in a semi-charged state. A lower reading than specified indicates a malfunction of the alternator.

10 If the above checks prove that the alternator is operating in a satisfactory manner, have the discharge warning light and relay circuit checked by your Toyota dealer as this is most probably at fault.

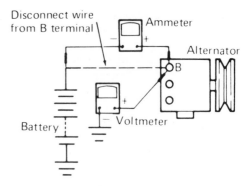

Fig. 12.3 Alternator check – connect voltmeter and ammeter as shown (Sec 7)

8 Alternator – removal and refitting

1 Disconnect the battery earth lead from the negative terminal.

2 Detach the wiring connector from the rear of the alternator (photo).

3 Undo the retaining nut and remove the wire from the stud on the rear of the alternator.

4 Unscrew and remove the pivot and adjustment bolts, disengage the drivebelt from the alternator pulley and withdraw the alternator.

5 Refitting is a reversal of the removal procedure. Semi-tighten the mounting and adjustment bolts, then adjust the drivebelt tension, as described in Chapter 2 (Section 7).

9 Alternator (UK models, and USA models up to 1984) – dismantling, servicing and reassembly

1 Undo the three through-bolts securing the two end frames together and withdraw the bolts. Insert a screwdriver in the notches in the drive end frame and carefully prise the drive end frame from the stator. Do not prise on the coil wires (Fig. 12.5).

2 Secure the rotor in a vice with soft jaws to prevent it turning then unscrew the pulley nut and remove it, together with the spring washer, spacer collar, pulley, fan and second spacer collar.

3 Withdraw the drive end frame from the rotor (Fig. 12.6).

4 Unscrew and remove the four nuts and the terminal insulators securing the rear end frame to the stator and rectifier holder.

5 Remove the noise suppression condenser and withdraw the rear end frame from the stator.

6 Withdraw the insulator from the rectifier holder studs and the rubber cushion from the brush holder.

7 Detach the stator leads from the rectifier holder by holding the rectifier terminal with a pair of long-nosed pliers whilst the leads are unsoldered. Take care to protect the rectifier from heat damage (Fig. 12.7).

8 Unsolder the IC leads of the regulator from the rectifier in a similar manner.

9 Test the rotor coil for an open circuit by connecting a circuit tester between the two slip rings located at the rear of the rotor. The indicated resistance should be: 2.8 to 3.0 ohm (Fig. 12.8).

10 Test the rotor for earthing by connecting a circuit tester between

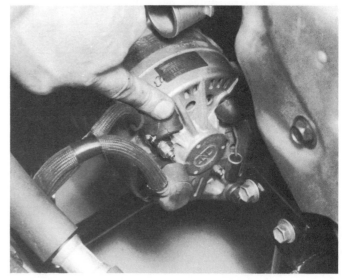

8.2 Rear face of alternator showing the wiring connections

the slip ring and rotor. If continuity exists the rotor must be renewed (Fig. 12.9).

11 Inspect the slip ring surfaces for signs of excessive wear, roughness or scoring and if defective renew the rotor.

12 Check the stator for open circuits by connecting an ohmmeter between the three wire connection point and the other leads (wires soldered). Renew the stator if there is no continuity (Fig. 12.10).

13 Check that there is no continuity between the stator core and the coil leads, again renew the stator if defective.

14 If more that one of the preceding tests proves negative then it will be economically sound to exchange the alternator complete for a factory reconditioned unit rather than renew more than one individual component.

15 Examine the brushes for wear. If worn down to or beyond the specified limit then they must be renewed. The old brushes will have to be unsoldered for removal. With the old brushes removed, insert the new brush wires through their springs, slide the brushes down into their holders and resolder the wire to the brush holder. Check that the brush exposed length is as specified as each one is fitted. Also check that the brushes can slide smoothly in their holders. Cut off any excess wire (Figs. 12.11, 12.12 and 12.13).

16 Finally check the front and rear bearings for excessive wear and renew if necessary. The rear bearing will have to be withdrawn from the

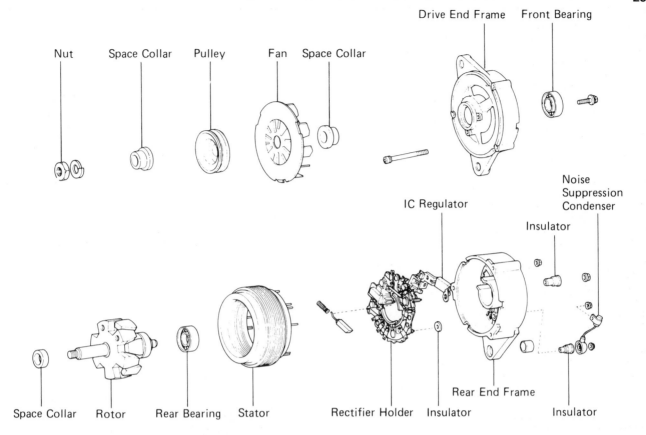

Fig. 12.4 Exploded view of the alternator as fitted to all UK models and USA models up to 1984 (Sec 9)

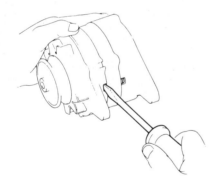

Fig. 12.5 Carefully prise free the drive end frame (Sec 9)

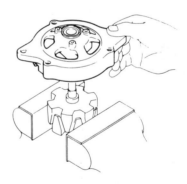

Fig. 12.6 Drive end frame removal from rotor (Sec 9)

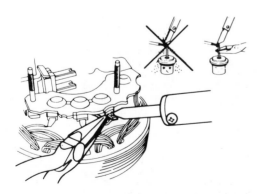

Fig. 12.7 Detach the stator leads from the rectifier holder (Sec 9)

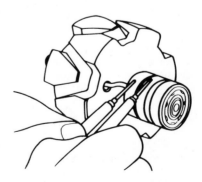

Fig.12.8 Checking the rotor coil for open circuits (Sec 9)

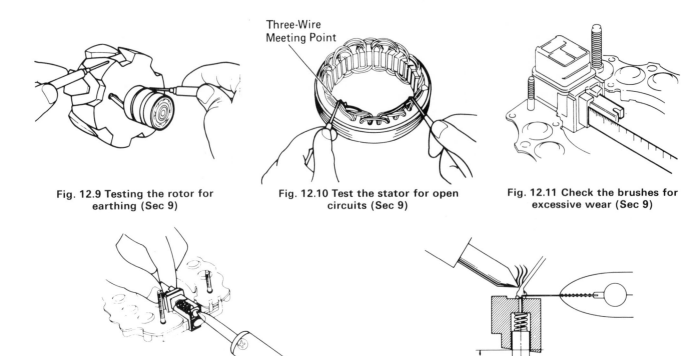

Fig. 12.9 Testing the rotor for earthing (Sec 9)

Three-Wire Meeting Point

Fig. 12.10 Test the stator for open circuits (Sec 9)

Fig. 12.11 Check the brushes for excessive wear (Sec 9)

Fig. 12.12 Unsolder the old brush and spring (Sec 9)

12.5 mm

Fig. 12.13 Solder the new brush wire to the holder to give the specified exposed brush length (Sec 9)

rotor shaft using a suitable puller. Press or drift the new bearing into position on the rotor shaft. Refit the front bearing and tighten the retainer screws.

17 Reassembly of the alternator is basically a reversal of the dismantling procedure, but the following special points should be noted.

18 When the rear end frame and the rectifier holder are reassembled, check that the wires are clear of the casing.

19 When refitting the rear end cover to the frame, fit two insulating washers onto the positive side stud followed by the condenser and retaining nut. The condenser lead then connects to the alternator B terminal (photo).

20 When fitting the fan pulley assembly the thinner spacer collar fits onto the rotor shaft first. The thicker spacer collar is fitted to the front side of the pulley on the shaft. Tighten the retaining nut to the specified torque setting (photo).

21 When assembling the drive end frame to the rectifier end frame, the rectifier lead wires must clear the rotor and may need to be bent back to achieve this. The brushes must be pushed back into their holders and held in this position temporarily by inserting a stiff wire through the access aperture in the frame (Fig. 12.14). When the drive end and rectifier end frames are assembled together, refit the three through-bolts and then withdraw the temporary brush retaining wire (Fig. 12.15).

22 On reassembly check that the rotor turns smoothly and then seal off the brush access hole to complete.

9.19 Alternator rear face showing the condenser and lead location

9.20 Tighten the alternator pulley nut to the specified torque

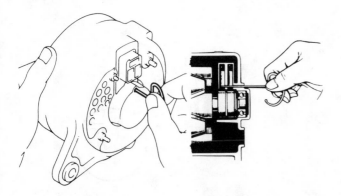

Fig. 12.14 Insert wire as shown to support brushes when assembling the end frames (Sec 9)

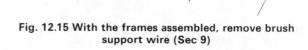

Fig. 12.15 With the frames assembled, remove brush support wire (Sec 9)

10 Alternator (1985 USA models) – dismantling, servicing and reassembly

1 Complete dismantling, testing and overhaul of this alternator is not recommended to the home mechanic. Special tools are required to remove the pulley nut, pulley and rear end frame in order to separate the rotor from the drive end frame. In view of this, apart from removing and inspecting the brushes, any more detailed dismantling, inspection and overhaul procedures must be entrusted to a Toyota dealer.

2 Undo the nut and remove the terminal insulator from the rear end cover, then undo the three retaining nuts and remove the end cover.

3 Undo the two securing screws and withdraw the brush holder and its cover.

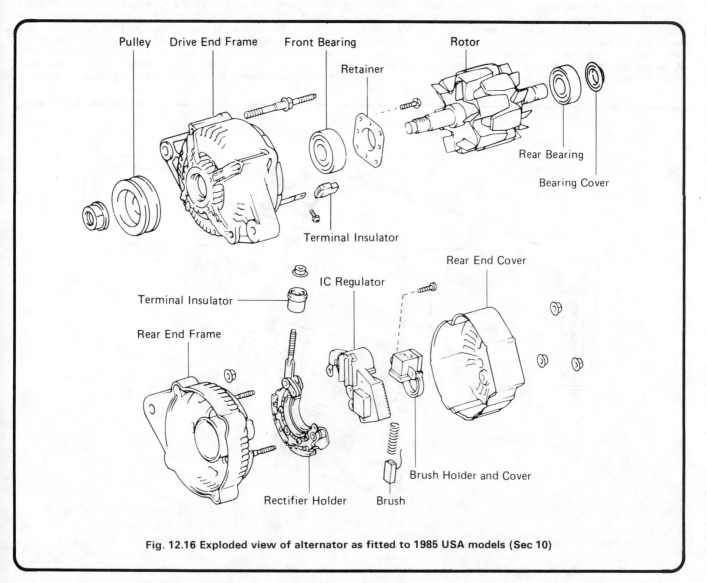

Fig. 12.16 Exploded view of alternator as fitted to 1985 USA models (Sec 10)

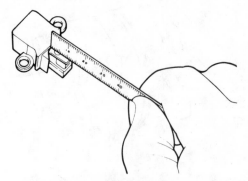

**Fig. 12.17 Check the brush lengths for excessive wear –
1985 USA models (Sec 10)**

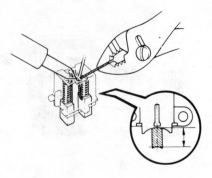

**Fig. 12.18 Solder new brush wire to give brush exposed
length of 10.5 mm (0.413 in) – 1985 USA models (Sec 10)**

4   If required, the IC regulator can also be removed by undoing the three retaining screws.
5   Check the exposed length of the brushes from the holder. If they have worn beyond the minimum limit specified they must be renewed (Fig. 12.17).
6   To renew the brushes, unsolder and detach the brush and spring.
7   Fit the new brush wire through the spring, insert the brush holder and solder the wire to the holder so that the exposed brush length from the holder is the length specified. On completion check that the brush slides freely in its holder and then cut off any excess wire (Fig. 12.18).
8   Reassembly of the brushes and, if applicable, the IC regulator is a reversal of the removal procedure.

11 Starter motor – general description

The starter operates on the principle of pre-engagement which, through the medium of a solenoid switch, meshes the starter drivegear with the ring gear on the flywheel (or torque converter – automatic transmission) fractionally in advance of the closure of the main starter motor contacts. This slight delay in energising the starter motor does much to extend the life of the starter drive and ring gear components. As soon as the engine fires and its speed or rotation exceeds that of the armature shaft of the starter motor, a built-in clutch mechanism prevents excessive rotation of the shaft and the release of the starter

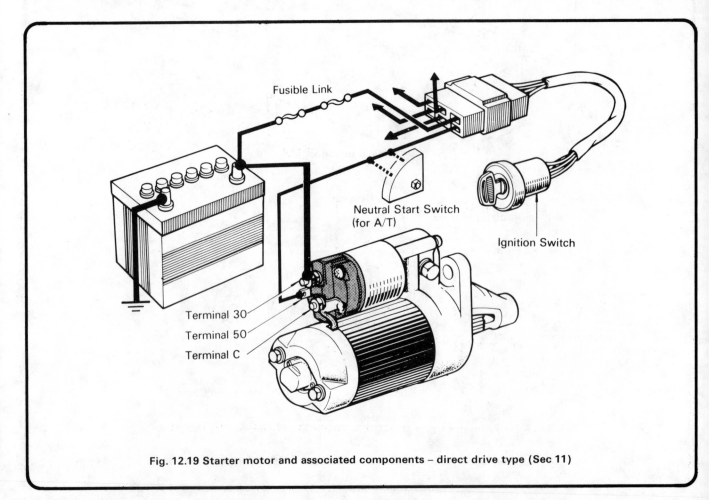

Fig. 12.19 Starter motor and associated components – direct drive type (Sec 11)

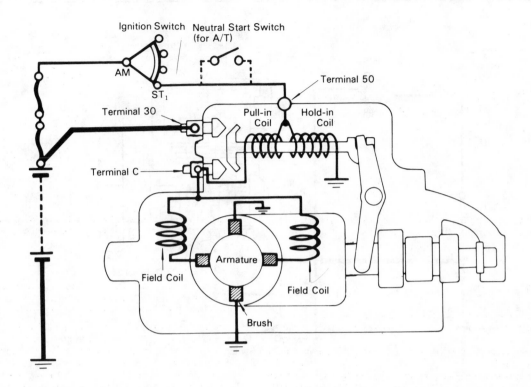

Fig. 12.20 Starter system wiring diagram – direct drive type (Sec 11)

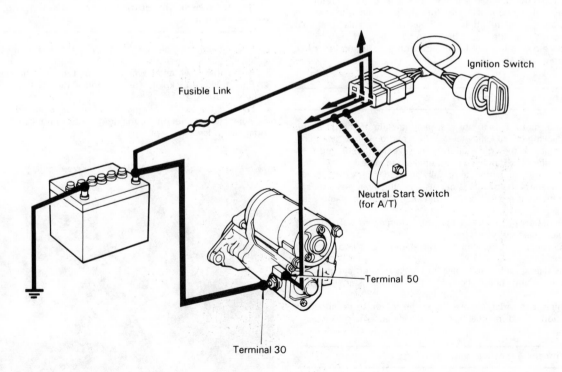

Fig. 12.21 Starter motor and associated components – reduction gear type (Sec 11)

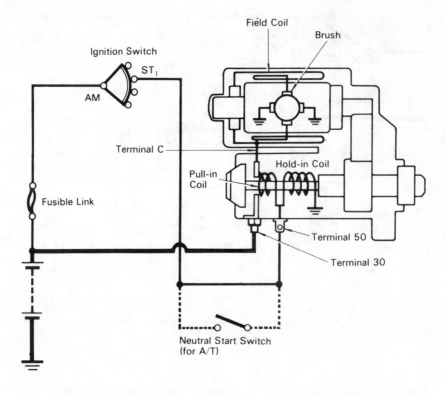

Fig. 12.22 Starter system wiring diagram – reduction gear type (Sec 11)

switch key causes the solenoid and drive engagement fork to return to their de-energised positions. The armature shaft is fitted with rear and central rotational speed retarding mechanisms to stop its rotational movement rapidly after the starter has been de-energised.

The starter motor fitted will be of reduction gear (direct drive) or non reduction gear design.

12 Starter motor – testing in vehicle

1 If the starter motor fails to operate, test the state of charge of the battery by checking the specific gravity with a hydrometer or switching on the headlamps. If they glow brightly for several seconds and then gradually dim, then the battery is in an uncharged state.
2 If the test proves the battery to be fully charged, check the security of the battery leads at the battery terminals, scraping away any deposits which are preventing a good contact between the cable clamps and the terminal posts.
3 Check the battery negative lead at its body frame terminal, scraping the mating faces clean if necessary.
4 Check the security of the cables at the starter motor and solenoid switch terminals.
5 Check the wiring with a voltmeter for breaks or short circuits.
6 Check the wiring connections at the ignition/starter switch terminals.
7 If everything is in order, remove the starter motor, as described in the next Section, and dismantle, test and service according to type.

13 Starter motor – removal and refitting

1 Disconnect the lead from the battery negative terminal.
2 Disconnect the cables from the starter solenoid terminals.
3 Unscrew and remove the starter motor securing bolts and withdraw the unit from the clutch bellhousing (or torque converter housing – automatic transmission) (photos).
4 Refitting is a reversal of removal.

14 Starter motor (direct drive type) – dismantling, overhaul and reassembly

1 Disconnect the field coil wire from the starter motor solenoid terminal.
2 Remove the two end cover screws and remove the cover (photo).
3 Prise free the lockplate (photo) and withdraw the washer, spring and seal (photos).
4 Remove the two securing screws from the solenoid and withdraw the solenoid far enough to enable it to be unhooked from the drive engagement lever fork (photo).

13.3A Undo the retaining bolts ...

13.3B ... and withdraw the starter motor

14.2 Direct drive starter motor dismantling: Remove the end cover screws (arrowed) and cover ...

14.3A ... remove the lockplate ...

14.3B ... washer and spring ...

14.3C ... and the seal

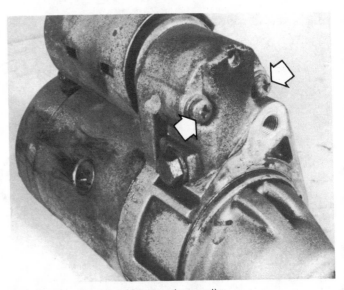

14.4 Remove the solenoid screws (arrowed)

14.5 Unscrew and withdraw the through-bolts

5   Unscrew and remove the two through-bolts and withdraw the commutator end frame (photo).
6   Pull out the brushes from their holders and remove the brush holder assembly.
7   Pull the yoke from the drive end frame.
8   Remove the engagement lever pivot bolt from the drive end frame and detach the rubber buffer and its backing plate. Remove the armature, complete with drive engagement lever, from the drive end frame.
9   With a piece of tubing, drive the pinion stop collar up the armature shaft far enough to enable the circlip to be removed and then pull the stop collar from the shaft, together with the pinion and clutch assembly.
10 Clean the respective components and lay them out for inspection.
11 The armature shaft bearings must be checked for wear. The shaft-to-bearing clearance must not exceed the specified limit.
12 Normally the bearings will require renewal by pressing out the old ones from the end frames and pressing in the new, but before doing this check that the armature shaft rotates smoothly. If it is worn, then a new armature will be required and it will be more economical to exchange the starter complete for a reconditioned unit.
13 Armature shaft bearings are available in standard sizes and undersizes where it is decided to have the original shaft turned down as the method of renovation.
14 Check the armature shaft for bend or ovality and renew if evident.
15 Check the commutator segments and undercut the mica insulators if necessary, using a hacksaw blade ground to correct thickness. If the commutator is burned or discoloured, clean it with a piece of fine glass paper (not emery or carborundum) and finally wipe it with a solvent moistened cloth (Fig. 12.23).
16 To test the armature is not difficult, but a voltmeter or bulb and 12 volt battery are required. The two tests determine whether there may be a break in any circuit winding or if any wiring insulation is broken down. The illustration (Fig. 12.24) shows how the battery, voltmeter and probe connectors are used to test whether (a) any wire in the windings is broken or (b) whether there is an insulation breakdown. In the first test the probes are placed on adjacent segments of clean commutator. All voltmeter readings should be similar. If a bulb is used instead it will glow very dimly or not at all if there is a fault. For the second test any reading or bulb lighting indicates a fault. Test each segment in turn with one probe and keep the other on the shaft. Should either test indicate a faulty armature the wisest action in the long run is to obtain a new starter. The field coils may be tested if an ohmmeter or ammeter can be obtained. With an ohmmeter, the resistance (measured between the terminal and the yoke) should be 6 ohm. With an ammeter, connect it in series with a 12 volt battery again

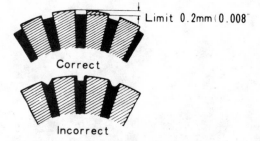

Fig. 12.23 Mica segment undercutting diagram – starter motor commutator (Sec 14)

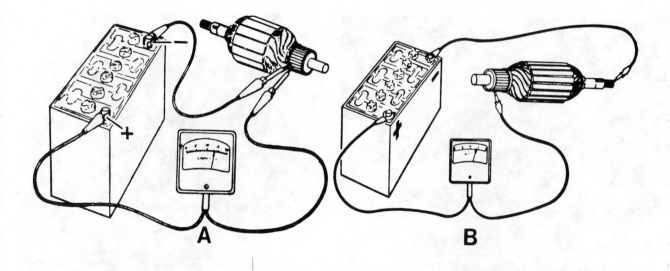

Fig. 12.24 Testing the starter motor armature (A) for open circuit and (B) for breakdown of wiring insulation (Sec 14)

from the field terminal to the yoke. A reading of 12 amps is normal. Zero amps or infinity ohm indicate an open circuit. More that 2 amps or less than 6 ohm indicates a breakdown of the insulation. If a fault in the field coils is diagnosed then a reconditioned starter should be obtained as the coils can only be removed and refitted with special equipment.

17 Check the insulation of the brush holders and the length of the brushes (photo). If these have worn to below the specified limit, renew them. Before fitting them to their holders, dress them to the correct contour by wrapping a piece of emery cloth round the commutator and rotating the commutator back and forth (Fig. 12.25).

18 Check the starter clutch assembly for wear or sticky action, or chipped pinion teeth and renew the assembly if necessary.

19 Check the centre bearing for excessive wear or damage and renew if necessary.

20 Check the solenoid (magnetic switch) by pushing the plunger as shown. When released the plunger should instantly return to its original position (Fig. 12.26).

21 Commence reassembly by refitting the centre bearing, clutch unit and new pinion stop collar and snap ring. With the snap ring engaged in its groove use a drift and tap the stop collar into position over the snap ring.

22 Locate the drive engagement lever to the armature shaft as shown in Fig. 12.27 or 12.28 (as applicable), with the spring towards the armature and the steel washer up against the clutch.

14.17 Check the brushes for wear

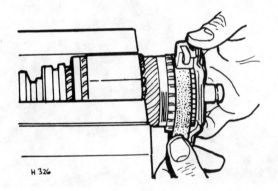

Fig. 12.25 Dressing the starter motor brushes to the correct shape (Sec 14)

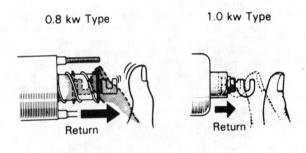

0.8 kw Type   1.0 kw Type

Return   Return

Fig. 12.26 Check the solenoid plunger returns after compression (Sec 14)

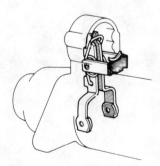

Fig. 12.27 Drive lever installation – 0.8 kW starter motor (Sec 14)

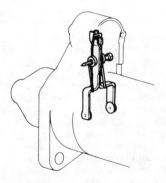

Fig. 12.28 Drive lever installation – 1.0 kW starter motor (Sec 14)

14.23 Refit the armature into the drive end frame

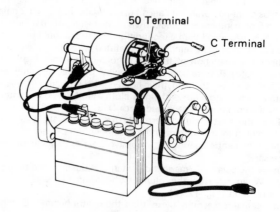
Fig. 12.29 Connect the starter motor as shown for testing (Sec 14)

23 Apply grease to all sliding surfaces and locate the armature assembly in the drive end frame. Insert the drive engagement lever pivot pin, well greased (photo).
24 Fit the rubber buffer aligning the yoke notch with the rubber plate tab. Then align and offer into position the yoke to the drive end frame.
25 Fit the brush holder to the armature and then insert the brushes.
26 Grease the commutator end frame bearing and then fit the end frame into position. Insert and tighten the two through-bolts.
27 Fit the washer, spring and lockplate and then measure the thrust clearance of the armature. If it exceeds the specified amount, an additional thrust washer must be fitted. Half pack the end cover with a multi-purpose grease and refit it securing with the two screws.
28 Install the solenoid switch making sure that its hook engages under the spring of the engagement lever fork.
29 Set up a test circuit similar to the one shown (Fig. 12.29).
30 To check the pinion clearance, move the pinion towards the armature to take up any slack and measure the pinion end-to-stop collar clearance (photo). If the clearance is not as specified, remove the solenoid switch and adjust the length of the switch mounting surface to stud end. Loosen the locknut and screw the stud in (to reduce the clearance) or out (to enlarge the clearance). Retighten the locknut.

14.30 Measure the pinion end-to-stop collar clearance

15 Starter motor (reduction type) – dismantling, overhaul and reassembly

1 One of two types of reduction starter motor may be fitted, the main components of each being shown in Figs. 12.30 and 12.31. The two types are similar in design, but where differences occur they will be mentioned in the following operations.
2 Disconnect the main lead wire at the solenoid switch (photo).
3 On the 1.4 kW type, unscrew the through-bolts and separate the starter housing complete with the reduction gears and clutch.
4 On the 1.0 kW type, unscrew the through-bolts and separate the starter housing, complete with idler gear and clutch.
5 Withdraw the felt seal from the bearing and, on the 1.4 kW type, remove the O-ring from the clutch holder periphery.
6 Unscrew and remove the setscrew and separate the housing from the clutch/reduction gear(s) assembly. Collect the ball and return spring, the ball being located in the clutch shaft bore.
7 Hook back the brush springs and extract the brushes from their respective holders (Figs. 12.32 and 12.33). On the 1.0 kW type you will have to remove the end cover for access to the brushes.
8 The armature can now be removed from the field frame.
9 Clean the components and lay them out for inspection.

15.2 Detach the solenoid switch lead (reduction starter motor)

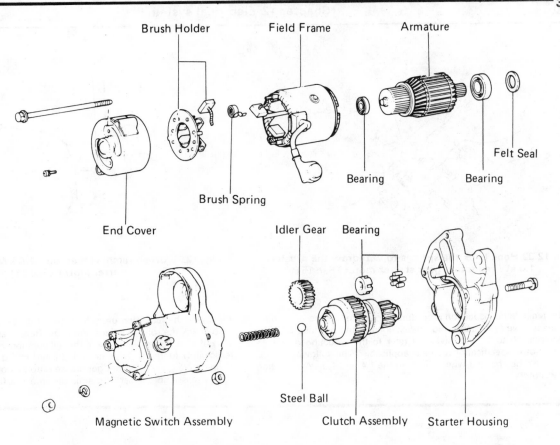

Fig. 12.30 Starter motor components – 1.4 kW reduction type (Sec 15)

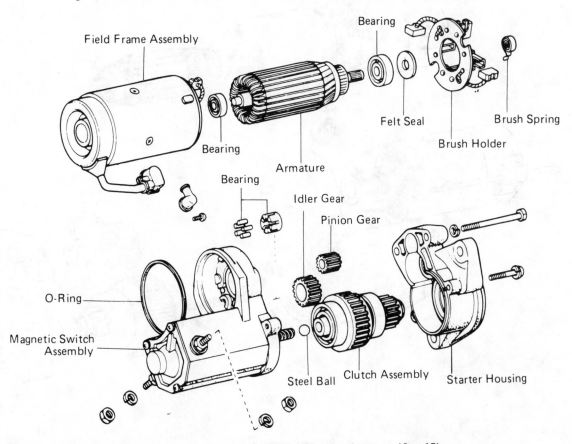

Fig. 12.31 Starter motor components – 1.0 kW reduction type (Sec 15)

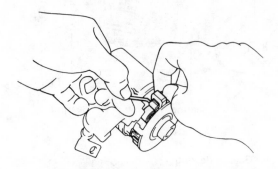

Fig. 12.32 Hook back the springs to withdraw the brushes – 1.0 kW reduction gear starter motor (Sec 15)

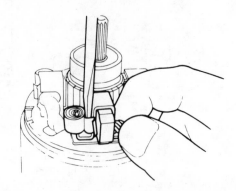

Fig. 12.33 Brush removal method – 1.4 kW reduction gear starter motor (Sec 15)

10 In general, the inspection procedures closely follow those given for the direct drive type starter motor described in the previous Section, paragraphs 10 to 17 inclusive, but refer to the reduction gear type starter motor specifications where applicable. The following items should also be checked when checking the 1.4 and 1.0 kW reduction starter motors.

11 Check the reduction gears for signs of excessive wear or damage. Also check the roller bearings and cage. Renew as necessary.
12 Before reassembling, ensure that all components are clean. During reassembly lubricate those items indicated in Fig. 12.34 with a high temperature grease. Do not get grease onto any other components.
13 To reassemble, insert the armature into the field frame and then

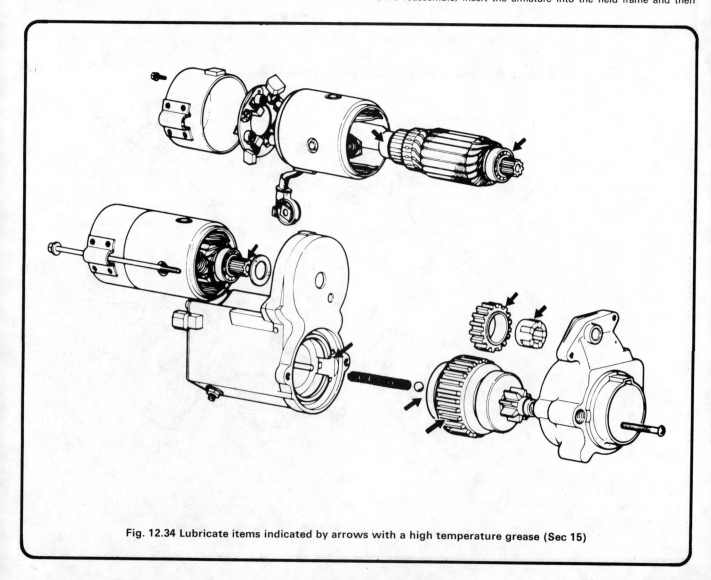

Fig. 12.34 Lubricate items indicated by arrows with a high temperature grease (Sec 15)

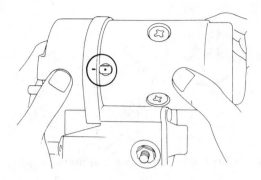

Fig. 12.35 Align bolt anchors with mark on housing – 1.4 kW type (Sec 15)

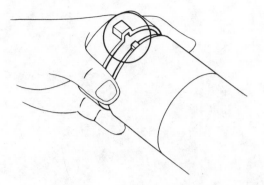

Fig. 12.36 Align yoke core and housing notches – 1.0 kW type (Sec 15)

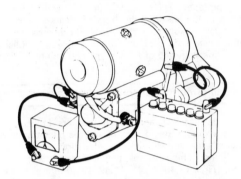

Fig. 12.37 Starter motor test connections (Sec 15)

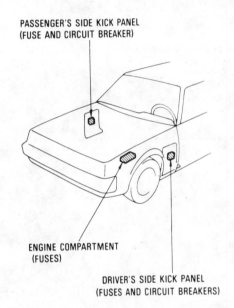

Fig. 12.38 Locations for the fuses, relays and circuit breakers – LHD (Sec 16)

locate the brush holder so that its tab aligns with the field frame notch. Hook back the brush springs and slide the brushes into their holders, then check that the positive leads are not earthed.

14 On the 1.4 kW type, locate a new O-ring over the brush holder, then refit the end cover.

15 Relocate the field washer, smeared with grease, against the bearing on the armature shaft.

16 Refit the armature/field frame unit to the solenoid switch housing assembly. On the 1.4 kW type, assemble so that the bolt anchors align with the mark on the solenoid switch housing as shown (Fig. 12.35). On the 1.0 kW type, align the yoke core and housing notches (Fig. 12.36).

17 Lubricate the ball-bearing with grease and insert it into the clutch shaft bore followed by the spring, then reassemble the idler gear/reduction gear unit.

18 Reconnect the solenoid switch wire.

19 Before refitting to the car you will find it beneficial to test the motor for satisfactory operation. To do this mount it securely in a vice and connect it up to a battery and ammeter, as shown in Fig. 12.37. The starter should rotate smoothly, the pinion disengage, and a maximum of 9.0 amps be drawn at 11.5 volts.

16 Fuses and fusible link

1 The main fuse block is located in the engine compartment, with further fuses being located in the driver's side and passenger side kick panels (Fig. 12.38 and photos). The fuse ratings and circuits vary according to model, but the fuse block for each is marked on the cover.

16.1A Main fuse block in the engine compartment (UK model)

16.1B Driver's side fuse block

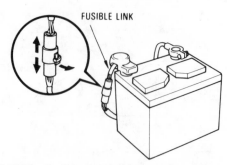

Fig. 12.39 The fusible link location at the battery (Sec 16)

2 A fuse 'pull out' removal tool is located on the inner face of the fusebox lid.

3 In the event of a fuse blowing, always find the reason and rectify the trouble before fitting the new one. Always renew a fuse with one of the same amperage rating as the original. For this reason it is a good idea to carry a spare set of fuses in the car at all times. A spare 7.5 or 10.5 amp fuse is supplied as standard with all models.

4 A double protection is provided for the electrical harness by fusible links installed in the lead running from the battery positive terminal (Fig. 12.39). The fusible links must never be bypassed and, should either melt, the cause of the circuit overload must be established before renewing the link with one of similar type and rating.

17 Relays and circuit breakers

1 The number of relays and circuit breakers fitted to individual vehicles depends upon the equipment and the operating territory.

2 Examples of relay and circuit breaker locations are shown and they may be positioned under the instrument panel or within the engine compartment (Figs. 12.40, 12.41, 12.42, 12.43 and photos).

3 In the event of failure of an electrical component, first check the fuse and then the bulb (where applicable).

4 Check the security of all connecting wires and terminals.

5 If a circuit breaker is suspect it can be checked easily. First check that the ignition is switched off then insert a needle or pin carefully into the hole in the front face of the circuit breaker until a click is heard. The component concerned should now operate. If the component does not operate or the circuit breaker switches off again, turn the component switch off and have the circuit concerned checked out by a Toyota dealer.

6 Relays and circuit breakers cannot be repaired and if faulty they must be renewed as a unit.

17.2A Defogger relay (shown with instrument panel removed)

17.2B Other relays and circuit breakers are located on the underside of the instrument and dash panels (UK model shown)

17.2C Passenger side panel relays and circuit breakers (UK model shown)

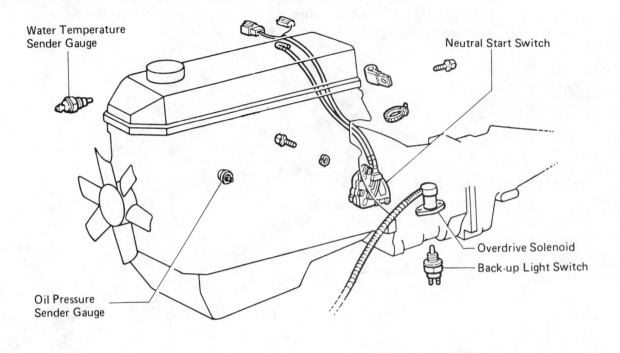

Water Temperature Sender Gauge

Neutral Start Switch

Overdrive Solenoid

Back-up Light Switch

Oil Pressure Sender Gauge

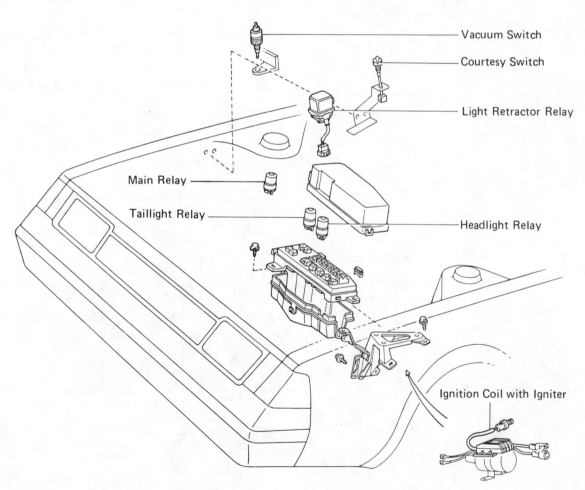

Vacuum Switch

Courtesy Switch

Light Retractor Relay

Main Relay

Taillight Relay

Headlight Relay

Ignition Coil with Igniter

Fig. 12.40 Location points for the switches and relays in the engine compartment (Sec 17)

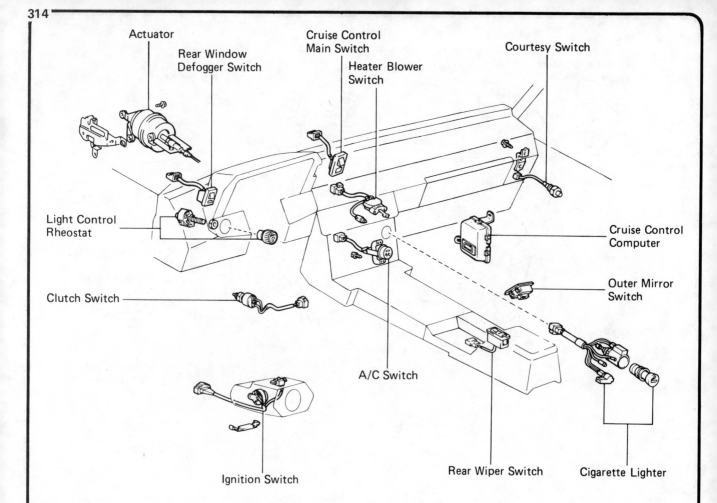

Actuator

Rear Window
Defogger Switch

Cruise Control
Main Switch

Heater Blower
Switch

Courtesy Switch

Light Control
Rheostat

Cruise Control
Computer

Clutch Switch

Outer Mirror
Switch

A/C Switch

Rear Wiper Switch

Cigarette Lighter

Ignition Switch

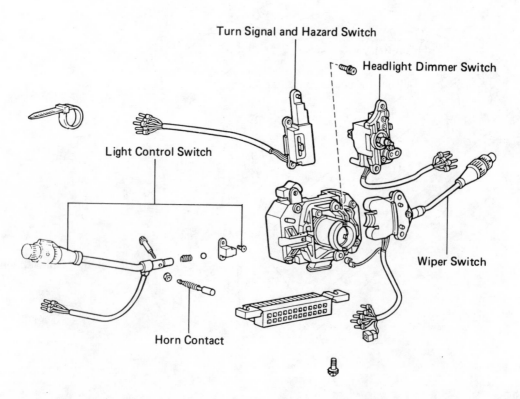

Turn Signal and Hazard Switch

Headlight Dimmer Switch

Light Control Switch

Wiper Switch

Horn Contact

Fig. 12.41 Switches and relay locations on the instrument panel and steering column (Sec 17)

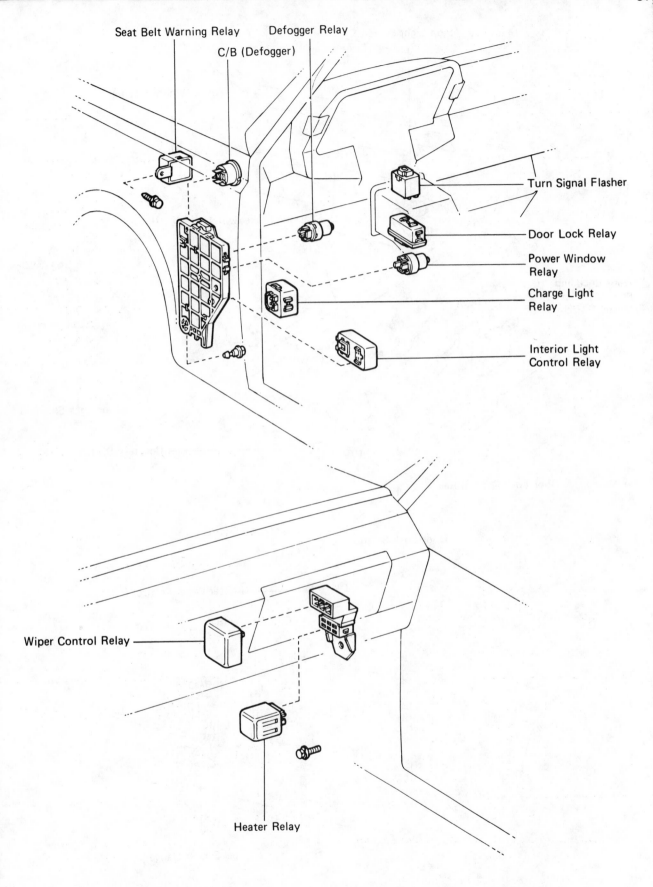

Seat Belt Warning Relay

C/B (Defogger)

Defogger Relay

Turn Signal Flasher

Door Lock Relay

Power Window Relay

Charge Light Relay

Interior Light Control Relay

Wiper Control Relay

Heater Relay

Fig. 12.42 Switches and relay locations in the passenger compartment (Sec 17)

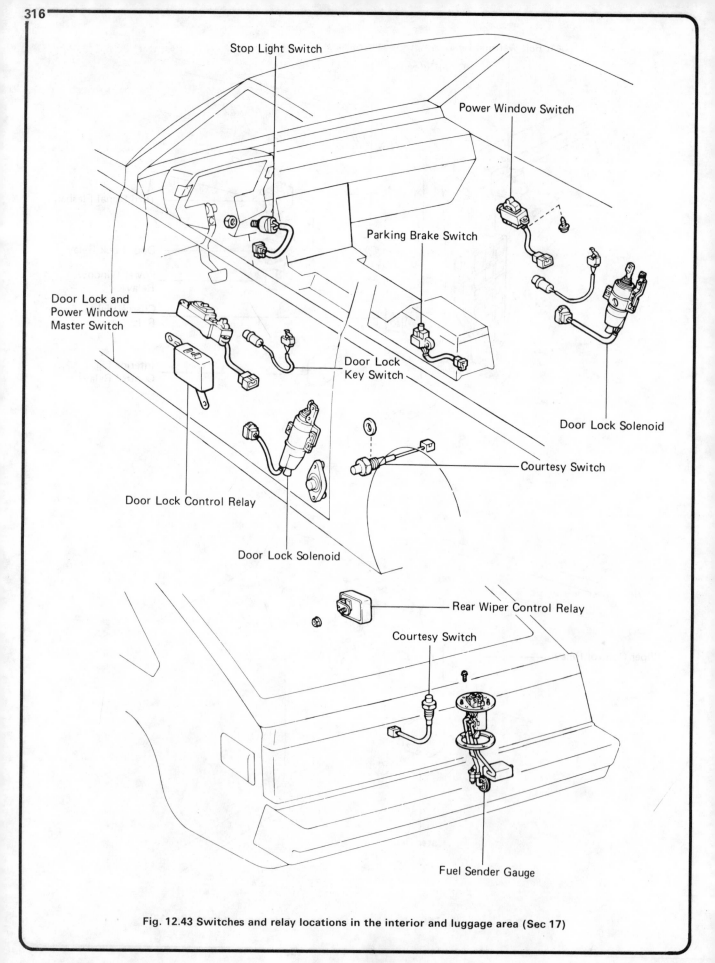

Stop Light Switch

Power Window Switch

Parking Brake Switch

Door Lock and
Power Window
Master Switch

Door Lock
Key Switch

Door Lock Solenoid

Door Lock Control Relay

Courtesy Switch

Door Lock Solenoid

Rear Wiper Control Relay

Courtesy Switch

Fuel Sender Gauge

Fig. 12.43 Switches and relay locations in the interior and luggage area (Sec 17)

18.2 Headlight unit surround screws (arrowed)

18.3 Headlight unit retaining screws

18 Headlight sealed beam unit – renewal

1 Raise the headlight units, but do not switch any lights on, then disconnect the fusible link (see Section 16), leaving the headlights raised. The fusible link is disconnected to avoid the possibility of the headlights suddenly retracting which could cause injury.
2 Undo the four headlight surround screws (two each side) and remove the surround (photo).
3 Undo the four headlight retaining frame securing screws and remove the frame (photo). Withdraw the headlight unit and detach the wiring connector. The connector may be tight, in which case hold the lock release and wriggle the connector free. Do not loosen the headlight beam adjuster screws.
4 Refit in the reverse order to removal. If renewing the unit, ensure that the correct type is fitted (regular or halogen) and check that the unit is correctly orientated (Fig. 12.44).
5 On completion, reconnect the fusible link and check the headlights for satisfactory operation and beam alignment (Section 22).

19 Headlight semi-sealed beam unit – bulb and unit renewal

Bulb renewal
1 The bulb can be renewed without removing the unit. Raise the bonnet, leave the headlight unit in the closed position and disconnect the fusible link (see Section 16).

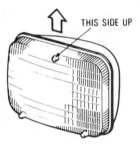

THIS SIDE UP

Fig. 12.44 Sealed beam unit orientation (Sec 18)

2 Detach the wiring connector from the rear of the unit (photo).
3 Remove the rubber cover then release the retaining ring and turn the bulb/holder anti-clockwise and withdraw it (photos). If a halogen type bulb is fitted take care not to touch the glass with your fingers, but if you do, wipe the glass clean with alcohol and a clean cloth.
4 Refitting the bulb is a reversal of the removal procedure. Align the bulb as shown according to type when inserting it into position (Fig. 12.45 or 12.46). Ensure that the correct replacement bulb is fitted.

19.2 Detach the headlight unit wiring connector

19.3A Release the bulb retaining clip ...

19.3B ... and withdraw the bulb and holder

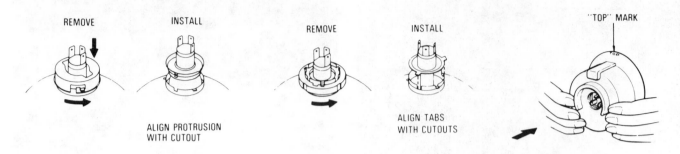

**Fig. 12.45 Headlight bulb renewal
– regular type bulb (Sec 19)**

**Fig. 12.46 Headlight bulb renewal
– halogen type bulb (Sec 19)**

**Fig. 12.47 Cover orientation mark
(Sec 19)**

When fitting the rubber cover, the top marking on it must be positioned upwards (Fig. 12.47).

Unit renewal

5   The unit is removed in the same manner as that described for the sealed beam type unit in Section 18.

20 Headlight (retractable) – manual operation

1   If a retractable headlight unit fails to raise or lower it can be operated manually. First turn off the ignition and headlight switches then disconnect the fusible link (Section 16).
2   Raise and support the bonnet. Remove the rubber cap from the manual operating knob on the headlamp unit concerned (photo).
3   Turn the knob in the direction of the arrow marking to raise the headlamp unit. When fully raised, check that the headlights are fully operational.
4   When lowering the headlight unit(s) manually, they should be closed fully to align with the surrounding bodywork.
5   Any faults concerning the operation of the retractable headlight units must be traced and repaired without delay. The headlight retraction motor on each side can easily be checked, as described in Section 21, but the motor will first need to be removed.

21 Headlight retraction motor – removal, testing and refitting

1   Disconnect the fusible link (Section 16).
2   Remove the front indicator and side lamp unit (Section 23).
3   Disconnect the wiring connector to the retraction motor (photo).
4   Undo the three motor retaining bolts and the lift arm nut, then withdraw the motor (photo).
5   To test the motor, connect up a wire between the motor wiring connector terminal No 1 to the battery positive terminal and a wire between the connector terminal No 2 to the battery negative terminal. The motor should operate. If the motor does not operate it must be renewed.
6   Refit in the reverse order of removal and on completion check the operation of the headlight units and their alignment (Section 22).

22 Headlight beam alignment – adjustment

1   Horizontal and vertical adjustment screws are located on the front face of the headlight units. These screws are accessible after removing the headlight unit surround and retaining frame. However, in view of the variation in regulations in different operating territories, specific adjustment details cannot be provided (Fig. 12.48).

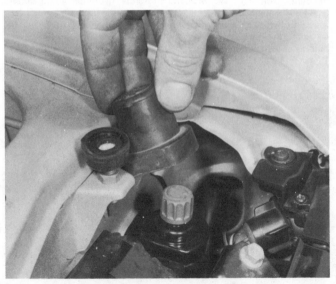

20.2 Remove rubber cap from headlamp operating knob (manual)

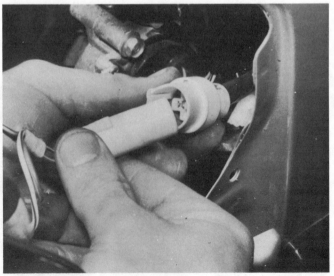

21.3 Disconnect the retraction motor wiring connector

21.4 Retraction motor and retaining bolts

2   A temporary adjustment can be made by turning the screws as necessary, for vertical adjustment and/or, for horizontal adjustment. A more accurate beam alignment check must be made at the earliest opportunity by your local garage or Toyota dealer using optical alignment equipment.

23 Light bulbs (exterior) – renewal

1   Whenever any bulbs are to be renewed, they must be replaced by the same type bulb and with the same wattage rating.

Front sidelight and indicators
2   Removal of the bulbs and holders is possible from the top with the bonnet raised, but access is restricted. It may be found easier to remove the light unit. To do this, bend back the bumper at the corner end by hand to unclip it from the side retainers (photo). Undo the side retaining screw and the upper retaining screw and withdraw the side/indicator light unit (photos). On some models the unit rim can also be removed by undoing the retaining screws.
3   Untwist the holder(s) and withdraw them, then remove the bulb(s) from the holder(s) for renewal (photo).

Side marker lights
4   Undo the retaining screws, remove the lens and extract the bulb for renewal (photo).

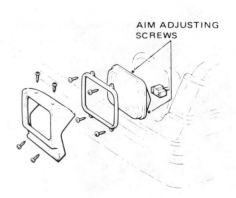

Fig. 12.48 Headlight beam adjustment screw positions (Sec 22)

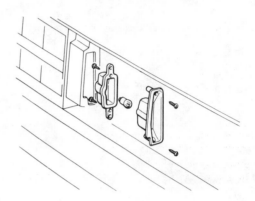

Fig. 12.49 Alternative licence plate light (Sec 23)

Rear combination lights
5   From the luggage compartment side, depress the plastic holder retaining clips and remove the holder from within the luggage area.
6   Remove the bulb from the socket concerned. If required the bulbholder sockets can be removed by undoing the retaining screws and withdrawing the clamps (photo).
7   To remove the unit completely, detach the multi-wiring socket connector.
8   To remove the lens, undo the two retaining screws from inside and withdraw it rearwards.

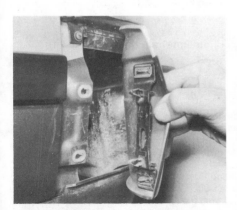

23.2A Prise free the bumper at the corner on the side concerned ...

23.2B ... undo the lower retaining screw ...

23.2C ... and the upper screw to remove the side/indicator light unit

23.3 Side/indicator bulbs and holders removal

23.4 Side marker light with lens removed

23.6 Rear combination lights

23.9 Reversing light bulb

23.10A Licence plate light: remove the retaining screws ...

23.10B ... and lens for access to the bulb

Reversing light
9   Unclip and hinge up the cover within the luggage compartment. Press/untwist and remove the bulb from its holder (photo).

Number plate light
10   Undo the two retaining screws, remove the lens and cover and extract the bulb from its holder (photos).

Refitting
11   In all instances, refitting is a reversal of the removal procedure. On completion check the lights for satisfactory operation.

24 Light bulbs (interior) – renewal

1   Whenever any bulbs are renewed they must be replaced with the same type of bulb and with the same wattage rating.
2   Interior light types vary according to model, but in most instances the bulb can be removed after removing the lens. According to type, the lens will either prise free (interior light), untwist (inspection light) or is secured by two retaining screws (personal and door courtesy lights) (photos).
3   For the renewal of the instrument, warning and switch illumination bulbs refer to the appropriate Section elsewhere in this Chapter.

25 Ignition switch and lock cylinder – removal and refitting

1   Disconnect the battery earth lead.
2   Undo the retaining screws and remove the upper and lower steering column shrouds.

Fig. 12.50 Inspection light bulb renewal (Sec 24)

3   Pull free and withdraw the switch illumination bulbholder. Withdraw the bulb from the holder if it is to be renewed (photo).
4   Undo the two screws and remove the illumination bezel (photos).
5   Set the ignition key in the ACC position then depress the inset retaining pin in the side of the unit and simultaneously pull on the key to withdraw the switch and lock unit (photos).
6   To remove the ignition switch wiring connector, undo the retaining screw, withdraw the unit from the column and detach the wiring from the multi connector (photo).
7   Refitting is a reversal of the removal procedure. On completion check the switch functions for satisfactory operation.

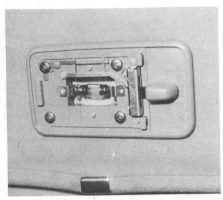
24.2A Courtesy light with lens removed

24.2B Typical door mounted light unit

24.2C Roof light and sunroof control switch with cover removed

25.3 Ignition switch illumination bulb and holder removal

25.4A Undo the retaining screws ...

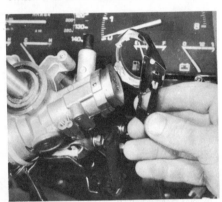
25.4B ... and remove the illumination bezel

25.5A Depress the retaining pin ...

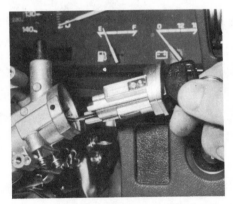
25.5B ... and withdraw the switch/lock unit

25.6 Ignition switch wiring connector

26 Steering column switches – removal and refitting

1 Disconnect the battery earth lead from the negative terminal.
2 Remove the steering wheel, as described in Chapter 10.
3 Undo the retaining screws and remove the lower and upper steering column shrouds.
4 Undo the four inset screws securing the switches, then withdraw the switches and disconnect the wiring connectors from the column on the underside (photos).
5 The individual switches can be renewed as follows.

Light control switch/headlight dimmer switch
6 Disconnect the terminals from the bulkhead connector by prising the lock lugs free with a screwdriver whilst pulling on the terminal (Fig. 12.52).

7 Remove the light control switch and the headlight dimmer switch.
8 Refit the dimmer switch, fit the spring into the lever and fit the lever, pin and E-ring.
9 Position the ball on the spring, and, with the lever positioned at H1, fit the plate (Fig. 12.54). Check that the switch operation is satisfactory.
10 Reconnect the terminals to the connector by pushing the terminal in so that the connector lug retains it. Pull the wire to confirm that it is secure (Fig. 12.53).

Turn signal/hazard warning switch and/or wiper/washer switch
11 Detach the terminals from the connector (see paragraph 6) then remove the switch unit from the main assembly.
12 Refit in reverse order to removal. Reconnect the wiring connector to the terminal referring to paragraph 10.

26.4A Undo the inset switch retaining screws ...

26.4B ... release the wiring connections and clips ...

26.4C ... and remove the column switches

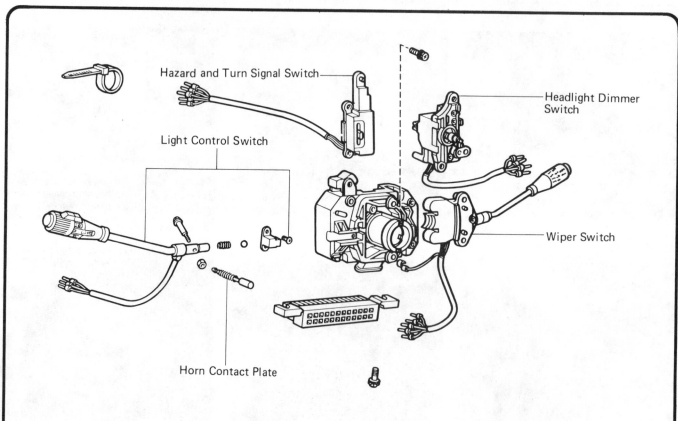

Hazard and Turn Signal Switch

Headlight Dimmer Switch

Light Control Switch

Wiper Switch

Horn Contact Plate

Fig. 12.51 Steering column combination switch assembly (Sec 26)

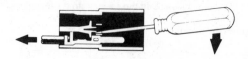

Fig. 12.52 Terminal removal from bulkhead connector:
Insert screwdriver between lock lugs and terminal
(Sec 26)

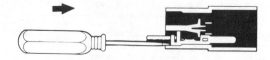

Fig. 12.53 Terminal refitting to bulkhead connector: Push
terminal in so that connector lug secures it (Sec 26)

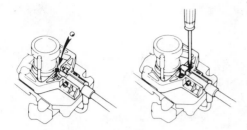

Fig. 12.54 Locate ball onto the spring and refit the plate (Sec 26)

27.3 Remove the rear cover ...

27 Rear window defogger (demister) control switch – removal and refitting

1 Disconnect the battery earth lead.
2 Remove the instrument panel facia, as described in Section 28.
3 Undo the two retaining screws within the facia and withdraw the defogger switch. Withdraw the rear cover (photo).
4 To renew the bulb, extract the holder and remove the bulb (photo).
5 To remove the switch from the housing, undo the three retaining screws, detach the wire securing clip and withdraw the unit.
6 Refitting is a reversal of the removal procedure. Check for satisfactory operation on completion.

28 Instrument panel cluster – removal and refitting

1 Disconnect the battery earth lead.
2 Undo the retaining screws and remove the lower and upper steering column shrouds.

3 Undo the screws securing the instrument cluster finisher panel, pull free the instrument cluster light control knob and remove the cluster finisher panel (photos).
4 Undo the four retaining screws and withdraw the instrument panel as far as possible. Reach behind the panel and detach the speedometer cable and the wiring connectors. Remove the panel (photo).
5 The warning and illumination bulbs with holders can be untwisted

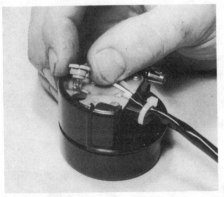

27.4 ... for access to the bulbholder. On some models, this unit also incorporates the rear window wiper/washer switch

28.3A Instrument cluster finisher panel upper screws removal

28.3B Remove the lower screws ...

28.3C ... and remove the light control knob

28.4A Instrument panel retaining screws

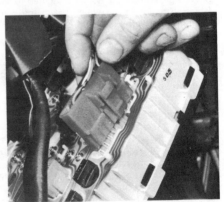

28.4B Disconnect the wiring connectors from the rear of the panel

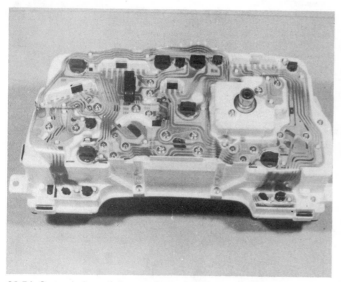

28.5A General view of the rear face of the instrument panel

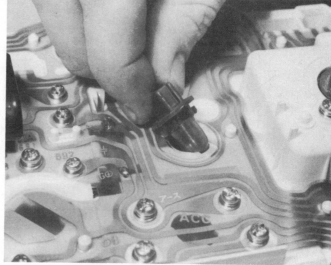

28.5B Bulb/holder removal from instrument panel

and withdrawn from the panel rear face for renewal as required. Take care not to damage the printed circuit (photos).
6 The testing and renewal of individual instruments and gauges should be entrusted to a Toyota dealer.
7 Refitting is a reversal of the removal procedure. On completion check for satisfactory operation of the various panel functions.

29 Instrument panel light control – removal and refitting

1 Remove the instrument cluster panel. Refer to paragraphs 1 to 3 in Section 28 for details.
2 Undo the retaining screws and detach the lower trim finisher panel on the driver's side.
3 Undo the retaining nut, remove the control switch unit from the support bracket and disconnect the wiring at the connector (photo).
4 Refit in the reverse order of removal.

29.3 Instrument panel light control bracket and retaining nut

30 Glovebox light – removal and refitting

1 Detach the battery earth lead.
2 Undo the five screws and remove the inner panel from the glovebox.
3 Withdraw the bulbholder from the panel and detach the wiring connector (photo). Renew the bulb if necessary.
4 Refit in the reverse order of removal.
5 The glovebox light switch is secured to a bracket behind the upper facia. To remove the switch, detach the wiring connector, undo the retaining bolt and remove the switch (photo).
6 Refit in the reverse order of removal.

31 Passenger side finisher panel (and speaker unit) – removal and refitting

1 Disconnect the battery earth lead.
2 Carefully prise free the speaker grille.
3 Undo the retaining screws and remove the side quarter panel.
4 Remove the glovebox. It is secured by four screws within the box and two hold the catch.
5 Remove the six screws from the panel lower edge and the single screw within the speaker recess.
6 Remove the screw at the side of the panel, withdraw the panel and detach the speaker wires.
7 Refit in the reverse order of removal.

30.3A Glovebox bulbholder and wiring connector

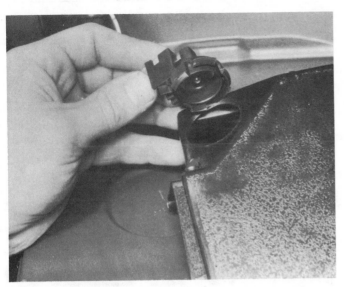

30.3B Glovebox bulbholder and location

30.5 Glovebox light switch

32 Driver's side finisher panel – removal and refitting

1   Disconnect the battery earth lead.
2   Pull free the instrument panel light control knob.
3   Undo the retaining screws and withdraw the panel. To remove the panel fully disconnect the speaker wires and the bonnet release cable.
4   Refit in the reverse order of removal.

33 Console panels – removal and refitting

1   Disconnect the battery earth lead.

Upper panel

2   Remove the ashtray and undo the lower retaining screws (photos).
3   Remove the heater control panel (Section 47) and undo the upper retaining screws. The panel can now be withdrawn partially for access to the cigar lighter and ashtray light, and if fitted the air conditioner control switch. Disconnect the switch and cigar lighter lead connectors to remove the panel fully (photos).

Forward console

4   Unclip and detach the gear lever gaiter for the console.
5   Remove the retaining screws each side at the front and rear, pull the console forwards and remove it. Disconnect any wiring connections (photos).

Rear console

6   Undo the retaining screw each side (towards the rear of the console). Remove the retaining screw from the cubby box and lift the console clear; guiding it over the handbrake lever.
7   Disconnect the switch wiring connections to remove the rear console fully.

Refitting

8   Refitting of the rear/forward consoles and the upper panel is a reversal of the removal procedure. Ensure that the wiring connections are correctly and securely made.

33.2A Remove the ashtray ...

33.2B ... for access to the console retaining screws

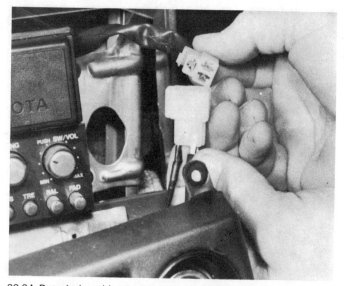

33.3A Detach the wiring connector ...

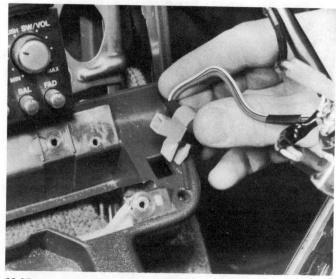

33.3B ... and the cigar lighter bulb lead

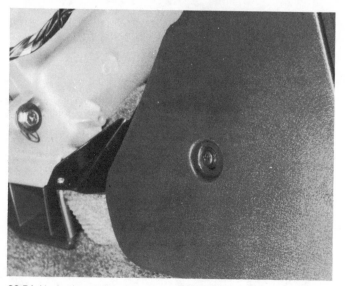

33.5A Undo the retaining screw each side at the front ...

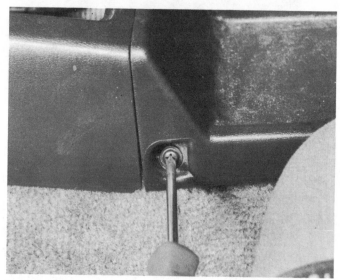

33.5B ... and at the rear ...

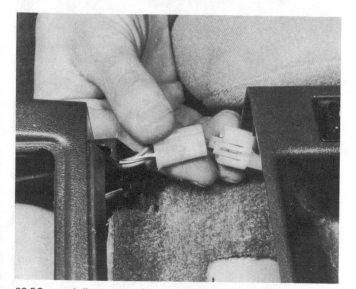

33.5C ... and disconnect wiring connectors as the console is removed

34 Cigar lighter and ashtray light – removal and refitting

1   Disconnect the battery earth lead.
2   Remove the upper panel, as described in Section 33.
3   Detach the wiring connector and bulb holder from the cigar lighter, and the ashtray light bulbholder (photo).
4   Unscrew the retainer and remove the light housing. Withdraw the cigar lighter from the front side of the panel (photo).
5   Refit in the reverse order of removal. Ensure that the wiring connections and bulbholders are secure.

35 Rocker switches – removal and refitting

1   Disconnect the battery earth lead.
2   Carefully prise free the switch from the panel concerned and withdraw the switch and detach the wiring connector (photo).
3   Where applicable, the switch bulb can be removed by withdrawing the holder and extracting the bulb from it (photo).
4   Refitting is a reversal of the removal procedure.

34.3 Bulbholder removal from cigar lighter

34.4 Cigar lighter components laid out in sequence of removal

35.2 Rocker switch removal

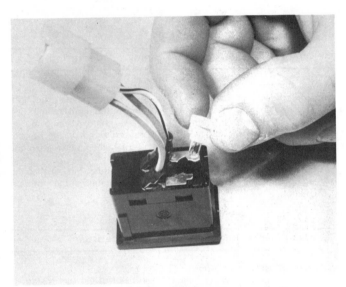

35.3 Bulb holder removal from rocker switch

36 Door courtesy light switch – removal and refitting

1 Disconnect the battery earth lead.
2 Prise back the rubber protector and unscrew the retaining nut (photo).
3 Remove the trim panel for access to the rear of the switch, detach the wiring connector and remove the switch.
4 Refit in the reverse order of removal.

37 Horns – removal and refitting

1 Disconnect the battery earth lead.
2 The horn(s) are located beneath the side-light/indicator units and are accessible from underneath (photo).
3 Disconnect the wire from the horn, undo the retaining bolt and remove the horn.
4 Refit in the reverse order of removal. Check for satisfactory operation on completion.

36.2 Door courtesy light switch unit

37.2 Horn location and attachment bolt

38.2 Remove the sunroof switch/roof light unit for access to the sunroof motor unit

38 Sunroof switch and motor – removal and refitting

1   Disconnect the battery earth lead.
2   Undo the retaining screw and remove the sunroof switch/roof light unit cover. Carefully prise free and remove the light/switch unit (photo). Disconnect the wiring connectors for complete removal.
3   Undo the sunroof motor retaining bolts and withdraw the sunroof motor so that the wiring connections can be detached then remove the motor.
4   Refitting is a reversal of the removal procedure. Ensure that the wiring connections are secure and check the operation of the motor on completion.

39 Wiper blades and arms – removal and refitting

Windscreen wiper blades
1   If the windscreen wiper blades are in need of renewal owing to wear or cracking they can be removed from the arm for replacement. To do this, pull the rubber, at the outer end, away from the arm so that the blade disengages from the end slot. Then pull the rubber along the line of the blade to withdraw it (Fig. 12.55).
2   To fit the new blade, feed the end with the small protrusions into the replacement aperture and slide the blade downwards along the blade frame slot. Once it is fully in position allow it to expand and fill in the end (Fig. 12.56).

Rear window wiper blade
3   Prise up the lockwire directly over the pivot point and detach the blade from the arm pivot. Refit in reverse and check that the blade is securely engaged on the pivot (Fig. 12.57).
4   On some models the rear wiper blade is removed by undoing the two retaining screws (photo).

Wiper arms and blades
5   To remove the wiper arm assembly, undo the pivot nut, mark or note the relative position of the arm and pivot shaft, and pull free the arm (photo).
6   Refit in reverse order to removal and check operation on completion. Check the wiping arc of the wiper blades on a wet screen and adjust the position of the arms if necessary by removing them and moving one or more splines in the appropriate direction.

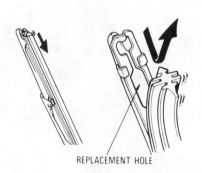

Fig. 12.55 Windscreen wiper blade removal (Sec 39)

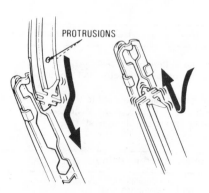

Fig. 12.56 Windscreen wiper blade replacement (Sec 39)

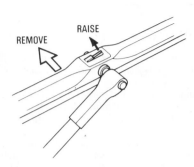

Fig. 12.57 Rear window wiper blade renewal (Sec 39)

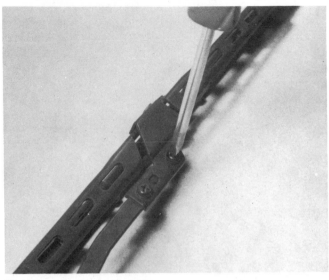

39.4 Wiper arm blade removal

39.5 Wiper arm retaining nut

40 Windscreen wiper motor and linkage – removal and refitting

1   Disconnect the battery earth lead.
2   Remove the windscreen wiper arms and blades if the linkages are to be removed. Refer to the previous Section.
3   Disconnect the wiring from the motor unit (photo).
4   Undo the four motor retaining bolts. Note that one bolt secures an earth lead.
5   Carefully release the grille panel(s) as required, taking care not to damage the grilles or the paintwork (photo).
6   Set the wiper linkages to the halfway position, reach through the grille aperture and support the link arm attached to the wiper motor then pull the motor from the bulkhead and detach the link balljoint (photo). Remove the motor unit.
7   To remove the linkages, undo the three retaining bolts at each pivot point. Separate the linkage joints (noting location and orientation) then remove the linkages (photo).

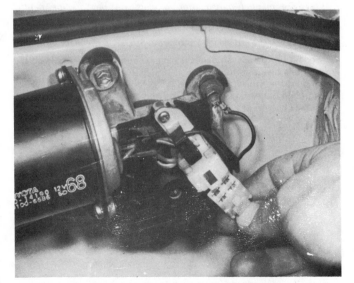

40.3 Disconnect the wiring from the wiper motor

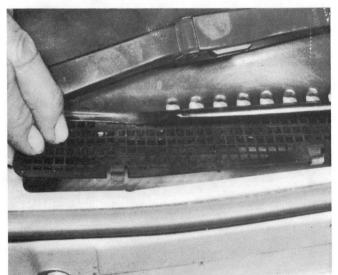

40.5 Remove the grille panel(s)

40.6 Disconnect the wiper motor link balljoint

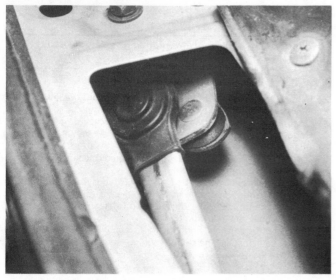

40.7 Wiper linkage joints and pivot bolts

8   Refitting is a reversal of the removal procedure. Lubricate the linkage pivots before assembly.
9   On completion, operate the windscreen washers, then check the windscreen wiper for satisfactory operation and the blades for correct travel and parking.

41 Rear window wiper washer (Liftback) – removal and refitting

1   Disconnect the battery earth lead.
2   Carefully remove the rear trim panel from the back door (tailgate).
3   Disconnect the wiring connector from the motor, undo the three retaining bolts and withdraw the motor and disengage it from the link arm.
4   To remove the link arm, remove the wiper arm and blade as described in Section 39, remove the pivot retaining nut and cap, then withdraw the link arm assembly.
5   Refitting is a reversal of the removal procedure. When the motor is bolted in position, reconnect the wiring and link arm, and then with the ignition switched on set the wiper to the AUTO-STOP position. The wiper arm can then be refitted in the parked position on the pivot and the ignition switched off.
6   Refit the inner panel and on completion, check the operation of the wiper.

42 Washer bottles and pumps – removal and refitting

Windscreen/headlight washer bottle(s) and pump
1   Disconnect the battery earth lead.
2   Syphon or drain the fluid from the reservoir bottle(s), detach the hose(s) from the bottle(s) and the wiring connection from the pump unit.
3   Undo the retaining bolts and lift out the reservoir bottle(s).
4   Refit in the reverse order to removal. Top up the reservoir and check for satisfactory operation and any signs of leakage from the pump and hose connections.
5   Always keep the fluid reservoir filled and do not operate the electric pump with a dry reservoir. In any case, operation of the washer pump should be limited to periods not exceeding 20 seconds.
6   It is recommended that a proprietary screen cleaning solvent is used in the reservoir and during very cold weather add some methylated spirit *but never engine anti-freeze,* as this will damage the vehicle paintwork.

Rear window washer bottle and pump
7   Remove the side trim panel for access to the washer bottle.
8   Proceed as described in paragraphs 1 to 6 above.

43 Cruise control – general

1   This system is fitted to USA models only, its function being to assist the driver on long distance driving by holding the speed of the vehicle at a selected level. The speed level can only be set at speeds above 25 mph (40 kph). It must not be used in heavy traffic conditions, on slippery (icy) roads, or on winding roads. When steep gradients are encountered, the cruise control should be cancelled.
2   The system is activated by depressing the main cruise control switch, this illuminates the switch indicator light, then when the required speed is obtained, the control knob on the column switch is turned downwards to the 'Set' position and released. The vehicle will now travel at the desired speed. If acceleration is required, for example to overtake, whilst the system is engaged, press the accelerator pedal in the normal manner as required. On releasing the accelerator pedal the system will take over again and the speed return to the set level (Fig. 12.58).
3   The system can be cancelled by depressing the brake pedal, depressing the clutch pedal (manual transmission) or by moving the selector lever to the N position (automatic transmission). If the vehicle slows below 25 mph, the system will automatically cancel.
4   The following precautions must be noted when using the system.

(a)   *On manual transmission models, do not engage neutral without first cancelling the system as this will cause the engine to race and overrevving will result*
(b)   *When the cruise control is not in use, keep the main switch off*

5   For further details on using the cruise control system consult the instructions given in the handbook supplied with the vehicle.
6   Should the cruise system develop a fault, first check the system wiring and connections for condition and security. The system wiring diagram is shown in Fig. 12.59.

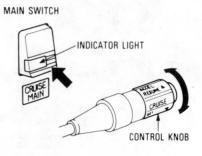

Fig. 12.58 Cruise control main switch and control knob (Sec 43)

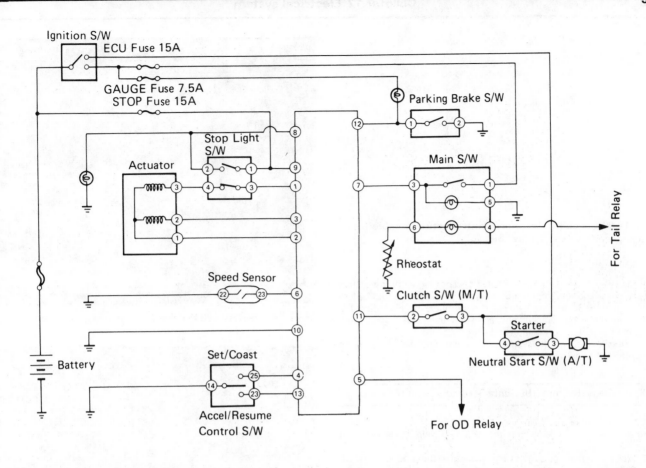

Fig. 12.59 Cruise control system wiring diagram and switch connections (Sec 43)

Fig. 12.60 Checking the cruise control actuator cable free play (Sec 43)

44.3A Radio/cassette unit retaining screws (typical installation)

7   If the system operates, but the speed deviates higher or lower than that set, check the actuator control cable for free play. It should be less than 10 mm (0.39 in). Adjustment can be made by loosening the locknut at the cable bracket and adjusting the cable as required. Retighten the locknut on completion (Fig. 12.60).
8   Any further tests on the system components and their renewal are best entrusted to a Toyota dealer.

44 Radio/cassette/amplifier units – removal and refitting

1   Disconnect the battery earth lead.
2   Remove the upper panel from the centre console, as described in Section 33.
3   Undo the retaining screws and withdraw the unit concerned. Detach the wiring/antenna lead as applicable to remove the unit(s) completely (photos).
4   Refitting is a reversal of the removal procedure.
5   To ensure optimum radio reception, adjust the antenna trimmer. To do this, fully raise the antenna, turn the radio volume and tone control to the maximum setting and set the dial to 1400 kHz (where there is no reception). Use a small screwdriver to adjust the trimmer to give the loudest static performance, then switch off the radio or turn down the volume and tune the radio to the required station (Fig. 12.61).

45 Speaker units – removal and refitting

1   Disconnect the battery earth lead.
2   Carefully prise free the grille panel from the front of the speaker (photo).
3   Remove the speaker unit by detaching the wiring connector to it, and undo the retaining screws. Where the retaining screws are behind the speaker, remove the trim panel for access (photos).
4   Refit in the reverse order of removal.

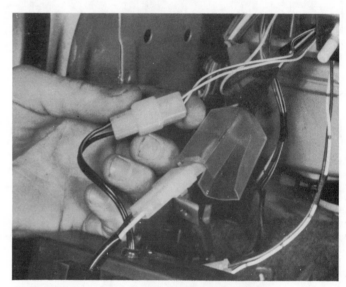

44.3B Radio/cassette unit wiring connections

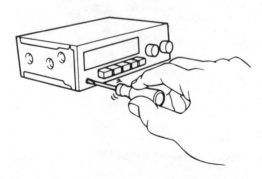

Fig. 12.61 Radio trimmer adjustment (Sec 44)

45.2 Speaker grille panel removal

45.3A Speaker unit and retaining screws (rear side fixing)

45.3B Speaker unit – alternative type with front mounting screws

46 Antenna – removal and refitting

1   Disconnect the battery earth lead.
2   Unscrew and remove the antenna set nut.
3   Remove the inner trim panel for access to the antenna motor unit.
4   Unscrew the retaining bolts, disconnect the wiring connector and remove the antenna unit, complete with the relay (photo).
5   Refit in the reverse order of removal and check for satisfactory operation on completion.

47 Heater control unit – removal and refitting

1   Disconnect the battery earth lead.
2   Remove the heater control knobs by pulling them free, then undo the panel securing screws and withdraw the panel (photo).
3   To renew the control panel bulbs, prise free the plastic retainer plate for access (photo).
4   Remove the upper console panel and the forward console, as described in Section 33.

46.4 Rear mounted antenna unit and relay

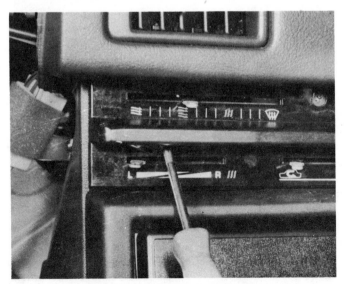

47.2 Remove the heater control panel ...

47.3 ... and the clear plastic retainer for access to the bulb

5   Undo the screw and bolts and detach one of the side metal pillar support brackets (photo).
6   Lower the control unit and disconnect the wiring connector and control cables then remove the unit.
7   Refitting is a reversal of the removal procedure. Adjust the controls if necessary as described in Section 50.

48 Heater blower unit – removal and refitting

1   Disconnect the battery earth lead.
2   Remove the glovebox and the passenger side lower trim panel (photo).
3   Undo the retaining screws and remove the centre duct between the blower unit and the matrix assembly. Disconnect the resistor wiring connector as it is withdrawn (photos).
4   To remove the resistor from the duct, undo the retaining screws, detach the wiring connector from the location bracket on top of the duct and remove the resistor unit (photos).
5   To remove the motor unit, undo the three retaining screws from underneath, detach the wiring connector and the flap valve control cable. Withdraw the unit (photo).

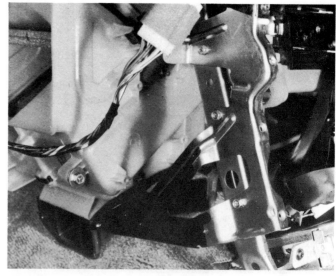

47.5 Metal side pillar support bracket

48.2 Glovebox retaining screws

48.3A Centre duct and retaining screws

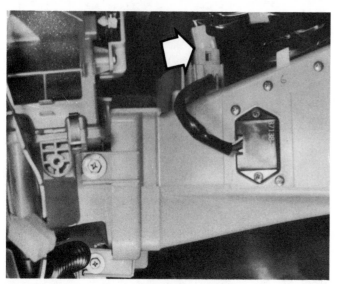

48.3B Detach the resistor wire connector (arrowed)

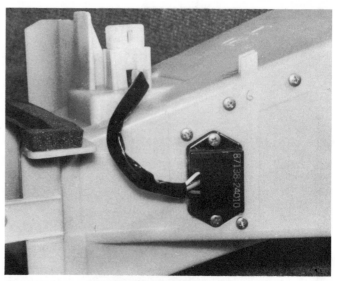

48.4A Resistor unit showing the retaining screws and wiring connector location on the top face of the duct

48.4B View of resistor within the duct

48.5 Blower motor unit wiring connector

6 To remove the blower motor from the housing, detach the hose, undo the retaining bolts and withdraw the motor unit (photo).

7 To separate the housing, undo the retaining screws, release the retaining clips and separate the housings (photo).

8 Refitting is a reversal of the removal procedure. Check for satisfactory operation on completion and if necessary adjust the controls, as described in Section 50.

49 Heater matrix – removal and refitting

1 Disconnect the battery earth lead.

2 Drain the cooling system, as described in Chapter 2, ensuring that the heater control is set to full heat.

3 Disconnect and remove the lower trim panel on the driver and passenger sides.

4 Remove the retaining screws, disconnect the wiring connectors and remove the centre duct between the blower unit and the matrix.

5 Remove the retaining screws or unclip (as applicable) and detach the remaining ventilation and heating ducts from the matrix housing.

6 Note their locations and disconnect the control cables from the control valve levers (photo).

48.6 Underside view of blower unit showing motor retaining screws

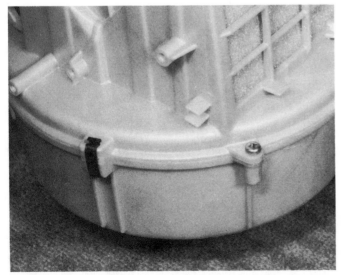

48.7 Housing retaining screws and clips

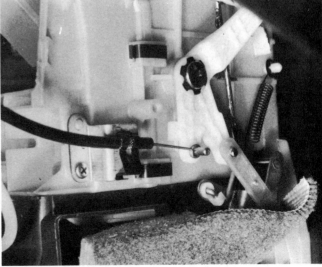

49.6 Disconnect the heater control valve cables

7 Undo the retaining nuts to the bulkhead (one each side and one at the top).
8 Detach the hoses from the inlet and outlet connections at the bulkhead on the engine compartment side.
9 Check that all connections are free then withdraw the matrix housing from the passenger side.
10 Undo the screws and release the clips to separate the casing and withdraw the matrix.
11 Refitting is a reversal of the removal procedure. Ensure that all seals and connections are securely made, particularly the inlet/outlet hoses at the bulkhead.
12 Before refitting the lower trim panels, top up the cooling system (Chapter 2) then check for signs of coolant leaks. Check the operation of the heater and ventilation and if necessary adjust the controls, as described in Section 50.

50 Heater controls – adjustment

1 If the heater or control units have been removed for any reason they should be adjusted as follows during reassembly.
2 Set the control lever to the 'fresh air' position then check that the air inlet damper is set accordingly (Fig. 12.62).
3 Set the model selector lever to the 'Vent' position and then check that the mode selector damper is set accordingly (Fig. 12.63).
4 Set the air mix lever to the 'Cool' position. The air mix damper

should be positioned as shown (Fig. 12.64).
5 Move the balance control lever to the central position, then set the damper centrally as shown (Fig. 12.65).
6 In each case above, move the outer cable casing in its retaining clamp as required to set the adjustment.
7 On completion, check the cables for satisfactory movement by moving them through their full range.

51 Heater control valve – removal and refitting

1 Drain the cooling system, as described in Chapter 2.
2 Disconnect the heater control valve cable from the lever and the securing clip.
3 Undo the retaining clips and detach the hoses from the valve (photo).
4 Unbolt and remove the valve unit from the bulkhead.
5 Refit in the reverse order of removal. When reconnecting the control cable, set the valve and the control lever to the 'Cool' position. Check for signs of coolant leakage on completion.

52 Air conditioning system – general description and maintenance

1 The optionally specified system comprises a heater and cooling

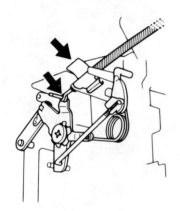

Fig. 12.62 Air inlet damper adjustment (Sec 50)

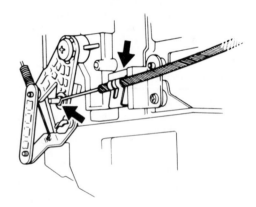

Fig. 12.63 Mode selector damper adjustment (Sec 50)

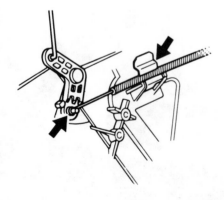

Fig. 12.64 Air mix damper adjustment (Sec 50)

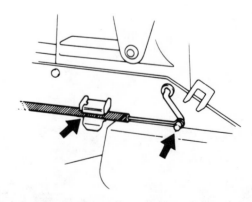

Fig. 12.65 Balance damper adjustment (Sec 50)

51.3 Heater control valve showing cable and hose connections

unit, a belt-driven compressor, a condenser and a receiver, together with the necessary temperature controls.

2   The oil filled compressor is driven from the crankshaft pulley   and incorporates a magnetic type clutch.

3   Servicing of the system is outside the scope of the home mechanic as special equipment is needed to purge or recharge the system with refrigerant gas, and dismantling of any part of the system must not be undertaken, in the interest of safety, without first having discharged the system pressure.

4   To maintain optimum performance of the system, the owner should limit his operations to the following:

> (a) Checking the tension of the compressor driving belt (Chapter 2)
> (b) Checking the security of all hoses and unions
> (c) Always keeping the ignition timing correctly set
> (d) Checking the security of the electrical connections
> (e) Regularly cleaning the air intake filter

5   Use a soft brush to remove accumulations of dust and flies from the condenser fins.

6   During the winter months, operate the air conditioning system for a few minutes each week to lubricate the interior of the compressor pump, as lack of use may cause deterioration in the moving parts.

53 Fault diagnosis – electrical system

Symptom	Reason(s)
Starter motor fails to turn engine	
No electricity at starter motor	Battery discharged
	Battery defective internally
	Battery terminal leads loose or earth lead not securely attached to body
	Loose or broken connections in starter motor circuit
	Starter motor switch or solenoid faulty
Electricity at starter motor: faulty motor	Starter brushes badly worn, sticking or brush wires loose
	Commutator dirty, worn or burnt
	Starter motor armature faulty
	Field coils earthed
Starter motor turns engine very slowly	
Electrical defects	Battery in discharged condition
	Starter brushes badly worn, sticking or brush wires loose
	Loose wires in starter motor circuit
Starter motor operates without turning engine	
Mechanical damage	Pinion or flywheel gear teeth broken or worn
Starter motor noisy or excessively rough engagement	
Lack of attention or mechanical damage	Pinion or flywheel gear teeth broken or worn
	Starter motor retaining bolts loose
Battery will not hold charge for more than a few days	
Wear or damage	Battery defective internally
	Electrolyte level too low or electrolyte too weak due to leakage
	Plate separators no longer fully effective
	Battery plates severely sulphated
Insufficient current flow to keep battery charged	Battery plates severely sulphated
	Drivebelt slipping
	Battery terminal connections loose or corroded
	Alternator not charging
	Short in lighting circuit causing continual battery drain
	Regulator unit not working correctly
Ignition light fails to go out, battery runs flat in a few days	
Alternator not charging	Drivebelt loose and slipping or broken
	Brushes worn, sticking, broken or dirty
	Brush springs weak or broken
	Faulty charge circuit relay

Fault diagnosis – electrical system (continued)

Symptom	Reason(s)
Regulator fails to work correctly	Regulator incorrectly set Open circuit in wiring of regulator unit

Failure of individual electrical equipment to function correctly is dealt with, item-by-item, under the headings list below:

Horn

Horn operates all the time	Horn push either earthed or stuck down Horn cable to horn push earthed
Horn fails to operate	Blown fuse Cable or cable connection loose, broken or disconnected Horn has an internal fault
Horn emits intermittent or unsatisfactory noise	Cable connections loose Horn faulty

Lights*

Lights do not come on	If engine not running, battery discharged Light bulb filament burnt out or bulbs broken Wire connections loose, disconnected or broken Light switch shorting or otherwise faulty Lighting circuit relay faulty
Lights come on but fade out	If engine not running battery discharged Light bulb filament burnt out or bulbs or sealed beam units broken Wire connections loose, disconnected or broken Light switch shorting or otherwise faulty
Lights give very poor illumination	Lamp glasses dirty Lamps badly out of adjustment Incorrect bulb with too low wattage fitted Existing bulbs old and badly discoloured
Lights work erratically – flashing on and off, especially over bumps	Battery terminals or earth connection loose Lights not earthing properly Contacts in light switch faulty
Headlight retractor(s) fail to operate	Retractor motor faulty Retractor operating circuit relay faulty

* **N.B.** *Disconnect the pink fusible link at the battery before making any repairs to the headlight units*

Wipers

Wiper motor fails to work	Blown fuse Wire connections loose, disconnected, or broken Brushes badly worn Armature worn or faulty Field coils faulty Circuit relay faulty
Wiper motor works very slowly and takes excessive current	Commutator dirty, greasy or burnt Armature bearings dirty or unaligned Armature badly worn or faulty Armature thrust adjuster screw overtightened
Wiper motor works slowly and takes little current	Brushes badly worn Commutator dirty, greasy or burnt Armature badly worn or faulty

Heater motor

Heater motor fails to work	Blown fuse Wire connections loose, disconnected, or broken Fault in motor Circuit relay faulty Faulty switch

Power windows

Windows fail to operate	Blown fuse (no windows operate) Circuit relay faulty (no windows operate) Wiring connections loose, disconnected or broken Switch faulty Motor faulty

Fault diagnosis – electrical system (continued)

Symptom	Reason(s)
Defogger	
Defogger fails to operate	Fuse blown
	Circuit wiring connections loose, disconnected or broken
	Circuit relay faulty
	Switch faulty
	Element faulty
Sunroof motor	
Sunroof motor fails to operate	Fuse blown
	Circuit wiring connections loose, disconnected or broken
	Sunroof switch faulty
	Sunroof motor faulty
Cruise control system	
System fails to operate, fails to reduce speed when coast switch activated, fails to accelerate when throttle switch activated, or fails to return to preset speed when resume switch activated	Fuse blown
	Circuit wiring connections loose, disconnected or broken
	Switch faulty
Vehicle speed higher or lower than set speed	Actuator incorrectly adjusted or faulty
	Wiring circuit fault
Setting speed fails to cancel when brake pedal depressed	Faulty stop light switch or wiring
Setting speed fails to cancel when handbrake applied	Faulty handbrake switch or wiring
Setting speed fails to cancel when clutch pedal depressed (manual transmission)	Faulty clutch pedal switch or wiring
Setting speed fails to cancel when N range engaged (automatic transmission)	Faulty neutral start switch or wiring
Cruise control fails to disengage below 20 kph or can be set before 20 kph	Faulty speed sensor or wiring

Wiring colour code

B	Black	GR	Grey	O	Orange	V	Violet
BR	Brown	L	Light blue	P	Pink	W	White
G	Green	LG	Light green	R	Red	Y	Yellow

If a wire is given two code letters the first is the main colour, the second the stripe

Wiring diagram abbreviations

A/T	Automatic transmission	C/P	Coupe	LH	Left-hand	S/W	Switch
CB	Circuit Breaker	IGN	Ignition	M/T	Manual transmission	TWC	Three-Way Catalyst
CIG	Cigarette Lighter	L/B	Lift Back	RH	Right-hand	VCS	Vacuum Control Switch
CMH	Cold Mixture Heater						

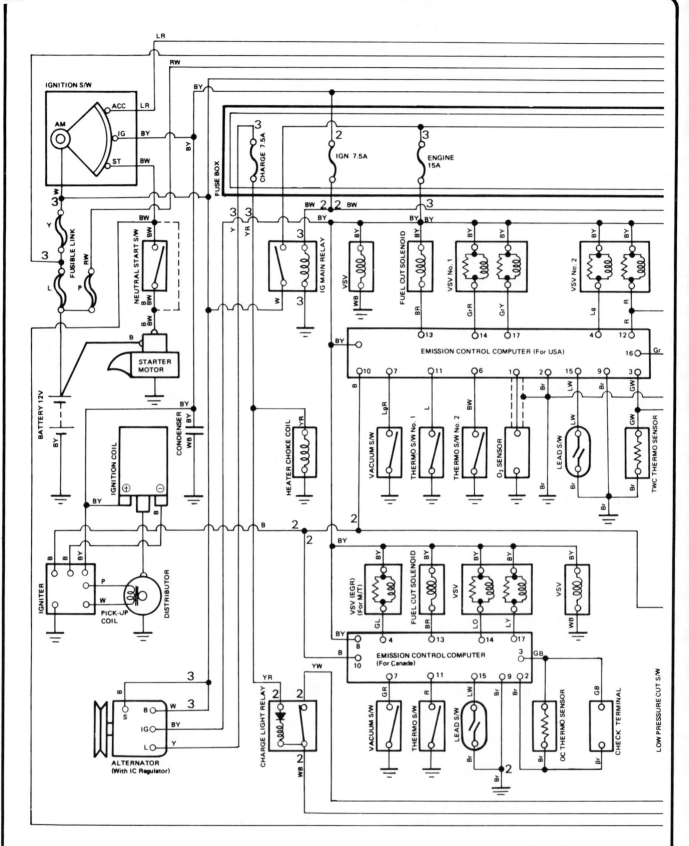

Fig. 12.66 Wiring diagram for all 1982 Toyota Celica models

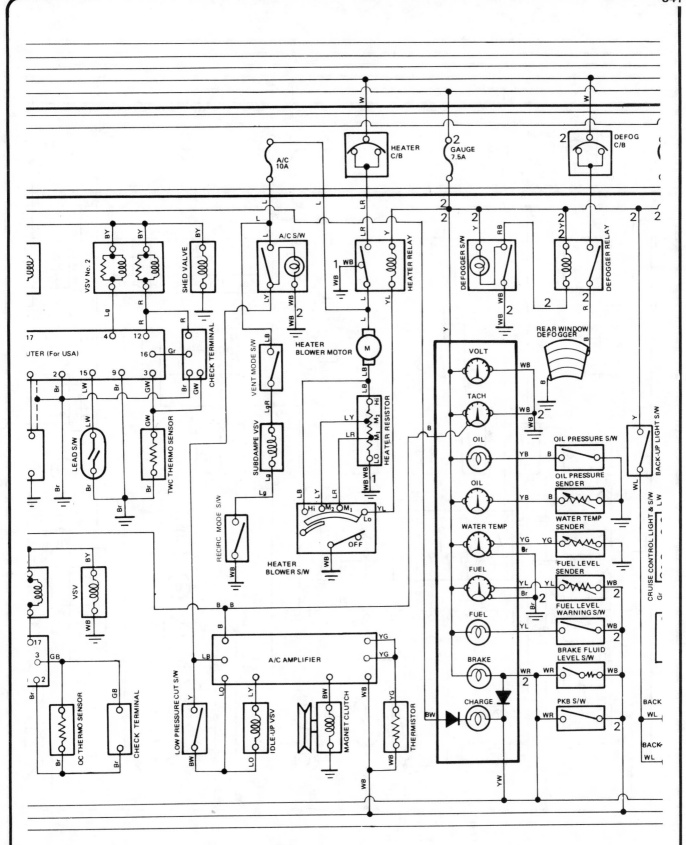

Fig. 12.66 Wiring diagram for all 1982 Toyota Celica models (continued)

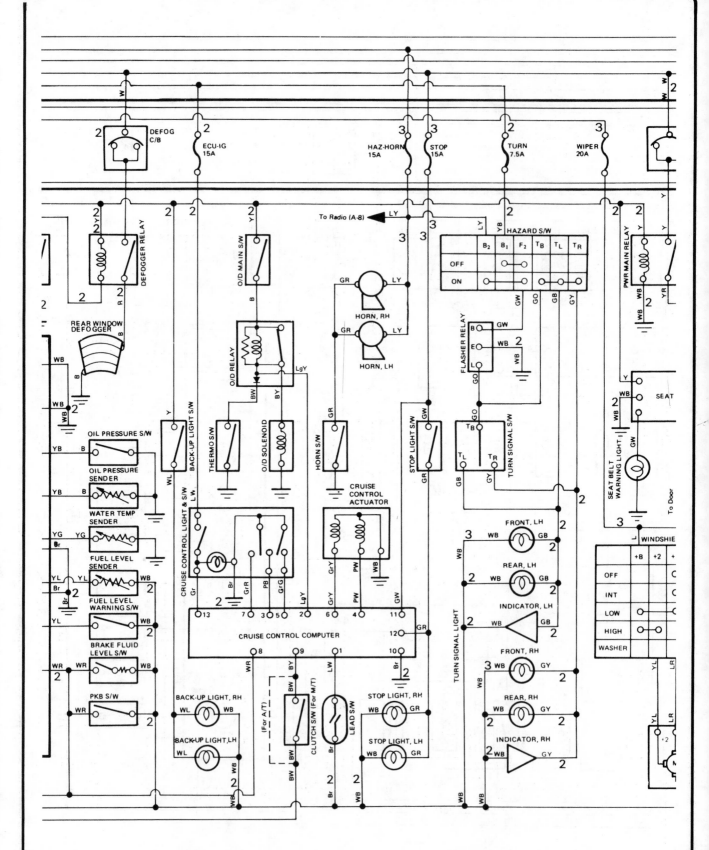

Fig. 12.66 Wiring diagram for all 1982 Toyota Celica models (continued)

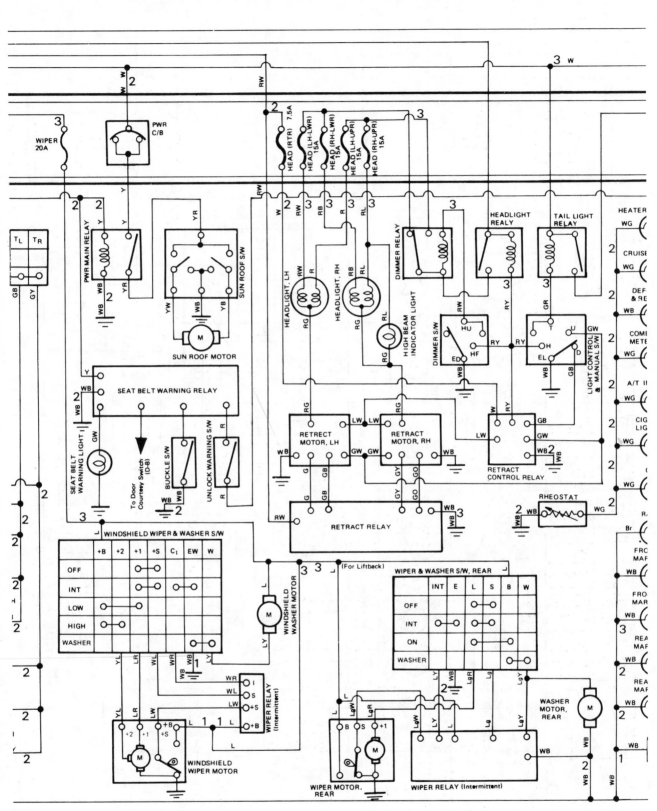

Fig. 12.66 Wiring diagram for all 1982 Toyota Celica models (continued)

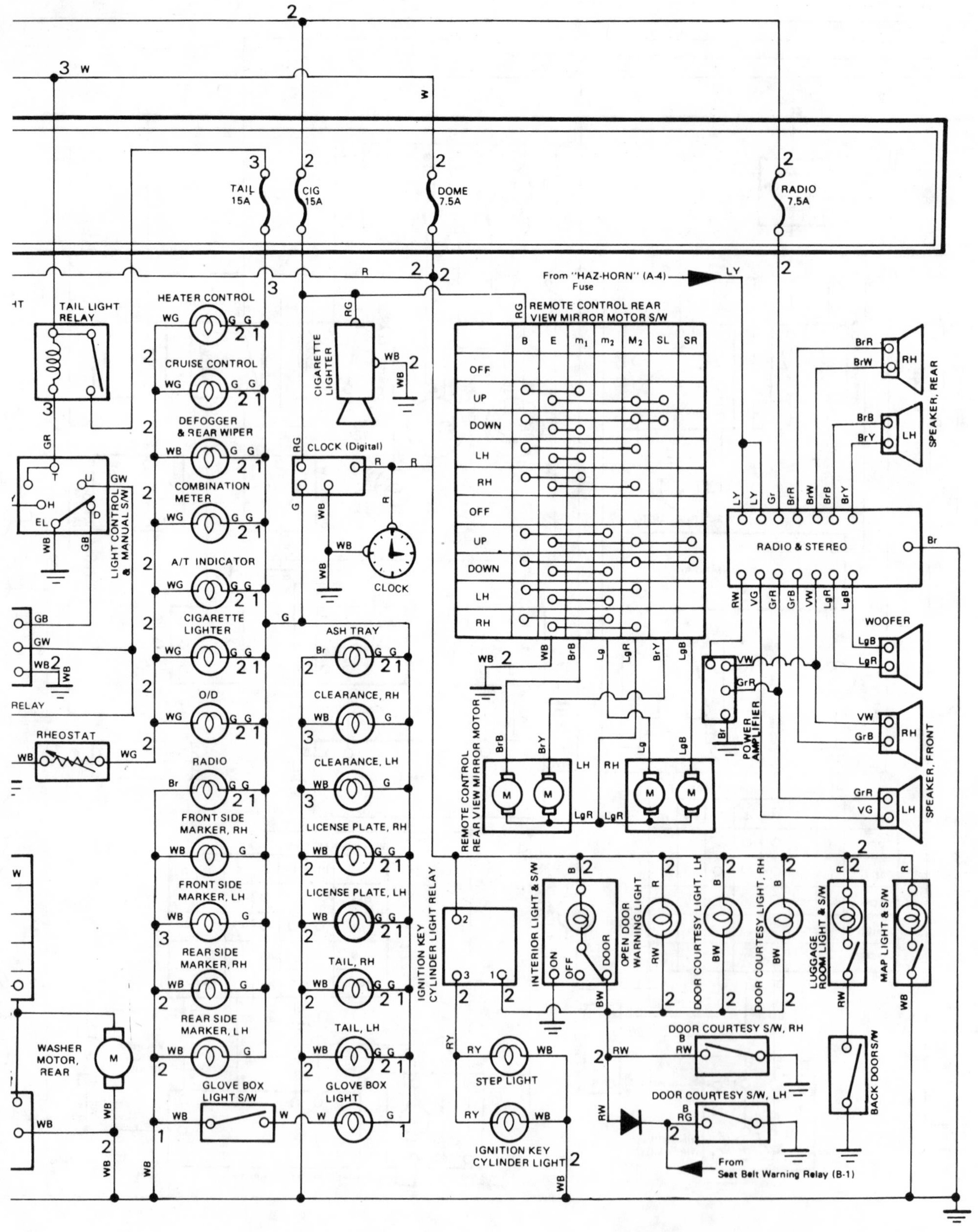

Fig. 12.66 Wiring diagram for all 1982 Toyota Celica models (continued)

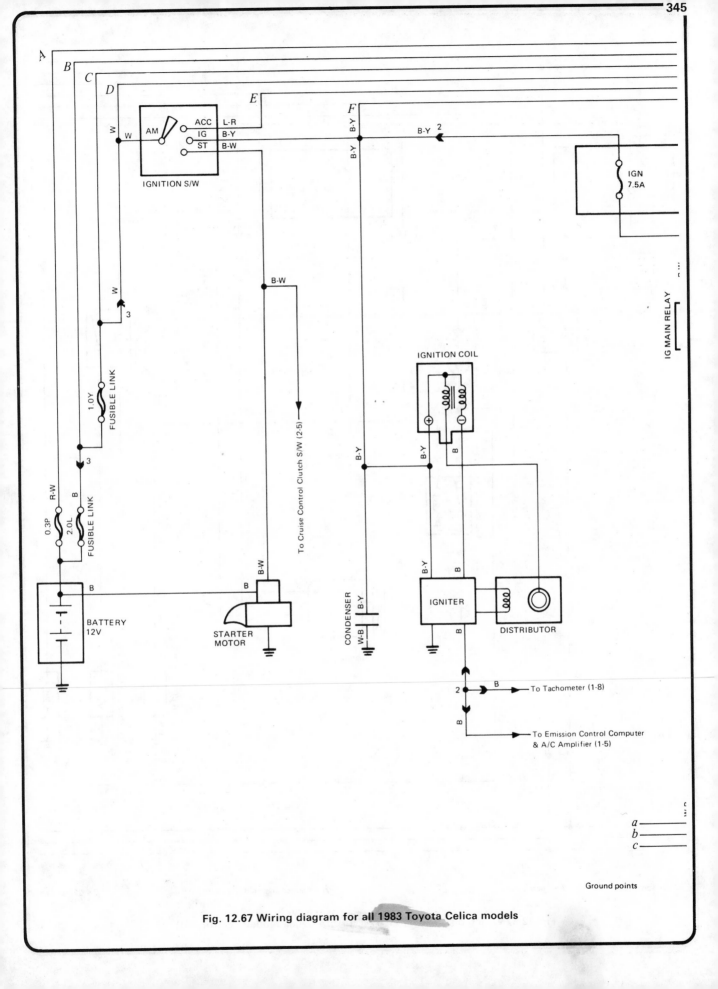

Fig. 12.67 Wiring diagram for all 1983 Toyota Celica models

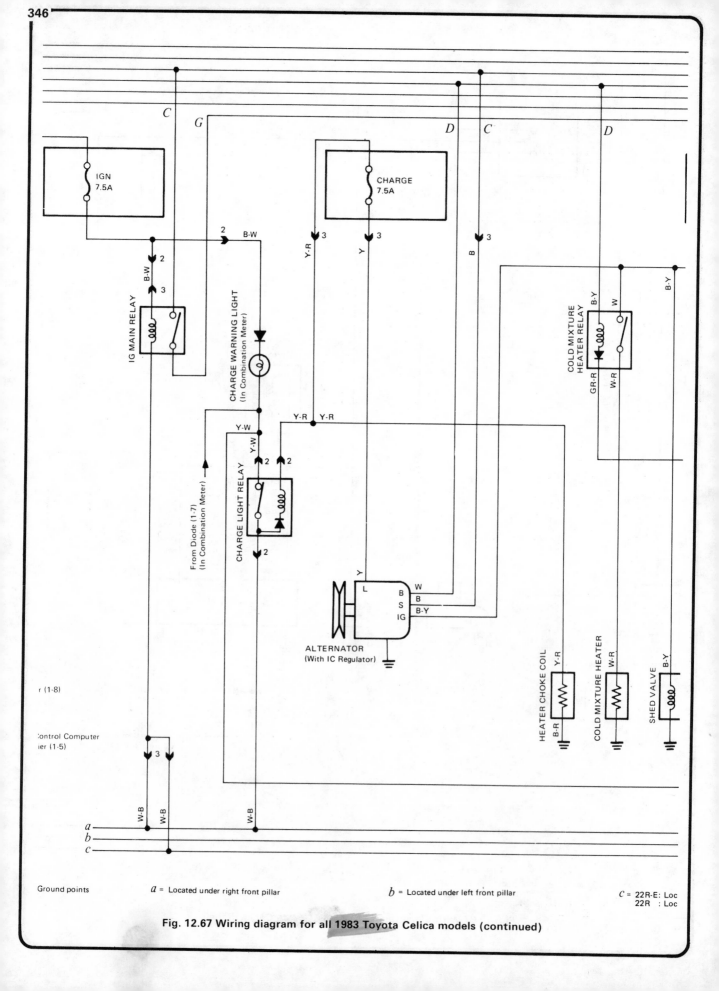

Fig. 12.67 Wiring diagram for all 1983 Toyota Celica models (continued)

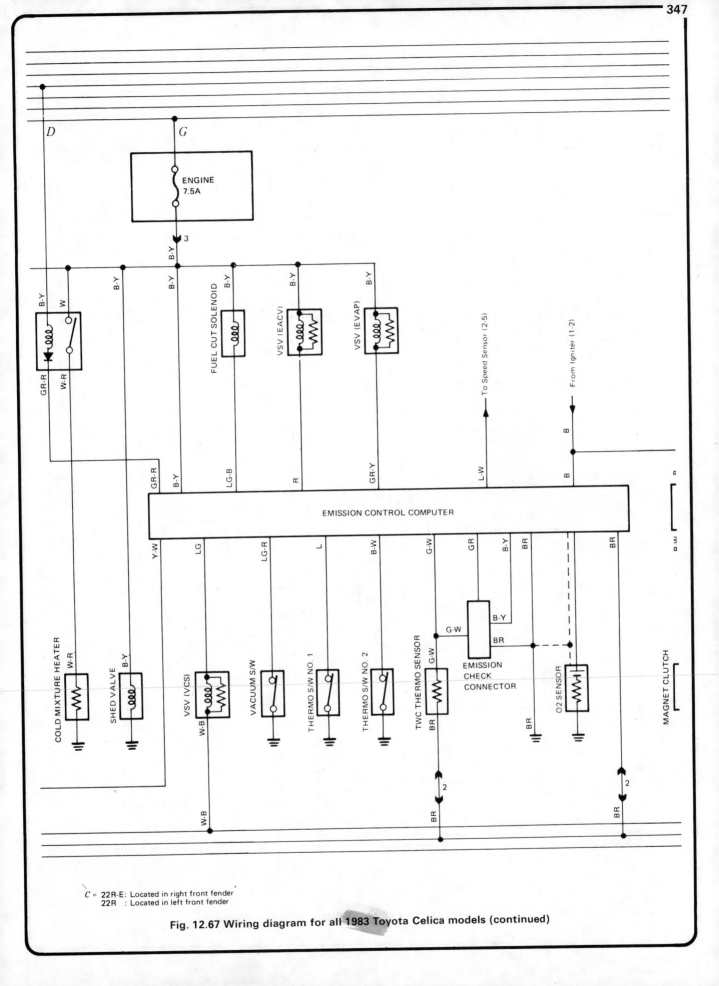

Fig. 12.67 Wiring diagram for all 1983 Toyota Celica models (continued)

C = 22R-E: Located in right front fender
22R : Located in left front fender

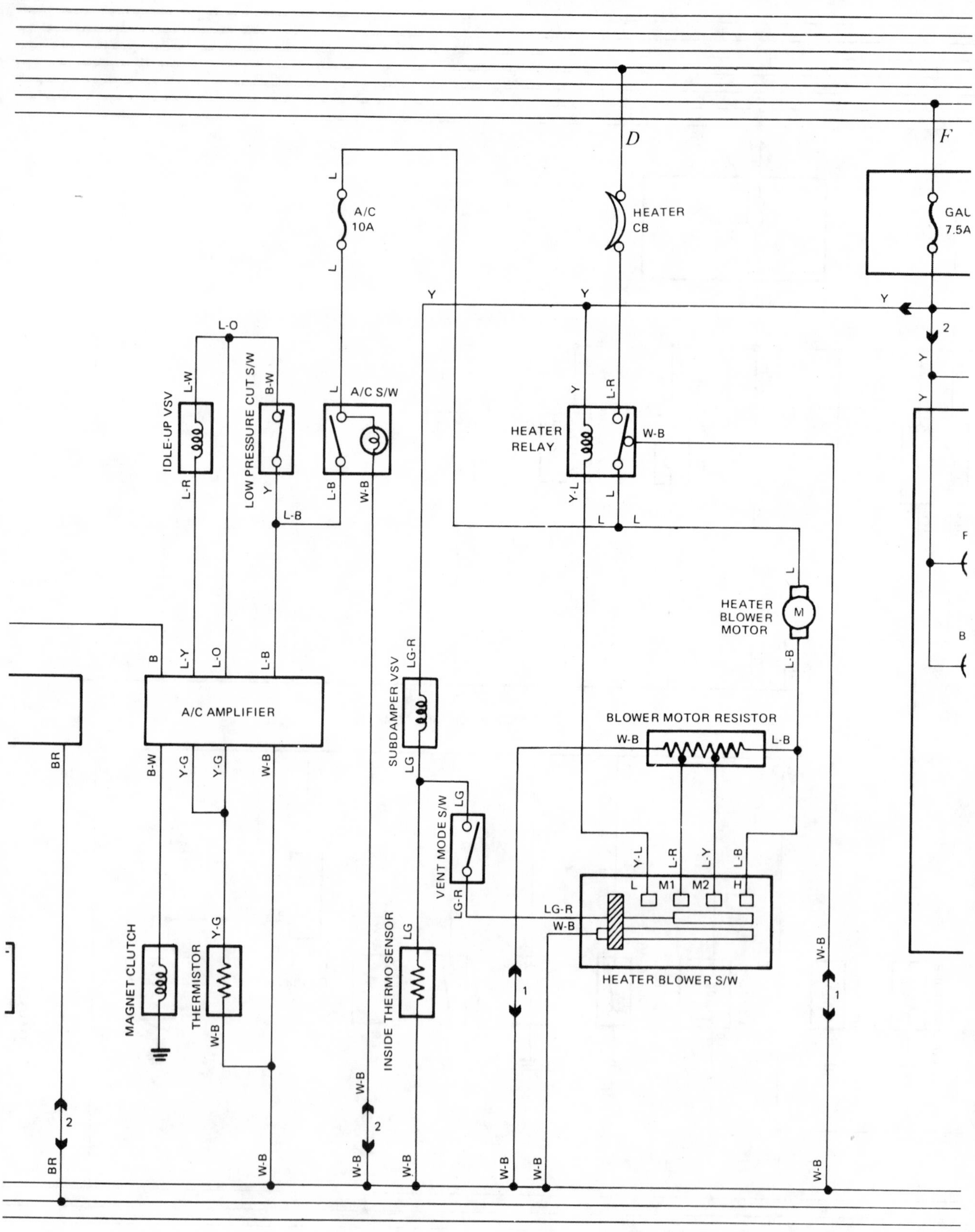

Fig. 12.67 Wiring diagram for all 1983 Toyota Celica models (continued)

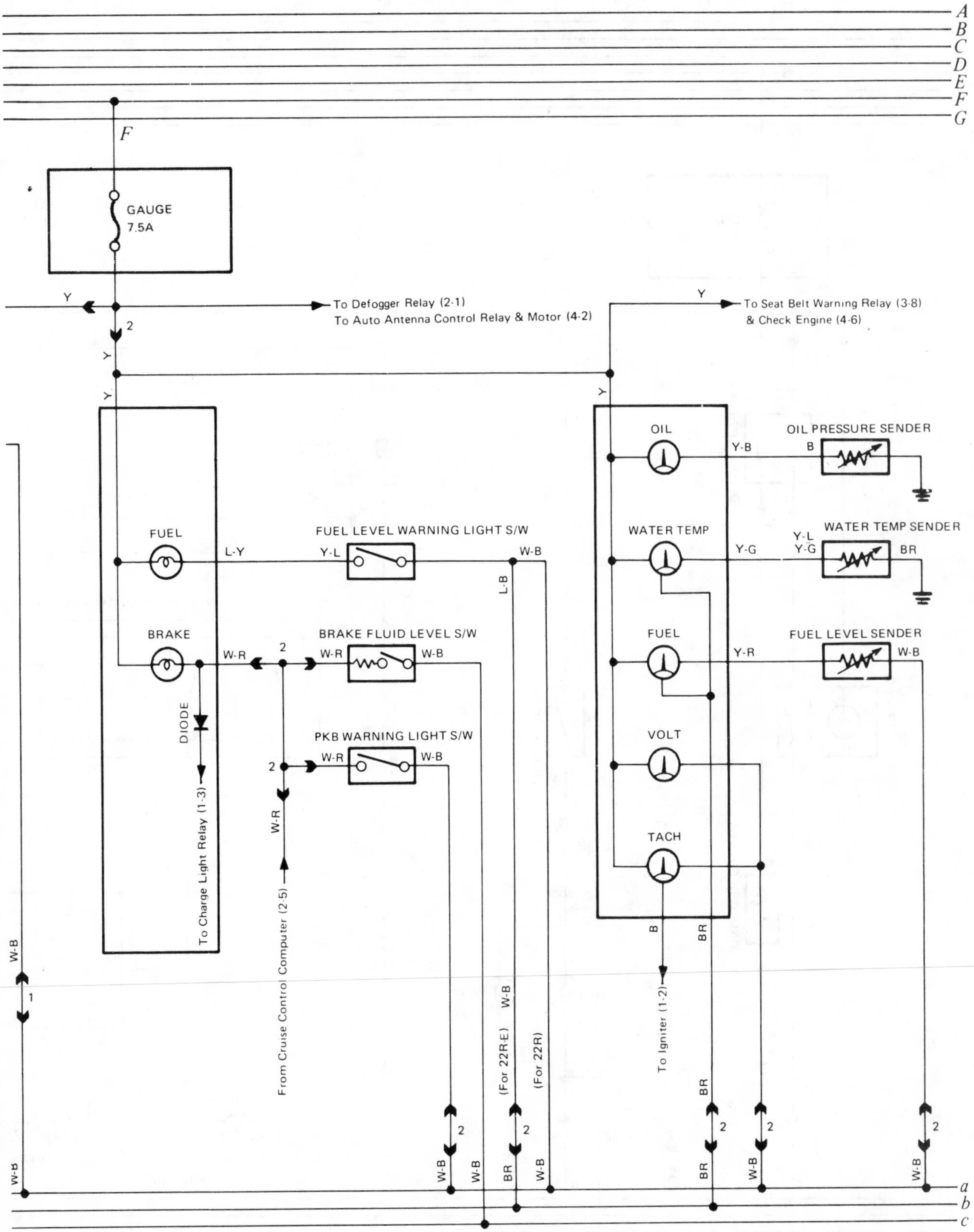

Fig. 12.67 Wiring diagram for all 1983 Toyota Celica models (continued)

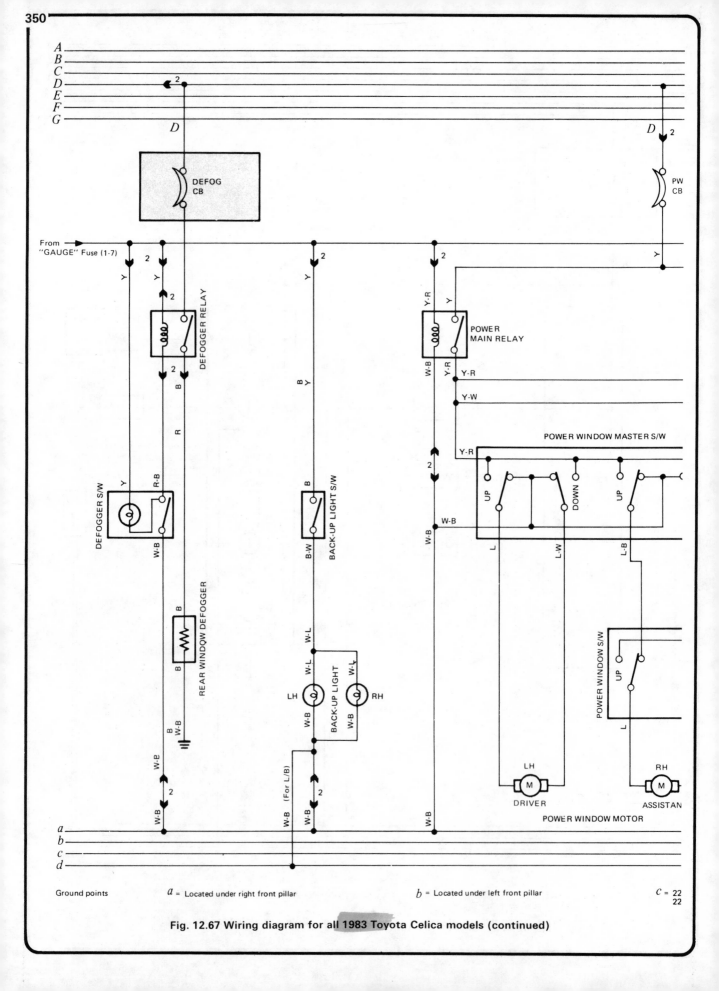

Fig. 12.67 Wiring diagram for all 1983 Toyota Celica models (continued)

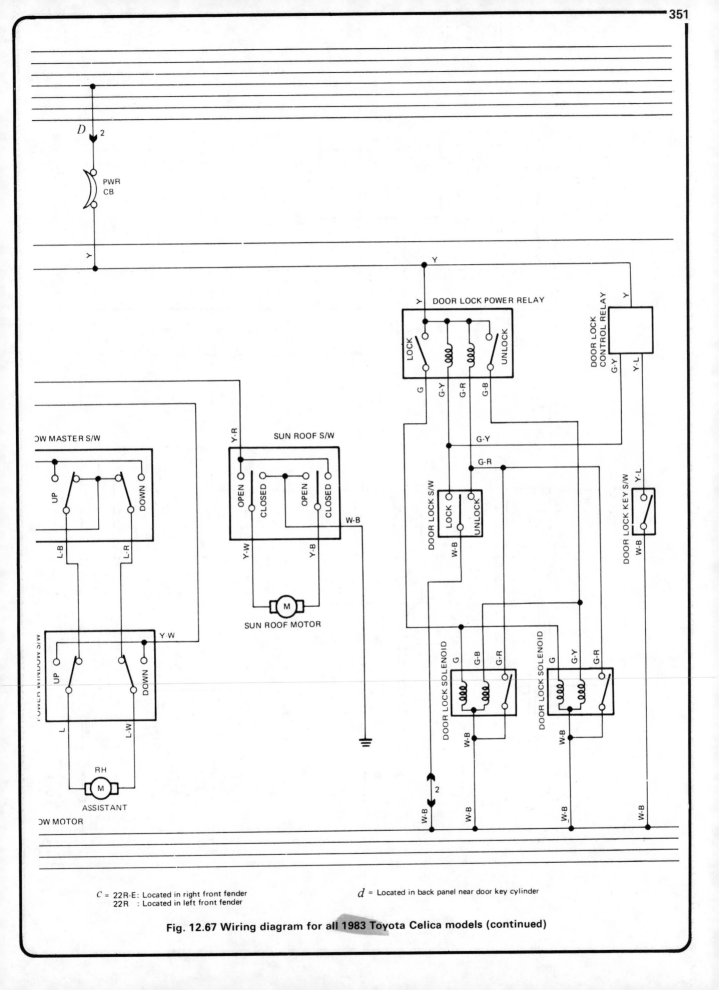

C = 22R-E: Located in right front fender
22R : Located in left front fender

d = Located in back panel near door key cylinder

Fig. 12.67 Wiring diagram for all 1983 Toyota Celica models (continued)

Fig. 12.67 Wiring diagram for all 1983 Toyota Celica models (continued)

Fig. 12.67 Wiring diagram for all 1983 Toyota Celica models (continued)

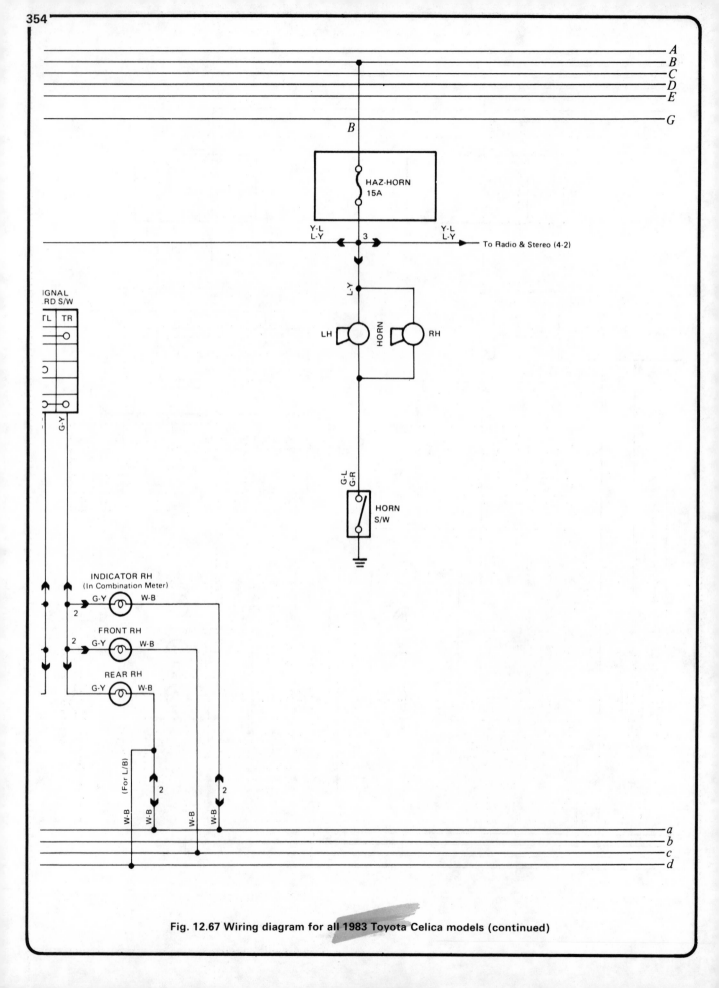

Fig. 12.67 Wiring diagram for all 1983 Toyota Celica models (continued)

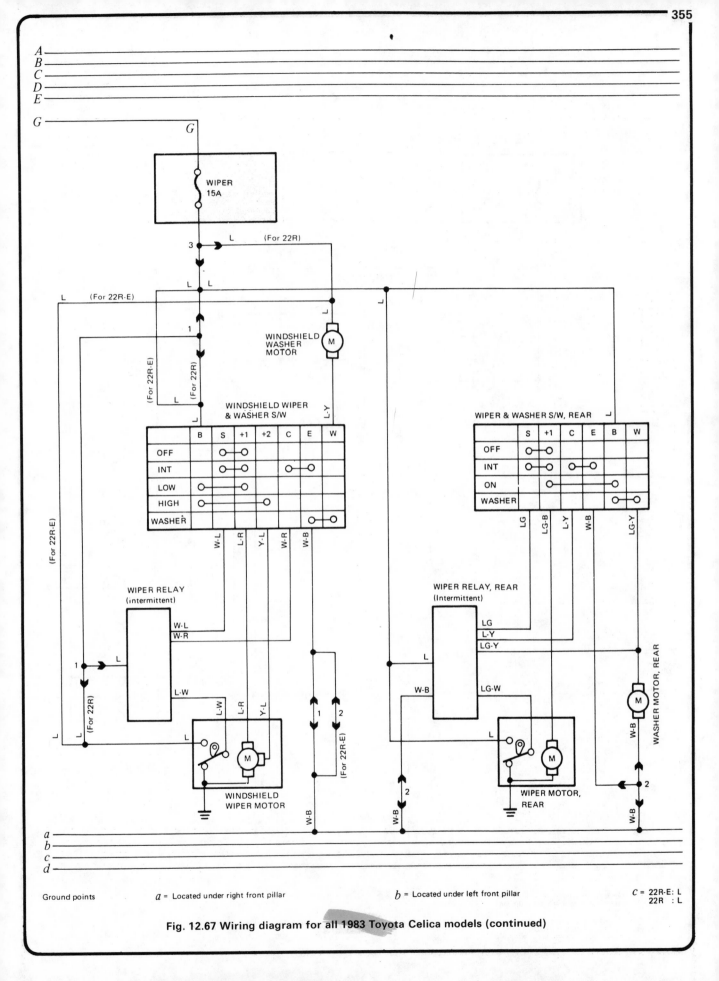

Fig. 12.67 Wiring diagram for all 1983 Toyota Celica models (continued)

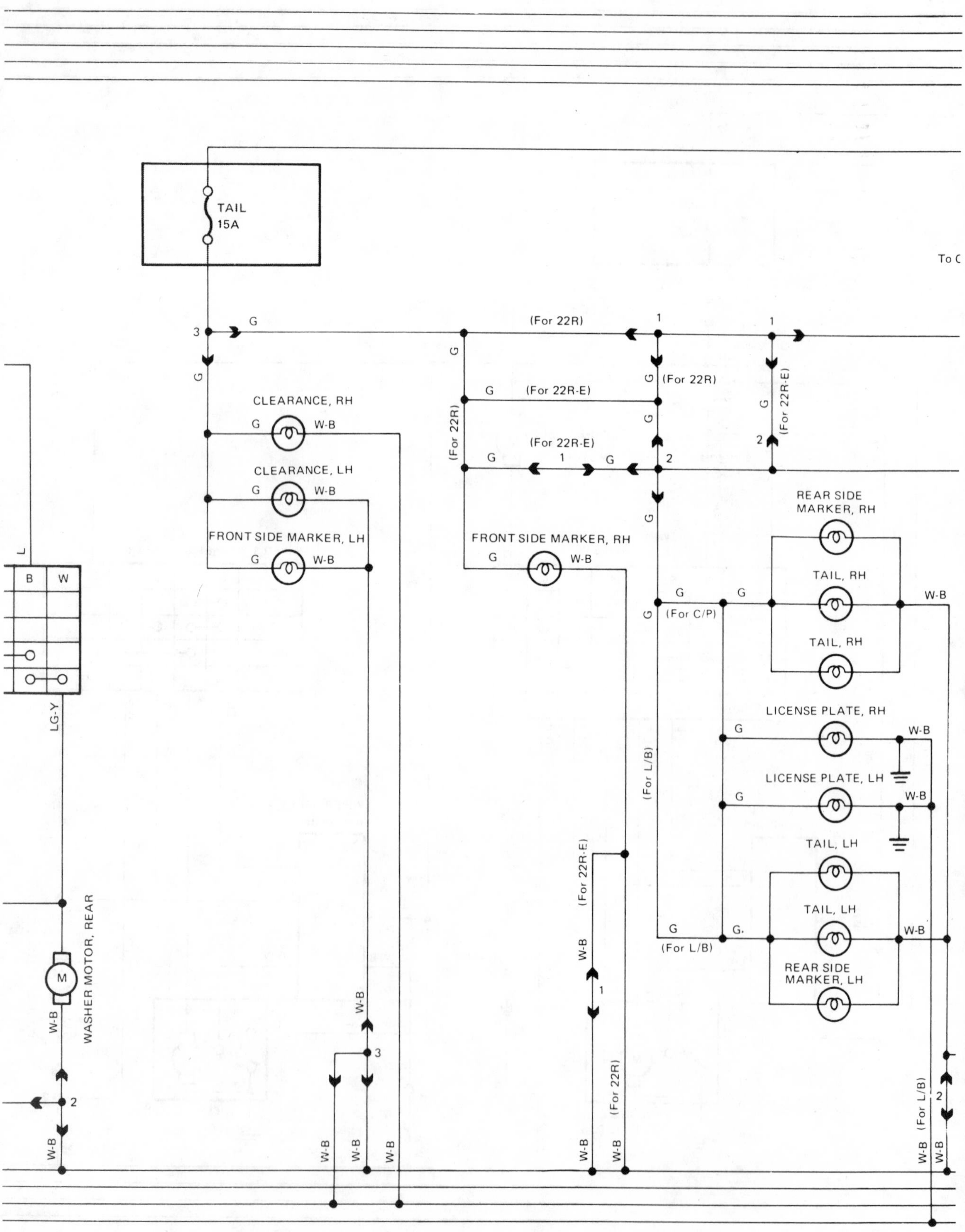

TAIL
15A

3   G   (For 22R)   1   1

G

CLEARANCE, RH
G   W-B   G   (For 22R-E)

CLEARANCE, LH   G   (For 22R)   G   G   (For 22R-E)
G   W-B

FRONT SIDE MARKER, LH   G   (For 22R-E)   1   G
G   W-B

REAR SIDE
MARKER, RH

FRONT SIDE MARKER, RH
G   W-B

G   G   TAIL, RH

G   (For C/P)   W-B

TAIL, RH

LICENSE PLATE, RH
G   W-B

LICENSE PLATE, LH
G   W-B

B   W

TAIL, LH

TAIL, LH
G   G.   W-B

LG-Y

REAR SIDE
MARKER, LH

WASHER MOTOR, REAR

W-B

W-B   (For 22R-E)   W-B

M

W-B   3

2   W-B   1

(For 22R)

2

W-B   W-B   W-B   W-B   W-B   W-B   W-B   W-B

C = 22R-E: Located in right front fender
    22R   : Located in left front fender

d = Located in back panel near door key cylinder

Fig. 12.67 Wiring diagram for all 1983 Toyota Celica models (continued)

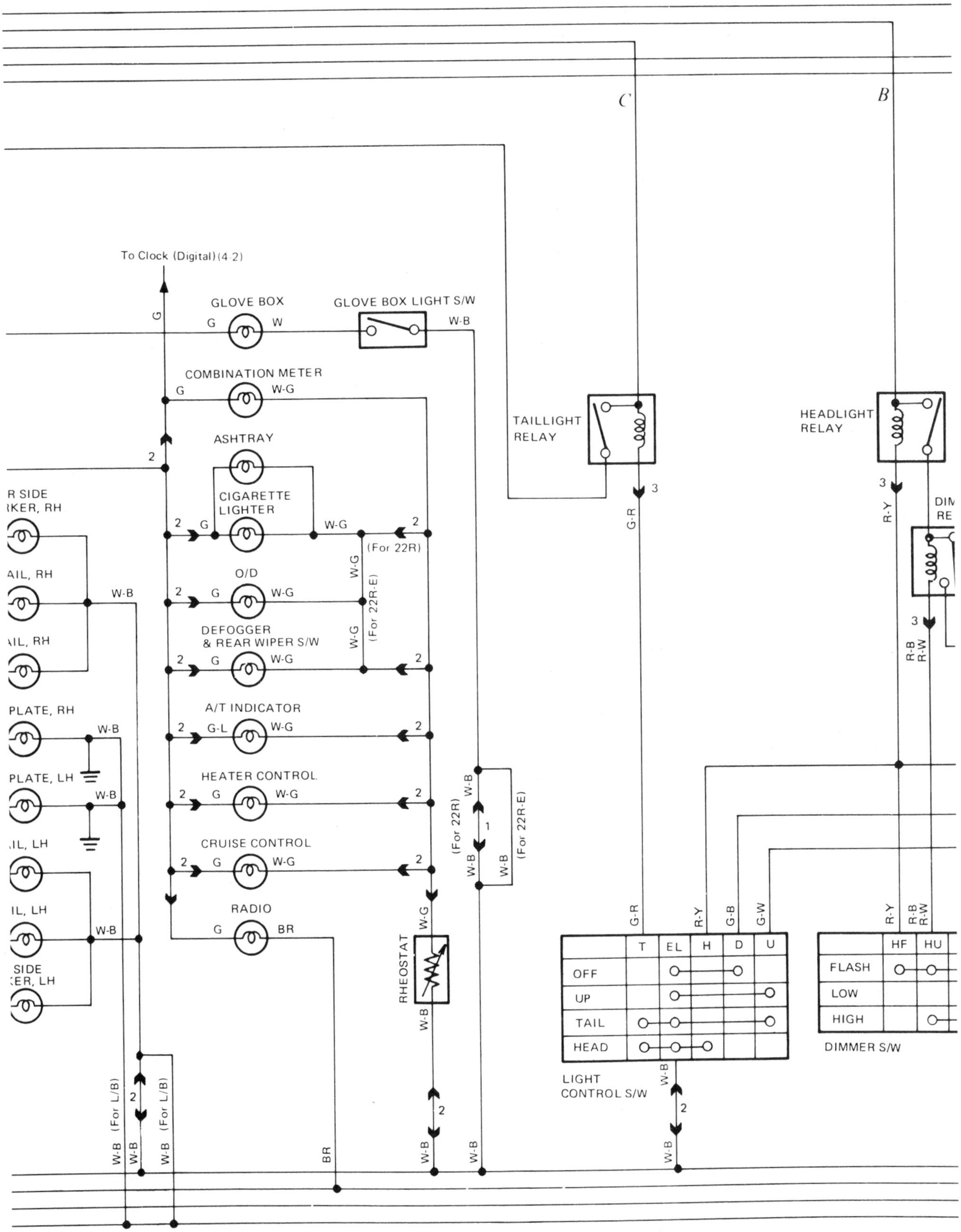

To Clock (Digital) (4·2)

GLOVE BOX
GLOVE BOX LIGHT S/W
G W W-B

COMBINATION METER
G W-G

ASHTRAY

CIGARETTE LIGHTER
2 G W-G 2
(For 22R)
W-G (For 22R-E)

O/D
2 G W-G 2

DEFOGGER & REAR WIPER S/W
2 G W-G 2

A/T INDICATOR
2 G-L W-G 2

HEATER CONTROL
2 G W-G 2

CRUISE CONTROL
2 G W-G 2

RADIO
G BR

RHEOSTAT
W-G
W-B

TAILLIGHT RELAY
G-R 3

HEADLIGHT RELAY
R-Y 3

DIM RE
R-B R-W 3

R SIDE RKER, RH

AIL, RH
W-B

AIL, RH

PLATE, RH
W-B

PLATE, LH
W-B

IL, LH

IL, LH
W-B

SIDE KER, LH

W-B (For L/B)
2
W-B
W-B (For L/B)

BR

W-B (For 22R)
W-B
1
W-B (For 22R-E)

W-B
2

W-B
2

G-R

	T	EL	H	D	U
OFF		○		○	
UP		○			○
TAIL	○	○			○
HEAD	○	○	○		

LIGHT CONTROL S/W

W-B
2

R-Y G-B G-W

R-Y R-B R-W

	HF	HU	
FLASH	○	○	
LOW			
HIGH		○	

DIMMER S/W

Fig. 12.67 Wiring diagram for all 1983 Toyota Celica models (continued)

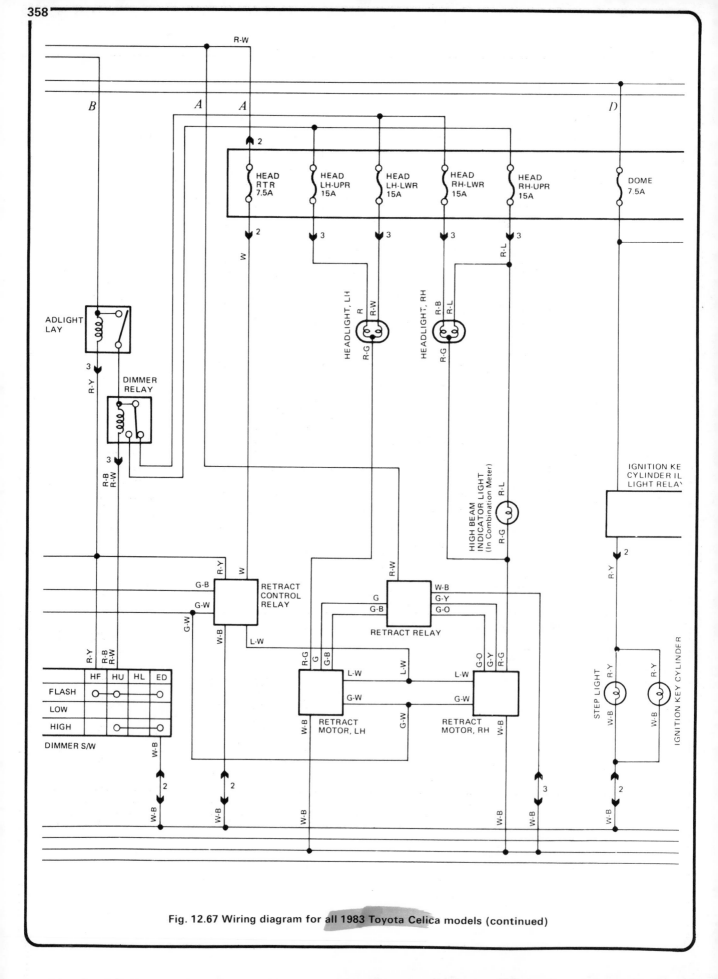

Fig. 12.67 Wiring diagram for all 1983 Toyota Celica models (continued)

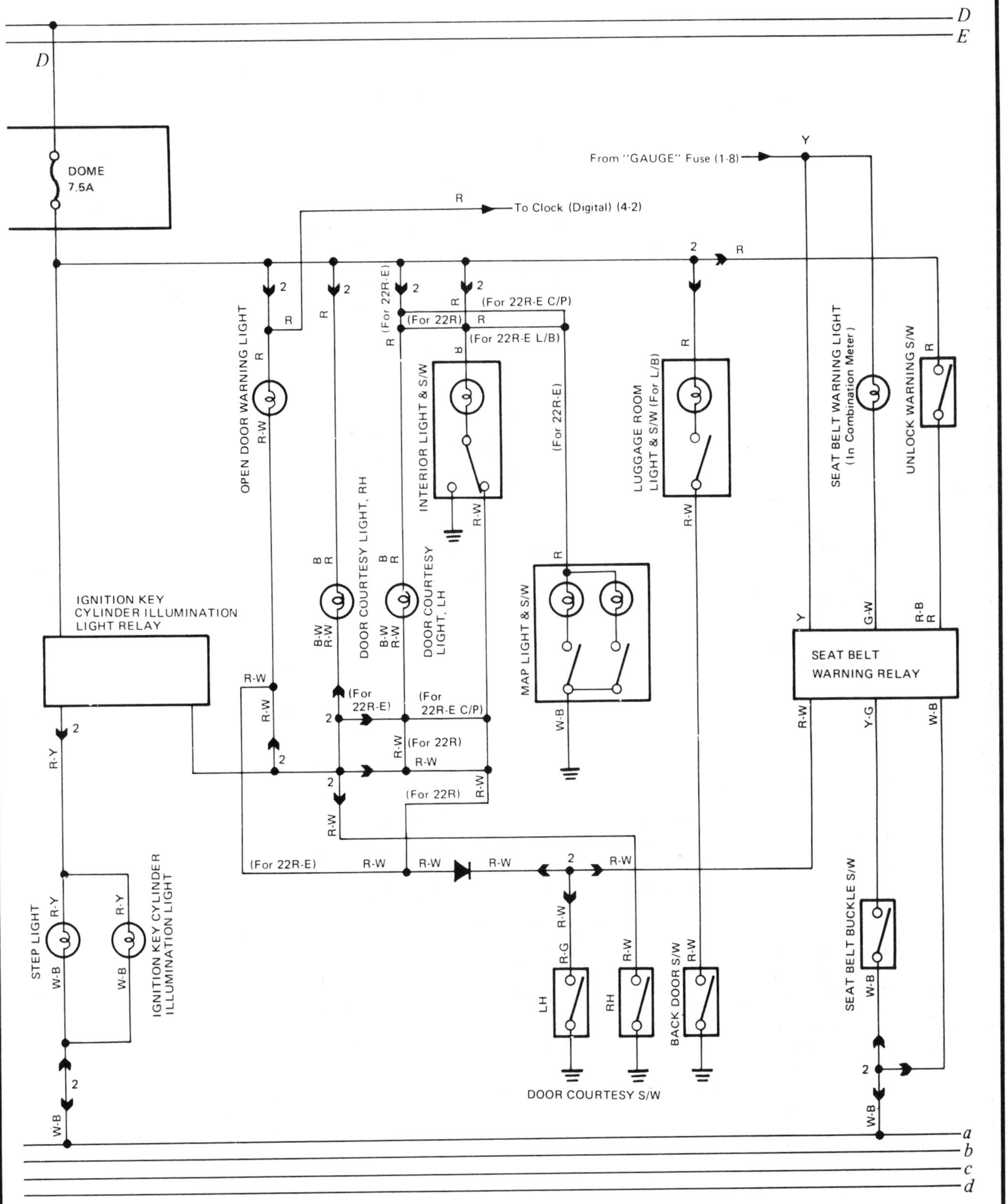

Fig. 12.67 Wiring diagram for all 1983 Toyota Celica models (continued)

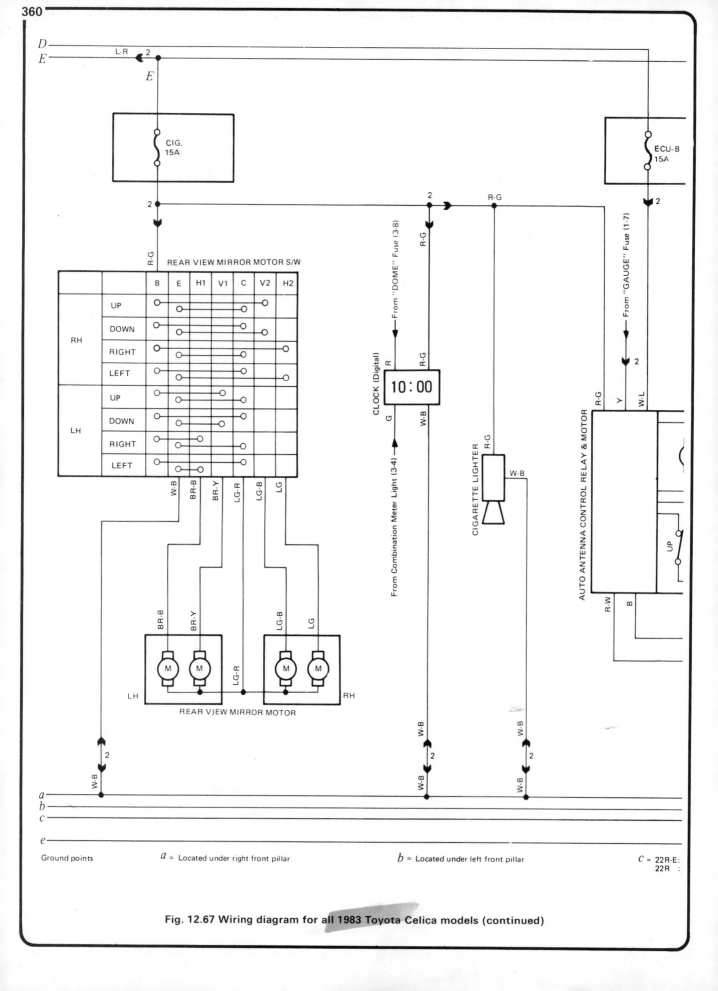

Fig. 12.67 Wiring diagram for all 1983 Toyota Celica models (continued)

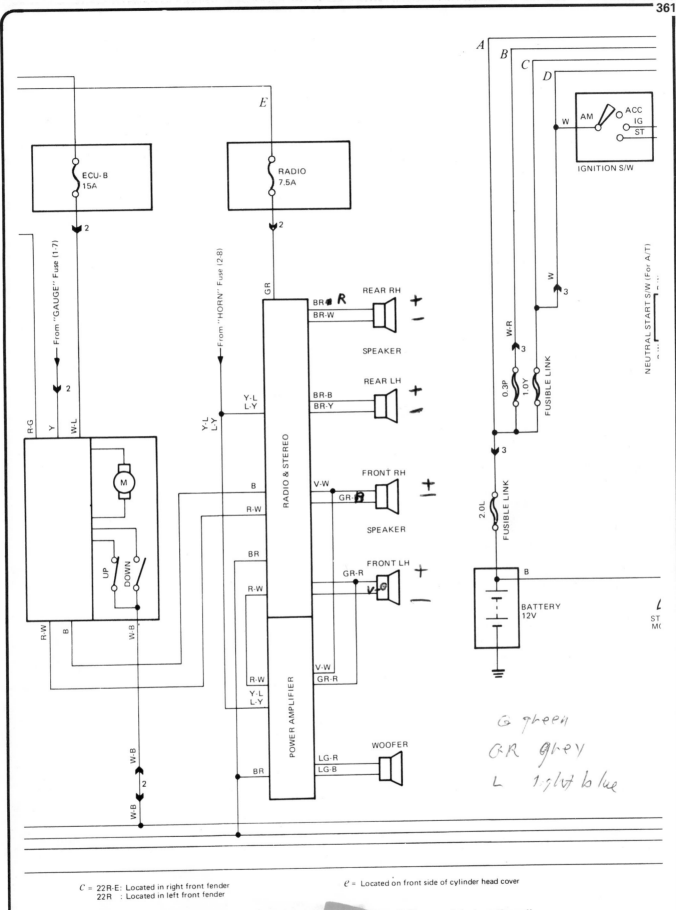

Fig. 12.67 Wiring diagram for all 1983 Toyota Celica models (continued)

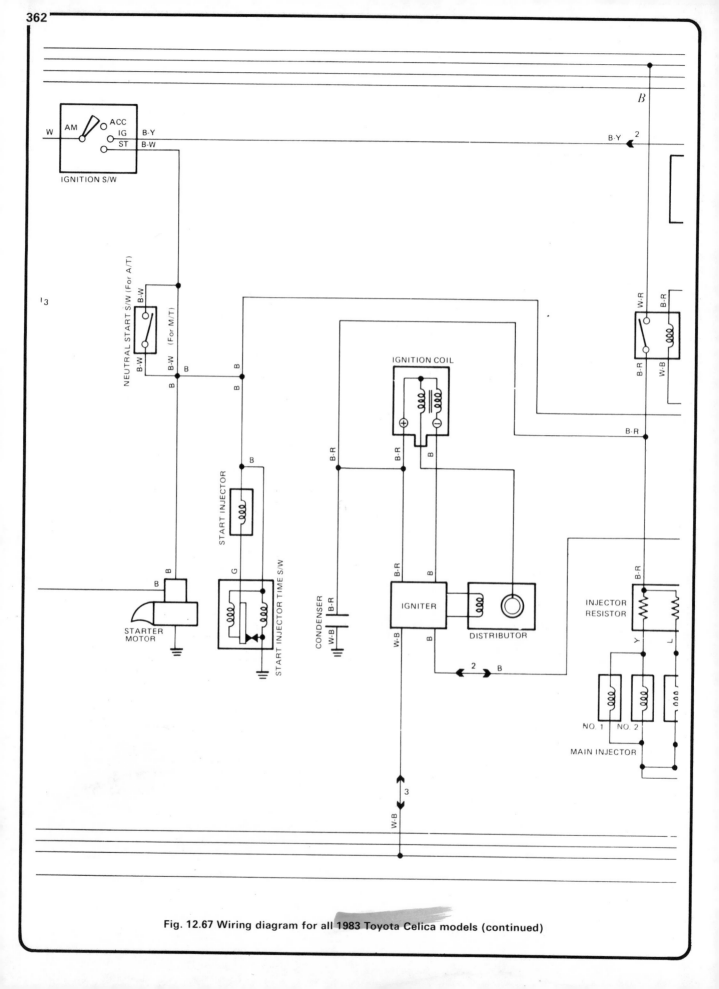

Fig. 12.67 Wiring diagram for all 1983 Toyota Celica models (continued)

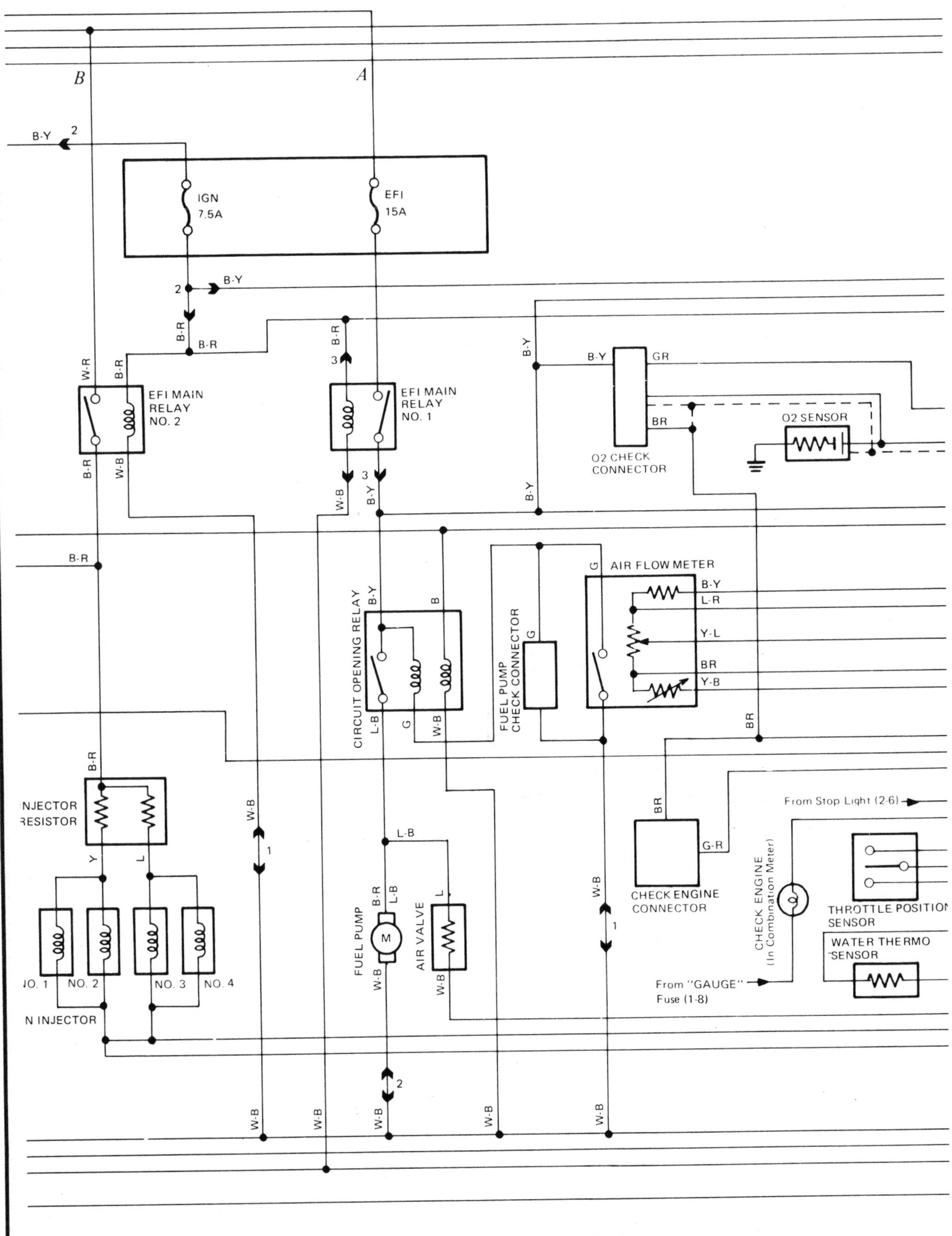

Fig. 12.67 Wiring diagram for all 1983 Toyota Celica models (continued)

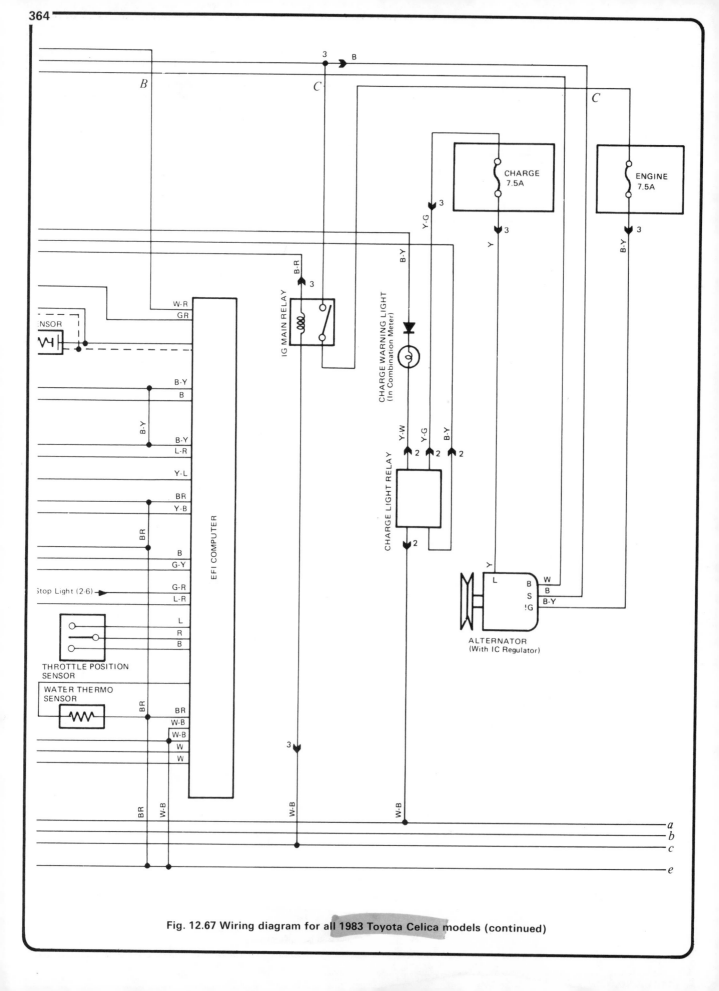

Fig. 12.67 Wiring diagram for all **1983 Toyota Celica models** (continued)

365

Fig. 12.68 Wiring diagram for all 1984/85 Toyota Celica models

Grounds points

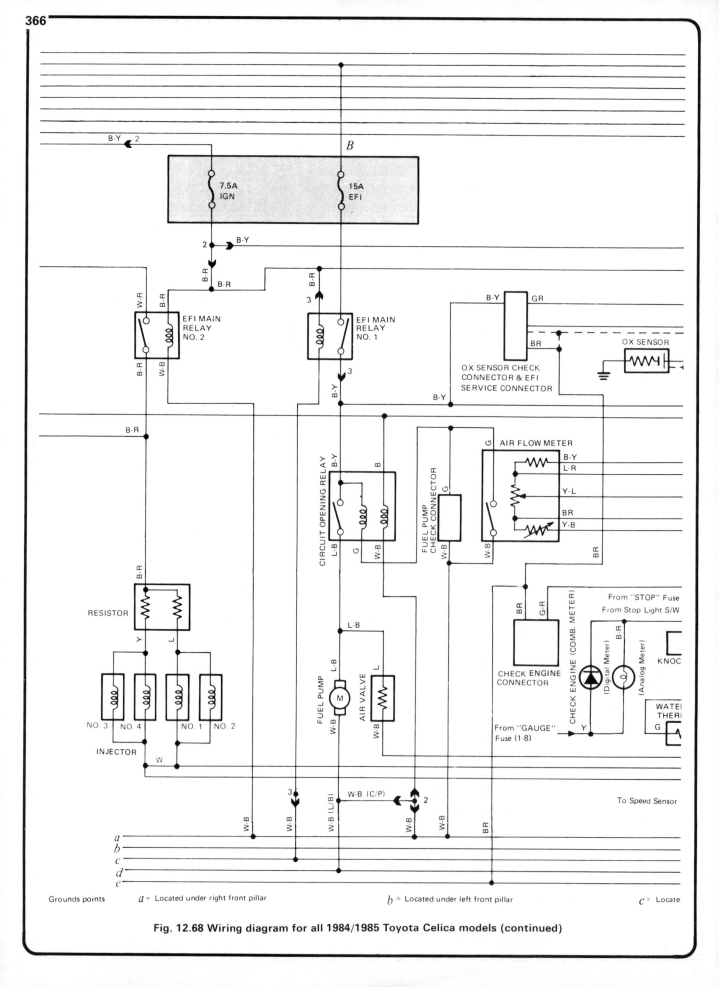

Fig. 12.68 Wiring diagram for all 1984/1985 Toyota Celica models (continued)

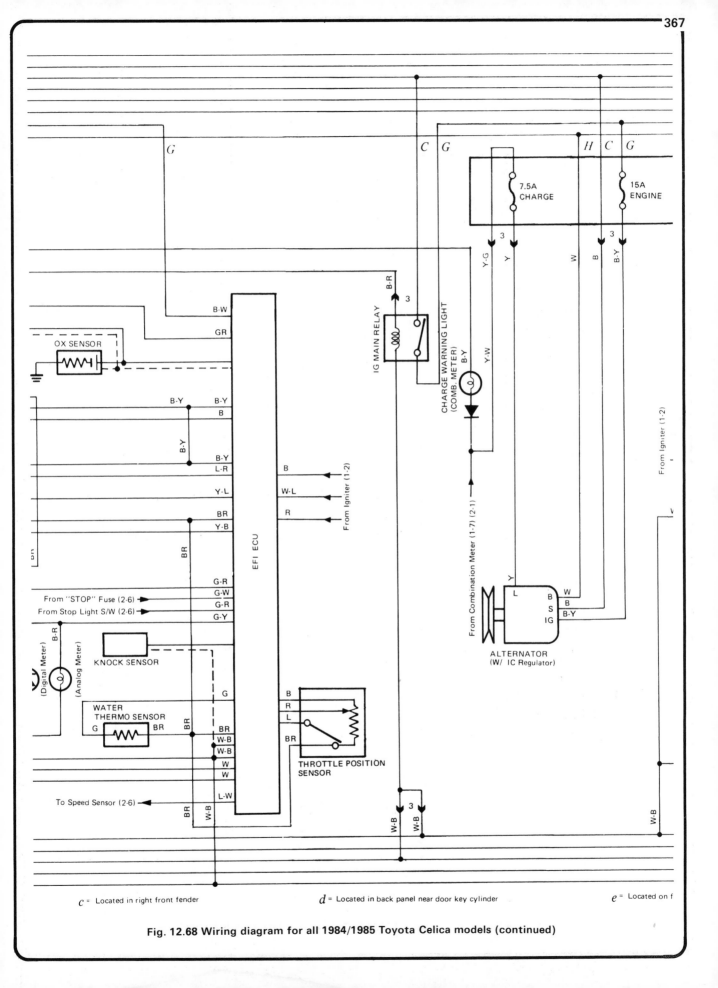

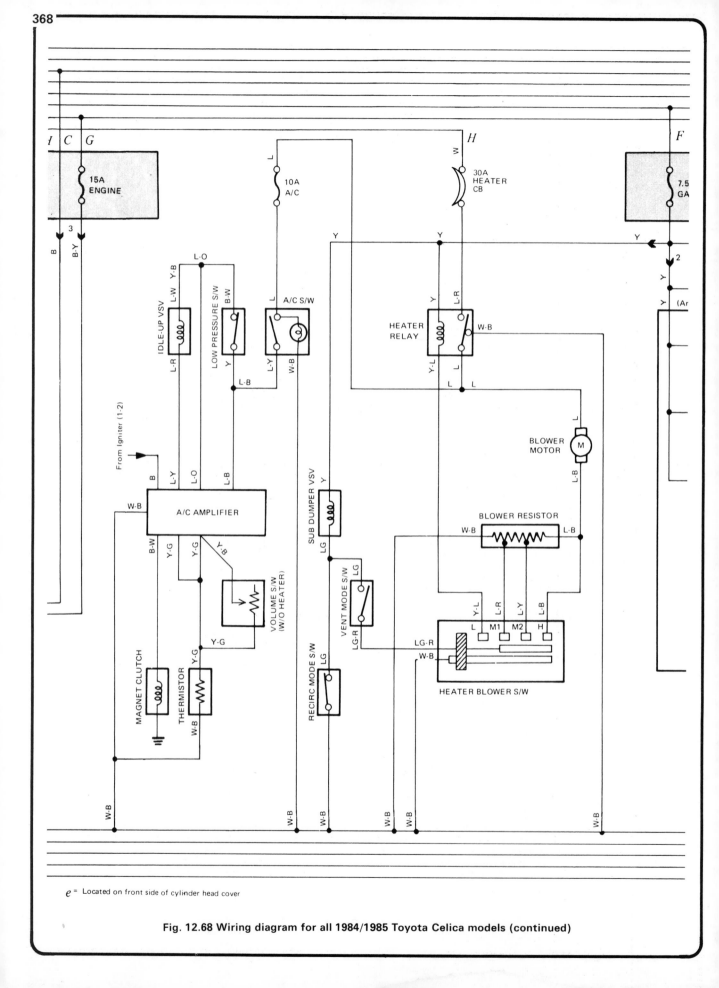

Fig. 12.68 Wiring diagram for all 1984/1985 Toyota Celica models (continued)

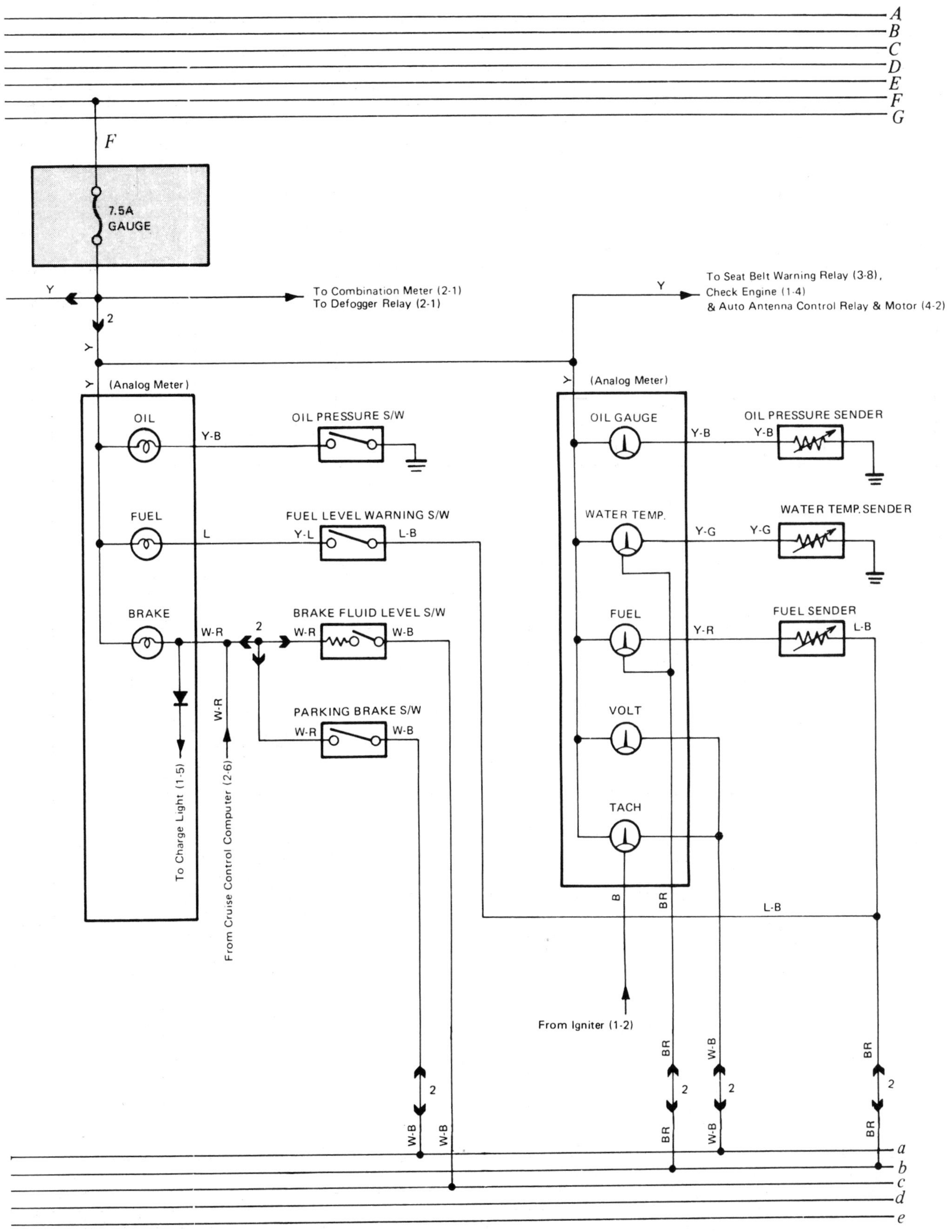

Fig. 12.68 Wiring diagram for all 1984/1985 Toyota Celica models (continued)

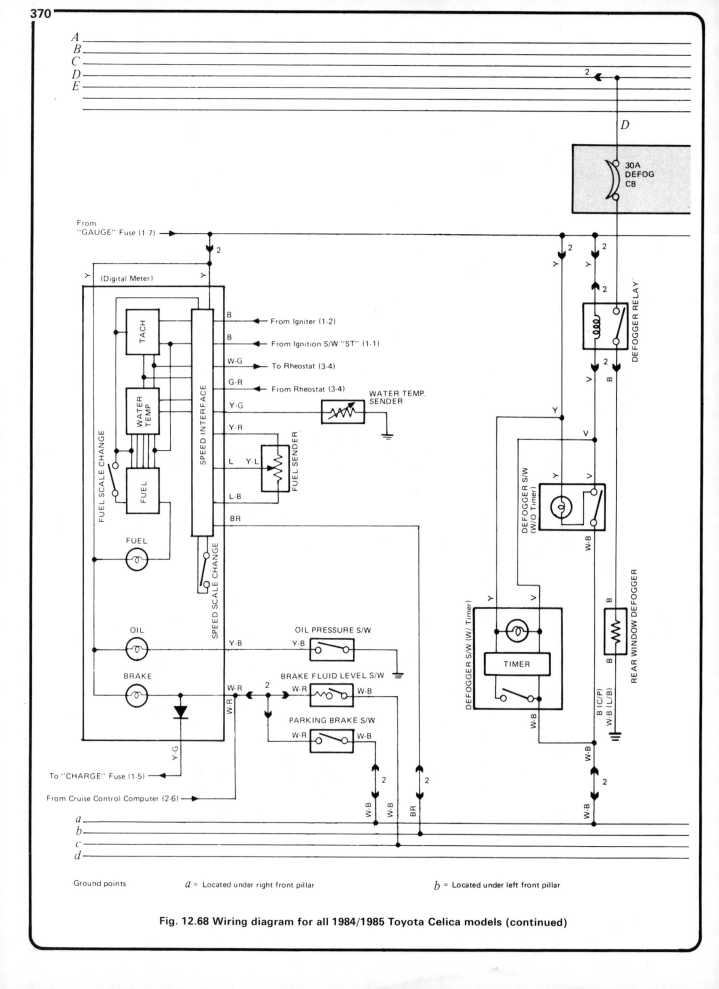

Fig. 12.68 Wiring diagram for all 1984/1985 Toyota Celica models (continued)

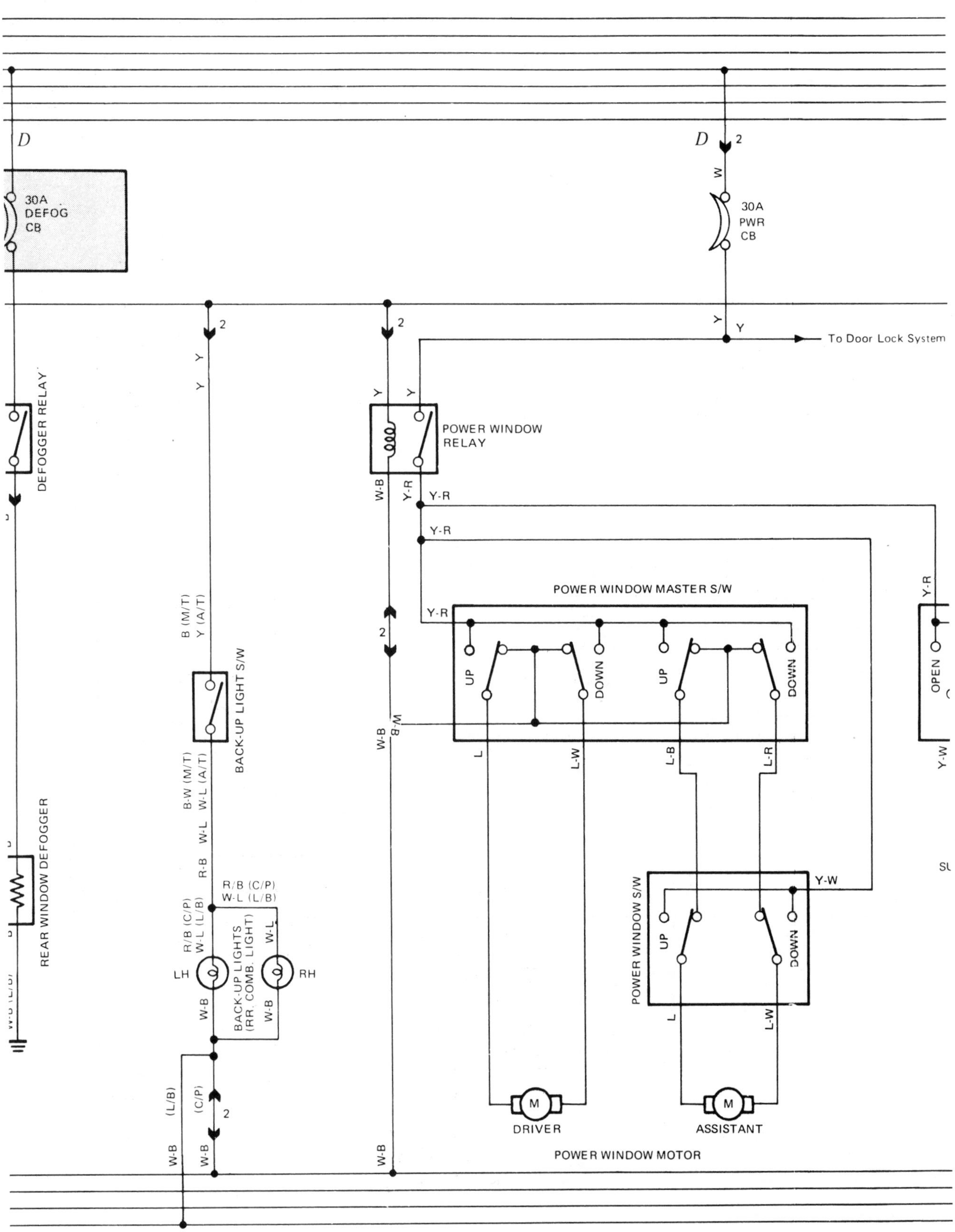

C = Located in right front fender

d = Located in back panel near door key cylinder

Fig. 12.68 Wiring diagram for all 1984/1985 Toyota Celica models (continued)

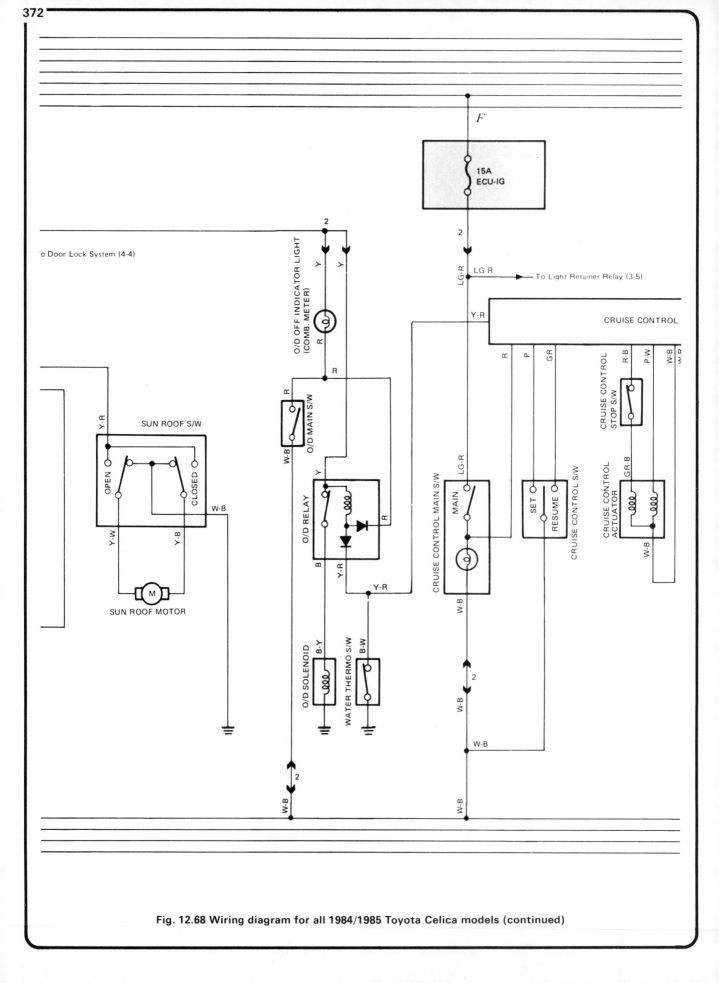

Fig. 12.68 Wiring diagram for all 1984/1985 Toyota Celica models (continued)

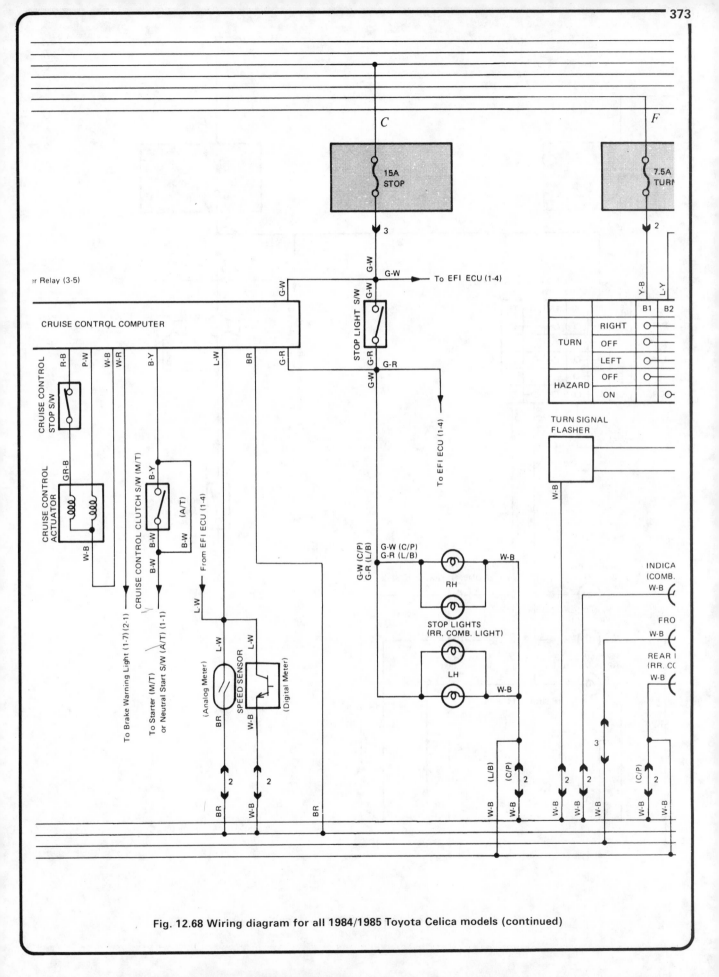

Fig. 12.68 Wiring diagram for all 1984/1985 Toyota Celica models (continued)

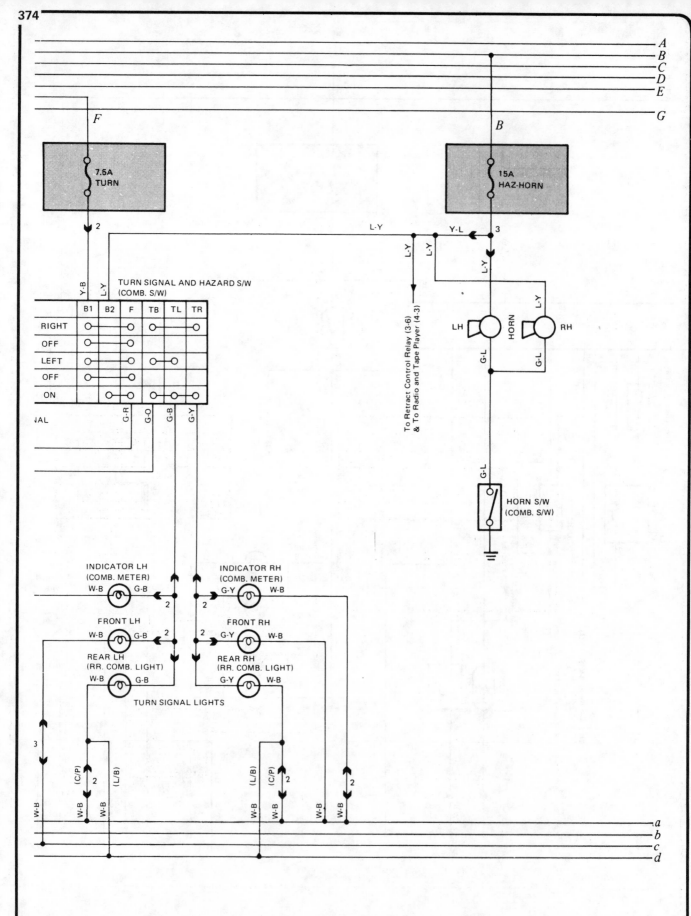

Fig. 12.68 Wiring diagram for all 1984/1985 Toyota Celica models (continued)

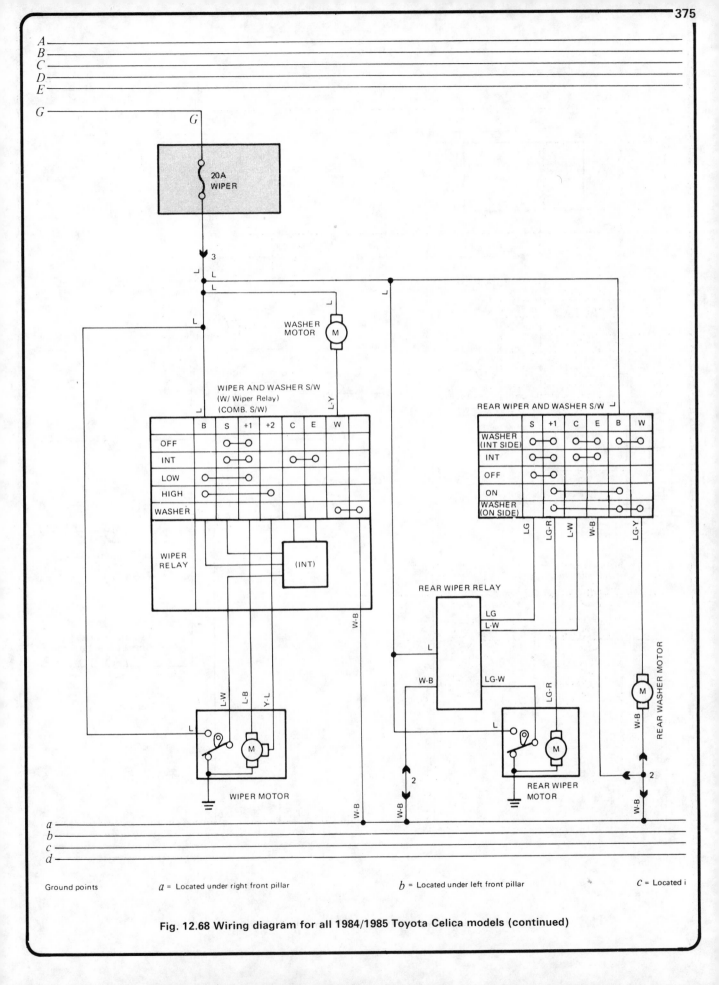

Fig. 12.68 Wiring diagram for all 1984/1985 Toyota Celica models (continued)

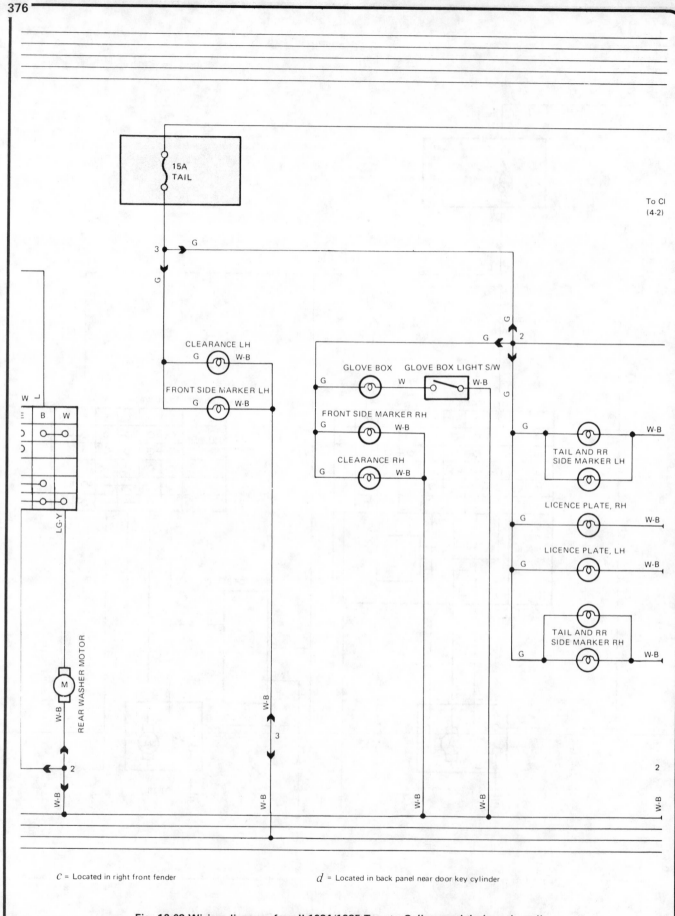

C = Located in right front fender

d = Located in back panel near door key cylinder

Fig. 12.68 Wiring diagram for all 1984/1985 Toyota Celica models (continued)

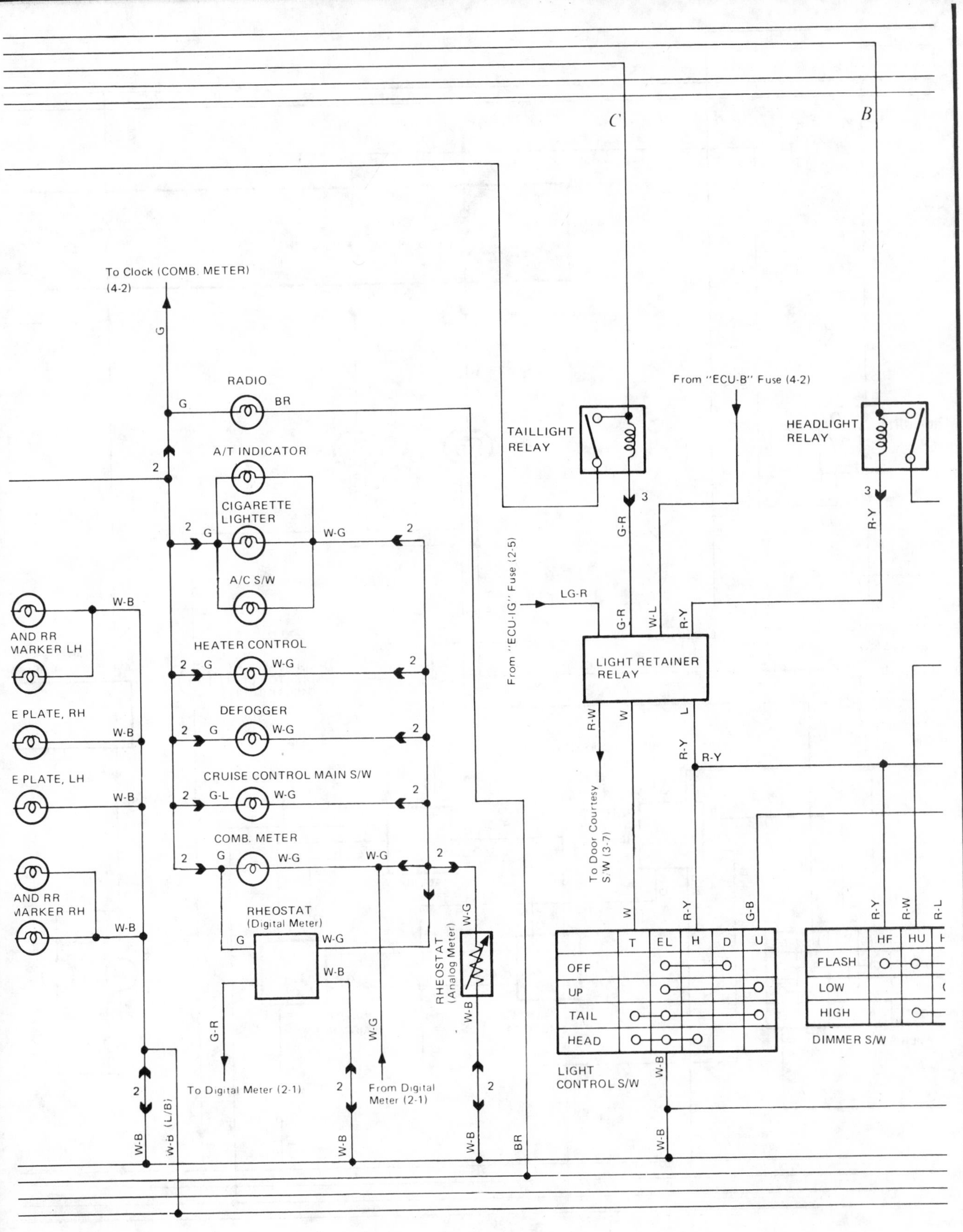

Fig. 12.68 Wiring diagram for all 1984/1985 Toyota Celica models (continued)

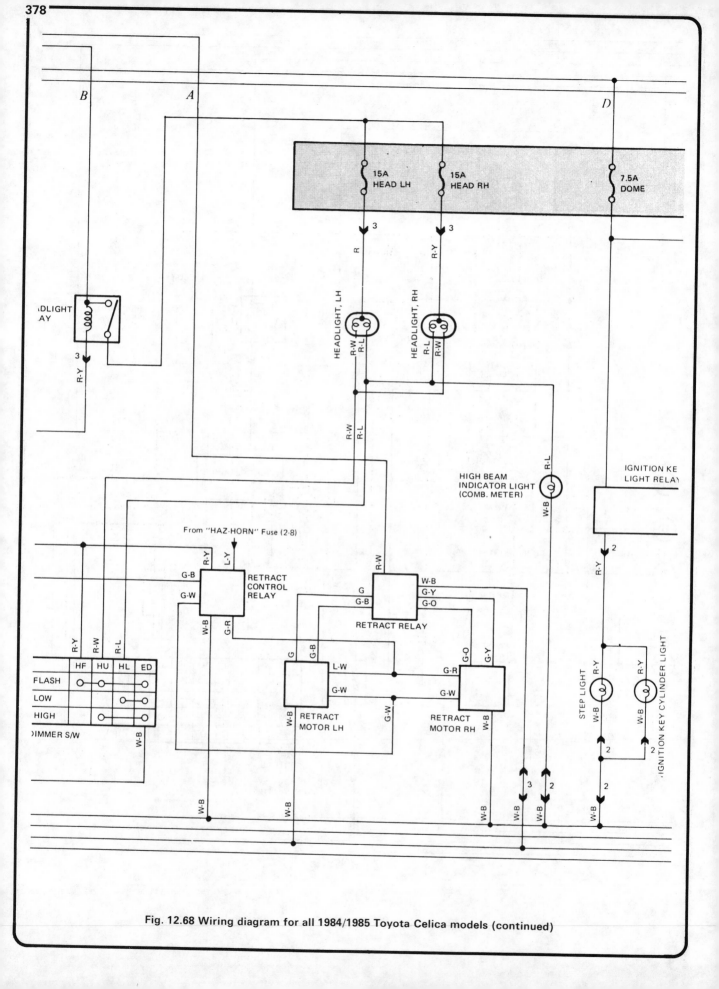

Fig. 12.68 Wiring diagram for all 1984/1985 Toyota Celica models (continued)

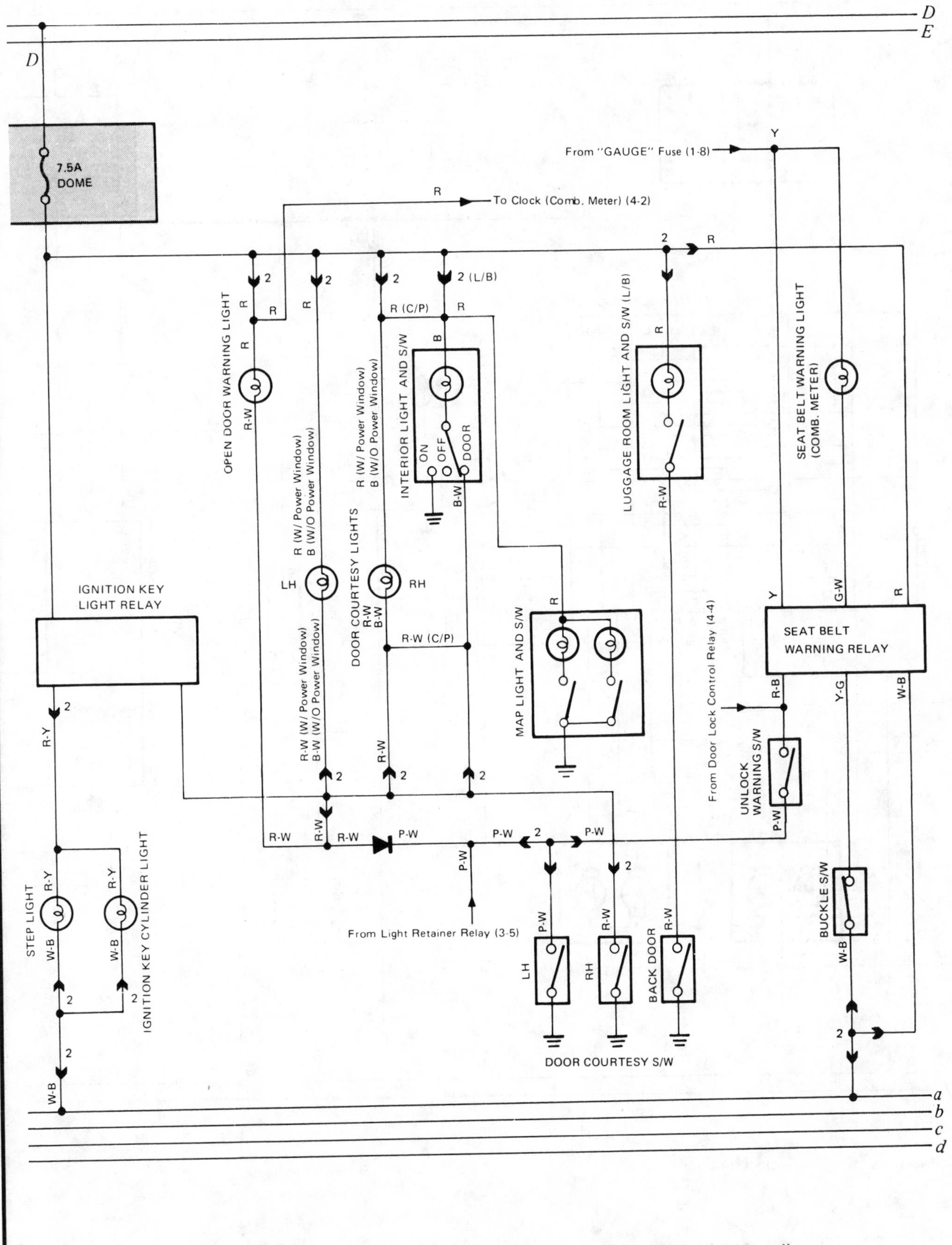

Fig. 12.68 Wiring diagram for all 1984/1985 Toyota Celica models (continued)

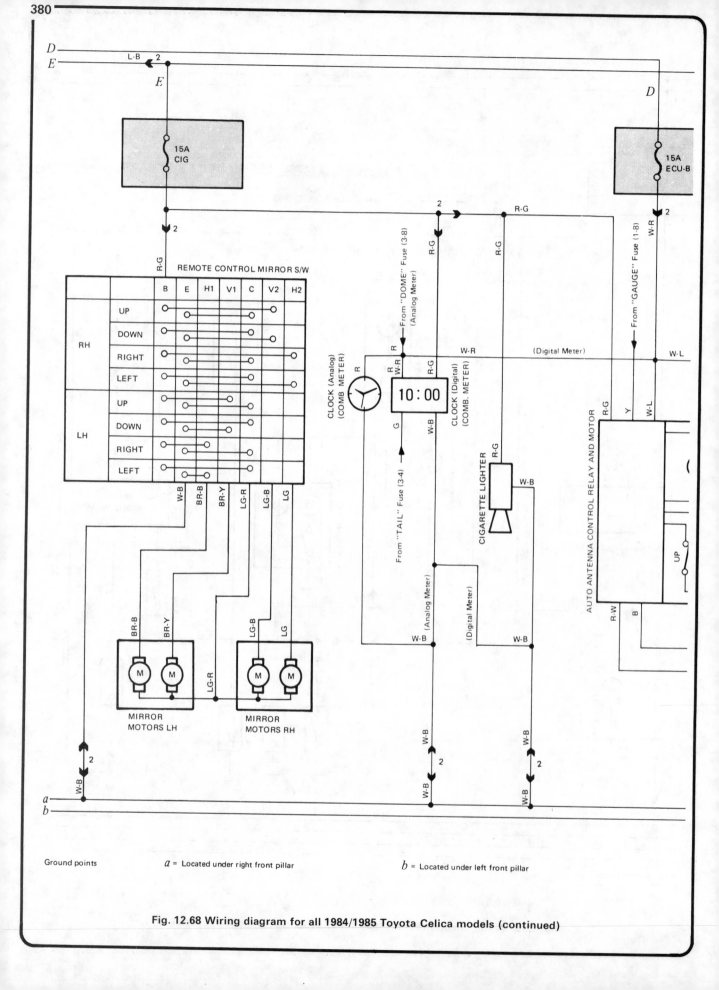

Ground points   *a* = Located under right front pillar   *b* = Located under left front pillar

Fig. 12.68 Wiring diagram for all 1984/1985 Toyota Celica models (continued)

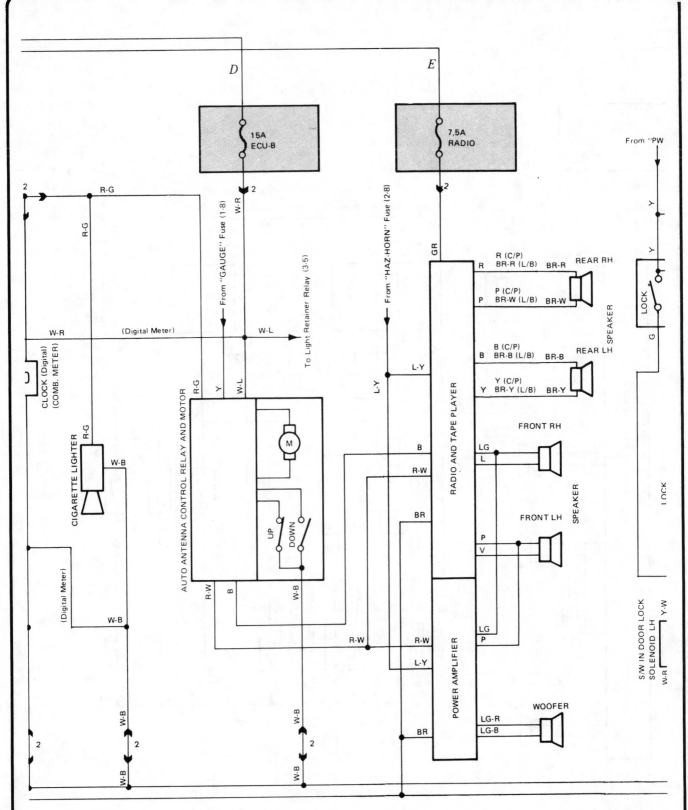

Fig. 12.68 Wiring diagram for all 1984/1985 Toyota Celica models (continued)

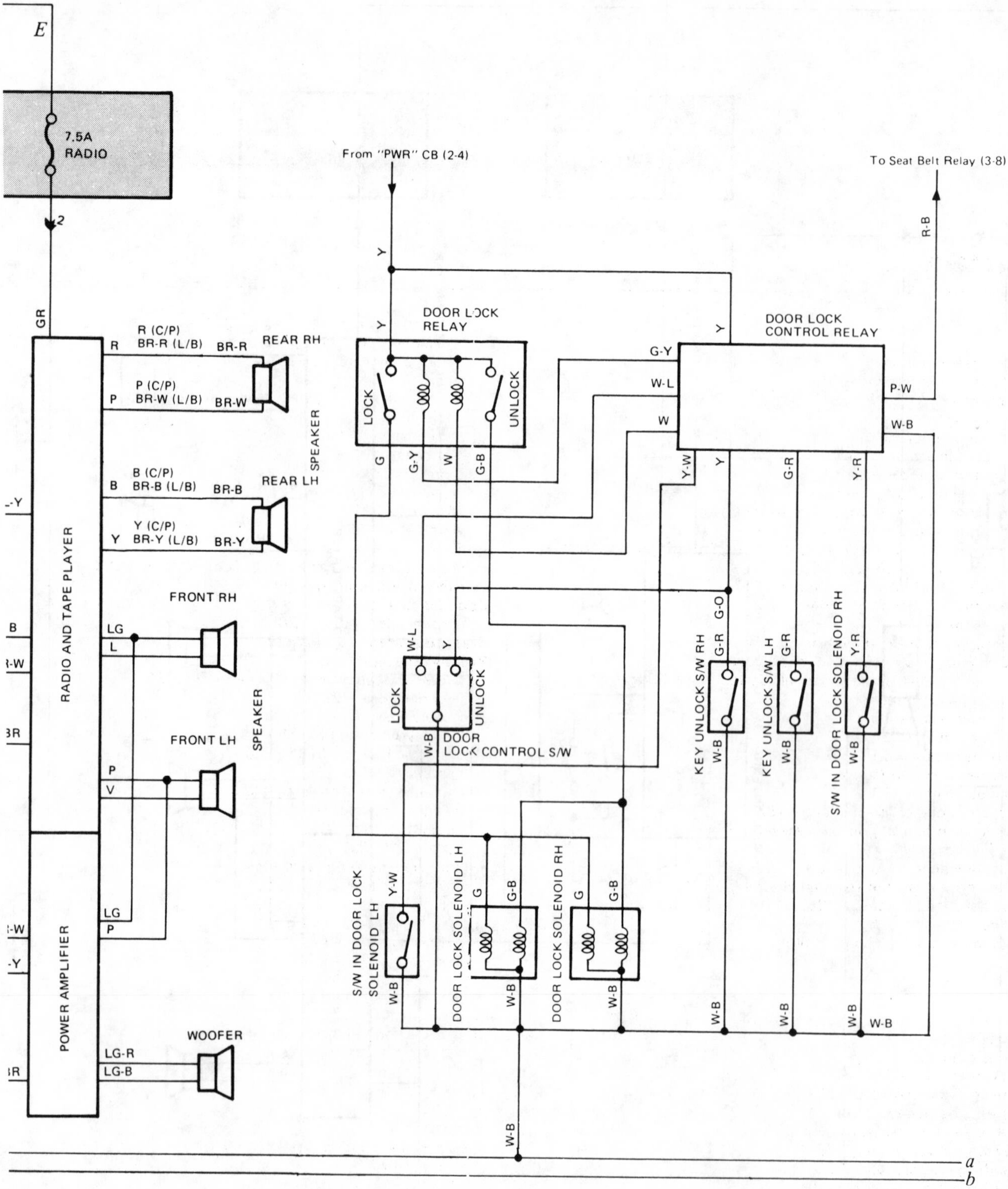

E

7.5A
RADIO

2

GR

RADIO AND TAPE PLAYER

R (C/P)
BR-R (L/B)   BR-R   REAR RH

R
P (C/P)
BR-W (L/B)   BR-W

P

SPEAKER

B (C/P)
BR-B (L/B)   BR-B   REAR LH

B
Y (C/P)
BR-Y (L/B)   BR-Y

Y

FRONT RH

LG
L

SPEAKER

FRONT LH

P
V

POWER AMPLIFIER

LG
P

LG-R   WOOFER
LG-B

From "PWR" CB (2-4)   To Seat Belt Relay (3-8)

Y   R-B

DOOR LOCK   DOOR LOCK
RELAY   CONTROL RELAY

Y   Y

G-Y   P-W

W-L

W   W-B

LOCK   UNLOCK

G   G-Y   W   G-B   Y-W   Y   G-R   Y-R

W-L   Y

LOCK   UNLOCK
W-B

DOOR
LOCK CONTROL S/W

KEY UNLOCK S/W RH   KEY UNLOCK S/W LH   S/W IN DOOR LOCK SOLENOID RH

G-R   G-O   G-R   Y-R

W-B   W-B   W-B

S/W IN DOOR LOCK   DOOR LOCK SOLENOID LH   DOOR LOCK SOLENOID RH
SOLENOID LH

Y-W   G   G-B   G   G-B

W-B   W-B   W-B   W-B   W-B   W-B   W-B

W-B

a
b

Fig. 12.68 Wiring diagram for all 1984/1985 Toyota Celica models (continued)

Index